CORPORATE LAW IN NIGERIA

Practice and Procedure

Second Edition

CORPORATE LAW IN NIGERIA

Practice and Procedure

Julius Onivehu Beida ••• King James Nkum

malthouse MP

Malthouse Press Limited

Lagos, Benin, Ibadan, Jos, Port-Harcourt, Zaria

Second Edition 2024
ISBN 978-978-60203-4-1

Published by Malthouse Press Limited
Lagos Port Harcourt Zaria

5 Adele Road, Off Warehouse Road, Apapa
Lagos Mainland, Nigeria
E-mail: malthouselagos@gmail.com
Facebook:@malthouselagos
Twitter:@malthouselagos
Instagram:@malthouselagos
Tel: 0802 600 3203

International Distributors
African Books Collective, Oxford, UK
Email: orders@africanbookscollective.com
Website: http://www.africanbookscollective.com

PREFACE

Authored by seasoned prolific authors, senior legal practitioners and university law dons, this book is a masterpiece on Corporate Law designed based on the most recent Companies and Allied Matters Act 2020 amendment, to meet the legal and educational needs of students, practitioners and corporate organisations. Its practical and incisive delivery is intended to enhance understanding of the subject by both those with legal background and the ordinary businessman/woman.

The book covers critical issues and topics, including:

- legal regime for corporate practice in Nigeria;
- administrative and regulatory institutions, classification of companies;
- forms of business organisations; incorporation of corporate bodies;
- incorporated trustees;
- business name registration;
- promoters and pre-incorporation contracts;
- post-incorporation matters;
- conversion of corporate bodies and alterations;
- corporate governance;
- company membership;
- meetings and resolutions;
- financial statements, audits and annual returns;
- majority rule and corporate sovereignty;

- company shares, debentures and securities;
- capital market practice and floatation of securities;
- internal restructuring;
- external options in corporate restructuring;
- company proceedings and investment dispute resolution;
- winding-up and dissolution of companies, business and non-business formation; and
- reliefs and incentives.

The material will be a great resource for corporate business practitioners such as CEOs, founders, company directors, firms, business executives, lawyers, Undergraduate and Law School Students, and other stakeholders in the business class.

King James Nkum
Julius Onivehu Beida

TABLE OF CASES

TABLE OF STATUTES

CONTENTS

Chapter 6: INCORPORATED TRUSTEES

Chapter 7: BUSINESS NAME REGISTRATION

Chapter 8: PROMOTERS AND PRE-INCORPORATION CONTRACTS

Chapter 9: POST-INCORPORATION MATTERS

Chapter 10: CONVERSION OF CORPORATE BODIES AND ALTERATIONS

Chapter 11: CORPORATE GOVERNANCE

Chapter 12: COMPANY MEMBERSHIP, MEETINGS AND RESOLUTIONS

Chapter 13: FINANCIAL STATEMENTS, AUDITS AND ANNUAL RETURNS

Chapter 14: MAJORITY RULE AND CORPORATE SOVEREIGNTY

Chapter 15: COMPANY SHARES, DEBENTURES AND SECURITIES

Chapter 16: CAPITAL MARKET PRACTICE AND FLOATATION OF SECURITIES

Chapter 19: COMPANY PROCEEDINGS AND INVESTMENT DISPUTE RESOLUTION

Chapter 20: WINDING-UP AND DISSOLUTION OF COMPANIES, BUSINESS AND NON-BUSINESS FORMATION

Chapter 21: RELIEFS AND INCENTIVES

Chapter 1

LEGAL REGIME FOR CORPORATE PRACTICE IN NIGERIA

INTRODUCTION

Previously, restrictions were imposed on aliens doing business in Nigeria before 1995. That policy was meant both to give Nigerians greater opportunity for participation in economic activities as well as to protect the economy. Prominent among these limiting statutes included the following:

(i) Nigerian Enterprises Promotion Acts of 1973 and 1989;
(ii) Industrial Development Coordination Act of 1988;
(iii) Immigration Act of 1963;
(iv) Exchange Control Act of 196;
(v) Securities and Exchange Commission Act of 1988.

The restrictions on foreigners were removed following the intractable economic problems of the 1980s and 1990s, with a view to encouraging foreign investment in line with the principles of globalization and liberalization of business practices around the world.

This limitation has however been lifted. Today, Nigeria is by and large a free enterprise country, with only a few restrictions on doing business regulations limited to those that are reasonably necessary in the national interest.

The business environment in Nigeria is governed by a number of company related laws. Prominent among them are these:

(i) Constitution of the Federal Republic of Nigeria 1999 (as amended);
(ii) Companies and Allied Matters Act 2004;
(iii) Investment and Securities Act, 2007;
(iv) Nigerian Investment Promotion Commission Act 2004;
(v) National Office for Technology Acquisition Promotion Act 2004;

(vi) Immigration Act 1963;
(vii) Banks and other Financial Institutions Act;
(viii) Asset Management Corporation Act, 2010;
(ix) Insurance Act 2007;
(x) National Industrial Court Act;
(xi) Federal Inland Revenue Service Act, 2007;
(xii) Foreign Exchange (Monitoring and Miscellaneous Provisions) Act 1995.

Some of the principal legal regimes are briefly highlighted below.

THE NIGERIAN CONSTITUTION

Nigeria's Constitution recognizes the need to encourage participation of the citizenry in economic activities as the basis for economic and national development. Accordingly, Section 16(1) expressly provides *inter alia* that the State shall protect the right of every citizen to engage in any economic activities outside the major sectors of the economy[1]. This provision is, however, without prejudice to the right of any person to participate in areas of the economy within the major sectors of the economy. This implies that every Nigerian citizen is at liberty to engage in any business as an individual or in partnership with others.

Nevertheless, this right is subject to any relevant laws limiting such freedom. An example of this limitation is the prohibition from investment or participation in commercial activities as contained in the "negative list" of the Nigerian Investment Promotion Commission Act.[2] The prohibited items on the list include:

(i) Production of arms and ammunition.
(ii) Production of military and paramilitary wear and accoutrement.
(iii) Production of and dealing in narcotics.
(iv) Such other items as the Federal Executive Council may determine from time to time.

Therefore, any person dealing in these items will be operating an illegal business, which amounts to criminal activity.

---

[1] Section 16(1) Constitution of the Federal Republic of Nigeria 1999 as amended
[2] Section 32 Nigerian Investment Promotion Commission Act

COMPANIES AND ALLIED MATTERS ACT (CAMA)

The Nigerian Company Law originated with the *Companies Ordinance* of 1912 as the first companies' statute in Nigeria. It provided for the first time in Nigeria, a procedure for incorporating a company by registration. The objects and reasons for the Ordinance were to provide for the formation of limited companies within the colony and protectorate. It was hoped thereby to foster the principles of cooperative trading and effort in the country. Subsequent to the foregoing was *the Companies Ordinance 1922*, which was first applied to the colony of Lagos and later extended to the rest of the country. In 1963, the 1922 ordinance was designated Companies Act and it continued to regulate companies until its repeal in 1968 by the Companies Act 1968. The *Companies Act 1968* was promulgated during the military era as Decree (Companies Decree No. 51 of 1968) and was re-designated in 1980 as the Companies Act. The promulgation of the Act was necessitated by an urgent need for a modern companies' legislation in view of the fact that the previous legislations had become largely inadequate to deal with growth of the economic activities in a developing country like Nigeria.

The current Companies and Allied Matters Act (CAMA) has made some revolutionary and landmark provisions for companies, for the registration of business names and for the incorporation of trustees. This was done in order to take care of emerging global trends in the conduct of business transactions.

(a) Innovations of CAMA

Some major innovations of the Act include the following as enumerated:

(i) Comprehensiveness of the Act, by the enactment of some relevant principles of common law and doctrines of equity; and by incorporation in the substantive enactment of many of the common and general provisions of the articles in table A of the Companies Act 1968;

(ii) More logical arrangement of the subject matter of the Act;

(iii) Establishment of a Corporate Affairs Commission to administer the Companies and Allied Matter Act;

(iv) Encouraging greater seriousness and commitment in the formation and registration of companies by requiring a minimum authorised share capital and minimum subscription;

(v)Prohibition of non-voting shares and of weighted votes;

(vi) Abolition of the common law rules on pre-incorporation contracts and the provision for ratification and adoption of such contracts;

(vii) Provision for greater and more effective participation in and control of, the affairs of the companies through improved provision in respect of meeting;

(viii) Expanded provisions for relief against illegal and oppressive acts including provision for derivative action relief against unfairly prejudicial conduct;

(ix) Provisions for greater accountability by directors;

(x) Provision for the appointment, qualification, duties and tenure of office of secretaries of public companies;

(xi) Improvement in the forms and contents of financial statements, classification of companies into small, and others for the purpose of greater financial disclosure, incorporation of accounting standards and provision for greater and more relevant disclosure in the Directors' Report;

(xii) More comprehensive provisions in respect of receivership;

(xiii) Provisions for the incorporation, authorisation and control of unit trust schemes;

(xiv) Provisions dealing with insider trading;

(xv) Provisions regulating mergers and take-över subject to the Securities and Exchange Commission Act. The administration of the Act itself, as is divided between the Corporate Affairs Commission which administers the whole of the Act [except part XVII, which is administered by Securities and Exchange Commission (SEC)].

In addition to the following, the revised CAMA 2020 makes the following significant changes among other things, after 30 years:

(xvi) It now allows a single member/shareholder company to be incorporated, rather than the previous minimum of two persons earlier provided;

(xvii) It now recognises digital transactions by providing for electronic filing, electronic share transfer, and e-meetings (via new media platforms such Whatsapp, Skype, Webinar, Zoom, etcetera) for private companies. Moreover, Certified True Copy (CTC) of electronically filed documents have been given judicial recognition as being admissible in court, with equal status as the original document;

(xviii) It prohibits duality of roles as Chairman/CEO to enhance protection of minority shareholders;

(xix) It allows for creation of Limited Liability Partnership (LLP), and Limited Partnership (LP), which incorporates the tax benefit of partnership business with the greater liability protection of private company owners;

(xx) It abolished the mandatory requirement for company common seal in line with global best practice;

(xxi) The appointment of company Secretary is no longer mandatory, but optional;

(xxii) It replaces the phrase "authorized share capital" with "minimum share capital to mitigate the cost of company registration;

(xxiii) Small companies are no longer mandated by law to hold an annual general meeting (AGM).

NIGERIAN INVESTMENT PROMOTION COMMISSION ACT AND RELATED LEGISLATIONS

The Act established the Nigerian Investment Promotion Commission (NIPC) for the purposes of *inter alia*:

(i) Coordinating investments;

(ii) Initiating and supporting investment policies;

(iii) Promoting investment;

(iv) Collecting and disseminating information on investment, among other functions.

The Commission's functions are carried out by a chairman and seven other members of the Agency.

Chapter 2

ADMINISTRATIVE AND REGULATORY INSTITUTIONS

INTRODUCTION

This chapter discusses the features and functions of the regulatory bodies and their relevance on corporate law practice in Nigeria. These institutional frameworks function by administering the relevant legal regimes. These include:

(i) Corporate Affairs Commission;
(ii) Securities Exchange Commission;
(iii) Nigerian Investment Promotion Commission;
(iv) One Stop Investment Centre;
(v) National Office for Technology Acquisition Promotion;
(vi) Asset Management Corporation of Nigeria;
(vii) National Insurance Commission;
(viii) Federal Inland Revenue Service;
(ix) Nigerian Immigration Service;
(x) Central Bank of Nigeria;
(xi) National Industrial Court;
(xii) Federal High Court.

THE CORPORATE AFFAIRS COMMISSION

(a) Establishment

The Corporate Affairs Commission (CAC) is the apex of the regulatory body for companies in Nigeria. The Companies and Allied Matters Act (CAMA) provides for the establishment of the Commission. The CAC is established as a body with full legal capacity like any other incorporated company. Thus, it has perpetual succession and a common seal, capable of suing and being sued in its corporate name, of acquiring, holding or disposing of any property, movable or immovable, for the purpose of carrying out its functions.

The establishment of the Corporate Affairs Commission as an autonomous body was due to the perceived inefficiency and ineffectiveness of the erstwhile Company Registry, a department within the Federal Ministry of Commerce and Tourism, which was then responsible for the registration and administration of the repealed Companies Act of 1968.

The Commission is the body charged with the responsibility of administering the Companies and Allied Matters Act 2004.

(b) Membership

The body is constituted by a membership of 15 persons representing a wide range of interests, namely:

(i) Business community;
(ii) Labour organisations;
(iii) Legal profession;
(iv) Accounting profession;
(v) Manufacturer's Association of Nigeria;
(vi) Association of Small Scale Industries;
(vii) Institute of Chartered Secretaries and Administrators;
(viii) Securities and Exchange Commission;
(ix) Ministries of Trade and Tourism, Finance and Economic Development, Justice, Industry, and Internal Affairs.

The chairman who is appointed by the President on the recommendation of the Minister of Trade and Commerce must be a person who is experienced in or has acquired specialised knowledge of corporate, industrial, commercial, financial or economic affairs and is thus able to make outstanding contributions to the work of the commission.

The Registrar-General of the commission must be a person qualified to practice law in Nigeria for not less than 10 years and he must have had experience in company law practice or administration for not less than 8 years. He is entitled to represent the Commission in legal proceedings in court.

Members of the Commission other than ex-officio members hold office for three years and are eligible for re-appointment for one further term of two years. With the exception of the Registrar, generally, they are all part-time members.

A member of the commission however ceases to hold office:

(i) If he becomes of unsound mind or is incapable of carrying out his duties;

(ii) If he becomes bankrupt or has made arrangement with his creditors;

(iii) If he is convicted of a felony or any offence involving dishonesty.

With the exception of representatives of the Ministries, the Securities and Exchange Commission, the Institute of Chartered Securities and Administrators and the Registrar-General, other members are entitled to such remuneration and allowances as the president may direct. The quorum for meetings of the Commission is five.

(c) Functions

The functions of the Commission include:

(i) Administration of the Act including the regulation and supervision of the formation, incorporation, regulation, management and winding up of companies;

(ii) Establishment and maintenance of companies registry and offices in all the states of the Federation;.

(iii) Conduct of investigation into the affairs of any company where the interest of the shareholders and the public so demand; and

(iv) Administration of the business names and incorporated trustees as provided for in parts B and C of the Act.

The chief executive of the commission is the Registrar General who must be a legal practitioner so qualified for not less than 10 years and who has not less than eight years experience in company law practice or administration. He is also the registrar of business names.

(d) Accreditation

The group of professionals accredited or authorised to transact business with the Commission in respect of part A of the Act include legal practitioners, chartered accountants and chartered secretaries. Only accredited professional individuals or firms are allowed to transact with the body.

Based on recent reforms at the Commission however, non-professional individuals are now allowed to transact with the Commission by registering their companies directly on the online portal.

In respect of registration of business names and incorporated trustees in part D and F, any other person and other non-professionals can be accredited to transact business with the Commission. Transacting business here means registering and incorporating companies on behalf of other people, preparing and filling of annual returns, conducting searches, etcetera.

The procedure for accreditation with the Commission are as enumerated hereunder:

(i) Pick up and fill Accreditation Form A or B;
(ii) Pay application fee of ₦5,000 for individuals ₦10,000 for firms
(iii) Return of completed application form accompanied by:

- Two passport photographs;
- Qualifying certificate (i.e. qualifying Certificate and Call to Bar Certificate).
- A copy of the current receipt of payment of the practicing fee for at least for the year of application;
- A copy of NYSC discharge or exemption certificate;
- A copy of registration receipt.

SECURITIES EXCHANGE COMMISSION

(a) Establishment and Purpose

The Securities and Exchange Commission (SEC) was established by the Investments and Securities Act (ISA) No 45 of 1999. This legislation originated in 1962, when the Capital Issues Committee, an arm of the

Central Bank of Nigeria, was set up to evaluate applications from companies wanting to raise capital from the market and recommend for approvals. That committee transmuted to the Capital Market Commission in 1973 and the Securities and Exchange Commission in 1978. The Investment and Securities Act No. 45 of 1999 finally sought to broaden the operation of the Commission and refocus it for more impact on economic growth. Thus, the ISA 2007 replaced ISA 1999.

The Securities and Exchange Commission (SEC) is the principal regulatory body for Nigeria's capital market, including the Nigerian Stock Exchange. The Commission is under supervision of the Federal Ministry of Finance. Similar to the exchange commission in other jurisdictions, the Commission supervises the operation of capital market transactions, ensuring that the relevant rules are complied with.

The business of capital formation and mobilisation is crucial to economic development. Capital markets drive capital mobilisation and allocation to businesses, in the push for economic growth. Through the capital market, companies and governments mobilise capital for investment, while offering opportunity to investors to seek profitable outlets for their funds. Because complex financial processes are often involved, and large numbers of investors participate, the need for guarding the mechanism for those transactions becomes apparent. Investors need to be protected, just as the process needs to be kept viable. This is where the role of SEC comes into play.

The corporate law is relevant to the Securities and Exchange Commission in the sense that it ensures orderly and transparent conduct, such that parties that take decisions, especially on investments, do it on the strength of good information and sound processes. By that, it is to attract more funds into the market and also attract more viable companies that could expand their operations.

(b) Membership

In terms of membership, the Commission is constituted by a Chairman appointed by the President and 10 other persons including 2 full-time Commissioners who must be 10 years post call and who must be persons with ability, experience and specialised knowledge in capital market matters. There is also a Director-General for the Commission who is appointed by the President and he is the Chief Executive of the Commission.

(c) Functions

Functions of the SEC as spelt out in the ISA include the under-listed:[1]

(i) Regulation of the investment and securities business in Nigeria;

(ii) Registration and regulation of the Capital Market Operators and their functions;

(iii) Registration of securities of public companies;

(iv) Maintenance of Register of foreign investment portfolios in Nigeria;

(v) Rendering of assistance to promoters and investors wishing to establish Securities Exchanges and Capital Trade Points;

(vi) Registration and regulation of the venture capital funds and collective investments schemes;

(vii) Protection of the integrity of the securities market;

(viii) Facilitation of the establishment of a nationwide system for securities trading in the Nigerian capital market;

(ix) Facilitation of the linking of all markets in securities through modern communication and data processing facilities;

(x) Review, approval and regulation of mergers, acquisitions and other forms of business combinations.

(d) Capital Market Registration

The category of persons allowed to transact with the capital market are experts or professionals, otherwise called Capital Market Operators (CMO). These professionals include Legal Practitioners, Accountants, Auditors, Engineers, Estate Valuers, Property Managers and others as determined by SEC. Individual partners on the other hand are required to possess five years post-call experience to qualify to be registered while sponsored individuals must possess two years post-call.

The procedure for registration with SEC as outline under the SEC Rules are as follows:[2]

---

[1] Section 9 ISA

(i) Send an application to the SEC by filling SEC Form 2 or 3.
(ii) Pay the application fees (Firm - ₦20,000, Principal partner- ₦ 5, 000, sponsored individual- ₦1, 000).
(iii) Submit the application Form with relevant documents:
- Bank statement of 3-6 months of the applicant with a minimum balance of Individual- ₦500,000, Firm- ₦2,000,000.00, Company Ltd. - ₦5,000,000.00;
- Curriculum vitae of at least two partners, if a Firm;
- Police clearance certificate;
- 4 copies of the Partnership Deed, if a partnership;
- Profile of the Firm;
- Sworn undertaken to keep proper records as specified by SEC;
- A copy of the receipt of payment of practicing fees;
- Professional indemnity insurance policy;

(iv) SEC will then visit the office of the applicant;
(v) The applicant is to participate in SEC training school;
(vi) Revalidate accreditation at SEC every 5 years.[3]

NIGERIAN INVESTMENT PROMOTION COMMISSION

(a) Establishment

This agency was established in 1995 as a body corporate with perpetual succession under the NIPC Decree, 1995. The commission shall encourage, promote and coordinate investment in the Nigerian economy.

(b) Functions

The establishment Act provides for the function of the Commission which include:

(i) Encouraging, promoting and coordinating investment in the Nigerian economy;
(ii) Coordinating and monitoring all investment promotion activities to which this Act applies;

---

[2] Rule 178 SEC Rules 2013
[3] Section 38 ISA, R.178 ISA Rules

(iii) Initiating and supporting measures which shall enhance the investment climate in Nigeria;

(iv) Promoting investments through effective promotional means;

(v) Collecting, collating, analysing and disseminating information about investment opportunities and sources of investment capital, and advise on request, the availability, choice or suitability of partners in joint-venture projects;

(vi) Registering and keeping records of all enterprises to which this Act applies;

(vii) Identifying specific projects and invite interested investors for participation in those projects;

(viii) Initiating, organising and participating in promotional activities, such as, exhibitions, conferences and seminars for the stimulation of investments;

(ix) Maintaining liaison between investors and Ministries, Government departments and agencies, institutional lenders and other authorities concerned with investments;

(x) Providing and disseminating up-to-date information on incentives available to investors;

(xi) Assisting incoming and existing investors by providing support services.

(xii) Evaluate the impact of the Commission in investments in Nigeria and make appropriate recommendations;

(xiii) Advise the Federal Government on policy matters designed to promote the industrialisation of Nigeria or the general development of the economy;

(xiv) Perform such other functions as are supplementary or incidental to the attainment of the objectives of this Act[4].

(c) Documents Required for Registration with NIPC

The mandatory requirements for application with the Commission includes the following documents:

(i) NIPC Form 1;

(ii) Receipt of purchase of NIPC Form 1;

---

[4] Section 4 NIPC Act

(iii) Payment of ₦5,000 fee;
(iv) Joint venture agreement (if any);
(v) Certified True Copy of the memorandum of association and article of association of the company;
(vi) Certificate of Incorporation;
(vii) Tax clearance certificate;
(viii) Certificate of capital importation;
(ix) Evidence of acquisition of business premises;
(x) Feasibility study report (if any);
(xi) Profile of expatriate personnel showing their qualifications, experience, positions to be held in the company and duration of each quota position.

(d) Procedure for Registration with NIPC

These includes the following steps:

(i) Obtain the NIPC Form 1.
(ii) Pay a non-refundable deposit of Ten Thousand Naira and obtain receipt.
(iii) Completed and submitted the Form at the NIPC Headquarters in Abuja or State Ministries of Trade with the following requirements:
I. Two copies of receipt of payment of ₦10,000
II. Incorporation Certificate of the applicant company.
III. Memorandum and articles of association of the company.
IV. Receipt of payment of stamp duties on the authorised share capital of the company as at the date of the application. (Minimum share capital is ₦10 million).
V. Tax clearance certificate of the applicant company.
VI. Partnership (Joint Venture) Agreement unless 100% foreign ownership.
(iv) Feasibility Report and Project Implementation Program of the company for its proposed business.
(v) Title deeds of land evidencing commitment to acquire requisite business premises for the company's operations.

(vi) Training program for Nigerian Staff or personnel policy of the company, incorporating management succession schedule for qualified Nigerians.

(vii) CTC of FORM CAC 2 & 7 (statement of share capital and return of allotment and particulars of Directors including non – resident directors "NRD").

(viii) Job title designations of expatriate quota positions required, and the academic and working experience required for the occupants of such positions.

(ix) Copies of Information Brochure on the foreign partner as testimony of Int'l expertise and credibility in the line of business.

(x) A copy of certificate of capital importation for wholly foreign companies.

(xi) After the submission of the NIPC Form 1, the Commission will register the applicant company within 14 days of the receipt of the application.

ONE STOP INVESTMENT CENTRE

(a) Establishment and Purpose

The One Stop Investment Centre (OSIC) otherwise known as One Stop Shop (OSS) was established on 21st March 2006. The initiative is part of the continuous effort to encourage Foreign Direct Investment (FDI) in the country.

Hitherto, the practice has been that company incorporation and foreign investment approvals are processed in different authorised government agencies. This process was characterised by delays usually caused by bureaucratic bottlenecks, which also stifled the smooth start-up of foreign businesses in the country. In a bid to ensure the timely incorporation of companies and grant of investment approvals, the government had in the early 1990's set up the Industrial Development Commission Committee (IDDC) to serve as a one stop agency for all pre-investment approvals. The IDDC had the statutory responsibility to grant Business Permits, Approved Status-in-Principle, Expatriate Quota, approvals on fiscal concessions, vet licensing and transfer agreements and generally advise the Federal Government on policy matters designed to promote the industrialisation of the country.

Although the law establishing the IDDC provided that every valid application received would be processed within two months, this expectation was rarely ever met in practice. The IDDC Act was subsequently repealed by the Nigerian Investment Promotion Commission (NIPC) Act 1995 which established the NIPC to encourage and promote investment in Nigeria. Companies with foreign participation are required to apply to NIPC for registration. Thus, the statute provides that within 14 days from the receipt of completed registration forms, NIPC shall register such companies or otherwise advise the applicant as appropriate.

(b) Features

In terms of it features, the OSIC is characterised thus:

(i) The participating agencies will maintain their existing mandates and responsibilities within the structure of OSIC.

(ii) Only statutory provisions will be administered at OSIC and not special applications;

(iii) Agencies will establish their presence at OSIC in phases;

(iv) Approval time for business entry approvals is 24 hours;

(v) OSIC covers investments into all sectors of the economy;

(vi) It is mandatory for all foreign investors to register with OSIC to facilitate;

(vii) It is involved with foreign direct investment ((FDI) tracking/investor tracking as provided in the NIPC Act.

(c) Functions

The OSIC is established with a mandate to achieve the following functions:

(i) Simplifying and curtailing the procedures and guidelines for issuing business approvals, permits and authorisations by eliminating bottlenecks faced by investors in establishing and running businesses in Nigeria;

(ii) Reducing the high cost of doing business;

(iii) Eliminating dealing with multiple agencies;
(iv) Eradicating the use of discretion and lack of transparency in granting approvals, licenses, permits;
(v) Eliminating over bureaucratisation in procedures and processes.
(vi) Eradicating poor service delivery;
(vii) Ensuring Foreign Direct Investment and investor tracking.

NATIONAL OFFICE FOR TECHNOLOGY ACQUISITION AND PROMOTION (NOTAP)

(a) Procedure of Applying for NOTAP Registration

(i) Complete a NOTAP Prescribed Form NOIP 1-84 with CTC of the contract, company documents and related information. The application form must be accompanied with the following documents:

I. Application fee;
II. Memorandum and articles of association of the company (certified true copies) and certificate of incorporation;
III. Two certified true copies of the agreement to be registered;
IV. Two copies of duly completed questionnaire;[5]
V. A copy of the relevant feasibility study;
VI. Annual audited accounts (if not a new company) and if it is a new company, a copy of the statement of affairs of the company accompanied with the certificate of incorporation.

(ii) Upon submission, NOTAP vets the agreement to determine its conformity with its evaluation criteria. If the agreement is approved, the Agency computes and advises the applicant on the fees payable as registration fees for the use of the technology and the duration approved for the agreement. The NOTAP Certificate of Approval is usually issued within a period of two weeks (maximum of 6 months) of the application and valid for a period of between 2-10 years.

---

[5] Revised NOIP 2-84

(iii) Both the transferor and transferee of such technology are responsible for registering the agreement. The registration is expected to be done within 60 days of execution or conclusion of the agreement. Non-registration with NOTAP does not render the contract void, only that repatriation of fees, profits, royalties through CBN is disallowed unless a certificate of approval of the registration with NOTAP accompanies the application to repatriate in respect of such contract.[6] Registrable contracts or agreements are listed in Section 4(d) NOTAP Act thus:

I. Use of trademarks;
II. Right to use patented inventions;
III. The supply of technical expertise;
IV. The supply of basic or detailed engineering drawing;
V. The supply of machinery and plants;
VI. The provision of operating staff or managerial assistance and training of personnel;
VII. Contract involving transfer of technology to Nigerian partners.

(b) Refusal by NOTAP to Register

The Agency may decline to register a technology for certain reasons, including:

(i) If the technology is available in Nigeria;
(ii) If the contract involves the transfer of obsolete technology;
(iii) If the price is not commensurate with the technology to be acquired;
(iv) If the transferee is obliged to submit to foreign jurisdiction in any controversy arising for decision concerning the interpretation or enforcement in Nigeria of any such contract.

NIGERIAN IMMIGRATION SERVICE

(a) Documents Required for Application with Immigration

(i) Completed Immigration Form T/1.

---

[6] Section 7 NOTAP Act

(ii) Certificate of incorporation.

(iii) Certified True Copies of particulars of directors, share allotment, and memorandum and articles of association of the company.

(iv) Current Tax Certificate.

(v) Rent, Lease or Certificate of Occupancy for operating premises.

(vi) Evidence of imported machineries with *proforma invoices*, Form M, etcetera, or evidence of work on hand with value attached to the contract.

(vii) Functional feasibility report.

(viii) Notary public confirmatory letter of office or site location.

(ix) Proposed salaries of expatriates to be received, designation and qualification.

(x) Training programme for Nigerians under studies.

(xi) Audit account.

Chapter 3

CLASSIFICATION OF COMPANIES

INTRODUCTION

There had existed some forms of economic activities within the region known as Nigeria prior to its colonization by the British. These include individuals trading within the towns and villages in articles of trade such as clothes, farm produce and other metal products. These business activities were peasant in nature, and revolved around the minimum needs for subsistence of the people. Trade by barter was the mode of exchange for goods and services. This largely subsistence and agrarian society transformed into modern trade, leading to the development of company law in the country.

With a population of over 200 million, Nigeria has a very large market as a destination for both local and foreign investment. With the right policies and legal regulations, its vast potentials could be harnessed.

Nigeria is essentially a free enterprise country. With the only restrictions on doing business being regulations and laws which are reasonably necessary and must be adhered to in the favour of national interest. The business environment in Nigeria is governed by a number of company related laws, including the Companies and Allied Matters Act 2004.[1]

This Chapter will consider the types or different kinds of companies or business organisations which can be formed to operate in Nigeria. These include:

(i) Registration of companies,

(ii) Registration of business names

---

[1] As revised 2020

(iii) Incorporated trustees

Under the Companies and Allied Matters Act (CAMA) which regulates the activities of companies, there are various types of businesses which shall be discussed below.

REGISTRABLE COMPANY

Nigeria is generally a free enterprise country, and any person can participate in its economy. This participation may be through sole proprietorship, partnerships, and unincorporated joint ventures, limited and unlimited liability companies.

The different types of business organisations that can be registered, their features and suitability are as follows:

(i) Sole trader/Proprietorship;
(ii) Partnership; and
(iii) Companies/Corporations.

There are also in addition, non-business or non-profit organisations such as:

(i) Company Limited by Guarantee;
(ii) Incorporated Trustees.

FACTORS THAT SHOULD DETERMINE THE TYPE OF COMPANY TO ESTABLISH

A number of factors are to be considered in determining the type of business organisation to be established. These include:

(i) The number of the membership;
(ii) The size and nature of the proposed business;
(iii) The cost/capital requirement of the business;
(iv) Restrictions on the issue and transfer of shares;
(v) The formalities and legal/statutory requirements to be complied with;
(vi) Extent of liability of members;
(vii) Commercial expediency;
(viii) The extent and sphere of operation;
(ix) The cost of registration and expenses;
(x) Speed of processing and completion of registration;

(xi) Post registration compliance and regulatory requirements;
(xii) The desire of the client himself;

These forms of business organisations will be discussed in subsequent Chapters.

Chapter 4

FORMS OF BUSINESS ORGANIZATIONS

INTRODUCTION

It is pertinent to consider the various forms of business organization in order to draw comparative merits of each type of organization and set the criteria to assess them. All business organizations must be assessed from these basic levels:

(i) Does it facilitate easy investment in the business? (This question borders on funding);

(ii) Does the business mitigate or minimize the risk involved in the venture? (This question seeks to determine the risk factor, since there is always no total assurance of success in any business); and

(iii) Does the organization have such a structure as to reduce friction or the disagreement amongst the investors and managers?

The basic types of business organization to be considered under this section are Sole Trader or Proprietorship and Partnership.

SOLE PROPRIETORSHIP

Sole trading is probably the oldest and commonest unit of business undertaking, also known as a one-man business. It is the most elementary type of business organization. The business involves only the individual himself going into business on his own, without the involvement of a partner. The sole proprietor runs his business solo, and may be assisted by members of his family, or employees.

As the business grows to a certain extent, he may engage the services of professionals like accountants and prevalent craftsmen to assist in the business. It is most suitable and prevalent in crafts work such as mechanics, schools, petty trading, supply manufacturing business, and firms among others. The trend is to register these forms of organisations as Business Names under Part E of the CAMA 2020.

Sole traders usually provide their own capital with their personal savings and sometimes, may obtain bank loans. In most cases they rely on friends and family to raise the initial capital, and are indeed limited in their activities due to limitation of capital.

The implements of their trade must be sourced by self-finance. They can only contract on their own with personal guarantee for all their dealings with third parties and their liability is personal. In effect, wherever the business is indebted to anybody, they must pay not only from the business but also from personal savings, and the creditors are entitled to levying execution not only on the business but also on the personal assets of the sole trader.

It is this lack of distinction between the personal assets of the sole trader and his business that makes this type of business organization unattractive. From the legal standpoint therefore, there is no distinguishing between the assets of the sole traders and that of the business.

As the business is just one individual, there is absolutely no risk of any disagreement and so there is no need for any serious organizational structure to prevent frictions and disagreement.

It is good for the sole trader to keep proper accounts, but where he does not, he is not responsible to anybody to keep proper accounts. However, for the purposes of tax he is taxed as a sole trader and nothing more, though he must obtain a business permit from the Local Government to operate as such within the cities.

The sole trader is therefore adequate for a single person with limited capital but is totally unsuitable for a large scale investment.

REQUIREMENT FOR REGISTRATION OF BUSINESS NAMES

The sole trader who desires to adopt a business name for his business must register the business name with the Corporate Affairs Commission[1]. Where however, the sole trader merely uses his real

[1] Section 814 CAMA 2020

name he does not need to register the business under the Act, but where he adopts another name that is different from his real name then he must register under the Act.

While registering the business, the sole trader must supply the following information to the Registrar:

(i) Filling of the prescribed form.
(ii) Name(s) business name proposed
(iii) General nature of the business
(iv) Full postal address of the principal place of business
(v) Full postal address of any other place of business
(vi) Personal information of the business proprietor (names, nationality, age, sex, residential address, and business occupation)
(vii) Date of commencement of business
(viii) Passport photograph of the sole trader (two copies).

As soon as the sole trader has complied with the legal requirements the Registrar will issue a certificate of registration to him.

PARTNERSHIP

A partnership is the relationship which subsists between two or more persons carrying on business in common with a view to make profit. The essential element common to all partnerships is the pooling together of resources.

The sole trader may in order to further expand or raise capital may consider involving investors or partners, who may desire to join in the business by bringing their own money into the business and thereby form partnership business. This may of course facilitate expansion of the business by increasing the capital available for business.

The Partnership Act of 1890 defines partnership as "the relationship which subsists between persons carrying on business in common with a view to make profit"[2].

As regards its mode of *formation*, a partnership may be formed in three ways

(i) By oral agreement or

---

[2] Section 1 Partnership Act of 1890

(ii) By written agreement or
(iii) It may be inferred from the conduct of the partners.

Where there is a written agreement it will specify the terms and conditions of the partnership. As such, there is no particular formal process of forming a partnership as it may be inferred from the conduct of the parties.

Partnership is sometimes sub-divided into limited and general partnership. Limited partnership shall not consist of more than twenty persons (except where it is firm of solicitors or accountants). It must consist of one or more persons called general partners who shall be liable for all debts and obligations of the firm.

In general partnership, the partners have the right to take part in the business and their liability for the firm's debts is unlimited. The general partner has power to bind the firm in respect of its management. The death, bankruptcy or mental disorder of a general partner may lead to the dissolution of the partnership.

The asset of the partnership belongs strictly to the partnership and not to the individual partners.

Where there is no partnership agreement or where the partnership agreement does not exclude the Partnership Acts/Laws, the law will govern the partnership. Each partner is entitled to participate in the partnership business. A partner is entitled to equal share in the profits of the business. No partner can be expelled by the others unless there is agreement to the contrary. A partnership will determine the death of a partner.

In order to avoid frictions and organizational problems, the partnership may modify the Partnership Act with a more complex agreement that will govern the partnership. Each is liable for the debt of the partnership, as each partner is jointly and severally liable for the debt of the partnership business. That is because unlike a company, a partnership lacks perpetual succession.

The law regulating the relationship between partners is enacted by each state. Sometimes an individual or a partnership carries on business under a business name. Such a name may be required to be registered under PART D of the CAMA.

DIFFERENCE BETWEEN PARTNERSHIPS AND COMPANIES

(i) Formation and existence of partnership depends on mutual trust and personal relationship. This is not required in the case of a company.

(ii) Partnership can be formed by oral agreement or from conduct, whereas you need a lot of formalities to bring a company into being.

(iii) Every partner is entitled to take part in the management of the firm's business whereas in a company ownership is separated from management.

(iv) Death or withdrawal may terminate the partnership, while death or withdrawal of a major shareholder does not terminate a company. Joint stock companies have perpetual succession.

(v) The liability of the partners is unlimited, and they are liable personally for the debts of the partnership jointly and severally. While the liability of the members of the company is limited only to their investment in the company.

Therefore, from the above two forms of business organization discussed above, the sole trader and partnership we discover that both are very popular, because they require little financial investment and they depend on the goodwill of the individuals involved. Most of the big industrial concerns today started from this modest level.

COOPERATIVE SOCIETIES

A number of statutory provisions exist for the formation and registration of co-operative societies. These societies are designed to assist the individual farmers, traders and producers of various goods to form cooperatives for producing or marketing of their goods. The society has the advantage that the registration makes it a corporation with perpetual succession and with power to hold property and enter into contracts.

LIMITED LIABILITY COMPANY

A registered company is called Limited Liability Company because the liability of the members is "limited by shares". That is, the liability of its members limited by the memorandum to such an amount as the members may respectively be liable thereby undertaking to contribute to the assets of the company in the event of its being wound up. The maximum number membership of a limited liability company is 50 excluding employees. The minimum number is now one person as against two, based on the recent amendment to the CAMA.

A registered company is the most important unit of business organisation for modern economic activities. This is because of its special features such as:

(i) Legal personality,
(ii) Perpetual succession,
(iii) Opportunity for investment and for raising capital, and
(iv) Strict legal control and protection of members and creditors.

Finally, the CAMA requires that the word "Limited or Ltd" must appear at the end of the name of the company.

We shall be looking at the company, incorporated trustee and company limited by guarantee more closely in subsequent chapters.

Chapter 5

INCORPORATION OF CORPORATE BODIES

INTRODUCTION

Incorporated companies are also referred to as body corporate or registered companies. They have legal personality, that is, they can sue and be sued because they are legal entities distinct and separate from the persons of which they consist upon registration.

This Chapter will focus on Limited Liability Company as a special consideration, because of its unique nature. Furthermore, it is the type of business most embarked upon in the country. The law requires that certain conditions be met or present before the commission may consider issuing a certificate of registration to any company. These conditions are statutory provided and cannot be negotiated or ignored.

The CAMA provides for the following types of Incorporated Companies under Part B, namely:

(i) Company limited by shares;

(ii) Company Limited by Guarantee/ltd/GTE;

(iii) Unlimited Liability Company/ULTD.

Any of the above companies may be a private company or a public company. This Chapter shall also discuss incorporation of non-profit organizations, with particular reference to Incorporated Trustees.

RIGHT AND CAPACITY TO ESTABLISH A COMPANY

The right to form a company is statutorily provided for under the Act. Any individual or more persons may form an incorporated company which could be private or public, as far as the requirements of the Act in respect of company registration are duly complied with.

However, a company, association or partnership consisting of more than 20 persons cannot be formed for the purpose of carrying out business for profit without being registered as a company under the Act. The only exceptions to this general rule are cooperative societies registered under any legal provisions, and partnerships for the purpose of carrying on practice as legal practitioners or as accountants by duly qualified persons.

As regards the capacity to form a company, any person can form a company with exceptions being person who are;

(i) Less than 18 years of age, unless there are two other persons of full age and capacity who have already subscribed to the memorandum;
(ii) Of unsound mind and has been so found to be by a court in Nigeria or elsewhere;
(iii) An undischarged bankrupt; or
(iv) Disqualified by the Act from being a director of a company.

Similarly, a bankrupted or liquidated corporate body cannot join in the formation of a company. An alien can join in the establishment of a company if he complies with the provisions of relevant applicable laws.

CLASSIFICATIONS OF COMPANIES

(a) Private Limited Company

A private company is one, which is stated in its memorandum to be a private company. It has the following features:

(i) It must by its articles restrict the transfer of its shares;
(ii) It has a minimum of one member and maximum of 50 (not including persons who are bona fide in the employment of the company);
(iii) Its minimum share capital is ₦100,000;
(iv) It is prohibited from inviting the members of the public to subscribe for any shares or debentures of the company; or to deposit money for fixed periods or payable on call, whether or not bearing interest, unless authorized by any law;
(v) Where two or more members hold share jointly, they shall be regarded as one member;
(vi) A private company is exempted from statutory meetings;

(b) Public Company

A public company is defined as any other company other than a private company and which is stated in its memorandum as a public company.

The features of a public company can be found in the difference between a private company and public company:

(i) Membership of a private company is limited to fifty while public is unlimited

(ii) Minimum share capital of a private company is currently N100,000 while a public company minimum is ₦2,000,000

(iii) A private company can commence business upon incorporation whilst a public company will have to wait until it has been issued with a certificate by the Registrar

(iv) Private companies are permitted to allot its shares without external control unless there is alien participation while a public company cannot do so without the prior approval of SEC

(v)The name of a private company must include "Ltd" while a public limited company is "Plc"

(vi) A private company cannot invite the public to subscribe for its shares or debentures or to deposit money with it unless authorised by law, but a public company can

(vii) A private company must by its articles restrict the transfer of its shares while a public company is not so restricted

(viii) Every public company must hold statutory meeting & file a statutory report within six months of its incorporation, while a private company is not so required

(ix) A person above the age of 70 years may, by a resolution via special notice, be appointed a director of a public company provided that the fact of his being 70 or above shall be disclosed to members at the general meeting. Such procedure is not required in a private company

(x) All resolutions of a public company must be passed at a general meeting otherwise they won't be effective but a written resolution signed by all the members entitled to attend & vote is as valid and effective as if passed in a general meeting in a private company

(xi) Company Secretary of a public company is qualified and has the requisite experience required while it is not so for a private company.

(c) Company Limited by Shares

This is the type of company where the liability of its members is limited by the memorandum, to the amount if any, as to the unpaid shares respectively held by them. It is the largest most common type of company normally employed for business purposes. The shares create very valuable security and the limitation of liability enables shareholders to determine the limit of their respective liability and indebtedness.

The shares, as the unit of holding, represent the involvement and commitment of the interest of the holders. Apart from special circumstances when the liability may be extended, for example, where a company carries on business with less than the minimum number of members or the authorized minimum share capital.

The company is to be registered with shares. The amount of the share capital stated in the memorandum to be registered shall not be less than the authorized minimum share capital and not less than 25 percent of that capital shall be taken by the subscribers of the memorandum.

Furthermore, the Act provides that no company having a share capital shall be registered with an authorised share capital less than the authorized minimum share capital.

The memorandum of the company, specifically its capital clause, must provide, inter alia that the share capital of the company is divided into "*shares of a fixed amount (i.e. N1 or 50 kobo each).*"

A person who has paid his shares in full cannot be held liable for any part of the liability of the company. On the other hand, where a shareholder has sums outstanding on his shareholding, he can be called upon to pay up and this is so whether or not the company is being wound-up.

Other features of a company limited by shares are that the liability of members of a company limited by shares may have to be implemented at any time during the active life of the company as well as during the winding-up. Moreover, it is usually incorporated for the purpose of making profits for distribution to members.

(d) Company Limited by Guarantee

This is a type of company without a share capital as it is most often a non-profit organisation. The liability of its respective members are limited by the memorandum to such amount that members have undertaken to contribute to the assets of the company in the event of liquidation.

Such companies are incorporated for purposes of promoting causes such as commerce, art, science, religion, and so on. The income and assets are applied for the promotion of the objects and not available for distributing to members as profits. A company limited by guarantee shall not be registered with a share capital.

All officers and members who are cognizant of the fact that it is so carrying on business shall be jointly and severally liable for the payment and discharge of all the debts and liabilities of the company incurred in carrying on such business, and the company and every such officer and member shall be liable to a fine not exceeding ₦100 for every day during which it carries on such business.

The total liability of the members of a company limited by guarantee to contribute to the assets of the company in the event of its being wound up should not at any time be less than ₦10,000. This is intended to give some assurance to third parties dealing with the company.

Again, the memorandum of such a company can only be registered with the authority of the Attorney-General of the Federation first having been sought and obtained.

(e) Unlimited Liability Company

As the name implies, this type of company has no limit on the liability of its members. Unlimited company is not common, being limited in its usefulness. It is like a partnership because every member is liable in full for the debts of the company while a member and does not have any limit on liability. This unlimited liability makes it unattractive for business purposes. It is used mainly by professionals who assume personal liability for their obligations.

Unlimited company is usually useful where the members are able to estimate the kind of liability or loss they are likely to incur in advance. For example, companies working on a patent and its development in terms of products, oil prospecting companies, etcetera.

The company must be registered with a share capital, and where an existing unlimited company has no share capital, it must, not later than the appointed day, alter its memorandum and articles so that it becomes an unlimited company having a share capital not below the minimum share capital permitted under Section 99 of the CAMA.

Other features of this company include the fact that there must be "Ultd" at the back of its name. Moreover, a private unlimited company cannot be converted into a public unlimited company.

PROCEDURE FOR COMPANY REGISTRATION

The procedural steps to be taken for incorporation of a company are as follows:

i. Ascertaining the particulars of the proposed company
ii. Preparation of the incorporation documents
iii. Filing of incorporation documents
iv. Registration of the company.

(a) Particulars of the Proposed Company

Anyone desirous of establishing a company has to decide on the particulars of the company in the light of the requirements of the Act and other relevant statutes.

The choice of the type of company will depend on the purpose for which it is being formed.

Other matters to be considered are the type of company, its structure, nature of business proposed, funding, organisation, and the memorandum and articles of association.

(b) Preparing the Incorporation Documents

A promoter or person forming the company will need to obtain particulars necessary for preparing the memorandum and articles of association, after deciding the type of company to be registered.

(i) Memorandum

Name: The name of the company should end with the words "Public Limited Company" in the case of a public company limited by shares; "Limited" in the case of a private company limited by shares; "Limited by Guarantee" in the case of a company limited by guarantee; and "Unlimited" in the case of an unlimited company. Certain names are prohibited while others can only be used with the consent of the Commission. Examples of prohibited names include words like "National", "Regional", "State", "Government". The name chosen must not be one already registered or misleading.

Objects: The object refers to the purposes for which a company is formed. The nature of the business or object(s) is to be stated in the memorandum.

Share Capital: This refers to the sum with which the company is registered. The share capital will depend largely on the type of company, nature of the business and the availability of other sources of working capital.

Registered Office: The Act mandates that the registered office of the company must be situated in Nigeria.

Limitation of Liability: This clause is inserted to determine if the company will be limited or unlimited, and if limited, whether by shares or guarantee.

Subscribers: Subscribers to the memorandum must take 25% of the authorised capital, but they need not be the true owners of the company and after incorporation, the shares may be transferred to the true owners.

(ii) Articles of Association

The Articles are for the internal workings of the company. The Act requires every company to file articles of association. Some of the matters to be considered in the articles are:

I. Shares: Detailed particulars should be obtained in respect of shares consisting of the structure of the shares (for example, classes of shares, issues and any special dealing with shares not contained in the Act).

II. Borrowing: Care should be taken to regulate the power as desired, although a trading company normally has power to borrow money for the purpose of its business.

III. Meetings: Special provisions required by the owners of the company should be considered in this section.

IV. Directors: Special instructions may be required as to their appointment, tenure of office, powers and duties, delegation of powers, use of company seal, the managing director, procedure of board meetings, etcetera.

V. Secretary: Instructions should be given as to the appointment, duties and powers, of secretaries, particularly where the Act did not provide for it.

VI. Accounts and Audit: Other special details not provided in the act may be added to the articles of association.

VII. Dividends: Instructions should be taken in respect of how dividends are to be dealt with. For instance, instructions should be taken for reserves and capitalization of profits and reserves.

VIII. Others: Such other matters important to the business should be considered. Additionally, special particulars may be required in the case of companies limited by guarantee and unlimited companies because of their peculiar nature.

EFFECT OF MEMORANDUM AND ARTICLES OF ASSOCIATION

Specifically, significance of this effect of the memorandum and articles of association is that:

(i) A shareholder may bring an action to enforce any personal right contained in the articles. In *Burdett v. Standard and Exploration Co*[1], the English Court held that a member was entitled to enforce compliance by the company with a clause in articles giving him a right to a share certificate;

(ii) The company is entitled to sue its members for the enforcement and to restrain the breach by them of its articles, and to treat as irregular anything which is done in contravention thereof, as was decided in *Blackpool v. Hampson*;[2]

(iii) A member or officer of the company is entitled to sue a member for the enforcement of his right in the articles. Such a member or officer may sue in a representative capacity on behalf of himself and all other members or officers who may be affected, particularly if any other member or officers is affected by the alleged breach of such obligation;

(iv) The company, directors and officers shall be treated as having entered into a contract in terms of the clause in the articles and are bound accordingly. In *Swabey* v. *Port Darwin Gold Mining Co*[3], it was held that the plaintiff was entitled to recover on the footing of an implied contract in the terms of the clause;

(v) The directors/officers of a company are bound by the articles and if they act otherwise than in accordance with the provisions of the articles, they may render themselves liable to an action at the instance of the members and if as a result of the breach of duty any loss is suffered by the company, the directors are liable to refund of the company any damage so suffered;

(vi) Where the memorandum or articles empower any person to appoint or remove any director or other officer, he cannot be prevented from doing so and such power shall be enforceable by that person notwithstanding that he is not a member or officer of the company;

---

[1] (1889) 16 TLR 112

[2] (1883) 23 Ch D 1

[3] 1889 1 Meg 385

(vii) Any alteration to the articles is, for the purpose specified under the CAMA is treated as if it were part of the original articles and will bind the company members and directors and officers of the company accordingly;

(viii) The contractual relations created by the articles have statutory operation, and the court cannot rectify them under its equitable jurisdiction even if it is proved that they do not reflect the intention of the parties;

(ix) All money payable by any member to the company under memorandum or articles shall be a debt due from him to the company and shall be of the nature of a specialty debt.

INCORPORATION DOCUMENTS

The CAMA makes provision for incorporation documents to include:

(i) *Memorandum and Articles of Association*: These refer to the two documents that traditionally form the constitution of the company. As stated above in details above, the memorandum sets out the structure and conditions of the company while articles contain the special regulations for the internal management of affairs of the company as long as they are provided in the Act;

(ii) *Notice of the Address of the Registered Office*: The notice must state the address of the registered office and the head office of the company. It must be a physical address. Private mail bag or postal box address is not acceptable;

(iii) *List, particulars and consent of the first directors*: This is a statement in a prescribed form containing the list and particulars together with the consent of the persons who are to be the first directors of the company;

(iv) *Statement of the authorised share capital*: The statement which is a form must show the authorised share capital divided into shares of a fixed amount and must be signed by at least one director;

(v) *Any other necessary document*: In practical terms, the Commission requires additional documents to be produced and filed. Examples of these documents as provided by the Act are 'the Commission's form' consenting to the use of the proposed name, and 'business and resident permit' in the case of an alien who is proposed as a director, secretary or subscriber to the memorandum;

(vi) *Statutory declaration of compliance*: After all the requirements of the law have been complied with, and these documents are produced to the commission, there must be made a statutory declaration in a prescribed form by a legal practitioner that the requirements for registration have been complied with. It should be noted that the Commission may accept or refuse the declaration, but if it refuses it, then it must within 30 days of receipt of the declaration send to the person applying (declarant) a notice of its refusal and the ground of such refusal. Any other person listed for accreditation under Part B can carry out this function, particularly with the current direct online registration system. But statutory declaration of compliance must be carried out by a lawyer and attested before the Commissioner of Oaths.[4]

STAMPING OF DOCUMENTS

The Act requires the stamping of memorandum and articles of association and share capital form presented to the Federal Commissioner of Stamp Duties for stamping. The documents required for stamping are:

(i) two copies of the memorandum and articles of association respectively;

(ii) two copies of statement of authorised share capital (form CAC 2) and return of allotment.

Once a company is registered, it becomes a going concern, and becomes entitled to all the rights and liabilities.

[4] Section 40(3) CAMA

Chapter 6

INCORPORATED TRUSTEES

Incorporated Trustees are non-business and non-profit-making organizations established to facilitate acquisition of corporate personality by a community of persons bound together by custom, religion, nationality or any association of persons established for religious, educational, literary, scientific, social developments, sporting or charitable purposes.[1]

Such organizations are registrable under Part F of the CAMA and can operate without registration. But it cannot take advantage of the corporate identity of the trustees without being incorporated or registered with the Commission.

However, in *The Registered Trustees of God's Kingdom Society v. Registrar*[2], a religious society registered under Part F as a religious society. Another group called Kingdom of God Society applied for registration. When they advertised, the Trustees of GKS raised an objection saying the names were too similar and they carry out the same objectives and the names would be confusing. The Registrar rejected this contention of GKS. They went to the Federal High Court to compel the Registrar not to register Kingdom of God Society. The judge refused the application as the work of both societies was to propagate the word of God. Thus except there is evidence of outright fraud, registration will go ahead. This shows the difference between incorporated trustees and companies working for profit.

---

[1] Section 823 CAMA

[2] [2012] eKLR

FEATURES OF INCORPORATED TRUSTEES

The following features characterise non-profit organisations:

(i) Two or more persons can register as an incorporated trustee.

(ii) The trustees are the only persons who obtain legal personality and not all the members.

(iii) The name starts with the words "Incorporated Trustees of…"

(iv) It does not do business and does not distribute profits.

(v) It receives income as grants or levies.

(vi) The income must be applied solely towards the promotion of its objects.

(vii) Income not distributable but (out of pockets) expenses can be paid to members.

(viii) Ownership of landed property or undertaking in lieu.

It may be dissolved by the Federal High Court upon petition by the governing council; or one or more members of the body of trustee; or not less than 50% of total members of the association; or by the Commission.

SPECIFIC INSTRUCTIONS FOR FORMATION OF INCORPORATED TRUSTEES

A Solicitor engaged to register a non-profit organization should take note of these:

(i) Name of the proposed body or organization

(ii) The aims and objectives of the body

(iii) Name, address, occupation, number and ages of the trustees

(iv) Powers, duties and tenure of office of trustees

(v) The use and custody of the common seal

(vi) Matters relating to meetings i.e. types of meeting and rules of proceedings

(vii) Procedure for disbursement of funds and accounting policies.

ITEMS IN CONSTITUTION OF INCORPORATED TRUSTEES

Section 825 of the CAMA provides for the inclusion of the following items in the Constitution of a non-profit organization:

(i) State the name or title of the association which shall not conflict with that of a company, or with a business name or trade mark registered in Nigeria;
(ii) State the supremacy of the constitution
(iii) Nature of the association
(iv) Registered address
(v) The aims and objects of the association
(vi) Appointment, powers, duties, tenure of office and replacement of the trustees
(vii) Use and custody of the common seal
(viii) Meetings of the association
(ix) Number of members of the governing body, if any, the procedure for their appointment and removal, and their powers
(x) Where subscriptions and other contributions are to be collected, the procedure for disbursement of the funds of the association, the keeping of accounts and the auditing of such accounts
(xi) Board of Trustees
(xii) Sources of fund
(xiii) Auditors
(xiv) Meetings
(xv) Amendments
(xvi) Special clause
(xvii) Officers of the Association
(xviii) Functions of the officers
(xix) Election of officers
(xx) Tenure of office of officers
(xxi) Vacation of office by officers
(xxii) Remuneration of officers
(xxiii) Executive committee
(xxiv) Powers and duties of Trustees
(xxv) Bye-election

The Constitution may be dated and signed by the Chairman or Secretary of the association. In practice, only items i-xv are included in the constitution, while the rest are incorporated into the by-laws of the organization.

CHECKLIST OF ITEMS FOR REGISTERING INCORPORATED TRUSTEES

A solicitor should check to ensure that the following items are available before proceeding to the Commission with the registration of a non-profit organization:

(i) A formal letter of application for registration of Incorporated Trustees signed by the Chairman and Secretary or Applicant's Solicitor.

(ii) CAC/IT Form 1 in triplicate which must contain, among other things: The full names, residence, occupation and signature of the Trustees of the Applicant Body.

(iii) The name of the proposed corporate body which must contain the words "Incorporated Trustees of ..."

(iv) Form CAC 1: Form for availability of name/search report.

(v) The rules of the Applicant incorporating its objects.

(vi) CAC/IT/Constitution: Two copies of the Applicant's Constitution (copies with Enclosure A-H).

(vii) Address and registered office of the body.

(viii) Minutes of the meeting where the Trustees were appointed. Copy of the extract of the minutes of the meeting must show:
   I. Appointed trustees
   II. List of member present and absent
   III. The voting pattern
   IV. Signature of the chairman and Secretary of the association

(ix) Minutes of the meeting where the Special Clause was adopted into the Constitution, showing the list of members in attendance and signed by the Chairman and Secretary.

(x) Publication of 28 days' notice in two National dailies calling for objections from members of the public (could be one national and one local but at least one must be a national newspaper). The publication must contain:
   I. Name of the organization
   II. Names of all trustees
   III. Aims and objectives of the organization

IV. Call for objections
V. Name of the announcer

(xi) Sworn affidavit by each Trustee in the IT Declaration Form that they are not disqualified from acting as Trustees CAC/IT/Form 2: Trustee Declaration form.

(xii) Original Receipt from the Court or Notary Public where the Trustee Declaration form was sworn to.

(xiii) Payment of the prescribed filing fee.

(xiv) Two passport photographs each of the Trustees (one attached to the Application form and the other attached to the IT Declaration Form).

(xv) Impression or Drawing of the Common Seal of the Association.

(xvi) Letter authorising the person effecting the registration for the applicant.

(xvii) Evidence of availability of landed property or undertaking in lieu Documents required.

DIFFERENCES BETWEEN COMPANIES LIMITED BY GUARANTEE AND INCORPORATED TRUSTEES

There exists some distinction between organisations Limited by Guarantee and Incorporated Trustees. These include the underlisted:

(i) Companies Limited by Guarantee may do business but cannot share the profit among members while Incorporated Trustees may not do business.

(ii) Registration requirements differ for both of them, i.e. guarantee company requires approval of its Memorandum of Association by the Attorney General of the Federation while Incorporated Trustee do not have such requirement.

(iii) Incorporated Trustees must fulfil the advertisement requirement before registration but Guarantee Company need not advertise.

(iv) Memorandum and Articles of association are required to register a Company Ltd/Gte, while Incorporated Trustees require a Constitution.

(v) Company Ltd/Gte is managed by a board of Directors while Incorporated Trustees operates with a board of Trustees.

(vi) Evidence of payment of stamp duties is required to register Company Ltd/Gte, but not required to register Incorporated Trustees.

SIMILARITIES BETWEEN COMPANIES LIMITED BY GUARANTEE AND INCORPORATED TRUSTEES

The following similarities can be found between a company limited by guarantee and an incorporated trustee:

(i) Both exist for charitable causes.

(ii) They have their profits not distributed (objects are non-profit oriented).

(iii) Both bodies enjoy tax exemptions.

(iv) Both bodies are regulated by the Corporate Affairs Commission.

(v) Both enjoy benefits of incorporation or winding up of these bodies, and upon settling all claims against it, all the remaining assets of the body shall be transferred to a body with a similar object as the body dissolved (on winding up assets are not shared by the members).

Chapter 7

BUSINESS NAME REGISTRATION

REGISTRATION OF BUSINESS NAME

The term Business Name refers to the name or style under which the business is carried on, registrable with the Commission. The business could be a sole proprietorship or a firm. A firm represents an incorporated body of two or more individuals and one or more corporations who or which have entered into partnership with one another with a view to carrying on a business for profit.

A business could commence prior to registration, provided it is incorporated within 28 Days. Where such a business is not registered within 28 days and a breach of contract ensues, the business cannot sue. This is in contrast to the case of a company, as it must be registered before the commencement of business. As regards incorporated trustees however, registration is not mandatory but desirable.

Registration of Business Name is not compulsory in the following instances:[1]

(i) For an individual, if he uses his full name, initial and surname or the surname without any addition;

(ii) Firm/partnership: if the partners use their full name, initial and surname of the partners without any addition;

(iii) Company/corporation: when it uses its corporate name without any addition;

(iv) Partners having the same surname: if there is an addition of an "S" at the end of the surname.

[1] Section 814 (2) (a)-(d) CAMA

Registration of Business Name is however compulsory under these circumstances:

(i) If true surname of individual is not used;
(ii) If mixed surname and forename of the partners is used;
(iii) If addition of "& sons", "& co", "enterprises", etc., is made;
(iv) Any addition or subtraction to company's registered name

CHECKLIST FOR REGISTRATION OF BUSINESS NAME

(i) The proposed business name and alternative name to be reserved for 60 days: Form CAC 1 to check availability and reservation of the business name.
(ii) The general nature of the business.
(iii) Full address of the principal place of business and the branches.
(iv) Full particulars and personal details of proprietors.
(v) Confirm whether or not a minor is to be involved as a partner.
(vi) Date of commencement of business (28 days rule).
(vii) Residential address of proprietor.
(viii) Certificate of proficiency from proprietors in the relevant field if the business is for professional services.
(ix) Two passport photos from each of the proprietors/partners.
(x) Evidence of name change (married women).
(xi) Result of availability check and reservation of name: Form CAC 1
(xii) Completed application form (CAC/BN/FORM1).
(xiii) In a case where a minor is involved, a statement in writing in prescribed form signed by the minor and counter signed by either a magistrate, legal practitioners or police officer of or above the rank of ASP (Assistant Superintendent of Police) is required. The Registrar General has absolute discretion as to whether to register the business name who has a minor as a partner or not. In all correspondence emanating from the sole proprietorship or partnership, the word 'minor' must be written so that anyone would know that there is a minor in the business.

PARTNERSHIP DEED

Partnership deed or agreement is not part of the document registrable at the Commission. A partnership agreement need not be in writing, although writing is advantageous for the following reasons:

(i) Ease of official transactions;
(ii) Ease of conflict resolution;
(iii) Clear terms of obligations, liability and privileges;
(iv) Avoidance of common law presumptions (for example, the presumption that property belongs to the partners; presumption of dissolution of partnership by death of a partner, equal sharing of profit and loss.

The specific instructions to take in preparation of partnership agreement include these:

(i) Name of the parties and addresses of partners;
(ii) Name of partnership (this will determine whether or not the name should be registered);
(iii) Nature of business (this will determine the extent of liability of the firm);
(iv) Place of business – (where the business will be situated);
(v) When to commence business (time or period when the business will commence);
(vi) The business (to determine if there is a need for proficiency);
(vii) Contribution (if there is no indication of the contribution, the common law presumption of equal contribution will apply).
(viii) Management (how the partnership agreement will be managed);
(ix) Premium (amount paid by a partner to be admitted into partnership);
(x) Salary (mode of salary and what each partner will be entitled to);
(xi) Partnership properties (mode of acquired properties);
(xii) Bankers (Bankers of the partnership);
(xiii) Accounts (who the signatories to the accounts will be);
(xiv) Retirement (where partnership is not for a fixed period, the retirement of any partner will dissolve the partnership. Where it is

for a fixed duration, no partner can retire except by the consent of other members);

(xv) Profit and loss sharing (normally indicated as per the capital contribution. Where there is no deed, it will be equal sharing);

(xvi) Remuneration (to show that those managing are entitled to remuneration. If nothing in the deed, then no remuneration);

(xvii) Suspension and expulsion (unless this is taken, they are all equal and one cannot suspend another for indiscipline, extent to which a minor can be involved);

(xviii) Admission of new partners (provision for bringing in new members);

(xix) Duration/dissolution (where no duration date is provided, the implication is that it could come to an end at any day);

(xx) Dispute resolution (alternative dispute resolution is suggested in order that the disputes are not in public domain).

Chapter 8

PROMOTERS AND PRE-INCORPORATION CONTRACTS

PROMOTERS

Before the formation of a contract, some people play key roles in relation to the proposed company. A promoter is anyone who undertakes to take part in forming a company with reference to a given project and to set it going and takes the necessary steps to accomplish that purpose or undertakes raising capital for it. Thus before incorporation, a person or group of persons may decide to raise capital or perform some duties in furtherance of the incorporation of a company.

Promotion activities are vital aspects of company formation. Certainly, all companies are brought to life through the activities of a set of persons who arrange for their formation. The idea of forming a company is usually conceived by a person or group of persons who, in furtherance of this idea, will begin to take necessary steps to incorporate the company. For example, they may have to source for funds, find directors, acquire properties, prepare the prospectus and may also have to pay for the printing and all other expenses incidental in bringing the company into the world. The law regards such persons as promoters of the company.

A promoter is statutorily defined *prima facie* (on face value) as a person who undertakes to take part in forming a company with reference to a given project and to set it going, and who takes the necessary steps to accomplish that purpose, or who, with regard to a proposed or newly formed company, undertakes a part in raising capital for it. Promoters can be natural or artificial persons. In other words, a promoter is a human agent, whose activities often give birth to the company as a legal entity[1].

However, a person acting in a professional capacity for persons engaged in procuring the formation of the company shall not thereby be deemed to be a promoter[2]. The import of this is that a solicitor or valuer does not become a promoter merely by acting in a professional capacity to a promoter. Thus in *Twycross* v. *Grant* Cockburn C.J. reiterated that a "promoter is one who undertakes to form a company with reference to a given project and to set it going and who takes the necessary steps to accomplish that purpose. They framed the scheme; they not only provisionally formed the company but also were to the end its creators. They found the directors and qualified them. They prepared the prospectus, they paid for the printing and advertised the undertaking before the world."

Similarly, in *Adeniji* v. *Starcola Ltd*,[3] Kazeem J. described a promoter as any person who undertakes to take part in forming a company or who with regard to a proposed or newly formed company undertakes a part in raising capital for it is prima facie a promoter of the company provided he is not acting in his professional capacity.

It should be noted further that a promoter also refers to someone who instructs a solicitor to prepare a Memorandum and Articles of Association and register a company for him. In *Spicer (Keith) Ltd.* v. *Mansell*,[4] the defendant and Mr. X decided to have a business in the form of a limited company. Prior to the incorporation, Mr. X ordered goods from the plaintiff's company (supplier) intending to use it in the company's business. The goods were delivered to the defendant's address. The defendant and Mr. X had opened an account in the name of the proposed company, but the account was never used by them. Mr. X subsequently become insolvent and the supplier sued the defendant for the price of the goods on the ground that the defendant and Mr. X were carrying on business together. The issue as formulated for

---

[1] (2002) FWLR (Pt. 121) 1837 at 1843
[2] *Adeniji* v. *Starcola (Nig.) Ltd* (1972) 1 SC 202
[3] Supra
[4] [1970] 1 All ER 462, [1970]

determination was whether parties who get together to form a company will be considered as partnership or not. The Court held that the fact that they were working together to set up a company does not make them doing business with a view of making profit, hence, there is no partnership agreement. The Court held further that a person who purchased a property expressly as trustee for an intended company would by so doing be deemed a promoter.

However, a solicitor who prepared the Articles and Memorandum of Association and registered a company for his client who paid him (the solicitor) his professional fees is not a promoter. A solicitor who drafts the Memorandum and Articles of Association in line with the promoters instructions and the accountant who values the assets of a business to be purchased are only giving expert or professional assistance to the promoters and will be paid for their services, they are not promoters as was held in *Re: Great Wheal Poolgooth Ltd.*[5]

If, however, the solicitor and accountant did more by way of helping his client to obtain directors for the company, they would be regarded as promoters. The law looks at the facts in determining whether or not a person is a promoter. Thus, the Court held in *Gluckstein* v. *Barnes*[6] that a person who purchased property for his own use and later decided to form a company to acquire the property became a promoter only from the time when he took steps to form the company. If a professional is interested in the new company personally, he is deemed to be a promoter, even if he rendered professional services. It is however, difficult to differentiate between a promoter and a professional as a professional is not a promoter[7].

A person may become a promoter of a company even after registration of a company. For instance, if he had assisted in procuring capital for the company to pay promotion expenses when the company was newly formed. A person becomes a promoter from the very moment he begins to take part in forming a company or in setting it

[5] (1883) 53 LJ CH 42
[6] [1900] AC 240
[7] See *Tyrrel* v. *Bank of London*(1862,10HL,case 26)

going. It should also be noted that an existing company may be a promoter for another new company.

Promoters play an important role in Foreign Direct Investment by acting as middlemen between the government of Nigeria and a foreign company, among other activities.

A promoter cannot be regarded as an agent or trustee of a company but he occupies a fiduciary relationship with the company, as was held in *Garba* v. *Sheba International (Nigeria) Ltd.*[8]

Similarly, an act of a promoter cannot bind an unincorporated company. Thus in *Orhobo* v. *Tarka*,[9] the 1st Defendant contracted on behalf of the 2nd defendant -a company which was unincorporated at the time for an assignment of the plaintiff's leasehold to the 2nd defendant. The 1st defendant had falsely represented to the plaintiff that the 2nd defendant company was already registered and that he was a director and shareholder to it. Acting on this misrepresentation, the plaintiff executed an assignment of the lease to the 2nd defendant company. When the plaintiff discovered that the 2nd defendant company was only incorporated after the assignment was made, he claimed a declaration that the assignment of the lease was void for misrepresentation. The defendants counter-claimed for specific performance of the agreement to assign on the ground of part performance. The court held that the crucial point to decide in this case was what became the effect of the agreement entered into by the plaintiff and the 1st defendant before the incorporation of the 2nd defendant company.

It must however be emphasized that a contractual obligation entered into on behalf of the company before its incorporation is not binding on the company but the promoter can agree to be personally bound on the contract. The law is that before its incorporation, a company has no capacity to contract. Consequently, in common law nobody can contract for it as agent because an act which cannot be done by the principal himself cannot be done by him through an agent,

---

[8] (2002) 1 NWLR (pt. 748,372 at 401

[9] (1976)11 CCHCJ262

nor can a pre-incorporation contract be ratified by the company after its incorporation. If a pre-incorporation contract is purported to be made by a company which does not exist, the contract is a nullity, and neither the company when formed, nor the promoter whose signature is added can sue or be sued on the contract. To make a contract valid there must be parties existing at the time who are capable of contracting. Both upon principle and upon authority, a non-existing company cannot be held liable under a contract entered into before its incorporation and it cannot take any benefit under it.

(a) Promoters Activities

As regards the *activities of promoters*, both at common law and as defined by CAMA, the term 'promoter' includes persons who assist in the formation of a company and setting it going.

An example of such relevant promotional activities required for pre-incorporation would include the following:

(i) Formation of companies, namely obtaining first directors, looking company secretary, shareholders, etcetera.
(ii) Negotiating an agreement.
(iii) Purchasing or otherwise acquiring property for the company.
(iv) Raising capital for the newly formed companies.
(v) Obtaining local registration.
(vi) Advertising and employing staff/workers of the company especially where highly skilled employees are involved (such as pilots, engineers, doctors, etcetera).
(vii) Deciding on the most suitable type of company to be formed.
(viii) Designating the directors of the company.
(ix) Inspection of business premises and making it suitable for operations.
(x) Engaging the services of relevant professionals (such as solicitors, accountant, licenses, estate valuers and surveyors, etcetera).
(xi) Applying for relevant permits/approvals to form the company where foreign partners are involved in the business.

(xii) Gathering relevant information from the subscribers and first directors.

(xiii) Entering in written contracts with the professionals to dispense their services to the company to be formed. The essence is to agree on the fee, give clear instructions etcetera.

(xiv) Taking care of all logistics, such as purchase of office equipment, machine, assessing internet services for the company etcetera.

(xv) Outsourcing of the market for the products to be sold.

(xvi) Sourcing for raw material.

(xvii) Acquiring the technology to be used in the company where one is required, such as entering into a transfer of technology contract.

(b) Duties of Promoters

Promoters stand in an advantageous position against the company. Consequently, the law imposes a duty on them. Thus, in *Erlanger* v. *New Sombrero Phosphate Company*,[10] where Lord Cairns observed that promoters have in their hands the creation and moulding of the company. They have the power of defining how and when and in what shape and under what supervision it shall start into existence and begin to act as a trading corporation.

The duties of promoters also goes with corresponding rights and liabilities:

(i) ***Duty of Fiduciary Relationship:*** The promoter stands in a fiduciary relationship to the company and must observe utmost good faith in transactions entered on behalf of the company. Accordingly, he shall observe the utmost good faith towards the company in any transaction with it or on its behalf and shall compensate the company for any loss suffered by reason of his failure to do so;

(ii) ***Duty of Accountability***: the promoter must account for any profit made from the use of information on property acquired in the course of his duty to the company. Thus, a promoter who acquired

[10] (1878) 3 App Cas 1218, 48 LJ Ch 73, 27 WR 65, [1874-80] All ER Rep 271, 39 LT 269

any property or information in circumstances in which it was his duty as a fiduciary to acquire it on behalf of the company shall account to the company for such property and for any profit which he may have made from the use of such property or information. In *Jubilee Cotton Mills* v. *Lewis*,[11] it was held that a promoter who received, by way of a secret reward for his part in promoting a company, an allotment of shares which had been allotted before a statement in lieu of prospectus, which was then required by law, has been filed was liable to account for the profit made on the resale of the shares. The transaction between the promoter and the company can be rescinded by the company except where after full disclosure by the promoter, such transaction is ratified on behalf of the company by either an independent Board of directors (that is, independent of the promoter) or at a General Meeting at which such promoter cannot vote or by all members of the company. In Erlanger's case, a syndicate of which he was the head, purchased an island in the West Indies said to contain valuable mines of phosphate for 55,000 pounds. He formed a company to buy this island and a contract was made between "X", a nominee of the syndicate, and the company for its purchase at 110,000 pounds. It was held that there had been no disclosure by the promoters of the profit they were making. Therefore, the company was entitled to rescind the contract and recover the purchase money from him and other members of the syndicate. Thus a promoter has a duty to disclose any property or information which he acquired on behalf of the company especially where he has used the information or property to gain a benefit. Similarly, he has a duty to account for money or properties received in the course of the promotion Activities;

(iii) Duty not to make secret profit; where made, it must be returned to the company;

(iv) Duty to disclose conflicting interests in transactions with the company;

[11] [1924] UKHL J0509-1

(v) Duty not to expose the company to loss.

(c) Remuneration of Promoters

A promoter is entitled to reward in view of the great skill, energy and ingenuity which the work of promoters involves. The reward for services employed in the promotion exercise may take a variety of forms. He may purchase a property and sell to the company at a profit, or he may negotiate a sale on commission.

The promoter may also take shares of the company which are credited as fully paid-up, in lieu of payment of remuneration and expenses. On the alternative, he may be given shares to be paid for within specified time at par where shares will normally have been appreciated.

In the event where a prospectus is issued, it must disclose the amount or benefit paid or given within the two preceding years or intended to be given to any promoter, as well as the consideration for the payment or the giving of the benefit[12]. Again, a promoter could enter into personal contracts with persons who ask him to form the company.

However, a promoter has no right against the company to pay for his promotion services and expenses unless *there is a valid contract for him to do so, as was held in Re English and Colonial Produce Company.* Moreover, since pre-incorporation contracts are not binding on, or enforceable by, or against the company, it may be difficult for promoters to have an enforceable contractual right to remuneration for their services and indemnify for their expenses. Thus, in Re National Motor Mail Coach Co. Ltd, it was held that the promoters were not entitled to prove or recover the expenses they incurred in incorporating the company.

The foregoing difficulty is more real in theory than in practice because recovery of preliminary expenses and remuneration does not present much difficulty. Usually, *the* Articles of Association will contain a provision authorising the directors to pay them though it does not go

---

[12] Section 50 (1) ISA

to the extent of constituting a contract between the company and the promoter(s). Unlike the common law position, a promoter can now recover remuneration by action against the company if the contract is ratified or adopted by the company after incorporation *by virtue of the provision for ratification as enabled by* CAMA. Thus, the Court in *Garba* v. *Sheba International Co,*[13] emphasized that the court held that it has always been the case that a promoter has no right against the company for payment of services rendered before the incorporation of the company and that a promise to pay him by the company is neither binding nor enforceable against the company because the consideration is a past consideration.

(d) Liabilities of Promoters

One of the liability of promoters is the duty to rescind the transaction except ratified by the company.

Where there is a breach of the duties imposed on a promoter, the company can take any of the following actions for redress:

(i) Action to render account of money or property received in the course of promotion activities.

(ii) Action to account for secret profits made which were discovered by the company.

(iii) Action for damages for wrongful exploitation of confidential information (fraudulent misrepresentation).

(iv) Refusal to ratify pre-incorporation contract tainted with conflict of interest.

(v) Action to rescind contracts perfected not by the Promoter.

It is important to note that there is no limitation period for a company to sue a promoter under this section. However, the court may give relief from liability to the promoter in whole or in part and on such terms as it thinks fit from liability hereunder if in all the circumstances, including lapse of time, the court thinks it equitable to do so.

The liability of promoters includes remedies for breach. There are basically three major remedies, viz.:

---

[13] Supra

(i) The company may sue the promoter for damages for breach of his fiduciary obligation to the company[14].

(ii) The company may rescind the contract and recover the purchase money paid where the promoter sold his own property to the company. The Court held in a decided case that the law requires the promoter to disclose such fact before he can be relieved of any liability for failure to disclose. Where he discloses such facts, it will no longer be regarded as secret profit and he may be allowed to keep it. Disclosure must be made to:

I. the Board of Directors who must be independent of the control of the promoters; or

II. Where no such Board exists then disclosure must be made to the shareholders either in a General Meeting or in a circular or prospectus issued by the promoters on behalf of the company[15].

(iii) The promoter may be compelled by the company to account for any profit he made.[16]

PRE-INCORPORATION CONTRACTS

The previous chapter discussed the registration of a company and the procedure involved. Sometimes before a company is registered, and in anticipation of registration, there is a need for a company to enter into some contracts. The contracts entered into between the anticipated company and other parties are known as pre-incorporation contracts. This section will therefore introduce pre-incorporation contracts and the legal implications of such contracts.

Pre-incorporation contract refers to various types of agreements which a proposed company enters into before its eventual registration. These are contracts purported to be made usually by promoters on behalf of a company before it is incorporated[17]. That is, before a company is formally registered, a promoter may have entered into some

---

[14] *Re Leeds & Hanley Theatres of Varieties, Ltd.* [1902] 2 Ch. 809

[15] *Erlanger* v. *New Sombrero Phosphate Ltd supra*

[16] *Gluckstein* v. *Barnes* supra

[17] *Sparka Electrics Nig. Ranor* v. *Ponmile* (1986) 2 NWLR (Pt. 23) 519 at 525

contracts on behalf of the company before incorporation. Most often than not, these contracts are initiated and executed by promoters. The law is that where a contract is entered into on behalf of a company not yet formed, the company will not be bound by the contract.

Similarly, the company cannot even sue on the contract, as was held in the case of *Caligara* v. *Sartori Company Limited*[18]. The issue for determination here was whether a contract entered into by a promoter of a company before its incorporation is enforceable. The facts are that sometimes in December 1956, Sartori (a promoter of the Defendant) approached the Plaintiff for a cash loan for the Defendant Company. At the time, unknown to the Plaintiff, the Defendant was not in existence. The plaintiff gave a cheque for 800 pounds in the name of the company to Sartori who cashed it on 9th January, 1957. The company was eventually incorporated on 24th January 1957. The court held that at the time the cheque was cashed, the defendant company was not in existence and it could not be said to have benefitted from the contract. The plaintiff's case failed.

In the same vein, the court held in *Kelnar* v. *Baxter*[19] that at Common Law, a pre-incorporation contract was not binding on the company because there was no principal on behalf of whom an agent could have contracted and that the company was not permitted to ratify or adopt it.[20]

However, if in the course of formation of the contract a promoter agreed in writing to be bound by a contract entered into before the company was formed, and then such a promoter will be bound. The argument here is that a company has no legal existence before its incorporation. Therefore it is not capable of entering into any valid contract itself.

However, a company can be bound by a pre-incorporation contract if after its incorporation it ratifies any contract entered into on

---

[18] (1963) 3 All N. L. R. page 543

[19] (1866) LR 2 CP 174

[20] *Trans Bridge Co Ltd.* v. *Survey Int'l Co. Ltd (1986) LCN/2265(SC); Edokpolor and Co. Ltd* v. *Sem-Edo Wire Industry Ltd (1989)LCN/0091(CA); Re English Colonial Produce 2 Ch. 435, 4 B. R. C. 748 (1906)*

its behalf prior to incorporation. The company can ratify a contract after its formation as if it were in existence when the contract was entered into; the company then becomes bound and entitled to the benefits thereof. Before such ratification of the contract, if there is no express agreement to the contrary, the promoter will personally be liable and can benefit from the contract.[21]

Apart from ratification, the only way in which the company could be party to the contract was to enter into a new contract in terms of the one purportedly entered into on his behalf. The reason for this is that such a company is not yet a person in the eyes of the law. A pre-incorporation contract at Common Law is, therefore, not binding on the company. Thus the Court in the case of *Caligara* v. *Giovanni Santore Ltd*[22] emphasized that a company cannot ratify or adopt a contract purported to have been entered into on its behalf by its promoters prior to its incorporation.

In any event, *Section 72* of CAMA has now modified this rule by providing that any contract or other transaction purporting to be entered into by the company or by any person on behalf of the company, prior to its formation, may be ratified by the company after its formation and thereupon the company shall be bound by and entitled to the benefit thereof as if it has been in existence at the date of such contract. The Supreme Court upheld this position when it held in *Societe Generale Bank (Nig) Ltd* v. *Societe Generale Favouriser & Ors*[23] after reviewing the common law position, that what has now changed in this country for the CAMA makes it possible for pre-incorporation contracts to be ratified by a company after its incorporation and thereby becoming bound by it and entitled to the benefit thereof. Essentially, the company can ratify after formation as if it were in existence when the contract was entered into. The company then becomes bound and entitled to the benefits therein.

The effect of ratification in this context is that the law merely treats the company as if it has been in existence at the date of such contract or

[21] (2005) 5 NWLR (PT. 917) 160 at 117
[22] Supra
[23] (1999) 11. NWLR (pt. 628) 521

other transaction and had been a party thereto. The theoretical basis of the power of ratification which companies are given under this section, is, obviously, predicated on agency principle by which a principal has the legal competence to ratify unauthorised acts of his agent. The power of ratification endowed upon incorporated companies in this section, it must be pointed out, is co-existence with that exercisable under normal agency relationship. Therefore, ratification may be expressed or implied.

The question whether or not the insertion of a pre-incorporation contract in the object clause of a memorandum of a company would make it binding on the company surfaced in the case of *Edokpolor and Company Ltd.* v. *Seme-Edo Wire Industries,*[24] where the Supreme court stated that the Object Clause is no more than a list of the objects the company may lawfully carry out. They are certainly not objects that the company must execute. The inclusion of the terms of the pre-incorporation contracts in the Memorandum of a company is an indication of a strong desire that the proposed company after incorporation should execute the terms of the agreement so included.

Finally as regards the *types of pre-incorporation contracts,* there are a variety of them, some of which include the underlisted:

(i) Joint Venture Agreement (especially between Nigerians and aliens)
(ii) Shareholders' Agreements
(iii) Contract for Payment of Promoters' expenses
(iv) Directors' service contract (appointment of the Managing Director)
(v) Contract Agreement for the acquisition of business or property (Takeover agreement)
(vi) Contract for Conversion of partnership to incorporated companies
(vii) Confidentiality/non-disclosure agreements
(viii) Employment contracts
(ix) Procurement contract
(x) Deed of assignment
(xi) Commercial Memorandum of understanding
(xii) Formation Agreement

---

[24] *Supra*

(xiii) Partnership Agreement
(xiv) Technology transfer agreement
(xv) Loan agreement.

Chapter 9

POST-INCORPORATION MATTERS

PRELIMINARY MATTERS BEFORE COMMENCEMENT OF BUSINESS

After the incorporation of a company into a going concern, certain steps are taken prior to the take-off of such business. These are steps or procedural arrangements undertaken after a business is incorporated but before it commences any business. They include preliminary matters before commencement of business and corporate searches.

Upon incorporation, a company has to put up some structure around itself before commencement of business by undertaking certain actions, some of which are required by law and hence must be complied with as of necessity. Two of such basic requirements are publication of name and statutory books.

PUBLICATION OF NAME

The publication of a company's name is a statutory requirement. The CAMA provides that every company, after incorporation shall:

(i) Paint or affix, and keep painted or affixed its name and registration number on the outside of every office or place in which its business is carried on, in a conspicuous position, in letters easily legible;

(ii) Have its name engraved in legible characters on its seals; and

(iii) Have its name and registration number mentioned in legible characters in all business letters of the company and in all notices, advertisements, and other official publications of the company, and in all bills of exchange, promissory notes, endorsements, cheques, and orders for money or goods purporting to be signed by or on behalf of the company, and in all bills or parcels, invoices, receipts, and letters of credit of the company.

It is worth mentioning here that non-compliance with the foregoing provision would make the company and its officers liable to a fine for every day that the default continues to survive. The officers of the company that allowed the name of the company to be used in any document would also be liable to pay a fine. This implies that the true names and nationality of all the operators of the company as well as the registration number of the company or business must be published in all trade catalogues, trade circulars and business letters in legible letters.

Corporate name refers to the name with which an incorporated company is registered with the Corporate Affairs Commission, and which the Certificate of Incorporation bears. Trade name on the other hand is the name style by which a Company conducts its affairs, that is the usual name by which the company is known by most. For example, United Bank of Africa PLC carries out business under the acronym "UBA".

A Company can seek to protect its trade name and corporate name as a company can mount its sign-point with its trade name if it is accompanied with its registration number. The publication of name in accordance with Section 548 (1) (a)–(c) is thus in three forms namely:

(i) Publication of name in name plate;
(ii) Publication of name in common seal; and
(iii) Publication of name in official documentation and bills of exchange.

The necessity for publication of names is aimed at identifying the true operators of the business.

STATUTORY BOOKS

These are books statutorily required to be kept by a Company preparatory to commencement of business to be used for various purposes in the course of the company's business transactions. The statutory books are these:

(a) Register of Members:

This register is to contain detailed information such as members –

(i) Names;
(ii) Addresses;
(iii) Ascriptions;
(iv) Number of shares;
(v) Class of shares;
(vi) Amount paid on the shares;
(vii) Whether cash or other considerations are paid on the shares; and
(viii) The date when the particular was registered as a member.

It is worth noting that the name of a member must be registered within 28 days of his acquiring the shares and in the case of a subscriber within 28 days of incorporating the company. The names of all the members of a company must be entered into the register of members, in fact it is not the subscription of shares that make a person a member of a company but the entering of the name into the register of members. This is kept in the registered office or other arranged accessible place within Nigeria. If kept outside the Registered Office, the Commission must be notified.

(b) Index of Members

The index of members is to contain a sufficient indication to enable the account of that member in the register to be readily found on the Register of Members. Where the company arranged that the Register of Members also include an index, there will be no need for a separate book as Index of Members. The index of members is only required where the membership of the company is more than 50. In essence, the Index of Members is meant only for public companies whose membership exceeds 50.

(c) Register of Substantial Interest in Shares

Public companies are required to keep this register in respect of those who acquire voting rights in the annual general meeting of a Public Company (namely, those who have up to 10 per cent and above of the total shares to notify the Company).

(d) Register of Charges

This register is used to keep copies of charges affecting property of the company. Securities or debentures charged on the properties of the company either on land, machinery or unpaid shares of the company or book debt of the company have to be included on the register and kept in the registered office for inspection. This requirement is applicable to both private and public companies.

(e) Register of Debenture Holders

Companies are mandated to keep a register of the names, addresses and particulars of the debenture holders, the principal of the debenture and the debentures held by each of them and the terms of the issue within 30 days of creation and 30 days of ceasing.

(f) Minutes Book

All companies are mandated to keep this book, which must contain the minutes of proceedings of general meetings, Directors (Board) meetings and Minutes of its Managers' Meeting. It is required to be open for inspection and kept in bound books or leaflets or in electronic storage devices easily retrievable and available for inspection. The Minutes Book shall prima facie be evidence of the proceedings. It should be noted that minutes are highlights of the proceedings of a meeting as opposed to record of proceedings of meetings, the latter being near verbatim record of the events at a meeting.

(g) Register of Directors' Share Holdings

This register is mandatory for all companies, as it records the shares and debentures of Directors in the company. It is open for inspection to the Commission always and between 14 days before and three days after the annual general meeting for members and debenture holders. A separate book is not kept for subsidiary companies that are wholly owned by the holding company.

(h) Register of Directors and Secretaries

This book is meant for all companies' types as it contains the names, residential address, nationality, date of birth and other particulars of other past and present Directors and Secretaries of companies and the Company is expected to notify the Commission within 14 days of appointment and ceasing.

Accounting Records

All companies are required to keep this book, which shall show and explain the transactions of the company. In other words, the financial position of the company and its assets and liabilities are to be kept sufficient to show and explain the transactions of the Company.

CORPORATE SEARCHES

Corporate search entails the verification of the particulars of a corporate body submitted to the Commission in view of the fact that all documents filed in the Companies Registry at the Commission are public records available for inspection. As such, any member of the public may obtain certified true copies on the payment of prescribed fees.

Corporate searches are usually conducted at the Commission's Headquarters in Abuja. However, in case of the searches relating to Business Names, they are conducted at the Zonal Headquarters where Business Names are registered.

(a) Reasons for Corporate Searches

There are several reasons for conducting corporate searches, some of which include:

(i) Confirmation of due incorporation/registration
(ii) Operation of a bank account
(iii) Granting of credit facilities
(iv) Due diligence/legal audit especially in the case of Banks
(v) Investigation of a company/organisation by CAC or other
(vi) Regulatory/Security agencies

(vii) Verification of corporate profile for award of contracts/projects etcetera.

(viii) Verify particulars of registered organizations

(ix) To obtain Certified True Copies of registered documents needed in court proceedings.

(b) Procedure for Conducting Corporate Search

(i) Obtain and complete CAC prescribed form for search from the Commission.

(ii) Payment of search fee and fees for Certified True Copy of documents requested for.

(iii) Evidence of payment of annual return up to date if application is made on behalf of the company or any of its directors or secretary.

(iv) Preparation of the search report and attaching the CTC of the relevant documents received from the Commission.

(c) Checklist for Content of Search Report

A report is expected to be written after conducting a search at the Commission. These are the checklist of items to be included in the report:

(i) Client's Name and address;

(ii) Date of search;

(i) Place of search;

(iv) Name of Company;

(v) Registered Certificate No (RC. No.);

(vi) Date of Incorporation;

(vii) Business/Object;

(viii) Subscribers.

Chapter 10

CONVERSION AND ALTERATIONS

CONVERSION AND RE-REGISTRATION OF COMPANIES

Conversion of companies occurs where a company which was originally registered under a particular type of company, changes its status by converting it to another type of company and re-registering it without incorporating a new company. This is done by following the laid down procedures and is subject to certain restrictions.

Of course, this does not imply that the company has changed its legal personality or that its former rights and liabilities are extinguished. As such, all its former rights and liabilities continue with it despite the conversion. For example, the recent ₦25 Billion recapitalisation policy of the Central Bank of Nigeria necessitated banks to change their status from private to public companies in order to increase their number of shareholders.

A private company can be converted to a public company and vice versa. Similarly, a company limited by shares may be converted to an unlimited company. An unlimited company may be converted to a company limited by shares. A statutory corporation may also be re-registered as a Company Limited by shares.

Apart from the above conversions, all other types of conversion and re-registration that are prohibited are:

(i) A private company previously re-registered as unlimited cannot re-register to a public company.

(ii) Where a company attained its limited liability by re-registration from unlimited status, it cannot re-register back to unlimited.

(iii) A public company or a company which has previously been re-registered as an unlimited company shall not be registered as unlimited.

(iv) A re-registered unlimited company cannot be re-registered as a Public Company or a company limited by guarantee.

(v) There is no provision for direct conversion from Public Company to Unlimited Company. It follows therefore that such a company must convert to a Private Company and then to Unlimited, but it cannot re-register back to Public Company.

The procedure for conversion depends on the type of company. Each of these has a slightly different method of re-registration.

PROCEDURE FOR RE-REGISTRATION OF PRIVATE COMPANY (LTD) TO PUBLIC COMPANY (PLC)

The procedure for re-registration of private company to public company is as follows:

(i) Board of directors' resolution proposing the conversion/re-registration.

(ii) Notice of meeting to members indicating that a special resolution is going to be passed at the general meeting.

(iii) Special resolution of the general meeting approving the conversion/re-registration.

(iv) Consequential alterations made in the Memorandum and Articles of association. For example:

- I. Name Clause,
- II. Type of Company Clause,
- III. Increase in Share Capital (if applicable),
- IV. Removal of restrictions on transfer of shares and regulations on appointment of Director and Secretary.

(v) Application to the Commission for re-registration with the following documents:

- I. Form CAC 1 (availability and reservation of name).
- II. Special resolution.
- III. Copy of Memorandum and Articles of association duly altered.
- IV. Written statement certified on oath by Directors and Secretary that paid up capital as at date of application is not less than 25% of authorised capital.

V. Statutory declaration by a Director and Secretary that the resolution has been passed and that the Company's assets are not less than the aggregate of the paid up capital and undistributed reserves.

VI. Copy of prospectus or statements in lieu of prospectus delivered within the preceding 12 months to the Securities and Exchange Commission (if applicable).

VII. Copy of balance sheet as at date of resolution or the preceding 6 months.

VIII. Evidence of up to date annual returns.

IX. Original Receipt of prescribed filing fees.

(vi) If satisfied with the requirements, CAC issues a new certificate, which serves as a prima facie evidence that all the requirements for conversion and re-registration have been complied with.

(a) Consequential Alterations to Memorandum of Association

(i) Alteration of name clause to end with PLC.

(ii) Alteration of authorised share capital clause to meet legal minimum for public company.

(iii) Alteration of type clause to show that it is a public company.

(b) Consequential Alterations to Articles of Association

(i) The name must be changed to end with PLC.

(ii) Removal of the restriction on the transfer of its shares.

(iii) Amendment of the qualification of Directors and appointment of those above 70 years old.

(iv) Amendment of the qualification of the company Secretary.

(v) Written Resolutions not to be allowed.

RE-REGISTRATION OF PUBLIC COMPANY TO PRIVATE COMPANY

The procedure for re-registration of public company to private company is as follows:

(i) Board of directors' resolution proposing the conversion/re-registration.

(ii) Notice for the general meeting is issued to pass a special resolution.

(iii) Special resolution by the general meeting approving the conversion/re-registration.

(iv) Consequential alterations made in the Memorandum and Articles of Association.

(v) Wait for 28 days for any application to cancel the resolution at the Federal High Court. Application can be brought by any member with not less than 5% of the nominal value of the company's issued capital or not less than 5% of the Company's members but not by a person who has consented to or voted in favour of the resolution.

(vi) If no application is made after 28 days, then the Company should deliver within 15 days to the CAC an application for re-registration with the relevant forms.

(vii) If application is made for cancellation, and the Federal High Court rejects the application, it is withdrawn, then the Company shall deliver to the CAC an application for re-registration within 15 days with the following documents:

I. Application in a prescribed form for the re-registration.
II. Copy of the Special resolution passed.
III. Certified True Copy of Court Order refusing cancellation of resolution (where applicable).
IV. Availability and reservation of Re-registration name in duly approved Form CAC 1.
V. Copy of Memorandum and Articles of association duly altered.
VI. Original receipt of payment of duly approved Form CAC 1.
VII. Evidence of filing of annual returns.

(viii) If application is made for cancellation and the Court confirms the cancellation, then submit to the Commission within 15 days the following documents:

I. Printed copy of the resolution.
II. CTC of the Court order.

(ix) If satisfied with the requirements, CAC issues a new certificate which serves as a *prima facie* evidence that all the requirements for conversion and re-registration have been complied with.

RE-REGISTRATION OF PRIVATE COMPANY LIMITED BY SHARES TO UNLIMITED COMPANY (LTD – ULTD)

The procedure for re-registration of Private Company to Unlimited Company is as follows:

(i) Board of Directors' Resolution proposing the conversion.

(ii) Subscription of the prescribed Form of Assent to the re-registration by all the members or on their behalf.

(iii) Statutory Declaration by all the Directors of the company that the persons who or on whose behalf, the form of assent is subscribed constitutes the whole membership of the company and that all persons who subscribed on behalf of a member did so with the members authority.

(iv) Pass a Special Resolution altering the Memorandum & Articles of the current status of the company.

(v) Stamp the altered memorandum and articles of association.

(vi) Apply to the Commission in the prescribed form with the following documents:

I. Form CAC 1A-Availability and reservation of new name duly approved.

II. Application in prescribed form setting out the alterations signed by a director and secretary or two known Directors.

III. A prescribed form of Assent of members in support of the re-registration.

IV. A statutory declaration made by the Directors of the Company.

V. Stamped Memorandum and Articles of association as altered.

VI. Receipt of filing fees.

VII. Evidence of filing Annual Returns up to date.

RE-REGISTRATION OF UNLIMITED COMPANY TO PRIVATE COMPANY LIMITED BY SHARES (ULTD – LTD)

The procedure for re-registration of Unlimited Company to Private Company Limited by Shares is as follows:

(i) Board meeting and Resolution to propose the conversion and re-registration.

(ii) General meeting passes a Special Resolution to convert and re-registration as LTD.

(iii) The Special Resolution shall state the proposed authorised share capital and the consequential alterations in the Memorandum and Articles of Association.

(iv) Application in the prescribed form signed by a Director and Secretary or two known Directors.

(v) Alteration of Memorandum and Articles of Association.

(vi) Payment of Registration fees.

(vii) Evidence of filing annual returns to date.

(viii) Filing of a copy of the Resolution and other documents at the Commission within 15 days of passing the Resolution.

It should be noted that the members are still liable on previous obligations of the company.

RE-REGISTRATION OF STATUTORY CORPORATION AS COMPANY LIMITED BY SHARES

A statutory corporation could be privatised and either unbundled into small companies or re-registered as public Limited by share. The essential features of the conversion are that:

(i) The company would cease to be a statutory corporation and be formally registered with the Commission accordingly.

(ii) The company will have Memorandum and Articles of Association which becomes its source of governance rather than the enabling laws which set up the corporation in the first instance.

(iii) The company ceases to enjoy status of statutory corporation being entitled to a Pre Action Notice. This is a written notice informing a corporation about an intention to sue it.

The procedure for re-registration of Statutory Corporation as Company Limited by Shares are as follows:

(i) Bureau of Public Enterprises (BPE) obtains a government white paper to commercialise and privatise the enterprise and arrange its sale.

(ii) The Bureau takes steps to incorporate the new company as a public limited liability company at the Commission and submits all approved documents.

(iii) The Bureau hands over the new company to its core investors.

It should be noted that it is only a public company converting to a private company or vice versa that can re-register without any restriction or prohibition.

CHANGE OF COMPANY NAME

The Act provides that if a company is registered under a name identical with that by which a company in existence is previously registered or so nearly resembling it as to be likely to deceive, the first mentioned company may, with the approval of the Commission, change its name. If the Commission so directs within six months of its being registered under that name, the company concerned shall change its name within a period of 6 weeks from the date of the direction or such longer period as the Commission may allow.

(a) Compulsory Change of Name

Some circumstances warrant compulsory change of name. A company may be directed by the Commission to compulsorily change its name under the following circumstances:

(i) Inadvertent registration of a new company by a name of an already existing company or so nearly resembling it as to be likely to deceive. An example of this is the case of *Niger*

Chemists v. Nigeria Chemist[1] where the parties operated on the same street and carried on the same business, the court held that there was passing off;

(ii) Later discovery that the company's name conflicts with an existing trade mark or business name registered in Nigeria without the consent of the owner of the trade mark.

After a successful Passing-off action, the court can direct the newly registered company to change its name as was demonstrated in *Halifax Plc* v. *Halifax Re-Possession Ltd & Ors.*[2]

(b) Voluntary Change of Name

The Procedure for change of name is provided for under the CAMA as follows:

(i) Pass Board Resolution approving the change.

(ii) Fill Form CAC 1 availability check and reservation of name, for approval of the name.

(iii) Notice of meeting specifying the intention to pass a resolution for change of name.

(iv) Pass Special Resolution for the change of the company name.

(v) Make consequential alterations on the Memorandum and Articles of Association.

(vi) Apply to the Commission for consent on the change of name attached with documents, viz.:

  I. Duly signed copies of the Special Resolution of the company and the Board Resolution.

  II. Stamped copies of the Memorandum and Articles reflecting the new name.

  III. The approved Form CAC 1.

  IV. Original Certificate of Incorporation for cancellation.

  V. Evidence of filing annual Returns.

  VI. Receipt of filing fees.

  VII. Advertisement of the name change by the Commission in its official Gazette.

---

[1](1961) 1 All NLR 171.

[2] (2002) EWCA Civ 1060

VIII. Issuance of a new Certificate of Incorporation by the Commission.

It should be noted that the Registered Company Number (RC No.) of the company is still maintained after the change of name.

ALTERATION OF OBJECT CLAUSE

The business or object clause in a company's Memorandum may be altered by Special Resolution at a meeting by which notice in writing was given to all members. As such, a company may alter its business or objects at any time and for any reason as long as the alteration is carried out by special resolution and there is no minority objection or if there is, the court has affirmed the resolution.

(a) Procedure for Alteration of Object Clause

The procedure for the alteration of object clause is as follows:

(i) Pass a Board of Directors Resolution to that effect.

(ii) Give 21 days' notice of meeting specifying in the notice the intention to pass a resolution as a Special Resolution. The notice of meeting must be sent to all members of the company and to all holders of debentures secured by floating charge of the company.

(iii) At the meeting, a Special Resolution must be passed by s of members voting in person or by proxy.

(b) Challenging the Alteration of Object Clause

The following category of persons can challenge the alteration of a company's business or object clause:

(i) Holders of not less than 15% of the paid up shares in the company's issued capital. For a company not limited by shares, 15% of its members.

(ii) Holders of not less than 15% of the company's debentures secured. Provided that such application shall not be made by any person who consented to or voted in favour of the alteration.

(iii) The Commission can refuse to approve a Resolution for alteration even though there is no objection by members or debenture holders, if it is not satisfied with the alteration.

The grounds for challenge of the alteration of the object clause are as follows:

(i) Minority and Creditor's protection.
(ii) Non–compliance with the condition precedents for the validity of resolution, such as:
  I. No or insufficient written notice of meeting to members or
  II. That the alteration was not based on Special Resolution.

It is important to emphasise that 'member' in this section includes any person financially interested in the company. The application may be made in representative capacity on a written appointment.

Where the alteration has not been properly made, application may be made to the court within 21 days of the passing of the resolution to have the alteration declared invalid. And any member can apply to have the resolution declared invalid notwithstanding the number of shares he has subscribed to.

ALTERATION OF SHARE CAPITAL CLAUSE

The alteration of capital as provided by the Act covers such changes as the alteration of share capital by consolidation, conversion and subdivision of shares, cancellation and reduction of shares, etcetera.

(a) Consolidation of Shares

With specific reference to the consolidation of shares, Section 100(1)(a) of the Act deals with consolidation of shares by providing that a company may consolidate and sub-divide its shares into larger amounts. For example, if a company has 100,000 shares of ₦1.00 each, it can consolidate the shares to 10,000 shares and sub-divide it to ₦2.00 each.

(b) Conversion of Shares

A company can convert paid-up shares into stock and to also reconvert stock into paid-up shares. A company however, cannot issue stock directly but can only convert paid up shares into stock, and any direct issue of stock is ultra vires.

(c) Subdivision of Shares

A company can sub-divide its shares or any of them into shares of smaller amounts. For instance, 5,000 shares of ₦2.00 each can again be subdivided into 10,000 shares of ₦1.00 each.

(d) Cancellation of Unissued Shares

A company may cancel shares which have not been issued because so long as the shares remain unissued to members, no member is committed to pay for them and if the shares are cancelled, no member will be prejudiced by doing so. Where a company takes steps in this regard, it must give notice to the Commission specifying, as the case may be, the shares consolidated, divided, converted, sub-divided, cancelled or the stock re-converted within one month of doing so.

There must however, be an offer and a valid acceptance before an agreement to take unissued shares would exist.

(e) Alteration of Increase in Share Capital

In accordance with the relevant statutory provision, a company limited by shares may in a General Meeting and not otherwise increase its share capital by creating new shares. This is done by Ordinary Resolution.

The procedure for increase are as listed hereunder:

(i) Board of Directors resolution to the effect that the capital of the company be increased and also authorising its Secretary to take necessary steps to effect the increase.

(ii) Notice of meeting must be given to members who are entitled to attend the General Meeting of the company. The notice must specify the amount of the proposed increase.

(iii) A General Meeting will be convened where an Ordinary Resolution to increase the capital of the company will be passed.

(iv) After the resolution is passed and within 15 days of the passing of the Resolution permitting the increase, the following documents must be delivered to the Commission:

I. A copy of the resolution authorising the increase.

II. A notice of increase stating the class or classes of shares involved and special rights attached to them, if any.

III. A statement of increase duly stamped (Form CAC 2). Two copies of the statement of increase must be taken to the Federal Commissioner of Stamp Duties for payment. The Commissioner for Stamp Duty will retain a copy of the statement of increase and return a stamped copy to the person applying, which the applicant will include in the documents to be filed with the Commission.

(v) Within 6 months of giving the notice of increase to the Commission, the company must issue to members not less than 25 per cent of the share capital including the increase has been issued and unless this is done, the increase cannot take effect.

(vi) The increase shall not take effect unless the Director's statutory declaration has been delivered to CAC. A statutory declaration verifying that 25% of the total share capital has been issued. Attach the statement of share capital and return of allotment.

(vii) A Certificate of Increase must be obtained from the Commission.

(viii) A copy each of the resolution and Certificate of Increase must be annexed to the Memorandum of the company.

(f) Reduction of Share Capital

A company limited by shares may reduce its capital by Special Resolution if authorised by its Articles and subject to confirmation by the court. As regards the modes of reduction, a company may:

(i) Extinguish or reduce the liability on any of its shares in respect of share capital not paid up; or

(ii) Either with or without extinguishing or reducing liability on any of its shares, cancel any paid-up share capital which is lost or unrepresented by available assets; or

(iii) Either with or without extinguishing or reducing liability on any of its shares, pay off any paid-up share capital which is in excess of the company's wants, and the company may, if and so far as is necessary, alter its memorandum by reducing the amount of its share capital and of its shares accordingly.

The ***mode of reduction of share capital*** can be done in three ways:

(i) The article must provide for it.

(ii) The company must pass a special resolution to reduce share capital.

(iii) The court must confirm the reduction of share capital.

The ***procedure for the reduction of share capital*** is as outlined below:

(i) Directors must meet to resolve that the share capital be reduced.

(ii) The scheme of reduction will be prepared.

(iii) The General Meeting has to be convened. The Notice of Meeting should be accompanied by explanatory circular and the scheme of reduction.

(iv) At the meeting, a Special Resolution must be passed reducing the capital and approving the scheme of reduction.

(v) Application must be made to the Court to confirm the reduction and also approve the Scheme of Reduction. If the court is satisfied that every creditor has duly consented or that adequate provisions have been made to discharge or secure their debts or claims or that the debts have been determined and the capital does not by this reduction fall below the authorised minimum, it may by order confirm the reduction. It should be noted that creditors who would be entitled to make a claim on the company are entitled to object to the reduction.

(vi) After the order of the court confirming the reduction, a copy of the order and a copy of the minutes approved by the Court showing particulars of the capital as altered (such as the amount of share capital, number of shares into which it is to be divided and the amount of each share, the amount at the date of registration deemed to be paid up on each share) must be delivered to the Commission.

(vii) Obtain a certificate of registration of the order and Minutes from the Commission.

(viii) The approved Minutes and order of reduction shall be annexed to the Memo of the company. The Minutes are deemed to be substituted for the corresponding part of the company's memorandum as well as an alteration of the memo of the company.

ALTERATION OF THE RESTRICTION OF THE POWERS OF THE COMPANY CLAUSE

The procedure to alter the restriction of the powers of the company clause is the same as that of the business/object clause. Alterations of provisions in the memorandum in certain cases deal with cases such as the restriction on the powers of directors. This can be altered by Special Resolution. However, if application is made to the court for the alteration to be cancelled, it will not have effect unless if confirmed by the court.

ALTERATION OF ARTICLES OF ASSOCIATION

A company has the power to alter or add to its Articles by Special Resolution but subject to the provisions of the Act and to the conditions or other provisions contained in the Memorandum of the company.

Any alteration made shall be as valid as if originally contained therein and be subject in like manner to alteration by Special Resolution. Thus, in *Andrews v. Gas Meter Co*[3] the original Articles contained no provision to issue preference shares. Nevertheless, the company by Special Resolution, altered its Articles so as to have power to issue preference shares accordingly. The alteration was held to be effective.

The *procedure for alteration of articles* is highlighted hereunder:

(i) Board meeting whereby a resolution will be passed to alter the Articles.

(ii) A notice of 21 days must be given to the Members accompanied with the proposed Special Resolution.

---

[3] (1884) LR 25 Ch D 320

(iii) A general meeting will be convened whereby a Special Resolution to alter the Articles will be passed.

(iv) The printed copies of the amended Articles and printed copy of the Special Resolution must be delivered to the CAC within 15 days of the passing of the resolution for registration.

(v) The resolution must be annexed to every copy of the Articles issued after the passing of the resolution.

The alteration must comply with the provision of the Act to the effect that a member of a company shall not be bound by any alteration made in the Memorandum or Articles of the company requiring him on or after the date of the alteration to:

(i) Take or subscribe for more shares than he held at the date on which he became a member; or

(ii) Increase his liability to contribute to the share capital of the company; or

(iii) Pay money by any other means to the company.

BUSINESS NAME CHANGES

The procedure for Change of Business Name under Part D of the CAMA is as follows:

(i) Conduct an availability check and reservation of name using Form CAC 1A

(ii) Write an application to the Corporate Affairs Commission to effect the change of name accompanied with the following documents:

   I. Form CAC 1A
   II. New filled Form CAC/BN/A1 (Application for business name registration).
   III. Original Certificate of Registration of the business name for cancellation.
   IV. Receipt of payment of the prescribed fees.
   V. Updated annual returns.

(iii) The Commission shall issue a new Certificate of Business name registration. The application for change of business name is to be done within 28 days of the actual change of the name.

(a) Change of Proprietors

The procedure for change of proprietor's name shall include the following steps–

(i) Duly completed application form
(ii) Evidence of change of name
(iii) Duly completed form
(iv) Formal application for change of name
(v) Original registration form for cancellation
(vi) Form of identification where necessary
(vii) Updated annual return
(viii) Payment of filing fees.

(b) Change of Business Nature

The procedure for change of nature of business shall include the following requirements:

(i) Duly completed application form
(ii) Duly completed form for change of nature of business
(iii) Formal application and proficiency certificate where applicable
(iv) Original certificate of registration and form for cancellation
(v) Form of identification where necessary
(vi) Updated annual return
(vii) Payment of filing fees.

(c) Change of Business Name Address

The procedure for change of business address shall include the following requirements:

(i) Duly completed application form.
(ii) Duly completed form for change of address.
(iii) Formal application for change of address.
(iv) Original certificate of registration and form for cancellation.
(v) Form of identification where necessary.

(vi) Updated annual return.
(vii) Payment of filing fees.

(d) Addition/Removal of Partner

The procedure for adding or removing a partner shall include the following requirements:

(i) Duly completed application form
(ii) Duly completed form for removal or addition of partner
(iii) Formal application for addition or removal of partner
(iv) Two passport-sized photographs for the new partner in case of individual and CTC of resolution together with photocopy of certificate of incorporation in case of company
(v) Copy of partnership agreement where applicable
(vi) Form of identification where necessary
(vii) Updated annual return
(viii) Payment of filing fees.

(e) Notice Business Cessation

The procedure of notice for cessation of business is as follows:

(i) Filing notice of cessation of business and removal of name from the register of business names shall include the following
    I. Notice of cessation of business by proprietor or personal representative of proprietor in case of deceased proprietor.
    II. Written consent of all partners in case of partnership.
    III. Submission of certificate and documents of registration for cancellation.
    IV. Updated annual return.
    V. Payment of filing fees.
(ii) The personal representative shall deliver the notice of cessation business to the Commission within 3 months of the cessation of the business.

ALTERATION OF INCORPORATED TRUSTEES

(a) Change of Name

The procedure for the change of name of an incorporated Trustee under Part F of the Act is as follows:

(i) Pass a Resolution approving the change by the Association (as provided for by the organization's Constitution).

(ii) Fill Form CAC 1- availability Check and reservation of name for approval.

(iii) Advertise the proposed change in 2 National Newspapers for objections to be made within 28 days.

(iv) An application is to be written to the CAC to effect the change attached with the following documents:

  I. Form CAC 1

  II. Resolution of the Association approving the Change duly certified by the trustees

  III. Two copies of the Newspaper advertisement

  IV. Original Certificate of Incorporation for cancellation

  V. Newly filled Form CAC/IT/1- Application for registration of Incorporated Trustees.

(v) The Commission will then issue a new Certificate of Incorporation reflecting the new name.

(b) Change of Objects and Amendment of Constitution

The procedure for the change of object and amendment of an organization's constitution is thus:

(i) Convene a General Meeting and pass a resolution.

(ii) Advertise the notice of application in the newspapers stating the Provisions of the Constitution to be amended and invite objections to the application within 28 days of the publication.

(iii) Make an application to CAC accompanied by the following documents:

  I. Duly completed application form.

  II. Formal application for change of objects and amendment of constitution signed by the chairman and secretary or the solicitor.

  III. Extracts of minutes of general meeting where change of objects and amendment of constitution was approved and signed by the chairman and secretary.

IV. Two copies of the constitution as amended and marked' Amended.

V. Copy of the public notice as pasted at the registered office of the association.

VI. Cuttings of publication page of notice of application for change of objects and amendment of the constitution in two daily newspapers.

VII. Updated annual returns.

VIII. Payment of fees.

(iv) Change of any other Provision of the Constitution is by a resolution passed by a simple majority of the members approved by the Commission.

(c) Replacement and Appointment of Additional Trustees

The procedure for replacement and appointment of additional trustees of an Incorporated Trustee is thus:

(i) Hold a general meeting adopting the proposed change – by resolution (depending on the provision of the organisation's Constitution).

(ii) Advertise notice of application for change of objects and amendment of the constitution in two daily newspapers within 28 days.

(iii) Make an application to CAC accompanied by the following documents:

I. Duly completed change of trustees form.

II. Formal application for change or appointment of additional trustees signed by the chairman or secretary or solicitor.

III. Extracts of minutes of general meeting where change or appointment of additional trustees was adopted signed by the Chairman and Secretary.

IV. Trustees declaration form duly deposed to by each of the new trustees in the High Court.

V. Photocopy of information page of international passport or national identity card for new trustee(s).

VI. Original certificate of incorporation (or CTC of certificate where applicable) for cancellation.

VII. Copy of the public notice as pasted at the registered office and every branch of the association.

VIII. Updated annual return.

IX. Payment of filing fee.

(iv) The extracts of minutes shall list members present and the voting pattern for outgoing and/or new trustees and state reasons for change or removal.

(v) Cuttings of publication page of notice of application for change or appointment of additional trustees in two daily newspapers

(vi) The notice published in the newspapers shall state names of old trustees indicating those to be removed, names of proposed trustees and shall invite objections to the application within 28 days of publication.

(vii) Thumb prints by an illiterate trustee or officer shall be accompanied by an illiterate jurat.

Chapter 11

CORPORATE GOVERNANCE

INTRODUCTION

Corporate governance refers to the system by which companies are directed and controlled. This system ensures protection of the interests of major stakeholders in a corporation through adequate checks and balances. Stakeholders in a corporation are the shareholders, directors, employees, customers, vendors/suppliers, creditors and the community as a whole.

The major components of corporate governance include corporate governance principles as captured in the codes related to key areas, namely: leadership, effectiveness, accountability, remuneration and relation with stakeholders.

Models of corporate governance include the following:

(i) Berle and means model (Agency theory)
(ii) Takeover model
(iii) German bank model
(iv) Leverage buyout
(v) Stakeholders model
(vi) Disclosure model
(vii) The co-determination model
(viii) Political model

The stakeholder model of corporate governance involves the following:

(i) Directors who are the managers of the company
(ii) Shareholders/members. They are the "owners" of the company; they ratify decisions of the board. They are the investors
(iii) Creditors e.g. debenture holders
(iv) Auditors

(v) Employees of the company: They run and see to the affairs of the company in order for their jobs to be secured

(vi) Experts, financial, branch managers who may not be directors of the company

(vii) They may constitute the management team as distinct from the Board of Directors. They are engaged by the Board and are accountable to the Board

(viii) Company Secretaries: They are the Returning Officers, Compliance Officers

(ix) Managers of the Company's Secretariat. They serve as a bridge between shareholders and the board.

It should be noted that there is no universally agreed Code of Good Corporate Governance. What obtains in practice is a set of rules laid down to be followed by Companies.

The Germans model operate a two tier of directorship, namely:

(i) Directors (*Vorstand*) who are directly managing the affairs of a company and

(ii) A Supervisory Board (*Aufsichsrat*) which oversees the acts of the Directors. This is embedded in the structure and management of public companies

COMPANY DIRECTORS

Directors are an important part of every company. Every company is constituted by a board of directors. They are the vehicle through which the objectives of the company are driven. The Act provides that a company shall act through its members in general meeting or its board of directors or through officers or agents, appointed by, or under authority derived from, the members in general meeting or the board of directors.

Directors registered under the Act are defined as persons duly appointed by the company to direct and manage the business of the company. The term 'director' includes any person occupying the position of director by whatever name called; and includes any person in whose directions or instructions the directors of the company are accustomed to act. However, the fact that a person in his professional capacity gives advice and a director acts on it shall not be construed to make such a person under this Act a person in accordance with whose directions or instructions the director of a company is accustomed to act.

There are implications of acting as director without being appointed as such. Where a person not duly appointed as director acts or holds himself out as having been duly appointed without the concurrence of the company:

(i) Under criminal liability, he shall be guilty of an offence and on conviction be liable to imprisonment for two years or to a fine for each day he so acts or holds out himself as a director, or to both such imprisonment or fine.

(ii) Under civil liability, his act shall not bind the company and he shall be personally liable for such action; provided that where it is not the company which held him out as director. If that is the case, then the company shall be bound by his acts. A Director is the alter ego of a company, as was held in *Yalaju Amaye* v. *Arec*'s case.

TYPES OF COMPANY DIRECTORS

(a) Executive Directors

These are full time or salaried directors who are appointed to take charge of day to day running of company affairs. They occupy dual status as alter ego as well as an employee of the company and thus have a contract of service. As an alter ego, an Executive Director sits at Board meetings formulating policy directions for the company, and as an employee, he is in charge of implementation of the policies of the company.

(b) Managing Directors/CEO

Such a director is usually either appointed from among the Board of Directors or from the employees of the company to oversee the management of the day-to-day business of the company. He occupies dual status as alter ego and as an employee of the company. The Board of Directors can delegate duties to him. The Managing Director is removable by the Board of Directors if appointed from amongst the directors but will still remain a director of the company unless he is removed in line with laid down procedure of the Act.

(c) Alternate Director

He is the Director who is appointed to take the position of another Director in the absence of the said Director. The Board of Directors are responsible for appointing him, but his appointment is subject to approval by the resolution of the General Meeting. A director can appoint an alternate director to attend board meetings when he cannot attend. It should be noted that there must be a provision in the Articles of Association of the company recognising the possibility of creating the position of an alternate director. He ceases to hold office whenever the substantive director ceases to hold office.

(d) Life Director

This refers to a person appointed a director for life as a director of the company. The import of this is that he is not subject to the rotation of directors but he is removable where he is disqualified or vacates the office.

(e) Nominee or Representative Director

Where a company is a Director in another company, the company is obliged to appoint a nominee to represent it in the Board for a fixed period. The company is obligated to file the name of the representative of the Director (company) upon filing returns at the Commission.

(f) Shadow Director

A Shadow Director is a person who is not expressly made a director of a company but in accordance with whose directions the real directors of the company are accustomed to act. An Exception to the above rule is professionals engaged by the company to advise the company on a particular issue.

(g) Chairman

He presides over the Board and General meetings of the company as he is also a director. The directors may elect a chairman for their meetings and determine the period for which he is to hold office. However, if no such chairman is elected or if at any meeting the chairman is not present within one hour after the time appointed for holding the same or he is unwilling to act, the directors present may choose one of their number to chair the meeting.

(h) Non-Executive Directors

A non-executive director is duly appointed and carries out affairs of the company. He is not involved in the day to day management and he is not an employee. He is a part-time director who is not entitled to remuneration but only reimbursement for his out of pocket expenses in carrying out the company affairs except as provided in the company's Articles of Association.

(i) First Directors

These are the pioneer directors of the company. Subject to the Act, the number of directors and the names of the first directors shall be determined in writing by the subscribers of the memorandum of association or a majority of them or the directors may be named in the articles.

(j) Casual Director

Where there is a vacancy arising out of death, resignation, retirement, or removal of a Director, the Board shall appoint new persons to fill any such casual vacancy subject to approval by the members in general meeting and if not approved, he shall cease to be a director. The new appointee steps into the shoes/tenure of the removed or dead or retired director. He merely enjoys the unexpired residue of the term of the initial director.

(k) Subsequent Directors

These are Directors appointed after the company is incorporated and while the company is operating in ordinary course of business. The procedure involves the re-election or appointment of new directors by the members at the annual general meeting. If the Articles excludes rotation rule, members can reject directors by removal. Upon appointment of subsequent directors, the company shall file Form CAC 7A (Change in Particulars of Directors) at the Commission within 14 days of the change, accompanied with the resolution of the appointment.

APPOINTMENT OF DIRECTORS AFTER DEATH OF ALL DIRECTORS AND SHAREHOLDERS

In the event of the demise of all the directors of a company, any of the personal representatives of the dead directors and shareholders shall apply to the Federal High Court for an order to convene a general meeting of all the personal representatives of the shareholders entitled to attend and vote at the general meeting to appoint new directors. Where they fail to convene the meeting, the creditors, if any, can do so. Similarly, the power can be conferred on an outsider to appoint or remove directors in the memorandum or articles and that power is enforceable.

The board of directors have the power to appoint new directors to fill any casual vacancy arising from death, resignation, retirement or removal of a director. Where a casual vacancy is filled by the directors, the person may be approved by the general meeting at the next annual general meeting, and if not so approved, he shall cease to be a director.

AGE OF DIRECTOR

To be eligible for directorship, a person must be above 18 years of age. Similarly, any person who is appointed or to his knowledge proposed to be appointed as a director of a public company and who is 70 years old or years old shall disclose this fact to the members at the general meeting.

The Act provides that any person who fails to disclose his age as required under this section shall be guilty of an offence and liable to a fine. A person may be appointed a director of a public company notwithstanding that he is 70 years or more of age but special notice shall be required of any resolution appointing or approving the appointment of such a director. The notice given to the company and by the company to its members shall state the age of the person to whom it relates.

NUMBER OF DIRECTORS

The minimum number of directors of a company is one or two. The directors may increase the number of directors so long as it does not exceed the maximum allowed by the articles. The general meeting shall have power to increase or reduce the number of directors generally and may determine in what rotation the directors shall retire, provided that such reduction shall not invalidate any prior act of the removed director.

It should be noted that the acts of a director wrongly appointed by a company are valid notwithstanding any defects in his appointment.

DISQUALIFICATION OF DIRECTORS

By the provision of the Act, the following persons cannot be appointed as directors of a company:

(i) Infants or under 18 years of age.

(ii) A lunatic or person of unsound mind.

(iii) Insolvent persons; persons guilty of fraud in relation to company; and vacation of office of a director.

(iv) A corporation other than its representative appointed to the board for a given term.

When someone is barred from being a director due to insolvency, or is found guilty of fraud in relation to the company, he is totally disqualified for that period.

VACATION OF OFFICE OF DIRECTOR

The office of director shall be vacated if the director:

(i) Shareholding disqualification (where articles provide for a person to hold particular number of shares to be a director); or

(ii) Becomes bankrupt or makes any arrangement or composition with his creditors generally; or

(iii) Becomes lunatic or person of unsound mind); or

(iv) Resigns his office by notice in writing to the company.

Furthermore, expiration of tenure is as fixed by the relevant regulatory body, such as the Central Bank of Nigeria's rule of 10 years for bank Chief Executive Officers.

The members in a general meeting may act in any matter if the members of the board of directors are disqualified or are unable to act because of a deadlock on the board or otherwise. Pursuant to this, any question arising at any meeting shall be decided by a majority of votes, and in case of an equality of votes, the chairman shall have a second or casting vote.

If any person, being an insolvent person, acts as director of or directly or indirectly takes part in or is concerned in the management of any company, he shall be guilty of an offence and liable on conviction to a fine, or to imprisonment for a term not less than six months or more than two years, or both.

RETIREMENT/ROTATION OF DIRECTORS

Except where the Articles of Association of a company makes provision on the retirement or rotation of directors, the provisions of the Act can apply viz:

(i) At the first Annual General Meeting (AGM), all the directors (excluding life directors) are to retire.

(ii) In subsequent AGMs, one-third (1/3) of the directors or if their number is not three or a multiple of three, then the number nearest one third shall retire from office.

(iii) Retirement is by rotation according to the number of years spent as director in office; those who have been longest in office since their last election shall retire.

(iv) The company at the meeting at which a director retires in the manner mentioned in (ii) and (iii) may fill the vacated office by electing a person to that office and in default, the retiring director shall, if offering himself for re-election, be deemed to have been re-elected, unless at such meeting it is expressly resolved not to fill such vacated office or unless a resolution for the re-election of such director shall have been put to the meeting and lost.

(v) No person other than a director retiring at the meeting shall, unless recommended by the directors, be eligible for election to the office of director at any general meeting unless not less than 3 nor more than 21 days before the date appointed for the meeting there shall have been left at the registered office or head office of the company notice in writing, signed by a member duly qualified to attend and vote at the meeting for which such notice is given, of his intention to propose such person for election, and also notice in writing signed by that person of his willingness to be elected.

(vi) Where a director presents himself for re-election, a record of his attendance at the meetings of the board during the preceding one year shall be made available to members at the general meeting where he is to be re- elected.

(vii) Where two or more directors appointed on the same day are to retire, deciding who to retire shall be by casting lot unless they agree among themselves who should retire.

(viii) Where a director at retirement presents himself for re-election then whether the company is silent or not, he is deemed to have been re-elected as a director, unless there is a resolution shifting the telling of vacancy or rejecting him or another director has been elected in his place. Where he is deemed to be re-elected as director, he is the newest in office.

(ix) A person appointed to replace a removed director continues the tenure of the person removed.

The exceptions to retirement and rotation rule above are as follows:

(i) If the Articles of Association exempt the rule.

(ii) Where it involves a life director.

REMOVAL OF DIRECTORS

A company may by ordinary resolution remove a director before the expiration of his period of office, notwithstanding anything in its articles or in any agreement between it and him. The process for the removal of directors is provided for under the Act.

Essentially, this procedure is invoked as a last resort. A company may by ordinary resolution remove a director before the expiration of his period of office, notwithstanding anything in its articles or in any agreement between it and him.

The *procedure for the removal of directors* is as follows:

(i) Issue a special notice (not less than 28 before the meeting to the company and company to send to members not less than 21 days before the meeting.

(ii) Send a copy of the Notice for his removal to the director concerned.

(iii) The director is to make representations in writing as to his defence on the grounds on which he is sought to be removed or if he failed to, he is to be allowed to be heard orally at the meeting of the company (whether or not he is a member of the company) where he is to be removed.

(iv) Where the representations are made in writing, the said director may request that such representations be made available to the members.

(v) The company shall inform the members (to whom notice of the meeting is sent) of the fact of such representation having been made and make the same available to members provided that: it is not received by it too late; they do not exceed a reasonable length.

(vi) Where the representations are not made available to members for reason of receiving it too late, the director can request for the written representation to be read. This does not derogate from his right to make oral representations.

(vii) Copies of the representations need not be sent out and the representations need not be read out at the meeting if, on the application either of the company or any other person who claims to be aggrieved, the court is satisfied that the rights conferred by this section are being abused to secure needless publicity for defamatory matter and the court may order the company's costs on an application under this section to be paid in whole or in part by the director, notwithstanding that he is not a party to the application.

(viii) Convene a meeting to pass an ordinary Resolution for his removal.

(ix) Secretary to fill Form CAC 7A (Particulars of Directors) containing the particulars of the directors of the company after the removal to be filed at the Commission within 14 days of the passage of the Resolution, attached with the Resolution.

(x) The company is to make the changes in its Register of Directors and Secretary.

The effect of non-compliance with the procedure for removal of a company's director is that it is rendered invalid, void and therefore set aside. It should be noted that a director cannot be suspended, as was held in Benard *Longe v. First Bank of Nigeria PLC*[1]. In that case, the Supreme Court held that a director cannot be removed otherwise than in compliance with the Act.

The replacement of a removed director can be done:

(i) At the same meeting by the members; or

(ii) By the directors filling the vacancy as a casual vacancy at the board of directors' meeting;

(iii) Calculation of tenure of office of an individual appointed in the place of a removed director.

REMEDIES FOR WRONGFUL REMOVAL OF A DIRECTOR

The remedies available in cases of wrongful removal of a director are listed thus:

(i) A declaration that the removal was wrongful hence void.

(ii) An Order of Court reinstating him as a director.

---

[1] (2010) 6 NWLR (Pt. 1189) 1

(iii) Prayer for an Order of compensation for breach of service contract.
(iv) Compensation for loss of office.
(v) Pressing for damages against the unlawful removal.
(vi) The company can approve a non-contractual compensation to the director wrongly removed.

REMUNERATION OF DIRECTORS AND MANAGING DIRECTOR

The general rule is that every director of a company is not entitled to remuneration for services rendered to the company except expressly stated in the Articles and Service Contracts or fixed by the General meeting. Where remuneration has been fixed by the articles, it shall be alterable only by a special resolution.

The remuneration of the directors shall, from time to time, be determined by the company in general meeting and such remuneration shall be deemed to accrue from day to day.

Directors may be paid for out of pocket expenses such as traveling, hotel and other expenses properly incurred in attending meetings or in connection with business of the company.

In essence, executive directors are employees, and thus have service contracts, which would provide for remuneration. Non-executive directors require express provision in the Articles or resolution to be able to earn remuneration.

Directors' remuneration is apportionable. Moreover, the amount of remuneration shall be a debt from the company. Accordingly, directors can sue the company on account of the debt or prove it in the liquidation. It is worth mentioning that a director who receives more money than he is entitled to shall be guilty of misfeasance and shall be accountable to the company for such money.

The Managing Director's remuneration is automatic upon appointment and is not subject to the Articles or general meeting of the company. A Managing Director shall receive such remuneration (whether by way of salary, commission, or participation in profits or partly in one way and partly in another) as the other directors may determine. He shall be entitled to payment on a *quantum meruit* where he performs some services without a contract. A managing director remuneration is taxable.

PUBLICATION OF DIRECTORS

The Act requires certain publications in respect of directors. These are as highlighted below.

(a) Register of Director's Shareholding

The Act provides that every company shall keep a register showing in respect of each Director the number, description and amount of any shares and/or Debentures of the company held by him or held in trust for him. The Register shall be kept at the company's registered address or Head office. It shall be open for inspection during business hours to members and debenture holders 14 days before the company's annual general meeting (AGM), and three days after the date of the AGM. The register shall always be open for inspection by the Commission.

(b) Register of Directors and Secretaries

Every company is required to keep a Register of its Directors and Secretaries, both past and present in accordance with the provision of the Act. The Register shall contain the following particulars:

(i) Present forename and surname
(ii) Residential address
(iii) Nationality
(iv) Occupation
(v) Date of Birth
(vi) Particulars of any other Directorship

(c) Particulars of Directors in Trade Catalogues

Every company is required to state in legible characters, in all trade circulars, show cards, and business letters in which the company's name appears and which are issued or sent to any person in Nigeria, the following particulars of every directors:

(i) Present forename or initials and surname

(ii) Any former forename and surname
(iii) Nationality if not Nigerian

DUTIES OF DIRECTORS

The basic legal position of directors is that they are trustees of the company as well as its agents. The duties of Directors are classified into two broad headings, namely, fiduciary duty and duty of care and skill.

(a) Fiduciary Duties

Directors owe fiduciary duties to the following persons:

(i) Company to which it must observe utmost good faith in any transactions with it or on its behalf.
(ii) Shareholders when acting as shareholders' agent.
(iii) Shareholder in any transaction affecting his interest.
(iv) Any person dealing with the company's securities.

The ***fiduciary duties of directors entails*** the duty –

(i) To ***act bona fide*** for the benefit of the company.
(ii) To ***exercise power for proper purpose*** and not for a collateral purpose (valid even if it incidentally affected a member adversely).
(iii) Not to ***fetter discretion*** *to vote* in a particular way. As trustee he shall not exercise his discretion to vote in a particular way without the consent of the company, being the beneficiary.
(iv) To ***avoid conflict of duty and personal interest***. A director who is in any way either directly or indirectly, interested in a contract or proposed contract with the company, shall declare the nature of his interest at a meeting of the directors of a company. Payments made to a director by way of compensation for loss of office or retirement must be disclosed to members in a General Meeting and approved by them. A director is prohibited from entering into guarantee or provision of security with the company. A director is restricted from the acquisition of non-cash assets of the company without approval by resolution of the General Meeting.
(v) ***Not to make secret profits*** by appropriating corporate assets or opportunities. A director shall not accept a bribe, a gift or

commission either in cash or kind from any person or a share in the profit of that person in respect of any transaction involving the company in order to introduce the company to deal with such a person. However, if the gift is unsolicited in the form of gratitude after the transaction has been completed, the director may be allowed to keep the gift provided he declares it before the Board.

In all circumstances, the interest of employees and members is to be considered with regard to the fiduciary duties of directors.

(b) Duties of Care and Skill

The duties of care and skill are measured according to the qualification and skill of the directors. Under the Common Law, a director need not exhibit the performance of his duties with a greater degree of skill than may reasonably be expected from a person of his knowledge and experience. He is not bound to give continuous attention to the affairs of his company, as was held in Re City Equitable Fire Insurance Company. This was a subjective standard of care and skill. A director could delegate his duty anyhow as he pleases. Director is not bound to give continuous attention to the affairs of his company

The Act however, introduced professionalism and objective standard of care and skill by mandating every director to exercise the powers and discharge his duties of his office honestly, in good faith, in the best interest of the company and to exercise that degree of care, diligence and skill which a reasonable, prudent director would exercise in comparable circumstances. This is an objective test, unlike the Common Law test, which is subjective in nature. Of course, a director can delegate his duties insofar as it does not amount to an abdication of duty.

There are consequences for failure to exercise duties of care and skill. First, failure to take reasonable care can ground an action against the director for negligence and breach of duty. Every Director is individually responsible for actions of the Board in which he is a member. His absence unless justified does not relieve him of such responsibility.

On the other hand, *directors' personal liabilities may arise in the following cases*:

(i) Misuse of loans collected by them for the company meant for some other projects.
(ii) When less than two (2) directors act and the company incurs debts
(iii) When the members of the company are less than two and the company incurs debt.

There are *remedies for failure to exercise duties of care and skill*. These are as enumerated below:

(i) Termination/Removal;
(ii) Injunction;
(iii) Damages;
(iv) Rescission and restoration of the company's assets.

It should be noted that any duty imposed on a director under this section shall be enforceable against the director by the company. Moreover the Act precludes any exemption from liability which may be inserted in the Articles or Resolution or contract of the company.

PROCEEDINGS OF DIRECTORS

The first meeting of the Board of directors is to be held within six months after incorporation of the company. The agenda of the first Board meeting should usually contain the following items:

(i) Appointment of the Chairman from amongst the directors;
(ii) Appointment of Auditor;
(iii) Appointment of Secretary;
(iv) Appointment of Managing Director;
(v) Appointment the company's Solicitor;
(vi) Adoption of the company's Common Seal;
(vii) Appointment of Bankers.

Every director shall be entitled to receive notice of the directors' meetings, unless he is disqualified by any reason under the Act from continuing with the office of director.

The mode of voting is by majority of votes and in a case of equality of votes, the Chairman shall have a second or casting vote. In all the directors' meetings, each director shall be entitled to one vote.

Therefore, directors in their Board meeting cannot vote by poll (that is, based on their number of shares).

A director may, and the secretary on the requisition of a director shall, at any time summon or call for a meeting of the directors. A resolution in writing, signed by all the directors for the time being entitled to receive notice of a meeting of the directors, shall be as valid and effectual as if it had been passed at a meeting of the directors duly convened and held. The length of Notice of Board meetings is 14 days' notice in writing unless otherwise provided in the articles.

The quorum of Board meetings is two if the directors are not more than six or 1/3 or 1/3 to the nearest number if they are more than six directors of the company, unless otherwise provided by the Articles. Where a committee of directors are appointed by the board of directors, the board shall fix its quorum, but where no quorum is fixed, the whole committee shall meet and act by a majority.

Where the board is unable to act because a quorum cannot be formed, the general meeting may act in place of the board and where a committee is unable to act because a quorum cannot be formed, the board may act in place of the committee. The members in general meeting may act in any matter if the members of the board of directors are disqualified or are unable to act because of a deadlock in the decision of board members or in a similar circumstance otherwise.

COMPANY SECRETARY

Every company is expected to have a secretary. Where a company has not yet appointed a secretary at the point of registration, a director can carry out an act that is required by law to be done by a company secretary. This does not extend to occasions where the law requires an act to be done by a director and secretary.

(a) Qualifications of Company Secretary

The directors are duty bound to take all reasonable steps to ensure that the secretary of the company is a person who appears to have the requisite knowledge and experience to discharge the functions as the secretary of the company. This is with particular reference to public companies.

A *person qualified to be appointed a company secretary* may be:

(i) A member of the Institute of Chartered Secretaries of Nigeria;

(ii) A Legal Practitioner within the meaning of the Legal Practitioners Act;

(iii) A member of the Institute of Chartered Accountants of Nigeria or such other bodies of accountants as are established from time to time by an Act or;

(iv) Any person who had held the office of the company secretary of a public company for at least three years of the five years preceding his appointment in a public company.

(v) A body corporate or a firm consisting of members each of whom is qualified under paragraphs i-iv.

(b) Appointment and Removal of Company Secretary

A company secretary is appointed and removed by the Board of Directors of the company. The procedure for the removal of [public] company secretaries is as follows:

i. Issue the affected secretary a Notice stating that the company is intending to remove him and the proposed grounds for his removal.

ii. The affected secretary is to make his defence within seven working days.

iii. The Secretary is given the option to resign within seven days.

iv. The Board may pass a Resolution for his removal if there is no reply from the Secretary and will report the same at the next general meeting.

v. Where he makes a defence and the defence is found to be insufficient by the board of directors, then the Board will remove him straight away on the grounds of fraud or serious misconduct and report it at the next General Meeting.

vi. If the grounds for the removal are on any other grounds except fraud, the Board will only suspend him and await the approval of the next General meeting for his removal.

Where a suspended secretary is removed by the general meeting, his removal takes effect from any time determined by the general meeting.

(c) Status and Acts by Secretary

A company secretary possesses a dual status. He can act as both a secretary and a director of the company, but he cannot execute company documents alone if it is required to be signed by a director and secretary.

As regards the binding nature of acts done by the secretary, a company secretary was previously regarded as a mere servant that cannot bind the company based on the case of Barnet *Hoares & Co* v. *South London Tramway & Co.*[2] The status of a company secretary has now been improved as he can now bind the company as an officer and alter ego of the company, as was held in *Panorama Dev. (Guilford) Ltd* v. *Fidelis Furnishing Fabrics.*[3]

(d) Duties of Company Secretary

There is no fiduciary duty on a company secretary except where he is acting as an agent. The regular duties of a corporate secretary are the following:

(i) Attend the meetings of; the company, the board of directors and its committees, rendering all necessary secretarial services in respect of the meetings and advising on compliance by the meetings with the applicable rules and regulations;

(ii) Maintaining the registers and other records required to be maintained by the company under this Act;

(iii) Rendering proper returns and giving notification to the Commission as required by this Act; and

(iv) Carrying out such administrative and other secretarial duties as directed by a director, or the Company.

---

[2] (1887) 18 QBD 815

[3] [1971] 2 QB 711

The secretary shall not without the authority of the board exercise any powers vested in the directors.

In specific terms, the duties of a company secretary before, during, and after the company meetings are enumerated below.

(i) ***Duties before meeting include:***

I. Serving out notice of meetings and the agendas on all members and officers of the company
II. Receiving the notice of proxies attendance within 48 hours to the meeting
III. Keeping the statutory records
IV. Ensuring that the venue of the meeting is secured
V. Publishing additional notice of meeting in at least two National Newspapers.

(ii) ***Duties during meetings include:***

I. Taking down the minutes of the meeting
II. Ensuring compliance with the Law (acting as Compliance Officer)
III. Assisting the Chairman

(iii) ***Duties after meeting include:***

I. Drafting resolutions of the meeting ready for filing at the Corporate Affairs Commission.
II. Preparing the minutes of the meetings for the Chairman/secretary to sign.
III. Filing statutory returns at the CAC required by Law
IV. Updating Statutory Records/ Registers kept by the company to reflect current Resolutions.

Chapter 12

COMPANY MEMBERSHIP, MEETINGS AND RESOLUTIONS

MEMBERSHIP

A member refers to a person who has subscribed to the memorandum of a company or any person who has agreed in writing to become a member of a company and whose name is entered in the register of members. An individual who subscribes to the Memorandum of a company becomes a member on incorporation of that company. He is deemed to have taken the shares set opposite his name. An infant can be a member of a company only if there are two other adult subscribers.

The minimum number of the members of a company is now one, whereas the maximum number depends on the type of company. There is no maximum limit for a public company, while that of a private company is not more than 50 members.

A company may take shares and be a member of another company and attend the meetings of the other company through a representative authorised by resolution of its directors. However, a company in liquidation is ineligible in becoming a member of a proposed company. An alien may join in forming a company or acquire shares in a company subject to compliance with the laws relating to alien participation.

(a) Membership Acquisition

An individual can become a member of a company through any of the following means:

(i) By subscription (only available to the first subscribers and promoters).

(ii) By allotment and being placed on the register of members. Allotment is the application for shares in a company by desirous members of the public. The company (board of directors) where it accepts the offer will allot shares to the person within 42 days via letter of allotment. After allotment, the company is mandated to issue a certificate of allotment to the member within two months. Thereafter, the subscriber's name is to be entered in the register of members.

(iii) By transfer or sale of shares from existing shareholders and being placed on the register of members. A member may transfer a part or the whole of the shares held by him in a company. Upon the transfer, steps are taken to register the transfer with the company so that the name of the transferor is substituted with the name of the transferee. A new certificate is to be issued to the transferee within three months. This process would necessitate rectification of the register of members. The transferee should first notify the company that he is the holder of the share in question. Where the company does not respond to the notification, the transferee may thereupon apply to the court (Federal High Court) for rectification of the register of members.

(iv) By transmission or inheritance, that is, by succeeding to the estate of a deceased, bankrupt member, and being placed on the register of members.

(v) By operation of law, which occurs where the shares of the deceased shareholder or shareholder who is bankrupt devolves or transmits to the successor in title or his personal representative. The protection of the beneficiary follows this process. When shares are given to a personal representative, the beneficiary is expected to file an affidavit of interest with the registrar of the company.

Every person other than subscribers must meet two conditions to become a member of a company, namely an agreement in writing to become a member and entry of his name in the register of members.

(b) Incidents and Rights of Membership

The following are the incidents and rights of a company membership:

(i) Right to dividends when declared
(ii) Right to bonus shares
(iii) Right to attend meetings
(iv) Right to receive notice of meetings
(v) Right to vote at meetings and be voted for
(vi) Right to demand poll
(vii) Right to appoint proxy
(viii) Right to requisition extra – ordinary general meeting.
(ix) Right to own shares
(x) Right to transfer shares.
(xi) Right to sell, mortgage or otherwise dispose of shares
(xii) Right to object to alteration of objects clause, shares etc.
(xiii) Right to take up minority action.
(xiv) Right to petition for investigation by CAC, SEC.
(xv) Right to petition for winding up.
(xvi) Right to copies of memo and Articles.
(xvii) Right to financial reports
(xviii) Right to inspect minutes of meetings.
(xix) Right to remain a member unless restructured out ordinary and shares acquired compulsory.

(c) Cessation of Membership

Membership of a company may be terminated by any of the following means:

(i) Transfer of all ones shares to another
(ii) Forfeiture of shares
(iii) Transmission of shares
(iv) Surrender of shares
(v) Liquidation of a company

(vi) Repudiation by an infant

MEETINGS

There are different types of general meetings of a company as discussed below.

(a) Statutory Meeting

Every public company is mandated to compulsorily hold a general meeting of the members of the company, within a period of six months from the date of its incorporation referred to as statutory meeting.

Notice must be sent to members at least 21 days before the meetings. A shorter notice is allowed if agreed to by majority holding not less than 95% in nominal value of the shares with right to attend and vote, and in the case of a company not having a share capital, together representing not less than 95 per cent of the total voting rights at that meeting of all the members.

As regards the business transacted at statutory meeting, the members of the company present at the meeting may:

(i) Discuss any matter relating to the formation of the company and commencement of business.

(ii) Consider the statutory report.

(iii) Consider matters arising from the statutory report.

The directors are expected to forward to every member of the company a statutory report at least 21 days before the day on which the statutory meeting is scheduled to be held. The statutory report shall be certified by not less than two directors or by a director and the secretary of the company. The directors shall also deliver a certified copy of the statutory report to the Commission.

The contents of statutory report are as follows:

(i) The total number of shares allotted, either as fully paid up, partly paid up or partly paid up in any form other than cash; for shares partly paid up the extent to which they are so paid up, or the consideration for which they have been allotted.

(ii) The total amount of cash received by the company in respect of all the shares allotted, distinguished as aforesaid.

(iii) The names, addresses and descriptions of the directors, auditors, managers, if any, and secretary of the company.

(iv) The particulars of any pre-incorporation contract together with the particulars of any modification or proposed modification.

(v) Any underwriting contract that has not been carried out and the reasons thereof.

(vi) The arrears, if any due on calls from every director.

(vii) The particulars of any commission or brokerage paid or to be paid on the issue or sale of shares or debentures to a director or manager.

(viii) An abstract of the receipts of the company and of the payments made from them up to a date.

It should be noted that the Statutory Report as it relates to shares and capital account (receipts and payment) shall be certified by the auditors.

The effect of failure to hold a statutory meeting or deliver a statutory report is that it would result firstly, to the Company and any officer in default being guilty of an offence and liable to a fine for every day during which the default continues. Secondly, it can constitute a ground for winding up of the company by the court. The Court can, at its discretion, make an order that the statutory meeting be held instead of winding up the company.

(b) Annual General Meeting

This type of meeting is compulsory for all companies. Every company shall in each year hold a general meeting as its annual general meeting in addition to any other meetings in that year. A company is expected to hold its first AGM within 18 months of incorporation. Subsequent AGMs should be held within a space of 15 months but as long as a company holds its first AGM within 18 months of its incorporation, it need not hold it in that year or in the following year. Apart from the first AGM, the Commission can extend the time of holding any subsequent AGM but the extension cannot be not more than three months.

Notice of the meeting must be sent to members at least 21 days before the meeting but shorter notice is allowed if agreed to by all the members entitled to attend and vote.

As regards the procedure to compel holding of AGM, a member can apply to the Commission urging it to call or direct the calling of a meeting. If a member's application is timely and the Commission grants the order to hold the meeting in that year, the meeting is deemed to be an AGM of that same year. However, where a meeting so held is not held in the year in which the default in holding the AGM occurred, the meeting is not to be treated as the company's AGM of the previous year, unless at that meeting the company resolves that it shall be so treated.

If the company resolves that it should be treated as its AGM of the previous year, a copy of the Resolution shall, within 15 days after the passage, be filed with the Commission. Non-compliance with the requirement to hold this meeting attracts a fine.

Two types of business are transacted at the AGM of the company. These are ordinary and special businesses. Ordinary business includes the following:

(i) Declaration of dividend.
(ii) Presentation of the Financial Statements – the Reports of Directors and Auditors
(iii) Election of directors in place of those retiring.
(iv) Appointment of Auditors.
(v) Fixing of remuneration of the auditors.
(vi) Appointment of members of the Audit committee.

Special business of AGM involves any other business not listed as ordinary business of AGM.

(c) Extraordinary General Meeting

Extraordinary General Meeting (EGM) is the General Meeting held at any time to transact business that cannot conveniently wait for the next AGM. An EGM can be held at any time and need not be held in Nigeria, unlike the other types of meeting.

The categories of persons who can convene an EGM are the following:

(i) Board of Directors.

(ii) Any Director if there are not sufficient Directors within Nigeria capable of acting to form a quorum.

(iii) Requisition by members holding not less than 1/10th of the paid up share capital of the company, or in the case of a company not having a share capital, members of the company representing not less than one tenth of the total voting rights of all the members having at the said date a right to vote at general meetings of the company. The directors shall on receipt of the requisition forthwith proceed duly to convene an extraordinary general meeting of the company, notwithstanding anything in its articles. The procedure for member's requisitioned EGM is as follows:

  I. The requisitioner is expected to deposit a signed requisition at the registered office of the company, stating "the objects of the meeting" and the Resolutions which they intend to propose.

  II. If the directors do not within 21 days from the date of the deposit of the requisition proceed duly to convene a meeting, the requisitioner, or any one or more of them, representing more than S of the total voting rights of all of them, may themselves convene a meeting. However, such a meeting must be convened within three months of the deposit of the requisition.

  III. Any reasonable expenses of the requisitioner in convening the meeting shall be repaid to the requisitioner by the company.

  IV. If no quorum is present at the requisitioned meeting, within one hour from the time appointed for the meeting, it is dissolved i.e. that would be the end of the matter, there would be adjournment.

Businesses transacted at an EGM shall be deemed to be special business. Accordingly, a matter which constitutes ordinary business cannot be discussed at EGM.

(d) Court-Ordered Meeting

The Federal High Court can upon an Application by an interested Party, order a company's meeting in the following circumstances:

(i) If for any reason, it is impracticable to call a meeting of the company or for the board of directors in any manner prescribed by the Articles or the Act.

(ii) Upon application of any director of the company or of any member of the company who would be entitled to vote at the meeting, the court can make all or any of the following orders:

   I. That the meeting be called, held and conducted in any manner the Court deems fit.

   II. Give such ancillary or consequential directions as it thinks expedient including a direction that one member of the company present in person or by proxy may apply to the Court for an order to take a decision which shall bind all the members.

(iii) The directions should be confined to matters that will facilitate the meeting and the court should not pronounce on matters raised for the meeting.

(iv) In the event of all the directors and shareholders dying, any of the personal representatives shall be able to apply to the court for an order to convene a meeting of all the personal representatives of the shareholders entitled to attend and vote at a general meeting to appoint new directors to manage the company, and if they fail to convene a meeting, the creditors if any, shall be able to do so.

RESOLUTIONS

Resolutions refer to decisions taken at the company meetings. These decisions are arrived at through voting, or unanimous agreement by members entitled to vote.

The two basic types of resolutions are ordinary resolution and special resolution. Ordinary resolution is a resolution passed by a simple majority of votes cast by members being entitled to vote either in person or by Proxy.

Special resolution on the other hand, is a resolution passed by not less than s of the votes cast by such members being entitled to vote either run person or by proxy, of which 21 days' notice, specifying the intention to propose the resolution as a special resolution has been duly given.

Examples of matters requiring special resolution include:

(i) Change of Name
(ii) Alteration of the Articles
(iii) Alteration of Objects
(iv) Reduction of Share Capital
(v) Voluntary winding up
(vi) Compulsory winding up
(vii) Re-registration of private company as public company
(viii) Re-registration of public company as private company
(ix) Alteration of memorandum to render unlimited the liability of directors or managers
(x) Re-registration of unlimited company as limited company
(xi) Variation of Class rights
(xii) Payment of interest out of capital

All resolutions shall be passed at general meeting and shall not be effective unless so passed. Provided that in the case of a private company, a written resolution signed by all the members entitled to attend and vote shall be as valid and effective as if passed in a general meeting.

As regards the date of passing resolution, resolutions passed at company meeting, holders of any class of shares of company meeting or directors of a company meeting even on adjourned meeting shall be treated as passed on the date on which it was actually passed and not an earlier date. For Written Resolution, it is deemed to be passed when the last signature is affixed to the resolution.

Members holding 1/20 of the total voting rights in a company can requisition a notice of their Resolution on an issue, and cause the company to circulate it to members entitled to attend the meeting in which the Resolution is proposed to be moved.

(a) Resolutions Requiring Special Notice

Special resolution deals with the number of votes to be cast for a decision. Special Notice on the other hand, deals with how to inform those entitled to attend and vote on the Resolution.

The procedure for the passing of a special resolution involves:

(i) Special Notice given by a member to the company of his intention at least 28 days before the date of the meeting at which he intends to move the Resolution. The resolution is enclosed on the Notice.

(ii) On receipt of the members notice, the company in turn will give the members 21 days' Notice as well as enclose the Resolution in the notice.

(iii) Where the company fails to call a meeting for a date 28 days less after the notice has been given, this will not invalidate the meeting.

The following are examples of resolutions that requires special notices:

(i) Appointment as Auditor any person other than a retiring Auditor.

(ii) Removing an Auditor before expiration of his term of office.

(iii) Appointing or re-appointing a Director aged more than 70 for a public company.

(iv) To Remove a Director from office.

(v) To appoint a new Director to replace a removed Director in the same meeting after removal.

(b) Registration of Resolution

Certain resolutions are required to be registered with the Commission. Printed copies of the following Resolution and Agreement must be forwarded to the Commission for registration within 15 days after its passage:

(i) Special resolution.

(ii) Unanimous resolution on issue, which requires special resolution.

(iii) Unanimous class resolution

(iv) Resolution requiring a company to be wound up voluntarily.

Chapter 13

FINANCIAL STATEMENTS, AUDITS AND ANNUAL RETURNS

FINANCIAL STATEMENTS

The financial statements of a company are its bills of health. It shows the annual state of affairs of the company. Financial statements are vital and of crucial importance not only to members of the company but also to third parties dealing with it.

The financial statements enable a member to know if his investments are growing or depreciating and whether to sell off or retain his shares in the company. The statements also provide a potential investor with information which would either persuade him to invest or dissuade him from investing in a particular company. Every company is mandated to keep accounting records as prescribed by the Act.

(a) Accounting Records

Accounting records form the basis of relevant information and data to be used in preparing financial statements and audited accounts of the company. The accounting records shall be *sufficient to show and explain the transactions* of the company and shall be such as to:

(i) Disclose with reasonable accuracy, at any time, the financial position of the company; and

(ii) Enable the directors to ensure that any financial statements prepared comply with the requirements of the Act.

As regards the *contents of accounting record*, the Act provides that it shall, in particular, contain the following items:

(i) Entries from day to day of all sums of money received and expended by the company, and the matters in respect of which the receipt and expenditure took place; and

(ii) A record of the assets and liabilities of the company.

Where the business of the company involves dealing in goods, the content of accounting records shall be:

(i) Statements of stocks held by the company at the end of each year of the company.

(ii) All statements of stock-takings from which any such statement of stock as is mentioned in paragraph (a) of this subsection has been or is to be prepared.

(iii) Except in the case of goods sold by way of ordinary retail trade, statements of all goods sold and purchased, showing the goods and the buyers and sellers in sufficient detail to enable all these to be identified.

(b) Preparation of Financial Statement

At the first meeting of the board, after incorporation, the directors must determine what date in each year the financial statements for the year would be prepared and inform the Commission within 14 days of such decision.

However, the Central Bank of Nigeria may, pursuant to its regulatory power, direct a Bank to fix a period to make financial statements, which may not be the same with the period agreed by board resolution of the Bank. Accordingly, banks are bound to comply despite the inconsistency with the powers conferred on the board. The financial year for financial institutions is 1st January - 31st December.

The Directors must prepare financial statements for the year in respect of each financial year of a company. This includes the following items:

(i) Statement of the accounting policies;

(ii) The balance sheet as the last day of the financial year;

(iii) A profit and loss account or, in the case of a company not trading for profit and income and expenditure account for the financial year;
(iv) Notes on the accounts;
(v) The auditor's report;
(vi) The director's report;
(vii) A statement of the source and application of fund;
(viii) A value added statement for the financial year;
(ix) A five year financial summary; and
(x) In the case of a holding company, the group financial statement.

It should be noted that financial statement of a private company need not include the following:

(i) Statement of the accounting policies;
(ii) Statement of the source and application of fund;
(iii) Value added statement for the financial year; and
(iv) A five-year financial summary.

(c) Publication and Delivery of Financial Statements

A company publishes its financial statements when the financial statements laid before the company in a General Meeting are delivered to the Commission. A company publishes its full account when the complete statements laid before the company in general meeting are also those delivered to the Commission.

Nevertheless, where a company is entitled to publish abridged financial statements, it needs to publish only the balance sheet or profit and loss account, otherwise than as part of full financial statements.

Where a company publishes full financial statements, it must publish the relevant auditor's report with them, and where appropriate, its group financial statements.

A company which contravenes this provision and any officer of it who is in default, shall be guilty of an offence and liable to a daily default fine.

In respect of each year, the directors must at a date not later than 18 months after incorporation of the company and subsequently at least once every year, lay before the company during the general meeting copies of the financial statements of the company made up to a date not exceeding nine months prior to the date of the meeting.

Similarly, the directors shall deliver to the Commission a copy of the balance sheet along with the annual returns, the profit and loss account and the notes on the statements, which were laid before the general meeting. A company's balance sheet and every copy of it which is laid before the company in general meeting or delivered to the Commission shall be signed on behalf of the board by two of the directors of the company.

The Penalty for laying or delivering defective financial statements is that a director of the company shall be guilty of an offence and in respect of each offence, be liable to a fine. In proceedings against a person for an offence under this section, it shall be a defence for him to prove that he took all reasonable steps to secure compliance with the requirements in question.

(d) Persons Entitled to Financial Statement

A copy of the company's financial statements for the financial year must be sent to each of the following persons not less than 21 days before the date of the meeting at which they are to be laid:

(i) Every member of the company (whether or not so entitled to receive notice of general meetings);

(ii) Every holder of the company's debentures (whether or not so entitled); and

(iii) All persons other than members and debenture holders, being persons so entitled.

With respect to a company not having a share capital, a copy of financial statement may not be sent to a member who is not entitled to receive notices of general meetings of the company, or to a holder of the company's debentures who is not so entitled.

Any person entitled but not given can demand for it and the company is obliged to give him a copy within seven days of demand otherwise the company and every officer is in default is guilty of an offence, and may be liable to pay a daily fine. Unlike in a case involving notice of meeting, failure to deliver a financial statement only attracts a penalty but does not affect the validity of the meeting or resolution reached thereafter.

AUDIT

Audit involves the examination of a company's books of accounts by external experts with a view to ascertaining its compliance with the accounting policy of incorporated bodies and accounting standard rules.

This process ensures that a company's accounting records, financial statements and practices comply with the law. The audited account must also show the financial status of the company, as it is the best way of showing the financial position of the company at any given time.

(a) Appointment and Removal of Auditors

An auditor is an external person, independent of the company who verifies and checks the compliance of accounting records of the company with basic accounting stands and legal requirements. A company has both external and internal auditors. An internal auditor is usually in the employment of the company.

According to the CAMA, every company shall at each annual general meeting appoint an auditor or auditors to audit the financial statements of the company, and to hold office from the conclusion of that meeting, until the conclusion of the next, annual general meeting. The first auditors of a company may be appointed by the directors at any time before the company is entitled to commence business and auditors so appointed shall hold office until the conclusion of the next annual general meeting.

The first Auditors appointed by the directors may be removed by the company at a General Meeting. The company can replace the affected Auditor with any other person who has been nominated for appointment by any members of the company and notice of his nomination must have been given to the members not less than 14 days before the date of the meeting.

Where the directors fail to appoint first auditors, the company may in a General meeting convened for that purpose appoint the first auditors. Such appointment of the Auditor by the General meeting terminates the powers of the Directors to appoint the Auditor.

Although an auditor is not a member of the company and must be truly independent of the company, the Auditor has the right to attend the company's meetings. A company's auditors shall be entitled to attend and be heard at any general meeting of the company and to receive all notices of and other communications relating to any general meeting.

Similarly, an Auditor of a company who has been removed shall be entitled to attend the general meeting at which his term of office would otherwise have expired and any general meeting at which it is proposed to fill the vacancy caused by his removal and to receive all notices.

The procedure for the removal of an auditor before the expiration of his term is enumerated hereunder.

(i) Issue a special notice to the company for his proposed removal stating the grounds.

(ii) At the AGM, pass an ordinary Resolution removing him from office as auditor.

(iii) The Notice of his removal is to be filed within 14 days of the resolution. If a company fails to give the notice to the Commission, the company and every officer of it who is in default shall be guilty of an offence and liable to a daily default fine.

(b) Qualification of Auditors

At any AGM, a retiring auditor however appointed shall be re-appointed without any resolution being passed unless:

(i) He is not qualified for reappointment; or

(ii) A resolution has been passed at that meeting appointing some other person instead of him or providing expressly that he shall not be reappointed;

(iii) He has given the company notice in writing of his unwillingness to be reappointed.

The following persons are prohibited from being appointed auditors:

(i) An officer or servant of the company;

(ii) A person who is a partner of or in the employment of an officer or servant of the company;

(iii) A body corporate.

However, a firm can be appointed as Auditor of a company if all its partners are qualified for appointment as auditors.

No person shall act as auditor of a company at a time when he knows that he is disqualified for appointment to that office and if an auditor of a company to his knowledge becomes so disqualified during his term of office, he shall thereupon vacate his office and give notice in writing to the company that he has vacated it by reason of that disqualification.

A person who acts as auditor in contravention of the above statutory provision or fails without reasonable excuse to give notice of vacating his office as required by that subsection, shall be guilty of an offence and liable to a fine and, for continued contravention, to a daily default fine.

(c) Resignation of Auditors

The procedure for the resignation of company auditor s is as follows:

(i) Auditor deposits notice of resignation in writing to that effect at the company's Registered Office.

(ii) Such notice shall bring his office to an end on the date of which the notice is deposited or a later date specified in the letter.

(iii) A copy of the Notice must be submitted at the Commission within 14 days of the deposit.

It is important to mention that an auditor's notice of resignation shall not be effective unless it contains either a statement to the effect that there are no circumstances connected with his resignation which he considers should be brought to the notice of the members or creditors of the company; or a statement of any such circumstances as are stated above.

Where an auditor's notice of resignation contains a statement of a circumstances which will be of interest to the creditor or member in notice of resignation, he may accompany the notice with a requisition calling on the directors to convene an extraordinary general meeting for the purpose of attending and considering the explanation of these circumstances connected with his resignation.

Where the auditor's notice of resignation contains a statement as mentioned above, the notice and statement shall be sent to the Commission and every person entitled to receive the financial statement of the company within 14 days.

The company or any other person aggrieved over the content of the statement made by the resigning Auditor, may within 14 days of the receipt of the notice, apply to the Federal High court on the ground that the Auditor is using the Resignation Notice to secure needless publicity for defamatory matter. The court where satisfied may order that copies of the notice need not be sent out and may further order the company's costs on the application to be paid in whole or in part by the auditor, notwithstanding that he is not a party to the application.

(d) Duties and Liabilities of Auditors

The Auditor of a company shall make a Report to the members on the account examined by him, on every balance sheet, profit and loss account and on all group financial statements. Copies of these reports are to be laid before the company in general meeting during the Auditor's tenure of office. In addition, an auditor shall in the case of a public company also make a report to an Audit Committee established by the company.

The duties of an auditor also goes with liabilities. As such, a company's auditor shall in the performance of his duties exercise all such care, diligence and skill as is reasonably necessary in each particular circumstance. Where a company suffers damage or loss because of the Auditor's breach of fiduciary duty, the Auditors shall be liable for negligence and the directors may institute an action for negligence against him in the court.

Where the Directors fail to institute the action against the auditor, any member may do so after the expiration of 30 days' notice to the company of his intention to institute such action. Similarly, an officer of a company who conveys information which is misleading, false or deceptive in a material particular to an auditor knowingly or recklessly, shall be guilty of an offence and liable to imprisonment for one year or to a fine, or both.

(e) Audit Committee

Every public company shall have a formally constituted Audit Committee, with a written term of reference. The Audit Committee shall consist of an equal number of directors and representatives of the shareholders of the company subject to a maximum of six members and shall examine the auditors' report and make recommendations thereon to the annual general meeting as it may think fit.

Nomination of a shareholder as a member of the Committee may be made by a member giving notice of such nomination to the company secretary at least 21 days before the AGM. A member appointed to the Audit Committee may be re-elected annually and shall not be entitled to remuneration, but shall be reimbursed for out of pocket expenses.

For a person to be appointed a member of the Audit Committee, he should possess qualities such as integrity, objectivity, accountability, intellectual honesty, and strong financial literacy skills.

The *objectives and functions of the Audit Committee* include:

i. Ascertaining whether the accounting and reporting policies of the company are in accordance with legal requirements and agreed ethical practices;
ii. Reviewing the scope and planning of audit requirements;
iii. Reviewing the findings on management matters in conjunction with the external auditor and departmental responses thereon;
iv. Keeping under review the effectiveness of the company's system of accounting and internal control;

v. Make recommendations to the Board in regard to the appointment, removal and remuneration of the external auditors of the company; and

vi. Authorise the internal auditor to carry out investigations into any activities of the company which may be of interest or concern to the committee.

ANNUAL RETURNS

Annual returns are to be filed once at least in every year at the Commission provided that a company need not make a return under this section either in the year of its incorporation or, if it is not required by section 213 of this Act to hold an annual general meeting during the following year, in that year. The time for filing annual returns is within 42 days after the AGM for the year.

The obligation to file Annual Return starts after incorporation of a company. The annual return shall be completed, signed by both a director and a Secretary.

The contents of annual returns of a company having share capital other than small company is as follows:

(i) Name and Registered Certificate Number (RC No) of the company;
(ii) Address of the Registered Office;
(iii) Situation of the Register of members and Register of Debenture holders;
(iv) Summary of Share Capital and Debentures;
(v) Particulars of Indebtedness;
(vi) List of past and present members;
(vii) Particulars of Directors and Secretary.

The documents to be annexed to annual return of a public company are:

(i) A written copy, certified by a director and the secretary of the company to be a true copy of every balance, and profit and loss account laid before the company in a General Meeting held in the year to which the return relates.

(ii) A copy certified by a director and secretary of the copy of the auditor's Report and the Report of the directors accompanying the balance sheet.

(iii) Where the balance sheet contains amendments, the fact that the copy has been so amended shall be stated on it.

In the case of a private company, the Annual Return shall be accompanied by a certificate by a director and the secretary to the effect that the company has not since the date of incorporation or last annual return, issued any invitation to the public to subscribe for any share or debenture of the company. Failure to file annual returns could attract penalties either in form of a fine, enforcement by the Commission, and striking off of a defunct company.

Chapter 14

MAJORITY RULE AND CORPORATE SOVEREIGNTY

MAJORITY RULE

It is important to determine what a majority implies in a company. Where voting is by show of hands, the majority is the number of people who raise their hands. If voting is by poll, the majority is based on the amount shareholding in the company.

The general rule in the *locus classicus* case of *Foss* v. *Harbottle*[1] is that only a company can sue to redress a wrong done to it or defend an action against the company.[2] The rule is also applicable in respect of non-business organizations.[3]

(a) Rationale for the Rule

The rationale for this rule are as follows:

(i) It prevents multiplicity of suits over one or similar incident; if each shareholder is allowed to sue over a single wrong done to the company, the company would be exposed to multiplicity of suits;

(ii) The members in the general meeting can ratify the wrongful acts of the director, if each individual shareholder could sue, this power to ratify would have been meaningless;

(iii) The company is a separate legal personality, thus should institute actions on its own;

(iv) It preserves the principle of majority rule;

---

1 (1843) 2 Hare 461, 67 ER 189
2 (1990)4 NWLR (Pt. 145) 422
3 [1998] 3 N WLR (Pt. 542) 456 at 471

(v) To protect courts of law from interfering in the internal affairs of a company.

(b) Exceptions to the Rule in Foss v. Harbottle

The exceptions to the rule on the protection of minority as exemplified by Foss' case are as follows:

(i) Injunction or declaration in certain cases;
(ii) Personal and representative action;
(iii) Derivative action;
(iv) Relief on grounds of unfairly prejudicial and oppressive conduct.

The Act provides exceptions to protect the minority shareholders who may be injured by the majority decisions of the company. Thus, the court, on the application of any member, may by injunction or declaration restrain the company from the following:

(i) Illegal or ultra vires acts of the company: The suitable action to take in redressing an illegal or ultra vires act of the company is a *derivative action* (that is, to sue in the name of the company) if the end of it will be for the benefit of the company or to get back the properties illegally taken. The rationale for this option is that if a direct action is to be used (namely, to sue in the name of the minority shareholder), it is only an order of injunction or declaration that can be given.

(ii) The company purports to do by ordinary Resolution, any act which the Act or the Articles of the company require a special Resolution (irregularity). The suitable way to redress an irregularity by the company is to take out a *member's direct action* seeking to declare the procedure as illegal and to be set aside.[4]

(iii) Infringement of personal rights of a member of the company. This includes breach of the member's personal right in the company (such as the right to attend meetings, to be paid dividend when

---

[4] *Williams* v. *Williams* - 120 Nev. 559, 97 P.3d 1124 (2004)

declared, to vote in meetings, to receive Notice of meetings etc.). The best course of action to take here is *members direct action.* A shareholder can sue to compel the company to record his vote. *Derivative action* may be used if the breach of the member's right will require him to recover money or property from the company (e.g. is where dividends on shares held were declared and is in arrears within 12 years of the declaration of the dividend) it is better to use a derivative action.

(iv) ***Commission of fraud on the company or the minority shareholders and the directors fail to take steps to redress it.*** An example of this ground is the *misappropriation* of the company's property/money by the directors or majority shareholders, as was held in *Cooks v. Deeks.* The suitable action to take in redressing this is a *derivative action* where the company must be the plaintiff and the wrongdoers the defendants. The fraud must be specially and adequately proved under this head, If the fraud cannot be adequately proved, it will be better to proceed under Section 300(f) of the Act that the directors have derived profits from their negligence or breach of duty.

(v) ***A company meeting cannot be practically called in time*** *to redress a wrong done to the company.* For example, where the directors have exceeded the borrowing limits and have mortgaged the prime asset of the company. The suitable action here is to make an application to the Commission **or** the Federal High Court to order a meeting of the company. The members holding one-tenth ($\frac{1}{10}$) of the paid-up capital can requisition a meeting.

(vi) ***Directors deriving profits or benefits from their negligence or breach of duty.*** For instance, a sale of company property at an under value[5]. The suitable type of action here is derivative action. This

[5] *Daniels* v. *Daniels* 30 A.D.2d 1039 (1968)

would enable a refund of the benefits so derived from the company to the company.

FORMS OF MINORITY PROTECTION ACTIONS

(a) Members Direct Action

Breach of the provision of the Act entitles a member/shareholder to bring a member's direct action to enforce his rights. The members' direct action can be brought either in a personal action or representative action.

As regards *personal action*, a member can institute a personal action to enforce a right due to him personally. Personal action is restricted to such infringements directed at the individual membership rights in the company e.g. entitlement to notice of meeting, voting, attendance to meetings, payment of dividend when declared etcetera.

On the other hand, members can bring action in a r*epresentative capacity* for the enforcement of personal rights due to them. Such members must nominate those who are members or members to bring action in a representative capacity for the enforcement of rights due to them. They can be named in the suit as their representatives and satisfy all the conditions for instituting representative actions in court.

With respect to *proper parties* to a member direct action, the member of the company sues in his name or in representative capacity as the plaintiff while the company and the directors are made defendants to the action.

The category of *persons who can bring a members direct action* are the following:

(i) Member;
(ii) Debenture holder secured by floating charge;
(iii) Shareholder;
(iv) Personal representative of a deceased member;
(v) Any person to whom shares have been transferred or transmitted.

The *reliefs* available to a person instituting a members direct action are:

(i) Declaration; or

(ii) Injunction restraining the company and/or directors from doing a particular act;

(iii) The cost for instituting the action may be awarded to the members whether or not his action succeeds.

The court may order that the member shall give security for costs. Where the act has been done, the member should seek for declarations. Where the act has not been done; the member should seek an injunction.

(b) Derivative Action

These are actions which ought to have been brought by the company through the directors. Therefore, the plaintiff's right of action derives from that of the company. The mode of instituting this type of action is that a member can commence a derivative action in the name of the company, or in a representative capacity on behalf of the company.

The following *persons* can apply for derivative action for a company:

(i) A registered holder (member) or beneficial owner (by Transfer or Transmission) and a former registered holder or beneficial owner of a company's security (debenture holder);

(ii) A director or officer or a former Director or Officer of a company;

(iii) Corporate Affairs Commission;

(iv) Any other person the Court may permit to make the application.

The *procedure* for bringing a derivative action is by obtaining leave of court by way of originating summons at the Federal High Court with an Affidavit in support and a written address.

The *conditions precedent* for application for derivative action are that the Affidavit in support of the Originating summons must show the following:

(i) That the wrong doers are the directors in control of the company who will not take the necessary steps to redress the illegality;

(ii) That a reasonable Notice of intention to seek redress in Court has been given to them;

(iii) The Applicant is acting in good faith; and

(iv) It appears to be in the best interest of the company that the action be brought, prosecuted, defended or discontinued.

It should be noted that all the conditions are *cumulative* and must be present.

The court may upon a successful derivative action grant general *reliefs* as well as specific reliefs as follows:

(i) An Order that the amount illegally collected from the company be returned to it;

(ii) An order authorising the applicant or any other person to control the conduct of the action;

(iii) An order directing that any amount adjudged payable by a defendant in the action shall be paid, in whole or in part, directly to former and present security holders of the company instead of to the company;

(iv) An order requiring the company to pay reasonable legal fees incurred by the Applicant;

(v) A direction that a Director of the company controls the action in Court to redress the illegal act or to recover the company's property;

(vi) Appointment of a receiver/manager of the property of the company;

(vii) Direct the company or its members to institute specific actions;

(viii) Vary or set aside a contract in which the company is a party;

(ix) Restrain a person from a specific action;

(x) Require a person to do a specific act or thing.

The *proper parties* in a derivative action should be the company and the Applicant as Plaintiffs/Applicants and the Directors, third party or wrongdoer as the Defendant/Respondent.

The difference between derivative action and members direct action is that members direct action seeks to protect the rights of members and shareholders whereas derivative action seeks to protect the company.

(c) Relief on Grounds of Unfairly Prejudicial and Oppressive Conduct

This has to do with a situation where the affairs of the company are being conducted in an illegal or oppressive manner or unfairly prejudicial or discriminatory against a member or members interest or in disregard of public interest.

The procedure for bringing this action is by the affected member filing a *petition* to the Federal High Court, proving pecuniary loss.[6]

The following persons have *locus standi* to institute action by Petition to the Federal High Court under:

(i) A member of the company;
(ii) The personal representative of a deceased member;
(iii) Any person to whom shares have been transferred or transmitted by operation of law;
(iv) Director or officer or former Director or Officer of the company;
(v) A Creditor;
(vi) Corporate Affairs Commission; or

i. Any other person who, in the discretion of the Court, is the proper to make the application.

It should be noted that only the Commission can petition on the ground that the affairs of the company are being conducted against the members in a manner which is in disregard to public interests. The others can bring action on the ground that it would unfairly would be oppressive or unfairly prejudicial to, or unfairly discriminatory against, or which is in a manner in disregard of the interests of that person.

The possible *reliefs or orders* the court can grant upon successful petition are:

(i) That the company be wound up;
(ii) For regulating the conduct of the affairs of the company in future;

---

[6] *Omololu Mulele v. Ijale Properties Co. Ltd* (2000) FWLR (Pt.5) 709.

(iii) For the purchase of the shares of any member by other members of the company;

(iv) For the purchase of the shares of any member by the company and for the reduction accordingly of the company's capital;

(v) Directing the company to institute, prosecute, defend or discontinue specific proceedings, or authorising a member or the company to institute, prosecute, defend or discontinue specific proceedings in the name or on behalf of the company;

(vi) Varying or setting aside a transaction or contract to which the company is a party and compensating the company or any other party to the transaction or contract;

(vii) Directing an investigation to be made by the Commission;

(viii) Appointing a receiver or a receiver and manager of property of the company;

(ix) Restraining a person from engaging in specific conduct or from doing a specific act or thing;

(x) Requiring a person to do a specific act or thing.

(d) Investigation of Company

The Commission may appoint one or more competent inspectors to investigate the affairs of a company and to report on them in such manner as it may direct. This represents an instance of lifting the veil.

The following circumstances can prompt such investigation:

(i) In case of a company having shares, on the application of members holding not less than one-quarter (¼) of the issued shares;

(ii) In the case of a company not having share capital, on the application of not less than one-quarter(¼) of members listed in the Register of members;

(iii) In any other case, on the application of the company.

(iv) By Court order directing that the affairs of the company be investigated.

It should be noted that the application must be supported by good reasons.

The commission may appoint one or more competent inspectors to investigate the affairs of the company. The inspectors shall have power to do any of the following:

(i) Demand for production of books or documents;
(ii) Demand the appearance of any officer;
(iii) Demand from the officers assistance for the investigation;
(iv) Call for Directors' bank accounts.

The circumstances warranting an application for investigation of company are that the Commission may order investigation if:

(i) The company's affairs are being or have been conducted with intent to defraud its creditors or the creditors of any other person, or in a manner which is unfairly prejudicial to some part of its members; or
(ii) Any actual or proposed act or omission of the company (including an act or omission on its behalf) is or would be so prejudicial; or
(iii) That the company was formed for any fraudulent or unlawful purpose; or
(iv) Persons concerned with the company's formation or the management of its affairs have in connection therewith been guilty of fraud, misfeasance or other misconduct towards it or towards its members;
(v) The company's members have not been given all the information with respect to its affairs, which they might reasonably expect.

Finally, as regards the uses of inspection report by the Commission, the Commission has power to:

(i) Bring civil proceedings on behalf of the company on the basis of the Inspector's Report;
(ii) Send the Inspector's Report to the Attorney General of the Federation for criminal prosecution or other proceedings;
(iii) Bring a winding up petition in respect of the company.

(e) Statutory Safeguards for Actions Commenced for Minority Protection

(i) Where court alters or adds to the memorandum or articles, such alteration shall have effect as if it had been duly made by a Resolution of the company. Hence, the company shall not have power, without the leave of court, to make further alteration to the memorandum and articles inconsistent with provisions of the court order.

(ii) Within 14 DAYS of altering the memo and articles by the court, a certified true copy of the Order should be delivered to the Commission and it is an offence to default.

(iii) A Derivative action shall not be stayed or dismissed by reason only that it is shown that an alleged breach of a right or a duty owed to the company has been or may be approved by the shareholders. However, evidence of approval by the shareholders may be taken into account by the court in making an order under the Act.

(iv) It is an offence not to comply with an order of the court made under the Act.

(f) Other Forms of Minority Protection

The Companies and Allied Matters Act also provides for other forms of minority protection as follows:

(i) Winding up where the court is of the opinion that it is just and equitable to do so. It is to file a petition for winding up in Court;[7]

(ii) If the company carries out a variation of class rights, 15 % holders of the issued shares of that class of shares of the company can apply to the Federal High Court to cancel the variation;

(iii) If the company is cancelling or altering the object/business of the company, 15% of the dissenting members as holders of nominal share capital or holders of 15% of the company's

---

[7] *Okeowo & Ors* v. *Migliore & Ors* (1979) 12 NSCC 210

debentures of the company can apply to the Court for its cancellation;

(iv) Upon the re-registration of a public company to a private company, 5% of the holders of the issued shares or 5% of company's members may apply to the Court to cancel it;

(v) Requisition of a meeting under the Act by the minority members notwithstanding the provisions in the articles.

(g) Payment of Dividends

Dividend refers to the money declared by a company as its distributable income to the members or shareholders of a company realised from the business of the company. It is customarily a portion of the after-tax profits of a company, which is distributed among the Shareholders of a company. Dividends are paid to shareholders after deduction of withholding tax at the prevailing rate currently fixed at ten per cent based on the existing tax legislation in Nigeria.

The distribution is done in the proportion of the shares that the shareholders hold in such a company, as a return on their investment in that company. In practice, a dividend is usually declared and paid at the end of a company's financial year. The Act however allows the directors of a company to recommend to its shareholders the payment of an Interim Dividend, out of the distributable profits of the company, for the financial year in which such distributable profits were made by the company.

By law, a company is not compelled to pay dividends but if it decides to, it must be from the profits of the company. The Board of Directors recommends the amount to be declared as dividends to the AGM, which may in turn reduce or approve it. The AGM cannot increase it. Once dividend has been approved or declared, it must be paid and it can be recovered as a debt by action in court within twelve (12) years of the dividend being in arrears.

Dividend policy is based on the fact that the Company aims to create a transparent and methodological dividend payout plan that ensures a balance between regular cash distribution to shareholders as a return on their investment and its corporate sustainability goals. The policy is formulated in accordance with the provisions of the Act, the Company's Articles of Association, Regulations of the Securities Exchange Commission, Nigerian Stock Exchange and other stock exchange where the company's shares are listed, as well as internationally recognized best practices and principles of good corporate governance.

Chapter 15

COMPANY SHARES, DEBENTURES AND SECURITIES

SHARES

Shares refers to a unit of a member's interest in a company which attaches to its rights and liabilities. A share is a bundle of rights and liabilities, which a person has in the capital of a company. The Supreme Court held in *Okoya* v. *Santili*[1] that shares represent a unit of the bundles of rights and liabilities which people hold in companies. It held further that shares is a chose in action and transferable property.

The *legal nature* of shares is informed by the fact that shares –

(i) Is personal property (a chose in action);
(ii) Is an intangible personal right, which a person has in a company;
(iii) Is *a res* in *persona;*
(iv) Confers a bundle of rights and liabilities.

(a) Rights and Liabilities on Shares

The following are inalienable rights that attach to shares in a company:

(i) Right to receive dividends when declared by the company;
(ii) Right to vote at the Annual General Meeting whether in person or by proxy;
(iii) Right to attend meetings;
(iv) Right to the balance sheet of the company;
(v) Right of access to the minute book;
(vi) Right to demand a poll;
(vii) Right to bonus;

[1] *Okoya v. Santili* (SC 327 of 1990) [1994] NGSC 4

(viii) Right to have name in register of members;
(ix) Right to a copy of memorandum and articles of association;
(x) Right to notice of meetings;
(xi) Right to petition for winding up;
(xii) Right to bring derivative action;
(xiii) Right to instigate the investigation of the company.

The following are liabilities that attaches to shareholders in a company:

(i) To pay for shares issued to him in the company;.
(ii) To forfeit his shares where calls are made for the shares and he is unable to pay within the time limit;
(iii) Liable to contribute to the company upon winding up – to the extent of the amount of shares unpaid held by the individual in the company (for limited liability companies);
(iv) Where the veil of the company is lifted and it is discovered that it is carrying on business with less than the statutory minimum, the directors and members are individually liable.

It should be noted that the rights of shareholders are the same as the rights of members. The rights and liabilities attaching to the shares of a company shall be dependent on the terms of issue and the terms in the Articles of Association.

(b) Duties on Shares

Similarly, certain duties are attached to shares, which are duty to effect payment of unpaid amount on shares when call is made, and repayment of unlawfully dividend received. The mode of payment for shares is either by cash or by payment/consideration other than in cash subject to the articles.

The procedure for valuation of shares other than cash is as follows:

(i) Appoint an independent valuer to determine the true value of the consideration and submit a valuation report to the company;

(ii) The valuer so appointed is entitled to any relevant information required from the officers of the company;

(iii) The company must forward the valuation report to the proposed purchaser informing it of its acceptance or non-acceptance of the consideration as payment or part-payment for its shares, within 3 days of receiving his valuation report;

(iv) Such consideration must be of the same value as the shares to be purchased before the company may accept it.

It should be noted that false or deceptive valuation by the valuer is an offence which attracts 12 months imprisonment or a fine of ₦1000, or both. A valuer could be:

(i) An auditor,
(ii) A valuer,
(iii) A surveyor,
(iv) An engineer or
(v) An accountant.

Persons who cannot be a valuer include those in the employment of the company, an agent or associate of the company, or any of the directors or officers of the company.

(c) Types/Classes of Shares

A company may issue classes of shares, where authorized to do so by its articles. Shares shall not be treated as being of the same class unless they rank equally for all purposes. The shares of a company may be classified into:

(i) Preference shares;
(ii) Equity or Ordinary Shares; and
(iii) Founders or Deferred shares.

(i) Preference Shares

Preference shares are a type of shares that entitles the holder to a *fixed preferential dividend.* This implies that the dividend payable by the company to the holder of such shares is fixed at a specific figure, for example 5%, 10%, 20% and so on. It only becomes payable when dividends are declared. The dividend must be paid before the ordinary shareholders receive their own dividends i.e. it has priority over ordinary shares.

However, they cannot participate in the profit of the company in excess of the fixed dividend. Preference shares may be –

- cumulative shares;
- non-cumulative shares;
- participating preference shares; or
- redeemable preference share.

The presumption is that preference shares are cumulative unless it is specifically stated as non-cumulative. Thus, if the company due to insufficient profits is unable to pay a dividend in one year, it must accumulate the arrears of dividend to the next year or subsequent years until they are fully paid from the profit of later years.

Non-cumulative preference shares do not carry the right to roll over unpaid dividends to the following financial year. Once the dividend is not paid in a particular year, that is the end of the matter.

Participating preference shares are preference shares which apart from receiving their fixed dividend in the usual way, also have the right to participate equally with the ordinary shareholders in surplus assets.

As regards redeemable preference shares, shares are generally not redeemable by the company without the court's consent nor can a company purchase its own shares. However, the Act allows a company limited by shares, on the authorisation of its articles to issue preference shares which are redeemable at the company's option.

The conditions for such redemption by the company are that the shares shall not be redeemed unless they are fully paid, and redemption shall be made only out of:

I. Profits of the company which would otherwise be available for dividend; or

II. the proceeds of a fresh issue of shares made for the purposes of the redemption.

(ii) Equity/Ordinary Shares

Ordinary shares are referred to as the Equity share capital of the company. They carry the remaining of distributed profits after the preference shares have been paid their fixed dividend. They are the risk bearing shares. They enjoy unrestricted right to participate in the surplus assets of the company.

(iii) Deferred Shares

deferred shares are also referred to as Founders' shares where they are issued to promoters or management shares if the issue is made to Directors. They customarily carry the right to the remaining of distributed profits after a certain fixed dividend has been paid to the ordinary shares.

(iv) Rights Issue

Rights issue refers to the first class of shares issued by the company. The existing members of a company have pre-emptive rights (right of first refusal) in the new issue of shares if it is authorised by the articles.

(v) Non-voting and Weighted Shares

A weighted share carries more than one voting right, whereas a non–voting share carries no right to vote. The CAMA has absolutely abolished non–voting shares. The Act also prohibits the issuance of weighted shares. The only exception is with reference to preference shares.

(d) Circumstances when Preference Shares Can Carry More than One Vote

Preference shares shall carry a right of more than one vote per share in the following circumstances, but not otherwise:

(i) Upon any resolution during such period as the preferential dividend or any part of it remains in arrear and unpaid, such period starting from a date not more 12 months or such lesser period as the articles may provide, after the due date of the dividend; or

(ii) Upon any resolution which varies the rights attached to such shares (e.g. changing cumulative preference shares to non-cumulative preference shares); or

(iii) Upon any resolution to remove an auditor of the company or to appoint another person in place of such auditor; or

(iv) Upon any resolution for the winding up of the company or during the winding up of the company.

(v) Any special resolution of a company increasing the number of shares of any class.

(e) Acquisition of Shares

The shares of a company can be acquired by any of the following:

(i) By subscribing to the Memorandum and Articles of Association of the company;

(ii) Allotment of shares;

(iii) Transfer of shares;

(iv) Transmission of shares.

(f) Allotment of Shares

The power to allot shares is vested in the company, which can delegate the same to the Board of Directors. The shares allotted by a company must not exceed the authorised share capital of the company.

The *procedure* for allotment of shares is as follows:

(i) Pass Board of Directors Resolution stipulating the number of shares to be allotted;

(ii) Issue prospectus and subscription list/register if a public company;

(iii) Receive application for allotment from interested persons and record them;

(iv) Convene a Board (allotment committee) meeting to pass a Resolution approving the allotment;

(v) Inform successful applicants of the allotment within 42 days, while for the unsuccessful applicants will be issued Letters of Regret with a cheque enclosed for the payment made on the unallotted shares;

(vi) Deal with Letters of Renunciation from those allotted shares;

(vii) Prepare and deliver Share Certificate on shares allotted within two months of the allotment while for shares transferred that should be done within three months of the transfer;

(viii) The allotees name and particulars must be entered in the Register of Members;

(ix) File a duly stamped Form CAC 2 (*Return of Allotment of Shares*) within one month of the allotment to the Commission and obtain a Certified True Copy;

(x) If the shares are issued for a consideration other than cash –

I. Have the consideration valued and obtain particulars of valuation;

II. If consideration involves capital investment of ₦20,000 or more apply under the Industrial Inspectorate Act;

III. Prepare and file along with Form CAC 2 –

- Agreement constituting the title of the allottee to the allotment;
- Agreement for sale of property or for services of other consideration; and
- Valuation report.

(g) Methods of Allotment

The method of application for allotment of shares depends on the type of company.

(i) In the case of a private company (private placement) or a public unquoted company, there shall be submitted to the company a written application signed by the person wishing to purchase shares and indicating the number of shares required to the company secretary;

(ii) In the case of a public company, subject to any conditions imposed by SEC there shall be returned to the company a form of application as prescribed in the company's articles, duly completed and signed by the person wishing to purchase shares.

(iii) Board of directors shall determine whether shares are available and whether or not shares should be allotted for the applicant.

When company advertises for allotment of shares usually for 30 days and subject to extension-

(i) Company must open register of allotment;

(ii) The application may be coordinated by stock brokers;

(iii) The company then processes the application;

(iv) When the application list is closed (offer closes) and the register will close;

(v) When the Register closes, the Board of directors will constitute a board on allotment. If they have more applications than the shares available on offer, then they determine how many they can allot and the remainder will get a letter of regret. This is accompanied by a bank cheque and by SEC Directive, accompanied by accrued benefit if it exceeds a certain amount of time, back to the applicant. So where such money attached for payment by a prospective allottee, such money must be repaid with appropriate bank interest;

(vi) When the Board resolves to allot shares to any applicant, within 42 days of taking this decision, the applicant shall receive a letter of notification of allotment, namely, specifying the allotment of a particular number of shares. A share certificate must be issued not less than 2 months;

(vii) From the time applicant is issued letter of notification of allotment, if applicant changes his mind, the applicant will write a letter of renunciation

(h) Transfer of Shares

This is where a shareholder of a company will alienate his interest in his shares to another. Private companies restrict the transfer of its shares.

The procedure for the transfer of all the shares held by a member is as follows:

(i) The transferor and the transferee execute A Deed of Transfer;
(ii) Stamp the Deed;
(iii) The transferor gives both the original Share Certificate and the Deed of Transfer to the transferee;
(iv) The transferee will lodge both with the company and he will be registered as the owner of the shares;
(v) A new Share Certificate will be issued to the transferee.

Until the name of the transferee is entered in the Register of members in respect of transferred shares, as far as the company is concerned, the transferor is deemed to remain a holder of the shares. Thus, all rights and liabilities of a shareholder would continue to be attached to the transferor as if the shares are still his own.

A company may refuse to register a transfer of shares on these grounds:

(i) If the shares are not fully paid up and the company does not approve the transfer;
(ii) The company has a lien on the shares;
(iii) Non-payment of requisite fees on instrument of transfer;
(iv) The instrument of transfer is not accompanied by share certificate or other evidence to show transferor's to make the transfer;
(v) The instrument is in respect of more than one class of shares.

The *remedies* for a person entitled to shares but not registered is as follows:

(i) Serve on the company a notice and affidavit of interest in the company's shares;
(ii) Apply to Federal High Court to rectify the company's register of members in his favour;
(iii) The transferee may bring an action against the transferor to account for the benefits derived within the period his interest was subsisting, especially dividend paid out within the period.

DEBENTURES

A debenture is a certificate issued by a company acknowledging the repayment of a loan obtained from the holder. It is a written acknowledgement of indebtedness (a debt instrument), which could also be a mortgage transaction between two companies. The Court has held in *Union Bank* v. *Tropics Foods Ltd*;[2] *General Auction Estate Co.* v. *Smith*;[3] and *Intercontractors (Nig.) Ltd. v. NPFMB*[4] that a company acquires the powers of a natural person of full capacity so the company can borrow money and mortgage its property for the repayment of such loan.

(a) Debenture Stock Certificate

The debenture or debenture stock certificate under the company's common seal must within 60 days after allotment or after registration of transfer of any debenture be delivered by the company to the registered holder.

Where the debenture or debenture stock certificate is lost, defaced or destroyed by the registered holder, he will be issued at his request, a certified true copy by the company on payment of a prescribed fee subject to the company's rights to be indemnified and payment of out of pocket expenses for investigating evidences where reasonably required.

A default by the company or officer attracts a fine and they can be compelled by court order to comply, on the application of the registered holder and can be responsible for all the costs of and incidental to the application.

(b) Types of Debentures

There are several types of debentures as highlighted hereunder.

(i) Perpetual Debenture

A debenture created with the intention that it will not be redeemed or it will only be redeemed upon the happening of a remote event or

---

2 (1986) 4 NWLR

3 [1891] 3 Ch 432)

4 1988 NWLR 280

contingency. On the face of it, the concept of perpetual debenture runs contrary to the general principle of mortgage (namely, once a mortgage is always a mortgage and there must be no clog on the equity of redemption). This statutory provision is an exception to these common law maxims, which creates a perpetually irredeemable debenture.

Thus, individuals who have high stakes in certain companies (such as Bill Gate or Dangote) can afford to stake everything as long as the company remains a going concern, since they are the alter ego of their respective companies.

(i) Convertible Debenture
This type of debenture is issued upon the terms that in lieu of redemption or repayment, it may be converted into shares in the company either at the option of the holder or the company upon terms as stated in the debenture instrument.

(ii) Secured or Naked Debenture
A debenture may either be secured by a charge over the company's property or may be unsecured by any charge. An unsecured charge is also known as naked debenture.

(iii) Redeemable Debenture
A company limited by shares may issue debentures which are or at the option of the company are to be liable, to be redeemed. As such, it is repayable at a fixed term as per terms of issues. Redeemable debentures can also be re-issued subject to the relevant provisions of the Act.

(iv) Bearer Debenture
As the name implies, Bearer debenture is a type of charge that is repayable to the holder of the instrument. Thus, a bearer debenture is a transferable negotiable instrument and payable to the holder in due course. It is transferable by mere delivery until due time for redemption.

(v) Registered Debenture

This debenture is repayable to only the Registered Holder of Instrument, that is the person whose name appears in Certificate and Register. Unlike bearer debenture, it is non-negotiable but it is transferable in a manner prescribed by the Debenture Instrument.

(vi) Syndicated Loan Debenture

A syndicated debenture involves a consortium of lenders having one asset charged and created in series, but with a *pari passu* clause, namely, that the later series created shall share equally with the earliest. The debenture is usually created where the value of the asset security outweighs the total loan advance. This is usually used to finance mega projects which would be difficult and risky for only one lender to lend such a huge sum. They rank equally in sharing in the event of enforcement of the security.

The separate legal personalities of the individual lenders are subsumed under and held by the Trustees of the Debenture holders appointed under the Trust Deed created by the consortium. Upon creation of *pari passu* mortgage debenture, the company shall within 90 days after execution of the Trust Deed file with Commission the under-listed particulars:

- Total amount secured by the whole series;
- Dates of resolution authorising the issue of the series;
- A general description of the property charged;
- Names of the trustees, if any, for the debenture holders; together with the deed containing the charge, or, if there is no such deed, one of the debentures of the series.

The *disqualification of trustee* for debentures are as follows:

I. Substantial shareholder;
II. Disqualified director;
III. Person less than 18 years of age;
IV. Person of unsound mind and has been so found by a court in Nigeria or elsewhere;
V. Undischarged bankrupt;
VI. Officer or employee of the company;

VII. If disqualified under the Act.

The Act limits the time within which to issue Debenture or Debenture Stock Certificate to holders to within 60 days whether it is by allotment or transfer.

(c) Contents of Debenture Deed

The contents or statements to be included in a debenture deed include:

(i) The principal amount borrowed;

(ii) The maximum discount allowed on the issue and the maximum premium at redemption;

(iii) The date of repayment of the principal sum;

(iv) The rate and the date of payment of interest;

(v) If a convertible debenture, the date and terms on which it shall be converted into the shares in the company;

(vi) The Charge securing the debenture and the condition to which the debenture are subject to the provisions of Section 168 of the Act.

(d) Types of Secured Debentures

Debenture may be secured by fixed or floating charges.

(i) Debenture secured on a fixed Charge, e.g. land/machinery of the company;

(ii) Debenture secured on a floating charge, for example cash in bank, unpaid shares *et cetera.*

(i) Fixed Charge

A fixed charge attaches to a particular piece of property when the charge is created. A fixed charge is normally legal or equitable in nature. The *advantage* of fixed charge is that the particular asset charged is earmarked and kept available to satisfy the charge's claims.

The company cannot dispose of the asset or create other change ranking in priority to the present charge. The disadvantage is that the Debenture holder is confined to the asset charged in the fixed charge and cannot proceed against other assets of the company.

It should be noted that a fixed charge on any property shall have priority over a floating charge affecting the same property until crystallisation and the person in whose favour the fixed charge is made has notice of such prohibition.

(ii) Floating Charge

A floating charge means an equitable charge over the whole or a specified part of the company's undertakings and assets including cash and uncalled capital of the company both present and future.

As regards the crystallization of a floating charge, a floating charge shall not preclude the company from dealing with such assets until:

I. The security becomes enforceable and the holder appoints a receiver or manager or enter into possession of such assets; or

II. The court appoints a receiver or manager of such assets on application of the holder;

III. The company goes into liquidation.

On the happening of any of the events stipulated above, the charge shall be deemed to crystallise and to become a fixed equitable charge on such of the company's assets as are subject to the charge.

The similarities between floating and fixed charges are that both are recognised securities and both are registrable. Both floating and fixed charges must be registered in the appropriate form of the Commission (CAC Form) for registration and Form CAC 9 for discharging the charge) within 90 days.

The distinction between floating and fixed charge are that first, a floating charge does not prevent or preclude the chargor from dealing with the charged property/asset adversely provided that it is in the normal course of business whereas the chargor in a fixed charge is precluded from dealing adversely with the object of a fixed charge in any situation. Secondly, in a floating charge, there is no crystallisation until the occurrence of certain events such as a breach, winding up and so on. The floating charge hovers over the charged assets until crystallisation. A crystallised floating charge has the same effect as a fixed charge.

(e) Procedure for Creation of Charges/Debentures

The procedure for creating charges or debentures is listed below.

(i) Convene a Board of Directors meeting and pass a Resolution authorising the loan.

(ii) Preparation, execution and stamping of the loan documents:

   I. Deed of mortgage (charge by way of legal mortgage debenture).

   II. Power of Attorney (if any).

   III. Debenture Trust Deed (if it involves a series of debentures, also a Trustees of the Debenture holders).

(iii) If a debenture is secured on the land of the company, obtain Governor's consent, stamp and register the Deed at the Lands Registry.

(iv) If the borrower (mortgagor) is a company, register it with the Commission by filing Form CAC 8 (Registration of Charges) within 90 days, attached with these documents:

- Original Debenture Deed/loan document;
- Resolution of the Board approving the Debenture;
- Valuation Report of the fixed charge;
- Trust deed.

(v) Collect a Certificate of Registration of Instrument from the Commission.

(vi) Keep copies of the certificate of the registration of Charges at the Registered office of the company.

(vii) Enter the details in the Register of Charges and Debenture holders of the company.

(viii) Obtain Certificate of Registration of charge from the CAC and have a copy of the charge endorsed on every debenture.

(ix) On the satisfaction of the charge, file a memorandum of satisfaction of charge (CAC Form 9) along with Deed of Release or other instrument.

(x) Notify the CAC of the appointment of a receiver/manager upon enforcement of the security.

The effect of failure to register debentures with the commission means that:

(i) The Debenture becomes void against the creditors and liquidators of the company;

(ii) The loan agreement is not *void ab initio* and the mortgagee can recover the loan;

(iii) The loan amount becomes repayable immediately as the debenture is rendered unsecured. The collateral is lost and the debt becomes a simple debt;

(iv) The interest of the mortgagee is then equitable and it loses priority over the debentures registered.

There is provision for extension of time to register/rectify debenture/charges if out of time under the following circumstances:

(i) The debenture holder/company may apply to the Federal High Court by Originating Motion supported by an affidavit to extend the time within which to register a Charge with the Commission;

(ii) Upon grant, go to the CAC with the Charge, Form CAC 8 and a CTC of the Order of the Court extending the time for registration;

(iii) Pay the fine or default fees;

(iv) Collect the Certificate of Registration of Charges.

The remedies of debenture holders for the default in repayment of the loan are as follows:

(i) Action in Court to recover the principal and interest;

(ii) Petition for winding-up of the company on the ground of its inability to pay its debt;

(iii) Specific performance;

(iv) Debenture holders' action.

Additional remedies for secured debentures include:

(v)Power of sale if it is a debenture secured on a fixed asset;

(vi) Foreclosure of the security property;

(vii) Debenture holders action to enforce security;

(viii) Appointment of receiver or manager over the company;

(ix) To take and enter possession of the security used for the loan;

(x) Valuation of security and providing proof of balance upon winding up.

Chapter 16

CAPITAL MARKET PRACTICE AND FLOATATION OF SECURITIES

CAPITAL MARKET

Simply put, capital floatation is the method by which a company can offer its securities to the public to raise money in accordance with the provisions of the Act. The Act also makes provisions for a company to borrow money.

The regulatory bodies for the capital Market include:

(i) Securities and Exchange Commission (SEC, main regulatory authority on public offer of companies' securities);
(ii) Nigerian Stock Exchange (NSE);
(iii) Corporate Affairs Commission;
(iv) Federal High Court of Nigeria;
(v) Central Bank of Nigeria;
(vi) Nigerian Investment Promotion Commission.

Similarly, the legal regime or applicable laws on capital market transactions are these:

(i) Investment and Securities Act (ISA) 2007;
(ii) Securities and Exchange Commission Consolidated Rules 2013;
(iii) Companies and Allied Matters Act 2004;
(iv) Nigeria Stock Exchange listing rules;
(v) Federal High Court Act.

(a) Financial Market and Capital Market

Financial market is the avenue by which companies and the government raise funds. There are two sources of funds, namely:

(i) the money market;

(ii) the capital market.

Money market is the forum where you can access funds from Banks and other financial institutions through negotiable instruments and bills. It is used to access short-term funds. Collaterals are usually required.

On the other hand, the capital market comprises all the arrangements that facilitate the buying and selling of securities. It is a forum where companies and governments may raise funds from the general public by trading securities on the Stock Exchange.

(b) Advantages of the Capital Market

The Capital market has two major advantages namely:

(i) It is believed to be a better option in terms of providing funds for companies as there is an unlimited access to funds there;

(ii) There is the absence of collateralization, since the company obtains money from the public without the members of the public requesting for collateral from the company.

(c) Role of the Capital Market

The *role* of the capital market outlined below also distinguishes between capital and money market thus:

(i) It provides opportunities for companies to borrow funds needed for long-term investment purposes;

(ii) It provides facilities that enable foreign businesses to offer their shares to the Nigerian market;

(iii) It encourages inflow of foreign capital when foreign companies or investors invest in domestic securities.

(iv) Government can carry out its privatisation exercise by offering its shareholdings in state owned enterprises to members of the public through the Stock exchange;

(v) It creates an avenue for the public to participate in the corporate sector of the economy and share in its wealth through ownership of securities;

(vi) It provides employment opportunities for the ever-growing labour force.

LEVELS OF THE NIGERIAN CAPITAL MARKET

The Nigerian capital market exists at two levels, namely at the primary and secondary levels.

(a) Primary Market

The primary market is a forum where companies can access funds for their shares, which have been newly listed or issued to the public[1]. It is also known as the *new issues market* since it provides an avenue for those wishing to raise funds from the market by selling their securities to the public (namely, from the company to the general public). Funds that are raised from the primary market go directly to the company.

The primary market may be in the form of Initial Public Offer (IPO) or Public Offer. An IPO takes place when a company invites members of the public for the very first time to subscribe for its shares or debentures. The offer represents the first entry of the shares or debentures into the capital market for the purpose of raising funds. Public offer on the other hand, refers to subsequent entries to the capital market to issue shares for the purpose of raising funds.

The *procedure* for public offer of securities is as follows:

(i) The bank must demonstrate need for public offer to SEC;

(ii) Pass Board of Directors resolution and special resolution authorising the public offer;

(iii) Prepare draft prospectus in line with relevant the relevant prescriptions of the rules and submit to SEC and NSE;[2]

(iv) File an application to SEC for approval in FORM SEC 6 through the issuing house accompanied by documents specified in Rule 279 (2) SEC Rules 2013 as required by Section 54 ISA;

(v) Upon approval, the final copy of the prospectus signed by all the directors accompanied by a registration statement; certified letters of consent; sworn declaration of full disclosure will be delivered to SEC within 48 hours for registration;[3]

---

[1] Rule 405 SEC Rules 2013

[2] Rule 288 SEC Rules; Section 73 and 79 ISA

[3] Section 80 ISA; Rule 279 (6); 280; 354 SEC Rules

(vi) The printed copy will be forwarded to NSE and CAC for record purposes.

Only public companies can offer their securities to the public, but only quoted public companies and government issuing Bonds can be listed at the Stock Exchange. Private companies and unquoted public companies can offer their securities through private placement but which must be registered with the SEC.

The following are the investment opportunities in the Nigerian capital market:

(i) Investment in Equities/shares;
(ii) Investment in Debentures;
(iii) Investment in Bonds;
(iv) Investment in Collective Investment Schemes;
(v) Investment in mortgage-backed securities.

(b) Secondary Market

The secondary market provides investors the opportunity to buy or sell securities that were earlier issued in the primary market. In other words, it is a sale of shares by the shareholder.

Secondary markets could be *organised or unorganised.* An organised secondary market is a stock market with physical location, trading in designated (quoted) securities, such as the Nigerian Stock Exchange. An unorganised secondary market has no physical trading location but transactions are conducted mainly through telephone calls and the computer. It is otherwise referred to as an Over-the-Counter Market (OTC). It trades in unquoted securities (CSCS).

It should be noted that funds raised in the secondary market do not go to the company but the proceeds go to the shareholder or investor. Meanwhile, transfer of shares applies only to sale of shares by a private person[4]. Accordingly, it does not apply to shares sold on the Stock Exchange.

[4] Section 157 ISA

(c) Public Offer of Securities

There are various methods for the offer of securities to the public. By virtue of Rule 279 of the SEC Rules, these methods are as follows:

(i) Direct Offer to the Public

In this category, the company offers its shares to the public through an issuing house. The issuing house merely acts as an official agent of the company as it packages and offers the shares to the public. The issuing house is a liaison between the company, the regulatory authorities and the public. The terms and conditions of the offer are all contained in the prospectus.

It is worth mentioning that the risk of failure of the issue is borne by the company and not the issuing house. Thus, to protect itself, the company usually arranges for the issue to be underwritten at an agreed commission.

(ii) Offer for Sale

Here, the company sells the whole issue of shares to an Issuing House, which in turn offers the shares to the public at a higher price. The issuing house bears the risk of failure of the issue, thus undertakes the responsibility of underwriting the issue. Thus in the event of failure, the issuing house indemnifies the company.[5]

The difference between *direct offer for sale* and *offer for sale* is as follows:

I. In a direct offer for sale, the Issuing house gets commission while in an offer for sale, the issuing house gets profits;
II. In a direct offer for sale, the company undertakes the responsibility for underwriting the shares; whereas in an offer for sale, the issuing house undertakes the responsibility of underwriting the shares.

(iii) ***Placing***

Here, an invitation is not made to the public whether directly or indirectly. The shares of a company is allotted to an issuing house who later sells the shares to a specialised client or institutional investors or

[5] Sections 69 (1), 70, 82, 315 ISA

pension funds, or cooperative bodies. The risk of failure is borne by the issuing house. Thus it sees the underwriting of the shares.

(iv) ***Placement***

Otherwise referred to as private placement, this is a method of offering shares by a public company which is not quoted on the stock exchange or by a private company upon application by members subject to its articles and SEC approval. A private company cannot allow private placements to more than 50 persons[6].

(v) ***Rights Issue***

This refers to the issue of shares by a company, which is directed only to existing shareholders who are expected to acquire the shares in the ratio at which they hold shares in the company[7]. Rights issue is meant to preserve the leverage or shareholding equilibrium.

It is important to note that no company can have rights issue of shares unless there is a pre-emptive rights clause in its Articles. As such, a company can have a pre-emptive rights clause in its Articles of Association (namely, the right to offer shares first to existing shareholders before transferring to the Public). A rights circular must be registered[8]. Rights issue should not be confused with Restriction of Transfer of Shares by a private company.

However, rights issue has a number of disadvantages which are as follows:

(i) Shares are sold at a lower price than it would have been sold in the market (could lead to insider trading);.
(ii) There could be the problem of the shareholders not having enough money to purchase the rights issue;
(iii) The precarious nature of the capital market or the problems associated with the management of the companies may make a shareholder reluctant to purchase new shares in the company.

---

[6] Rule 340 SEC Rules
[7] Rule 234-338
[8] Rule 326 ISA; Section 54 ISA

(vi) ***Others***

The other methods of public offer of securities are as follows:

- Hybrid offer (comprising rights issue and offer of shares to the public);
- debt/equity conversion [this is not issued by companies only[9].
- Offer by Introduction (used to secure securities admitted to the stock exchange);
- Bonus Issue [this does not require a prospectus.[10]

(d) Documents Required for Registration of Securities

(i) Duly completed Form SEC 6.

(ii) A CTC of the resolution(s) by the general meeting authorising the offer.

(iii) Two CTCs of the altered Memorandum and Articles of Association.

(iv) A CTC of certificate of incorporation of the issuer.

(v) A signed copy of audited accounts for the preceding five years or number of years for which the issuer company has been in operation, (if less than five years) or audited statement of affairs (in the case of a new company).

(vi) Two copies each of the draft prospectus/rights circular/placement memorandum and abridged prospectus.

(vii) Two copies of the draft underwriting agreement and sub-underwriting agreement, where applicable.

(viii) Two copies of draft vending agreement, between issuer and the issuing house.

(ix) Letters of consent given by the parties to the issue, sworn to before a Notary Public or Commissioner for Oaths.

(x) Evidence of technical agreement (if any) reached between the issuer and technical partner(s), advisers/consultants.

(xi) CTC of CAC FORM 7 (particulars of directors).

(xii) A copy of the mandate letter by the issuer to the issuing house.

---

[9] Rule 279 (5) SEC Rules

[10] Section 69 (2) ISA

(xiii) Evidence of payment of registration and filing fees.
(xiv) A certificate of exemption from a recognised stock exchange (where applicable.

(e) Procedure for Issuance and Publication of Prospectus

The procedure for issuing and publishing prospectus of a company involves the following:

(i) Prepare a draft Prospectus in accordance with Rule 288 SEC rules 2013.[11]

(ii) Submit to the NSE for approval/ listing if it is an initial public offer. If the issuer of the shares is already listed, obtain an Exemption Certificate from the NSE.

(iii) File an application to SEC for registration through the issuing house (FORM SEC 6) accompanied by the approved draft prospectus and other documents prescribed in Rule 279 (2) SEC Rules 2013.

(iv) Get letters of consent from all the experts involved in preparation of prospectus and attach to the application.

(v) Print the approved prospectus and have it duly executed by all the directors named in the prospectus accompanied by a registration statement and a sworn declaration of full disclosure of material facts [Section 80 ISA; Rule 279(6), 280, 354 SEC Rules 2013)].

(vi) Deliver the duly executed printed prospectus to SEC for registration within 48 hours and to CAC and NSE for record purposes.

(vii) Publish the prospectus in the abridged form specified in Rule 290 SEC Rules and advertise to the public in line with the rules in Rule 284 SEC Rules.

(f) Registration of Securities with SEC

All forms of securities (including shares, debentures, GDR, bonds etcetera) and Collective investment schemes to be offered to the public

[11] Section 73 and 79(1) ISA

by public companies and government and its agencies must be approved and registered by SEC and the provision of ISA & SEC rules duly complied with.[12]

Registrable securities are securities issue (ordinary share, bonus share, debentures, preference shares, right issue, unit of an investment trust scheme and asset backed securities). Others include-issue of securities offered to the public, state or local government bonds, investment contracts or participation in the oil or gas sector of the economy.

The liability for non-registration of securities is a fine of ₦1,000,000 or three years imprisonment or both.[13] The liability for non-issuance of prospectus is ₦500,000 for corporate bodies and ₦100,000 for individuals.[14] Other liabilities are also provided for under the Investment and Securities Act and SEC Rules[15]. Those liable include director, person consenting to be named, employee, issuing house and principal officers.[16]

(g) Role of Solicitor in Public Offer of Securities

(i) Ensuring the company is a public company. If it is a private company, the solicitor must ensure the proper procedures are followed for conversion from private to public company.

(ii) Ensure that the shares to be issued are within the nominal share capital of the company.

(iii) Ensure that all requirements of the Regulatory bodies are

(iv) Prepare the appropriate prospectus

(v) Ensure that the Prospectus makes all the required disclosures.

(vi) Getting all written consents, including his own and that of other experts that may be mentioned in the Prospectus.

(vii) Ensuring that the Prospectus carries the signature of all directors named in the Prospectus as directors.

(viii) Register the prospectus.

---

[12] Section 54 (1), (5), (6) ISA; Rule 106 SEC Rules

[13] Section 54 (6) ISA

[14] Section 67 (2)

[15] Section 80 (6), 85, 86 ISA; Rule 292 and 293 SEC Rules

[16] Section 85 (2)

(ix) Make sure there are no untrue or misleading statements in the prospectus.

(x) Advising on the opening of subscription lists before any allotment.

(xi) Seeking the initial and final approval of SEC and the Stock Exchange to the issue.

(xii) Ensuring that the issue conforms to all necessary laws and regulations.

FLOATATION OF BONDS

Bonds are fixed income securities issued as debt instruments with low interest yield. It is a loan instrument used to raise long-term capital for infrastructural development. Bonds are negotiable debt instruments. There cannot be a perpetual bond, as the maximum life span is 25 years. Any amount to be sold through bonds must not be more than half of the total income of the company in the preceding financial year. The two main types of bonds are Government bonds and Corporate bonds.

(a) Corporate Bonds

These bonds can be issued by any public company, foreign public companies and supranational bodies (Rule 567).

The *condition* for the issuance of bonds by public companies and supranational bodies is as follows:

(i) Eligibility of Debt Offering

- Any public company, foreign public company or supranational body is eligible to issue.
- All necessary approvals (where applicable) in relation to the issue, from other regulatory authorities shall be obtained and filed with the Commission together with the registration statement.
- All issues of corporate bonds shall be rated by a rating agency (optional for private placements.

- No Issuer shall offer bond if it is in default of payment of interest or repayment of principal in respect of previous debts issuance for a period of more than six months.

(ii) Mode of issue
Corporate bonds may be issued by way of an offer for subscription, rights issue or private placement.

(iii) Resolution
There shall be a resolution by the Board of Directors authorising the issue of the bond and a resolution of the general meeting resolution shall be required in the circumstances below:

- The amount to be borrowed is beyond the specified limit on the borrowing powers of directors in the Memorandum and Articles of Association of the issuer;
- The bond to be issued is convertible.

(b) Procedure for Disclosure and Creation of Charge
The procedure for disclosure and creation of charge in respect of bond issue are thus:

(i) Summon a Board of Director meeting and pass a resolution authorising the bond issue;

(ii) Pass a resolution passed at the General Meeting if the amount to be borrowed is beyond the issuing companies borrowing limit or the bond is a convertible bond;

(iii) The company shall file a registration statement accompanied by the following documents:

1. Duly completed SEC Form 6;
2. Appropriate filing and registration fees;
3. Two copies of the board resolution authorising the issue of the bond or special resolution if needed;
4. Two copies of the Memorandum and Articles of Association (CTC) of the Issuer;
5. A copy of certificate of incorporation of the issuer certified by the company secretary;

6. A signed copy of the Issuers latest audited accounts for the preceding three years, with the latest account not more than nine months old at the time of filing with the SEC;
7. Reporting accountant report;
8. Consent letters of the parties to the offer;
9. Two copies of the draft vending agreement between the issuer and the issuing house;
10. Draft underwriting agreement (where applicable);
11. Rating report by a registered rating agency;
12. A letter of "*No Objection*" from the relevant regulatory body (where applicable);
13. Two copies of draft trust deed;
14. A draft prospectus, right circular, placement memorandum or any form of information Memorandum with specified contents in Rule 567(n) (i-xi) of SEC Rules;
15. Declaration by the issuer on compliance with all requirements of the Act.

(c) Government Bonds

By the provision of Section 222 of the Investment and Securities Act, Government bonds can be issued by the following:

- The Federal Government;
- Federal Government Agencies;
- State Government and their agencies;
- The Federal Capital Territory and its agencies;
- Local Governments;
- Any company which is wholly owned by the Federal, State, FCT and Local Government.

Federal Government issued bonds are known as *sovereign bonds.* States, local governments, government agencies issue *revenue bonds*, while cities within local governments issue *municipal bonds.* The debt management office is part of the Federal Ministry of Finance, which oversees the issue of government securities in collaboration with the SEC.

The laws regulating Government bonds in Nigeria are:

(i) Trustee Investment Act;
(ii) Debt Management Office (Establishment) Act;
(iii) Investment and Securities Act (ISA) and SEC Rules 2013.

(d) Conditions for Issue of Government Bonds

The following are the conditions and requirements for the issuance of government bonds:

(i) There must be a law passed by the National Assembly, State House of Assembly or Local Government authorising the issuance of bonds;
(ii) The bond instrument must bear crest of the government body and be signed by the minister, commissioner or chairman or other appropriate officer of the body raising the loan;[17]
(iii) The total amount of out-standing loan and the bond of the issuer should not *exceed* more than half of its actual revenue for the preceding financial year;[18]
(iv) The bond issue must be registered with the SEC;[19]
(v) Redemption date shall not exceed 25 years from the date of issuance of the bond;[20]
(vi) Letter of authority of guarantee by the Accountant General of state or federation stating that the bond shall be paid and to deduct at source from the statutory allocation due to the issuer in the event of default or failure to meet its payment obligations;
(vii) A sinking fund is required to be opened by the Accountant General of the state or federation to deposit money overtime to make up for the payment of the bonds at the required date;[21]
(viii) A separate sinking fund shall be established for each loan raised;[22]

---

[17] Section 241 (1) ISA
[18] Section 223 (1) (a) ISA; Rules 565 (2) SEC Rules
[19] Section 224 (1) ISA; Rule 564 SEC Rules
[20] Section 226 (2) ISA
[21] Section 224 (4) ISA
[22] Section 251 ISA)

(ix) The bond holders must pay full purchase price before registration;[23]

(x) Bond Certificates must be issued to bondholders by the registrar within two months of the issue;[24]

(xi) A trustee (usually a company) is to be appointed to act on behalf of the bondholders [Section 232 ISA; Rule 565 (5) SEC Rules];

(xii) Registered Bonds may be designated in any denominations approved by SEC [Section 241(1) ISA].

(e) Procedure for Registration of Government Bonds

The process of registering Government bond is by fill application Form SEC 6 with the following documents attached:

(i) A copy of the Law authorising the issue of the bond by the State Government, etcetera, or a Resolution of either the House of Assembly (or the Senate if it is by the Federal Government) or the State (Federal) Executive Council in lieu of a formal Law;

(ii) Copies of the draft trust deed (where applicable);

(iii) An irrevocable Letter of authority issued by the Accountant-General of the State to the Accountant General of the Federation to deduct at source from the statutory allocation to it (the issuer) into the sinking fund(note-waiver);

(iv) Evidence of technical agreement (if any) reached between the issuer and technical partner(s), advisers/consultants;

(v) A feasibility report on the project to be financed;

(vi) Copies of the draft underwriting agreement and sub-underwriting agreement;

(vii) A copy of a rating report by a rating agency;

(viii) The latest audited accounts shall not be more than twelve months old for states, local governments and Federal Government agencies and Supranational bodies;

(ix) Publication of annual financial statements in two daily newspapers;

(x) Details of sinking fund;

---

[23] Section 231

[24] Section 232 ISA; Rule 565 (5) SEC Rules

(xi) Evidence of payment of registration and filing fees.[25]

(f) Registration of Government Owned Company and Agency Bond

Where it involves an agency of the Government or a company wholly owned by the Government, the procedure for registration will be to fill and file application Form SEC 6 attached with the following documents attached:

(i) Copy of the Law or instrument establishing the Agency or company;

(ii) Copy of the Law/Resolution authorising the Agency or company to issue the bond;

(iii) A rating Report;

(iv) An irrevocable letter of Guarantee of repayment issued by the Federal/ State Government that owns the Agency or company etc.

GLOBAL DEPOSITORY RECEIPT

Global Depository Receipt (GDR) is the acknowledgment of purchase of shares on the floor of the stock exchange authorising the bond. It has to do with the re-issuing of shares of a foreign company already issued in that country, in Nigeria. In this case, the country issues receipts to investors who are interested in owing shares in the foreign company.

A GDR is denominated in the foreign currency and is listed on the stock exchange of that foreign country. Other features of GDR include the fact that no share certificate is given, and only listed companies can enjoy the issuance of GDR.

COLLECTIVE INVESTMENTS SCHEMES

Collective Investment Schemes (CIS) refers to a pooled investment by a group of persons with no membership nor participatory rights. It is under a third party management and control.

Essentially, CIS is any form of arrangement which may involve:

---

[25] Section 224 (3) ISA; Rule 565 (1) SEC Rules

(i) A situation where investors share the risk and benefit of investment in proportion to their participatory interest; or

(ii) Where investors share the risk and benefit of investment as determined in the deed.

As such, CIS is a scheme in whatever form, in pursuance of which members of the public are invited to invest money or other assets in a portfolio, such as cooperative societies among other types of scheme.[26]

The main features of a collective investment scheme include these:

(i) Pooling of funds by participants for the purpose of sharing profit and the participants do not have day to day control over the management of the property underlying the arrangement;

(ii) The pooled fund is usually managed by a designated professional fund manager;

(iii) The participants in a CIS merely have a participatory interest in the scheme and they are not members of any company in which their funds are invested;

(iv) The participants do not enjoy membership rights of a company;

(v) Participants in a CIS are designated as unit holders.

(a) Types of Collective Investment Schemes

There are different types of CIS depending on the purpose, and they include the following:

(i) Unit Trust Scheme

This scheme is an arrangement made for the purpose of providing facilities for participation of the public as beneficiaries under a trust, in profits or income arising from acquisition, management or disposal of securities or any other property.[27]

It is usually administered as a Limited Liability Company (private or public) approved by SEC with the main objective to pool resources of small savers in order to build a portfolio of securities to earn income and capital gains for the investors (unit holders) and managed by Fund/Portfolio Managers.

---

[26] Section 153 ISA

[27] Section 152 and 315 ISA

A Trustee is also appointed whose responsibility is to register and hold investments in trust for the unit holders. The Trustee is also to ensure that the terms of the trust as contained in the Trust Deed executed with the Fund Managers are strictly observed.

The *conditions* for the authorisation or licencing of a unit trust scheme are:

(i) No Unit Trust Scheme can be issued or made available unless it is registered and authorised by SEC;[28]

(ii) The fund manager must be an incorporated company with a profile of dealing with business.

(iii) Independence of the fund manager must be evident on the face of the scheme;

(iv) The share capital of the manager must be in line with the authorised capital as prescribed by SEC;

(v) The Trustee must be an incorporated company with the authorised share capital;

(vi) The designation or name of the UTS must not be absurd and must be acceptable to the SEC;

(vii) There must be evidence of non – interference between the managers and trustees.

(ii) Investment Trust Fund/Ethical Mutual Investment

An Investment Trust Fund and Ethical Mutual Investment is a socially responsive fund which complies with ethical or moral principles of investment. It is usually packaged as a specialised unit trust scheme whereby the Unit Holders define in advance what type of securities their money would be invested in. For example, IBTC Ethical Fund clearly excluded Alcoholic and Cigarette producing companies from the investments of the trust scheme.

(iii) Real Estate Investment Trust

A Real Estate Investment Trust (REIT) is established solely for the purpose of acquiring intermediate or long term interest in real estate or

---

[28] Section 152 and 315 ISA

property development and may raise funds from the capital market through the issuance of securities in favour of the pooled investors that contributed to the scheme[29].

Some features of this Scheme include the presence of unit, unit holders, trustees, fund managers and trust deeds. It also involves the contribution of money and profit.

However, the scheme does not envisage the allotting of lands to the unit holders. It is merely an interest in real estate.

(iv) Cooperative/Community Savings Scheme

This Scheme involves the pooling of small funds from certain members of a group within a community. It requires approval and registration from the SEC for statistical purposes.

(v) Closed-Ended Scheme

This scheme is a publicly traded investment company that raises a fixed amount of capital through an initial public offering (IPO). The fund is then structured, listed and traded like a stock on a stock exchange.

Unlike regular stocks, closed-end fund stock represents an interest in a specialised portfolio of securities that is actively managed by an investment advisor and which typically concentrates on a specific industry, geographic market, or sector. The stock prices of a closed-end fund fluctuate according to market forces (supply and demand) as well as the changing values of the securities in the fund's holdings.

A Close-ended Scheme does not re-issue nor redeem additional issues of new units (shares). It is often listed and traded on the Stock Exchange and its price is determined by market forces. The scheme issues all the shares from the onset, with such shares usually being tradable between investors thereafter.

(vi) Open-Ended Investment Company

An Open-ended Investment Company is one with an authorised share capital whose Articles of Association authorise the acquisition of its

---

[29] Section 193 ISA; Rule 502-508 SEC Rules

own shares structured in such a manner that it provides for the re-issuing of different classes of shares to investors, each class of shares representing a separate portfolio with a distinct investment policy.[30]

The normal practice is for an investor to purchase shares in the fund directly from the fund itself rather than from the existing shareholders. This type continually issues and redeems units or shares after IPO. The price is based on the net asset value, which is the sum of the fund less all liabilities as at the date of acquisition or redemption.

(vii) Venture Capital Fund

A Venture Capital Fund is a profit seeking scheme set up by entrepreneurs. Their main aim is making funds available to new and growing businesses towards long term profit. It is usually an initial stage of financing new and developing companies seeking to develop quickly. Institutional investors, affluent individuals among others, are sources of the fund. A very striking feature of this scheme is that the risk of return is high.

(viii) Specialised fund

This is a mutual fund that invests in securities of a particular sector, industry or geographical location. Like Venture Capital Fund, this type of scheme is also notable for high risks and returns when compared to other funds due to lack of diversification of the portfolio of investment.

It should be noted that in addition to the schemes discussed above, there are other types designated as CIS in the *Gazette*.

(b) Procedure for Registration of Collective Investment Scheme

The procedure for the Registration of Collective Investment Scheme includes an application in Form SEC 6A attached with the following:

(i) Copies of draft prospectus;
(ii) Copies of draft Trust Deed;
(iii) The proposed portfolio mix and experts;
(iv) Notarised letters of consent of the prospective parties to the schemes;

---

[30] Section 152 and 315 ISA

(v) Copies of the CTC of the Memorandum and Articles of the Fund;

(vi) Manager company;

(vii) Copies of the CTC of the Memorandum and Articles of the Trustee company;

(viii) A sworn undertaken to file evidence of maintenance of a separate fund account in a reputable Bank;

(ix) Copies of the CTC of the particulars of Directors (Form CAC 7) of the managers and trustees of the company;

(x) Evidence that the minimum paid-up capital of the managers and trustees of the CIS complies with the requirements of SEC thus:

I. Fund Manager – ₦150 million (20 million)

II. Trustee company- ₦300 million (40 million).[31]

(c) Differences between Company and CIS

The following distinctions can be made between a company and a collective investment scheme:

(i) Members of a company are called shareholders while the participants in CIS are called unit holders;

(ii) Shareholders are entitled to dividends whereas unit holders are entitled to profit pro rata;

(iii) The Board of Directors manage a company while the CIS is managed by the Fund managers, trustees;

(iv) Shareholders have and exercise membership rights while unit holders do not take decisions in the running of the company;

(v) Shareholders have a definite number of shares as against funds invested whereas funds contributed by unitholders' individualism are not representative of individual contributions made.

In conclusion, the capital market sector of the economy is technical and that is why it is unpopular. Hence the need to have sound knowledge about the operations, procedures, rules and regulations governing it.

---

[31] Rule 41 (1) SEC Rules

Chapter 17

INTERNAL RESTRUCTURING

MEANING OF RESTRUCTURING

Restructuring generally means designing or repositioning a company either internally or externally. *Internal restructuring* involves the company alone with its members or creditors while external *restructuring* deals with the company and other third parties.

It is normal for companies in business to restructure when the need arises, either to mitigate loss or stem a downward trend. Restructuring could also be due to reckless management of resources of a company by its directors.

(a) Reasons and Rationale for Restructuring

The reasons for corporate restructuring include these:

(i) The need to reposition itself to make more profit;

(ii) To gain more control in the market;

(iii) To expand its sphere of coverage;

(iv) To reduce or arrest losses and downward sliding;

Whereas the rationale for internal restructuring are:

(i) To survive economic hardship/financial trauma without losing corporate identity;

(ii) To eliminate superfluous shares/securities no longer represented by a company's assets through negotiation with company's creditors to accept money's worth;

(iii) To reduce likelihood of fraud.

It should be noted that internal restructuring is used when a company has a large debt profile and the company desires that it should not be wound up.

(b) Options for Internal Restructuring

The options or methods available to the company to salvage the it from collapse and keep the company afloat as a going concern are as enumerated hereunder:

(i) Buy out e.g. shareholders buy out, management /employee buy-out;[1]
(ii) Arrangement and compromise;
(iii) Arrangement on sale;
(iv) Increase of share capital;
(v) Reduction of Share capital;
(vi) Share consolidation and reconstruction;
(vii) Conversion and re-registration of the company in order to take advantage of the capital market;
(viii) Salary Adjustment (downsizing, involves cut down in salaries);
(ix) Redundancy scheme or voluntary withdrawal (a type of labour scheme).

(c) Signposts for Determining Best Internal Restructuring Option

The markers for determining best internal restructuring options to adopt are outlined thus:

(i) *Arrangement and Compromise* is appropriate for determining indebtedness of creditors and preference shareholders where the company does not want to be wound up;
(ii) Arrangement on sale is the best option for a solvent company selling whole or part of assets (voluntary winding up);
(iii) *Reduction of shares capital* is for bloated shares (issued shares);
(iv) *Buy-out of controlling shares* is a good directors/employees intervention;

[1] Rule 499 SEC Rules

(v) *Increase of share capital* by raising money at the capital market is an option to settle debts);
(vi) *Share reconstruction* will enable a company to raise the value of shares and raise more capital if it wants to target plenty of participants;
(vii) *Cancellation* is appropriate where shares are unissued.

(d) Arrangement or Compromise

This is a negotiated agreement by a company for its creditors, members or a class of them to accept an amount less than what the company is owing or accept a settlement other than cash as full and final settlement of the company's indebtedness under the arrangement. This is done under an instrument.

In an arrangement and compromise situation, the company alters the rights of its members and creditors only. For instance, an agreement with the preferred shareholders to cancel their dividends in arrears, etcetera. An arrangement is the alteration of the obligation of a company by negotiation with those entitled to what the company is owing, such as members, debenture holders, creditors or a class of them.

The *forms* of arrangement or compromise include:

(i) Arrangement or compromise with creditors;
(ii) Debt equity swap; and
(iii) Arrangement or compromise with members/creditors.

Arrangement or compromise with creditors involves the following:

(i) A proposal to create successive legal mortgages where possible;
(ii) An arrangement to accept a lesser amount than that which it is entitled to;
(iii) A compromise with creditors to relinquish their security;
(iv) A compromise to reschedule the time for redemption of the loans;
(v) Conversion of convertible debentures into shares;
(vi) An arrangement to create a high ranking or *pari passu* charge;

(vii) An arrangement with creditors to accept shares or debt instruments in lieu of cash payments for satisfaction of debt.

Debt Equity Swap (otherwise called *convertible debenture* in form of debt equity swap) is a mode whereby the company negotiates with its creditors to propose a relinquishment of their security, or to undertake to pay them off prior to the reconstruction or convince them to take shares or part shares or part cash in satisfaction of their debts. This mode is suitable because the creditors are made to accept less than what they are ordinarily entitled to as full satisfaction of its obligation. It is also suitable because it enables a company to alter the rights of its creditors with the sanction of the court thus modifying the rights of the creditors involved.

The scheme is the document that embodies the proposed compromise, namely, variation/reduction of the obligation) – how much the company is owing, who it is owing, what the company is offering and in what way has the creditors responded to it.

Arrangement or compromise with members/shareholders first, involves an agreement for variation of class rights as follows:

- Persuade the ordinary shareholders to relinquish part of their shares to preference;
- Propose an agreement with preference shareholders for:
  1. Cancellation of their dividend arrears;
  2. Reduction of the fixed rate of dividend;
  3. Conversion of their preference shares to ordinary shares;
  4. Acceptance of ordinary shares in lieu of dividend arrears;

- Secondly, members may be persuaded to pass a resolution for the Increase and Reduction of Share Capital of the company;
- Thirdly, the company may also make calls on shares or demand the shareholder to pay up for the shares issued to them that have remained unpaid by them;

The *procedure* for arrangement or compromise are as follows:

- Board resolution sanctioning proposed scheme of arrangement;

- When a scheme of arrangement is proposed, either the company or the creditors may approach the Federal High Court for an order to sanction the scheme of arrangement. When the court is approached, the court will order a meeting of the creditors, debenture holders, members or a class of them;
- Notice of meeting should be served on members accompanied with a statement showing the effect of the arrangement on the directors as creditors/shareholders;
- 75 per cent or a majority of the shareholders/creditors should vote in favour of the scheme and a written report of it made to the Court;
- The Federal High Court refers the scheme to the SEC to investigate its fairness or otherwise of the scheme;
- The SEC appoints inspectors to investigate it and reports to the Court;
- If the court is satisfied with the fairness of the scheme, the Court will make an Order sanctioning the scheme and the scheme becomes binding on all affected creditors/shareholders;
- The order shall have no effect until a certified true copy of the order has been delivered by the company to the Commission for registration and a copy of the Court order should be annexed to every copy of the Memorandum of the company.

(e) Arrangement on Sale

This restructuring method is a process of voluntary winding up of a company and liquidators appointed and authorised to sell the whole or part of its undertaking or assets to another corporate body.

In this regard, the consideration for the sale may be cash, shares, debentures or policies, which would be distributed to members of the companies in accordance with their rights in liquidation. Alternatively, the money realised could be used in the floatation of a new company or as equity contribution in any scheme of arrangement for restructuring such as merger.

Arrangement on Sale is one of the options that could be adopted for the internal restructuring for a company whose assets outweigh its liabilities. This gives rise to the resurrection of the company in another form either as a new company or providing funds for another restructuring scheme. In essence, the company will not be brought to a permanent end upon winding up as a result of its liabilities and liquidation. Hence, it will still exist and operate but in another form.

This is an option in corporate restructuring, which may be wholly internal or commence as an internal restructuring and end as an external restructuring. Internal restructuring is one that does not require cooperation of more than one corporate entity. It is used when a company is doing well and has no financial difficulty in meeting its obligations. Thus, it is an option available to a solvent company, namely, where its assets exceed its liabilities.

The procedure for arrangement on sale is as follows:

(i) Board resolution adopting draft scheme of arrangement on sale;

(ii) Statutory declaration of solvency by board of directors basis for the voluntary winding-up;

(iii) Notice of Extraordinary General Meeting will be issued to members of the company;

(iv) Special Resolution passed by members authorising members voluntary winding up and to appoint a liquidator to sell the assets to another company in consideration for cash or shares in the company;

(v) The liquidator convenes a meeting of the shareholders/creditors to approve/consider the scheme of arrangement;

(vi) A dissenting member can write the liquidator within 30 days of the passing of the Resolution asking him to either:

- Abstain from carrying out the Resolution; or
- Purchase his own shares at a price to be determined by an agreement if it is a private company with no alien or SEC if a Plc or a private company with alien participation.

(vii) If all assets are sold, the proceeds of the sale will be distributed amongst members in order of priority of a company in liquidation;

(viii) The liquidator will convene a final dissolution meeting where the accounts of the winding up would be considered by the members;

(ix) The arrangement will be valid if there is no objection after one year under:

- unfairly prejudicial and oppressive conduct; or
- an order of the Court for a creditors' winding-up.

However, where the mandate is that the liquidator is to sell part of the assets or undertaking of the company, it is an *internal option* but where the mandate is to sell all the assets and undertaking and invest it in another company. This then becomes an external option.

Finally, the difference between arrangement on sale and arrangement or compromise is as follows:

(i) In an arrangement on sale, the company is solvent (its assets are in excess of its liabilities) and to demonstrate this, the directors are required to make a solemn declaration of solvency which is not required in arrangement or compromise.

(ii) Arrangement or compromise is more suitable where a company is in financial trauma, whereas an arrangement on sale is usually used when a company is solvent.

(f) Increase and Reduction in Share Capital

As an internal option in restructuring, a company facing financial difficulty may opt to increase its share capital and then place it on the capital market for purchase. Alternatively, a company which is financially buoyant may opt to reduce its share capital realised for other investments.

A company may need to reduce its share capital if the assets of the company is no longer represented by a portion of its shares. The shares become superfluous, that is, not proportional to the assets of the company. Thus reduce the share capital as to what is fully represented. Special resolution at a general meeting of a company but for private companies, if all members entitled to attend and vote unanimously by written resolution and reduction will be approved by the Court. Copy of resolution, order of court and memo and article as altered will be filed with the Commission. Every memo will now bear indications that the share capital has been reduced.

As regards increase of share capital, this involves the injection of more funds to the capital base of the company so the company can do more business and make more profit. The procedure is by convening a meeting of the company by the company secretary. An ordinary resolution is passed at the meeting, after which Form CAC 2.1 for alteration of share capital is filed at the Commission.

(g) Share Reconstruction and Reconsolidation

The shares of a company can be reconstructed or consolidated, added together and subdivided into several numbers than they originally were or cancelled entirely. Similarly, a company may cancel issued but unpaid shares.

The aim is to dissolve the shares into one whole lump and subdivide the shares into stocks or shares of larger numbers that it was or subdivide into fewer numbers of shares provided that in either case, the amount paid by the shareholders is not tampered with. As such, the total amount represented by all the shares must be unchanged.

The *procedure* for this option is to prepare and file Form CAC 2A and Scheme of Reconstruction (authorised share capital and ratio for reconstruction). Prior to this, the company shall give the Commission one-month Notice.

(h) Buy-Out

The buy-out option is an agreement or arrangement where certain interest groups within a company acquire the interest in shares of others in a company. It involves an acquisition of the totality or a controlling percentage of a company's equity or shares by stakeholders within or outside the company. These stakeholders may be the employees, management, pension scheme, creditors or other external groups interested in the equities of the company. They decide to leverage or take advantage of the special relationship they have with the company.

With specific reference to employees buy-out, the employees may decide to buy out a company because of their job securities or attachment to the company. They can do this by pooling their salaries together and buying out the management of the company.

Leverage Buy-out or Management Buy-out on the other hand, is the acquisition by a management team (directors/employees) of a company of controlling shares of that company or its subsidiaries by buying controlling shares.[2]

As a form of internal restructuring, it involves restructuring of the ownership of the company. The shareholders are divested and replaced with the management who also become the owners of the equity of the company as well as the managers of the company. A buy-out is regulated by the SEC as a neutral party. It regulates the amount to be paid as value for the share.

However, where an external company (its management/board of directors) acquires the controlling equities or all the equities of another company, this is called management buy-in, and thus falls under the ambit of external restructuring.

The *procedure* for management buy-out is as follows:[3]

(i) An application for the approval of a management buy-out completed by the management team, attached with –
   - A Resolution of the shareholders approving the management buy-out;
   - Resolution of the management team to undertake the management buy-out;
   - A copy of the Certificate of Incorporation of the company;
   - A copy of the Memorandum of Association and Articles of Association of the company;
   - Two copies of the prospectus containing -
     - ➢ Profile of the company;

[2] Section 118 ISA; Rule 449 SEC Rules
[3] Rule 499 SEC Rule

- Profile of the management team buying over the company;
- Objectives of the management buy-out;
- Five years audited financial statement of the company (or if less than five years, the statement of affairs for the number of years in existence);
- Claims and litigation.

(ii) Sale agreement between the company and the management team containing these items:

- Terms and conditions of sale;
- Indemnity against contingent liabilities by the seller to third-parties, and pay tax not provided for in the account;
- If employees of the target company operate a pension scheme, the agreement should have a clause on the continuation of the scheme;
- Sale and purchase of assets;
- Contracts and creditors;
- *Employees*: the liabilities and obligations under the existing contract of employment will pass to the buyer with accrued contractual and statutory rights unaffected;
- *Debtors*: the agreement should reflect that monies owed the seller by its debtors should be paid to the seller unless assigned to the buyer. The purchase price must reflect the fact that the debts are assigned;
- The agreement should state whether the buyer or seller would like to carry on the business under the existing name. Where a new name would be used, it should be so stated and copies of relevant documents shall be filed with SEC:
- Trust Deed (where applicable);
- Any other document that may be required by the Commission from time to time.[4]

[4] See Rule 449 (b) (vi) (a-h) of SEC Rules

Chapter 18

EXTERNAL OPTIONS IN CORPORATE RESTRUCTURING

EXTERNAL RESTRUCTURING

External restructuring is the opposite of internal restructuring, as it involves the company and other third parties. Every merger acquisition or external restructuring between or among companies shall be subject to the prior review and approval of the SEC.[1]

The SEC Rules provide general requirements for other forms of external restructuring. It refers to the combination of corporate effort by two or more companies coming together to collaborate, synergise and combine efforts.

REGULATORY BODIES AND LEGAL FRAMEWORK FOR EXTERNAL RESTRUCTURING

The following *regulatory bodies* are involved external restructuring options with their roles:

(i) Securities and Exchange Commission (the apex regulatory body of capital market operations. It grants pre-merger consent, clears scheme documents and approves the merger. It also grants authority to proceed in a take-over bid);

(ii) Central Bank of Nigeria (it gets involved in merger and acquisition, where banking institutions are involved in the merger scheme. The prior consent of the CBN Governor must be sought and obtained before any such agreement;[2]

---

[1] Rule 423 SEC Rule

[2] Section 7 Banks and Other Financial Institutions Act (BOFIA)

(iii) Federal High Court of Nigeria (issues Orders, deals with objections to shareholders' meeting or to merger, and sanctions merger – the merger becomes effective from the date the order is given);

(iv) Nigeria Stock Exchange (it is a self-regulatory organization that regulates listed public companies and secondary market transactions. It must be notified by listed companies of intention to merge);

(v) Corporate Affairs Commission (responsible for filing and certification of corporate resolutions and documents to be filed with SEC, filing of sanction, and de-registration of dissolved companies);

(vi) Nigeria Deposit Insurance Corporation (insures depositors' funds in event of bank liquidation);

(vii) Asset Management Corporation of Nigeria (manages the assets of a company in liquidation).

The laws and Rules guiding merger are:

(i) Investment and Securities Act 2007;

(ii) Central Bank of Nigeria (CBN) Act;

(iii) Banks and Other Financial Institutions Act 1991 (as amended);

(iv) Federal High Court Act;

(v) Nigerian Deposit Insurance Commission (NDIC) Act (for banks);

(vi) Asset Management Commission of Nigeria (AMCON) Act;

(vii) Securities and Exchange Commission, SEC (Consolidated) Rules 2013;

(viii) Federal High Court Rules;

(ix) Insurance Act;

(x) National Insurance Commission Act;

(xi) Investment and Securities Tribunal Rules;

(xii) Arbitration and Conciliation Act 2004.

External restructuring takes various forms as discussed in the sections below.

PURCHASE AND ASSUMPTION

This option is a device in contemporary corporate investment to save ailing companies so that their investments will not be totally lost. It involves purchase of the assets and assumption of the liabilities therein. The option allows another company/investors to purchase the liabilities of the failing company and assume ownership of its assets, usually at auction price.

Purchase and assumption may involve cherry picking, wherein the healthy company is not taking up the liabilities of the failed company but is allowed to inspect the books and assets, operations and business activities of the failed company with a view to picking out those aspects they could save by integrating them into its own operations.

(a) Implications of Purchase and Assumption

The implications of the adopting this option are as follows:

(i) It serves to save the interest of shareholders or creditors of ailing companies especially so that they can exercise their rights against the offeror company;

(ii) It provides a window for investment for both companies;

(iii) There is loss of corporate personality of the purchased company;

(iv) Management restructuring is inevitable and in most cases this does not favour the purchased company;

(v) The purchasing company will inevitably obtain the trade secrets of the company as well as the assets of the company and liabilities.

(b) Procedure for Purchase and Assumption

The procedure for the option of purchase and assumption is as follows:

(i) Board and General Meeting resolution by both assumed and purchasing company or government whitepaper approving the proposed arrangement and preparation of deed of purchase and assumption;

(ii) Licensed valuer to value the assets of the moribund company;

(iii) Negotiation btw regulatory bodies (e.g. NDIC, CBN) and purchaser company;

(iv) The transaction is perfected (signing of deed by the parties);

(v) The perfected documents are filed along with the court process for judicial sanction at the FHC;

(vi) The assumed company is dissolved through a judicial sale of its assets and liabilities to the purchasing company;

(vii) Upon successful purchase, the assumed company takes up the status of the purchasing company through a judicial assent.

The documents required for perfection during purchase and assumption are:

(i) Duly executed deed of purchase and assumption;

(ii) Board of directors and General Manager's resolutions or Government whitepaper (in case of a government owned company or company taken over by a regulatory agency, namely NDIC, AMCON or CBN).

MERGER AND ACQUISITION

Merger takes place when a viable company takes over another company or two companies decide to merge to form a new company or to maintain the earlier names of one of the companies.

An Acquisition on the other hand refers to the purchase by one company of all or substantial interest of another company, such that the acquired company becomes a subsidiary or division of the acquiring company. For an Acquisition to amount to a merger, it must be a purchase of more than one half of the issued share capital of a company.

(a) Reasons for Merger and Acquisition

The following reasons account for the preference of this external restructuring option:

(i) ***Risk Diversification*** (where a company diversifies into an unrelated line of business, the costs and risks involved in developing and maintaining a new product line may be avoided or reduced through the acquisition of the company);

(ii) ***Economies of Scale*** (the amalgamation of entities brings about expanded productive capacity in the surviving or evolving entity);

(iii) ***Corporate Leverage*** (a company seeking to improve its debt or equity ratio may utilise the option of merging with another company for this purpose);

(iv) ***Technological Drive*** *(*a company which is unable to have easy access to the required technology to enhance its operations may merge with another which has the technological advantage over it);

(v) ***Management Expertise*** (a company that lacks the requisite personnel with high level, technical or managerial skills to achieve its corporate objective may decide to merge or be acquired by another company);

(vi) *Desire for growth and increased market share* also constitutes a reason for mergers;

(vii) *Survival of regulatory requirements for consolidation* (the desire to remain in business in the face of stringent requirements for consolidation in a particular business line, may force a company to go for merger or acquisition);

(viii) *Stock Exchange Quotation* (a private company desirous of public quotation may integrate with a publicity quoted company in order to achieve this aim).

(b) Classification of Mergers

Mergers and acquisitions are broadly classified into three types, viz: horizontal, vertical and conglomerate.

(i) Horizontal Merger

This involves the combination of enterprises or companies operating in the same geographical location, same market at the same level in the business/market. An example is where two banks both in Nigeria or

Africa, looking for customers and same service to customers, such as between Stanbic and IBTC bank.

(ii) Vertical Merger

A vertical merger involves the fusion of companies in the same market but operating at different levels of production or service provision in a complimentary manner. For instance, a goods manufacturing enterprise and a distributor company could merge to consolidate on their gains.

(iii) Conglomerate Merger

This type of merger has to do with the combination of two business concerns in a completely unrelated line of operations. The objective of the merger is to diversify, dominate the market and expand their sphere of control of the market. An example will be an oil company with a telecoms company.

(c) Categories of Merger

The prescribed categories or threshold are based on either a combination of assets and turnover or combined annual turnover or assets as follows:[3]

(i) Small Merger

This can be done with a capital less than ₦1 billion or equal to ₦500 million. Parties to a small merger are not required to notify the SEC and may implement the merger without approval unless the SEC expressly requires notification.[4]

The SEC may within 6 months after a small merger is commenced, require the parties to notify it of the merger where it forms the opinion that the merger may substantially prevent or lessen competition or cannot be justified on public interest grounds.[5]

The *procedure* for a small merger is as outlined below.

I. Parties notify SEC of the merger (if required).[6]

---

[3] Section 120 ISA; Rule 427 SEC Rule

[4] Section 122 ISA; Rule 424 SEC Rules.

[5] Section 122 (3) ISA

[6] [(Section 122 (1) and (2)

- Within 20 working days of such notification, SEC may extend the period in which to consider the merger by a single period not exceeding 40 working days, and in that case it must issue an extension certificate to the parties. After considering the merger in terms of section 121 of ISA, the SEC shall notify the parties in a prescribed form of its approval/conditional approval or prohibition of the merger.[7]
- Upon the expiration of the 20 working days or the expiration of the extension, if SEC has not notified the parties of its decision, the merger shall be deemed to have been approved.[8]
- The SEC shall thereupon, publish a notice of its decision in the Gazette; and issue written reasons for the decision if it prohibits or conditionally approves the merger, or requested to do so by a party to the merger.[9]
- If the merger is approved the parties shall apply to the court for the merger to be sanctioned and when so sanctioned, it becomes binding on the companies.[10]
- Within six months of the implementation of a small merger, SEC may require notification on the grounds in Section 122(3) of ISA.

(ii) Intermediate Merger and Large Merger

An Intermediate Merger requires a capital between ₦1 billion and up to ₦5 billion. Whereas a Large Merger a capital projection of above ₦5 billion.

The *procedure* for obtaining approval for Large and Intermediate Merger is as summarized below:[11]

- Submit pre-merger notification to SEC for evaluation accompanied by clearance of scheme documents with the information set out in Rule 426 of SEC Rules;

---

7 Section 122 (5)
8 Section 122 (11)
9 Section 122 (12)
10 Section 122(6)]
11 Rule 425 SEC Rules

- File application with Federal High Court seeking an order to convene a court ordered meeting;
- Both companies pass separate board resolutions agreeing to merge;
- Following the resolution of the shareholders after the court ordered meeting, the applicants shall file with the SEC a formal application of the merger;
- If it is an intermediate/ large merger, the companies are to inform the Trade Unions or its employees of the merger;[12]
- Pre-merger notice for large merger shall be referred to the Court;[13]
- Statement shall be made to court within 40 working days;
- Letters of consent must be written by the merging companies under oath;[14]
- The merging companies will wait for 20/40 working days after submitting the application for SEC to issue a certificate of approval or refusal;
- If after 20/40 days nothing is heard of its approval from the SEC, it is deemed approved;
- The SEC shall then give an approval in principle for the companies to proceed;
- An application shall be made to the Federal High Court for an order to convene simultaneous separate meetings of shareholders of merging companies;[15]
- Pass a special resolution at the separate court ordered meetings approving the merger;
- The parties shall then return to the Court to obtain sanction of the merger;
- Both companies shall make an application to the SEC for formal approval attached with these documents:[16]

---

[12] Section 123 ISA
[13] Section 126 ISA
[14] Rule 428 (1) ISA
[15] Rule 425 (b) SEC Rules

- Two duly signed copies of the merger scheme documents;
- Extracts of the minutes of the Court ordered meeting approving merger scheme duly signed by director and secretary. The extract shall capture the consideration as approved by majority shareholders, representing not less than three–quarter in value of the shares of members being present and voting either in person or by proxy;
- Resolutions passed at the Separate court ordered meetings;
- Scrutinizer's report showing votes for and against the schemes;
- Stamped Power of Attorney of absent directors at the separate Court-ordered meetings (where applicable);
- Amended Copy of Memorandum and Article of Association of the resultant company;
- Clearance letter from Federal Inland Revenue Service;
- Form CA7/7A (directors);
- Form CAC2/2A (allotment of share capital);
- Evidence of payment of prescribed processing fees;
- Relevant SEC Forms.

- The companies must comply with all post approval requirements in line with Rule 430 of SEC Rules;
- A post-merger inspection will be carried out by the SEC within 3 months after the approval to assess how the resultant (merged) company is fairing;[17]
- The company shall forward the requisite documents to the Corporate Affairs Commission for registration.

(d) Post-merger Compliance

Post-merger compliance is usually effected after the final SEC approval and Court order sanctioning the scheme[18].

---

[16] Rule 429 SEC Rules
[17] Rule 431 SEC Rules)
[18] Rule 430 SEC Rules

It involves filing the following documents:

(i) Copy of the court order sanctioning the scheme within seven days.

(ii) Copy of newspaper publication of Court Order

(iii) Statement of the actual cost of the scheme.

(iv) Notification of completion of merger or otherwise within three months of Court's Order.

(v) Summary reports of the scheme in respect of the following:

- Arrangement relating to employees of the acquired company;
- Settlement of shareholders;
- Utilization of monies injected into the company (if any);
- Treatment of dissenting shareholders;
- Submission of gazetted copy of the court sanction;
- Evidence of allotment of shares;
- Evidence of settlement of severance benefits of employees (where applicable);
- Statement of the actual cost of the scheme.

(e) Post-merger Inspection

Post-merger inspection involves the scrutiny or perusal of these documents:

- The board minutes book;
- Original Certificate of incorporation of the resultant company (where applicable);
- Copy of the amended Memorandum and Articles of Association (where applicable);
- Severance benefits of employees of the dissolved companies;
- Final settlement of shareholders;
- Dispatch of share certificates;
- Settlement of debts;
- Report of shareholders representatives on the merger;
- Any other document that may be required by the SEC from time to time.

(f) Refusal of Merger Application

An application for merger may be refused by the relevant authorities on these grounds:

(i) If it will cause a substantial restraint in competition;

(ii) If it has the tendency to create a monopoly in any line of business of the merging companies;

(iii) It is otherwise obnoxious to public policy.

(g) Revocation of Merger Approval

The SEC may revoke its own decision to approve or conditionally approve a small, intermediate or large merger on these grounds:[19]

(i) If the decision was based on incorrect information for which a party to the merger is responsible;

(ii) If the approval was obtained by deceit;

(iii) If a company concerned in the merger has breached an obligation attached to the decision.

It should be noted that the SEC may, where the business practice of a company substantially prevents or lessens competition, order the breakup of the company into separate entities and re-register them.[20] The order shall be referred to court for sanctioning.

TAKE-OVER

Take-over is an external restructuring process which results in the acquisition or purchase of substantial interest or shares by an individual or company in another company known as the target company sufficient enough to give the offeror substantial control over either management and/or overall affairs of the target company [the company whose shares are the subject of a take-over bid, namely the company that is to be taken over.[21]

In terms of the modalities for takeover, the Target Company and the Offeror company (the persons or company making the take-over bid - a document that packages the take–over) would form a single

---

[19] Section 127 ISA
[20] Section 128 ISA
[21] Section 131 ISA

group in which the bigger and stronger company (offeror) becomes the *Holding company* and the weaker or smaller (target) becomes the subsidiary. However, for acquisition to take over the share acquired must not be less than 30 per cent.

Hostile takeover is a systematic takeover to bypass the normal process of going through the Board of directors and members of the company. It means to gradually acquire the shares of the company in the stock exchange market or purchase shares of existing shareholders at a premium to acquire 30 per cent to 50 per cent of the shares. Another means is to instigate other shareholders in the company to vote out the Board of Directors and vote in a Board that the company can persuade to allot shares that would lead the company to take-over the target company.

Companies that cannot be taken over include the following:

(i) A company with less than 20 shareholders representing 60 per cent of the members of the target company;[22]

(ii) Shares of a private company.[23]

(a) Take-over Procedure

Takeover is commenced by takeover bid (an invitation or offer) and is follows:

(i) Offeror companies will take steps to acquire (30-50) the shares;[24]

(ii) The offeror or acquiring company passes a Board Resolution to bid for the shares in another company signed by at least one director and Secretary;[25]

(iii) In addition to the take-over bid, other documents to be filed at the SEC;

(iv) If the SEC refuses to register the bid, the applicant can within 30 days of the refusal, by notice in writing, request SEC to refer the fact of the refusal for review at the Investment and Securities Tribunal;

---

[22] Rule 445 (3)

[23] Section 133(4) ISA; Rule 445 (3) (b) and 104 SEC Rules

[24] Rule 433-439 SEC Rules

[25] Rule 445(2) SEC Rules; Section 137(2) ISA].

(v)An authority to proceed is issued by SEC to last for 3 months subject to renewal within 14 days to the expiration of the authority;[26]

(vi) Proposed bid shall be registered with the SEC before dispatch accompanied by documents in Rule 448 (5) of SEC Rules;

(vii) Upon the receipt of authority to proceed with a takeover bid, the following documents shall be filed with the SEC:[27]

- Two draft copies of the takeover bid;
- consent letters of directors and other parties to the transaction;
- CTC of particulars of directors of offeror company;
- Copy of draft of financial service agreement and any other agreement btw the financial adviser and offeror company;
- Annual report and account of offeror company for last five years or years in business if less than five years;
- Evidence of payment of application fees and requisite SEC fees (based on values of shares involved in the takeover);
- A draft newspapers publication of the proposed takeover;
- Evidence of source of funds and any other document that may be required by the SEC;

(viii)Upon approval, the offeror company will dispatch the bid itself or through a Capital Market Operator simultaneously to SEC, each director of the offeree company and each shareholder of the offeree company;[28]

(ix) The offeror company Board of directors shall make preparation to dispatch a takeover bid with contents as set out in Section 136 of ISA and Rule 446 SEC of Rules;

(x) Takeover bid shall be dispatched simultaneously by the Board of directors of offeror company to the directors of the offeree company, shareholders and the SEC (otherwise it could constitute a ground to invalidate a takeover bid);

---

[26] Rule 447(2) Sec Rules; Section 134 (8) ISA

[27] Rule 448 (5) SEC Rules; Section 135 ISA

[28] Section 138 ISA

(xi) Advertise the takeover bid in at least two newspapers;[29]

(xii) The target company calls a meeting to consider the bid and not less than 90 per cent of the paid up shares subject to acquisition shall be accepted;

(xiii)The offeror company must within seven days of the conclusion of the offer file with the SEC forward a schedule of target company shareholders accepting the offer containing the volume and value of the respective share and settlement of the consideration;[30]

(xiv) The offerror company shall give notice to dissenting shareholders within one month of the acceptance of the bid to elect either to be paid like other consenting shareholders or require their shares to be valued;[31]

(xv) The dissenting shareholders are to communicate their acceptance or otherwise within 20 days, if not they would be deemed to have accepted to be paid like others who accepted the bid;

(xvi) The SEC will carry out a post takeover inspection not less than three months after registration of the bid;[32]

(xvii) Make consequential filings with the Corporate Affairs Commission.

---

[29] Rule 445 (4) SEC Rules)

[30] Rule 448 (6) SEC Rules

[31] Section 146 -147 ISA

[32] Section 448 (7) ISA

Chapter 19

COMPANY PROCEEDINGS AND INVESTMENT DISPUTE RESOLUTION

COMPANY PROCEEDINGS

Company proceedings deal with the proceedings of a company with the Federal High Court having exclusive jurisdiction on company proceedings and administration of the Companies and Allied Matters Act (CAMA).All offences under the act may be tried by the Court in the place where the offence is alleged to have been committed.

The Federal High Courtis one court with judicial division in states of the federation. The judicial division of the Court that has jurisdiction in any matter is where the registered office of the company is situated, subject to the overriding interest of *forum conveniens.*

(a)Laws and Rules Governing Company Proceedings

The *laws and rules* governing company proceedings in Nigeria are these:

(i) Constitution of the Federal Republic of Nigeria 1999 (as Amended);
(ii) Companies Proceeding Rules 1992 (as amended);
(iii) Companies Winding-Up Rules 2001;
(iv) Federal High Court (Civil Procedure) Rules 2009;
(v) Federal High Court Act;
(vi) Investment and Securities Act (ISA) 2007;
(vii) Companies and Allied Matters Act (CAMA)2004;
(viii) Securities and Exchange Commission (Consolidated) Rules 2013;
(ix) Investment and Securities Tribunal Procedure Rules 2003.

(b) Courts and Tribunals in Company Proceedings

The *Courts and Tribunals* in company proceedings are:

(i) Federal High Court;

(ii) Investment and Securities Tribunal (IST);

(iii) IST-ADR centre;

(iv) Administrative Proceedings Committee annexed to IST.

(c) Modes of Commencing Corporate Litigation

The various *modes of commencing* corporate litigation are as enumerated hereunder:

(i) Originating Summons;

(ii) Originating motion;

(iii) Petition;

(iv) Writ of Summons;

(v) Originating Application (exclusively at Investment and Securities Tribunal, IST).

ORIGINATING SUMMONS

The default mode of commencement of action in corporate litigation is by originating summons. It involves interpretation clarification or declaration of legal/documentary prescriptions. Actions commenced by originating summons dispense with exchange of pleadings and calling of witnesses and thus saves time. Application to be supported by affidavit and all annexures attached together with a written address.

An originating summons under the Rule shall be in Form 1as specified in the schedule to the Companies Proceedings Rule 1992. It can be on Notice or *Exparte.* Again, an application under section 317 CAMAmay be made by ex-parte originating summons.[1]

An application is to be made by originating summons except where it is specified by the rules to be made by originating motions.[2] It contains a mixture of law and fact and is generally used when needed to remedy an error or omission from a set rules. Similarly, an application

---

[1]Rules 2 and 3

[2] Rule 3

is to be made by originating summons except where it is expected to be made by petition.[3]

ORIGINATING MOTION

An Originating Motion contains a mixture of both law and disputed facts. In corporate litigation, originating motion is mostly used where there is a need to remedy an error or omission or benefit from set rules. Its aim is to bring an original application in the circumstances specified by statute.

Applications to be made by originating motions under the Companies and Allied Matters Act are these:[4]

(i) Relief from consequences of default in complying with the conditions of a limited liability company;
(ii) Extension of time to file documents at the Commission;
(iii) Rectification of Company's Register of Members;
(iv) Appointment of Inspector to investigate a company;
(v) Inquiry into refusal to produce documents or respond to summons;
(vi) Termination of imposition of restrictions on shares;
(vii) Order for a declaration of dissolution of company which has not been wound up to have been void.

The notice of an originating motion must be given in Form 2 of the Rules, and it shall include a concise statement of the nature of the claim made or the relief or remedy sought.

WRIT OF SUMMONS

A Writ isused for proceedings concerning the operations of the CAMA where noprovision is made by these Rules. As such, the Federal High Court (Civil Procedure) Rules would apply most with Writ of Summons.[5]

---

[3] Rule 4
[4] Rule 3 (a)-(g)
[5] Order 3 Rule 1 Federal High Court (Civil Procedure) Rules 2009

ORIGINATING APPLICATION

Originating Application is used in proceedings involving investment and securities matters at the Tribunal. The SEC Rules prescribes Originating Application as the originating process for use at the IST.[6]

PETITION

A Petition as a mode of commencing proceedings is brought in the cases which are specifically provided in the Rules. For a proceeding to be made by way of Petition, it must be in respect of winding-up of companies and used where no provision is made in Company Proceeding Rules.

Applications to be made by originating petition under the Rules and Act shall be (Order 4 Companies Proceedings Rules):

(i) An order for cancellation of a company's amended objects;
(ii) Cancellation or alteration of Memorandum;
(iii) Cancellation of a special resolution to re-register public companies as private companies;
(iv) To confirm a reduction of the share premium account of a company;
(v) Application to confirm issue of shares at a discount;
(vi) To confirm a reduction of the capital redemption reserve fund of a company;
(vii) Confirmation of reduction of share capital;
(viii) Cancellation of variation of right attached to class of shares.
(ix) Relief on ground that affairs of the company are being conducted in an illegal and oppressive conduct;
(x) For an order restoring the name of a company to the register, when the application is made in conjunction with an application for the winding-up of the company;
(xi) To sanction a scheme of merger between two or more companies;
(xii) For relief from liability of an officer of a company or a person employed by a company as auditor.

---

[6] Rule 5 and 6(1) SEC Rules

(a) Procedure for Bringing Petition

The procedure has to do with *summons for direction*in regards to petition under Form 3 thus:

(i) Presentation of the petition by the Petitioner:[7]

(ii) After the presentation, the petitioner shall apply for direction as in Form 5, except where the application is made under the CAMAor section 100(3) of ISA to sanction a compromise or arrangement;[8]

(iii) On the hearing of the summons, the court may give such direction, as to the proceedings to be taken before the hearing of the petition, as it deems fit;[9]

(iv) When the application made by the petition is to confirm a reduction of share capital,or of the share premium account of the capital redemption reserve fund of a company, the court may give additional directions for inquiry as to debts of and claims against the company, and also as to the proceedings to be taken for settling the list of creditors entitled to object to the reduction and fixing the date of the list.[10]

This section has to do with inquiry as to debts, thus:

1. where an inquiry is ordered as to the debts, the company must, within 14 days, file in the court, an affidavit made by a competent officer of the company verifying a list of creditors.[11]
2. The company must give notice of the list of creditors, and advertise a notice of the list in the newspaper.[12]
3. With regard to claims by creditors, the company must also file an affidavit made by the company's solicitor and a competent officer of the company.[13]

---

[7]Rule 4 Companies Proceedings Rules
[8] Ibid Rule 5
[9]Ibid Rule 5 (3)
[10] Ibid Rule 5 (4)
[11] Ibid Rule 6 and 7
[12] Ibid Rule 8 and 9
[13] Ibid Rule 10

4. Where there is dispute as to the entitlement of creditors to be entered in the list, the dispute is to be adjudicated upon and settled by the court.[14]
5. The list of creditors entitled to object to the reduction must be certified and the certificate filed by the Court Registrar.[15]

Every originating summons, originating motion and petition by which company proceedings are begun and all affidavits, notice and other documents in those proceedings shall be titled accordingly.

(b) Hearing of Petition

Hearing of the petition happens for instance, where a petition is for the confirmation of a reduction under Rule 5(4) and the Court had directed an inquiry as above, the petition shall not be heard before the expiration of at least eight clear days after the filing of the certificate.[16] Before the hearing, a notice of the day appointed for the hearing must be published in the newspaper as the court directs.[17]

The effect of commencing an action by a wrong mode is that it will not invalidate proceedings except it will lead to substantial injustice.[18]

(c) Service of Court Process and Other Documents

Service of court processes on companies is very important to know as this goes to the jurisdiction. The legal consequence of non-service or invalid service renders the entire proceedings null and void. Non-compliance with the rules of issuance of the process renders proceedings ineffectual as was held in *Integrated Builders* v. *Domzaq Ventures (Nig) Ltd.*[19]

Accordingly, the court process is to be served on a company in accordance with the provisions of the applicable rule of the CAMA. Court processes to be served on the principal officers of the company:

(i) Managing Director;

---

[14] Ibid Rule 11-13
[15] Ibid Rule 12
[16] Ibid Rule 14
[17] Ibid Rule 14 (2)
[18] *Agip (Nigeria) Ltd.* v *Agip Petroleum International & 7 Ors.* (2010) Lcn/4180(Sc)
[19] (2005) 2 NWLR (Pt. 909) 97

(ii) Directors heading various departments;

(iii) Company Secretary; or

(iv) by leaving it at the registered office of the company.

All other documents other than a court process are to be served by posting it to the company, leaving it at the registered office of the company or leaving it with a principal member of the company.[20]

ALTERNATIVE DISPUTE RESOLUTION IN CORPORATE DISPUTE

Alternative Dispute Resolution (ADR) is an informal dispute resolution process in which the parties meet with a professional third party who helps them resolve their dispute in a way that is less formal and often more consensual than is done in the courts.

The Investment and Securities Tribunal has an ADR centre designed to provide sessions for various ADR options such as Negotiation, mediation, arbitration and other hybrid processes. The tribunal issues directives for ADR Proceedings and the effective management and resolution of dispute brought before the centre pursuant to the enabling provision of the Rules.[21]

The *advantages* of ADR in disputes involving companies include:

(i) It is generally faster and less expensive;

(ii) It is based on more direct participation by the disputants, rather than being run by lawyers, judges, and the state;

(iii) This type of involvement is believed to increase people's satisfaction with the outcomes, as well as their compliance with the agreements reached;

(iv) Most Alternative Dispute Resolution (ADR) processes are based on an integrative approach;

(v) They are more cooperative and less competitive than adversarial court-based methods like litigation. For this reason, ADR tends to generate less escalation and ill-will between parties.

---

[20] [Order 6 Rule 8 Federal High Court (Civil Procedure) Rules 2009]

[21] Rule 34 (1), 3 (2) and 4 IST (Procedure) Rules 2003

RESOLUTION OF INVESTMENT DISPUTES

The resolution of investment disputes in Nigeria is done by the institutions below.

(a) Federal High Court

The Federal High Court has limited jurisdiction in investment disputes except for enforcement of IST awards and application for an order for the revocation of registration of a capital market operator.[22]

(b) SEC Administrative Proceedings Committee

The Administrative Proceedings Committee (APC) of the Securities and Investment Commission (SEC) is a body established pursuant to the Investments and Securities Act for the purpose of resolving disputes between parties to a capital market dispute.

A party who is not satisfied with the decision of the Committee as confirmed by the Commission may appeal to the Investments and Securities Tribunal (IST) within 30 days of the receipt of the decision.[23]

(c) Investments and Securities Tribunal

The Investments and Securities Tribunal (IST) was established under Section 224 of Investments and Securities Act (ISA) 1999 now Section 274 ISA 2007. The IST is a tribunal established by an Act of National Assembly to give expeditious hearing of capital market issues. The IST is deemed to be a civil court. It has both appellate and original jurisdiction. It has an appellate from the administrative proceedings committee annexed to IST. It has jurisdiction on capital market disputes.

The *aims and objectives* of the Tribunal are:

(i) To provide expedient and affordable dispute resolution mechanisms;

(ii) To Protect the integrity of the capital market and stable economy;

(iii) To avoid delays and technicalities;

---

[22]Section 51 and 293 (3) ISA

[23]Rule 18 Administrative Proceedings Committee Rules of Procedure).

(iv) To ensure efficient resolution of investments and capital market disputes with fairness, flexibility and transparency.

In terms of its jurisdiction, the IST has exclusive original jurisdiction over disputes arising from the administration, management and operation of collective investment schemes.[24] The Tribunal is also empowered to adjudicate on pensions disputes in Nigeria by virtue of the Pension Act.[25]

As regards the scope of its jurisdiction, the Tribunal may also adjudicate in the matters as set out below:

(i) Interpretation of any law or regulations to which the Act applies;
(ii) Disputes between SEC and a Securities Exchange or capital Trade Point;
(iii) Disputes between capital market operators and the securities exchange or capital trade point;
(iv) Disputes between capital market operators;
(v) Disputes between capital market operators and their clients; and
(vi) Disputes between quoted companies and the regulators of the securities exchange.

The Proceeding of IST is judicial and shall be deemed to be a civil court.[26] The IST is flexible in adherence to the rules of evidence, and other technicalities in proceedings. A party may appear before the Tribunal either in person or by counsel.[27]

The mode of commencing action in IST is by an Originating Application. The Tribunal's powers include:[28]

(i) Power to summon/compel attendance of any person;
(ii) Power to require discovery and production of documents;
(iii) Power to decide matters ex *parte*;
(iv) Power to dismiss applications in default;
(v) Power to call for the examination of witnesses or documents;
(vi) Power to review its decisions.

[24]Section 284 & 294 ISA
[25]Section 93 Pension Reform Act 2004
[26]Section 290 ISA
[27]Section 291 ISA)
[28]Section 290 (2) (a)-(h) ISA

The IST is required to conclude any proceedings before it within 90 days of commencement of the action. The decision of the Tribunal is enforced as a judgment of the Federal High Court by registering it with the Federal High Court.[29]

Any appeal against its judgment lies directly to the Court of Appeal on points of law only. Any issue of fact is not appellable as deemed to have been resolved by the best experts in the field.[30]

[29]Section 293 (2) ISA
[30]Section 295 & 297 ISA

Chapter 20

WINDING-UP AND DISSOLUTION OF COMPANIES, BUSINESS AND NON-BUSINESS FORMATION

COMPANIES WINDING-UP

A company's winding-up is the process of liquidation of the assets of a company for the benefits or distribution to its creditors, members and employees in accordance with certain rules of priority.

The court with jurisdiction to wind up a company shall be the Federal High Court. The judicial division of the Federal High Court with jurisdiction to handle the matter would be the one closest to the registered or head office of the company or the one where it has maintained registered office for the past six months preceding the presentation of the petition.

(a) Commencement of Winding-Up Proceedings

The commencement of winding-up proceedings of a company depends on the type of winding up as follows:

(i) If a members' Resolution to wind up was passed, it is commenced at the time of passing the Resolution: i.e. for voluntary members' winding up; or

(ii) If it is a Petition to wind up that is filed, at the time of presentation of the Petition (in any other case).

The effect of commencement of winding up proceedings is:

(i) No attachment of a company's property is allowed

(ii) No judgment debt can be claimed

(iii) No more carrying on of the business of the company and

(iv) Its properties cannot be disposed of nor can its shares be transferred unless such is sanctioned by the Court.

As regards the effect of winding up proceeding on the legal personality of a company, the winding up of a company or the appointment of liquidator does not by itself result in the death of the corporate body thereby removing its legal personality. A company under a winding up proceedings has not died, it is still alive though sick. A company only "dies" on its dissolution, as was held in *C. S. (Nig.) Plc* v. *Mbakwe.*[1]

The effect of a winding–up order is that:

(i) Action or proceedings against the company must be with the leave of Court;

(ii) Employees are automatically laid off;

(iii) Any disposition of the company's property and transfer of its shares after the commencement of a winding up is void;

(iv) The directors' power to run the company ceases to exist

TYPES OF WINDING-UP

There are three basic way of winding-up companies, viz.:

(i) Compulsory winding-up by order of court;

(ii) Voluntary winding-up, members or creditors;

(iii) Winding up subject to the supervision of the court.

(a) Compulsory Winding-Up by Court

The grounds for winding-up compulsorily by the court could be when one or more of the conditions below are present:

(i) The company has by special resolution resolved that the company be wound up by the court;

(ii) Default is made in delivering the statutory report to the CAC or holding the statutory meeting;

(iii) The number of members is reduced below two;

(iv) The company is unable to pay its debts;

---

[1] (2002) 3 NWLR (Pt. 755) 523 at 527 – 528

(v) The Court is of the opinion that it is just and equitable that the company should be wound-up.

The procedure for a members special resolution for compulsory winding-up is as follows:

(i) Pass board Resolution and company special Resolution to wind up the company;

(ii) Send Notice of the Resolution to the Corporate Affairs Commission, the Security and Exchange Commission, and the Nigerian Stock Exchange (if it is a quoted company);

(iii) Present a Petition for winding up to the Federal High Court accompanied with these documents:

I. Verifying affidavit ;

II. Copy of the Resolution;

(iv) The Court shall thereupon appoint a liquidator;

(v) After the liquidation, the Court will give a winding-up order

(vi) The company is then dissolved upon application to the Court;

As regards compulsory winding up by Court due to default made in delivering statutory report, the petition can only be brought by a shareholder and it must be before the expiration of 14 days after the last day on which the meeting should have been held. The court may, instead of making a winding-up order, direct that a meeting be held or the report be delivered, and make orders as to costs as it deems fit. This ground is only applicable to public companies.

As regards the reduction of members to a number below two, the position of the law is that a company cannot be incorporated with less than two persons. A company which is in default of this would be wound-up by the court in addition to other sanctions as to liability. This is one of the cases where a contributory is expressly authorised to bring a petition for winding-up.

With respect to inability to pay debt, a company would be deemed to be unable to pay its debts if the creditor to whom it is indebted in a sum exceeding ₦2,000 by a notice in writing demanded for the debt to be paid; the company has for a period of three weeks thereafter neglected to pay, then the company is unable to pay its debts. This was the decision of the Court in *Ado Ibrahim & Co Ltd* v. *B.C.C. Ltd.*[2]

Another instance is with respect to execution or other processes issued on a judgment or order of any court in favour of a creditor of the company is returned unsatisfied in whole or in part. The court, taking into account any contingent or prospective liability of the company, is satisfied that the company is unable to pay its debts.

As exceptions to this rule, a company will not be deemed to be unable to pay its debt if:

(i) The debt to a creditor is not due;
(ii) No evidence of due demand for payment was made;
(iii) If there is a *bona fide* dispute of the debt;
(iv) There is no evidence that the company is insolvent.

It is important to emphasise that demand must be made by an officer of the company. Thus in the case of *Nigerian Commercial & Industrial Enterprises Ltd.* v. *Registrar of Companies*,[3] the Court held that a demand made by the solicitor to a company for payment of debt was not a demand made by an officer of the company.

The Demand is a statutory document and not a mere letter of correspondence, and should be formally titled as a Statutory Demand for Payment, and clearly set out the amount owed and a request to pay within three weeks and a Notice that upon expiration, the creditor would take steps to wind up the company.

Finally, the grounds upon which the court may order winding up under just and equitable grounds are:

(i) The substratum of the company has disappeared, such as the inability of the company to achieve its object clause or the company is deeply indebted;
(ii) The company is formed for fraudulent purpose;
(iii) The company is a "bubble" as it has no business or asset or never intended to carry on business in a proper manner;

---

[2] (2009) 15 NWLR (Pt.891) 543, (2004) 8 NSCQR
[3] (1973) 1 FRCR 249

(iv) Unfairly prejudicial or discriminatory act against the minority or other members, culminating in lack of confidence in the management of the company's affairs by those in control of the company;

(v) If the company is small, grounds that would justify dissolution of partnership on just and equitable ground is enough, such as deadlock.

The factors guiding Courts discretion in winding-up under is the consideration as to whether it is just and equitable to wind-up a company. It depends on the facts which are available to the court at the time of hearing of the application as set out in the petition. Nevertheless, it was held that a petition on just and equitable grounds should not be dismissed solely because the petitioner has some other remedies since the motive of the petitioner is irrelevant.

(i) Procedure for Compulsory Winding-Up

The procedure for compulsory winding-up requires an application made to the Court for the winding-up of a company which must be in the form of a petition. Every petition shall be in any of the Forms 2, 3, or 4 in the Appendix thus:

I. Filing of the Petition for winding-up along with a verifying affidavit;
II. Service of the Petition and Affidavit on the respondent with proof of Service;
III. Obtain leave of court to advertise petition and advertise;
IV. Petitioner will File Memorandum of Compliance;
V. The Respondent shall file a Notice of intention to appear, Memorandum of Appearance and an affidavit in opposition to the petition;
VI. The petitioner files a Reply to the Respondent's processes;
VII. Appointment of Provisional Liquidator;
VIII. Filing and hearing of Summons for Security for Costs;
IX. Filing of List of Persons Appearing (creditors);
X. Hearing of Petition;
XI. Making of winding-up order;

XII. Service of winding-up order to the Commission;
XIII. Application for dissolution and the order of dissolution made;
XIV. Appeals from the order of dissolution and enforcement.

The Act empowers the Federal High Court to stay winding-up proceedings even after the order is made. This is not a form of Appeal, but a review of the entire proceedings that led to the order. This may be on the application of either a liquidator or official receiver, a creditor or contributory.

(ii) Appointment and Powers of Liquidator

The Federal High Court may appoint a liquidator for the purpose of conducting the proceedings in winding-up a company. On the making up of a winding-up order, if no liquidator is appointed, the official receiver shall become the liquidator by virtue of his office.

The liquidator in a winding-up by Court, exercises some powers, as sanctioned by the Court or the Committee of Inspection. These powers include:

(i) The power to bring or defend any action in the name and on behalf of the company;
(ii) The power to carry on the business of the company as may be necessary for the purpose of the beneficial winding-up;
(iii) The power to appoint relevant professionals or legal practitioner to assist him in the performance of his duties;
(iv) The power to pay all classes of creditors in full;
(v) The power to make any compromise or arrangement with creditors or persons claiming to be creditors;
(vi) The power to compromise all calls, debts and liabilities capable of resulting in debts.

(b) Voluntary Winding-Up

A company may be wound up voluntarily under any of these circumstances:

(i) When the period, if any fixed for the duration of the company by the articles expires, or the event, if occurs, on occurrence of which the articles provided the company is to be dissolved; or

(ii) If the company resolves by special resolution that company will be wound up voluntarily. If a company passes a resolution for voluntary winding up, it shall within 14 days after the passing of the resolution –

I. Give notice of the resolution by advert in the Gazette; or
II. Advertise in two daily newspaper; and
III. Give notice to the Commission.

It is worth mentioning that the passing of the resolution is deemed to commence the voluntary winding up.

The types of voluntary winding-up are namely:

(i) Members voluntary winding-up; and
(ii) Creditors voluntary winding-up.

Members' voluntary winding-up is where a statutory declaration of solvency shall be made by the directors to the effect.

The procedure for members' voluntary winding-up is as follows:

(i) Company passes Board and company Resolution to wind up the company and to appoint a liquidator to wind up the company;
(ii) Gives notice of the special Resolution and appointment of liquidator passed to CAC and the public within 14 days of its passage and advertises it in the Gazette or two daily newspapers;
(iii) Make a Statutory Declaration of Solvency that the company can pay its debts within 12 months of winding-up is made by the Directors within five weeks of passing the Resolution to wind up voluntarily and is delivered to the Commission;
(iv) Liquidator holds meeting if the process of winding-up last more than one year;
(v) Liquidator holds meetings to adopt the audited accounts of the winding-up and send copies to members;
(vi) Liquidator holds final meetings upon liquidation of the company and sends a copy of the accounts/ return of the meeting to the Commission within seven days of the meeting;
(vii) Liquidator sends to the members the audited accounts and he is required to preserve all the books/papers of the company on his activities as liquidator for a period of five years before destruction;

(viii) Liquidators apply for Dissolution Order and send the Order to the Commission. The company is deemed dissolved after three months of the registration of the accounts/returns with the Commission.

Creditors' voluntary winding-up, on the other hand, takes place where the directors are not able to make a declaration of solvency at the Commission.

The circumstances where members' voluntary winding-up will be converted to creditors winding-up is as follows:

(i) Where there is no Statutory Declaration of Solvency made and filed in support of the Resolution for winding-up;

(ii) The liquidator is of the opinion that the company will not be able to pay its debts within the 12 months stated in the declaration of solvency.

The procedure for creditors' voluntary winding-up is as follows:

(i) Both the company and its creditors hold separate meetings to propose for a winding-up of the company. The creditors' meeting shall be held a couple of days prior to the company meeting;

(ii) The notice of both meetings must be sent simultaneously. The notice is to be published in the Gazette and two newspapers. The publication of the notice amounts to a declaration of insolvency;

(iii) The meeting of the creditors is to be presided over by one of the directors who shall be appointed from one of them;

(iv) The directors lay before the creditors' meeting a full statement of the company's affairs with a list of the creditors of the company. A breach of this is an offence;

(v) Liquidators and a Committee of inspectors are to be appointed by the creditors and the company, but if the creditors reject the persons appointed by the company they stand disqualified;

(vi) Upon appointment of Liquidator, all powers of the Directors shall cease except as sanctioned by the Committee of Inspection or in its absence the creditors;

(vii) The liquidator should within 14 days of his appointment, publish it in the gazette and two daily Newspapers and he is to deliver to the Commission for registration a Notice of his Appointment;

(viii) The resolution to wind-up the company and appointment of liquidator are given to the Corporate Affairs Commission and published in the Gazette and two newspapers within 14 days;

(ix) A general meeting of the company and creditors is to be summoned if the winding up continues for more than one year within three months of the end of the first year and every succeeding year;

(x) The final meeting and dissolution of the company is held to enable the liquidator to lay the account and give explanation;

(xi) After the meeting, the liquidator shall send a copy of the account and return of the holding of the meeting to the CAC for registration within seven days;

(xii) The company is deemed dissolved after three months of the registration of the accounts and returned to the Commission;

(xiii) Nevertheless, the Court upon an application by the liquidator or a person interested (a creditor) can void the dissolution order within two years.

It is worth noting that where separate persons are nominated as liquidators at the separate meetings, the person nominated by the creditors would be the liquidator. Nonetheless, a director, member or the company may apply to Court within seven days for an order that the person nominated by the company shall be the liquidator, if the creditors did not nominate, the company's nominee would be the liquidator.

The consequences of a voluntary winding-up are:

(i) The company shall cease to carry on its business except so far as may be required for the beneficial winding-up thereof;

(ii) The corporate status and powers of the company shall notwithstanding anything to the contrary in its articles, continue until it is dissolved;

(iii) Any transfer of shares not made with the sanction or approval of the liquidator shall be void;

(iv) Any alteration in the status of members of the company made after the commencement of the voluntary winding-up shall also be void;

(v) On the appointment of a liquidator, all the powers of the directors shall cease, except so far as the company in general meeting or the liquidator sanctions the continuance thereof;

(vi) In a creditor's voluntary winding-up, the powers of the directors shall also cease, except so far as the committee of inspection or if there is one, the creditors sanction the continuance;

(vii) A voluntary winding up will operate as a discharge of employees if the company is wound up because it is insolvent just as it will in the case of a compulsory winding up.

(c) Winding-Up Subject to Court Supervision

Winding-up subject to Court supervision as provided under the Act, occurs when a company passes a special Resolution for winding-up backed by a Petition filed to the Court to wind up the company subject to its supervision.

The Court appoints the liquidator and the winding-up is deemed to be a winding-up by the court. Where an order is made for a winding up subject to court supervision, the court may by the same or any subsequent order appoint an additional liquidator. The Court is also empowered to remove any liquidator so appointed by it and may fill any vacancy, occasioned by the removal, resignation or death.

The procedure for a winding-up subject to the supervision of the Court includes:

(i) Passing a special Resolution for winding up of the company; and

(ii) Filing a Petition supported with a verifying affidavit requesting the Court to wind up the company subject to its supervision.

The effect of an order for winding-up subject to the supervision of the Court is thus:

(i) The liquidator so appointed is free to exercise all his powers without the sanction or intervention of the court;

(ii) The liquidator shall not exercise the powers to pay all classes of creditors in full; the power to make any compromise or arrangement with creditors or persons claiming to be creditors; and the power to compromise all calls, debts and liabilities capable of resulting in debts respectively, except with the sanction of the Court;

(iii) A winding-up subject to the supervision of the court does not amount to winding-up by the court for the purpose of the provisions of CAMA.

The order or priority of payments of liabilities upon winding-up of a company are as enumerated hereunder:

(i) All costs including the remuneration of the liquidator are paid out;

(ii) Outstanding local rates and charges due from the company and payable within 12 months next before the date of the winding-up Order or its commencement are paid;

(iii) Pay all PAYEE (Pay As You Earn) tax deductions, assessed taxes, land taxes, properties or income taxes from the company not exceeding one year before the winding-up Order or its commencement;

(iv) Pay salaries of junior staff or servants of the company for services rendered to the company and deductions under the National Provident Fund Act;

(v) Settle claims of creditors and members. Secured creditors with fixed/floating charges are paid first before the unsecured debentures;

(vi) Settle preferential shareholders;

(vii) Distribute the remaining assets to the ordinary shareholders.

It should be noted that a company in receivership is a company which has appointed a receiver to manage the debts of the company. The company may still bounce back as an effective going concern.

MAJOR OFFICERS OF WINDING-UP

The major officers in respect of a winding-up procedure are the following:

(a) Liquidator

A liquidator is a person appointed by the company or court to wind up the affairs of the company and to distribute its assets among the creditors and contributories in accordance with the articles. A liquidator represents the interest of the creditors, especially the unsecured creditors. Thus upon appointment all powers of the directors of a company shall cease.

He shall, within 14 days after his appointment publish in the gazette and in two daily newspapers and deliver to the commission for registration a notice of his appointment.

Other powers and duties of a liquidator which are:

(i) Power to sell the property of the company by public auction or private arrangement;

(ii) Power to do all acts and to execute in the name and on behalf of the company, all deeds, receipts and other documents;

(iii) Power to prove, rank and claim in the bankruptcy, insolvency or sequestration of any contributory;

(iv) Power to draw, accept, make and indorse any bill of exchange or promissory note in the name and on behalf of the company;

(v) Power to raise any money required on the security of the assets of the company;

(vi) Power to appoint an agent to do any business which the liquidator is unable to do himself

The following are persons who are incompetent to be appointed or to act as liquidator whether in winding up by, or under the supervision of the court or in a voluntary winding up:

(i) An infant;

(ii) Anyone found by the court to be of unsound mind;

(iii) A body corporate;

(iv) An undischarged bankrupt;

(v) Any director of the company under liquidation;

(vi) Any person convicted of any offence involving fraud, dishonesty, official corruption or moral turpitude and in respect of whom there is a subsisting order to restraint fraudulent persons.

It should be noted that an appointment made in contravention of the above shall be void.

(b) Official Receiver

An official receiver is the Deputy Chief Registrar to the Federal High Court or any other officer designated for that purpose by the Chief Judge of the Federal High Court, whose duty is to receive the statement of Affairs of the company and to collate information about the company in winding up.

(c) Provisional Liquidator

A Provisional Liquidator is appointed by the Court before the making of a winding up Order and the formal appointment of a liquidator. An official receiver may be a provisional liquidator when the winding up order is made in a compulsory winding up until the appointment of a liquidator. He continues to act wherever there is vacancy in the office of a liquidator.

(d) Receiver

This is a person appointed by the secured creditors under the power contained in the debenture instrument, executed by the company and the creditors. A receiver need not get involved in the management of the company. His focus is usually on the income and expenditure of the company in order to realise assets and pay off the debt due to the creditors.

(e) Receiver Manager

He is not only concerned to realise the assets of the company but takes over the management of the affairs of the company to stabilise it to make profit and pay off the creditors and then handover the company to the members. He stands in a fiduciary relationship to the company and observes utmost good faith towards it in any transaction with it or on its behalf.

The powers of the Receiver Manager include power to:

(i) Carry on the business of the company;
(ii) Use the company's seal;
(iii) Appoint other professionals to assist him;
(iv) Sell and dispose of the property;
(v) Establish subsidiaries of the company;
(vi) Raise or borrow money and grant security due over the property of a company.

(f) Special Manager

A special manager is an officer appointed by the Chief Judge of the Federal High Court to assist the Deputy Chief Registrar (Official Receiver) in the winding up of a company by the order of the court.

DISSOLUTION OF COMPANY

The effect of a dissolution order is that a company loses its legal entity and ceases to exist or dies once fully wound-up and dissolved. The incorporated name cannot be used any longer.

A major difference between winding-up and dissolution of a company is that in a winding-up, the company can still sue in its corporate name during liquidation. A company in liquidation is a company in the process of winding up. However, it cannot be a member of a new company. Conversely, during dissolution of a company, the company no longer exists in its corporate entity as it is now dead.

(a) Procedure for Dissolution

The procedure for dissolution of a company is as follows:

(i) Winding up must have been completed;
(ii) The application is made to court by the liquidator for a dissolution Order;

(iii) Notice of the Order of dissolution made is to be given to the Commission within 14 days of the order;

(iv) CAC shall record the dissolution of the company in its books.

The liquidator or any other interested person may apply to the court to make an order deferring the date of the dissolution. Even where the company is deemed to be dissolved, the court may, on application by the liquidator or any other interested person, within two years of the dissolution void the dissolution. That person must deliver the order to the Commission within seven days after making the order.

Failure to comply with the provision by the liquidator will attract a fine daily for the breach.

DISSOLUTION OF SOLE PROPRIETORSHIP

The death of a sole proprietor will lead to dissolution of a sole proprietor except provision in his will for a Personal Representative to carry on the business for a certain period of time.

The Procedure for dissolution of a sole proprietorship upon death of sole proprietor are these:

(i) Evidence of the death of the sole proprietor;

(ii) Within a period of three months of the death, the personal representatives shall submit to the Registrar General, the evidence of death together with the original certificate of the business name and particulars of registration for cancellation (also attach letter of probate/administration);

(iii) Upon the payment of requisite fees, filing fees for cancellation;

(iv) Evidence of payment of annual returns up to date or payment of the annual returns.

DISSOLUTION OF PARTNERSHIP

The dissolution of a partnership can be caused by any of the partners in the ways discussed below.

(a) By Act of the Parties

This can be done by any of these ways:

(i) Giving notice of intention to dissolve the partnership (could be provided for in the agreement); or
(ii) In the event of an ill-health of one partner which rendered that partner permanently incapacitated, and as a result, the partnership is unable to continue;
(iii) Where a partner creates a charge on his or her share of the partnership property; or
(iv) By providing for a clause like power of expulsion in the partnership agreement/deed

(b) By Operation of Law

Dissolution of partnership would be by operation of law if –
(i) It is for a fixed term, at the expiration of the term;
(ii) It is for an undertaking, after the performance of the undertaking and sharing of the proceeds;
(iii) It is supervening illegality;
(iv) It is for death or bankruptcy or insanity of a partner (namely, where a partner has lost legal capacity).

(c) By Order of Court

Dissolution by order of Court is one in which a partner can apply that the partnership be dissolved based on these grounds:
(i) Persistent breach of agreement;
(ii) Mental illness;
(iii) Where it is obvious that a partner is permanently incapable of continuing with the partnership;
(iv) Where business is carrying on at a loss; or
(v) On any equitable ground.

(d) Procedure for Dissolution of Partnership

The procedure for the dissolution of a partnership is as follows:
(i) The business will cease to be in existence by either a Resolution by the partners or by a Court order or death of a sole proprietor;

(ii) The partners shall file a Notice to the Commission within three months of the cessation of the business, stating that the firm/ individual has ceased to do business under a business name with evidence attached:

I. A copy of the court order or evidence of consent of the partners must be annexed to the notice;.

II. The original particulars of the business registration should be surrendered for cancellation (certificate of registration and other particulars);

III. Pay the prescribed fees for filing the Notice;

(iii) Upon delivery of the notice to the Registrar of Business Name, the Registrar may remove the firm, company or individual from the register;

(iv) If the Registrar has reasonable cause to believe that the firm, company or individual is not carrying on business, the Registrar may send a notice to the firm, company or individual enquiring whether or not business is being carried on.

Where there is no response within two months, or the firm, company or individual responds and admits that no business is being carried on, the Registrar may remove the business name from the Register.

DISSOLUTION OF INCORPORATED TRUSTEES

The dissolution of non-business organisations, particularly incorporated trustees or associations, takes a different format from the dissolution of business organizations discussed above.

The Federal High Court is the court with jurisdiction over dissolution of Incorporated Trustees. The Petition for its dissolution can be brought by any of the following persons:

(i) The Governing Body or Board of Trustees;

(ii) One or more trustees of the association;

(iii) Members of the Association constituting not less than 50% of the total membership;

(iv) The Corporate Affairs Commission as a monitoring agency. Members of the public can write to the Commission if the Incorporated Trustee is doing something against public policy. The Commission will investigate and can petition for dissolution if the organisation is encouraging something illegal or against public policy.

(a) Grounds for Dissolution

The grounds for the dissolution of Incorporated Trustees are not conjunctive but disjunctive. Hence, any of the following grounds would suffice:

i. That the aims and objects for which it was established have been fully realised and no useful purpose would be served by keeping the corporation alive;

ii. That the body corporate is formed to exist for a specified period and that the period has expired (effluxion of time);

iii. That all the aims and objects of the association have become illegal or otherwise contrary to public policy;

iv. That it is just and equitable in all the circumstances that the body corporate be dissolved [for example, fraud or crime, oppressive acts by the organisation's trustees acting in a manner prejudicial to other members, organisation is frustrated by financial constraints, high indebtedness (namely, liabilities outweighing assets of the organisation, conflict of interest, rancour and misunderstanding in the board of trustees)].

(b) Procedure for Dissolution

The grounds for the dissolution of Incorporated Trustees are these:

(i) It is dissolved voluntarily by an ordinary Resolution passed by not less than 50 % of the members on any of the grounds stated above;

(ii) File a Petition to the Court for a formal and effectual dissolution;

(iii) All the persons likely to be affected by the dissolution (e.g. creditors/trustees) shall be put on Notice. A formal advertisement of the hearing of the petition following an Order of Court will suffice as Notice.

(c) Assets Distribution

The distribution of the assets of a dissolved incorporated trustee is to be done in accordance with the Special Clauses in its Constitution as follows:

i. Satisfaction of all its just debts and liabilities of the organisation or association;

ii. If the properties remain after the payment of liabilities, they are not to be distributed among the members of the Association but to be transferred to some other institutions having similar objects of the organisation as will be determined by the members of the association at or before the time of dissolution;

iii. If there is no institution with similar objects, the remaining property shall be transferred to some charitable objects.

Chapter 21

RELIEFS AND INCENTIVES

INTRODUCTION

Various incentives and reliefs in the form of tax rebate and concession have been designed by the Federal government to boost industrial and agricultural production for export. These reliefs and incentives are discussed below.

PIONEER STATUS

Tax exemption is granted for a period of between five to seven years under the Industrial Development (Income Tax Relief) Act.

(a) Eligibility

To be eligible for this relief:

(i) The investment must be in respect of industry or products designated as pioneer, particularly, sectors where Nigeria is lacking pioneer products as outlined by the NIPC;

(ii) The investment must be up to ₦500 million;

(iii) The application for pioneer status must be submitted within one year the applicant starts commercial production;

(iv) NIPC Form 1 must be purchased, completed and returned with the original purchase receipt, accompanied with evidence of:

I. Acquisition of landed property and installation of requisite equipment, as development carried out at factory site; and

II. That the industry is not being carried out in Nigeria on a scale suitable to the economic development and requirements of Nigeria or at all or that there are favourable prospects for further developments in Nigeria of such industry.

(b) Procedure for Obtaining Reliefs and Incentives

The procedure begins with approaching the desk officer at the One Stop Investment Centre (OSIC) or NIPC to make enquiries. Meanwhile, the Inspectorate Division of the Ministry of Trade and Investment, looks at where the acquisitions are, the land acquired, the equipment that was acquired, manufacturing and so on.

If it is up to the threshold, an applicant is given a provisional certificate based on his proposal. Furthermore, an applicant needs to find out how long it will take to recoup his capital investment. This is because pioneer status is to help to defray an investor's capital expenditure. While trying to recoup capital expenditure, the company is exempted from company tax.

An applicant may apply for extension, although the whole time cannot be more than five (5) years under the law. In extreme circumstances, a further two years could be granted.

TAX RELIEF ON DOUBLE TAXATION TREATY

This relief obtains in circumstances where a Nigerian company is liable to Tax in a Commonwealth or other country having double taxation agreement with Nigeria. There is also relief from payment of double taxation if there are bilateral agreements with other countries.

For example there are Double Taxation Relief Treaties between Nigeria and the Governments of the United Kingdom, Northern Ireland, Canada, France, Pakistan, Romania and Belgium, etcetera.

TAX RELIEF ON FOREIGN LOAN

The Companies Income Tax Act provides for tax exemption/relief on foreign loans. However, the following conditions are attached:

(i) The loan must not be less than One Hundred and Fifty Thousand Naira (₦150,000)

(ii) The loan must be granted by a foreign company to any person carrying on trade, business, profession in Nigeria

(iii) If the loan is to be repaid after 10 years, the interest is exempted from tax

(iv) If the loan is to be repaid between five to 10 years, then the tax the interest accruing should be half of the chargeable tax must be made within a maximum of two years from the date of exportation

INVESTMENT TAX CREDIT

This relief is for research and development carried out in Nigeria Companies engaged in research and development activities for commercialisation are allowed a certain percentage of investment tax credit on their qualifying expenditure.

The Companies Income Tax Act provides that a company which engages wholly in the fabrication of spare parts for local consumption and export shall be allowed 25% investment tax credit on its qualifying capital expenditure.

Similarly, a company which purchases a locally manufactured plant, machinery or equipment for use in its business shall be allowed 15% investment tax credit.

Moreover, expenses incurred on research and development including the amount paid to the national Science and Technology Fund are allowed as deductible expenses.

RURAL INVESTMENT ALLOWANCE

The CITA provides graduated allowances for capital expenditure on such facilities as electricity, water, tarred road and telephone located at least 20 kilometres away from such facilities provided by the government.

The rural investment allowance is tied to the profits of the year in which the date of completion of the investment falls and should not be carried over to the next year.

TAX EXEMPTION ON PROFIT UNDER COMPANIES INCOME TAX ACT

This refers to profit exempted from taxation. The Act lists corporate bodies exempt from taxation, including co-operative societies, religious/charitable organisation, sporting activities, among others.

Similarly the profits of any Nigerian company in respect of goods exported from Nigeria are exempted from taxation, provided that the proceeds from such export are repatriated to Nigeria and are used exclusively for the purchase of raw materials, plants, equipment and spare parts.

Interests payable on bank loans granted for agricultural trade and business also enjoy tax concession. Bank loans granted to a company engaged in agricultural business and fabrication of local plant and machinery also enjoys concession.

Deposit accounts or domiciliary accounts of a foreign non-residence company are also exempted from taxation provided that the account consists mainly of foreign currencies imported into Nigeria on or after 1st January 1990 through the CBN or any other authorised bank. Moreover, bank loans granted for manufacture of goods for export are also tax-free.

DUTY DRAWBACK AND SUSPENSION SCHEME

This incentive is meant to encourage importation of raw materials in Nigeria to be used in manufacturing goods for export. The Customs and Excise Management Act and also the Customs Duty Drawback Scheme/Regulation provides for the refund of import duties by companies in manufacturing on:

(i) Raw materials including packaging materials used in manufacturing goods that are exported - 100% of import duty;

(ii) Paper used for the manufacture of goods supplied for educational purposes to educational establishments recognised by the Federal Adviser on Education 100% of import duty;

(iii) Goods exported in the same state as that in which they were imported.

EXPORT INCENTIVES UNDER THE EXPORT (INCENTIVES AND MISCELLANEOUS PROVISIONS) ACT

This relief is granted in respect of the following:

(i) Incentives to a company engaged in the utilisation of associated gas under the Petroleum Profits Tax Act;
(ii) Investment in the Export Processing Zone: The profits or gain of a 100% export oriented undertaking established within and outside an Export Free Zone shall be exempted from tax for the first three consecutive assessment years provided, (among other conditions) it manufactures, produces and exports articles during the relevant year and the export proceeds from 75% of its turnover;
(iii) Investment in economically disadvantaged areas - 100% tax relief for seven years;
(iv) Intensive local raw materials utilisation;
(v) Investment in solid minerals - A new company going into mining of solid minerals shall be exempted from tax for the first three years of its operation, which may be extended for another further period of two years. While Section 18 has to do with capital allowances, Section 19 for exemption from customs duties and other benefits.

ECOWAS TRADE LIBERALIZATION SCHEME

This relief or incentive is designed for trade liberalization aimed towards the integration among member countries of the Economic Community of West African States (ECOWAS).

FISCAL INCENTIVES

This covers servicing foreign loan/repatriation of profit and capital/procuring foreign exchange from the CBN/capital importation without limit. The Foreign Exchange (Monitoring & Miscellaneous Provisions) Act mandates the importation of such money through an authorised dealer and holding a certificate of capital importation.

There is no limit on how much he can bring into the country. An authorized dealer can obtain foreign currency from the CBN at an official rate and repatriate the profit from such investment to the foreign country. Can repatriate your capital without any restriction.

INCENTIVES UNDER THE LOCAL CONTENT ACT

The Local Content Act 2011 and the Petroleum Industry Bill provides for incentives for investors in the Oil and gas sector.

LABOUR INTENSIVE MODE OF PRODUCTION

This refers to tax concessions granted to industries with high labour/capital ratio. These are industries with plants, equipment and machinery, which essentially are operated with minimal automation. The rate of tax concession here is graduated, in that a company employing 1000 persons or more enjoy 15% tax concession, an industry employing 200 persons will enjoy 7%, 100 persons enjoy 6% *et cetera.*

BONUS FOR FILING OF ANNUAL RETURNS ON TIME

Under the CAMA, 1% bonus is allowed for companies complying with early payment of tax by FIRS.

OTHER RELIEFS AND INCENTIVES

In addition to the above mentioned, others include inter alia:

(i) Investment in Agriculture, Education, Research and Development;
(ii) Statutory undertaking on non-indigenisation.

APPENDIX

COMPANIES AND ALLIED MATTERS ACT, 2020

COMPANIES AND ALLIED MATTERS ACT, 2020

ARRANGEMENT OF SECTIONS *Section*:

PART A : CORPORATE AFFAIRS COMMISSION

PART B: INCORPORATION OF COMPANIES AND INCIDENTAL MATTERS CHAPTER 1—FORMATION OF COMPANY

MEMORANDUM OF ASSOCIATION

NAME OF COMPANY

457. Notification of appointment.
458. Invalid appointment and indemnity.

APPOINTMENT OF ADMINISTRATION BY COMPANY OR DIRECTORS OUT OF COURT

459. Power to appoint by company or directors.
460. Restrictions on power to appoint.
461. Effect of moratorium on the appointment of administrator.
462. Effect of non-disposal of winding-up petition on appointment of administrator.
463. Notice of intention to appoint.
464. Filing of notice of intention to appoint.
465. Requirements of sections 463 and 464 to be complied with.
466. Filing of notice of appointment.
467. Offence in relation to section 464.
468. Where person not entitled to notice of intention to appoint.
469. Commencement of appointment under section 459.
470. Notification of administrator of his appointment.
471. Effect of administration order on appointment.

ADMINISTRATION—SPECIAL CASES

472. Application by holder of floating charge.
473. Intervention by holder of floating charge.
474. Application where company in liquidation.
475. Administration application by liquidator.
476. Effect of receivership based on appointment by a holder of a fixed charge.

EFFECT OF ADMINISTRATION

477. Dismissal of pending winding-up petition.
478. Vacation of office by receiver.
479. Company in administration.
480. Moratorium on other legal process.
481 Where administration application or administration order not yet granted.
482. Details to be stated on documents.

PROCESS OF ADMINISTRATION

483. Announcement of administrator's appointment.
484. Administrator to be provided with statement of affairs of company.
485. Period within which to submit statement of affairs.
486. Administrator's proposals.
487. Creditors' meeting.
488. Requirement for initial creditors' meeting.
489. Restrictions on summoning of initial creditors' meeting.
490. Business and result of initial creditors' meeting.
491. Revision of administrator's proposal.
492. Failure to obtain approval of administrator's proposals.
493. Further creditors' meetings.

798. Application for registration.
799. Certificate of registration.
800. Registration of changes in partnership.
801. Notice of change in status of general partner or assignment of share of limited partner.
802. Name of limited partnership.
803. Reservation of name and change of name of limited partnership.
804. Penalty for improper use of words "limited partnership" or "LP".
805. Commission to keep register.
806. Modification of general law in case of limited partnerships.
807. Application of Part C.
808. Law as to private partnerships to apply where not excluded by this Act.
809. Inspection, etc. of documents. 810. Liability for false statement.

PART E : BUSINESS NAMES

CHAPTER 1—ESTABLISHMENT OF BUSINESS NAMES REGISTRY : APPOINTMENT AND FUNCTIONS OF HEAD OF OFFICE AND OTHER OFFICERS

811. Establishment of business names registry in each state.
812. Appointment of head of office and other officers of business names registry.
813. Functions of the head of office.

CHAPTER 2—REGISTRATION OF BUSINESS NAMES

814. Registration of business names.
815. Procedure for registration.
816. Entry of business name in the register.
817. Certificate of registration. 818. Registration of changes.

CHAPTER 3 — REMOVAL OF BUSINESS NAME FROM REGISTER

819. Removal of name from register.

CHAPTER 4—MISCELLANEOUS AND SUPPLEMENTAL

820. Publication of true name.
821. Liability of person in default.
822. Annual returns.

PART F : INCORPORATED TRUSTEES

CHAPTER 1—INCORPORATED TRUSTEES

823. Incorporation of trustees of certain communities, bodies and associations.
824. Classification of associations.
825. Method of application.
826. Qualification of trustees.
827. Constitution.
828. Advertisement and objections.
829. Registration and certificate.
830. Effect of registration and certificate.
831. Related associations.

COMPANIES AND ALLIED MATTERS ACT, 2020ACT No. 3

AN ACT TO REPEAL THE COMPANIES AND ALLIED MATTERS ACT, CAP. C20, LAWS OF THE FEDERATION OF NIGERIA, 2004 AND ENACT THE COMPANIES AND ALLIED MATTERS ACT, 2020 TO PROVIDE FOR THE INCORPORATION OF COMPANIES, LIMITED LIABILITY PARTNERSHIPS, LIMITED PARTNERSHIPS, REGISTRATION OF BUSINESS NAMES TOGETHER WITH INCORPORATION OF TRUSTEES OF CERTAIN COMMUNITIES, BODIES, ASSOCIATIONS ;
AND FOR RELATED MATTERS

[7th Day of August, 2020]

ENACTED by the National Assembly of the Federal Republic of Nigeria—

PART A—CORPORATE AFFAIRS COMMISSION

1.—(1) There is established the Corporate Affairs Commission (in this Act referred to as “the Commission”).

(2) The Commission—

(a) is a body corporate with perpetual succession and a common seal ; (b) may sue and be sued in its corporate name ; and

(c) may acquire, hold or dispose of any property, movable or immovable, for the purpose of performing its functions.

(3) The headquarter of the Commission shall be in the Federal Capital Territory, Abuja, and there shall be established an office of the Commission in each State of the Federation.

2.—(1) There is established for the Commission, a Governing Board (in this Act referred to as “the Board”) which shall be responsible for performing the functions of the Commission.

(2) The Board shall consist of—

(a) a chairman who is appointed by the President on the recommendation of the Minister, and who, by reason of his ability, experience or specialised knowledge of corporate, industrial, commercial, financial or economic matters, business or professional attainment, is capable of making outstanding contributions to the work of the Commission ;

(b) one representative of the—

(i) business community, appointed by the Minister on the recommendation of the Nigerian Association of Chambers of Commerce, Industries, Mines and Agriculture,

(ii) legal profession, appointed by the Minister on the recommendation of the Nigerian Bar Association,

(iii) accountancy profession, appointed by the Minister after consultation with professional bodies of accountants as are established by Acts of the National Assembly,

(iv) Institute of Chartered Secretaries and Administrators of Nigeria, appointed by the Minister on the recommendation of the Institute,

(v) Nigerian Association of Small and Medium Enterprises, appointed by the Minister on the recommendation of the Association,

(vi) Manufacturers Association of Nigeria, appointed by the Minister on the recommendation of the Association,

(vii) Securities and Exchange Commission not below the rank of a Director or its equivalent, and

(viii) each of the Federal Ministries of Industry, Trade and Investment, Justice and Finance who shall not be below the rank of Director ; and (*c*) the Registrar-General of the Commission.

(2) The Minister may, with the approval of the President, at any time remove any member of the Board from office if the Minister is of the opinion that it is not in the interest of the Commission for the member to continue in office and shall notify the member in writing to that effect.

(3) The members of the Board except the Registrar-General shall be part-time members of the Board.

(4) A member of the Board ceases to hold office if—

(a) he resigns his appointment as a member of the Board by three months' notice under his hand and addressed to the Minister ;

(b) he becomes of unsound mind or is incapable of discharging his duties ;

(c) he becomes bankrupt or has made arrangement with his creditors ;

(d) he is convicted of a felony or any offence involving fraud or dishonesty ;

(e) he is guilty of serious misconduct relating to his duties ; or

(f) in the case of a person who possesses professional qualifications, he is disqualified or suspended from practising his profession in any part of Nigeria by an order of any competent authority made in respect of him personally.

(5) There is vacancy on the Board if a member—

(a) dies ;

(b) is removed from office in accordance with subsection (2) ;

(c) resigns from office in accordance with subsection (4) (*a*) ; or

(d) completes his tenure of office ; or

(e) ceases to hold office in accordance with paragraphs (*b*) to (*f*) of subsection (4).

(6) A vacancy on the Board shall be filled by the appointment of another person to the vacant office in accordance with the provisions of this Act, as soon as it is reasonably practicable after the occurrence of such vacancy.

(7) Where a vacancy on the Board is created as a result of death, removal or resignation of a member of the Board, a replacement of the immediate past member shall be appointed to complete the unexpired period of his predecessor's term of office.

4. The Board shall—
(a) review and provide general policy guidelines for performing of the functions of the Commission in accordance with international commercial best practice ;
(b) have general oversight on the administration of the Commission ;
(c) review and approve the strategic plans of the Commission ;
(d) receive and consider management reports and advise the Minister on the reports ;
(e) determine the terms and conditions of service of employees of the Commission ;
(f) fix the remuneration, allowances and benefits of employees of the Commission, in consultation with the National Salaries, Income and Wages Commission ;
(g) ensure compliance with the provisions of this Act ; and
(h) do such other things as are necessary to ensure the effective and efficient performance of the functions of the Commission.
5. Members of the Board appointed under section 2 (2) (a)-(b) shall be paid such remuneration and allowances as the Minister may, from time to time, direct.
6.—(1) Subject to this section and section 27 of the Interpretation Act, the Board may make standing orders regulating its proceedings.
(2) The Chairman shall preside at every meeting of the Board but, in his absence, the members present shall elect one of them present to preside at the meeting.
(3) The quorum for meetings of the Board is five.
(4) The Board may appoint any of its officers to act as secretary at any of its meetings.
7.—(1) A member of the Board who is directly interested in any company or enterprise, the affairs of which are being deliberated upon by the Board, or is interested in any contract made or proposed to be made by the Board shall, as soon as possible after the relevant facts have come to his knowledge, disclose the nature of his interest at a meeting of the Board.
(2) A disclosure, under subsection (1), shall be recorded in the minutes of the Board, and the member shall—
(a) not take part, after such disclosure, in any deliberation or decision of the Board with regard to the subject matter in respect of which his interest is disclosed ; and
(b) be excluded for the purpose of constituting a quorum of the Board for any such deliberation or decision.
8.—(1) The functions of the Commission shall be to—
(a) administer this Act, including the registration, regulation and supervision of—
(i) the formation, incorporation, management, striking off and winding up of companies,
(ii) business names, management and removal of names from the register, and
(iii) the formation, incorporation, management and dissolution of incorporated trustees ;
(b) establish and maintain a company's registry and office in each State of the Federation suitably and adequately equipped to perform its functions under this Act or any other law ;
(c) arrange or conduct an investigation into the affairs of any company, incorporated trustees or business names where the interest of shareholders,
members, partners or public so demands ;

(d) ensure compliance by companies, business names and incorporated trustees with the provisions of this Act and such other regulations as may be made by the Commission ;

(e) perform such other functions as may be specified in this Act or another law ; and

(f) undertake such other activities as are necessary or expedient to give full effect to the provisions of this Act.

(2) Nothing in this section affects the powers, duties or jurisdiction of the Securities and Exchange Commission under the Investments and Securities Act (or any amendment thereto or re-enactment thereof).

9.—(1) The Commission shall appoint a Registrar-General who—

(a) is qualified to practice as a legal practitioner in Nigeria ;

(b) has been so qualified for at least 10 years ; and

(c) in addition, has had experience in company law practice or administration for at least eight years.

(2) The Registrar-General—

(a) is the Chief Executive of the Commission ;

(b) is subject to the directives of the Board and shall hold office on such—

(i) terms and conditions as may be specified in his letter of appointment, and

(ii) other terms and conditions as may be determined by the Board with the approval of the President.

(3) The Registrar-General is the accounting officer for the purpose of controlling and disbursing amounts from the Fund established under section 13.

10. The Commission may appoint such other staff as it may deem necessary for the efficient performance of the functions of the Commission under this Act.

11. Notwithstanding the provisions of any enactment to the contrary, a person appointed to the office of Registrar-General under section 9 of this Act or a person appointed under section 10 of this Act who is a legal practitioner shall, while so appointed, be entitled to represent the Commission as a legal practitioner for the purpose and in the course of his employment.

12.—(1) Service in the Commission shall be approved service for the purpose of the Pensions Reform Act (or any amendment thereto or re-enactment thereof) and accordingly, officers and other persons employed in the Commission are, in respect of their service in the Commission entitled to pensions, gratuities and other retirement benefits as determined in the Commission's conditions of service.

(2) Nothing in this Act shall prevent the appointment of a person to any office on terms in the Commission which preclude the grant of pension contributions or gratuity.

13. The Commission shall establish a fund (in this Act referred to as "the Fund") which shall consist of—

(a) money as may be allocated to it by the Federal Government ; and

(b) such other money as may accrue to it in the performance of its functions.

14. The Commission may apply the proceeds of the Fund—

(a) to the cost of administration of the Commission ;

(b) for reimbursing members of the Board or any Committee set up by the Board for such expenses as may be authorised or approved by the Board, in accordance with the rate approved in that behalf by the Minister ;

(c) to the payment of salaries, fees or other remuneration or allowances, pensions and gratuities payable to the employees of the Commission ;
(d) for the maintenance of any property acquired or vested in the Commission ; and
(e) for any purpose related to the functions of the Commission under this Act.

15.—(1) The financial year of the Commission starts on the 1st day of January and end on the 31st day of December of the same year or any time as may be prescribed by Financial Regulations issued by the Federal Government of Nigeria.
(2) The Commission shall keep proper accounts and records in relation thereto and shall prepare in respect of each year a statement of accounts in such form as may be prescribed by the Financial Reporting Council of Nigeria.
(3) The accounts of the Commission shall be audited, not later than six months after the end of the year, by auditors appointed by the Commission from the list and in accordance with guidelines issued by the Auditor-General for the Federation, and the fees of the auditors and the expenses of the audit generally shall be paid from the funds of the Commission.
(4) The Commission shall, not later than 30th September in each year, cause to be prepared an estimate of the expenditure and income of the Commission during the next succeeding year and shall be submitted to the Minister.

16. The Commission shall, not later than 30th June in each year, submit to the Minister a report on the activities of the Commission during the immediate preceding year, in such form as may be prescribed by the Minister and shall include in such report the audited accounts of the Commission.

17.—(1) A suit shall not be commenced against the Commission before the expiration of 30 days after a written notice of intention to commence the suit is served upon the Commission by the intending plaintiff or his agent.
(2) The notice referred to in subsection (1) shall clearly state the—
(a) cause of action ;
(b) particulars of the claim ;
(c) name and place of abode of the intending plaintiff ; and(*d*) relief sought.

PART B—INCORPORATION OF COMPANIES AND INCIDENTAL MATTERS

CHAPTER 1—FORMATION OF COMPANY

18.—(1) As from the commencement of this Act, any two or more persons may form and incorporate a company by complying with the requirements of this Act in respect of registration of the company.
(2) Notwithstanding subsection (1), one person may form and incorporate a private company by complying with the requirements of this Act in respect of private companies.
(3) A company may not be formed or incorporated for an unlawful purpose.

19.—(1) No association, or partnership consisting of more than 20 persons shall be formed for the purpose of carrying on any business for profit or gain by the association, or partnership, or by the individual members thereof, unless it is registered as a company under this Act, or is formed in pursuance of some other enactments in force in Nigeria.
(2) Nothing in this section shall apply to—
(a) any co-operative society registered under the provisions of any enactment in force in Nigeria ; or

(b) any partnership for the purpose of carrying on practice—
(i) as legal practitioners, by persons each of whom is a legal practitioner, or
(ii) as accountants by persons each of whom is entitled by law to practise as an accountant.
(4) If at any time the number of members of an association or partnership exceeds 20 in contravention of this section and it carries on business for more than 14 days while the contravention continues, each person who is a member of the company, association or partnership during the time it so carries on business is liable to a fine as prescribed by the Commission for every day during which the default continues.

20.—(1) Subject to subsection (2), an individual shall not join in the formation of a company under this Act if he is—
(a) less than 18 years of age ;
(b) of unsound mind and has been so found by a court in Nigeria or elsewhere ;
(c) an undischarged bankrupt ; or
(d) disqualified under sections 281 and 283 of this Act from being a director of a company.
(2) A person shall not be disqualified under subsection (1) (*a*), if two other persons not disqualified under that subsection have subscribed to the memorandum.
(3) A corporate body in liquidation shall not join in the formation of a company under this Act.
(4) Subject to the provisions of any enactment regulating the rights and capacity of aliens to undertake or participate in trade or business, an alien or a foreign company may join in forming a company.

21.—(1) An incorporated company may be a company—
(a) having the liability of its members limited by the memorandum of association to the amount, if any, unpaid on the shares respectively held by them (in this Act referred as "a company limited by shares") ;
(b) having the liability of its members limited by the memorandum of association to such amount as the members may respectively undertake to contribute to the assets of the company in the event of its being wound up (in this Act referred to as "a company limited by guarantee") ; or
(c) not having any limit on the liability of its members (in this Act referred to as "an unlimited company").
(2) A company of any of these types may either be a private company or a public company.

22.—(1) Private company is one which is stated in its memorandum of association to be a private company.

(2) Subject to the provisions of the articles, a private company may restrict the transfer of its shares and also provide that—
(a) the company shall not, without the consent of all its members, sell assets having a value of more than 50% of the total value of the company's assets ;
(b) a member shall not sell that member's shares in the company to anon-member, without first offering those shares to existing members; and (*c*) a member, or a group of members acting together, shall not sell or agree to sell more than 50% of the shares in the company to a person who is not then a member, unless that non-member has offered to buy all the existing members' interests on the same terms.

(3) The total number of members of a private company shall not exceed50, not including persons who are *bona fide* in the employment of the company, or were, while in that employment and have continued after the determination of that employment, to be members of the company.

(4) Where two or more persons hold one or more shares in a company jointly, they shall, for the purpose of subsection (3), be treated as a single member.

(5) A private company shall not, unless authorised by law, invite the public to—

(a) subscribe for any share or debenture of the company ; or

(b) deposit money for fixed periods or payable at call, whether or not bearing interest.

of the provisions of section 22 of this Act in respect of a private company, the company shall cease to be entitled to the privileges and exemptions conferred on private companies by or under this Act and this Act shall apply to the company as if it were not a private company.

(2) If a Court, on the application of the company or any other person interested, is satisfied that the failure to comply with the provisions of section 22 of this Act was accidental or due to inadvertence or to some other sufficient cause or that on other grounds it is just and equitable to grant relief, the court may, on such terms and conditions as may seem to be just and expedient, order that the company be relieved from the consequences mentioned in subsection (1).

24. Any company other than a private company shall be a public company and its memorandum of association shall state that it is a public company.

25. An unlimited company shall be registered with a share capital not below the minimum issued share capital permitted under section 27 (2) (*a*) of this Act.

26.—(1) Where a company is to be formed for the promotion of commerce, art, science, religion, sports, culture, education, research, charity or other similar objects, and the income and property of the company are to be applied solely towards the promotion of its objects and no portion thereof is to be paid or transferred directly or indirectly to the members of the company except as permitted by this Act, the company shall not be registered as a company limited by shares, but may be registered as a company limited by guarantee.

(2) Any provision in the memorandum or articles of association or in any resolution of the company purporting to give any person a right to participate in the divisible profits of the company or purporting to divide the company's undertaking into shares or interest is void.

(3) A company limited by guarantee shall not be incorporated with the object of carrying on business for the purpose of making profits for distribution to members.

(4) The memorandum of a company limited by guarantee shall not be registered without the authority of the Attorney-General of the Federation.

(5) The Attorney-General of the Federation shall, within 30 days, grant authority to the promoters of a company limited by guarantee where there are no objections to the memorandum or other cogent reason for not granting approval to register the company as one limited by guarantee.

(6) Where further information is required by the Attorney-General of the Federation from the promoters of a company limited by guarantee, the 30 days period shall be begin on receipt of all relevant information.

(7) Where all valid documents are furnished by the promoters of a company limited by guarantee and no decision has been made by the Attorney-General of the Federation within the 30 days period—

(*a*) the promoters shall—

(i) place an advertisement in three national daily newspapers, and

(ii) invite objections, if any, to the incorporation of the company ;

(b) an objection shall state the grounds on which it is made and shall be forwarded to the Commission within 28 days from the date of the last publications in the newspapers, where there is objection to the incorporation of the company ;

(c) the Commission—

(i) shall consider the objection and may require the applicant to furnish further information or documentation, and

(ii) may uphold or reject the objection as it deems fit and inform the applicant accordingly.

(8) If the Commission is satisfied that the memorandum and articles of association have complied with the provisions of this section, it shall cause the application to be advertised, in the prescribed form, in three national daily newspapers.

(9) The advertisement referred to in subsection (8) shall invite objections, if any, to the incorporation of the company and the objection shall state the grounds on which it is made and shall be forwarded to the Commission within 28 days of the date of the last publications in the newspapers, and, if the objection is made, the Commission–

(a) shall consider it and may require the applicant to furnish further information or documentation ; and

(b) may uphold or reject the objection as it deems fit and inform the applicant accordingly.

(10) If—

(a) after the advertisement, no objection is received within the period specified in subsection (9) or, where any objection is received, the same is rejected, the Commission, having regard to all the circumstances, may assent to the application or withhold its assent ; and

(b) the Commission assents to the application, it shall register the company and issue a certificate of incorporation.

(11) If a company limited by guarantee carries on business for the purpose of distributing profits to its members, all officers and members who are cognisant of the fact that it is so carrying on business shall jointly and severally be liable for the payment and discharge of all the debts and liabilities of the company incurred in carrying on such business, and the company and every such officer and member shall be liable to penalty as prescribed by the Commission for every day during which it carries on such business.

(12) The total liability of a member of a company limited by guarantee to contribute to the assets of the company in the event of its being wound up shall not at any time be less than ₦100,000.

(13) Subject to compliance with subsection (11), the articles of association of a company limited by guarantee may provide that a member can retire or be removed from membership of the company by a special resolution duly filed with the Commission.

(14) If in breach of subsection (12), the total liability of the members of any company limited by guarantee is at any time less than ₦100,000, every director and member of the company who is cognisant of the breach is liable to a penalty as prescribed by the Commission for every day during which the default continues.

(15) Subject to section 117 (4) (*d*) of this Act, if upon the winding-up of a company limited by guarantee, there remains, after the discharge of all its debts and liabilities, any property of the company, the same shall not be distributed among the members but shall be transferred to some other company limited by guarantee having objects similar to the objects of the company or applied to some charitable object and such other company or association shall be determined by the members prior to dissolution of the company.

27.—(1) The memorandum of association of every company shall state—

(a) the name of the company ;

(b) that the registered office of the company shall be situated in Nigeria ;

(c) the nature of the business or businesses which the company is authorised to carry on, or, if the company is not formed for the purpose of carrying on business, the nature of the object or objects for which it is established ;

(d) the restriction, if any, on the powers of the company ;

(e) that the company is a private or public company, as the case maybe ; and

(f) that the liability of its members is limited by shares, by guarantee or unlimited, as the case may be.

(2) If the company has a share capital—

(a) the memorandum of association shall also state the amount of the minimum issued share capital which shall not be less than ₦100,000.00 in the case of a private company and ₦2,000,000.00, in the case of a public company, with which the company proposes to be registered, and the division thereof into shares of a fixed amount ; and

(b) each subscriber shall write opposite his name the number of shares he takes.

(3) A subscriber of the memorandum who holds the whole or any part of the shares subscribed by him in trust for any other person shall disclose that fact and the name of the beneficiary in the memorandum of association.

(4) The memorandum of association of a company limited by guarantee shall also state that—

(a) the income and property of the company shall be applied solely towards the promotion of its objects, and that no portion thereof shall be paid or transferred directly or indirectly to the members of the company except as permitted by, or under this Act ; and

(b) each member undertakes to contribute to the assets of the company in the event of its being wound up while he is a member or within one year after he ceases to be a member for payment of debts and liabilities of the company, and of the costs of winding-up, such amount as may be required not exceeding a specified amount and the total of which shall not be less than ₦100,000.

(5) The memorandum of association shall be signed by each subscriber in the presence of at least one witness who shall attest the signature.

(6) The memorandum shall be stamped as a deed.

NAME OF COMPANY

28. Subject to the provisions of section 27 of this Act, the form of memorandum of association of— (*a*) a company limited by shares,

(b) a company limited by guarantee, and

(c) an unlimited company, shall be in such form as may be prescribed by regulations issued by the Commission.

29.—(1) The name of a private company limited by shares shall end with the word, "Limited".

(2) The name of a public company limited by shares shall end with the words, "Public Limited Company".

(3) The name of a company limited by guarantee shall end with the words, "Limited by Guarantee".

(4) The name of an unlimited company shall end with the word, "Unlimited".

(5) A company may use the abbreviations, "Ltd", "PLC" "Ltd/Gte" and "Ultd" for the words, "Limited", "Public Limited Company", "Limited by Guarantee" and "Unlimited" respectively in the name of the company.

30.—(1) If a company, through inadvertence or otherwise, on its first registration or on its registration by a new name, is registered under a name identical with that by which a company in existence is previously registered, or nearly resembling it to be likely to deceive, the first-mentioned company may, with the approval of the Commission, change its name, and if the Commission directs, the company concerned shall change its name within six weeks from the date of the direction or such longer period as the Commission may allow.

(2) If a company defaults in complying with a direction under subsection (1), such company shall, without prejudice to any other lawful action which the Commission may take against it, be liable to a penalty as prescribed by the Commission, for every day during which the default continues.

(3) Any company may, by special resolution and with the approval of the Commission signified in writing, change its name, provided that no such approval shall be required where the only change in the name of a company is the substitution of the words, "Public Limited Company", for the word, "Limited" or vice versa on the conversion of a private company into a public company or a public company into a private company in accordance with this Act.

(4) Nothing in this Act precludes the Commission from requiring a company to change its name if it discovers that such a name conflicts with an existing trade mark or business name registered in Nigeria prior to the registration of the company and the consent of the owner of the trade mark or business name was not obtained.

(5) Where a company changes its name, the Commission shall enter the new name on the register in place of the former name, and issue a certificate of incorporation altered to meet the circumstances of the case.

(6) The change of name does not affect any right or obligation of the company, or render defective any legal proceeding by or against the company, and any legal proceeding that could have been continued or commenced against or by it in its former name, may be continued or commenced against or by it in its new name.

(7) Any change made in the name of a company under this section shall be published periodically by the Commission in a national daily newspaper and on its website.

Reservation

31.—(1) The Commission may, upon receipt of an application delivered of name. to it in hard copy or through electronic communication and on payment of the prescribed fees, reserve a name pending registration of a company or change of name by a company upon confirmation of the availability of such name.

(2) The reservation mentioned in subsection (1) shall be determined upon receipt of the application under subsection (1), and shall be valid for such period as the Commission may deem fit not exceeding 60 days, and during the period of reservation no other company shall be registered under the reserved name or under any name which, in the opinion of the Commission nearly resembles the reserved name.

(3) Notwithstanding the provisions of subsections (1) and (2), the Commission may at any time before a certificate of incorporation is issued, withdraw or cancel a reserved name if it discovers that such name is identical with that by which a company in existence is already registered, or so nearly resembles it as to be likely to deceive.

(4) If any name becomes available in the event of a change of name or otherwise, the Commission shall have the power to approve the name for use by another company after 60 days from the date of approval of such change of name.

(5) The Commission may withdraw or cancel approval for reservation of name where it is discovered that the approval was fraudulently, unlawfully or improperly procured.

32.—(1) A company shall have articles of association prescribing regulations for the company.

(2) Unless it is a company to which model articles apply by virtue of section 34 it shall register articles of association.

(3) Articles of association registered by a company shall be—

(a) contained in a single document, and

(b) divided into paragraphs numbered consecutively.

(4) Reference in this Act to a company's "articles" are to its articles of association.

33.—(1) The Minister may by regulations prescribe model articles of association for companies.

(2) Different model articles may be prescribed for different descriptions of companies.

(3) A company may adopt all or any of the provisions of model articles.

(4) Any amendment of model articles by regulations does not affect a company registered before the amendment takes effect.

(5) In this section, "amendment" includes addition, alteration or repeal.

34.—(1) On the formation of a limited company if articles are—

(a) not registered ; or

registered, in so far as they do not exclude or modify the relevant model articles, the relevant model articles form part of the company's articles in the same manner and to the same extent as if those articles expressly included the relevant model articles in the form in which those articles had been duly registered.

(2) In this section, the "relevant model articles" means the model articles prescribed by the Commission for a company of that description as in effect at the date on which the company is registered.

35.—(1) Unless a company's articles specifically restrict the objects of the company, its objects are unrestricted.

(2) Where a company amends its articles to add, remove or alter a statement of the company's objects—

(a) it shall give notice to the Commission ;

(b) on receipt of the notice, the Commission shall register it ; and

(c) the amendment is not effective until after the entry of that notice in the register.

(3) Any such amendment does not affect any right or obligation of the company or render defective any legal proceeding by or against it.

REGISTRATION OF COMPANIES

36.—(1) The memorandum of association shall be delivered to the Commission together with an application for registration of the company, the documents required by this section and a statement of compliance.

(2) The application for registration shall state—

(a) the company's proposed name ;

(b) the registered office address and head office address if different from the registered office address ;

(c) whether the liability of the members of the company is to be limited and, if so, whether it is to be limited by shares or by guarantee ; and (*d*) whether the company is to be a private or a public company.

(3) If the application is delivered by a person as agent for the subscribers to the memorandum of association, it shall state the name and address of that agent.

(4) The application shall contain—

(a) in the case of a company that has a share capital, a statement of initial issued share capital and initial shareholdings ;

(b) in the case of a company that is limited by guarantee, a statement of guarantee ;

(c) a statement of the company's proposed directors ;

(d) a statement of the proposed registered office of the company ; and

(e) a copy of the proposed articles of association to the extent that these are not supplied by the default application of model articles.

37.—(1) The statement of initial issued share capital and initial shareholdings required to be delivered in the case of a company that has a share capital shall state—

(*a*) the total number of shares of the company to be taken on formation by the subscribers to the memorandum of association ;

(b) the aggregate nominal value of those shares ;

(c) for each class of shares—

(i) prescribed particulars of the rights attached to the shares,

(ii) the total number of issued shares of that class, and

(iii) the aggregate nominal value of issued shares of that class ; and

(*d*) the amount to be paid up and the amount (if any) to be unpaid on each share (whether on account of the nominal value of the share or by way of premium).

(2) The statement of initial issued share capital and initial shareholdings shall—

(a) contain such information as may be prescribed for the purpose of identifying the subscribers to the memorandum of association ; and

(b) with respect to each subscriber to the memorandum—

(i) the number, nominal value (of each share) and class of shares to be taken by him on formation, and

(ii) the amount to be paid up and the amount (if any) to be unpaid on each share (whether on account of the nominal value of the share or by way of premium).

(3) Where a subscriber to the memorandum is to take shares of more than one class, the information required under subsection (2) (*b*) is required for each class.

(4) The total fees payable to the Commission in connection with the filing or increase of a company's issued share capital under this Part of this Act shall be as the Minister may by regulation specify.

38.—(1) The statement of guarantee required to be delivered in the Statement of case of a company that is limited by guarantee shall— guarantee.

(a) contain such information as may be prescribed for the purpose of identifying the subscribers to the memorandum of association ; and

(b) that each member undertakes that, if the company is wound up while he is a member, or within one year after he ceases to be a member, he shall contribute to the assets of the company such amount as may be required for—

(i) payment of the debts and liabilities of the company contracted before he ceases to be a member, payment of the costs, charges and expenses of winding-up, and

39.—(1) The statement of the company's proposed directors required to be delivered to the Commission shall contain the required particulars of—

(a) the person who is, or persons who are, to be the first director or directors of the company ; and

(b) where applicable, the person who is, or persons who are, to be the first secretary or joint secretaries of the company.

(2) The required particulars are the particulars that are required to be stated in the case of a—

(a) director, in the company's register of directors and register of directors' residential addresses ; and

(b) secretary, in the company's register of secretaries.

(3) The statement shall also contain a consent by each of the persons named as a director, as secretary or one of joint secretaries, to act in the relevant capacity but if all the partners in a firm are to be joint secretaries, consent may be given by one partner on behalf of all of them.

40.—(1) The statement of compliance required to be delivered to the Commission is a statement by the applicant or his agent that the requirements of this Act as to registration have been complied with.

(2) The Commission may accept the statement of compliance as sufficient evidence of compliance.

(3) Nothing in this section prevents the Commission from accepting declaration of compliance which is signed by a legal practitioner and attested before the commissioner for oaths or notary public.

41.—(1) The Commission shall register the memorandum and articles unless in its opinion—

(a) they do not comply with the provisions of this Act ;

(b) the business which the company is to carry on, or the objects for which it is formed, or any of them, are illegal ;

(c) any of the subscribers to the memorandum is incompetent or disqualified in accordance with section 20 of this Act ;

(d) there is non-compliance with the requirement of any other law as to registration and incorporation of a company ; or

(e) the proposed name conflicts with or is likely to conflict with an existing company, trade mark or business name registered in Nigeria.

(f) adjustment of the rights of the contributories among themselves, not exceeding a specified amount.

(2) Any person aggrieved by the decision of the Commission under subsection (1), may give notice to the Commission requiring it to apply to the Court for directions and the Commission shall, within 21 days of the receipt of such notice, apply to the court for the directions.

(3) The Commission may, in order to satisfy itself as provided in subsection(1) (*c*), by instrument in writing, require a person subscribing to the memorandum to make and lodge with the Commission, a statutory declaration to the effect that he is not disqualified under section 20 of this Act from joining in forming a company.

(4) Steps to be taken under this Act to incorporate a company shall not include any invitation to subscribe for shares or on the basis of a prospectus.

(5) Upon registration of the memorandum and articles, the Commission shall certify under its seal—

(a) that the company is incorporated ;

(b) in the case of—

(i) a limited company, that the liability of the members is limited by shares or by guarantee, or

(ii) an unlimited company, that the liability of the members is unlimited ; and

(*c*) that the company is a private or public company, as the case may be.

(6) The certificate of incorporation shall be *prima facie* evidence that all the requirements of this Act in respect of registration and matters precedent and incidental to it have been complied with and that the association is a company authorised to be registered and duly registered under this Act.

(7) The Commission may withdraw, cancel or revoke a certificate of incorporation issued under this Act where it is discovered that the certificate was fraudulently, unlawfully or improperly procured.

(8) The Commission may cause the publication of the withdrawal, cancellation or revocation of certificates of incorporation periodically in the Federal Government *Gazette*.

42. As from the date of incorporation mentioned in the certificate of Effect of incorporation, the subscriber of the memorandum together with such other registration. persons as may become members of the company, shall be a body corporate by the name contained in the memorandum, capable of exercising all the powers and performing all functions of an incorporated company including the power to hold land, and having perpetual succession, but with such liability on the part of the members to contribute to the assets of the company in the event of its being wound up as is mentioned in this Act.

CAPACITY AND POWERS OF COMPANIES

43.—(1) Except to the extent that the company's memorandum or any enactment otherwise provides, every company shall, for the furtherance of its business or objects, have all the powers of a natural person of full capacity.

(2) A company shall not have or exercise power either directly or indirectly to make a donation or gift of any of its property or funds to a political party or political association, or for any political purpose, and if any company, in breach of this subsection makes any donation or gift of its property to a political party or political association, or for any political purpose, the officers in default and any member who voted for the breach shall be jointly and severally liable to refund to the company the sum or value of the donation or gift and in addition, every such officer or member commits an offence and is liable to a fine equal to the amount or value of the donation or gift.

44.—(1) A company shall not, carry on any business expressly prohibited by its memorandum and shall not exceed the powers conferred upon it by its memorandum or this Act.

(2) A breach of subsection (1), may be asserted in any proceeding under sections 344-358 of this Act or under subsection (4) of this section.

(3) Notwithstanding the provisions of subsection (1), no act of a company, conveyance or transfer of property to or by a company shall be invalid by reason of the fact that such act, conveyance or transfer was not done or made for the furtherance of any of the authorised business of the company or that the company was otherwise exceeding its objects or powers.

(4) On the application of—(*a*) any member of the company, or

(*b*) the holder of any debenture secured by a floating charge over all or any of the company's property or by the trustee of the holders of any such debentures, the Court may prohibit, by injunction, the doing of, any act, conveyance or transfer of any property in breach of subsection (1).

(5) If the transactions sought to be prohibited in any proceeding under subsection (4) are being, or are to be performed or made pursuant to any contract to which the company is a party, the Court may, if it deems the same to be equitable and if all the parties to the contract are parties to the proceedings, set aside and prohibit the performance of such contract, and may allow compensation to the company or to the other parties to the contract for any loss or damage sustained by them by reason of the setting aside or prohibition of the performance of such contract but no compensation shall be allowed for loss of anticipated profits to be derived from the performance of such contract.

45.—(1) Where there is provision in the memorandum of association of a company restricting the powers and capacity of the company to carry on its authorised business or object, the restriction may be relied on and have effect only for the purpose of proceedings—

(a) against the company by a director or member of the company, or where the company has issued debentures secured by a floating charge over all or any of the company's property, by the holder of any of the debentures or the trustee for the holders of the debentures ;

(b) by the company or a member of the company against the present or former officers of the company for failure to observe any such restriction ;

(c) by the Commission or a member of the company to wind up the company ; or
(d) for the purpose of restraining the company or other person from acting in breach of the memorandum or directing the company or such person to comply with the same.

(2) A person may not in the proceedings referred to in subsection (1) (*a*), (*b*) or (*c*), rely on a restriction of the power or capacity of the company contained in the memorandum in any case where he voted in favour of, or expressly or by conduct agreed to the doing of an act by the company or the conveyance by or to the company of property which, it is alleged in the proceedings, was or would be contrary to the restriction.

46.—(1) Subject to the provisions of this Act, the memorandum and articles, when registered, shall have the effect of a deed between the company and its members and officers and between the members and officers themselves whereby they agree to observe and perform the provisions of the memorandum and articles, as altered in so far as they relate to the company, its members, or officers.

(2) All money payable by any member to the company under the memorandum or articles shall be a debt due from him to the company and shall be of the nature of a specialty debt.

(3) Where the memorandum or articles empower any person to appointor remove any director or other officer of the company, such power shall be enforceable by that person notwithstanding that he is not a member or officer of the company.

(4) In any action by any member or officer to enforce any obligation owed under the memorandum or articles to him and any other member or officer, such member or officer may, if any other member or officer is affected by the alleged breach of such obligation, with his consent, sue in a representative capacity on behalf of himself and all other members or officers who may be affected other than any who is a defendant and the provisions of Chapter 13 of this Act shall apply.

47.—(1) A company shall, on being so required by any member, send to him a copy of the memorandum and articles, and a copy of any enactment which alters the memorandum, subject to payment, in the case of a copy of the memorandum and of the articles, of the cost of producing the said documents (such cost not to exceed ₦500 or such other amount that the Commission may prescribe) or such lesser sum as the company may prescribe and, in the case of a copy of an enactment, of such sum not exceeding the published price thereof as the company may require.

(2) If a company defaults in complying with this section, the company and every officer of the company who is in default is liable to such penalty as the Commission shall prescribe by regulation.

48.—(1) Where an alteration is made in the memorandum of a company, every copy of the memorandum issued after the date of the alteration shall be in accordance with the alteration.

(2) Where any such alteration has been made, the company at any time after the date of the alteration issues any copy of the memorandum which is not in accordance with the alteration, it shall be liable to such penalty as the Commission shall prescribe by regulation for each copy so issued, and every officer of the company who is in default is liable to the like penalty.

49.—(1) A company may not alter the conditions contained in its memorandum except in the cases and in the manner and to the extent for which express provision is made in this Act.

(2) Only those provisions which are required by section 27 or by any other specific provision contained in this Act, to be stated in the memorandum of the company concerned, are deemed to be conditions contained in its memorandum.

50.—(1) The name of the company shall not be altered except with the consent of the Commission in accordance with section 30.

(2) The business which the company is authorised to carry on or, if the company is not formed for the purpose of carrying on business, the objects for which it is established, may be altered or added to in accordance with the provisions of section 51.

(3) Any restriction on the powers of the company may be altered in the same way as the business or objects of the company.

(4) The share capital of the company may be altered in accordance with the provisions of sections 128-130, but not otherwise.

(5) Subject to section 54, any other provision of the memorandum maybe altered in accordance with section 51, or as otherwise provided in this Act.

51.—(1) Where a company has stated its business or objects in its memorandum, such a company may, at a meeting of which notice in writing has been duly given to all members (whether or not they are entitled to), by special resolution alter the provisions of its memorandum with respect to the business or objects of the company :

Provided that if an application is made to the Court in accordance with this section for the alteration to be cancelled, it shall not have effect except in so far as it is confirmed by the Court.

(2) An application under this section may be made to the Court by the holders of not less—

(a) in the aggregate, than 15% in nominal value of the company's issued share capital or any class thereof or, if the company is not limited by shares,

not less than 15% of the company's members ; or

(b) than 15% of the company's debentures entitling the holders to object to alterations of its objects :

Provided that any such application shall not be made by any person who has consented to or voted in favour of the alteration.

(3) An application under this section shall be made not later than 28 days after the date on which the resolution altering the company's business or objects was passed, and may be made on behalf of the persons entitled to make the application by such one or more of them as they may appoint in writing for that purpose.

(4) On an application under this section, the Court may make an order confirming the alteration either wholly or in part and on such terms and conditions as it deems fit, and may adjourn the proceedings in order that an arrangement may be made to the satisfaction of the Court for the purchase of the interest of dissenting members, and the Court may give such directions and make such orders as it considers expedient for facilitating or carrying into effect any such arrangement, but that no part of the capital of the company shall be expended in any case.

(5) The debentures entitling the holders to object to alterations of a company's business or objects shall be any debenture secured by a floating charge.

(6) The special resolution altering a company's business or objects requires the same notice to the holders of such debentures as to members of the company, and in default of any provision regulating the giving of notice to any debenture holder, the provisions of the company's articles regulating the giving of notice to members shall apply.

(7) Where a company passes a resolution altering its business or objects and—

(*a*) application is thereafter made to the Court for its confirmation under this section, the company shall forthwith give notice to the Commission of the making of the application, and thereafter there shall be delivered to the Commission within 15 days from the date of its making—

(i) a certified true copy of the order, in the case of refusal to confirm the resolution, and

(ii) a certified true copy of the order, in the case of confirmation of the resolution together with a printed copy of the memorandum as altered ; and

(*b*) no application is made with respect to confirmation to a Court under this section, the company shall, within 15 days from the end of the period for making such an application, deliver to the Commission a copy of the resolution as passed.

(8) If the Commission—

(a) is satisfied, a printed copy of the memorandum as altered by the resolution shall forthwith be delivered to it ;

(b) is not satisfied, it shall give notice in writing to the company of its decision and an appeal from its decision shall thereafter lie to the Court at the suit of any person aggrieved and such appeal shall be made within 21 days from the date of the receipt by the company of the notice of rejection, or within such extended time as the Court may allow.

(9) The Court may at any time extend the time for the delivery of documents to the Commission under subsection (7) (*a*) for such period as the Court may consider proper.

(10) If a company defaults in giving notice or delivering any document to the Commission as required by subsection (7), the company and every officer of the company who is in default is liable to such penalty as the Commission shall prescribe by regulation, and for every day during which the default continues.

(11) The validity of an alteration of the provision of a company's memorandum with respect to the business or objects of the company shall not be questioned on the ground that it was not authorised by subsection (1) except in proceedings taken for the purpose (whether under this section or otherwise) before the expiration of 21 days after the date of the resolution in that behalf, and where such proceedings are taken otherwise than under this section, subsections (6), (7), (8) and (9) of this section shall apply in relation thereto as if they had been taken under this section, and as if any order declaring the alteration invalid were an order cancelling it and as if any order dismissing the proceedings were an order confirming the alteration.

(12) For the purpose of this section only, any reference to "member" includes any person financially interested in the company within the context of subsection (2) (*b*).

52.—(1) Subject to the provisions of section 49 and of this section and of any part of Part B (which preserves the rights of minorities in certain cases) any provision in a company's memorandum, which might lawfully have been in articles of association instead of in the memorandum, may be altered by the company by special resolution, but if an application is made to the court for the alteration to be cancelled, the alteration does not have effect except in so far as it is confirmed by the Court.

(2) This section does not apply where the memorandum itself provides for or prohibits the alteration of all or any of the said provisions, and shall not authorise any variation or abrogation of the special rights of any class of members.

(3) Section 51 (2), (3), (4), (7), (8) and (9) (which relate to mode of alteration of business or objects) except subsection (2) (*b*) thereof, shall apply in relation to any alteration and application made under this section as they apply in relation to alterations and to applications made under that section.

(4) This section applies to a company's memorandum, whether registered before or after the commencement of this Act.

53.—(1) Subject to the provisions of this Act and to the conditions or other provisions contained in its memorandum, a company may, by special resolution, alter or add to its articles, including deletion or modification of the provisions stated in section 27 (1) (*a*)-(*d*).

(2) Any alteration or addition made in the articles shall, subject to the provisions of this Act, be as valid as if originally contained therein and be subject, in like manner, to alteration by special resolution.

54. Except to the extent to which a member of a company agrees in writing at any time to be bound thereby, and anything to the contrary in the memorandum or articles notwithstanding, the member shall not be bound by any alteration made in the memorandum or articles of the company requiring him on or after the date of the alteration to—

(a) take or subscribe for more shares than he held at the date on which he became a member ;

(b) increase his liability to contribute to the share capital of the company; or pay money by any other means to the company.

CHAPTER 2—RE-REGISTRATION OF COMPANIES

55. A company may by re-registration under this Part alter its status from—

(a) a private company to a public company ;

(b) a public company to a private company ;

(c) a private limited company to an unlimited company ;(*d*) an unlimited company to a limited company ; or (*e*) a public limited company to an unlimited company.

56.—(1) A private company (whether limited or unlimited) may be reregistered as a public company limited by shares if—

(a) a special resolution that it should be so re-registered is passed ;

(b) the conditions specified under subsection (2) are met, and

(c) an application for re-registration is delivered to the Commission in accordance with section 60, together with—

(*i*) the other documents required by that section, and (*ii*) a statement of compliance.

(2) The conditions are—

(a) that the company has a share capital ;

(b) that the requirements of section 57 are met as regards its share capital ;

(c) that the requirements of section 58 are met as regards its net assets ;

(d) if section 59 applies, that the requirements of that section are met ; and

(e) that the company has not previously been re-registered as an unlimited company.

(3) The company shall make such changes to its name and articles, as are necessary in connection with its becoming a public company.

(4) If the company is unlimited it shall also make such changes in its articles as are necessary in connection with its becoming a company limited by shares.

57.—(1) The following requirements shall be met at the time the special resolution is passed that the company should be re-registered as a public company—

(a) the nominal value of the company's allotted share capital shall be not less than the minimum specified in section 27 (2) ;

(b) the company's allotted shares shall be paid up at least one-quarter of the nominal value of that share and the whole of any premium on it ;

(c) if any share in the company or any premium on it has been fully or partly paid up by an undertaking given by any person that he or another should work or perform services (whether for the company or any other person), the undertaking shall have been performed or otherwise discharged ; or

(d) if shares have been allotted as fully or partly paid up as to their nominal value or any premium on them otherwise than in cash, and the consideration for the allotment consists of, or includes, an undertaking to the company (other than one to which paragraph (*c*) applies), then either—

(i) the undertaking shall have been performed or otherwise discharged, or

(ii) there shall be a contract between the company and some person pursuant to which the undertaking is to be performed within five years from the time the special resolution is passed.

(2) Shares allotted in pursuance of an employees' share scheme, by reason of which the company would, but for this subsection, be precluded under subsection (1) (*b*) from being re-registered as a public company, shall not be regarded for the purpose of determining whether the requirements in subsection (1) (*b*), (*c*) and (*d*) are met.

(3) No more than one-tenth of the nominal value of the company's allotted share capital is to be disregarded under subsection (2) and for this purpose the allotted share capital is treated as not including shares disregarded under the subsection.

(4) Shares disregarded under subsection (2) are treated as not forming part of the allotted share capital for the purposes of subsection (1) (*a*).

(5) A company shall not be re-registered as a public company if it appears to the Commission that—

(a) the company has resolved to reduce its share capital ;

(b) the reduction is supported by a solvency statement in accordance with regulations made by the Minister ; and

(c) the effect of the reduction is, or will be, that the nominal value of the company's allotted share capital is below the minimum specified in section 27 (2).

58.—(1) A company applying to re-register as a public company shall obtain—

(a) a balance sheet prepared as at a date not more than seven months before the date on which the application is delivered to the Commission ;

(b) an unqualified report by the company's auditor on that balance sheet ; and

(c) a written statement by the company's auditor that, in his opinion at the balance sheet date, the amount of the company's net assets was not less than the aggregate of its called-up share capital and undistributable reserves.

(2) Between the date of the balance sheet and the date on which the application for re-registration is delivered to the Commission, there shall be no change in the company's financial position that results in the amount of its net assets becoming less than the aggregate of its called-up share capital and un-distributable reserves.
(3) In subsection (1) (*b*), an "unqualified report" means—
(a) if the balance sheet was prepared for a financial year of the company, a report stating without material qualification the auditor's opinion that the balance sheet has been properly prepared in accordance with the requirements of this Act ;
(b) if the balance sheet was not prepared for a financial year of the company, a report stating without material qualification the auditor's opinion that the balance sheet has been properly prepared in accordance with the provisions of this Act which would have applied if it had been prepared for a financial year of the company.
(4) For the purpose of an auditor's report on a balance sheet that was not prepared for a financial year of the company, the provisions of this Act apply with such modifications as are necessary.
(5) For the purposes of subsection (3), a qualification is material unless the auditor states in his report that the matter giving rise to the qualification is not material for the purpose of determining (by reference to the company's balance sheet) whether at the date of the balance sheet, the amount of the company's net assets was not less than the aggregate of its called-up share capital and un-distributable reserves.
(6) In this Part—
(a) "*net assets*" means the aggregate of the company's assets less the aggregate of its liabilities, and
(b) "*un-distributable reserves*" are its—
(i) share premium account, and
(ii) capital redemption reserve ;
(c) the amount by which its accumulated or unrealised profits (so far as not previously utilised by capitalisation) exceed its accumulated or unrealised losses (so far as not previously written off in a reduction or reorganisation of capital duly made) ; and
(d) any other reserve that the company is prohibited from distributing by any enactment (other than one contained in this Part) or by its articles.
(7) The reference in subsection (6) (*c*) to capitalisation does not include a transfer of profits of the company to its capital redemption reserve.
59.—(1) This section applies where the shares are allotted—
(a) by the company in the period between the date the balance sheet required by section 58 is prepared and the passing of the resolution that the
company should re-register as a public company ; and
(b) as fully or partly paid up as to their nominal value or any premium on them otherwise than in cash.
(2) The Commission shall not entertain an application by the company for re-registration as a public company unless the requirements of section 57 have been complied with, or the allotment is in connection with— (*a*) a share exchange as described in subsections (3)-(5) ; or
(*b*) a proposed merger with another company as described in subsection (6).
(3) An allotment is in connection with a share exchange if—
(*a*) the shares are allotted in connection with an arrangement under which the whole or part of the consideration for the shares allotted is provided by—

(i) the transfer to the company allotting the shares of shares (or shares of a particular class) in another company, or

(ii) the cancellation of shares (or shares of a particular class) in another company ; and

(*b*) the allotment is open to all the holders of the shares of the other company in question (or, where the arrangement applies only to shares of a particular class, to all the holders of the company's shares of that class) to take part in the arrangement in connection with which the shares are allotted.

(4) In determining whether a person is a holder of shares for the purposes of subsection (3), there shall be disregarded—

(a) shares held by, or by a nominee of, the company allotting the shares ; and

(b) shares held by, or by a nominee of—

(i) the holding company of the company allotting the shares,

(ii) a subsidiary of the company allotting the shares, or

(iii) a subsidiary of the holding company of the company allotting the shares.

(5) It is immaterial, for the purposes of deciding whether an allotment is in connection with a share exchange, whether or not the arrangement in connection with which the shares are allotted involves the issue to the company allotting the shares of shares (or shares of a particular class) in the other company.

(6) There is a proposed merger with another company if one of the companies concerned proposes to acquire all the assets and liabilities of the other in exchange for the issue of its shares or other securities to shareholders of the other.

(7) For the purposes of this section—

(a) the consideration for an allotment does not include any amount standing to the credit of any of the company's reserve accounts, or of its profit and loss account, that has been applied in paying up (to any extent) any of the shares allotted or any premium on those shares ; and

(b) "arrangement" means any agreement, scheme or arrangement pursuant to Chapter 27.

60.—(1) An application for re-registration as a public company shall contain—

(a) a statement of the company's proposed name on re-registration; and

in the case of a company without a secretary, a statement of the company's proposed secretary.

(2) The application shall be accompanied by—

(a) a copy of the special resolution that the company should re-register as a public company ;

(b) a copy of the company's memorandum and articles as proposed to be amended ;

(c) a copy of the balance sheet and other documents referred to in section 58 (1) ; and

(d) if section 59 applies, a copy of the valuation report (*if any*) under subsection (2) (*a*) of that section.

(3) The statement of compliance required to be delivered together with the application is a statement that the requirements of this Part as to reregistration as a public company have been complied with.

(4) The Commission may accept the statement of compliance as sufficient evidence that the company is entitled to be re-registered as a public company.

61.—(1) The statement of the company's proposed secretary shall contain the required particulars of the person or persons who is or are to be the secretary or joint secretaries of the company.

(2) The required particulars are those required to be stated in the company's register of secretaries.

(3) The statement shall also contain consent by the person named as secretary, or each of the persons named as joint secretaries, to act in the relevant capacity and if all the partners in a firm are to be joint secretaries, consent may be given by one partner on behalf of all of them.

62.—(1) If, on an application for re-registration as a public company, the Commission is satisfied that the company is entitled to be re-registered, the company shall be re-registered accordingly.

(2) The Commission shall issue a certificate of incorporation altered to meet the circumstances of the case.

(3) The certificate shall state that it is issued on re-registration and the date on which it is issued.

(4) Upon the issue of the certificate—

(a) the company by virtue of the issue of the certificate becomes a public company ;

(b) the changes in the company's name, memorandum and articles take effect ; and

(c) where the application contained a statement of proposed secretary, the person or persons named in the statement as secretary or joint secretaries of the company are deemed to have been appointed to that office.

(5) The certificate is *prima facie* evidence that the requirements of this Act as to re-registration have been complied with.

63.—(1) A public company may be re-registered as a private limited company if—

(*a*) a special resolution that it should be so re-registered is passed ; (*b*) the conditions specified under this section are met ; and

(*c*) an application for re-registration is delivered to the Commission in accordance with section 66, together with—

(*i*) the other documents required by that section, and (*ii*) a statement of compliance.

(2) The conditions are that—

(*a*) where no application under section 64 for cancellation of the resolution has been made—

(i) having regard to the number of members who consented to, or voted in favour of, the resolution, no such application may be made, or

(ii) the period within which such an application could be made has expired ; or

(*b*) where such an application has been made—

(i) the application has been withdrawn, or

(ii) an order has been made confirming the resolution and a copy of that order has been delivered to the Commission.

(3) The company shall make such changes—

(a) in its name ; and

(b) in its memorandum and articles, as are necessary in connection with its becoming a private company limited by shares or, as the case may be, by guarantee.

64.—(1) Where a special resolution by a public company to be reregistered as a private limited company has been passed, an application to the Court for the cancellation of the resolution may be made—

(a) by the holders of at least 5% in nominal value of the company's issued share capital or any class of the company's issued share capital (disregarding any shares held by the company as treasury shares) ;
(b) if the company is not limited by shares at least 5% of its members; or
(c) by at least 50 members of the company, but not by a person who has consented to or voted in favour of the resolution.
(2) The application shall be made within 28 days after the passing of the resolution and may be made on behalf of the persons entitled to make it by such one or more of their number as they may appoint for that purpose.
(3) On the hearing of the application, the Court shall make an order either cancelling or confirming the resolution.
(4) The Court may—
(a) make that order on such terms and conditions as it deems fit ;
(b) if it deems fit, adjourn the proceedings in order that an arrangement may be made to the satisfaction of the Court for the purchase of the interests of dissenting members ; and
(c) give such directions, and make such orders, as it considers expedient for facilitating or carrying into effect any such arrangement.
(5) The Court order may, if the Court deems fit—
(a) provide for the purchase by the company of the shares of any of its members and for the reduction accordingly of the company's capital ; and
(b) make such alteration in the company's memorandum articles as maybe required in consequence of that provision.
(6) The Court order may, if the Court deems fit, require the company not to make amendment to its articles without the leave of the Court.

65.—(1) On making an application to the Court to cancel the resolution, the applicants, or the person making the application on their behalf, shall immediately give notice to the Commission, without prejudice to any provision of rules of court as to service of notice of the application.
(2) On being served with notice of any such application, the company shall immediately give notice to the Commission.
(3) Within 15 days of the making of the Court order on the application, or such longer period as the Court may at any time direct, the company shall deliver to the Commission a copy of the order.
(4) If default is made in complying with subsections (2) and (3), the company and each officer of the company is liable to such penalty as the Commission shall prescribe by regulation for every day during which the default continues.

66.—(1) An application for re-registration as a private limited company shall contain a statement of the company's proposed name on re-registration. (2) The application shall be accompanied by a copy of the—
(a) resolution that the company should re-register as a private limited company ; and company's memorandum and articles as proposed to be amended.
(3) The statement of compliance required to be delivered together with the application is a statement that the requirements of this Part as to reregistration as a private limited company have been complied with.
(4) The commission may accept the statement of compliance as sufficient evidence that the company is entitled to be re-registered as a private limited company.

67.—(1) If, on an application for re-registration as a private limited company, the Commission is satisfied that the company is entitled to be so reregistered, the company shall be re-registered accordingly.

(2) The Commission shall issue a certificate of incorporation altered to meet the circumstance.

(3) The certificate shall state that it is issued on re-registration and the date on which it is issued.

(4) Upon the issue of the certificate—

(a) the company by virtue of the issue of the certificate becomes a private limited company ;

(b) the changes in the company's name, memorandum and articles take effect.

(5) The certificate is *prima facie* evidence that the requirements of this Act as to re-registration have been complied with.

68.—(1) A private limited company may be re-registered as an unlimited company if—

(a) all the members of the company have assented to its being so reregistered ;

(b) the condition specified under subsection (2) is met ; and

(c) an application for re-registration is delivered to the Commission in accordance with section 69, together with—

(*i*) the other documents required by that section, and (*ii*) a statement of compliance.

(2) The condition is that the company has not previously been reregistered as limited.

(3) The company shall make such changes in its name and its memorandum and articles—

(a) as are necessary in connection with its becoming an unlimited company ; and

(b) if it is to have a share capital, as are necessary in connection with its becoming an unlimited company having a share capital.

(4) For the purposes of this section—

(i) a trustee in bankruptcy of a member of the company is entitled, to the exclusion of the member, to assent to the company's becoming unlimited ; and

(ii) the personal representative of a deceased member of the company may assent on behalf of the deceased.

(5) In subsection (4) (*a*), "a trustee in bankruptcy of a member of the company" includes—

(a) a permanent trustee or an interim trustee on the sequestrated estate of a member of the company ; and

(b) a trustee under a protected trustee deed granted by a member of the company.

69.—(1) An application for re-registration as an unlimited company shall contain a statement of the company's proposed name on re-registration.

(2) The application shall be accompanied by—

(a) the prescribed form of assent to the company's being re-registered as an unlimited company, authenticated by or on behalf of all the members of the company ; and

(b) a copy of the company's memorandum and articles as proposed to be amended.

(3) The statement of compliance required to be delivered together with the application is a statement that the requirements of this Part as to reregistration as an unlimited company have been complied with.

(4) The statement shall contain a statement by the directors of the company—

(a) that the persons by whom or on whose behalf the form of assent is authenticated constitute the whole membership of the company ; and

(b) if any of the members has not authenticated that form himself, that the directors have taken all reasonable steps to satisfy themselves that each person who authenticated it on behalf of a member was lawfully empowered to do so.

(5) The Commission may accept the statement of compliance as sufficient evidence that the company is entitled to be re-registered as an unlimited company.

70.—(1) If, on an application for re-registration of a private limited company as an unlimited company the Commission is satisfied that the company, is entitled to be so re-registered, the company shall be re-registered accordingly.

(2) The Commission shall issue a certificate of incorporation altered to meet the circumstance.

The certificate shall state that it is issued on re-registration and the date on which it is issued.

(4) Upon the issue of the certificate—

(a) the company by virtue of the issue of the certificate becomes an unlimited company ; and

(b) the changes in the company's name, memorandum and articles take effect.

(5) The certificate is conclusive evidence that the requirements of this Act as to re-registration have been complied with.

71.—(1) An unlimited company may be re-registered as a private limited company if—

(a) a special resolution that it should be re-registered is passed ;

(b) the condition specified under subsection (2) is met ; and

(c) an application for re-registration is delivered to the Commission in accordance with section 72, together with—

(*i*) the other documents required by that section, and (ii) a statement of compliance.

(2) The condition is that the company has not previously been reregistered as unlimited.

(3) The special resolution shall state whether the company is to be limited by shares or by guarantee.

(4) The company shall make such changes—

(a) in its name ; and

(b) in its memorandum and articles, as are necessary in connection with its becoming a company limited by shares or, as the case may be, by guarantee.

72.—(1) An application for re-registration as a limited company shall contain a statement of the company's proposed name on re-registration.

(2) The application shall be accompanied by—

(a) a copy of the resolution that the company should re-register as a private limited company ;

(b) if the company is to be limited by guarantee, a statement of guarantee ; and

(c) a copy of the company's memorandum and articles as proposed tobe amended.

(3) The statement of guarantee required to be delivered in the case of a company that is to be limited by guarantee shall state that each member undertakes that, if the company is wound up while he is a member, or within one year after he ceases to be a member, he will contribute to the assets of the company to such amount as may be required for—

(a) payment of the debts and liabilities of the company contracted before he ceases to be a member ;

(b) payment of the costs, charges and expenses of winding-up ; and

(c) adjustment of the rights of the contributories among themselves, not exceeding a specified amount.

(4) The statement of compliance required to be delivered together with the application is a statement that the requirements of this Part as to reregistration as a limited company have been complied with.

(5) The Commission may accept the statement of compliance as sufficient evidence that the company is entitled to be re-registered as a limited company.

73.—(1) If, on an application for re-registration of an unlimited company as a limited company, the Commission is satisfied that the company is entitled to be so re-registered, the company shall be re-registered accordingly.

(2) The Commission shall issue a certificate of incorporation altered to meet the circumstances of the case.

(3) The certificate shall state that it is issued on re-registration and the date on which it is so issued.

(4) Upon the issue of the certificate—

(a) the company by virtue of the issue of the certificate becomes a limited company ; and

(b) the changes in the company's name, memorandum and articles take effect.

(5) The certificate is *prima facie* evidence that the requirements of this Act as to re-registration have been complied with.

74.—(1) A company which on re-registration under section 71 has already allotted its share capital, shall within 15 days after the re-registration deliver a statement of the share capital to the Commission.

(2) This does not apply if the information which would be included in the statement has already been sent to the Commission in a statement of—

(*a*) capital and initial shareholdings ; or (*b*) capital contained in an annual return.

(3) The statement of capital shall state with respect to the company's share capital on re-registration—

(a) the total number of shares of the company ;

(b) the aggregate nominal value of those shares ;

(c) for each class of shares—

(i) prescribed particulars of the rights attached to the shares,

(ii) the total number of shares of that class, and

(iii) the aggregate nominal value of shares of that class ; and

(*d*) the amount paid up and the amount (if any) unpaid on each share (whether on account of the nominal value of the share or by way of premium).

(4) If default is made in complying with this section, the company and each officer of the company are liable to such penalty as the Commission shall prescribe by regulation for every day during which the default continues.

75.—(1) A public company limited by shares may be re-registered as an unlimited company with a share capital if—

(a) all the members of the company have assented to its being so reregistered ;

(b) the condition specified under subsection (2) is met ; and

(c) an application for re-registration is delivered to the registrar in accordance with section 76, together with—

(*i*) the other documents required by that section, and (*ii*) a statement of compliance.

(2) The condition is that the company has not previously been reregistered as —

(*a*) limited ; or (*b*) unlimited.

(3) The company shall make such changes—

(a) in its name ; and

(b) in its memorandum and articles, as are necessary in connection with its becoming an unlimited company.

(4) For the purposes of this section—

(a) a trustee in bankruptcy of a member of the company is entitled, to the exclusion of the member, to assent to the company's re-registration ; and

(b) the personal representative of a deceased member of the company may assent on behalf of the deceased.

(5) In subsection (4) (*a*), "a trustee in bankruptcy of a member of the company" includes—

(a) a permanent trustee or an interim trustee on the sequestrated estate of a member of the company ; and

(b) a trustee under a protected trustee deed granted by a member of the company.

76.—(1) An application for re-registration of a public company as an unlimited company shall contain a statement of the company's proposed name on re- registration.

(2) The application shall be accompanied by—

(a) the prescribed form of assent to the company's being re-registered as an unlimited company, authenticated by or on behalf of all the members of the company ; and

(b) a copy of the company's memorandum and articles as proposed to be amended.

(3) The statement of compliance required to be delivered together with the application is a statement that the requirements of this Part as to reregistration as an unlimited private company have been complied with.

(4) The statement shall contain a statement by the directors of the company—

(a) that the persons by whom or on whose behalf the form of assent is authenticated constitute the whole membership of the company ; and

(b) if any of the members has not authenticated that form himself, that the directors have taken all reasonable steps to satisfy themselves that each person who authenticated it on behalf of a member was lawfully empowered to do so.

(5) The Commission may accept the statement of compliance as sufficient evidence that the company is entitled to be re-registered as an unlimited company.

77. (1) If, on an application for re-registration of a public company as an unlimited company, the Commission is satisfied that the company is entitled to be so re-registered, the company shall be re-registered accordingly.

(2) The Commission shall issue a certificate of incorporation altered to meet the circumstances of the case.

(3) The certificate shall state that it is issued on re-registration and the date on which it is so issued.

(4) Upon the issue of the certificate the —

(a) company, by virtue of the issue of the certificate, becomes an unlimited company ; and

(b) changes in the company's name, memorandum and articles take effect.

(4) The certificate is *prima facie* evidence that the requirements of this Act as to re-registration have been complied with.

CHAPTER 3—FOREIGN COMPANIES

78.—(1) Subject to sections 80-83 of this Act, every foreign company which before or after the commencement of this Act was incorporated outside Nigeria, and having the intention of carrying on business in Nigeria, shall take all steps necessary to obtain incorporation as a separate entity in Nigeria for that purpose, but until so incorporated, the foreign company shall not carry on business in Nigeria or exercise any of the powers of a registered company and shall not have a place of business or an address for service of documents or processes in Nigeria for any purpose other than the receipt of notices and other documents, as matters preliminary to incorporation under this Act.

(2) Any act of the company in contravention of subsection (1) is void.

(3) Nothing in this section affects the status of any foreign company—

(*a*) which before the commencement of this Act was granted exemption from compliance under the provisions of any preceding Companies Acts that had been applicable in Nigeria before the commencement of this Act ; and (*b*) exempted under any treaty to which Nigeria is a party.

79. If any foreign company fails to comply with the requirements of section 80 of this Act in so far as they may apply to the company, the company commits an offence and is, in addition to being liable to prosecution, also liable to such penalty as the Commission shall specify by regulation, and every officer or agent of the company who authorises or permits the default or failure to comply is, whether or not the company is also convicted of any offence, liable on conviction to such penalty as the Commission shall specify by regulation, and where the offence is a continuing one, the company and every officer or agent of the company are liable to a further penalty as the Commission shall specify by regulation for every day during which the default continues.

80.—(1) A foreign company may apply to the Minister for exemption from the provisions of section 78 of this Act if that foreign company belongs to one of the following categories, that is—

(a) foreign companies other than those specified in paragraph (*d*), invited to Nigeria by or with the approval of the Federal Government to execute any specified individual project ;

(b) foreign companies which are in Nigeria for the execution of specific individual loan projects on behalf of a donor country or international organisation ;

(c) foreign government-owned companies engaged solely in export promotion activities ; and

(d) engineering consultants and technical experts engaged on any individual specialist project under contract with any of the governments in the Federation or any of their agencies or with any other body or person, where such contract has been approved by the Federal Government.

(2) An application for exemption under this section shall be in writing addressed to the Minister and shall set out—

(a) the name and place of business of the foreign company outside Nigeria ;

(b) the name and place of business or the proposed name and place of business of the foreign company in Nigeria ;

(c) the name and address of each director, partner or other principal officer of the foreign company ;

(d) a certified copy of the charter, statutes, or memorandum and articles of association of the company, or other instrument constituting or defining the constitution of the company and if the instrument is not written in the English language, a certified translation thereof ;

(e) the names and addresses of one or more persons resident in Nigeria authorised to accept, on behalf of the foreign company, service of processes and any notice required to be served on the company ;

(f) the business or proposed business in Nigeria of the foreign company and the duration of such business ;

(g) particulars of any project previously carried out by the company as an exempted foreign company ; and

(h) such other particulars as may be required by the Minister or Secretary to the Government of the Federation.

(3) Where the Minister, upon the receipt of an application for exemption, is of the opinion that the circumstances are such as to render it expedient that such an exemption should be granted, the Minister, subject to such conditions as he may prescribe, exempt the foreign company from the obligations imposed by or under this Act.

(4) Every exemption granted under this section shall specify the period or, as the case may be, the project or series of projects, for which it is granted and shall lapse at the end of such period or upon the completion of such project or series of projects.

(5) The Minister may at any time revoke any exemption granted to any company if he is of the opinion that the company has contravened any provision of this Act or has failed to meet any condition contained in the exemption order or for any other good or sufficient reason.

(6) The Minister shall cause to be published in the Federal Government *Gazette* the name of any company—

(a) to which an exemption has been granted and the period or, as the case may be, the project or series of projects for which the exemption is granted ; and

(b) which exemption has been revoked and the effective date of such revocation.

(7) Every exempted company shall deliver to the Commission upon payment of a prescribed fee a notice of its exemption within 30 days of the grant of such exemption.

(8) If an exempted company fails to comply with the provisions of subsection (7), it is liable to such penalty as the Commission shall specify by regulation for every day during which the default continues.

81. (1) Every exempted foreign company shall deliver to the Commission, in every calendar year, a report in the form prescribed by the Commission.

(2) An exempted foreign company that fails to comply with the provisions of subsection (1), is liable to such penalty as the Commission shall specify by regulation, for every year of default.

82. Subject to this Act and save as may be stated in the instrument of exemption, a foreign company exempted pursuant to this Act shall have the status of an unregistered company and accordingly, the provisions of this Act applicable to an unregistered company shall apply in relation to such an exempted company as they apply in relation to an unregistered company under this Act.

83.—(1) A person who, for the purpose of obtaining an exemption or of complying with any of the provisions of section 80 of this Act, makes any statement or presents any instrument which is false commits an offence unless he proves that he has taken all reasonable steps to ascertain the truth of the statement made or contained in the instrument so presented.

(2) Any person who contravenes subsection (1) commits an offence under this section is liable on conviction to a fine or imprisonment as the Court deems fit.

84. Except as provided under sections 80, 81 and 82 of this Act—

(*a*) nothing shall be construed as authorising the disregard by any exempted foreign company of any enactment or rule of law ; and

(*b*) nothing in this Chapter shall be construed as affecting the rights or liability of a foreign company to sue or be sued in its name or in the name of its agent.

CHAPTER 4—PROMOTERS

85. Any person who undertakes to take part in forming a company with reference to a given project and set it going and who takes the necessary steps to accomplish that purpose, or who, with regard to a proposed or newly formed company, undertakes a part in raising capital for it, is deemed a promoter of the company: Provided that a person acting in a professional capacity for persons engaged in procuring the formation of the company shall not be deemed to be a promoter.

86.—(1) A promoter stands in a fiduciary relationship to the company and shall observe utmost good faith towards the company in any transaction with it or on its behalf and shall compensate the company for any loss suffered by reason of his failure to do so.

(2) A promoter, who acquires any property or information in circumstances in which it was his duty as a fiduciary to acquire it on behalf of the company, shall account to the company for such property and for any profit which he may have made from the use of such property or information.

(3) Any transaction between a promoter and the company may be rescinded by the company unless, after full disclosure of all material facts known to the promoter, such transaction shall have been entered into or ratified on behalf of the company by —

(a) the company's board of directors independent of the promoter ;

(b) all the members of the company ; or

(c) the company at a general meeting at which neither the promoter nor the holders of any share in which he is beneficially interested shall vote on the resolution to enter into or ratify that transaction.

(4) No period of limitation shall apply to any proceeding brought by the company to enforce any of its rights under this section but in any such proceeding the Court may relieve a promoter in whole or in part and on such terms as it deems fit from liability if in all the circumstances, including lapse of time, the Court deems it equitable to do so.

CHAPTER 5—ACTS BY OR ON BEHALF OF THE COMPANY IN EXERCISE OF COMPANY'S POWERS

87.—(1) A company shall act through its members in general meeting or its board of directors or through officers or agents appointed by, or under authority derived from, the members in general meeting or the board of directors.

(2) Subject to the provisions of this Act, the respective powers of the members in general meeting and the board of directors shall be determined by the company's articles.

(3) Except as otherwise provided in the company's articles, the business of the company shall be managed by the board of directors who may exercise all such powers of the company as are not by this Act or the articles required to be exercised by the members in general meeting.

(4) Unless the articles otherwise provide, the board of directors, when acting within the powers conferred upon them by this Act or the articles, is not bound to obey the directions or instructions of the members in general meeting provided that the directors acted in good faith and with due diligence.

(5) Notwithstanding the provisions of subsection (3), the members in general meeting may—

(a) act in any matter if the members of the board of directors are disqualified or unable to act because of a deadlock on the board or otherwise ;

(b) institute legal proceedings in the name and on behalf of the company, if the board of directors refuse or neglect to do so ;

(c) ratify or confirm any action taken by the board of directors ; or

(d) make recommendations to the board of directors regarding action to be taken by the board.

(6) No alteration of the articles invalidates any prior act of the board of directors which would have been valid if that alteration had not been made.

88. Unless otherwise provided in this Act or in the articles, the board of directors may—

(a) exercise its powers through committees consisting of such members of their body as they think fit ; or

(b) from time to time, appoint one or more of its members to the office of managing director and may delegate all or any of its powers to such managing director.

LIABILITY FOR ACTS OF THE COMPANY

89. Any act of the members in general meeting, the board of directors, or a managing director while carrying on in the usual way the business of the company, shall be treated as the act of the company itself and the company is criminally and civilly liable to the same extent as if it were a natural person : Provided that—

(a) the company shall not incur civil liability to any person if that person had actual knowledge at the time of the transaction in question that the general meeting, board of directors, or managing director, as the case may be, had no power to act in the matter or had acted in an irregular manner or if, having regard to his position with or relationship to the company, he ought to have known of the absence of such power or of their irregularity ; and

(b) if in fact a business is being carried on by the company, the company shall not escape liability for acts undertaken in connection with that business merely because the business in question was not among the business authorised by the company's memorandum.

90. (1) Except as provided in section 89 of this Act, the acts of any officer or agent of a company shall not be deemed to be acts of the company, unless—

(a) the company, acting through its members in general meeting, board of directors, or managing director, shall have expressly or impliedly authorised such officer or agent to act in the matter ; or

(b) the company, acting as mentioned in paragraph (*a*), shall have represented the officer or agent as having its authority to act in the matter, in which event the company shall be civilly liable to any person who has entered into the transaction in reliance on such representation unless such person had actual knowledge that the officer or agent had no authority or unless having regard to his position with or relationship to the company, he ought to have known of such absence of authority.

(2) The authority of an officer or agent of the company may be conferred prior to any action by him or by subsequent ratification, and knowledge of such action by the officer or agent and acquiescence by all the members of the company or by the directors or by the managing director for the time being, shall be equivalent to ratification by the members in general meeting, board of directors, or managing director, as the case may be.

(3) Nothing in this section shall derogate from the vicarious liability of the company for the acts of its servants while acting within the scope of their employment.

91.—(1) Any provision, whether contained in the articles of the company or in any contract with a company or otherwise, for exempting any officer of the company or any person employed by the company as auditor from, or indemnifying him against any liability which by virtue of any rule of law would otherwise attach to him in respect of any negligence, default, or breach of trust of which he may be guilty in relation to the company, is void.

(2) Notwithstanding the provisions of subsection (1), (*a*)—

(a) person shall not be deprived of any exemption or right to be indemnified in respect of anything done or omitted to be done by him while any such provision as mentioned in that subsection was in force ; and

(b) company may, in pursuance of any such provision as mentioned in subsection (1), indemnify any such officer or auditor against any liability incurred by him in defending any proceeding, whether civil or criminal, in which judgment is given in his favour or in which he is acquitted or in connection with any application under section 740 of this Act in which relief is granted to him by the Court.

92. Except as mentioned in section 223 of this Act, regarding particulars in the register of particulars of charges, a person is not deemed to have knowledge of the contents of the memorandum and articles of a company or of any other particulars, documents, or the contents of documents merely because such particulars or documents are registered by the Commission or referred to in the particulars or documents so registered, or are available for inspection at an office of the company.

93. A person dealing with a company or with someone deriving title under the company, is entitled to make the following assumptions and the company and those deriving title under it shall be estopped from denying their truth that—

(a) the company's memorandum and articles have been duly complied with ;

(b) every person described in the particulars filed with the Commission pursuant to sections 36 (4) (*c*), 319 and 337 of this Act as a director, managing director or secretary of the company, or represented by the company, acting through its members in general meeting, board of directors, or managing director, as an officer or agent of the company, has been duly appointed and has authority to exercise the powers and discharge the duties customarily exercised or performed by a director, managing director, or secretary of a company carrying on business of the type carried on by the company or customarily exercised or performed by an officer or agent of the type concerned ;

(c) the secretary of the company, and every officer or agent of the company having authority to issue documents or certified copies of documents on behalf of the company, has authority to warrant the genuineness of the documents or the accuracy of the copies so issued ; and

(d) a document has been duly sealed by the company if it bears what purports to be the seal of the company attested by what purports to be the signatures of two persons who, in accordance with paragraph (*b*), can be assumed to be a director and the secretary of the company :

Provided that a person shall not be entitled to—

(i) make such assumptions, if he had actual knowledge to the contrary or if, having regard to his position with or relationship to the company, he ought to have known the contrary, and

(ii) assume that any one or more of the directors of the company have been appointed to act as a committee of the board of directors or that an officer or agent of the company has the company's authority merely because the company's articles provided that authority to act in the matter that may be delegated to a committee, an officer or agent.

94. Where, in accordance with sections 89-93 of this Act, a company would be liable to a third party for the acts of any officer or agent, the company shall, except where there is collusion between the officer or agent and the third party, be liable notwithstanding that the officer or agent has acted fraudulently or forged a document purporting to be sealed by or signed on behalf of the company.

COMPANY'S CONTRACTS

95.—(1) Contracts on behalf of a company may be made, varied or discharged as follows—

(a) any contract which if made between individuals would be by law required to be by deed, or which would be varied, or discharged only by deed may be made, varied or discharged, as the case may be, in writing as a deed in the name or on behalf of the company ;

(b) any contract which if made between individuals would be by law required to be in writing, signed by the parties to be charged therewith, or which could be varied or discharged only by writing or written evidence signed by the parties to be charged, may be made, varied or discharged, as the case may be, in writing signed in the name or on behalf of the company ; and

(c) any contract which if made between individuals would be valid although made orally only and not reduced into writing or which could be varied or discharged orally, may be made, varied or discharged, as the case may be, orally on behalf of the company.

(2) A contract made according to this section shall be effectual in law, and shall bind the company and its successors and all other parties thereto, their heirs, executors, or administrators, as the case may be; and may be varied or discharged in the same manner in which it is authorised by this section to be made.

96.—(1) Any contract or other transaction purporting to be entered into by the company or by any person on behalf of the company prior to its formation may be ratified by the company after its formation and thereupon the company shall become bound by and entitled to the benefit thereof as if it has been in existence at the date of such contract or other transaction and had been a party thereto.

(2) Prior to ratification by the company, the person who purported to act in the name or on behalf of the company shall, in the absence of express agreement to the contrary, be personally bound by the contract or other transaction and entitled to the benefit thereof.

97.—(1) A bill of exchange or promissory note is deemed to have been made, accepted, or endorsed on behalf of a company if made, or expressed to be made, accepted, or endorsed in the name of the company, or if expressed to be made, accepted or endorsed on behalf or on account of the company by a person acting under its authority.

(2) The company and its successors shall be bound thereby if the company is, in accordance with sections 89-91, liable for the acts of those who made, accepted or endorsed it in its name or on its behalf or account, and a signature by a director or the secretary on behalf of the company shall not be deemed to be a signature by procuration for the purposes of section 25 of the Bills of Exchange Act.

98. A company may have a common seal but need not have one, and where a company has a common seal, the design and use of that seal shall be regulated by the company's articles and it shall have its name engraved in legible characters on the seal.

99.—(1) A company whose objects require or comprise the transaction of business in foreign countries may, if authorised by its articles, have for use in any territory, district, or place outside Nigeria, an official seal, the design and use which shall be regulated by the company's articles, and shall indicate on its face of the name of every territory, district, or place where it is to be used.

(2) A company having such an official seal may, by deed, authorise any person appointed for the purpose in any territory, district, or place outside Nigeria, to affix the same to any deed or other document to which the company is party in that territory, district, or place.

(3) The authority of any such agent shall, as between the company and any person dealing with the agent, continue during the period, if any, mentioned in the instrument conferring the authority, or if no period is there mentioned, then until notice of the revocation or determination of the agent's authority has been given to the person dealing with him.

(4) The person affixing any such official seal shall, by writing under his hand, on the deed or other document to which the seal is affixed, certify the date on which and place at which it is affixed.

(5) In the case of companies that have a common seal, a deed or other document to which an official seal is duly affixed shall bind the company as if it has been sealed with the common seal of the company.

respect of any specified matter, as its attorney, to execute deeds on its behalf in any place within or outside Nigeria.

(2) A deed signed by a person empowered as provided in subsection (1) shall bind the company and have the same effect as it would have if it were a deed signed by the company.

AUTHENTICATION AND SERVICE OF DOCUMENTS

101. A document or proceeding requiring authentication by a company may be signed by a director, secretary, or other authorised officer of the company, and need not be signed as a deed unless otherwise so required in this Part and that an electronic signature is deemed to satisfy the requirement for signing under this section.

102.—(1) A document is validly executed by a company as a deed for the purposes of this Act, if it is duly executed by the company and it is delivered as a deed.

(2) A company may execute a document described or expressed as a deed without affixing a common seal on the document by signature on behalf of the company by —

(a) a director of the company and the secretary of the company ;

(b) at least two directors of the company ; or

(c) a director of the company in the presence of at least one witness who shall attest the signature.

(3) A document mentioned in subsection (2) that is signed on behalf of the company in accordance with that subsection has the same effect as if the document was executed under the common seal of the company.

(4) Where a document is to be signed by a person on behalf of more than one company, the document shall not be considered to be signed by that person for the purposes of subsection (2) or (3), unless the person signs the document separately in each capacity.

(5) This section applies in the case of a document mentioned in subsection (2) that is executed by the company in the name or on behalf of another person, whether or not that person is also a company.

103. Where any written law or rule of law requires any document to beunder or executed under the common seal of a company, or provides for consequences for not sealing, the document is deemed to have satisfied the provisions of that written law or rule of law if the document is signed in the manner set out in sections 101 and 102.

104. A court process shall be served on a company in the manner provided by the rules of court and any other document may be served on a company by leaving it at, or sending it by post to, the registered office or head office of the company.

CHAPTER 6—MEMBERSHIP OF THE COMPANY

105.—(1) A subscriber of the memorandum of a company shall be deemed to have agreed to become a member of the company, and on its registration shall be entered as the member in its register of members.

(2) Every other person who agrees in writing to become a member of a company, and whose name is entered in its register of members, is a member of the company.

(3) In the case of a company having a share capital, each member is a shareholder of the company and shall hold at least one share, except in relation to a company that has only one shareholder.

106.—(1) As from the commencement of this Act, an individual is not capable of becoming a member of a company if he is—

(a) of unsound mind and has been so found by a court in Nigeria or elsewhere ; or

(b) an undischarged bankrupt.

(2) A person under the age of 18 years shall not be counted for the purpose of determining the legal minimum number of members of a company.

(3) A corporate body in liquidation is not capable of becoming a member of a company.

(4) Where, at the commencement of this Act, any person falling within the provisions of subsection (1) is a member of a company by reason of being a shareholder of the company, his share vests in his committee or trustee, as the case may be.

(5) Where, after the commencement of this Act, any shareholder purports to transfer any share or shares to a person falling within the provisions of subsection (1), the purported transfer shall not vest the title in the shares in that person, but the title remains in the purported transferor or his personal representative who holds the shares in trust for that person during the period of his incapacity.

107. Every member shall, notwithstanding any provision in the articles, have a right to attend any general meeting of the company and to speak and vote on any resolution before the meeting :

Provided that the articles may provide that a member shall not be entitled to attend and vote unless all calls or other sums payable by him in respect of shares in the company have been paid.

108. If a person falsely and deceitfully impersonates any member of a company and thereby obtains or endeavours to obtain any benefit due to any such member, he commits an offence and is liable on conviction to—

(a) imprisonment for a term of not more than seven years or a fine as the court deems fit;

(b) pay such additional fines as the Commission may specify by regulation ; and

(c) account to the aggrieved member for any benefit which he directly or indirectly derived as a result of his act of impersonation.

109.—(1) Every company shall keep a register of its members and enter in the register the—

(a) names and addresses of the members, and in the case of a company having a share capital, a statement of the shares and class of shares, if any, held by each member, distinguishing each share by its number so long as the share has a number, and of the amount paid or agreed to be considered as paid on the shares of each member ;

(b) date on which each person was registered as a member ; and(*c*) date on which any person ceased to be a member.

(2) The entry required under subsection (1) (*a*) or (*b*) shall be made within 28 days of the conclusion of the agreement with the company to become a member or, in the case of a subscriber of the memorandum, within 28 days of the registration of the company.

(3) The entry required under subsection (1) (*c*), shall be made within 28 days of the date on which the person concerned ceased to be a member, or if he ceased to be a member other than as a result of action by the company, within 28 days of producing to the company evidence satisfactory to the company of the occurrence of the event whereby he ceased to be a member.

(4) Where a company defaults in complying with the provisions of this section, the company and each officer of the company is liable to— (*a*) such penalties as the Commission shall specify by regulation ; and

(b) an additional daily default fine that the Commission shall specify by regulation.

(5) Liability incurred by a company from the making or deletion of an entry in its register of members, or from a failure to make or delete any entry, is not enforceable after the expiration of 20 years from the date on which the entry was made or deleted or, in the case of any such failure, from the date on which the failure first occurred.

110.—(1) The register of members shall be kept at the registered office of the company, except if the—

(a) work of making it up is done at another office of the company, it maybe kept at that other office ; or

(b) company arranges with some other person for the making up of the register to be undertaken on behalf of the company by that person, it may be kept at the office of that other person at which the work is done, but the register shall not be kept in the case of a company registered in Nigeria at a place outside Nigeria.

(2) Every company shall send notice to the Commission of the change in location of the register, and a company is not bound to send notice under this subsection where the register has at all times since it came into existence or, in the case of a register in existence at the commencement of this Act, at all times since then, been kept at the registered office of the company.

(3) Where a company fails to comply with the provisions of subsection (2) within 28 days of the change of the location of the register, the company and every one of its officers are liable to—

(a) such penalties as the Commission shall specify by regulation ; and

(b) an additional daily default fine that the Commission shall specify by regulation.

111.—(1) Every company having more than 50 members shall, unless the register of members is in such a form as to constitute in itself an index, keep an index of the names of the members of the company.

(2) Where a company makes any alteration in the register of members, the company shall, within 14 days after the date which the alteration is made, make such necessary alterations in the index.

(3) The index shall, in respect of each member, contain sufficient indication to enable the account of that member in the register to be readily found.

(4) The index shall, at all times, be kept at the same place as the register of members.

(5) If default is made in complying with the provisions of this section, the company and every officer of the company are liable to such penalties as the Commission shall specify by regulation.

112.—(1) Except when the register of members is closed under the provisions of this Act, the register and the index of members' names shall be open during business hours (subject to such reasonable restrictions as the company in general meeting may impose, that not less than two hours in each day shall be allowed for inspection) to the inspection of any member of the company without charge.

(2) A member or any person may, with the permission of the company which permission shall not be unreasonably withheld require a copy of the register, or of any part, on payment of such amount the Commission may prescribe or such lesser amount the company may prescribe for every page required to be copied, and the company shall cause any copy required by any person to be duly endorsed by an officer of the company and sent to that person within a period of 10 days commencing on the day after the day on which the requirement is received by the company :

Provided that the Commission may require such copy without any restriction or charge.

(3) If any inspection required under this section is refused, or if any copy required under this section is not sent within the prescribed period, the company and every officer of the company is liable in respect of each default to such penalties as the Commission shall specify by regulation.

(4) Notwithstanding the provisions of subsection (3), the Court may by order compel an immediate inspection of the register and index or direct that the copies required shall be sent to the persons requiring them.

113. Where, by virtue of section 110 (1) (*b*), the register of members is kept at the office of some person other than the company, and by reason of any default of that person, the company fails to comply with subsections 112 (1) or (2), or with any requirements of this Act as to the production of the register, that other person is liable to the same penalties as if the person were an officer of the company who was in default, and the power of the Court under section 112 (4) shall extend to the making of orders against that other person and his officers and servants.

(2) Where any contribution has become due and payable by reason of a call, validly made by the company, pursuant to the articles or where, under the terms of any agreement with the company, a member has undertaken personal liability to make future payments in respect of shares issued to him, the liability of the member shall continue notwithstanding that the shares held by him are subsequently transferred or forfeited under a provision to that effect in the articles, but his liability ceases if and when the company have received payment in full of all such money in respect of the shares.

(3) Subject to subsections (1) and (2), no member or past member shall be liable to contribute to the assets of the company, except in the event of its being wound up.

(4) In the event of a company being wound up, every present or past member shall be liable to contribute to the assets of the company to an amount sufficient for payment of its debts and liabilities and for the costs, charges and expenses of the winding-up and the adjustment of the rights of the members and past members among themselves, but subject to the following qualifications—

(a) a past member is not liable to contribute if he has ceased to be a member for a period of one year or upwards before the commencement of the winding-up ;

(b) a past member is not liable to contribute unless it appears to the Court that the existing members are unable to satisfy the contributions required to be made by them in pursuance of this section ;

(c) in the case of a company limited by shares, no contribution is required from any member or past member exceeding the amount, if any, unpaid on the shares in respect of which he is liable as a present or past member ;

(d) in the case of a company limited by guarantee, no contribution is required from any member or past member exceeding the amount undertaken to be contributed by him to the assets of the company in the event of its being wound up ; and

(e) any sum due from the company to a member or past member, in his capacity as member, by way of dividends or otherwise shall not be set- off against the amount for which he is liable to contribute in accordance with this section but any such sum is to be taken into account for the purposes of final adjustment of the rights of the members and past members amongst themselves.

(5) For the purposes of this section, the expression "past member" includes the estate of a deceased member and where any person dies after becoming liable as a member or past member, such liability shall be enforceable against his estate.

(6) Except as contained in this section, a member or past member is not liable as a member or past member for any of the debts and liabilities of the company.

118. If a public company or a company limited by guarantee carries on business or its objects, without having at least two members and does so for more than six months, every director or officer of the company, during the time that it so carries on business with only one or no member, is liable jointly and severally with the company for the debts of the company contracted during that period.

DISCLOSURE OF PERSONS WITH SIGNIFICANT CONTROL

119.—(1) Notwithstanding the provisions of section 120, every person with significant control over a company shall, within seven days of becoming such a person, indicate to the company in writing the particulars of such control.

(2) A company after receiving or coming into possession of the information required under subsection (1), shall, not later than one month from the receipt of the information or any change therein, notify the Commission of that information provided that a company shall in every annual return, disclose the information required under subsection (1) in respect of the year for which the return is made.

(3) The Commission shall maintain a register of persons with significant control in which it shall enter the information received from the company or any change therein under subsection (2).

(4) A company shall inscribe against the name of every member in the register of members the information received in pursuance of the requirements of this section.

(5) If default is made by any person or company in complying with subsections (1), (2) and (4), the person or company and every officer of the company are liable to such fines as the Commission may prescribe by regulation for every day during which the default continues.

120.—(1) A person who is a substantial shareholder in a public company shall give notice in writing to the company stating his name, address and full particulars of the shares held by him or his nominee (naming the nominee) by virtue of which he is a substantial shareholder.

(2) A person is a substantial shareholder in a public company if he holds himself or by his nominee, shares in the company which entitle him to exercise at least 5% of the unrestricted voting rights at any general meeting of the company.

(3) A person required to give a notice under subsection (1), shall do so within 14 days after that person becomes aware that he is a substantial shareholder.

(4) The notice shall be given notwithstanding that the person has ceased to be a substantial shareholder before the expiration of the period referred to in subsection (3).

(5) The company shall, within 14 days of receipt of the notice or of becoming aware that a person is a substantial shareholder give notice in writing to the Commission of this fact.

(6) If any person or company fails to comply with the provisions of this section, the person or the company is liable to such fines as the Commission may prescribe by regulation for each day the default continues.

121.—(1) A person who ceases to be a substantial shareholder in a public company shall give notice in writing to the company stating his name and the date on which he ceased to be a substantial shareholder and give full particulars of the circumstances by reason of which he ceased to be substantial shareholder.

(2) A person required to give notice under subsection (1), shall do so within 14 days after he becomes aware that he has ceased to be substantial shareholder.

(3) The company shall within 14 days of receipt of the notice or of becoming aware that a person has ceased to be a substantial shareholder, give notice in writing to the Commission of this fact.

(4) If any person or company fails to comply with the provisions of this section, the person or the company is liable to such fines as the Commission may prescribe by regulation for each day the default continues.

122.—(1) A public company shall keep a register in which it shall enter—

(a) in alphabetical order, the names of persons from whom it has received a notice under section 121 ; and

(b) against each name so entered, the information given in the notice, and where it receives a notice under section 121, the information given in that notice.

(2) The register shall be kept at the place where the register of members required to be kept under section 110 is kept and subject to the same right of inspection as the register of members.

(3) The Commission may, at any time in writing, require the company to furnish it with a copy of the register or any part of the register and the company shall furnish the copy within 14 days after the day on which the requirement is received.

(4) If the company ceases to be a public company, it shall continue to keep the register until the end of the period of six years beginning with the day following that on which it ceases to be such a company.

(5) A company shall not, by reason of anything done for the purposes of this section, be affected with notice of, or put on enquiry as to, a right of a person to or in relation to a share in the company.

(6) If default is made in complying with this section, the company and every officer of the company are liable to—

(a) such fine as the Commission may prescribe by regulation ; and

(b) additional daily default fine that the Commission shall specify by regulation.

123. The matter relating to beneficial interests in shares required by section 120 shall be entered in a different part of the register of interests which shall be so made up that the entries inscribed in it appear in chronological order.

CHAPTER 7—SHARE CAPITAL

24. (1) Where, after the commencement of this Act, a memorandum delivered to the Commission under section 36 states that the association to be registered is to be registered with shares, the amount of the share capital stated in the memorandum to be registered shall not be less than the minimum issued share capital.

(2) No company having a share capital shall, after the commencement of this Act, be registered with a share capital less than the minimum issued share capital.

(3) Where, at the commencement of this Act, the issued share capital of an existing company is less than the minimum issued share capital, the company shall, not later than six months after the commencement of this Act, issue shares to an amount not less than the minimum issued share capital.

(4) Subject to subsection (3), where a company is registered with shares, its issued capital shall not at any time be less than the minimum issued share capital.

(5) Where a company to which subsections (3) and (4) apply fails to comply with the applicable subsection, the company is—

(a) liable to such fine as the Commission may prescribe by regulation ; and

(b) in addition, liable to a daily default fine as the Commission shall specify by regulation for every day during which the default continues.

ALTERATION OF SHARE CAPITAL

125. A company having a share capital may in general meeting and not otherwise, alter the conditions of its memorandum to—

(a) consolidate and divide all or any part of its share capital into shares of larger amount than its existing shares; and

(b) subdivide its shares or any of them, into shares of smaller amount than is fixed by the memorandum, but in the subdivision the proportion between the amount paid and the amount unpaid on each reduced share shall be the same as it was in the case of the share from which the reduced share is derived.

126.(1)If a company having a share capital has—

(a)consolidated and divided its share capital into shares of larger amount than its existing shares, or

(b) subdivided its shares or any of them,

The company shall within one month after so doing, give notice of it to the Commission specifying, the shares consolidated, divided, or subdivided.

(2) If default is made in complying with this section, the company and every officer of the company are liable to such fine as the Commission may prescribe by regulation, for everyday during which the default continues.

127. (1) A company having a share capital, may in general meeting and not otherwise, increase its issued share capital by the allotment of new shares of such amount as it considers expedient.

(2) Where a company increased its share capital, it shall, within 15 days after the passing of the resolution authorising the increase, give to the Commission notice of the increase and the Commission shall record the increase.

(3) Where, in connection with the increase of shares, any approval is required to be obtained under any enactment other than this Act, the company shall give notice of that fact to the Commission within 15 days after the passing of the resolution authorising the increase, together with an affidavit sworn to by a director of the company to that effect, and upon receipt of the notice and affidavit by the Commission, the period of 15 days stated in subsection (2) is deemed extended, for a period terminating no later than 10 days after receipt of the approval is required to be obtained by the company under an enactment other than this Act.

(4) If the company has not obtained the required approval under an enactment other than this Act within 48 days of the date on which it notified the Commission under subsection (3), the company shall file another notice and affidavit to that effect with the Commission, and shall do so for every successive period of 48 days that elapses after the date on which it first notified the Commission under subsection (3).

(5) If the Company fails to obtain the approval that is required to be obtained under an enactment other than this Act within nine months from the date on which it first

notified the Commission under subsection (3), the resolution increasing the company's issued share capital becomes null and void.

(6) The notice to be given under this section includes the particulars prescribed with respect to the classes of shares affected and the condition subject to which the new shares have been or are to be issued and the notice shall be accompanied by a printed copy of the resolution authorising the increase.

(7) If default is made in complying with the provisions of this section, the company in default is liable to such fine as the Commission may prescribe by regulation for everyday during which the default continues.

(8) Where a company increases its share capital, it shall be by an ordinary resolution and shall amend its memorandum and articles of association to reflect the new issued share capital.

128.—(1) Where a company allots new shares, thereby increasing its issued share capital, the increase shall not take effect unless—

(a) at least 25% of the share capital including the increase has been paid-up ; and

(b) the directors have delivered to the Commission a statutory declaration verifying that fact.

(2) Where a company fails to comply with the applicable subsection, it shall be liable to such fine as the Commission may prescribe by regulation for every day during which the default continues.

129. If an unlimited company resolves to be re-registered as a limited company under this Act, it may—

(a) increase the nominal amount of its issued share capital by increasing the nominal amount of each of its shares, but subject to the condition that no part of the increased issued capital shall be capable of being called up except in the event and for the purpose of the company being wound up ; or

(b) provide that a specified portion of its uncalled share capital shall not be capable of being called up except in the event and for the purposes of the company being wound up.

REDUCTION OF SHARE CAPITAL

130. (1) Except as authorised by this Act, a company having a share capital shall not reduce its issued share capital.

(2) For the purposes of this section and other sections relating to reduction of share capital, any issue of share capital shall include the share premium account and any capital redemption reserve account of a company, and "issued share capital" shall be construed accordingly.

131.—(1) Subject to confirmation by the Court, a company having share capital may, if so authorised by its articles, by special resolution reduce its share capital in any way.

(2) In particular, and without prejudice to subsection (1), the company may—

(a) extinguish or reduce the liability on any of its shares in respect of share capital not paid up,

(b) either with or without extinguishing or reducing liability on any of its shares, cancel any paid-up share capital which is lost or unrepresented by available assets, or

(c) either with or without extinguishing or reducing liability on any of its shares, cancel any paid-up share capital which is in excess of the company's wants, and the company may, if and so far as is necessary, alter its memorandum by reducing the amount of its share capital and of its shares accordingly.

(3) A special resolution under this section shall in this Act be referred to as "a resolution for reducing share capital".

132.—(1) Where a company has passed a resolution for reducing share capital, it may apply to the court for an order confirming the reduction.

(2) If the proposed reduction of share capital involves either—

(a) diminution of liability in respect of unpaid share capital ; or

(b) subject to subsection (6), the payment to a shareholder of any paid-up share capital, and in any other case if the Court so directs, subsection (3), (4) and (5) shall have effect.

(3) Every creditor of the company who, at the date fixed by the court, is entitled to any debt or claim which, if that date were the commencement of the winding-up of the company, would be admissible in proof against the company, is entitled to object to the reduction of capital.

(4) The Court shall settle a list of creditors entitled to object, and for that purpose—

(a) shall ascertain, as far as possible without requiring an application from any creditor, the names of those creditors and the nature and amount of the debts or claims ; and

(b) may publish notices fixing a day or days within which creditors not entered on the list are to claim to be so entered or are to be excluded from the right of objecting to the reduction of capital.

(5) If a creditor entered on the list whose debt or claim is not discharged or has not been determined does not consent to the reduction, the Court may, if it deems fit, dispense with the consent of that creditor, on the company securing payment of his debt or claim by appropriating (as the Court may direct) the following amount if the company—

(a) admits the full amount of the debt or claim or, though not admitting it, is willing to provide for the full amount of the debt or claim ; or

(b) does not admit, and is not willing to provide for, the full amount of the debt or claim, or if the amount is contingent or not ascertained, then an amount fixed by the court after the like enquiry and adjudication as if the company were being wound up by the Court.

(6) If a proposed reduction of share capital involves either the diminution of any liability in respect of unpaid share capital or the payment to any shareholder of any paid-up share capital, the Court may, if having regard to any special circumstance of the case it considers proper to do so, direct that subsections (3) - (5) shall not apply as regards any class or classes of creditors.

133.—(1) The Court, if satisfied—

(*a*) with respect to every creditor of the company who under section 132 is entitled to object to the reduction of capital, that either—

(i) his consent to the reduction has been obtained, or

(ii) his debt or claim has been discharged or determined or secured ; and

(*b*) that the share capital does not by this reduction fall below the minimum issued share capital, may make an order confirming the reduction on such terms and conditions as it deems fit.

(2) Where the Court so orders, it may also—

(a) if for any special reason it considers it proper to do so, make an order directing that the company shall, during such period (commencing on or at any time after the date of the order) as is specified in the order, add to its name as its last words "and reduced" ; and

(b) make an order requiring the company to publish (as the court directs) the reasons for reduction of capital or such other information in regard to it as the court considers expedient with a view to giving proper information to the public and (if the court deems fit) the causes which led to the reduction.

(3) Where the company is ordered to add to its name the words, "and reduced", those words shall, until the expiration of the period specified in the order, be deemed to be part of the company's name.

134. (1) The Commission, on delivery to it the order of the court confirming the reduction of a company's share capital, and minutes of the meeting of the company (approved by the Court) showing, with respect to the company's share capital as altered by the order—

(a) the amount of the share capital ;

(b) the number of shares into which it is to be divided, and the amount of each share ; and

(c) the amount (if any) at the date of the registration deemed to be paid-up on each share, shall register the order and minutes.

(2) On the registration of the order and minutes, the resolution for reducing share capital as confirmed by the order so registered shall take effect.

(3) A notice of the registration shall be published in such manner as the Court may direct.

(4) The Commission shall certify the registration of the order and minutes, and the certificate—

(a) may be either signed by the Registrar-General or authenticated by its official seal ; and

(b) shall be prima facie evidence that all the requirements of this Act with respect to the reduction of share capital have been complied with, and that the company's share capital is as stated in the minutes.

(5) The minutes, when registered, is deemed substituted for the corresponding part of the company's memorandum, and valid and alterable as if it had been originally contained in it.

(6) The substitution of such minutes for part of the company's memorandum shall be deemed an alteration of the memorandum.

135.—(1) Where a company's share capital is reduced, a member of the company (past or present) is not liable in respect of any share to any call or contribution exceeding in amount the difference (if any) between the amount of the share as fixed by the minutes and the amount paid on the share or the reduced amount (if any), which is deemed to have been paid on it, as the case may be.

(2) Subsections (3) and (4) shall apply if—

(a) a creditor entitled in respect of a debt or claim, to object to the reduction of share capital, by reason of his ignorance of the proceedings for reduction of share capital, or of their nature and effect with respect to his claim, is not entered on the list of creditors ; and

(b) after the reduction of capital, the company is unable (within the meaning of section 572) to pay the amount of the creditor's debt or claim.

(3) Every person who was a member of the company at the date of the registration of the order for reduction and minutes, is liable to contribute for the payment of the debt or claim in question an amount not exceeding that which he would have been liable to contribute if the company had commenced to be wound up on the day before that date.

(4) If the company is wound up, the Court, on application of the creditor in question and proof of ignorance referred to in subsection (2) (*a*), may, if it deems fit, settle a list of persons so liable to contribute, and make and enforce calls and orders on the contributories settled on the list, as if they were ordinary contributories in a winding-up.

(5) Nothing in this section affect the rights of the contributories among themselves.

136. If an officer of the company—

(a) wilfully conceals the name of a creditor entitled to object to the reduction of capital,

(b) wilfully misrepresents the nature or amount of the debt or claim of any creditor, or

(c) aids, abets or is privy to any concealment or misrepresentation, he commits an offence and is liable on conviction to such fines as the Commission shall specify by regulation.

MISCELLANEOUS MATTERS RELATING TO CAPITAL

137.—(1) Where the net assets of a public company are half or less of its called-up share capital, the directors shall, not later than 30 days from the earliest day on which that fact is known to a director of the company, duly convene an extraordinary general meeting of the company, for a day not later than 60 days from that day for the purpose of considering whether any, and if so, what steps should be taken to deal with the situation.

(2) If there is a failure to convene an extraordinary general meeting as required by subsection (1), each of the directors of the company who— (*a*) allows the failure, or

(*b*) after the expiry of the period during which that meeting should have been convened, allows the failure to continue, is liable to such fines as the Commission shall specify by regulation.

(3) Nothing in this section authorises the consideration, at a meeting convened in pursuance of subsection (1), of any matter which could have been considered at that meeting apart from this section.

CHAPTER 8—SHARES AND NATURE OF SHARES

138. Subject to the provisions of this Act, the rights and liabilities attaching to the shares of a company or any class thereof shall—

(a) be dependent on the terms of issue or the company's articles ; and

(b) notwithstanding anything to the contrary in the terms or the articles, include the right to attend any general meeting of the company and vote at such a meeting.

139. The shares or other interests of a member in a company are personal property transferable in the manner provided in articles of association of the company.

140.—(1) Unless otherwise provided by any other enactment, any share issued by a company shall carry the right on a poll at a general meeting of the company to one vote in respect of each share, and no company may by its articles or otherwise authorise the issue of shares which carry more than one vote in respect of each share or which do not carry any right to vote.

(2) If a company contravenes any of the provisions of this section, the company and any officer in default are liable to a daily default fine as the Commission shall specify by regulation and any resolution passed in contravention of this section shall be void.

(3) Nothing in this section shall affect any right attached to a preference share under section 168.

ISSUE OF SHARES

141. Subject to any limitation in the articles of a company with respect to the number of shares which may be issued, and any pre-emptive rights prescribed in the articles in relation to the shares, a company has the power, at such times and for such consideration as it shall determine to issue shares.

142.—(1) A company shall not in any event allot newly issued shares unless they are offered in the first instance to all existing shareholders of the class being issued in proportion as nearly as may be to their existing holdings.

(2) The offer to existing shareholders shall be by notice specifying—(*a*) the number of shares to which the shareholder is entitled to subscribe ; (*b*) the price ; and

(*c*) a reasonable time period after the expiration of which the offer, if not accepted, will be deemed to be declined.

(3) On the receipt of notice from the shareholder that he declines toaccept the shares offered or after the expiration of the specified time, the board of directors may, subject to the terms of any resolution of the company, dispose of the shares at a price not less than that specified in the offer, in such manner as they think most beneficial to the company.

(2) Shares shall not be treated as being of the same class unless they rank equally for all purposes.

144. Without prejudice to any special rights previously conferred on the holders of existing shares or class of shares, any share in a company may be issued with such preferred, deferred or other special rights or such restrictions, whether with regard to dividend, return of capital or otherwise, as the company may determine by ordinary resolution.

145.—(1) Shares of a company may be issued at a premium.

(2) Where a company issues shares at a premium, whether for cash or otherwise, a sum equal to the aggregate amount or value of the premium on those shares shall be transferred to, "the share premium account".

(3) The provisions of this Act relating to the reduction of the share capital of a company shall, except as provided in this section, apply as if the share premium account were paid-up share capital of the company.

(4) Notwithstanding anything to the contrary in subsection (2), the share premium account may be applied by the company in—

(a) paying up unissued shares of the company to be issued to members of the company as fully-paid bonus shares ;

(b) writing off the preliminary expense of a newly incorporated company ;

(c) writing off the expenses of, or the commission paid on any issue of shares of the company ; or

(d) providing for the premium payable on redemption of any redeemable share of the company.

146. It is unlawful for a company to issue shares at a discount.

147.—(1) No company limited by shares shall, after the commencement of this Act issue any preference shares which are irredeemable.

(2) A company limited by shares may, if so authorized by its articles, issue preference shares which are liable to be redeemed subject to such conditions as may be prescribed in the terms of issue or in the articles of the company.

148.—(1) Where a company has purported to issue or allot shares and the issue or allotment of those shares was invalid by reason of any provision of this Act or any other enactment, of the articles or the terms of issue or allotment were inconsistent with or unauthorised by any such provision, the company may within 30 days of an application made by a holder, mortgagee of those shares or by a creditor of the company, and by special resolution, validate the issue or allotment of those shares or confirm the terms of the issue and allotment, as the case may be.

(2) Where a company refuses to validate the issue or allotment of the shares or confirm the terms of the issue and allotment, the Court may, upon application made by a holder, a mortgagee of those shares or by a creditor of the company, and upon being satisfied that in all the circumstances it is just and equitable to do so, validate the issue, allotment of those shares or confirm the terms of the issue and allotment, as the case may be.

(3) In every case where the court validates an issue, allotment of shares or confirms the terms of an issue or allotment in accordance with subsection (1), it shall make, upon payment of the prescribed fees, an order which is proof of the validation or confirmation and upon the issue of the order, those shares are deemed to have been issued or allotted upon the relevant terms of issue or allotment.

ALLOTMENT OF SHARES

149.—(1) The power to allot shares is vested in the company, and, in relation to a private company, this power may be delegated to the directors, subject to any condition or direction that may be imposed in the articles or by the company in general meeting.

(2) The power to allot shares of a public company is subject to the provisions of the Investment and Securities Act.

(3) The powers to allot the shares of a company are not exercised by the directors of a company unless express authority to do so has been vested in the board of directors by—

(*a*) the company in a general meeting ; or (*b*) the company's articles.

(4) In this section, the reference to shares includes any right to subscribe for, or to convert any security into, shares in the company other than shares so allotted.

(5) The authorisation to the directors under this section may be given to be exercised in a particular instance, or to be exercised generally, and may be unconditional or subject to conditions.

150.—(1) Without prejudice to the provisions of the Investment and Securities Act, the following provisions apply in respect of an application for an allotment of issued shares of a company—

(a) in the case of a private company or a public company where the issue of shares is not public, there shall, if so required by the company, be submitted to the company a written application signed by the person wishing to purchase shares indicating the number of shares required ;

(b) in the case of a public company, subject to conditions imposed by the Securities and Exchange Commission where the issue of shares is public, there shall be returned to the company a form of application as prescribed in the company's articles, duly completed and signed by the person wishing to purchase the shares; and

(c) upon the receipt of an application, a company shall, where it wholly or partly accepts the application, make an allotment to the applicant and within 42 days after the allotment notify the applicant of the fact of allotment and the number of shares allotted to him.

(2) An applicant under this section shall have the right at any time before allotment, to withdraw his application by written notice to the company.

151. An allotment of shares made and notified to an applicant in accordance with section 150 is an acceptance by the company of the offer by the applicant to purchase its shares and the contract takes effect on the date on which the allotment is made by the company.

152. Subject to the provisions of sections 160 – 163 of this Act, a company may, in its articles, make provision with respect to payments on allotment of its shares.

153.—(1) An allotment made by a public company before the holding of the statutory meeting to an applicant in contravention of the provisions of this Act, is voidable at the instance of the applicant—

(a) within one month after the holding of the statutory meeting of the company and not later, or

(b) where the allotment is made after the holding of the statutory meeting, within one month after the date of the allotment, and not later :

Provided that the allotment shall be so voidable notwithstanding that the company is in the course of being wound up.

(2) If any director of a company knowingly contravenes, permits or authorises the contravention of any of the provisions of this Act with respect to allotment, he is liable to compensate the company and the allottee respectively for any loss, damages or costs which the company or the allottee may have sustained or incurred thereby, but proceedings to recover any such loss, damages, or costs shall not be commenced after the expiration of two years from the date of the allotment.

154.—(1) Whenever a company limited by shares makes any allotment Return as to of its shares, the company shall within one month thereafter deliver to the allotment. Commission for registration—

(a) a return of the allotments in the prescribed form, stating—

(i) the number and nominal value of the shares comprised in the allotment,

(ii) the names, addresses and description of the allottees, and

(iii) the amount, if any, paid or due and payable on each share, whether on account of the nominal value of the shares or by way of any premium payable in relation to such shares ;

(b) in the case of shares allotted as fully or partly paid up otherwise than in cash—

(i) a contract in writing, constituting the title of the allottee to the allotment together with any contract of sale, or for services or other consideration in respect of which that allotment was made, such contracts being duly stamped,

(ii) a return stating the number and nominal amount of shares so allotted, the extent to which they are to be treated as paid up, and the consideration for which they have been allotted, and

(iii) with respect to public companies, particulars of the valuation of the consideration in accordance with section 162 ; and

(c) such other documents and particulars as may be required by the Commission, but where the Commission requires that additional documents or particulars be submitted it shall grant the company additional time of at least seven days within which to provide the additional documents and particulars, and the additional time granted is deemed to be an extension of the one month period in subsection (1).

(2) If default is made in complying with this section, each officer of the company is liable to such penalty as the Commission shall specify in the regulation for every day during which the default continues.

(3) In case of default in delivering to the Commission within one month after the allotment any document required to be delivered by this section, the company or any officer liable for the default, may apply to the court for relief, and the court, if satisfied that the omission to deliver the document was accidental or due to inadvertence or that it is just and equitable to grant relief, may make an order extending the time for the delivery of the document for such period as the Court may consider proper.

155.—(1) Except as provided in section 156, no company shall apply any of its shares or capital money either directly or indirectly in payment of any commission, discount or allowance to any person in consideration of his subscribing or agreeing to subscribe, whether absolutely or conditionally, for any share in the company, or procuring or agreeing to procure subscriptions, whether absolute or conditional, for any share in the company, whether the shares or capital money are so applied by being added to the purchase money of any property acquired by the company or to the contract price of any work to be executed for the company, or any such money is paid out of the nominal purchase money or contract price, or otherwise.

(2) Nothing in this section affects the payment of any brokerage or agency fees agreed between the company and a broker or agent of the company, for services provided by such broker or agent in connection with the raising of the capital by the company.

(3) A vendor to, promoter of, or other person who receives payment in money or shares from a company, shall have and is deemed always to have had power to apply any part of the money or shares so received in payment of any commission, the payment of which, if made directly by the company, would have been legal under this section.

156.—(1) A company may pay a commission to any person in consideration of his subscribing or agreeing to subscribe, whether absolutely or conditionally, for any share in the company or procuring or agreeing to procure subscription, whether absolute or conditional, for any share in the company if—

(a) the payment of the commission is authorised by the articles ;

(b) the commission paid or agreed to be paid does not exceed 10% of the price at which the shares are issued or the amount or rate authorised by the articles, whichever is lesser ;

(c) the amount or rate per cent of the commission paid or agreed to be paid is—

(i) in the case of shares offered to the public for subscription, disclosed in the prospectus, or

(ii) in the case of shares not offered to the public for subscription, disclosed in the statement in lieu of prospectus, or in a statement in the prescribed form signed in like manner as a statement in lieu of prospectus, and delivered to the Commission for registration before the payment of the commission, and where a circular or notice, not being a prospectus inviting subscription for the shares is issued, also disclosed in that circular or notice ; and

(d) the number of shares which persons have agreed for a commission to subscribe absolutely is disclosed in the manner specified in this section.

(2) If default is made in delivering any document required to be delivered to the Commission under this section, the company and every officer in default is liable to such penalty as the Commission shall specify in the regulation.

157.—(1) Where a company has paid any amount by way of commission in respect of any shares in the company, the amount so paid or so much of it as has not been written off, shall be stated in every balance sheet of the company until the whole amount has been written off.

(2) If default is made in complying with this section, the company and every officer of the company is liable to such penalty as the Commission shall specify by regulation for every day during which the default continues.

CALL ON AND PAYMENT FOR SHARES

158.—(1) Subject to the terms of the issue of the shares and of the articles, the directors may make calls upon the members in respect of any money unpaid on their shares (whether on account of the nominal value of the shares or by way of premium) and not by the conditions of allotment of the shares made payable at fixed times:

Provided that no call shall exceed one fourth of the nominal value of the share or be payable at less than one month from the date fixed for the payment of the last preceding call, and each member shall (subject to receiving at least 14 days' notice specifying the time or times and place of payment) pay to the company at the time or times and place so specified the amount called on his shares, so however that a call may be revoked or postponed as the directors may determine.

(2) A call is deemed to have been made at the time when the resolution of the directors authorising the call was passed, and may be required to be paid by instalments.

(3) The joint holders of a share are jointly liable to pay all calls in respect of the share.

(4) If a sum called in respect of a share is not paid before or on the day appointed for payment, the person from whom the sum is due shall pay interest on the sum from the day appointed for payment to the time of actual payment at such rate not exceeding the current bank rate per annum, as the directors may determine, but the directors are at liberty to waive payment of such interest wholly or in part.

(5) A sum which by the terms of issue of a share becomes payable on allotment or at any fixed date, whether on account of the nominal value of the shares or by way of premium shall, for the purposes of these provisions, is deemed to be a call duly made and payable on the date on which by the terms of issue the same becomes payable, and in case of non- payment, all the relevant provisions of this Act as to payment of interest and expenses, forfeiture or otherwise apply as if such sum had become payable by virtue of a call duly made and notified.

(6) The directors may, if they think fit, receive from any member willing to advance the same, all or any part of the money uncalled and unpaid upon any share held by him, and upon all or any of the money so advanced may (until the same would, but for

such advance, become payable) pay interest at such rate not exceeding the current bank rate per annum as may be agreed upon between the directors and the member paying such sum in advance (unless the company in general meeting otherwise directs).

159. A company limited by shares may, by special resolution determine that any portion of its share capital which has not been already called up are not capable of being called up except in the event and for the purposes of the company being wound up and thereupon, that portion of its share capital shall not be capable of being called up, except in the event and for the purposes specified in this section.

160. Subject to the provisions of sections 161 and 162, the shares of a company and any premium on them shall be paid up in cash, or where the articles so permit, by a valuable consideration other than cash or partly in cash and partly by a valuable consideration other than cash.

161.—(1) Shares are not deemed to have been paid for in cash except to the extent that the company shall have actually received cash for them at the time of, or subsequently to, the agreement to issue the shares.

(2) Where shares are issued to a person who has sold or agreed to sell property or rendered or agreed to render services to the company or to persons nominated by him, the amount of any payment made for the property or services shall be deducted from the amount of any cash payment made for the shares and only the balance (if any) shall be treated as having been paid in cash for such shares notwithstanding any exchange of cheques or other securities for money.

162.—(1) Where a public company agrees to accept payment for its shares otherwise than wholly in cash, it shall appoint an independent valuer who shall determine the true value of the consideration other than cash and prepare and submit to the company a report on the value of the consideration.

(2) The valuer is entitled to require from the officers of the company such information and explanation as he thinks necessary to enable him to carry out the valuation or make the report under subsection (1).

(3) The company shall, not more than three days after it receives the valuer's report, send a copy of the report to the proposed purchaser of shares, and indicate to the proposed purchaser whether or not it intends to accept the consideration as payment or part payment for its shares.

(4) A public company shall not accept as payment or part payment for its shares consideration other than cash unless the cash value of the consideration as determined by the valuer is worth at least as much as may be credited as paid up in respect of the shares allowed to the proposed purchaser.

(5) A valuer who, in his report or otherwise, knowingly or recklessly makes a statement which is misleading, false or deceptive in a material particular, commits an offence and is liable to imprisonment for a term of 12 months or a fine as shall be imposed by the court, or both.

(6) For the purposes of this section, "valuer" means an auditor, a valuer, surveyor, an engineer or accountant not being a person in the employment of the company nor an agent or associate of the company or any of its directors or officers.

163. Where it is authorised by its articles, a company may—

(a) make arrangements on the issue of shares for a difference between the shareholders in the amounts and times of payment of calls on their shares ;

(b) accept from any member the whole or a part of the amount remaining unpaid on any shares held by him, although no part of that amount has been called up ; or

(c) pay dividends in proportion to the amount paid up on each share where a larger amount is paid up on some shares than on others.

164.—(1) A company has a first and paramount lien on every share, (not being a fully paid share) for all money (whether currently payable or not) called or payable at a fixed time in respect of that share, and the company also has a first and paramount lien on all shares (other than fully paid shares) standing registered in the name of a single person for all money presently payable by him or his estate to the company, but the directors may at any time declare any share to be wholly or in part exempt from the provisions of this subsection.

(2) A company's lien, if any, on a share shall extend to all dividends payable on, and any bonus shares issued in relation to such share.

(3) A company may sell, in such manner as the directors think fit, any share on which the company has a lien, but no sale shall be made unless a sum in respect of which the lien exists is currently payable, nor until the expiration of 14 days after a notice in writing, demanding payment of such part of the amount in respect of which the lien exists as is currently payable, has been given to the registered holder of the shares, or the person entitled to them by reason of his death or bankruptcy.

(4) For the purpose of giving effect to any such sale, the directors may authorise a person to transfer the shares sold to the purchaser of the shares and the purchaser shall be registered as the holder of the shares comprised in any such transfer.

(5) The purchaser is not bound to see to the application of the purchase money and his title to the shares is not affected by any irregularity or invalidity in the proceedings in reference to the sale.

(6) The proceeds of the sale of any share pursuant to this section shall be received by the company and applied in payment of such part of the amount in respect of which the lien exists as is presently payable, and the residue, if any, shall (subject to a like lien for sums not presently payable as existed upon the shares before the sale) be paid to the person entitled to the shares at the date of the sale.

165.—(1) If a member fails to pay any call or instalment of a call on the day appointed for payment, the directors may, thereafter during such time as any part of the call or instalment remains unpaid, serve a notice on him requiring payment of the sum of the call or instalment as is unpaid, together with any interest which may have accrued.

(2) The notice shall state a further day (not earlier than the expiration of14 days from the date of service of the notice) on or before which the payment required by the notice is to be made, and it shall state that in the event of non-payment at or before the time appointed, the shares in respect of which the call was made are liable to be forfeited.

(3) If the requirements of the notice as is mentioned in subsections (1) and (2) are not complied with, any share in respect of which notice was given may, at any time thereafter, before the payment required by the notice is made, be forfeited by a resolution of the directors to that effect.

(4) A forfeited share may be sold or otherwise disposed of on such terms and in such manner as the directors think fit, and at any time before a sale or disposition, the forfeiture may be cancelled on such terms as the directors think fit.

(5) A person whose shares have been forfeited ceases to be a member in respect of the forfeited shares, but shall, notwithstanding, remain liable to pay to the company all money which, at the date of forfeiture, were payable by him to the company in respect of the shares, but his liability ceases when the company receives payment in full of all money in respect of the shares.

(6) A statutory declaration that the declarant is a director or the secretary of the company, and that a share in the company has been duly forfeited on a date stated in the declarations, is *prima facie* evidence of the facts stated in it as against all persons claiming to be entitled to the shares.

(7) The company may receive the consideration, if any, given for the share on any sale or disposition of it and may execute a transfer of the share in favour of the person to whom the share is sold or disposed of, and he shall thereupon be registered as the holder of the share, and is not bound to see to the application of the purchase money, if any, nor shall his title to the share be affected by any irregularity or invalidity in the proceedings in reference to the forfeiture, sale or disposal of the share.

(8) The provisions of this section as to forfeiture apply in the case of non-payment of any sum which, by the terms of issue of a share, becomes payable at a fixed time, whether on account of the nominal value of the share or by way of premium, as if the same had been payable by virtue of a call duly made and notified.

CLASSES OF SHARES

166.—(1) If at any time the share capital of a company is divided into Power to different classes of shares under section 143, the rights attached to any class vary rights (unless otherwise provided by the terms of issue of the shares of that class) may, whether or not the company is being wound up, be varied—

(a) in accordance with the provision in the company's articles for the variation of those rights ; or

(b) where the company's articles contain no such provision, with the consent, in writing, of the holders of three- quarters of the issued shares of that class, or with the sanction of a special resolution passed at a separate general meeting of the holders of the shares of the class.

(2) To every such separate general meeting as mentioned in subsection (1), the provisions of this Act relating to general meetings apply, but the necessary quorum shall be two persons at least holding or representing by proxy one- third of the issued shares of the class and that any holder of shares of the class present in person or by proxy may demand a poll.

(3) The rights conferred upon the holders of the shares of any class issued with preferred or other rights are not, unless otherwise expressly provided by the terms of issue of the shares of that class, be deemed to be varied by the creation or issue of further shares ranking *pari passu* with them.

(4) Any proposed amendment of a provision contained in a company's articles for the variation of the rights attached to a class of shares, or the insertion of any such provision into the articles, shall be treated as a variation of those rights and shall require the consent, in writing, of the holders of three quarters of the issued shares of that class, or the sanction of a special resolution passed at a separate general meeting of the holders of the shares of the class, before the procedure for the amendment of the articles can proceed.

167.—(1) Where in pursuance of section 166, the rights attached to any class of shares are at any time varied, the holder of at least 15% of the issued shares of that class, being persons who did not consent to or vote in favour of the resolution for the variation, may apply to the Court to have the variation cancelled, and, where any such application is made, the variation shall not have effect, unless it is confirmed by the court, and for the purpose of this section, any share in the company's share capital that are held by the company as treasury shares shall not be taken into account for the purpose of computing the aggregate per cent of shares held by holders seeking to make an application to the Court.

(2) An application to the court under this section shall, in a proper case, be made within 21 days after the date on which the consent was given or the resolution was passed, as the case may be, and may be made on behalf of the shareholders entitled to make the application or by such one or more of them as they may appoint in writing for the purpose.

(3) If on any such application the court, after hearing the applicant and any other persons applying to it to be heard and appearing to be interested in the application, is satisfied that the variation would unfairly prejudice the shareholders of the class represented by the applicant, the Court, having regard to all the circumstances of the case, may disallow the variation, and shall, if not satisfied, confirm the variation.

(4) The decision of the Court on any such application is final.

(5) The company shall, within 15 days after the making of an order by the Court on an application to it under this section, forward a copy of the order to the Commission and if default is made in complying with the provisions of this subsection, the company and each officer of the company is liable to such fine as the Commission shall specify in the regulation for every day during which the default continues.

(6) In this section, "variation" includes abrogation, and cognate expressions are construed accordingly.

168.—(1) Notwithstanding the provisions of section 140, the articles may provide that preference shares issued after the commencement of this Act shall carry the rights to attend general meetings and on a poll at the meetings, to more than one vote per share in the following circumstances, but not otherwise, but upon any resolution—

(a) during such period as the preferential dividend or any part of it remains in arrears and unpaid, such period starting from a date not more than 12 months or such lesser period as the articles may provide, after the due date of the dividend ;

(b) which varies the rights attached to such shares ;

(c) to remove an auditor of the company or to appoint another person in place of such auditor ; or

(d) for the winding-up of the company or during the winding-up of the company.

(2) Notwithstanding the provisions of section 140, any special resolution of a company increasing the number of shares of any class, may validly resolve that any existing class of preference shares shall carry the right to such votes additional to one vote per share as is necessary in order to preserve the existing ratio which the votes exercisable by the holders of such preference shares at a general meeting of the company bear to the total votes exercisable at the meeting.

(3) For the purposes of subsection (2), a dividend is deemed to be due on the date appointed in the articles for the payment of the dividend for any year or other

period, or if no such date is appointed, upon the day immediately following the expiration of the year or other period, and whether or not such dividend shall have been earned or declared.

169. In construing the provisions of a company's articles in respect of the rights attached to shares, the following rules of construction shall be observed—

(a) unless the contrary intention appears, no dividend is payable on any shares unless the company resolves to declare such dividend ;

(b) unless the contrary intention appears, a fixed preferential dividend payable on any class of shares is cumulative, and no dividend shall be payable on any share ranking subsequent to them until all the arrears of the fixed dividend have been paid ;

(c) unless the contrary intention appears, in a winding-up arrears of any cumulative preferential dividend, whether earned or declared or not, are payable up to the date of actual payment in the winding-up ;

(d) if any class of shares is expressed to have a right to a preferential dividend, then, unless the contrary intention appears, such class has no further right to participate in dividends;

(e) if any class of shares is expressed to have preferential rights to payment out of the assets of the company in the event of winding-up, then, unless the contrary intention appears, such class has no further right to participate in the distribution of assets in the winding-up;

(f)) in determining the rights of the various classes to share in the distribution of the company's property on a winding-up, no regard shall be given, unless the contrary intention appears, to whether or not such property represents accumulated profits or surplus which would have been available for dividend while the company remained a going concern ; and

(g) subject to this section, all shares rank equally in all respects unless the contrary intention appears in the company's articles.

NUMBERING OF SHARES

170. Each share in a company having a share capital shall be distinguished by its appropriate number:

Provided that, if at any time all the issued shares in a company, or all of its issued shares of a particular class, are fully paid up and rank *pari passu* for all purposes, none of those shares need thereafter have a distinguishing number so long as it remains fully paid up and ranks *pari passu* for all purposes with all shares of the same class for the time being issued and fully paid up.

SHARE CERTIFICATES

171.—(1) Every company shall, within two months after the allotment of any of its shares and within three months after the date on which a transfer of any such shares is lodged with the company, complete and have ready for delivery the certificates of all shares allotted or transferred, unless the conditions of issue of the shares otherwise provide.

(2) Every person whose name is entered as a member in the register of members is entitled, without payment, to receive within three months of allotment or lodgment of transfer or within such other period as the conditions of issue provide, one

certificate for all his shares or several certificates each for one or more of his shares upon payment of a fee as the directors shall determine.

(3) Every certificate issued by a company shall be under the company's seal (where the company has a common seal) or otherwise signed as a deed by the company and shall specify the shares to which it relates and the amount paid up on them :
Provided that in respect of shares held jointly by several persons, the company is not bound to issue more than one certificate, and delivery of a certificate for shares to one of several joint holders shall be sufficient delivery to all such holders.

(4) If a share certificate is defaced, lost or destroyed, it may be replaced on such term, as to evidence and indemnity and the payment of out-of-pocket expenses of the company of investigating evidence as the directors think fit.

(5) If any company on which a notice has been served requiring it to make good any default in complying with the provisions of subsection (1), fails to make good the default within 10 days after the service of the notice, the Court may, on the application of the person entitled to have the certificate delivered to him, make an order directing the company and any officer of the company to make good the default within such time as may be specified in the order, and the order may provide that all costs of and incidental to the application shall be borne by the company or by any officer of the company responsible for the default.

(6) If default is made in complying with this section, the company and each officer of the company is liable to such penalty as the Commission shall specify in the regulation for every day during which the default continues.

172.–(1) A certificate, under the common seal of the company (where the company has a common seal) or otherwise signed as a deed by the company, specifying any share held by any member, is a prima facie evidence of the title of the member to the shares.

(2) If any person changes his position to his detriment in good faith on the continued accuracy of the statements made in a certificate, the company shall be estopped from denying the continued accuracy of such statements and shall compensate the person for any loss suffered by him in reliance on them and which he would not have suffered had the statements been or continued to be accurate.

(3) Nothing in subsection (2) shall derogate from any right the company may have to be indemnified by any other person.

173. The production to a company of any document which is by law sufficient evidence of probate of the will, or letters of administration of the estate, or confirmation as executor, of a deceased person having been granted to some person, shall be accepted by the company as sufficient evidence of the grant, notwithstanding anything in its articles to the contrary.

174.—(1) No company has the power to issue bearer shares.

(2) For the purposes of this Act, a "bearer share" means a share which is represented by a certificate, warrant or other document (in any form or by whatever name called) which states or indicates that the bearer of the certificate is the owner of the shares.

TRANSFER AND TRANSMISSION

175.—(1) The transfer of a company's shares shall be by instrument of transfer and except as expressly provided in the articles, transfer of shares shall be without restrictions, and instruments of transfer shall include electronic instrument of transfer.

(2) Notwithstanding anything in the articles of a company, a company shall not register a transfer of shares in the company, unless a proper instrument of transfer has been delivered to the company:

Provided that nothing in this section shall prejudice any power of the company to register as shareholder, any person to whom the right to any share in the company has been transmitted by operation of law.

(3) The instrument of transfer of any share shall be executed by or on behalf of the transferor and transferee, and the transferor is deemed to remain a holder of the share until the name of the transferee is entered in the register of members in respect of the share.

(4) Subject to any restrictions of a company's articles as may be applicable, any member may transfer all or any of his shares by instrument in writing in any usual or common form or any other form which the directors may approve.

176.—(1) On the application of the transferor of any share or interest in a company, the company shall enter, in its register of members, the name of the transferee in the same conditions as if the application for the entry were made by the transferee, and register of transfer includes electronic register of transfer.

(2) Until the name of the transferee is entered in the register of members in respect of the transferred shares, the transferor is, so far as it concerns the company, deemed to remain the holder of the shares.

(3) The company may refuse to register the transfer of a share (not being a fully paid share) to a person of whom they do not approve, and may also refuse to register the transfer of a share on which the company has a lien.

(4) The company may refuse to recognise any instrument of transfer unless—

(a) a fee, as the company may determine, is paid to the company in respect of the instrument ;

(b) the instrument of transfer is accompanied by the certificate of the shares to which it relates and such other evidence as the directors may reasonably require to show the right of the transferor to make the transfer ; and

(c) the instrument of transfer is in respect of only one class of shares.

177.—(1) If a company refuses to register a transfer of any share, it shall, within two months after the date on which the transfer was lodged with it, send notice of the refusal to the transferee.

(2) If default is made in complying with this section, the company and each officer of the company is liable to such penalty as the Commission shall specify in the regulation.

178. A transfer of the share or other interest of a deceased member of a company made by his personal representative is, although the personal representative is not himself a member of the company, as valid as if he had been such a member at the time of the execution of the instrument of transfer.

179.—(1) In case of the death of a member, the survivor or survivors where the deceased was a joint holder, or the legal personal representative of the deceased where he was a sole holder, is the only person recognised by the company as having any title to his interest in the shares, but nothing in this section shall release the estate of a deceased joint holder from any liability in respect of any share which had been jointly held by him with other persons.

(2) Any person becoming entitled to a share in consequence of the death or bankruptcy of a member may, upon such evidence being produced as may be required by the directors and subject to this section, elect either to be registered himself as holder of the share, or to have a person nominated by him registered as the transferee of the share, but the company shall, in either case, have the same right to decline or suspend registration as they would have had in the case of a transfer of the share by that member before his death or bankruptcy, as the case may be.

(3) If the person becoming entitled elects to be registered himself, he shall deliver or send to the company a notice in writing signed by him stating that he so elects, and if he elects to have another person registered, he shall testify his election by executing to that person a transfer of the share in the prescribed form.

(4) All the limitations, restrictions and provisions of this Act and the company's articles relating to the rights to transfer and the registration of transfers of share, are applicable to any such notice or transfer as mentioned in subsection (3) as if the death or bankruptcy of the member had not occurred and the notice or transfer were a transfer signed by that member.

(5) A person becoming entitled to a share by reason of the death or bankruptcy of the holder, is entitled to the same dividends and other advantages to which he would be entitled if he were the registered holder of the share, except that he is not, unless the articles otherwise provide, before being registered as a member in respect of the share, entitled in respect of it to exercise any right conferred by membership in relation to meetings of the company :

Provided that the directors may at any time give notice requiring any such person to elect either to be registered himself or to transfer the share, and if the notice is not complied with within 90 days, the directors may thereafter withhold payment of all dividends, bonuses or other money payable in respect of the share until the requirements of the notice have been complied with.

180.—(1) Any person claiming to be interested in any share, dividend or interest on them, may protect his interest by serving on the company concerned a notice of his interest.

(2) The company shall enter, on the register of members, the fact that such notice has been served and shall not register any transfer or make any payment or return in respect of the shares contrary to the terms of the notice until the expiration of 42 days' notice to the claimant to the proposed transfer or payment.

(3) In the event of any default by the company in complying with this section, the company shall compensate any person injured by the default.

181.—(1) When the holder of any share of a company wishes to transfer to any person only a part of the shares represented by one or more certificates, the instrument of transfer together with the relevant certificates shall be delivered to the company with a request that the instrument of transfer be recognised and registered and a certificate of transfer shall include a certificate issued in electronic form.

(2) A company to which a request is made under subsection (1), may recognise the instrument of transfer by endorsing on it the words, "certificate lodged" or words to the like effect.

(3) The recognition by a company of any instrument of transfer of shares in the company shall be taken as a representation by the company to any person acting on the faith of the recognition that there have been produced to the company such

documents as on the face of them show a prima facie title to the shares in the transferor named in the instrument of transfer, but not as a representation that the transferor has any title to the shares.

(4) Where any person acts on the faith of a false recognition by a company made negligently, the company shall be under the same liability to that person as if the recognition has been made fraudulently.

(5) For the purposes of this section—

(a) an instrument of transfer is deemed to be recognised if it bears the words, "certificate lodged" or words to the like effect ;

(b) the recognition of an instrument of transfer is deemed to be made by a company if—

(i) the person issuing the instrument is a person authorised to issue certificated instruments of transfers on the company's behalf; and

(ii) the recognition is signed by a person authorised to recognise transfers of shares on the company's behalf or by any officer or servant either of the company or of a body corporate so authorised ; and

(c) a recognition is deemed to be signed by any person if—

(i) it purports to be authenticated by his signature or initials (whether handwritten or not), and

(ii) it is not shown that the signature or initials was or were placed there by any person other than him or a person authorised to use the signature or initials for the purpose of transfers on the company's behalf.

TRANSACTIONS BY COMPANY IN RESPECT OF ITS OWN SHARES

182.—(1) The provisions of this section apply with respect to the redemption by a company of any redeemable preference share issued by it under section 147.

(2) The shares are not redeemed unless they are fully paid, and redemption shall be made only out of—

(a) profits of the company which would otherwise be available for dividend ; or

(b) the proceeds of a fresh issue of shares made for the purposes of the redemption.

(3) Before the shares are redeemed, the premium, if any, payable on redemption, shall be provided for out of the profits of the company or out of the company's share premium account.

(4) Where shares are redeemed otherwise than out of the proceeds of afresh issue, there shall, out of profits which would otherwise have been available for dividend, be transferred to a reserve fund, to be called "the capital redemption reserve account", a sum equal to the nominal amount of the shares redeemed, and the provisions of this Act relating to the reduction of the share capital of a company shall, except as provided in this section, apply as if the capital redemption reserve fund were paid-up share capital of the company.

(5) Subject to the provisions of this section, the redemption of preference shares may be effected on such terms and in such manner as are provided by the articles of the company or in the terms of issue of the relevant preference shares.

(6) The redemption of preference shares under this section by a company shall not be taken as reducing the amount of the company's share capital.

(7) The capital redemption reserve fund may, notwithstanding anything in this section, be applied by the company in paying up unissued shares of the company to be issued to members of the company as fully paid bonus shares.

(8) Any redeemable share issued by a company is regarded as a preference share and the provisions of this Act with respect to preference shares shall apply to all redeemable shares.

183.—(1) In this section—

(a) "*financial assistance*" means a gift, guarantee, any form of security or indemnity, a loan or any form of credit or any other financial assistance given by a company, the net assets of which are thereby reduced by up to 50%, or which has no net assets ;

"*net assets*" means the aggregate of the company's assets, less the aggregate of its liabilities ("*liabilities*" to include any charges or provision for liabilities in accordance with the applicable accounting standards applied by the company in relation to its accounts).

(2) Subject to the provisions of this section—

(a) where a person is acquiring or is proposing to acquire shares in a company, it shall not be lawful for the company or any of its subsidiaries to give financial assistance directly or indirectly for the purpose of that acquisition before or at the same time as the acquisition takes place ; and

(b) where a person has acquired shares in a company and any liability has been incurred (by that or any other person), for the purpose of this acquisition, it shall not be lawful for the company or any of its subsidiaries to give financial assistance directly or indirectly for the purpose of reducing or discharging the liability so incurred.

(3) Nothing in subsection (1) of this section shall be taken to prohibit—

(a) the lending of money by the company in the ordinary course of its business, where the lending of money is part of the ordinary business of a company ;

(b) the provision by a company, in accordance with any scheme for the time being in force, of money for the purchase of, or subscription for, fully paid shares in the company or its holding company, being a purchase or subscription by trustees of or for shares to be held by or for the benefit of employees of the company, including any director holding a salaried employment or office in the company ;

(c) the making by a company of loans to persons, other than directors, bona fide in the employment of the company with a view to enabling those persons to purchase or subscribe for fully-paid shares in the company or its holding company, to be held themselves by way of beneficial ownership ;

(d) any act or transaction otherwise authorised by law including—

(*i*) a distribution of a company's assets by way of dividend lawfully made or a distribution made in the course of the company's winding-up, (*ii*) the allotment of bonus shares,

(iii) a reduction of capital confirmed by order of the court under this Act, and

(iv) a redemption or purchase of shares ;

(e) anything done in pursuance of an order of the court under a scheme of arrangement ; a scheme of merger or any other scheme or restructuring of a company done with the sanction of the Court ; or

(f) an assistance given by a company where its principal purpose in giving the assistance is not to reduce or discharge any liability incurred by a person for the purpose of the acquisition of shares in the company or its holding company, or the reduction or discharge of any such liability, but an incidental part of some larger purpose of the company, and the assistance is given in good faith in the interests of the company.

(4) This section does not prohibit a private company from giving financial assistance in a case where the acquisition of shares in question is or was an acquisition of shares in the company or, if it is a subsidiary of another private company, in that other company, provided that—

(a) the financial assistance may only be given if the company has net assets which are not thereby reduced or to the extent that they are reduced, if the assistance is provided out of distributable profits ;

(b) the giving of assistance under this section must be approved by special resolution of the company in general meeting ; and

(c) the directors of the company proposing to give the financial assistance and, where the shares acquired or to be acquired are shares in its holding company, the directors of that holding company shall, before the financial assistance is given, make a statutory declaration in a form prescribed by the Commission.

(5) If a company acts in contravention of this section, the company and every officer of the company who is in default shall be liable to such penalty as the Commission shall specify by regulation.

(6) A Company may accept from any shareholder, a share in the Company, surrendered to it as a gift, but may not extinguish or reduce a liability in respect of an amount unpaid on any such share, except in accordance with section 131 of this Act.

184.—(1) A limited liability company may purchase its own shares including redeemable shares provided that—

(a) a company may only purchase its own shares if so permitted by its articles ;

(b) the shareholders shall, by special resolution, approve the acquisition by the company of the shares that it intends to purchase ;

(c) only fully paid up shares of a company may be purchased by the company, and the terms of purchase shall provide for payment for the purchase ;

(d) within seven days after the passing of the special resolution referred to in paragraph (*b*), the company shall cause to be published in two national newspapers, a notice of the proposed purchase by the company of its own shares ;

(e) within 15 days after the publication in two national newspapers, the directors of the company shall make and file with the Commission, a statutory declaration of solvency, to the effect that the company is solvent and can pay its debts as they fall due, and that after the purchase of its shares, the company shall remain solvent and can pay its debts as they fall due ;

(f) a company may not under this section purchase its shares if, as a result of the purchase, there would no longer be any issued shares of the company other than redeemable shares or shares held as treasury shares.

(2) Within a period of six weeks following the publication in two national newspapers, any of the company's creditors may make an application to the Court for an order cancelling the resolution and a dissenting shareholder who did not vote in favour of the share buyback shall also have the right to seek an order of court cancelling the resolution.

(3) The ability of the company to proceed with the share buyback shall depend on the order of the court, where applicable.

(4) For the purpose of determining a company's creditors under this section, service providers whose fees are not yet due shall be excluded.

(5) Where a company holds shares as treasury shares, the company shall be entered in the register of members as the member holding those shares.

185. Where a company buys back its shares, payment for the share buyback shall be made from the distributable profits of the company.

186. A company may buy back its shares—

(a) from the existing shareholders or security holders on a proportionate basis ;

(b) from the existing shareholders in a manner permitted pursuant to a scheme of arrangement sanctioned by the court ;

(c) from the open market ; and

(d) by purchasing the securities issued to employees of the company pursuant to a scheme of stock option or any other similar scheme.

187.—(1) A company shall not hold more than 15% of the nominal value of the issued share capital of any class of its shares as treasury shares.

(2) Where a company buys back more than 15% of the issued share capital of any class of its shares, the company shall, before the end of 12 months beginning with the date on which that contravention occurs—

(a) reissue,

(b) cancel, or reissue and cancel such number of shares that will ensure that the company holds not more than 15% of the issued share capital of any class of its shares as treasury shares upon the completion of the transaction.

(3) Notwithstanding anything contained in section 142, a company shall not exercise any right in respect of the treasury shares (including any right to attend or vote at meetings) and any purported exercise of such a right shall be void.

(4) No dividend shall be paid, and no other distribution (whether in cash or otherwise) of the company's assets (including any distribution of assets to members on a winding-up) shall be made to the company, in respect of the treasury shares.

(5) Nothing in this section prevents an allotment of shares as fully paid bonus shares in respect of the treasury shares, or the payment of any amount payable on the redemption of the treasury shares (if they are redeemable shares).

(6) Shares allotted as fully paid bonus shares in respect of the treasury shares shall be treated as if purchased by the company at the time they were allotted.

188.—(1) A contract with a company providing for the acquisition by the company of shares in the company is specifically enforceable against the company, except to the extent that the company cannot perform the contract without thereby being in breach of the provisions of section 184.

(2) In any action brought on a contract referred to in subsection (1), the company shall have the burden of proving that performance of the contract is prevented by the provisions of section 184.

189. Where shares are held as treasury shares, the company may at any time—

(a) sell the shares (or any of them) for a cash consideration, or

(b) transfer the shares (or any of them) for the purpose of or pursuant toan employees' share scheme.

190.—(1) A company which is a subsidiary may acquire shares in its holding company where the subsidiary company is concerned as personal representative or trustee, unless the holding company or any subsidiary of it is beneficially interested otherwise than by way of security for the purposes of a transaction entered into by it in the ordinary course of a business which includes the lending of money.

(2) A subsidiary which is, at the commencement of this Act, a holder of shares of its holding company or a subsidiary which acquired shares in its holding company before it became a subsidiary of that holding company, may continue to hold such shares but, subject to subsection (1), shall have no right to vote at meetings of the holding company or any class of shareholders of the holding company and shall not acquire any future shares in it except on a capitalisation issue.

(3) Where a public company, or a nominee of a public company, acquires shares in the company, and those shares are shown in a balance sheet of the company as an asset, an amount equal to the value of the shares shall be transferred out of profits available for dividend to a reserve fund and shall not be available for distribution.

CHAPTER 9—DEBENTURES - CREATION OF DEBENTURE AND DEBENTURE STOCK

191. A company may borrow money for the purpose of its business or objects and may mortgage or charge its undertaking, property and uncalled capital, or any part thereof, and issue debentures, debenture stock and other securities whether outright or as security for any debt, liability or obligation of the company or of any third party.

192.—(1) Every company shall, within 60 days after the allotment of any of its debentures or after the registration of the transfer of any debentures, deliver to the registered holder thereof, the debenture or a certificate of the debenture stock under the common seal of the company (if the company has a common seal) or otherwise executed as a deed by the company.

(2) If a debenture or debenture stock certificate is defaced, lost or destroyed, the company, at the request of the registered holder of the debenture, shall issue a certified copy of the debenture or renew the debenture stock certificate on payment of a fee as the company may determine and on such terms as to evidence and indemnity and the payment of the company's out-of- pocket expenses of investigating evidence, as the company may reasonably require.

(3) If default is made in complying with this section, the company and any officer of the company who is in default, is liable to such fine as the Commission shall specify in the regulation, and on application by any person entitled to have the debentures or debenture stock certificate delivered to him, the Court may order the company to deliver the debenture or debenture stock certificate and may require the company and any such officer to bear all the costs of and incidental to the application.

193. Every debenture shall include a statement on the following matters—

(a) the principal amount borrowed ;

(b) the maximum discount which may be allowed on the issue or reissue of the debentures, and the maximum premium at which the debentures may be made redeemable ;

(c) the rate of and the dates on which interest on the debentures issued shall be paid and the manner in which payment shall be made ;

(d) the date on which the principal amount shall be repaid or the manner in which redemption shall be effected, whether by the payment of instalments of principal or otherwise ;

(e) in the case of convertible debentures, the date and terms on which the debentures may be converted into shares and the amounts which may be credited as paid up on those shares, and the dates and terms on which the holders may exercise any right to subscribe for shares in respect of the debentures held by them ; and

(f) the charges securing the debenture and the conditions subject to which the debenture shall take effect.

194.—(1) Statements made in debenture or debenture stock certificates is *prima facie* evidence of the title to the debentures of the person named therein as the registered holder and of the amounts secured thereby.

(2) If any person changes his position to his detriment in reliance in good faith on the continued accuracy of any statement made in the debenture or debenture stock certificate, the company shall be estopped in favour of such person from denying the continued accuracy of such statements and shall compensate such person for any loss suffered by him in reliance thereon, which he would not have suffered had the statement been or continued to be accurate, but nothing in this subsection shall derogate from any right the company may have to be indemnified by any other person.

195. A contract with a company to take up and pay for any debenture of the company may be enforced by an order for specific performance.

TYPES OF DEBENTURES

196. A company may issue perpetual debentures, and a condition contained in any debenture, or in any deed for securing any debentures, shall not be invalid by reason only that the debentures are made irredeemable or redeemable only on the happening of a contingency, however remote, or on the expiration of a period, however long, any rule of equity to the contrary notwithstanding.

197. Debentures may be issued upon the terms that in lieu of redemption or repayment, they may, at the option of the holder or the company, be converted into shares in the company upon such terms as may be stated in the debentures.

198.—(1) Debentures may either be secured by a charge over the company's property or may be unsecured by any charge.

(2) Debentures may be secured by a fixed charge on certain of the company's property or a floating charge over the whole or a specified part of the company's undertaking and assets, or by both a fixed charge on certain property and a floating charge.

(3) A charge securing debentures shall become enforceable on the occurrence of the events specified in the debentures or the deed securing the same.

(4) Where legal proceedings are brought by a debenture holder to enforce the security of a series of debentures of which he holds part, the debenture holder shall sue in a representative capacity on behalf of himself and all other debenture holders of that series.

199. A company limited by shares may issue debentures which are, or at the option of the company are, liable to be redeemed.

200.—(1) Where either before or after the commencement of this Act, a company has redeemed any debenture previously issued, unless—

(a) any provision, express or implied, to the contrary is contained in the articles or in any contract entered into by the company ; or

the company has, by passing a resolution to that effect or by some other act, manifested its intention that the debentures shall be cancelled, the company shall have, and shall be deemed always to have had, power to re-issue the debentures, either by re-issuing the same debentures or by issuing other debentures in their place.

(2) On a re-issue of redeemed debentures, the person entitled to the debentures, shall have, and shall be deemed always to have had, the same priorities as if the debentures had never been redeemed.

(3) Where a company has, either before or after the commencement of this Act, deposited any of its debentures to secure advances, from time to time, on current account or otherwise, the debenture shall not be deemed to have been redeemed by reason only of the account of the company having ceased to be in debit, whilst the debentures remained so deposited.

(4) The re-issue of a debenture or the issue of another debenture in its place under this section shall be treated as the issue of a new debenture for the purposes of stamp duty, but it shall not be so treated for the purposes of any provision limiting the amount or number of debentures to be issued.

(5) Any person lending money on the security of a debenture re-issued under this section which appears to be duly stamped, may give the debenture in evidence in any proceeding for enforcing his security without payment of the stamp duty or any penalty in respect thereof, unless he had notice of, or but for his negligence, might have discovered, that the debenture was not duly stamped, but in any such case the company is liable to pay the proper stamp duty and penalty.

(6) Nothing in this section shall prejudice any power to issue debentures in place of any debenture paid off or otherwise satisfied or extinguished which, by its debentures or the securities for the same, is reserved to a company.

201.—(1) The trustee of a debenture trust deed shall hold all contracts, stipulations and undertakings given to him and all mortgages, charges and securities vested in him in connection with the debentures covered by the deed, or some of those debentures, exclusively for the benefit of the debenture holders concerned (except in so far as the deed otherwise provides) and the trustee shall exercise due diligence in respect of the enforcement of those contracts, stipulations, undertakings, mortgages, charges and securities and the fulfilment of his functions generally.

(2) A debenture holder may sue—

(a) the company which issued the debentures he holds for payment of any amount payable to him in respect of the debentures ; or

(b) the trustee of the debenture trust deed covering the debentures he holds for compensation for any breach of the duties which the trustee owes him, and in any such action, it shall not be necessary for any other debenture holder of the same class, or if the action is brought against the company, the trustee of the covering trust deed, to be joined as a party.

(3) This section applies notwithstanding anything contained in a debenture or trust deed or other instrument, but a provision in a debenture or trust deed is valid and binding on all the debenture holders of the class concerned in so far as it enables a meeting of the debenture holders by a resolution supported by the votes of the holders of at least three quarters in value of the debentures of that class in respect of which votes are cast on the resolution to—

(a) release any trustee from liability for any breach of his duties to the debenture holders which he has already committed, or generally from liability for all such breaches (without necessarily specifying them) upon his ceasing to be trustee ;

(b) consent to the alteration or abrogation of any of the rights, powers or remedies of the debenture holders and the trustee of the debenture trust deed covering their debentures (except the powers and remedies under section 233 ; or

(c) consent to the substitution for the debentures of a different class issued by the company or any other company or corporation, or the cancellation of the debentures in consideration of the issue to the debenture holders of shares credited as fully paid in the company or any other company.

202.—(1) The terms of any debenture or trust deed may provide for the convening of general meetings of the debenture holders and for the passing, at such meetings, of a resolution binding on all the holders of the debentures of the same class.

(2) Whether or not the debenture or trust deed contain such provisions as are referred to in subsection (1), the Commission may at any time direct a meeting of the debenture holders of any class to be held and conducted in such manner as the Commission deems fit to consider ancillary or consequential direction as it shall deems fit.

(3) Notwithstanding anything contained in a debenture trust deed, or in any debenture, contract or instrument, the trustee of a debenture deed shall, on the requisition of persons holding, at the date of the deposit of the acquisition debentures covered by the trust deed which carry at least one-tenth of the total voting rights attached to all the issued and outstanding debentures of that class, proceed to convene a meeting of that class of debenture holders.

FIXED AND FLOATING CHARGES

203.—(1) A "*floating charge*" means an equitable charge over the whole or a specified part of the company's undertakings and assets, including cash and uncalled capital of the company both present and future, but so that the charge shall not preclude the company from dealing with such assets until—

(a) the security becomes enforceable and the holder thereof, pursuant to a power in that behalf in the debenture or the deed securing the same, appoints a receiver or manager or enters into possession of such assets ; or

(b) the Court appoints a receiver or manager of such assets on the application of the holder ; or

(c) the company goes into liquidation.

(2) On the happening of any of the events mentioned in subsection (1), the charge shall be deemed to crystallise and become a fixed equitable charge on such of the company's assets as are subject to the charge, and if a receiver or manager is withdrawn with the consent of the chargee, or the chargee withdraws from possession before the charge has been fully discharged, the charge shall thereupon be deemed to cease to be a fixed charge and again to become a floating charge.

204. A fixed charge on any property shall have priority over a floating charge affecting that property, unless the terms on which the floating charge was granted prohibits the company from granting any later charge having priority over the floating charge and the person in whose favour such later charge was granted had notice of that prohibition at the time when the charge was granted to him:

Provided that a person is deemed to have notice of such prohibition in a floating charge where a notice indicating the existence of such prohibition is registered with the Commission.

205.—(1) Whenever a fixed or floating charge has become enforceable, the Court may appoint a receiver and in the case of a floating charge, a receiver and manager of the assets subject to the charge.

(2) In the case of a floating charge, the Court may, notwithstanding that the charge has not become enforceable, appoint a receiver or manager if it is satisfied that the security of the debenture holder is in jeopardy, and the security of the debenture holder shall be deemed to be in jeopardy if the Court is satisfied that events have occurred or are about to occur which render it unreasonable in the interests of the debenture holder that the company should retain power to dispose of its assets.

(3) A receiver or manager shall not be appointed as a means of enforcing debentures not secured by any charge.

206. Where a receiver or manager is appointed by the Court, advertisement to this effect shall be made by the receiver or the receiver and manager in the Federal Government *Gazette* and in two daily newspapers.

207.—(1) Where a receiver is appointed on behalf of the holders of any debenture of a registered company secured by a floating charge, or possession is taken by, or on behalf of those debenture holders of any property comprising of subject to the charge, then if the company is not at the time in the course of being wound up, the debts which in every winding-up are under the provisions relating to preferential payments in section 657 to be paid in priority to all other debts, shall be paid out of any assets coming to the hands of the receiver or other person taking possession in priority to any claim for principal or interest in respect of the debentures.

(2) In the application of the provisions relating to preferential payments—

(a) section 657 shall be construed as if the provision for payment of accrued holiday remuneration becoming payable on the termination of employment before or by the effect of the winding-up order or resolution, were a provision for payment of such remuneration becoming payable on the termination of employment before or by the effect of appointment of the receiver or possession being taken ; and

(b) the periods of time mentioned is reckoned from the date of the appointment of the receiver or of possession being taken, as the case may be, and if such date occurred before the commencement of this Act, the provisions relating to preferential payments which would have applied but for this Act, shall be deemed to remain in full force.

(3) Any payment made under this section shall be recouped as far as maybe out of the assets of the company available for payment of general creditors.

(4) Notwithstanding any provision in this Act or any other law to the contrary, the holder of a fixed charge shall have priority over other debts of the company including preferential debts.

DEBENTURE TRUST DEED

208.—(1) Every company which offers debentures to the public for subscription or purchase shall, before issuing any of the debentures, execute a debenture trust deed in respect of them and procure the execution of the deed by the trustee for the debenture holders appointed by the deed.

(2) No debenture trust deed shall cover more than one class of debentures, whether or not the trust deed is required by this section to be executed.

(3) Where a trust deed is required to be executed by this section but has not been executed, the Court, on the application of a debenture holder concerned, may—

(a) order the company to execute a trust deed ;
(b) direct that a person nominated by the Court to be appointed as a trustee ; and
(c) give such consequential directions as it deems fit, as to the contents of the trust deed and its execution by the trustee.
(4) For the purposes of this Act, debentures shall belong to different classes if different rights attach to them in respect of—
(a) the rate of, or dates for payment of, interest ;
(b) the dates when, or the instalments by which, the principal of the debenture shall be repaid, unless the difference is solely that the class of debentures shall be repaid during a stated period of time and particular debentures may be repaid at different dates during that period according to selections made by the company or by drawings, ballot or otherwise ;
(c) any right to subscribe for or convert the debentures into shares in, or other debentures of, the company or any other company ; or
(d) the powers of the debenture holders to realise any security.
(5) Debentures further belong to different classes, if they do not rank equally for payment when any security invested in the debenture holders under any trust deed is realised or when the company is wound up, if, in the circumstances mentioned in subsection (4) the subject matter of any such security or the proceeds, or any assets available to satisfy the debentures, is or are not to be applied in satisfying the debentures strictly in proportion to the amount of principal, premiums and arrears of interest to which the holders of them are respectively entitled.
(6) A debenture is covered by a trust deed if the holder of the debenture is entitled to —
(a) participate in any money payable by the company under the deed ; or
(b) the benefit of any mortgage, charge or security created by the deed, whether alone or together with other persons.
(7) If a company issues debentures in circumstances in which this section requires a debenture trust deed to be executed, without such a deed having been executed in compliance with this section, or if the company issues debentures under a trust deed which covers two or more classes of debentures, the directors of the company who are in default commit an offence and are liable jointly on conviction to such fine as the court deems fit and in addition, the directors of the company shall be jointly severally liable to such fines as the Commission shall specify in the regulation.

209.—(1) Every debenture trust deed, whether required by section 208 or not, shall state—
(a) the maximum sum which the company may raise by issuing debentures of the same class ;
(b) the maximum discount which may be allowed on the issue or reissue of the debentures, and the maximum premium at which the debentures may be made redeemable ;
(c) the nature of any asset over which a mortgage, charge or security is created by the trust deed in favour of the trustee for the benefit of the debenture holders equally, and except where such a charge is a floating charge, the identity of the assets subject to it ;

(d) the nature of any asset over which a mortgage, charge or security has been or will be created in favour of any person other than the trustee for the benefit of the debenture holders equally, and except where such a charge is a floating charge, the identity of the assets subject to it ;

(e) whether the company has created or will create any mortgage, charge or security for the benefit of some, but not all, of the holders of debentures issued under the trust deed ;

(*f*) any prohibition or restriction on the power of the company to issue debentures or create mortgages, charges or any security on any of its assets ranking in priority to, or equally with the debentures issued under the trust deed ;

(g) whether the company has power to acquire debentures issued under the trust deed before the date of their redemption and to re-issue the debentures ;

(h) the rate of, and the dates on which, interest on the debentures issued under the trust deed shall be paid and the manner in which payment may be made ;

(i) the date or dates on which the principal or the debentures issued under the trust deed shall be repaid or redeemed, and unless the whole principal is to be repaid to all the debenture holders at the same time, the manner in which redemption is effected, whether by the payment of equal instalments of principal in respect of each debenture, or by the selection of debentures for redemption by the company, or by drawing, ballot, or otherwise ;

(j) in the case of convertible debentures, the dates and terms on which the debentures may be converted into shares and the amounts which may be credited as paid up on those shares in the right of the debentures held by them ;

(k) the circumstances in which the debenture holders are entitled to realise any mortgage, charge or security vested in the trustee or any other person for their benefit (other than the circumstances in which they are entitled to do so by this Act);

(l) the powers of the company and the trustee to call meetings of the debenture holders and the rights of debenture holders to require the company or the trustee to call such meetings ;

(m) whether the rights of debenture holders may be altered or abrogated and if so, the conditions which shall be fulfilled, and the procedure which shall be followed, to effect such an alteration or abrogation ;

(n) the amount or rate of remuneration to be paid to the trustee and the period for which it is paid, and whether it is paid in priority to the principal, interest and costs in respect of debentures issued under the trust deed; and (*o*) provisions for the replacement of the trustee if required.

(2) If debentures are issued without a covering debenture trust deed being executed, the statements required by subsection (1) shall be included in each debenture or in a note forming part of the same document or endorsed thereon, and in applying that subsection references to the debenture trust deed shall be construed as references to all or any of the debentures of the same class.

(3) Subsection (2) shall not apply if the debenture is the only debenture of the class to which it belongs which has been or may be issued, and the rights of the debenture holder may not be altered or abrogated without his consent.

(4) Any director who issues a debenture in violation of the provisions of this section is liable to such fines as the Commission shall specify in the regulation.

210.—(1) Every debenture covered by a debenture trust deed shall state, either in the body or in a note forming part of the same document or endorsed therein—

(a) the matters required to be stated in a debenture trust deed by section209 (1) (*a*), (*b*), (*f*), (*h*), (*i*), (*j*), (*l*) and (*m*) ;

(b) whether the trustee of the covering debenture trust deed holds the mortgages, charges and securities vested in him by the trust deed in trust for the debenture holders equally, or in trust for some only of the debenture holders, and if so, which debenture holders ; and

(c) whether the debenture is secured by a floating charge vested in the trustee of the covering debenture trust deed or in the debenture holders.

(2) A debenture issued by a company shall state on its face in legible print, that it is unsecured if no mortgage, charge or security is vested in the holder of the debenture or in any other person for his benefit as security for payment of principal or interest.

(3) Any director of a company who issues a debenture in violation of the provisions of subsections (1) and (2) is liable to such fines as the Commission shall specify in the regulation.

211.—(1) Whether or not a debenture is secured by a charge over the company's property, there may be created in relation to such debenture, a trust deed appointing trustees for the debenture holders.

(2) It is the duty of such trustee to safeguard the rights of the debenture holders and, on behalf of and for the benefit of the debenture holders, exercise the rights, powers and discretions conferred upon him by the trust deed.

(3) Charges securing the debentures may be created in favour of the debenture holders by vesting them in the trustees.

(4) Any provision contained in a trust deed or in any contract with the holders of debentures secured by a trust deed is void if it would have the effect of exempting a trustee from, or indemnifying him against, liability for any breach of trust or failure to show the degree of care and diligence required of him as trustee having regard to the powers, authorities or discretions conferred on him by the trust deed.

(5) In subsection (4), nothing is deemed to invalidate any release otherwise validly given in respect of anything done or omitted to be done by a trustee on the agreement to such release of a majority of at least three quarters in value of the debenture holders present in person, or where proxies are permitted, by proxy at a meeting summoned for the purpose.

(6) Notwithstanding any provision contained in the debentures or trust deed, the Court may, on the application of any debenture holder or of the Commission, remove any trustee and appoint another in his place if satisfied that such trustee has interests which conflicts or may conflict with those of the debenture holders or that for any reason it is undesirable that such trustee should continue to act :

Provided that where any such application is made by a debenture holder, the Court if it deems fit, may order the applicant to give security for the payment of the costs of the trustee and may direct that the application be heard in Chambers.

212.—(1) A person is not qualified for appointment as a trustee of a debenture trust deed if he is—

(a) an officer or employee of the company which issues debentures covered by the trust deed or of a company in the same group of companies as the company issuing debentures ;

(b) less than 18 years of age ;
(c) of unsound mind and has been so found by a court in Nigeria or elsewhere ;
(d) an undischarged bankrupt ; or
(e) disqualified under section 283 from being appointed as a director of a company, but a corporation shall not be disqualified from being appointed as a trustee.

(2) If a trustee becomes subject to any of the disqualifications mentioned in subsection (1) after he has been appointed, he shall immediately cease to be qualified to act as a trustee of the debenture trust deed.

(3) Any person who acts as a trustee of a debenture trust deed whose appointment is invalid under subsection (1) or who is disqualified from acting under subsection (2), commits an offence and is liable on conviction as the Court deems fit, or to such fines as the Commission shall specify in the regulation.

213.—(1) Subject to the provisions of this section, anything contained in a trust deed for securing an issue of debentures, or in any contract with the holders of debentures secured by a trust deed, is void if it would have the effect of exempting a trustee from or indemnifying him against liability for breach of trust, where he fails to show the degree of care and diligence required of him as trustee, having regard to the provisions of the trust deed conferring on him any power, authorities or discretion.

(2) Subsection (1) does not invalidate—
(a) any release validly given in respect of anything done or omitted to be done by a trustee before the giving of the release ; or
(b) any provision enabling such a release to be given—
(i) on the agreement of a majority of not less than three quarters in value of the debenture holders present and voting in person or, where proxies are permitted, by proxy at a meeting summoned for that purpose, and
(ii) either with respect to specific acts or omissions or on the trustee dying or ceasing to act.

(3) Subsection (1) does not operate to—
(a) invalidate any provision in effect at the commencement of this Actin any such trust deed or contract, provided that any person entitled to the benefit of that provision, or afterwards given the benefit thereof under subsection (4), remains a trustee of the trust deed in question ; or
(b) deprive any person of any exemption or right to be indemnified in respect of anything done or omitted to be done by him, while any such provision was in effect.

(4) While any trustee of a trust deed remains entitled to the benefit of a provision exempted by subsection (3), the benefit of that provision may be given—
(a) to all trustees of the deed, present and future ; or
(b) to any named trustee or proposed trustee, by a resolution, passed bya majority of at least three-quarters in value of the debenture holders present in person or, where proxies are permitted by proxy at a meeting summoned for that purpose in accordance with the provisions of the trust deed or, if the trust deed makes no provision for summoning meetings, a meeting summoned for that purpose in any manner approved by the Court.

214.—(1) Except as expressly provided in the terms of any debenture, debentures shall be transferable without restriction by a written transfer in any usual or common form, or any other form which the directors of the company may approve, and that the transferee is entitled to the debenture and to the money secured thereby without regard to any equity, set-off or cross claim between the company and the original, or any intermediate, holder.

(2) The terms of any debenture may impose restrictions of any nature on the transferability of debentures, including power for the company to refuse to register any transfer and provisions for compulsory acquisition or rights of first refusal in favour of other debenture holders, or members or officers of the company:

Provided that if any restriction is imposed on the right to transfer any debenture, notice of the restriction shall be endorsed on the face of the debenture or debenture stock certificate and in the absence of such endorsement, the restriction shall be ineffective as regards any transferee for value, whether or not he has notice of the restriction.

PROVISIONS AS TO COMPANY'S REGISTER OF CHARGES, DEBENTURE HOLDERS AND AS TO COPIES OF INSTRUMENTS CREATING CHARGES

215. Every company shall cause a copy of every instrument creating any charge requiring registration under this Part to be kept at the registered office of the company, but, in the case of a series of uniform debentures, a copy of one debenture of the series is sufficient.

216.—(1) Every company shall keep, at the registered office of the company, a register of charges and enter therein all charges specifically affecting property of the company and all floating charges on the undertaking or any property of the company, giving in each case a short description of the property charged, the amount of the charge, and, except in the case of securities to bearer, the names of the persons entitled thereto.

(2) If any officer of the company knowingly and wilfully authorises or permits the omission of any entry required to be made under this subsection, he is liable to such fines as the Commission shall specify in the regulation.

217.—(1) The copies of instruments creating any charge requiring registration under this Part with the Commission and the register of charges kept under section 216 of this Act, shall be open during business hours (but subject to such reasonable restrictions as the company in general meeting may impose, so that at least two hours in each day shall be allowed for inspection) to inspection by any creditor or member of the company without fee and the register of charges shall also be open to inspection by any other person on payment of such fee as the Commission shall determine or such less sum as may be prescribed by the company for each inspection, as the company may prescribe:

Provided that the Commission may request for and obtain such copy without any restriction or charge.

(2) If inspection of copies of instruments creating charges or of the register is refused, each officer of the company who is in default is liable to such fines as the Commission shall specify in the regulation for every day during which the refusal continues.

(3) If any such refusal occurs, the Court may by order compel an immediate inspection of the copies of instruments or register.

218.—(1) A company which issues or has issued debentures shall maintain a register of the holders.

(2) The register shall contain the—

(a) names and addresses of the debenture holders ;

(b) principal of the debentures held by each of them ;

(c) amount or the highest amount of any premium payable on redemption of the debentures ;

(d) issue price of the debenture and the amount paid up on the issue price ;

(e) date on which the name of each person was entered on the register as a debenture holder ; and

(*f*) date on which each person ceased to be a debenture holder.

(3) The entry required under this section shall be made within 30 days of the conclusion of the agreement with the company to become a debenture holder or within 30 days of the date at which he ceases to be one.

219.—(1) Every register of holders of debentures of a company shall, except when duly closed (but subject to such reasonable restrictions as the company may in general meeting impose, so that at least two hours in each day shall be allowed for inspection), be open to the inspection of the registered holder of such debentures or any holder of shares in the company without fee, and of any other person on payment of such fee as the Commission shall determine or such less sum as may be prescribed by the company:

Provided that the Commission may at any time during working hours request for and obtain such copy without any restriction or charge.

(2) Any such registered holder of debentures or any other person may require a copy of the register of the holders of debentures of the company or any part thereof on payment of such fee as the Commission shall determine or such less sum as may be prescribed by the company.

(3) A copy of any trust deed for securing any issue of debentures shall be duly endorsed by an officer of the company and forwarded to every holder of such debentures at his request on payment in the case of a printed trust deed, of the sum of such fee as the Commission shall determine or such less sum as may be prescribed by the company, or, where the trust deed has not been printed, on payment of such fee as the Commission shall determine or such less sum as may be prescribed by the company for every page required to be copied.

(4) If inspection is refused, or a copy is refused or not forwarded, the company and every officer of the company who is in default is liable to such fine as the Commission shall specify in the regulation for every day during which the default continues.

(5) Where a company is in default, a Court may by order compel an immediate inspection of the register or direct that the copies required shall be sent to the person requiring them.

(6) For the purposes of this section, a register is deemed to be duly closed in accordance with provisions contained in the articles or in the debentures or, in the case of debenture stock, in the stock certificates, or in the trust deed or other document securing the debentures or debenture stock, during such periods, not exceeding in the whole 30 days in any year, as may be therein specified.

220. On the application of the transferor of any debenture in a company, the company shall enter in its register of debenture holders the name of the transferee in the same manner and subject to the same conditions as if the application for the entry were made by the transferee.

221.—(1) If a company refuses to register a transfer of any debenture, the company shall, within two months after the date on which the transfer was lodged with the company, send to the transferee notice of the refusal.

(2) If any default is made in complying with the provisions of this section, the company and each officer of the company are liable to such fine as the Commission shall specify by regulation.

222.—(1) Subject to the provisions of this Part, every charge created by a company, being a charge to which this section applies, shall, so far as any security on the company's property or undertaking is conferred, be void against the liquidator and any creditor of the company, unless the prescribed particulars of the charge (including any provisions in a floating charge that prohibits or restricts the company from granting any further charge ranking in priority to or *pari passu* with the floating charge) together with the instrument, if any, by which the charge is created or evidenced, have been or are delivered to or received by the Commission for registration in the manner required by this Act or by any enactment repealed by this Act within 90 days after the date of its creation, but without prejudice to any contract or obligation for repayment of the money thereby secured, and when a charge becomes void under this section, the money thereby secured shall immediately become payable and registration under this section shall give rise to constructive notice of the matters stated in the particulars of charge.

(2) The provisions of this section apply to a —

(a) charge for the purpose of securing any issue of debentures ;

(b) charge on uncalled share capital of the company ;

(c) charge created or evidenced by an instrument which if executed by an individual would require registration as a bill of sale ;

(d) charge on land, wherever situate, or any interest therein, but not including a charge for rent or other periodical sum issuing out of land ; (*e*) charge on book debts of the company ;

(*f*) floating charge on the undertaking or property of the company ;

(g) charge on calls made but not paid ;

(h) charge on a ship or aircraft or any share in a ship ; and(*i*) charge on goodwill, or on any intellectual property.

(3) Where a charge affects or relates to property situate in Nigeria and in addition to registration under subsection (1), registration elsewhere in Nigeria is necessary to make the charge valid or effectual, it shall, subject to this subsection, be sufficient evidence of compliance with the requirements of subsection (1), if, instead of delivery of the original instrument creating or evidencing the charge, there is delivered to and received by the Commission within the prescribed period of 90 days, or such extended time as the Court may allow, a true copy of it duly certified as such by the secretary to the company.

(4) A reference in any enactment to the date of execution of an instrument for the purposes of computation of time within which registration is to be effected with or without penalty, shall be construed as a reference to the date of presentation of a copy of the instrument to the Commission under this Act, and time shall be computed accordingly, and if a certified copy is delivered to the Commission under this subsection, the original of it shall be produced to the Commission for inspection and comparison, if the Commission so requires.

(5) In the case of a charge created out of Nigeria, affecting or in relation to property situate outside Nigeria, the delivery to and the receipt by the Commission of a copy verified in the prescribed manner of the instrument by which the charge is created or evidenced, shall have the same effect for the purposes of this section as the delivery and receipt of the instrument itself, and 90 days after the date on which the instrument or copy could, in due course of post, and if dispatched with diligence, have been received in Nigeria shall be substituted for 90 days after the date of the creation of the charge as the time within which the particulars and instrument or copy are to be delivered to the Commission.

(6) Where a charge is created in Nigeria but affects or relates to property outside Nigeria, the instrument creating or purporting to create the charge may be sent for registration under this section, notwithstanding that further proceedings may be necessary to make the charge valid or effectual according to the law of the country in which the property is situate.

(7) Where a negotiable instrument has been given to secure the payment of any book debts of a company, the deposit of the instrument for the purpose of securing an advance to the company shall not, under this section, be treated as a charge on those book debts.

(8) The holding of debentures entitling the holder to a charge on land is not, for the purposes of this section, deemed to be an interest in land.

(9) Where a series of debentures containing, or giving by reference to any other instrument, any charge to the benefit of which the debenture holders of that series are entitled *pari passu* is created by a company, it is, for the purposes of this section, sufficient if there are delivered to or received by the Commission within 90 days after the execution of the deed containing the charge or, if there is no such deed, after the execution of any debenture of the series, the following particulars—

(a) the total amount secured by the whole series ;

(b) the dates of the resolutions authorising the issues of the series and the date of the covering deed, if any, by which the security is created or defined ;

(c) a general description of the property charged ; and

(d) the names of the trustees, if any, for the debenture holders, together with the deed containing the charge, or, if there is no such deed, one of the debentures of the series:

Provided that, where more than one issue is made of debentures in the series, there shall be sent to the Commission, for entry in the register, particulars of the date and amount of each issue, but an omission to do this does not affect the validity of the debentures issued.

(10) Where any commission, allowance or discount has been paid or made either directly or indirectly by a company to any person in consideration of his subscribing or agreeing to subscribe, whether absolutely or conditionally, for any debenture of the company, or procuring or agreeing to procure subscriptions, whether absolute or conditional, for such debentures, the particulars required to be sent for registration under this section shall include particulars as to the amount or rate percent of commission, discount or allowance paid or made, but an omission to do this does not affect the validity of the debentures issued.

(11) The deposit of any debenture as security for any debt of the company shall not, for the purposes of subsection (10), be treated as the issue of the debentures at a discount.

(12) The total fees payable to the Commission in connection with the filing, registration or release of a charge with the Commission under this Part shall not exceed 0.35% of the value of the charge or such other amount as the Minister may specify in the Federal Government *Gazette*.

(13) In this Part—"*charge*" includes mortgage ;

"*book debt*", for the purposes of subsection (2) (*e*), means a debt due or to become due to the company at some future date on account of or in connection with a profession, trade or business carried on by the company, whether entered in a book or not, and includes a reference to a charge on a future debt of the same nature although not incurred or owing at the time of the creation of the charge, but does not include a reference to a charge on a marketable security or on a negotiable instrument ;

"*intellectual property*", for the purposes of this section, means any patent or a licence under a patent, any registered design or design right or a licence, any trademark or licence under a trademark, or any copyright or a licence under a copyright ;

"*security financial collateral arrangement*" means an agreement or arrangement, evidenced in writing, where :

(a) the purpose of the agreement or arrangement is to secure the relevant financial obligations owed to the collateral-taker ;

(b) the collateral-provider creates or there arises a security interest in financial collateral to secure those obligations ;

(c) the financial collateral is delivered, transferred, held, registered or otherwise designated so as to be in the possession or under the control of the collateral-taker or a person acting on its behalf; any right of the collateral-provider to substitute equivalent financial collateral or withdraw excess financial collateral shall not prevent the financial collateral being in the possession or under the control of the collateral-taker ; and

(d) the collateral-provider and the collateral-taker are both non-natural persons.

(14) This section does not apply in relation to a security financial collateral arrangement or any charge created or otherwise arising under a security financial collateral arrangement.

223.—(1) The Commission shall keep, with respect to each company, a register in the prescribed form of all the charges requiring registration under this Part and shall, on payment of such fee as may be specified by regulations made by the Commission, enter in the register with respect to such charges in the case of—

(a) a charge to the benefit of which the holders of a series of debentures are entitled, such particulars as are specified in section 222 (9) ; and

(b) any other charge—

(i) if the charge is a charge created by the company, the date of its creation, and if the charge was a charge existing on property acquired by the company, the date of its creation and the date of the acquisition of the property,

(ii) the amount secured by the charge,

(iii) short particulars of the property,

(iv) the persons entitled to the charge, and

(v) or a floating charge, a notice indicating the existence of any provisions in the charge that prohibit or restrict the company from granting any further charge ranking in priority to or *pari passu* with the floating charge.

(2) Where a charge is registered under this Part, the Commission shall issue a registration certificate setting out the parties to the charge, the amount thereby secured, with such other particulars as the Commission may consider necessary, and the certificate is *prima facie* evidence of due compliance with the requirements as to registration under this Part.

(3) The register kept in pursuance of this section shall be open to inspection by any person on payment of such fees as may be prescribed by the Commission.

224.—(1) It is the duty of a company to send to the Commission for registration, the particulars of every charge created by the company and of the issues of debentures of a series requiring registration under section 222, but registration of any such charge may be effected on the application of any person interested therein.

(2) Where registration is effected on the application of a person other than the company, that person is entitled to recover from the company the amount of any fees properly paid by him to the Commission on the registration.

(3) If any company defaults in sending to the Commission for registration, the particulars of any charge created by the company or of the issues of debentures of a series requiring registration, unless the registration has been effected on the application of some other person, the company and each officer of the company who is in default commits an offence and are liable to such penalty as may be prescribed by the Commission.

225.—(1) Where a company acquires any property which is subject to a charge of any such kind as would, if it has been created by the company after the acquisition of the property, have been required to be registered under this Part, the company shall cause the prescribed particulars of the charge, together with a copy (certified in the prescribed manner to be a correct copy) of the instrument, if any, by which the charge was created or is evidenced, to be delivered to the Commission for registration in the manner required by this Act within 90 days after the date on which acquisition is completed :

Provided that, if the property is situate and the charge was created outside Nigeria, 90 days after the date on which the copy of the instrument could in due course of post, and if despatched with due diligence, have been received in Nigeria shall be substituted for 90 days after the completion of the acquisition, as the time within which the particulars and the copy of the instrument are to be delivered to the Commission.

(2) If default is made in complying with this section, the company and each officer of the company are liable to such penalty as may be prescribed by the Commission for every day during which the default continues.

(3) It is sufficient compliance with this section in any case affecting land registered under any enactment in a State, where the charge is registered before the land is acquired by the company, if a true copy of the charge duly certified by the Registrar of Land is delivered to the Commission within the time prescribed by this section.

226.—(1) Where, at the date of commencement of this Act, a company has property on which there is a charge, particulars of which would require registration if it had been created by the company after the date of such commencement, then, unless the charge has been discharged or the property has ceased to be held by the company prior to the expiration of six months from the date of such commencement, the company shall, within that time, cause particulars of the charge as prescribed by section 222 to be delivered to the Commission for registration together with the document, if any, by which the charge was created or a copy thereof, certified as required by that section.

(2) Failure to comply with the provisions of this section does not affect the validity of the charge.

227. Where a charge, particulars of which require registration under section 222, is expressed to secure all sums due or to become due or some other uncertain or fluctuating amount, the particulars required under section 222 (9) shall state the maximum sum deemed to be secured by such charge (being the maximum sum covered by the stamp duty paid thereon) and such charge is void, so far as any security on the company's property is thereby conferred, as respects any excess over the stated maximum :

Provided that, if additional stamp duty is subsequently paid on such charge; and at any time thereafter prior to the commencement of the winding-up of the company, amended particulars of the said charge stating the increased maximum sum deemed to be secured thereby (together with the original instrument by which the charge was created or evidenced) are delivered to the Commission for registration, then, as from the date of such delivery, the charge, if valid, is effective to the extent of such increased maximum sum except as regards any person who, prior to the date of such delivery, has acquired any proprietary rights in, or a fixed or floating charge on, the property subject to the charge.

228.—(1) The company shall cause a copy of every certificate of registration given under section 223 to be endorsed on every debenture or certificate of debenture stock which is issued by the company and the payment of which is secured by the charge so registered :

Provided that nothing in this subsection shall be construed as requiring a company to cause a certificate of registration of any charge given to be endorsed on any debenture or certificate of debenture stock issued by the company before the charge was created.

(2) If any person authorises or permits the delivery of any debenture or certificate of debenture stock which under the provisions of this section is required to have endorsed on it a copy of a certificate of registration without the copy being so endorsed upon it, he is, without prejudice to any other liability, liable to such penalty as may be prescribed by the Commission.

229. If the Commission is satisfied with respect to any registered charge that—

(a) the debt for which the charge was given has been paid or satisfied in whole or in part ; or

(b) part of the property or undertaking charged has been released from the charge or has ceased to form part of the company's property or undertaking, the company may, enter on the register a memorandum of satisfaction to the extent necessary to give effect thereto and, where it enters a memorandum of satisfaction it shall, if required, furnish the company with a copy of the entry, and any such entry shall have effect, subject to the requirement of any other enactment as to registration.

230. The court, on being satisfied that—

(a) the omission to register a charge within the time required by this Actor that the omission or misstatement of any particular with respect to any such charge or in a memorandum of satisfaction was—

(i) accidental, or due to inadvertence or to some other sufficient cause, or

(ii) is not of a nature to prejudice the position of creditors or shareholders of the company ; or

(b) that on other grounds it is just and equitable to grant relief, may, on the application of the company or any person interested and on such terms and conditions as seems to the court just and expedient, order that the time for registration is extended or, as the case may be, that the omission or misstatement shall be rectified.

231.—(1) If any person obtains an order for the appointment of a receiver or manager of the property of a company, or appoints such a receiver or manager under any power contained in any instrument, he shall, within seven days from the date of the order or the appointment under the said powers, give notice of the fact to the Commission and the Commission shall, on payment of such fee as may be specified by regulations, enter the fact in the register of charges.

(2) Where a person appointed receiver or manager of the property of a company under the powers contained in any instrument, ceases to act as such receiver or manager, he shall, on so ceasing, give the Commission notice to that effect, and the Commission shall enter the notice in the register of charges.

(3) If any person makes default in complying with the requirements of this section, he is liable to such penalty as the Commission shall specify by regulation.

REALISATION OF SECURITY

232.—(1) A debenture holder is entitled to realise any security vested in him or in any other person for his benefit if—

(a) the company fails to pay any instalment of interest, or the whole, part of the principal or any premium, owing under the debenture or the debenture trust deed covering the debenture, within one month after it becomes due ;

(b) the company fails to fulfil any of the obligations imposed on it by the debentures or the debenture trust deed ;

(c) the circumstance occur whereby the terms of the debentures or debenture trust deed entitled the holder of the debenture to realise his security ; or

the company is wound up.

(2) A debenture holder whose debenture is secured by a floating charge vested in him or the trustee of the covering debenture trust deed, or any other person, is additionally, entitled to realise his security if—

(a) any creditor of the company issues a process of execution against any of its assets or commences proceedings for winding-up of the company by order of any court of competent jurisdiction ;

(b) the company ceases to pay its debts as they fall due ; or

(c) the company ceases to carry on business ;

(d) the company suffers, after the issue of debentures of the class concerned, losses or diminutions in the value of its assets which in the aggregate amount to more than one half of the total amount owing in respect of debentures of the class held by the debenture holder who seeks to enforce his security and debentures whose holder ranks before him for payment of principal or interest ; or

(e) the circumstances occur which entitle a debenture holder who ranks for payment of principal or interest in priority to the debentures secured by the floating charges to realise his security.

233.—(1) At any time after a debenture holder or a class of debenture holders, becomes entitled to realise his or their security, a receiver of any asset subject to a mortgage, charge or security in favour of the class of debenture holders or the trustee of the covering trust deed, or any other person, may be appointed by—
(a) that trustee ;
(b) the holders of debentures of the same class containing power to appoint;
(c)debenture holders having more than one half of the total amount owing in respect of all the debentures of the same class ; or (*d*) the court on the application of the trustee.
(2) Subject to any condition imposed in the debenture or debenture trust deed, a debenture holder, or a trustee in the case of a trust deed, may—
(a) bring an action in a representative capacity against the company for payment and enforcement of the security ; or
(b) realise his security by—(*i*) bringing a foreclosure action, or (*ii*) commencing a winding-up proceeding.
(3) A receiver appointed under this section has, subject to the order made by the court, power to take possession of the assets subject to the mortgage, charge or security and sell those assets and, if the mortgage, charge or security extends to such property collect debts owed to the property enforce claims vested in the company, compromise, settle and enter into arrangements in respect of claims by or against the company, on the company's business with a view to selling it on the most favourable terms, grant or accept leases of land and licences in respect of patents, designs, copyright or trademarks and recover any instalment unpaid on the company's issued shares.
(4) Where a representative action is being brought under subsection (2)(*a*), the approval of the court shall be obtained where the company is being wound up.
(5) The remedies given by this section are in addition to, and not in substitution for, any other powers and remedies conferred on the trustee of the debenture trust deed or on the debenture holders, by the debentures or debenture trust deed, and any power or remedy which is expressed in any instrument to be exercisable if the debenture holders become entitled to realise their security, is exercisable on the occurrence of any of the events specified under section 232 (1) of this Act or, in the case of a floating charge in section 203 of this Act, but a manager of the business or of any of the assets of a company may not be appointed for the benefit of debenture holders unless a receiver has also been appointed and has not ceased to act.
(6) The provisions of sections 550-563 of this Act shall apply to receivers and managers under this Part.
(7) No provision in any instrument which purports to exclude or restrict the remedies given by this section is valid.

234. Subject to the provisions of this Part of this Act and unless the context otherwise admits, the provisions of sections 171, 172, 175, 177, 180 and 181 of this Act relating to share certificates and transfer of shares shall apply in respect of shares as if "debentures" were substituted for "shares" and "debenture holders" for "shareholders".

CHAPTER 10—MEETINGS AND PROCEEDINGS OF COMPANIES

235.—(1) Every public company shall, within a period of six months from the date of its incorporation, hold a general meeting of the members of the company (in this Act referred to as "the statutory meeting").

(2) The directors shall, at least 21 days before the day on which the statutory meeting is held, forward to every member of the company a copy of the statutory report.

(3) The statutory report shall be certified by not less than two directors or by a director and the secretary of the company and shall state—

(a) the total number of shares allotted, distinguishing shares allotted as fully or partly paid-up than in cash, and stating in the case of shares partly paid-up, the extent to which they are paid up, and the consideration for which they have been allotted ;

(b) the total amount of cash received by the company in respect of all the shares allotted, distinguished as aforesaid ;

(c) the names, addresses and descriptions of the directors, auditors, managers, if any, and secretary of the company ;

(d) the particulars of any pre-incorporation contract together with the particulars of any modification or proposed modification ;

(e) any underwriting contract that has not been carried out and the reasons therefor ;

(f) the arrears, if any, due on calls from every director ; and

(g) the particulars of any commission or brokerage paid or to be paid in connection with the issue or sale of shares or debentures to any director or to the manager.

(4) The report shall contain an abstract of the receipts of the company and the payments made from them up to a date within seven days of the date of the report, exhibiting under distinctive headings the receipts of the company from shares, debentures and other sources, the payments made from such receipts and particulars concerning the balance remaining in hand, and an account or estimate of the preliminary expenses of the company.

(5) The statutory report shall, so far as it relates to the shares allotted by the company, and to the cash received in respect of such shares, and to the receipts and payments of the company on capital account, be certified as correct by the auditors.

(6) The directors shall cause a copy of the statutory report, certified as required by this section, to be delivered to the Commission for registration within 14 days after the sending of copies to the members of the company.

(7) The directors shall cause a list, showing the names, descriptions and addresses of the members of the company and the number of shares held by them respectively, to be produced at the commencement of the meeting and to remain open and accessible to any member of the company during the continuance of the statutory meeting.

(8) The members of the company present at the statutory meeting are at liberty to discuss any matter relating to the formation of the company, its commencement of business or arising out of the statutory report.

(9) Any member who wishes a resolution to be passed on any matter arising out of the statutory report shall give further 21 days' notice from the date on which the statutory report was received to the company of his intention to propose such a resolution, in which case, the statutory meeting shall not be held until the expiration of the 21 days' notice given to the company by the member.

(10) The statutory meeting may be adjourn and at any adjourned meeting any resolution of which notice has been given in accordance with the articles, either

before or subsequently to the former meeting, may be passed, and the adjourned meeting shall have the same powers as the original meeting.

236. Without prejudice to the provisions of section 567 of this Act, if a company fails to comply with the requirements of section 235 of this Act, the company and any officer in default commits an offence and are liable to a fine for everyday during which the default continues in such amount as the Commission shall specify in its regulations.

GENERAL MEETING

237.—(1) Except in the case of a small company or any company having a single shareholder, every company shall in each year hold a general meeting as its annual general meeting in addition to any other meeting in that year, and specify the meeting as such in the notices calling it; and not more than 15 months shall elapse between the date of one annual general meeting of a company and the next :

Provided that—

(a) so long as a company holds its first annual general meeting within 18 months of its incorporation it need not hold it in that year or in the following year ; or except for the first annual general meeting, the Commission shall have power to extend the time within which any annual general meeting shall be held, by a period not exceeding three months so that not more than 18 months shall elapse between the date of the last annual general meeting and the date of any meeting so extended.

(2) If default is made in holding a meeting of a company in accordance with subsection (1), the Commission, may, on its own or on the application of any member of the company call, or direct the calling of a general meeting of the company and give such ancillary or consequential directions as the Commission considers expedient, including directions modifying or supplementing, in relation to the calling, holding, conducting of the meeting, the operation of the company's articles, and that the directions that may be given under this subsection shall include a direction that one member of the company present in person or by proxy may apply to the court for an order to take a decision which binds all the members.

(3) A general meeting held in pursuance of subsection (2) is, subject to any direction of the Commission, deemed to be an annual general meeting of the company, but, where a meeting so held is not held in the year in which the default in holding the company's annual general meeting occurred, the meeting so held shall not be treated as the annual general meeting for the year in which it is held unless, at that meeting, the company resolves that it shall be so treated.

(4) Where a company resolves that a meeting shall be treated as its annual general meeting, a copy of the resolution shall, within 15 days after the passing, be filed with the Commission.

(5) If default is made in holding a meeting of the company in accordance with subsection (1), or in complying with any direction of the Commission under subsections (2) and (3), or in complying with this subsection, the company and every officer of the company are liable to a penalty in such amount as the Commission shall specify in its regulations.

238. All businesses transacted at annual general meetings are deemed special business, except declaring a dividend, presentation of the financial statements and the reports of the directors and auditors, election of directors in the place of those retiring, the appointment, fixing of the remuneration of the auditors, appointment of members of the audit committee and disclosure of remuneration of managers of a company, which are ordinary business.

EXTRAORDINARY GENERAL MEETING

239.—(1) The board of directors may convene an extraordinary general meeting whenever they deem fit, and if at any time they are not within Nigeria, sufficient directors capable of acting to form a quorum, any director may convene an extraordinary general meeting.

(2) An extraordinary general meeting of a company may be requisitioned by any member or members of the company holding at the date of the requisition not less than one-tenth of the paid up capital of the company as at the date of the deposit carrying the right of voting, or in the case of a company not having a share capital, members of the company representing not less than one tenth of the total voting rights of all the members having at the said date a right to vote at general meetings of the company, and the directors shall on receipt of the requisition immediately proceed to convene an extraordinary general meeting of the company, notwithstanding anything in its articles.

(3) The requisition shall state the objects of the meeting, and be signed by the requisitionists and deposited at the registered office of the company, and the requisition may consist of several documents in like form each signed by one or more requisitionists.

(4) If the directors do not within 21 days from the date of the deposit of the requisition proceed to convene a meeting, the requisitionists, or any one or more of them representing more than one half of the total voting rights of all of them, may themselves convene a meeting but any meeting so convened shall not be held after the expiration of three months from that date.

(5) A meeting convened under this section by a requisitionist or requisitionists shall be convened in the same manner, as nearly as possible, as that in which meetings are to be convened by directors.

(6) Any reasonable expenses incurred by the requisitionist or requisitionists by reason of the failure of the directors to convene a meeting, shall be repaid to the requisitionists by the company.

(7) For the purpose of this section, the directors are, in the case of a meeting at which a resolution is to be proposed as a special resolution, deemed not to have duly convened the meeting if they do not give such notice as is required by section 241 of this Act.

(8) All businesses transacted at an extraordinary general meeting are deemed special.

240.—(1) With the exception of small companies and companies having a single shareholder, all statutory and annual general meetings shall be held in Nigeria.

(2) A private company may hold its general meetings electronically provided that such meetings are conducted in accordance with the articles of the company.

NOTICE OF MEETINGS

241.—(1) The notice required for all types of general meetings is 21 days from the date on which the notice was sent out.

(2) A general meeting of a company, notwithstanding that it is called by a shorter notice than that specified in subsection (1), is deemed to have been duly called if it is so agreed in the case of—

(a) a meeting called as the annual general meeting, by all the members entitled to attend and vote ; and

(b) any other general meeting, by a majority in number of the members having a right to attend and vote at the meeting, being a majority together holding at least 95% in nominal value of the shares giving a right to attend and vote at the meeting or, in the case of a company not having a share capital, together representing at least 95% of the total voting rights at that meeting of all the members.

242.—(1) The notice of a meeting shall specify the place, date and time of the meeting, and the general nature of the business to be transacted in sufficient detail to enable those to whom it is given to decide whether to attend or not, and where the meeting is to consider a special resolution, set out the terms of the resolution.

(2) In the case of notice of an annual general meeting, a statement that the purpose is to transact the ordinary business of an annual general meeting is deemed to be a sufficient specification that the business is for the declaration of dividends, presentation of the financial statements, reports of the directors and auditors, the election of directors in the place of those retiring, fixing of the remuneration of the auditors, and, if the requirements of sections 409 and 410 of this Act are complied with, the removal and election of auditors and directors.

(3) No business may be transacted at any general meeting unless notice of it has been duly given.

(4) In every case in which a member is entitled, pursuant to section 254 of this Act, to appoint a proxy to attend and vote instead of him, the notice shall contain, a statement that a member has the right to appoint a proxy to attend and vote instead of him and that the proxy need not be a member of the company, and if default is made in complying with this subsection as respects any meeting, each officer of the company is liable to a penalty in such amount as the Commission shall specify in its regulations.

(5) An error or omission in a notice with respect to the place, date, time or general nature of the business of a meeting shall not invalidate the meeting, unless the officer of the company responsible for the error or omission acted in bad faith or failed to exercise care and diligence provided that in the case of accidental error or omission, the officer responsible shall effect the necessary correction either before or during the meeting.

243.—(1) The following persons are entitled to receive notice of a general meeting—

(a) every member ;

(b) every person upon whom the ownership of a share devolves by reason of his being a legal representative, receiver or a trustee in bankruptcy of a member ;

(c) every director of the company ;

(d) every auditor for the time being of the company ; and

(e) the secretary, and Commission in the case of public companies.

(2) No other person is entitled to receive notice of general meetings.

244.—(1) A notice may be given by the company to any member either personally or by sending it by post to him or to his registered address, or (if he has no registered address within Nigeria) to the address, supplied by him to the company for the giving of notice to him.

(2) Where a notice is sent by post, service of the notice is deemed to be effected by properly addressing, prepaying, and posting a letter containing the notice, and to

have been effected in the case of a notice of a meeting at the expiration of seven days after the letter containing the same is posted, and in any other case at the time at which the letter would be delivered in the ordinary course of post.

(3) In addition to the notice given personally or by post, notice may also be given by electronic mail to any member who has provided the company an electronic mail address.

(4) A notice may be given by the company to the joint holders of a share by giving the notice to the joint holder first named in the register of members in respect of the share.

(5) A notice may be given by the company to the persons entitled to a share in consequence of the death or bankruptcy of a member by sending it through the post in a prepaid letter addressed to them by name, or by the title of representatives of the deceased, or trustee of the bankrupt, or by any like description, at the address, if any, within Nigeria supplied for the purpose by the person claiming to be so entitled, or until such an address has been so supplied by giving the notice in any manner in which the same might have been given if the death or bankruptcy had not occurred.

(6) In this section, "registered address", means any address whether physical or electronic supplied by a member to the company.

245.—(1) Failure to give notice of any meeting to a person entitled to receive it invalidates the meeting unless such failure is an accidental omission on the part of the person giving the notice.

(2) Failure to give notice to a person entitled to it, due to a misrepresentation or misinterpretation of the provisions of this Act, or the articles, shall not amount to an accidental omission for the purposes of subsection (1).

246. In addition to the notice required to be given to those entitled to receive it in accordance with the provisions of this Act every public company shall, at least 21 days before any general meeting, advertise a notice of such meeting in at least two daily newspapers.

247.—(1) If for any reason it is impracticable to call a meeting of a company or of the board of directors in any manner in which meetings of that company or board may be called, or to conduct the meeting of the company or board in the manner prescribed by the articles or this Act, the Court may, either of its own motion or on the application of any director of the company or of any member of the company who would be entitled to vote at the meeting, in the case of the meeting of the company, and of any director of the company, in case of the meeting of the board, order a meeting of the company or board, as the case may be, to be called, held and conducted in such manner as the Court deems fit, and where any such order is made, may give such ancillary or consequential directions as it deems expedient.

(2) The directions that may be given under subsection (1) include a direction that one member of the company present in person or by proxy in the case of a meeting of the company, and one director in the case of the board may apply to the Court for an order to take a decision which shall bind all the members.

(3) Any meeting called, held and conducted in accordance with an order under subsection (1), is for all purposes deemed to be a meeting of the company or of the board of directors duly called, held and conducted.

VOTING

248.—(1) At any general meeting, a resolution put to the vote shall be decided on a show of hands, unless a poll is (before or on the declaration of the result of the show of hands) demanded by—

(a) the chairman, where he is a shareholder or a proxy ;

(b) at least three members present in person or by proxy ;

(c) a member or members present in person or by proxy and representing at least one tenth of the total voting rights of all the members having the right to vote at the meeting ; or

(d) any member or members holding shares in the company conferring a right to vote at the meeting being shares on which an aggregate sum has been paid up equal to at least one-tenth of the total sum paid up on all the shares conferring that right.

(2) Unless a poll is so demanded, a declaration by the chairman that a resolution has on a show of hands been carried unanimously or by a particular majority, or lost, and an entry to that effect in the book containing the minutes of the proceedings of the company, is a conclusive evidence of the fact, without proof of the number or proportion of the votes recorded in favour of, or against, the resolution.

249.—(1) Any provision contained in a company's articles is void if it would have the effect of—

(a) excluding the right to demand a poll at a general meeting on any question other than the election of the chairman of the meeting or the adjournment of the meeting ; or

(b) making ineffective a demand for a poll on any such question which is made by any of the persons mentioned in section 248 of this Act.

(2) The instrument appointing a proxy to vote at a meeting of a company is also deemed also to confer authority to demand or join in demanding a poll, and for the purposes of subsection (1), a demand by a person as proxy for a member is the same as a demand by the member.

(3) Notwithstanding section 248 of this Act and subsections (1) and (2) of this section, there shall be no right to demand a poll on the election of members of the audit committee under section 404 of this Act.

250.—(1) On a poll taken at a meeting of a company, or a meeting of any class of members of a company, a member entitled to more than one vote, if he votes, need not use all his votes or cast all the votes he uses in the same way.

(2) Except as provided in subsection (4), if a poll is duly demanded, it shall be taken in such manner as the chairman directs, and the result of the poll is deemed to be the resolution of the meeting at which the poll was demanded.

(3) In the case of an equality of votes, whether on a show of hands or on a poll, the chairman of the meeting at which the show of hands takes place or at which the poll is demanded, shall be entitled to a second or casting vote.

(4) A poll demanded on the election of a chairman or on a question of adjournment is taken immediately, and on any other question is taken at such time as the chairman of the meeting directs, and any business other than that upon which a poll has been demanded may be proceeded with pending the taking of the poll.

251.—(1) Subject to section 252 of this Act, every member has a right to attend any general meeting of the company in accordance with the provisions of section 107.

(2) In the case of joint holders, the vote of the senior joint holder who tenders a vote, whether in person or by proxy, shall be accepted to the exclusion of the votes of the

other joint holders, and for this purpose seniority is determined by the order in which the names stand in the register of members.

(3) A member of unsound mind, or in respect of whom an order has been made by any court having jurisdiction in lunacy, may vote, whether on a show of hands or on a poll, by his committee, receiver, *curator bonis*, or other person in the nature of a committee, receiver or *curator bonis* appointed by that court, and any such committee, receiver, *curator bonis* or other person may vote by proxy.

2 Every person who is entitled to receive notice of a general meeting of the company as provided under section 251 of this Act, is entitled to attend such a meeting.

3 No objection shall be raised to the qualification of any voter except at the meeting or adjourned meeting at which the vote objected to is given or tendered, and every vote not disallowed at such meeting is valid for all purposes and any such objection made in due time shall be referred to the chairman of the meeting, whose decision is final and conclusive.

254.—(1) Any member of a company entitled to attend and vote at a meeting of the company is entitled to appoint another person (whether a member or not) as his proxy to attend and vote instead of him, and a proxy appointed to attend and vote instead of a member has the same right as the member to speak at the meeting, and unless the articles provide, this section shall not apply in the case of a company not having a share capital.

(2) In every notice calling a meeting of a company having a share capital, there shall appear a statement that a member entitled to attend and vote is entitled to appoint a proxy or, where that is allowed, two or more proxies, to attend and vote instead of him, and that a proxy need not be a member and if default is made in complying with this subsection as respects any meeting, each officer of the company is liable to a penalty in such amount as the Commission shall specify in its regulations.

(3) Any provision contained in a company's articles is void in so far as it would have the effect of requiring the instrument appointing a proxy or any other document necessary to show the validity of the appointment of a proxy, to be received by the company or any other person more than 48 hours before a meeting or adjourned meeting in order that the appointment may be effective at the meeting.

(4) If, for the purpose of any meeting of a company, invitations to appoint as proxy a person or one of a number of persons specified in the invitations are issued at the company's expense only to some of the members entitled to receive notice of the meeting and to vote by proxy at the meeting, each officer of the company who authorises or permits their issue is liable to a penalty in such amount as the Commission shall specify in its regulations:

Provided that an officer is not liable under this subsection by reason only of the issue to a member at his request in writing of a form of appointment naming the proxy or a list of persons willing to act as proxy if the form or list is available on request in writing to every member entitled to vote at the meeting by proxy.

(5) A vote given in accordance with the terms of an instrument of proxy is valid notwithstanding the previous death, insanity of the principal, revocation of the proxy or of the authority under which the proxy was executed, the transfer of the share in respect of which the proxy is given, where no intimation in writing of such death, insanity, revocation or transfer is received by the company before the commencement of the meeting or adjourned meeting at which the proxy is used.

(6) The instrument appointing a proxy shall be in writing, under the handoff the appointer or his attorney duly authorised in writing and, if the appointer is a corporation, either by deed, or under the hand of an officer or attorney duly authorised.

(7) The instrument appointing a proxy and the power of attorney or other authority, under which it is signed or a certified copy of that power or authority is deposited at the registered office or head office of the company or at such other place within Nigeria as is specified for that purpose in the notice convening the meeting, at least 48 hours before the time for holding the meeting or adjourned meeting, at which the person named in the instrument proposes to vote, or, in the case of a poll, at least 24 hours before the time appointed for the taking of the poll, and if defaulted, the instrument of proxy shall not be treated as valid.

(8) This section applies to meetings of any class of members of a company as it applies to general meetings of the company.

255.—(1) A corporation, whether a company within the meaning of this Act or not, may if it is—

(a) a member of another corporation, being a company within the meaning of this Act, by resolution of its directors or other governing body, authorise such person as it deems fit to act as its representative at any meeting of the company or at any meeting of any class of members of the company ; or

(b) a creditor (including a holder of debentures) of another corporation, being a company within the meaning of this Act, by resolution of its directors or other governing body, authorise such person as it deems fit to act as its representative at any meeting of any creditors of the company held in pursuance of this Act or of any rule made thereunder or in pursuance of the provisions contained in any debenture or trust deed, as the case may be.

(2) A person authorised as provided in subsection (1), is entitled to exercise the same powers on behalf of the corporation which he represents as that corporation might exercise if it were an individual shareholder, creditor or holder of debentures of that other company.

256.—(1) Except in the case of a company with one member or provided in the articles, no business shall be transacted at any general meeting unless a quorum of members is present at the time when the meeting proceeds to business and throughout the meeting.

(2) Except in the case of a company with one member or provided in the articles, the quorum for the meeting of a company is one third of the total number of members of the company or 25 members (whichever is less) present in person or by proxy, but where the number of members is not a multiple of three, then the number nearest to one third, but where the number of members is six or less, the quorum is two members and for the purpose of determining a quorum, all members or their proxies shall be counted.

(3) Where a member withdraw from the meeting for what appears to the chairman to be insufficient reasons and for the purpose of reducing the quorum, and the quorum is no longer present, the meeting may continue with the number present, and their decision bind all the shareholders but where there is only one member, he may seek direction of the Court to take a decision.

(4) Where there is a quorum at the beginning, but no quorum later due to some shareholders leaving for what appears to the chairman to be sufficient reasons, the meeting shall be adjourned to the same place, and time, in a week's time, and if there is no quorum still at the adjourned meeting, the members present are then the quorum and their decision shall bind all shareholders and where only one member is present, he may seek direction of the Court to take a decision.

(2) A resolution is a special resolution when it has been passed by at least three-fourths of the votes cast by members of the company as, vote in person or by proxy at a general meeting of which 21 days' notice, specifying the intention to propose the resolution as a special resolution, has been duly given :

Provided that, if it is so agreed by majority in number of the members having the right to attend and vote at any such meeting, being a majority together holding at least 95% in nominal value of the shares giving that right or, in the case of a company not having a share capital, together representing at least 95% of the total voting rights at that meeting of all the members, a resolution may be proposed and passed as a special resolution at a meeting of which less than 21 days' notice has been given.

(3) At any meeting in which a special resolution is submitted to be passed, a declaration of the chairman that the resolution is carried is, unless a poll is demanded, conclusive evidence of the fact without proof of the number or proportion of the votes recorded in favour of or against the resolution.

(4) In computing the majority of a poll demanded on the question that a special resolution be passed, reference shall be had to the number of votes cast for and against the resolution.

(5) For the purposes of this section, notice of a meeting is deemed to be duly given and the meeting to be duly held when the notice is given and the meeting held in the manner provided by this Act or the articles.

(6) A company may, by its articles, provide that any matter not required by the articles or this Act to be passed by a special resolution, shall be passed by an ordinary resolution.

259. All resolutions shall be passed at general meetings and are not effective unless so passed, but in the case of a private company a written resolution signed by all the members entitled to attend and vote are as valid and effective as if passed in a general meeting.

260.—(1) Subject to provisions of this section, it is the duty of a company, on the requisition in writing of such number of members as specified in this section and (unless the company otherwise resolves) at the expense of the company to—

(a) give to members of the company entitled to receive notice of the next annual general meeting notice of any resolution submitted by a member which may properly be moved and is intended to be moved at that meeting ; and

(b) circulate to members entitled to receive notice of general meeting any statement of not more than 1,000 words with respect to the matter referred to in any proposed resolution or the business to be dealt with at that meeting, and where the statement has more than 1,000 words to circulate a summary of it.

(2) The number of members necessary for a requisition under subsection (1) shall be—

(a) any one or more members representing at least one-twentieth of the total voting right of all the members having at the date of the requisition a right to vote at the meeting to which the requisition relates ; or

(b) at least 100 members holding shares in the company on which there has been paid up an average sum, per member, of at least ₦500.

(3) Notice of any such resolution shall be given, and any such statement shall be circulated, to members of the company entitled to receive notice of the meeting, by serving a copy of the resolution or statement on each such member in any manner permitted for service of notice of the meeting, and notice of such resolution is given to any other member of the company by giving notice of the general effect of the resolution in any manner permitted for giving notice of meetings of the company:

Provided that the copy is served, or notice of the effect of the resolution is given, as the case may be, in the same manner and at the same time as notice of the meeting and, where it is not practicable for it to be served or given at that time, it shall be served or given as soon as practicable.

(4) A company is not bound under this section to give notice of any resolution or to circulate any statement unless—

(a) a copy of the requisition signed by the requisitionists (two or more copies which between them contain the signatures of all the requisitionists) is deposited at the registered office of the company—

(i) in the case of a requisition requiring notice of a resolution, at least six weeks before the meeting, and

(ii) in the case of any other requisition, at least one week before the meeting ; and

(b) there is deposited or tendered with the requisition, a sum reasonably sufficient to meet the company's expenses in giving effect to it, but if, after a copy of a requisition requiring notice of a resolution has been deposited at the registered office of the company, an annual general meeting is called for a date six weeks or less, the copy, though not deposited within the time required by this subsection, is deemed to have been properly deposited for that purposes.

(5) The company is also not bound under this section to circulate any statement if, on the application of the company or any other person who claims to be aggrieved, the court is satisfied that the rights conferred by this section are being abused to secure needless publicity for defamatory matter, and the Court may order the company's costs on an application under this section to be paid in whole or in part by the requisitionist, notwithstanding that the requisitionist is not party to the application.

(6) Notwithstanding anything in the company's articles, the business which may be dealt with at an annual general meeting includes any resolution of which notice is given in accordance with this section and for purposes of this subsection, notice is deemed to have been given, notwithstanding the accidental omission in giving it to one or more members.

(7) Where there is default in complying with the provisions of this section, each officer of the company is liable to a penalty in such amount as the Commission shall specify in its regulations.

261. Where by any provision contained in this Act, special notice is required of a resolution, the resolution is not effective unless notice of the intention to move it has been given to the company at least 28 days before the meeting at which it is to be moved, and the company shall give its members notice of any such resolution at the same time and in the same manner as it gives notice of the meeting, or if that is not practicable, shall give them notice thereof, either by advertisement in a newspaper having an appropriate circulation, or in any other mode allowed by the articles, at least 21 days before the meeting:

Provided that if, after notice of the intention to move such a resolution has been given to the company, a meeting is called for a date 28 days or less after the notice has been given, the notice, though not given within the time required by this section, is deemed to have been properly given.

262.—(1) Subject to section 51 (7) (*b*) of this Act, a printed copy of every resolution or agreement to which this section applies shall, within 15 days after the passing or making of the resolution or agreement, be forwarded to the Commission.

(2) Where, pursuant to the provisions of sections 49-52 of this Act, a company by special resolution alters the provisions of its memorandum and the Commission is satisfied that the alteration is not in compliance with the applicable provisions of those sections, it may refuse to file a copy of the resolution in its records and shall notify the company, and any person aggrieved by the refusal may appeal to the court within 21 days from the receipt of the notification.

(3) A copy of every such resolution or agreement shall be embodied inor annexed to every copy of the articles issued after the passing of the resolution or making of the agreement.

(4) This section applies to—

(a) special resolutions ;

(b) resolutions which have been agreed to by all the members of a company, but which, if not so agreed to, would not have been effective, unless they had been passed as special resolution ;

(c) resolutions or agreements which have been agreed to by all the members of any class of shareholders but which, if not so agreed to, would not have been effective, unless they had been passed by some particular majority or in some particular manner, and all resolutions or agreements which effectively bind all the members of any class of shareholders though not agreed to by all those members ; and

(d) resolutions requiring a company to be wound up voluntarily, passed under section 620 (1) (a) of this Act.

(5) If a company fails to comply with subsection (1), the company and each officer of the company are liable to a penalty in such amount as the Commission shall specify in its regulations.

(6) If a company fails to comply with subsection (3), the company and each officer of the company are liable to a penalty for each copy in respect of which default is made in such amount as the Commission shall specify in its regulations.

(7) For the purposes of subsections (5) and (6), a liquidator is deemed to be an officer of the company.

263. Where a resolution is passed at an adjourned meeting of—

(a) a company,

(b) the holders of any class of shares in a company, or

(c) the directors of a company, the resolution shall, for all purposes be treated as having been passed on the date on which it was in fact passed, and not be deemed to have been passed on any earlier date.

MISCELLANEOUS MATTERS RELATING TO MEETINGS AND PROCEEDING

264.—(1) The chairman may, with the consent of any meeting at which a quorum is present (and shall if so directed by the meeting), adjourn the meeting from time to time and place to place, but no business shall be transacted at any adjourned meeting other than the business left unfinished at the meeting from which the adjournment took place.

(2) When a meeting is adjourned for 30 days or more, notice of the adjourned meeting and the business to be transacted shall be given as in the case of an original meeting, but if otherwise it shall not be necessary to give any notice of an adjournment or of the business to be transacted at an adjourned meeting.

(3) If within one hour from the time appointed for the meeting a quorum is not present, the meeting if convened upon the requisition of members shall be dissolved, but in any other case, it shall stand adjourned to the same day in the next week, at the same time and place or to such other day and at such other time and place as the chairman, and in his absence the directors, may direct.

(4) If a meeting stands adjourned under subsection (3) any two or more members present at the place and time to which it so stands adjourned shall form a quorum and their decision shall bind all shareholders, and where only one member is present, he may seek the direction of the Court to take a decision.

(5) The provisions of this section do not apply to a company with one member.

265.—(1) The chairman, of the board of directors shall preside as chairman at every general meeting of the company, and if there is no such chairman, if he is not present within one hour after the time appointed for the holding of the meeting or is unwilling to act, the directors present shall elect one among themselves to be chairman of the meeting.

(2) If at any meeting no director is willing to act as chairman or no director is present within one hour after the time appointed for holding the meeting, the members present shall choose one among themselves to be chairman of the meeting.

(3) The duties and powers of the chairman includes a duty to—

(a) preserve order and power to take such measures as are reasonably necessary to do so ;

(b) see that proceedings are conducted in a regular manner ;

(c) ensure that the true intention of the meeting is carried out in resolving any issue that arises before it ;

(d) ensure that all questions that arise are promptly decided ; and(*e*) act in the interest of the company.

(4) The Chairman shall cast his vote in the interest of the company as a whole, but if he is a shareholder, he may cast it in his own interest.

(5) The Chairman has power to adjourn a meeting in accordance with section 264 (1) of this Act.

(6) The chairman of a public company shall not act as the chief executive officer of such company.

266.—(1) With the exception of a company having a single member, every company shall cause minutes of all proceedings—

(a) of general meetings,

(b) at meetings of its directors, and

(c) at meetings of its managers, to be entered in books kept for that purpose.

(2) Any such minute if purported to be signed by the chairman of the meeting at which the proceedings were held, or by the chairman of the next succeeding meeting, is *prima facie* evidence of the proceedings.

(3) Where minutes have been made, in accordance with the provisions of this section, of the proceedings at any general meeting of the company, meeting of directors or managers, then, until the contrary is proved, the meeting is deemed to have been duly held and convened, and all proceedings had at the meeting to have been duly had, and all appointments of directors, managers or liquidators are deemed to be valid.

(4) In the case of a company that has only one member—(*a*) where that single member takes any decision that—

(i) may be taken by the company in general meetings, and

(ii) has effect as if agreed by the company in general meeting, he shall provide the board with details of that decision ; and

(*b*) if a person fails to comply with this section he commits an offence and is liable to a penalty for each day the default continues in such amount as the Commission shall specify in its regulations, and failure to comply with this section does not affect the validity of any decision taken by that single member.

(5) If a company fails to comply with subsection (1), the company and every officer of the company are liable to a penalty for every day the default continues in such amount as the Commission shall specify in its regulations.

267.—(1) The books containing the minutes of proceedings of any general meeting of a company held on or after the commencement of this Act, shall be kept at the registered office of the company, and shall during business hours (subject to such reasonable restrictions as the company may by its articles or in general meeting impose, but so that at least six hours in each day be allowed for inspection) be open to inspection by members without charge.

(2) Any member is entitled to be furnished within seven days after receipt of his request in that behalf to the company, with a copy of any such minutes certified by the secretary at a charge not exceeding ₦100 for every page.

(3) If any inspection required under this section is refused or if any copy required under this section is not sent within required time, the company and every officer of the company are liable in respect of each default to a penalty in such amount as the Commission shall specify in its regulations.

(4) In the case of any such refusal or default, the Court may by order compel an immediate inspection of the books in respect of all proceedings of general meetings, or direct that the copies required be sent to the person requiring them.

where expressly excluded by this Act.

CHAPTER 11—DIRECTORS

269.—(1) A Director of a company registered under this Act is a person duly appointed by the company to direct and manage the business of the company.

(2) There is a rebuttable presumption in favour of any person dealing with the company that all persons who are described by the company as directors, whether as executive or otherwise, is duly appointed.

(3) Where a person not duly appointed acts or holds himself out as a director, he commits an offence and is liable on conviction to imprisonment for a term of two years or a fine as the Court deems fit for each day he so acts or holds out himself as a director or both and shall be restrained by the company.

(4) If it is the company that holds him out as a director, it is liable to a fine in such amount as the Commission shall specify in its regulations for each day it holds him

out, and he and the company may be restrained by any member from so acting until he is duly appointed.

270.—(1) Without prejudice to the provisions of sections 269 and 276 of this Act, and for the purposes of sections 279, 301 and 307 of this Act, "director" shall include any person on whose instructions and directions the Directors are accustomed to act.

(2) Subject to sections 301, 306 and 307 of this Act, nothing contained in section 276 of this Act is deemed to derogate from the duties or liabilities of the duly appointed directors.

(3) Where a person in his professional capacity gives advice and a director acts on it , that shall not be construed to make such a person under this Act a person in accordance with whose directions or instructions the director of a company is accustomed to act.

APPOINTMENT OF DIRECTORS

271.—(1) Every company, not being a small, company shall have at least two directors.

(2) Subject to subsection (1), any company whose number of directors falls below two shall, within one month of its so falling, appoint new directors and shall not carry on business after the expiration of one month, unless such new directors are appointed.

(3) A director or member of a company, not being a small company, who knows that a company carries on business after the number of directors has fallen below two for more than 60 days is liable for all liabilities and debts incurred by the company during that period when the company so carried on business.

272. Subject to section 271 of this Act, the number of directors and the names of the first directors shall be determined in writing by the subscribers of the memorandum of association or a majority of them or the directors may be named in the articles.

273.—(1) The members at the annual general meeting may re-elect or reject directors and appoint new ones.

(2) In the event of all the directors and shareholders dying, any of the personal representatives apply to the Court for an order to convene a meeting of all the personal representatives of the shareholders entitled to attend and vote at a general meeting to appoint new directors to manage the company, and if they fail to convene a meeting, the creditors, if any, may do so.

274.—(1) The Board of directors may appoint new directors to fill any casual vacancy arising out of death, resignation, retirement or removal.

(2) Where a casual vacancy is filled by the directors, the person may be approved by the general meeting at the next annual general meeting, and if not so approved, he shall immediately cease to be a director.

(3) The directors may increase the number of directors if it does not exceed the maximum allowed by the articles, but the general meeting may increase or reduce the number of directors generally, and may determine in what rotation the directors shall retire, provided that such reduction shall not invalidate any prior act of the removed director.

275.—(1) A public company shall have at least three independent directors.

(2) In a public company, any person who nominates candidates for the board who would comprise a majority of the members of the board shall nominate at least three persons who would be independent directors.

(3) In this section, "independent director" means a director of the company who, or whose relatives either separately or together with him or each other, during the two years preceding the time in question—

(a) was not an employee of the company ;

(b) did not—

(i) make to or receive from the company payments of more than₦20,000,000, or

(ii) own more than a 30% share or other ownership interest, directly or indirectly, in an entity that made to or received from the company payments of more than the amount stated in subparagraph (*i*) or act as a partner, director or officer of a partnership or company that made to or received from the company payments of more than such amount ;

(c) did not own directly or indirectly more than 30% of the shares of any type or class of the company, and

(d) was not engaged directly or indirectly as an auditor for the company.

276. Where a person not duly appointed as a director acts as such on behalf of the company, his act does not bind the company and he is personally liable for such action, but where it is the company which holds him out as director, the company is bound by his acts.

277.—(1) The shareholding qualification for directors may be fixed by the articles of association of the company and unless so fixed no shareholding qualification shall be required.

(2) It is the duty of every director who is by the articles of the company required to hold a specified share qualification, and who is not already so qualified, to obtain qualification within two months after his appointment.

(3) The office of director of a company is vacated if the director does not, within two months from the date of his appointment, obtain his qualification or after the expiration of the said period, he ceases at any time to hold his shareholding qualification.

(4) A person vacating office under this section is incapable of being reappointed a director of the company until he has obtained his shareholding qualification.

(5) If, after the expiration of the period, any unqualified person acts as a director of the company, he is liable to a penalty in such amount as the Commission shall specify in its regulations for every day between the expiration of the said period or the day on which he ceased to be qualified, as the case may be, and the last day on which it is proved that he acted as a director.

278.—(1) Any person who is appointed or to his knowledge proposed to be appointed director of a public company and who is 70 or more years old shall disclose this fact to the members at the general meeting.

(2) Any person who is proposed to be appointed a director of a public company shall disclose any position he holds as a director in any other public company at the meeting in which he is proposed for appointment as a director.

(3) Any person who fails to disclose his age or multiple directorship as required under this section shall, without prejudice to the provisions of section 307 (4) of this Act, be liable to a penalty in such amount as the Commission shall specify in its regulations.

279.—(1) If any person, being an insolvent person, acts as director of or directly or indirectly takes part in, or is concerned in the management of any company, he commits an offence and is liable on conviction to a fine as the Court deems fit, or imprisonment for a term of at least six months but not more than two years, or both.

(2) In this section, "company" includes an unregistered company.

280.—(1) Where—

(a) a person is convicted by a High Court of any offence in connection with the promotion, formation or management of a company, or

(b) in the course of winding-up a company, it appears that a person—

(i) has been guilty of any offence for which he is liable (whether he has been convicted or not) under sections 668-670 of this Act, or has been guilty of any offence involving fraud, the court shall make an order that that person shall not be a director of or in any way, whether directly or indirectly, be concerned or take part in the management of a company for a specified period not exceeding 10 years.

(2) The period of disqualification referred to in subsection (1) shall commence after the sentence for the offence has been served or on the date the fine for the offence is paid.

(3) In this section, the "High Court and the court", where used in relation to the making of an order against any person by virtue of subsection (1) (*a*), includes the court before which he is convicted, as well as any court having jurisdiction to wind up the company, and in relation to the granting of leave means any court having jurisdiction to wind up the company as respects which leave is sought.

(4) A person intending to apply for the making of an order under this section by the court having jurisdiction to wind-up a company shall give at least 10 days' notice of his intention to the person against whom the order is sought, and on the hearing of the application, the last mentioned person may appear in person and give evidence or call witnesses.

(5) An application for the making of an order under this section by the court having jurisdiction to wind-up a company, may be made by the official receiver, the liquidator of the company or person who is or has been a member or creditor of the company, and on the hearing of any application for an order under this section by the official receiver or the liquidator, or of any application for leave under this section by a person against whom an order has been made on the application of the official receiver or liquidator, the official receiver or liquidator shall appear and call the attention of the court to any matter which seem to him to be relevant, and may himself give evidence or call witnesses.

(6) An order may be made by virtue of subsection (1) (*b*) (*ii*), notwithstanding that the person concerned may be criminally liable in respect of the matters on the ground of which the order is to be made, and for the purposes of the said paragraph (*b*) (*ii*), "*officer*" includes any person in accordance with whose directions or instructions the directors of the company have been accustomed to act.

(7) If any person acts in contravention of an order made under this section, he commits an offence and in respect of each offence, is liable on conviction to a fine as the Court deems fit or to imprisonment for a term of at least six months or more than two years, or both.

281. A person may be appointed a director for life provided that he shall be removable under section 288 of this Act.

282. Subject to the provisions of this Act, a person may be appointed a director of a public company notwithstanding that he is 70 years or more of age but special notice shall be required of any resolution appointing or approving the appointment of such a director for the purposes of this section, and the notice given to the company and by the company to its members shall state the age of the person to whom it relates.

283. The following persons shall be disqualified from being director—

(a) an infant, that is, a person under the age of 18 years ;

(b) a lunatic or person of unsound mind ;

(c) a person suspended or removed under section 288 of this Act ;

(d) a person disqualified under sections 279, 280, 284 of this Act ; and

(e) a corporation other than its representative appointed to the board fora given term.

284.—(1) The office of director shall be vacated if the director—

(a) ceases to be a director by virtue of section 277 of this Act ;

(b) becomes bankrupt or makes any arrangement or composition with his creditors ;

(c) becomes prohibited from being a director by reason of any order made under sections 280-281 of this Act ;

(d) becomes of unsound mind ; or

(e) resigns his office by notice in writing to the company.

(2) Where a director presents himself for re-election, a record of his attendance at the meetings of the board during the preceding one year shall be made available to members at the general meeting where he is to be re-elected.

285.–(1) Unless the articles provide, at the first annual general meeting of the company all the directors shall retire from office, and at the annual general meeting in every subsequent year one third of the directors or if their number is not three or a multiple of three, then the number nearest one-third shall retire from office.

(2) The directors to retire in every year are those who have been longest in office since their last election, but as between persons who became directors on the same day those to retire are (unless they agree among themselves) determined by lot.

(3) The company at the meeting at which a director retires in the manner mentioned in subsections (1) and (2), may fill the vacated office by electing a person to that office and in default, the retiring director is, if offering himself for re-election, deemed to have been re-elected, unless at such meeting it is expressly resolved not to fill such vacated office or unless a resolution for the re-election of such director have been put to the meeting and lost.

(4) No person other than a director retiring at the meeting is, unless recommended by the directors, eligible for election to the office of director at any general meeting unless not less than three nor more than 21 days before the date appointed for the meeting there shall have been left at the registered office or head office of the company notice in writing, signed by a member duly qualified to attend and vote at the meeting for which such notice is given, of his intention to propose such person for election, and also notice in writing signed by that person of his willingness to be elected.

286. The acts of a director, manager, or secretary are valid notwithstanding any defect that may afterwards be discovered in his appointment or qualification.

287.—(1) At a general meeting of a company other than a private company, a motion for the appointment of two or more persons as directors of the company by a single resolution shall not be made, unless resolution that it shall be made has first been agreed to by the meeting without any vote being given against it.

(2) A resolution moved in contravention of this section is void, whether or not its being so moved was objected to at the time :

Provided that—

(a) this subsection shall not be taken as excluding the operation of section286 of this Act ; and

(b) where a resolution so moved is passed, no provision for automatic-appointment of retiring directors in default of another appointment applies.

(3) For the purposes of this section, a motion for approving a person's appointment or for nominating a person for appointment is treated as a motion for his appointment.

(4) Nothing in this section applies to a resolution altering the company's articles.

REMOVAL OF DIRECTORS

Removal of directors. **288.**—(1) A company may by ordinary resolution remove a director before the expiration of his period of office, notwithstanding anything in its articles or in any agreement between the company and him.

(2) A special notice is required of any resolution to remove a director under this section, or to appoint some other person instead of a director so removed, at the meeting at which he is removed, and on receipt of notice of an intended resolution to remove a director under this section, the company shall immediately send a copy of the notice to the director concerned and (whether or not he is a member of the company) and is entitled to be heard on the resolution at the meeting.

(3) Where notice is given of an intended resolution to remove a director under this section and the director concerned makes, with respect to it, representations in writing to the company (not exceeding a reasonable length) and requests their notification to members of the company, the company shall, unless the representations are received by it too late for it to do so—

(a) in any notice of the resolution given to members of the company, state the fact of the representations having been made ; and

(b) send a copy of the representations to every member of the company to whom notice of the meeting is sent (whether before or after receipt of the representations by the company), and if a copy of the representations is not sent as required in this section because it is received too late or because of the company's default, the director may (without prejudice to his right to be heard orally) require that the representations are read out at the meeting :

Provided that copies of the representations need not be sent out and the representations need not be read out at the meeting if, on the application either of the company or any other person who claims to be aggrieved, the court is satisfied that the rights conferred by this section are being abused to secure needless publicity for defamatory matter and the court may order the company's costs on an application under this section to be paid in whole or in part by the director, notwithstanding that he is not a party to the application.

(4) A vacancy created by the removal of a director under this section, if not filled at the meeting at which he is removed, may be filled as a casual vacancy.

(5) A person appointed director in place of a person removed under this section is treated, for the purpose of determining the time at which he or any other director is

to retire, as if he had become director on the day on which the person in whose place he is appointed was last appointed a director.

(6) Nothing in this section is taken as depriving a person removed under it of compensation or damages payable to him in respect of the termination of his appointment as a director or of any appointment terminating with that as director, or as derogating from any power to remove a director which may exist apart from this section.

PROCEEDINGS OF DIRECTORS

289.—(1) The directors may meet together for the dispatch of business, Proceedings adjourn and otherwise regulate their meetings as they think fit, and the first of directors. meeting of the directors shall be held not later than six months after the incorporation of the company.

(2) Unless the articles provide otherwise, any question arising at any meeting is decided by a simple majority of votes, and in case of an equality of votes, the chairman has a second or casting vote.

(3) A director may, and the secretary on the requisition of a director shall, at any time summon a meeting of the directors.

(4) The directors may elect a chairman of their meetings and determine the period for which he is to hold office, but if no such chairman is elected or if at any meeting the chairman is not present within five minutes after the time appointed for holding same, the directors present may choose one of them to be chairman of the meeting.

(5) The directors may delegate any of their powers to a managing director or to committees consisting of such member or members of their body as they think fit and the managing director or any committee so formed shall, in the exercise of the powers so delegated, conform to any regulations that may be made by the directors.

(6) A committee may elect a chairman of its meeting, and if no such chairman is elected, or if at any meeting the chairman is not present within five minutes after the time appointed for holding the same, the members present may choose one of them to be chairman of the meeting.

(7) A committee may meet and adjourn as it deems proper, and any question arising is determined by a majority of votes of the members present, and in the case of equality of votes the chairman has a second or casting vote.

(8) A resolution in writing, signed by all the directors for the time being entitled to receive notice of a meeting of the directors, is as valid and effectual as if it had been passed at a meeting of the directors duly convened and held. (9) In all the directors' meetings, each director is entitled to one vote.

290.—(1) Unless the articles provide otherwise, the quorum necessary for the transaction of the business of directors are two where there are not more than six directors, but where there are more than six directors, the quorum is one-third of the number of directors, and where the number of directors is not a multiple of three, then the quorum is one third to the nearest number.

(2) Where a committee of directors is appointed by the board of directors, the board shall fix its quorum, but where no quorum is fixed, the whole committee shall meet and act by a majority.

291. Where the board is unable to act because a quorum cannot be formed, the general meeting may act in place of the board and where a committee is unable to act because a quorum cannot be formed, the board may act in place of the committee.

292.—(1) Every director is entitled to receive notice of the directors' meetings, unless he is disqualified by any reason under the Act from continuing with the office of director.

(2) There shall be given 14 days' notice in writing to all directors entitled to receive notice unless provided in the articles.

(3) Failure to give notice in accordance with subsection (2) invalidates the meeting.

(4) Unless the articles provide otherwise, it is not necessary to give notice of a meeting of directors to any director absent from Nigeria, but if he has given an address in Nigeria, the notice shall be sent to such an address.

REMUNERATION AND OTHER PAYMENTS

293.—(1) The remuneration of the directors is determined by the company in general meeting and such remuneration is deemed to accrue from day-to-day.

(2) The directors may also be paid travelling, hotel and other expenses properly incurred by them in attending and returning from meetings of the directors, committee of the directors, general meetings of the company or in connection with the business of the company.

(3) Where remuneration has been fixed by the articles, it is alterable only by a special resolution.

(4) A company is not bound to pay remuneration to directors, but where the company agrees to pay, the directors shall be paid such remuneration out of the fund of the company.

(5) The amount of remuneration is a debt from the company so that if directors take office on the basis of the articles, they shall be able to sue the company on account of the debt or prove it in liquidation.

(6) A director who receives more money than he is entitled to, is guilty of misfeasance and is accountable to the company for such money.

(7) The remunerations of directors is apportionable.

294.—(1) A managing director receives such remuneration (whether by way of salary, commission, participation in profits, or partly in one way and in another) as the directors may determine.

(2) Where a managing director is removed for any reason under section 288 of this Act, he may claim for breach of contract if there is any or where a contract could be inferred from the terms of the articles.

(3) Where he performs some services without a contract, he is entitled to payment on a *quantum merit.*

295.—(1) It is not lawful for a company to pay a director remuneration (whether as director or otherwise) free of income tax, or calculated by reference to or varying with the amount of his income tax, or at or with the rate or standard rate of income tax, except under a contract which was in effect at the commencement of this Act, and provides expressly, and not by reference to the articles, for payment or remuneration.

(2) Any provision contained in a company's articles or in any contract other than such a contract as mentioned in subsection (1), or in any resolution of a company or of a company's directors for payment to a director of remuneration as mentioned in subsection (1), shall have effect as if it provided for payment, as a gross sum subject to income tax, of the net sum for which it actually provides.

(3) This section does not apply to remuneration due before this Act comes into effect or in respect of a period before it comes into effect.

296.—(1) It is not lawful for a company to make a loan to any person who is its director or a director of its holding company, or to enter into any guarantee or provide any security in connection with a loan made to such a person as earlier mentioned by any other person :

Provided that nothing in this section applies—

(a) subject to subsection (2), to anything done to provide any such person as mentioned in this subsection with funds to meet expenditure incurred or to be incurred by him for the purposes of the company or for the purpose of enabling him to properly discharge his duties as an officer of the company ; or

(b) in the case of a company whose ordinary business includes the lending of money or the giving of guarantees in connection with loans made by other persons, to anything done by the company in the ordinary course of that business.

(2) Subsection (1)(*a*) does not authorise the making of any loan, or the entering into any guarantee, or the provision of any security except—

(a) with the prior approval of the company given at a general meeting at which the purposes of the expenditure, the amount of the loan or the extent of the guarantee or security, are disclosed ; or

(b) on condition that, if the approval of the company is not given as in subsection (2)(*a*) at or before the next annual general meeting, the loan shall be repaid or the liability under the guarantee or security shall be discharged, within six months from the conclusion of that meeting.

(3) Where the approval of the company is not given as required by any such condition, the directors authorising the making of the loan, the entering into the guarantee or the provision of the security, are jointly and severally liable to indemnify the company against any loss arising from it.

297. A company shall not make to any director of the company any payment by way of compensation for loss of office, or as consideration for or in connection with his retirement from office, unless particulars with respect to the proposed payment and the amount have been disclosed to members of the company and the proposal is approved by the company.

298.—(1) If in connection with the transfer of the whole, or any part of the undertaking or property of a company, it is proposed to make any payment to a director of the company by way of compensation for loss of office, or as consideration for or, in connection with his retirement from office, the payment is unlawful unless particulars with respect to the proposal and the amount have been disclosed to members of the company and the proposal is approved by the company.

(2) Where a payment declared by this section to be illegal is made to a director of a company, the amount received is deemed to have been received by him in trust for the company.

299.—(1) Where, in connection with the transfer to any person of all or any of the shares in a company, being a transfer resulting from—

(a) an offer made to the general body of shareholders,

(b) an offer made by or on behalf of some other body corporate with a view to the company becoming its subsidiary or a subsidiary of its holding company,

(c) an offer made by or on behalf of an individual with a view to his obtaining the right to exercise or control the exercise of at least one-third of the voting power at any general meeting of the company, or

(d) any other offer which is conditional on acceptance to a given extent payment is to be made to a director of the company by way of compensation for loss of office, or as consideration for or in connection with his retirement from office, it is the duty of that director to do all things reasonably necessary to secure that particulars with respect to the proposed payment and the amount, are included in or sent with any notice of the offer made for their shares which is given to any shareholder.

(2) If—

(a) any such director fails to do all things reasonably necessary as mentioned in this section, or

(b) any person who has been properly required by any such director to include the said particulars in or send them with any such notice fails so to do, he is liable to a penalty in such amount as the Commission shall specify in its regulations.

(3) If—

(a) the requirements of subsection (1) of this section are not complied with in relation to any such payments ; or

(b) the making of the proposed payment is not, before the transfer of any share in pursuance of the offer, approved by a meeting summoned for the purpose of the holders of the shares to which the offer relates and of other holders of shares of the same class as any of the said shares, any sum received by the director on account of the payment is deemed to have been received by him in trust for any person who has sold his shares as a result of the offer made, and the expenses incurred by him in distributing that sum amongst those persons shall be borne by him and not retained out of that sum.

(4) Where the shareholders referred to in subsection (3) (*b*) are not all the members of the company and no provision is made by the articles for summoning or regulating such a meeting as is mentioned in that paragraph, the provisions of this Act and of the company's articles relating to general meetings of the company, for that purpose, apply to the meeting either without modification or with such modification as the Commission on the application of any person concerned may direct for the purpose of adapting them to the circumstances of the meeting.

(5) If at a meeting summoned for the purpose of approving any payment as required by subsection (3) (*a*), a quorum is not present and, after the meeting has been adjourned to a later date, a quorum is again not present, the payment is, for the purposes of that subsection be deemed to have been approved.

300.—(1) Where, in proceedings for the recovery of any payment which has been received by any person in trust by virtue of section 298 and 299 (1) and (3) of this Act, it is shown that—

(a) the payment was made in pursuance of any arrangement entered into as part of the agreement for the transfer in question, or within one year but before two years after that agreement or the offer leading thereto ; and

(b) the company or any person to whom the transfer was made was privy to that arrangement, the payment is deemed, except in so far as the contrary is shown, to be one to which the subsections apply.

(2) If in connection with any such transfer mentioned in sections 298 and 299 of this Act—

(a) the price to be paid for any share held by a director of the company whose office is to be abolished or who is to retire from office in the company held by him is in excess of the price obtainable at the time by other holders of the like shares ; or

(b) any valuable consideration is given to any such director, the excess or the money value of the consideration, as the case may be, shall, for the purposes of that section, be deemed to have been a payment made to him by way of compensation for loss of office, or as consideration for or in connection with his retirement from office.

(3) References in sections 297-299 of this Act to payments made to any director of a company by way of compensation for loss of office or as consideration for or in connection with his retirement from office does not include any *bona fide* payment by way of damages for breach of contract or by way of pension in respect of past services and for the purposes of this subsection, "pension" includes any superannuation allowance, superannuation gratuity or similar payment.

(4) Nothing in section 298 or 299 of this Act shall be taken to prejudice the operation of any rule of law requiring disclosure to be made with respect to any such payments as are mentioned there, or with respect to any other like payments made, or to be made, to the directors of a company.

DISCLOSURE OF DIRECTORS' INTERESTS

301.—(1) Every company shall keep a register showing as respects each director of the company (not being its holding company) the number, description and amount of shares in, debentures of the company or any other body corporate, being the company's subsidiary, holding company, or a subsidiary of the company's holding company, which are held by or in trust for him or of which he has any right to become the holder: Provided that the register need not include shares in anybody corporate which is the wholly owned subsidiary of another body corporate, and for this purpose, a body corporate is wholly-owned subsidiary of another if it has no members but that other and that other's wholly-owned subsidiaries and its or their nominees.

(2) Where any share or debenture fail to be or cease to be recorded in the said register in relation to any director by reason of a transaction entered into after the commencement of this Act and while he is a director, the register shall also show the date of, and price or other consideration for the transaction: Provided that where there is an interval between the agreement for any such transaction and the completion thereof, the date is that of the agreement.

(3) The nature and extent of a director's interest or right in or overshares or debentures recorded in relation to him in the said register shall, if he so requires, be indicated in the register.

(4) The company shall not by virtue of anything done for the purposes of this section, be affected with notice of, or put upon inquiry as to the rights of any person in relation to shares or debentures.

(5) The said register shall, subject to the provisions of this section, bekept at the company's registered or head office and be open to inspection during business hours (subject to such reasonable restrictions as the company may by its articles or in general meeting impose, so that at least two hours in each day be allowed for inspection)—

(a) during the period beginning 14 days before the date of the company's annual general meeting and ending three days after the date of its conclusion, it shall be open to the inspection of any member or holder of debentures of the company ; and

(b) during that or any other period, it shall be open to the inspection of any person acting on behalf of the Commission.

(6) In computing the 14 days and the three days mentioned in subsection (5), any day which is a Saturday, Sunday or a public holiday is disregarded.

(7) Without prejudice to the rights conferred by subsection (5), the Commission may, at any time, request for the production to it of a copy of the register, or any part thereof.

(8) The register shall also be produced at the commencement of the company's annual general meeting and remain open and accessible during the continuance of the meeting to any person attending the meeting.

(9) If default is made in complying with subsection (1) or (2), or if any inspection required under this section is refused, or any copy required is not sent within a reasonable time, the company and each officer of the company are liable to a penalty in such amount as the Commission shall specify in its regulations, and if default is made in complying with subsection (8), the company and every officer of the company are liable to a penalty in such amount as the Commission shall specify in its regulations.

(10) If any inspection required under this section is refused, the Court may, by order, compel an immediate inspection of the register.

(11) For the purposes of this section—

(a) any person, in accordance with whose directions or instructions the directors of a company are accustomed to act, is deemed to be a director of the company ; and

(b) a director of a company is deemed to hold or to have any interest or right in or over, any share or debenture, if a permanent representative of the body corporate other than the company holds them or has that interest or right in or over them, and either—

(i) that permanent representative is accustomed to act in accordance with his directions or instructions, or

(ii) he is entitled to exercise or control the exercise of one third or more of the voting power at any general meeting of that body corporate.

302.—(1) It is the duty of any director of a company to give notice to the company of such matters relating to himself as may be necessary for the purposes of sections 301 and 303 of this Act except so far as it relates to loans made by the company or by any other person under a guarantee from or on a security provided by the company, to an officer.

(2) Any notice given for the purposes of this section, shall be in writing and if it is not given at a meeting of the directors, the director giving it shall do all things reasonably necessary to secure that it is brought up and read at the next meeting of directors after it is given.

(3) Subsection (1) shall, to the extent to which it applies in relation to directors, apply to the like extent for the purposes of—

(a) section 303 of this Act in relation to officers other than directors, and

(b) section 303 of this Act in relation to persons who are or have at anytime during the preceding five years been officers of the company.

(4) Any person who makes default in complying with the provisions of this section is liable to a penalty in such amount as the Commission shall specify in its regulations.

303.—(1) Subject to the provisions of this section, it is the duty of a director of a company who is in any way, whether directly or indirectly, interested in a transaction or a proposed transaction with the company, to immediately notify the directors of such company in writing, specifying particulars of the director's interest.

(2) For the purpose of this section, a general notice given to the directors of a company by a director to the effect that he is a member of a specified company or firm and is to be regarded as interested in any transaction which may, after the date of the notice, be made with that company or firm, shall not be deemed to be a sufficient declaration of interest in relation to any transaction so made unless the particulars of the transaction are also disclosed by that director to the board upon being known to that director, and that the director does all things reasonably necessary to be sure that it is brought up and read at the next meeting of the directors after it is given.

(3) Any director who fails to comply with the provisions of this section commits an offence and is liable to a fine in such amount as the Commission shall specify in its regulations.

(4) Nothing in this section shall be taken to prejudice the operation of any rule of law restricting directors of a company from having any interest in contracts with the company.

304.—(1) Every company to which this section applies shall, in all trade circulars, show cards and business letters on or in which the company's name appears and which are issued or sent by the company to any person in Nigeria, state in legible characters with respect to every director—

(a) his present forename or the initials, and present surname ;

(b) any former forename and surname ; and

(c) his nationality, if not a Nigerian: provided that, if special circumstances exist which the Commission is of the opinion render it expedient that such an exemption should be granted, the Commission may, subject to such conditions as it may prescribe by notice published in the Federal Government *Gazette*, exempt a company from the obligations imposed by this subsection.

(2) This section applies to every company incorporated under this Act, or any enactment repealed by it.

(3) If a company defaults in complying with this section, every officer of the company is liable to a penalty in such amount as the Commission shall specify in its regulations.

(4) For the purposes of this section—

(a) "*initials*" includes a recognised abbreviation of a forename ;

(b) references to a former forename or surname in the case of a married woman do not include the name or surname by which she was known previous to the marriage ; and

(c) "*show cards*" means cards containing or exhibiting articles dealt with, or samples or representations.

305.—(1) A director of a company stands in a fiduciary relationship directors. towards the company and shall observe utmost good faith towards the company in any transaction with it or on its behalf.

(2) A director owes fiduciary relationship with the company where— (*a*) a director is acting as agent of a particular shareholder; or

(*b*) though, he is not an agent of any shareholder, such a shareholder or other person is dealing with the company's securities.

(3) A director shall act at all times in what he believes to be the best interests of the company as a whole so as to preserve its assets, further its business, and promote the purposes for which it was formed, and in such manner as a faithful, diligent, careful and ordinarily skilful director would act in the circumstances and, in doing so, shall have regard to the impact of the company's operations on the environment in the community where it carries on business operations.

(4) The matters to which a director of a company is to have regard in the performance of his functions include the interests of the company's employees in general, as well as the interests of its members.

(5) A director shall exercise his powers for the purpose for which he is specified and shall not do so for a collateral purpose, and the power, if exercised for the right purpose, does not constitute a breach of duty, if it, incidentally, affects a member adversely.

(6) A director shall not fetter his discretion to vote in a particular way.

(7) Where a director is allowed to delegate his powers under any provision of this Act, such a director shall not delegate the power in such a way and manner as may amount to an abdication of duty.

(8) No provision, whether contained in the articles, resolutions of a company, or any contract, shall relieve any director from the duty to act in accordance with this section or relieve him from any liability incurred as a result of any breach of the duties conferred upon him under this section.

(9) Any duty imposed on a director under this section is enforceable against a director by the company.

306.—(1) The personal interest of a director shall not conflict with any of his duties as a director under this Act.

(2) A director shall not—

(a) in the course of management of affairs of the company, or

(b) in the utilisation of the company's property, make any secret profit or achieve other unnecessary benefits.

(3) A director is accountable to the company for any secret profit made by him or any benefit derived by him contrary to the provisions of subsection (2).

(4) The inability or unwillingness of the company to perform any function or duty under its articles and memorandum does not constitute a defence to any breach of duty of a director under this Act.

(5) The duty not to misuse corporate information does not cease by a director or an officer having resigned from the company, and he is still accountable and can be restrained by an injunction from misusing the information received by virtue of his previous position.

(6) Where a director discloses his interests before the transaction and before the secret profits are made before the general meeting, which may or may not authorise any resulting profits, he may escape liability, but he does not escape liability if he discloses only after he has made the secret profits, and in this case, he shall account for the profits.

307.—(1) The fact that a person holds more than one directorship shall not derogate from his fiduciary duties to each company, including a duty not to use the property, opportunity or information obtained in the course of the management of one company for the benefit of the other company, or to his own or other person's advantage.

(2) Subject subsection (3), a person shall not be a director in more than five public companies.

(3) Any person who is a director in more than five public companies shall, at the next annual general meeting of the companies after the expiration of two years from the commencement of this Act, resign from being a director from all but five of the companies.

(4) Any person who acts as a director of a public company in contravention of the provisions of this section is liable to a daily penalty in such amount as the Commission shall specify in its regulations and shall refund to each of the companies every remuneration and allowances paid to him as a director in each of the companies.

308.—(1) Every director of a company shall exercise the powers and discharge the duties of his office honestly, in good faith and in the best interests of the company, and shall exercise that degree of care, diligence and skill which a reasonably prudent director would exercise in comparable circumstances.

(2) Failure to take reasonable care in accordance with the provisions of this section, is a ground for an action for negligence and breach of duty.

(3) Each director is individually responsible for the actions of the board in which he participated, and the absence from the board's deliberations, unless justified, does not relieve a director of such responsibility.

(4) The same standard of care in relation to the director's duties to the company shall be required for both executive and non-executive directors: Provided that additional liability and benefit may arise under the master and servant law in the case of an executive director if there is an express or implied contract to that effect.

309.—(1) Directors are trustees of the company's money, properties and their powers and as such shall account for all the money over which they exercise control, refund any money improperly paid away, and shall exercise their powers honestly in the interest of the company and all the shareholders, and not in their own or sectional interests.

(2) A director may, when acting within his authority and the powers of the company, be regarded as agents of the company under Part III of this Act.

PROPERTY TRANSACTIONS BY DIRECTORS

310.—(1) Subject to the exceptions provided by section 311 of this Act, a company shall not enter into an arrangement whereby— relating to the transaction and if the director, controlling member or connected person is a director of its holding company or a person connected with such a director or controlling member, by a resolution in general meeting of the holding company after being informed of all material facts relating to the transaction.

(2) For the purpose of subsection (1), a non-cash asset is of the requisite value if, at the time the arrangement in question is entered into, its value is not less than an amount the Commission may by regulation prescribe".

(3) A person is a controlling member of a company if that person, either alone or in an understanding with other persons, has more than 50% of the voting power to elect or remove directors of the company.

(4) For the purposes of this section and sections 311 and 312 of this Act, a shadow director is treated as a director.

311.—(1) No approval shall be required to be given under section 310 of this Act by any body corporate unless it is a company within the meaning of this Act, or if it is a wholly-owned subsidiary of anybody corporate.

(2) Section 309 of this Act does not apply to an arrangement for the acquisition of a non- cash asset if—

(a) the asset is to be acquired by a holding company from any of its wholly-owned subsidiaries or from a holding company by any of its wholly owned subsidiary of a holding company from another wholly-owned subsidiary of that same holding company ; or

(b) the arrangement is entered into by a company which is being wound-up, unless the winding-up is a member's voluntary winding-up.

(3) Section 310 (1) (*a*) does not apply to an arrangement whereby a person is to acquire an asset from a company of which he is a member, if the arrangement is made with that person in his character as a member.

312.—(1) An arrangement entered into by a company in contravention of section 310 of this Act and any transaction entered into in pursuance of the arrangement (whether by the company or any other person), is voidable at the instance of the company or voidable by a court on its decision on a claim by members, unless one or more of the conditions specified in subsection (2) is satisfied.

(2) The conditions are that—

(a) restitution of any money or other asset which is the subject-matter of the arrangement or transaction is no longer possible or the company has been indemnified in pursuance of this section by any other person for the loss or damage suffered by it ;

(b) any right acquired *bona fide* for value and without actual notice of the contravention by any person who is a party to the arrangement or transaction would be affected by its avoidance ; or

(c) the arrangement is, within a reasonable period, ratified and affirmed in full accordance with the requirements for advance approval set out in section 311 of this Act.

(3) If an arrangement is entered into with a company by a director of the company or its holding company or a person connected with him in contravention of section 310 of this Act, that director, controlling member and person so connected, and any other director of the company who authorises the arrangement or any transaction entered into in pursuance of such an arrangement, commits an offence and liable—

(a) to account to the company for any gain which he has made and any loss or damage suffered by the company, directly or indirectly by the arrangement or transaction,

(b) directly and derivatively to members of the company for any loss or damage suffered by them,

(c) jointly and severally with any other person liable under this subsection, to indemnify the company for any loss or damage resulting from the arrangement or transaction, where found guilty and convicted of an offence guilty of the office, disqualified to serve as a director of the company.

(4) In any action referred to in this section the plaintiff has the right to obtain any relevant documents from the defendant and the witnesses at trial, and may request categories of documents from such person without identifying specific documents.

(5) This section is without prejudice to any liability imposed than by this section, and is subject to subsections (6)-(7) and the liability under subsection (3) arises whether or not the arrangement or transaction entered into has been avoided under subsection (1) of this section.

(6) If an arrangement is entered into by a company and a person connected with a director of the company or its holding company in contravention of section 310 of this Act, that director is not liable under subsection (3) if he shows that he took all reasonable steps to secure the company's compliance with that section.

(7) This section has effect with respect to references in sections 310,311 and 312 of this Act to a person being "connected" with a director of a company, and to a director being "associated with" or "controlling" a body corporate.

(8) A person is connected with another person if he is—

(a) that other person's spouse, child or step-child, including illegitimate child ;

(b) a body corporate with which the person is associated ; or

(c) a person acting in his capacity as trustee of any trust, the beneficiaries of which include—

(i) the director, his spouse, any children or step-children, or

(ii) a body corporate with which he is associated, or of a trust whose terms confer a power on the trustees that may be exercised for the benefit of the person, his spouse or any children or step-children of his, or any such body corporate ; or

(d) a person acting in his capacity as partner of that director or of any person who, by virtue of paragraphs (*a*), (*b*) or (*c*), is connected with that director.

313.—(1) A director shall not accept a bribe, a gift, or commission either in cash or kind from any person or a share in the profit of that person in respect of any transaction involving his company in order to introduce his company to deal with such a person.

(2) If a director contravenes the provisions of subsection (1), he commits a breach of duty and the company shall recover from the director the actual gift and sue him and the other person for damages sustained without any deduction in respect of what the director has returned.

(3) Where the gift is made after the transaction has been completed in a form of unsolicited gift as a sign of gratitude, the director may be allowed to keep the gift, provided he declares it before the board and that fact shall also appear in the minutes book of the directors.

(4) In all cases concerning secret benefits, the plea that the company benefited or that the gift was accepted in good faith is not a defence.

MISCELLANEOUS MATTERS RELATING TO DIRECTORS

314.—(1) In a limited company the liability of the directors, managers or managing director, may, if so provided by the memorandum, be unlimited.

(2) In a limited company in which the liability of a director, manager is unlimited, the directors and managers of the company and the member who proposes a person for election or appointment to the office of director or manager, shall add to that

proposal a statement that the liability of the person holding that office is unlimited, and before the person accepts the office or acts therein, notice in writing that his liability are unlimited is given to him by the promoters of the company, the directors of the company, any managers of the company and the Secretary of the company.

(3) If any director, manager, or promoter makes default in adding such a statement, or if any promoter, director, manager or secretary makes default in giving such a notice, he shall is liable to a penalty in such amount as the Commission shall specify in its regulations and is also liable for any damage which the person so elected or appointed may sustain from the default.

315.—(1) A limited company, if so authorised by its articles, may, by special resolution, alter its memorandum so as to render unlimited the liability of its directors or managers, or of any managing director.

(2) Upon the passing of any such special resolution, the provisions of it are as valid as if they had been originally contained in the Memorandum.

316. Where a company—

(a) receives money by way of loan for specific purpose ;

(b) receives money or other property by way of advance payment for the execution of a contract or project ; or

(c) with intent to defraud, fails to apply the money or other property for the purpose for which it was received, every director or other officer of the company who is in default is personally liable to the party from whom the money or property was received for a refund of the money or property so received and not applied for the purpose for which it was received and nothing in this section affects the liability of the company itself.

317.—(1) The provisions of this section apply in respect of any term of an agreement where a director's employment with the company of which he is a director or, where he is the director of a holding company, his employment within the group, is to continue or may be continued, than at the instance of the company (whether under the original agreement entered into in pursuance of it or not), for more than five years during which the employment—

(*a*) cannot be terminated by the company by notice ; or (*b*) can be so terminated only in specified circumstances.

(2) References in subsection (1) to employment being continued (or its potential to be continued) are references to its being continued (or its potential to be continued) whether under the original agreement concerned or under a new agreement entered into in pursuance of the original agreement concerned prior to the expiration of the original agreement or within 6 months of the expiration of the original agreement.

(3) A company shall not incorporate, in an agreement, such a term as is mentioned in subsection (1) unless the term is first approved by a resolution of the company in general meeting and in the case of a director of a holding company, by a resolution of that company in general meeting.

(4) No approval is required to be given under this section by anybody corporate unless it is a company within the meaning of this Act, or if it is a wholly-owned subsidiary of any body corporate.

(5) A resolution of a company approving such a term as is mentioned in subsection (1), shall not be passed at a general meeting of the company unless a written

memorandum setting out the proposed agreement incorporating the term is available for inspection by members of the company both—

(*a*) at the company's registered office for at least 15 days ending with the date of the meeting ; and (*b*) at the meeting itself.

(6) A term incorporated in an agreement in contravention of this section is to the extent that it contravenes the section, void, and that agreement and in a case where subsection (2) applies, the original agreements is deemed each to contain a term entitling the company to terminate it at any time by the giving of reasonable notice.

(7) In this section—

(*a*) "*employment*" includes employment under a contract for services ; and (*b*) "*group*" in relation to a director of a holding company, means the group which consists of that company and its subsidiaries and for purposes of this section, a shadow director shall be treated as a director.

318.—(1) Every company shall keep a register of its directors. Register of directors.

(2) The register shall contain the required particulars of each person who is a director of the company.

(3) The register shall be kept available for inspection at the company's registered office.

(4) The company shall give notice to the Registrar—

(a) of the place at which the register is kept available for inspection, and

(b) of any change in that place, unless it has at all times been kept at the company's registered office.

(5) The Register shall be open to the inspection of any—

(a) member of the company without charge, and

(b) other person on payment of such fee as may be prescribed.

(6) If default is made in complying with subsection (1), (2) or (3) or if default is made for 14 days in complying with subsection (4), or if an inspection required under subsection (5) is refused, the company and each officer of the company is each liable to a penalty in such amount as the Commission shall specify in its regulations.

(7) In the case of a refusal of inspection of the register, the Court may upon application by any person aggrieved, by order compel an immediate inspection of it.

319.—(1) A company's register of directors shall contain, in the case of an individual—

(a) full name and any former name or names ;

(b) service address ;

(c) nationality ;

(d) business occupation (if any) ;

(e) date of birth ;

(*f*) phone number ; and (*g*) email address.

(2) For the purposes of this section a "former name" means a name by which the individual was formerly known.

(3) The register contain particulars of a former name where the former name—

(a) was changed or disused before the person attained the age of 18 years, or

(b) has been changed or disused for 20 years or more.

(4) A person's service address may be stated to be the company's registered office.

320.—(1) Every company shall keep a register of directors' residential addresses.

(2) The register shall state the usual residential address of each of the company's directors.

(3) If a director's usual residential address is the same as the service address (as stated in the company's register of directors), the register of directors' residential addresses need only contain an entry to that effect provided the service address is not the company's registered office.

(4) If default is made in complying with this section, the company and each officer of the company are each liable to a penalty in such amount as the Commission shall specify in its regulations.

321.—(1) A company shall, within 14 days from—

(a) a person becoming or ceasing to be a director ; or

(b) the occurrence of any change in the particulars contained in its register of directors or residential addresses, give notice to the Commission of the change and of the date on which it occurred.

(2) Notice of a person having become a director of the company shall—

(a) contain a statement of the particulars of the new director that are required to be included in the company's register of directors and its register of directors' residential addresses ; and

(b) be accompanied by a consent, by that person, to act in that capacity.

(3) Where—

(a) a company gives notice of a change of a director's service address as stated in the company's register of directors ; and

(b) the notice is not accompanied by notice of any resulting change in the particulars contained in the company's register of directors' residential addresses, the notice shall be accompanied by a statement that no such change is required.

(4) If default is made in complying with this section, the company and each officer of the company are liable to a penalty for every day during which the default continues.

PARTICULARS OF DIRECTORS TO BE REGISTERED AND NOTIFIED TO THE COMMISSION

322. The Minister may by regulations, vary particulars required to be contained in a company's register of directors and to notify the Commission.

RESTRICTION ON USE OR DISCLOSURE OF DIRECTORS' ADDRESSES

323.—(1) This Chapter makes provision for protecting, in the case of a company director who is an individual—

(a) information as to his usual residential address ; and

(b) the information that his service address is his usual residential address.

(2) Information in subsection (1) is referred to in this Part as "protected information".

(3) Information does not cease to be protected information on the individual ceasing to be a director of the company, and references in this Chapter to a director include, to that extent, a former director.

324.—(1) A company shall not use or disclose protected information about any of its directors, except—

(a) for communicating with the director concerned,

(b) in order to comply with any requirement of this Act as to particulars to be sent to the registrar, or

(c) in accordance with section 328.

(2) Subsection (1) does not prohibit any use or disclosure of protected information with the consent of the director concerned.

325.—(1) The Commission shall omit protected information from the material on the register that is available for inspection where—

(a) it is contained in a document delivered to the director in which such information is required to be stated ; and

(b) in the case of a document having more than one part, it is contained in a part of the document in which such information is required to be stated.

(2) The Commission is not obliged—

(a) to check other documents or (as the case may be) other parts of the document to ensure the absence of protected information ; or

(b) to omit from the material that is available for public inspection anything registered before this Chapter comes into effect.

(3) The Commission shall not use or disclose protected information except—

(*a*) as permitted by section 326 ; or (*b*) in accordance with section 327.

326.—(1) The Commission may use protected information for communicating with the director in question.

(2) The Commission may disclose protected information—

(*a*) to a public authority specified for the purposes of this section by regulations made by the Minister ; or (*b*) to a credit reference agency.

(3) The Minister may make provision by regulations—

(a) specifying conditions for the disclosure of protected information in accordance with this section ; and

(b) providing for the charging of fees.

(4) The Minister may make provision by regulations requiring the Commission, on application, to refrain from disclosing protected information relating to a director to a credit reference agency.

(5) Regulations under subsection (4) may make provision as to—

(a) who may make an application ;

(b) the grounds on which an application may be made ;

(c) the information to be included in and documents to accompany an application ; and

(d) how an application is to be determined.

(6) Provision under subsection (5) (*d*) may in particular—

(a) confer a discretion on the Commission ; and

(b) provide for a question to be referred to a person other than the Commission for the purposes of determining the application.

(7) In this section—

(a) "*credit reference agency*" means a person carrying on a business comprising the furnishing of information relevant to the financial standing of individuals, being information collected by the agency for that purpose ; and

(b) "*public authority*" includes any person or body having functions of a public nature.

327.—(1) The court may make an order for the disclosure of protected information by the company or by the Commission if—

(a) there is evidence that service of documents at a service address other than the director's usual residential address is not effective to bring them to the notice of the director ; or

(b) it is necessary or expedient for the information to be provided in connection with the enforcement of an order or decree of the Court and the Court is satisfied that it is appropriate to make the order.

(2) An order for disclosure by the Commission is to be made only if the company—

(*a*) does not have the director's usual residential address ; or (*b*) has been dissolved.

(3) The order may be made on the application of a liquidator, creditor or member of the company, or any other person appearing to the court to have a sufficient interest.

(4) The order shall specify the persons to whom, and purposes for which, disclosure is authorised.

328.—(1) The Commission may put a director's usual residential address on the public record if—

(a) communications sent by the Commission to the director and requiring a response within a specified period remain unanswered ; or

(b) there is evidence that service of documents at a service address provided in place of the director's usual residential address is not effective to bring them to the notice of the director.

(2) The Commission shall give notice of the proposal—

(a) to the director ; and

(b) to every company of which the Commission has been notified that the individual is a director.

(3) The notice shall—

(a) state the grounds on which it is proposed to put the director's usual residential address on the public record, and specify a period within which representations may be made before that is done ; and

(b) be sent to the director at his usual residential address, unless it appears to the Commission that service at that address may be ineffective to bring it to the director's notice, in which case it may be sent to any service address provided in place of that address.

(4) The Commission shall take account of any representations received within the specified period.

329.—(1) The Commission, on deciding that a director's usual residential address is to be put on the public record, shall proceed as if notice of a change of registered particulars had been given—

(a) stating that address as the director's service address ; and stating that the director's usual residential address is the same as his service address.

(2) The Commission shall give notice of having done so—

(*a*) to the director ; and (*b*) to the company.

(3) On receipt of the notice the company shall—

(a) enter the director's usual residential address in its register of directors as his service address ; and

(b) state in its register of directors' residential addresses that his usual residential address is the same as his service address.

(4) If the company has been notified by the director in question of a more recent address as his usual residential address, it shall—

(a) enter that address in its register of directors as the director's service address ; and

(b) give notice to the registrar as on a change of registered particulars.

(5) If a company fails to comply with subsection (3) or (4), the company and each officer of the company are liable to a penalty for every day during which the default continues in such amount as the Commission shall specify in its regulations.

(6) A director whose usual residential address has been put on the public record by the Commission under this section may not register a service address other than his usual residential address for five years from the date of the Commission's decision.

CHAPTER 12—SECRETARIES

330.—(1) Except in the case of a small company, every company shall have a secretary.

(2) Where at the commencement of this Act a public company has not appointed a secretary, the company shall not later than six months after the commencement of this Act appoint a secretary.

(3) Anything required or authorised to be done by or of the secretary may, if the office is vacant or there is for any other reason no secretary capable of acting, be done by or of any assistant or deputy secretary or, if there is no assistant or deputy secretary capable of acting, by or of any officer of the company authorised generally or specially by the directors.

(4) If a public company contravenes the provisions of this section, the company and the directors of the company are liable to a fine in such amount as the Commission shall specify and, in the case of continued contravention, to a daily penalty in such amount as the Commission shall specify.

331. A provision requiring or authorising a thing to be done by or of a director and the secretary is not satisfied by its being done by or of the same person acting both as director and as, or in place of the secretary.

332. It is the duty of a director of a company to take all reasonable steps to ensure that the secretary of the company is a person who appears to have the requisite knowledge and experience to discharge the functions of a secretary of a company, and in the case of a public company, he shall be—

(a) a member of the Institute of Chartered Secretaries and Administrators ;

(b) a legal practitioner within the meaning of the Legal Practitioners Act ;

(c) a member of any professional body of accountants established from time to time by an Act of the National Assembly ;

(d) any person who has held the office of the secretary of a public company for at least three years of the five years immediately preceding his appointment in a public company ; or

(e) a body corporate or firm consisting of members each of whom is qualified under paragraph (*a*), (*b*), or (*c*).

333.—(1) A secretary is appointed by the directors and, subject to the provisions of this section, may be removed by them.

(2) Where it is intended to remove the secretary of a public company, the board of directors shall give him notice—

(a) stating that it is intended to remove him ;

(b) setting out the grounds on which it is intended to remove him ;

(c) giving him a period at least seven working days within which to make his defence ; and

(d) giving him an option to resign his office within seven working days.

(3) Where, following the notice prescribed in subsection (2), the secretary does not within the given period resign his office or make a defence, the board may remove

him from office and shall make a report to the next general meeting, but where the secretary, without resigning his office, makes a defence and the board does not consider it sufficient, if the ground—

(a) on which it is intended to remove him is fraud or serious misconduct, the board may remove him from office and shall report to the next general meeting ; and

(b) is other than fraud or serious misconduct, the board shall not remove him without the approval of the general meeting, but may suspend him and shall report to the next general meeting.

(4) Notwithstanding any provision of law, where a secretary suspended under subsection (3) (*b*) is removed with the approval of the general meeting, the removal may take effect from such time as the general meeting may determine.

334. A secretary does not owe fiduciary duties to the company, but where he is acting as its agent he owes fiduciary duties to it, and as such is liable to the company where he makes secret profits or lets his duties conflict with his personal interests, or uses confidential information he obtained from the company for his own benefit.

335.—(1) The duties of a secretary include—

(a) attending the meeting of the company, the board of directors and its committees, rendering all necessary secretarial services in respect of the meeting and advising on compliance, by the meetings, with the applicable rules and regulations ;

(b) maintaining the registers and other records required to be maintained by the company under this Act ;

(c) rendering proper returns and giving notification to the Commission required under this Act ; and

(d) carrying out such administrative and other secretarial duties as directed by the director or the company.

(2) The secretary shall not, without the authority of the board exercise any power vested in the directors.

336. Every public company shall maintain a register of secretaries which shall contain the particulars set out in section 337 of this Act.

337.—(1) A company's register of secretaries shall contain the following particulars in the case of an individual—

(a) full name and any former name or names ;

(b) address ; and(*c*) email address.

(2) For the purposes of this section a "former name" means a name by which the individual was formerly known.

(3) The register may not contain particulars of a former name where the former name—

(a) was changed or disused before the person attained the age of 18 years ; or

(b) has been changed or disused for 20 years or more.

(4) The address required to be stated in the register is a service address which may be stated to be the company's registered office.

338.—(1) A company's register of secretaries shall contain the following particulars in the case of a body corporate, or a firm—

(a) corporate or firm name ;

(b) registered or principal office ; and (*c*) email address.

(2) If all the partners in a firm are joint secretaries it is sufficient to state the particulars that would be required if the firm were a legal person and the firm had been appointed secretary.

339.—(1) A company shall, within 14 days, from—

(a) a person becoming or ceasing to be a secretary, or

(b) the occurrence of any change in the particulars contained in its register of secretaries, give notice to the Commission of the change and of the date on which it occurred.

(2) Notice of a person having become a secretary of the company shall—

(a) contain a statement of the particulars of the new secretary that are required to be included in the company's register of secretaries ; and

(b) be accompanied by a consent, by that person, to act in that capacity.

(3) If default is made in complying with this section, the company and each officer of the company are liable to a penalty for every day during which the default continues in such amount as the Commission shall specify in its regulations.

340. The Minister may, by regulations vary particulars required to be contained in a company's register of secretaries and to be notified to the Commission.

CHAPTER 13—PROTECTION OF MINORITY AGAINST ILLEGAL AND OPPRESSIVE CONDUCT ACTION BY OR AGAINST THE COMPANY

341. Subject to the provisions of this Act, where an irregularity is made in the course of a company's affairs or any wrong is done to the company, only the company can sue to remedy that wrong and only the company can ratify the irregular conduct.

342.—(1) For the purposes of this section, "major asset transaction" means a transaction or related series of transactions which includes the—

(a) purchase or other acquisition outside the usual course of the company's business ; and

(b) sale or other transfer outside the usual course of the company's business, of the company's property or other rights the value of which, on the date of the company's decision to complete the transaction, is 50% or more of the book value of the company's assets based on the company's most recently compiled balance sheet.

(2) In undertaking a major asset transaction—

(a) the board of directors of the company shall recommend the transaction and direct that it be submitted for approval to an annual or extraordinary general meeting of members ;

(b) notice of the transaction, stating that a purpose of the meeting is to consider the transaction and including a summary of the transaction and of the recommendation of the board of directors on the transaction, shall be given to all members entitled to notice of or to attend the meeting or to vote on the transaction ; and

(c) at the meeting the members shall approve the transaction by a special resolution, unless the company's memorandum of association provides for its approval by an ordinary resolution, in which case it is approved by an ordinary resolution.

343. Without prejudice to the rights of members under sections 346-351 and sections 353-355 of this Act or any other provisions of this Act, the Court, on the application of any member, may by injunction or declaration restrain the company or its officers from—

(a) entering into any transaction which is illegal or ultra vires ;

(b) purporting to do by ordinary resolution any act which by its articles or this Act required to be done by special resolution ;
(c) any act or omission affecting the applicant's individual rights as a member ;
(d) committing fraud on either the company or the minority shareholders where the directors fail to take appropriate action to redress the wrong done ;
(e) where a company meeting cannot be called in time to be of practical use in redressing a wrong done to the company or to minority shareholders ;
(f) where the directors are likely to derive a profit or benefit, or have profited or benefited from their negligence or from their breach of duty ; and
(g) any other act or omission, where the interest of justice so demands.

344.—(1) Where a member institutes a personal action to enforce a right due to him personally, or a representative action on behalf of himself and other affected members to enforce any right due to them, he or they are subject to subsection (2), entitled to—
(a) damages for any loss incurred on account of the breach of that right ; or
(b) declaration or injunction to restrain the company or the directors from doing a particular act.
(2) Where, in proceedings brought under this section, the Court finds the directors or any of them liable for any wrongdoing, the erring director is personally liable in damages to the aggrieved member.
(3) Where any member institutes an action under this section, the Court may award costs to him personally whether or not his action succeeds.
(4) In any proceeding by a member under section 343 of this Act, the Court may, if it deems fit, order that the member shall give security for costs.

345. For the purpose of sections 343 and 344 of this Act, "*member*" includes—
(a) the personal representative of a deceased member ; and
(b) any person to whom shares have been transferred or transmitted by operation of law.

346.—(1) Subject to the provisions of subsection (2), an applicant may apply to the Court for leave to bring an action in the name or on behalf of a company or a company's subsidiary, or to intervene in an action to which the company or the company's subsidiary is a party, for the purpose of prosecuting, defending or discontinuing the action on behalf of the company or the company's subsidiary.
(2) No action may be brought and no intervention may be made under subsection (1), unless the Court is satisfied that—
(a) a cause of action has arisen from an actual or proposed act or omission involving negligence, default, breach of duty or trust by a director or a former director of the company ;
(b) the applicant has given reasonable notice to the directors of the company of his intention to apply to the Court under subsection (1) ;
(c) the directors of the company do not bring, diligently prosecute, defend or discontinue the action ;
(d) the notice contains a factual basis for the claim and the actual or potential damage caused to the company ;
(e) the applicant is acting in good faith ; and
(f) it appears to be in the best interest of the company that the action be brought, prosecuted, defended or discontinued.

(3) An action under this section may be against the director or any other person (or both).

(4) In any action referred to in this section the plaintiff shall have the right to obtain any relevant documents from the defendant and the witnesses at trial, and may in pursuance of that right request categories of documents from such person without identifying specific documents.

347.—(1) In connection with an action brought or intervened under section 346 of this Act, the Court may, at any time, make any such order or orders as it deems fit.

(2) The Court may make an order—

(a) authorising the applicant or any other person to control the conduct of the action ;

(b) giving directions for the conduct of the action ;

(c) directing that any amount adjudged payable by a defendant in the action is paid, in whole or in part, directly to former and present security holders of the company instead of to the company ; and

(d) requiring the company to pay reasonable legal fees incurred by the applicant in connection with the proceedings.

348. An application made or an action brought or intervened in under section 6 shall not be stayed or dismissed by reason only that it is shown that an alleged breach of a right or a duty owed to the company has been or may be approved by the shareholders of such company, but evidence of approval by the shareholders may be taken into account by the Court in making an order under section 347.

349. An application made or an action brought or intervened in under section 346 shall not be stayed, discontinued, settled or dismissed for want of prosecution without the approval of the Court given upon such terms as the Court deems fit and, if the Court determines that the rights of any applicant may be substantially affected by such stay, discontinuance, settlement or dismissal, the Court may order any party to the application or action to give notice to the applicant.

An applicant shall not be required to give security for costs in any application made or action brought or intervened in under section 346 of this Act.

350. An application made or an action brought or intervened in under section 6 shall not be stayed or dismissed by reason only that it is shown that an alleged breach of a right or a duty owed to the company has been or may be approved by the shareholders of such company, but evidence of approval by the shareholders may be taken into account by the Court in making an order under section 347.

351. An application made or an action brought or intervened in under section 346 shall not be stayed, discontinued, settled or dismissed for want of prosecution without the approval of the Court given upon such terms as the Court deems fit and, if the Court determines that the rights of any applicant may be substantially affected by such stay, discontinuance, settlement or dismissal, the Court may order any party to the application or action to give notice to the applicant.

An applicant shall not be required to give security for costs in any application made or action brought or intervened in under section 346 of this Act

352. An application made or an action brought or intervened in under section 6 shall not be stayed or dismissed by reason only that it is shown that an alleged breach of a right or a duty owed to the company has been or may be approved by the shareholders of such company, but evidence of approval by the shareholders may be taken into account by the Court in making an order under section 347.

353. An application made or an action brought or intervened in under section 346 shall not be stayed, discontinued, settled or dismissed for want of prosecution without the approval of the Court given upon such terms as the Court deems fit and, if the Court determines that the rights of any applicant may be substantially affected by such stay, discontinuance, settlement or dismissal, the Court may order any party to the application or action to give notice to the applicant.

An applicant shall not be required to give security for costs in any application made or action brought or intervened in under section 346 of this Act.

354.—(1) An application for relief on the ground that the affairs of a company are being or have been conducted in an illegal or oppressive manner may be made to the Court by petition.

(2) An application to the Court by petition for an order under this section in relation to a company may be made by—

(a) a member of the company who alleges that—

(i) the affairs of the company are being or have been conducted in a manner that is oppressive or unfairly prejudicial to, or unfairly discriminatory against, a member or members, or in a manner that is or has been in disregard of the interests of a member or the members as a whole, or

(ii) an act or omission or a proposed act or omission, by or on behalf of the company or a resolution, or a proposed resolution, of a class of members, was, is or would be oppressive or unfairly prejudicial to, or unfairly discriminatory against, a member or members or was, is or would be in a manner which is in disregard of the interests of a member or the members as a whole ;

(b) any of the persons mentioned under section 353 (1) (*b*), (*c*) and (*e*) who alleges that—

(i) the affairs of the company have been or are being conducted in a manner oppressive or unfairly prejudicial to or discriminatory against or in a manner in disregard of the interests of that person, or

(ii) an act or omission, or a proposed act or omission was, is or would be oppressive or unfairly prejudicial to, or unfairly discriminatory against, or was or is in disregard of the interests of that person, or

(c) the Commission in a case where it appears to it in the exercise of its powers under the provisions of this Act or any other enactment that—

(i) the affairs of the company were or are being conducted in a manner that was or is oppressive or unfairly prejudicial to, or unfairly discriminatory against a member or members, or was or is in disregard of the public interest, or

(ii) any actual or proposed act or omission of the company, including an act or omission on its behalf which was, is or would be oppressive, or unfairly prejudicial to, or unfairly discriminatory against a member or members in a manner which was or is in disregard of the public interest.

355.—(1) If the Court is satisfied that a petition under sections 353 and 354 is well founded, it may make such order or orders as it deems fit for giving relief in respect of the matter complained of.

(2) Without prejudice to the generality of subsection (1), the Court may make an order—

(a) that the company be wound up ;

(b) for regulating the conduct of the affairs of the company in future;

(c) for the purchase of the shares of any member by other members of the company ;

(d) for the purchase of the shares of any member by the company and for the reduction accordingly of the company's capital ;

(e) directing the company to institute, prosecute, defend or discontinue specific proceedings, or authorising a member or the company to institute, prosecute, defend or discontinue specific proceedings in the name or on behalf of the company;

(f) varying or setting aside a transaction or contract to which the company is a party and compensating the company or any other party to the transaction or contract ;

(g) directing an investigation to be made by the Commission ;

(h) appointing a receiver or a receiver and manager of property of the company ;

(i) restraining a person from engaging in specific conduct or from doing a specific act or thing ; or

(j) requiring a person to do a specific act or thing.

(3) Where an order that a company be wound up is made under this section, the provisions of this Act relating to winding-up of companies shall apply, with such modifications as are necessary, as if the order had been made upon an application duly filed in the Court by the company.

(4) Where an order under this section makes any alteration or addition to the memorandum or articles of a company, notwithstanding anything in any other provision of this Act, but subject to the provisions of the order, the company does not have power, without the leave of the Court, to make any further alteration or addition to the memorandum and articles inconsistent with the provisions of the order but, subject to this subsection, the alteration or addition shall have effect as if it had been made by a resolution of the company.

(5) A certified true copy of an order made under this section altering or giving leave to alter a company's memorandum or articles shall, within 14 days from the making of the order or such longer period as the Court may allow, be delivered by the company to the Commission for registration, and if the company defaults in so complying, the company and each officer of it are liable to a penalty as the Commission shall specify in its regulations.

356. Any person who contravenes or fails to comply with an order made under section 355 that is applicable to him, commits an offence and is liable to a penalty as the Commission shall specify in its regulations.

357.—(1) The Commission may appoint one or more competent inspectors to investigate the affairs of a company and to report on them in such manner as it may direct.

(2) The appointment may be made—

(a) in the case of a company having a share capital, on the application of members holding at least one-tenth of the class of shares issued ;

(b) in the case of a company not having a share capital, on the application of at least one-tenth in number of the persons on the company's register of members ; and

(c) in any other case, on the application of the company.

(3) The application shall be supported by such evidence as the Commission may require for the purpose of showing that the applicant or applicants have good reason for requiring the investigation.

(4) Where a company's employee, in compliance with an inspector's request, provides the inspector with any information concerning the company's affairs, the company

shall protect the employee from any form of discrimination or other unfair treatment.

(5) Any employee relieved of his employment without any just cause, other than for reason of disclosure made pursuant to the provision of this section, is entitled to a compensation which is calculated as if he had attained the maximum age of retirement or had served the maximum period of service, in accordance with his terms of employment or conditions of service to the company.

358.—(1) The Commission shall appoint one or more competent inspectors to investigate the affairs of a company and report on them in such manner as it directs, if the Court, by order declares that its affairs ought to be investigated.

(2) Notwithstanding the provisions of sections 357 and subsection (1) of this section, the Commission may appoint one or more competent inspectors to investigate the affairs of a company and report on them in such manner as it directs, if it appears to it that there are circumstances suggesting that—

(a) the company's affairs are being or have been conducted with intent to defraud its creditors or the creditors of any other person, or in a manner which is unfairly prejudicial to some part of its members ;

(b) any actual or proposed act or omission of the company (including an act or omission on its behalf) is or would be so prejudicial, or that the company was formed for any fraudulent or unlawful purpose ;

(c) persons concerned with the company's formation or the management of its affairs have in connection therewith been guilty of fraud, misfeasance

or other misconduct towards it or towards its members ; or

(d) the company's members have not been given all the information with respect to its affairs which they might reasonably expect.

(3) Subsections (1) and (2) are without prejudice to the powers of the Commission under section 366, and the power conferred by subsection (2) is exercisable with respect to a body corporate, notwithstanding that it is in a course of being voluntarily wound up.

(4) Reference in subsection (2) to a company's member, includes—(*a*) any of the personal representatives of a deceased member ; and

(c) any person to whom shares have been transferred or transmitted by operation of law.

359.—(1) If an Inspector appointed, under section 357 or 358, to investigate the affairs of a company thinks it necessary for the purposes of his investigation to investigate the affairs of another body corporate which is or at any time been the company's subsidiary or holding company, or a subsidiary of its holding company or a holding company of its subsidiary, he shall report on the affairs of the other body corporate so far as he thinks that the results of his investigation of its affairs are relevant to the investigation of the affairs of the company first mentioned above.

(2) An inspector appointed under either section 357 or 358 may at any time in the course of his investigation, without the necessity of making an interim report, inform the Commission of matters coming to his knowledge as a result of the investigation tending to show that an offence has been committed.

360.—(1) When an inspector is appointed under section 357 or 358, it is the duty of both past and present officers and agents of the company, and all past and present officers and agents of any other body corporate whose affairs are investigated under section 359, to—

(a) produce to the inspector all information, books and documents of or relating to the company or, as the case may be, the other body corporate, which are at their disposal, in their custody or power ;

(b) appear before the inspector when required to do so ; and

(c) give the inspector all assistance in connection with the investigation which he is reasonably able to give.

(2) If the inspector considers that a person other than an officer or agent of the company or other body corporate is or may be in possession of information concerning its affairs, he may require that person to produce to him such information, books or documents at his disposal, under his custody or power relating to the company or other body corporate, to appear before him and give him all assistance in connection with the investigation which he is reasonably able to give, and it is that person's duty to comply with the requirement.

(3) An inspector may examine on oath the officers and agents of the company or other body corporate, and any such person as is mentioned in subsection (2) in relation to the affairs of the company or other body, and administer an oath accordingly.

(4) In this section, a reference to officers or to agents includes past and present officers or agents, as the case may be, and "agent" in relation to a company or other body corporate, includes its bankers and solicitors and persons employed by it as auditors, whether these persons are or are not officers of the company.

(5) An answer given by a person to a question put to him in exercise of powers conferred by this section (whether as it has effect in relation to an investigation under any of sections 357-359 as applied by any other section in this Act) may be used in evidence against him.

(6) Where any officer or agent of the company, or any other person refuses to answer any question put to him by the inspector, or provide any information, books or documents at his disposal, under his custody or power with respect to the affairs of the company, or other body corporate, the inspector may apply to Court for contempt proceedings against the officer, agent or person.

361.—(1) If an inspector has reasonable grounds for believing that a director, or past director, of the company or other body corporate whose affairs he is investigating maintains or has maintained a bank account of any description, whether alone or jointly with another person and whether in Nigeria or elsewhere, into or out of which there has been paid—

(a) the emoluments or part of the emoluments of his office as such director, particulars of which have not been disclosed in the financial statements of the company or other body corporate for any financial year, contrary to the provisions of Part V of the Second Schedule to this Act (in relation to particular in accounts of directors) ;

(b) any money which has resulted from or been used in the financing of an undisclosed transaction, arrangement or agreement ; or

(c) any money which has been in any way connected with an act or omission or series of acts or omissions, which on the part of that director constituted misconduct whether fraudulent or not towards the company or body corporate or its members, the inspector may require the director to produce to him all documents in the director's possession, or under his control, relating to that bank account.

(2) For purposes of subsection (1) (*b*) of this section, an "undisclosed" transaction, arrangement or agreement is one the particulars of which have not been disclosed in the financial statement of any company or in a statement annexed thereto for any financial year, including the disclosure of contracts between companies and their directors.

362.—(1) When an inspector is appointed under section 357 or 358 to investigate the affairs of a company, the following applies in the case of—

(a) any officer or agent of the company ;

(b) any officer or agent of another body corporate whose affairs are investigated under section 359 ; and any such person as is mentioned in section 360 (2).

(2) Section 360 (4) applies with regards to references in subsection (1) to an officer or agent.

(3) If that person—

(a) refuses to produce any book or document which it is his duty under section 360 or 361 to produce, or

(b) refuses to appear before the inspector when required to do so, the inspector may certify the refusal in writing and apply to the Court for contempt proceedings against the person.

(4) The Court may thereupon enquire into the case, and after hearing any witness who may be produced against or on behalf of the alleged offender and after hearing any statement which may be offered in defence, the Court may punish the offender in like manner as if he had been guilty of contempt of the Court.

363.—(1) The inspector may, and if so directed by the Commission shall, make interim reports to the Commission, and on the conclusion of his investigation shall make a final report to it and any such report shall be written or printed, as the Commission may direct.

(2) The Commission may direct that a copy of the inspector's report be forwarded to the company at its registered or head office.

(3) Where an inspector is appointed under section 357 in pursuance of an order of the Court, the Commission shall furnish a copy of any of its reports to the Court.

(4) In any other case, the Commission may, if it deems fit—

(*a*) furnish a copy on request and on payment of the prescribed fee to—

(i) any member of the company or other body corporate which is the subject of the report,

(ii) any person whose conduct is referred to in the report,

(iii) the auditors of that company or body corporate,

(iv) the applicants for the investigation, and

(v) any other person whose financial interests appear to the Commission to be affected by the matters dealt with in the report, whether as creditors of the company or body corporate, or otherwise ; and (*b*) cause any such report to be printed and published.

364.—(1) If, from any report made under section 363, it appears to the Commission that any civil proceeding ought in the public interest to be brought by the company or anybody corporate, the Commission may itself bring such proceedings in the name and on behalf of the company or the body corporate.

(2) The Commission shall indemnify the body corporate against any costs or expenses incurred by it in or in connection with proceedings brought under this section, and

any costs or expenses so incurred shall, if not otherwise recoverable, be defrayed out of the Consolidated Revenue Fund.

365.—(1) If, from any report made under section 363, it appears that any person has, in relation to the company or anybody corporate whose affairs have been investigated by virtue of section 359, been guilty of any offence for which he is criminally liable, the report shall be referred to the Attorney General of the Federation.

(2) If the Attorney-General of the Federation considers that the case referred to him is one in which a prosecution ought to be instituted, he shall direct action accordingly, and it is the duty of all past and present officers and agents of the company or other body corporate, (other than the defendant in the proceedings), to give all assistance in connection with the prosecution which they are reasonably able to give.

(3) If, from any report made under section 363, it appears to the Commission that proceedings ought, in the public interest, to be brought by any body corporate dealt with by the report for the recovery of damages in respect of any fraud, misfeasance or other misconduct in connection with the promotion or formation of that body corporate or the management of its affairs, or for the recovery of any property of the body corporate which has been misapplied or wrongfully retained, it may refer the case to the Attorney-General of the Federation for his opinion as to the bringing of proceedings for that purpose in the name of the body corporate and if proceedings are brought, it shall be the duty of all past and present officers and agents of the company or other body corporate (other than the defendants in proceedings), to give him all assistance in connection with the proceedings which they are reasonably able to give.

(4) Costs and expenses incurred by a body corporate in or in connection with any proceedings brought by it under subsection (3) shall, if not otherwise recoverable, be defrayed out of the Consolidated Revenue Fund.

366. If, in the case of any body corporate liable to be wound up under this Act, it appears to the Commission from a report made by an inspector under section 363 that it is expedient in the public interest that the body corporate should be wound up, the Commission may (unless the body corporate is already wound up by the Court) present a petition for it to be wound up if the Court considers it just and equitable to do so.

367.—(1) The expenses of, and incidental to, an investigation by an inspector appointed by the Commission under the provisions of this Act, are defrayed in the first instance out of the Consolidated Revenue Fund, but the following persons are, to the extent mentioned, liable to make repayment,—

(a) any person who is convicted on a prosecution instituted, as a result of the investigation by the Attorney-General of the Federation, or who is ordered to pay damages or restore any property in proceedings brought under section 365 (3), may, in the same proceedings, be ordered to pay the said expenses to such extent as are specified in the order ;

(b) any body corporate in whose name proceedings are brought under section 365 (3) is liable to the extent of the amount or value of any sums or property recovered by it as a result of those proceedings ; or

(c) unless, as the result of the investigation, a prosecution is instituted by the Attorney-General of the Federation, the applicants for the investigation, where the inspector was appointed under section 357, are liable to such extent, if any, as the Commission may direct, and any amount for which a body corporate is liable under paragraph (*b*), shall be a first charge on the sums or property mentioned in that paragraph.

(2) For the purposes of this section, any costs or expenses incurred by the Commission in or in connection with proceedings brought by virtue of section 364 (2), is treated as expenses of the investigation giving rise to the proceedings.

(3) Expenses to be defrayed by the Commission under this section are, so far as not recoverable are to be paid out of the Consolidated Revenue Fund.

368.—(1) A copy of any report of an inspector appointed under sections 357 and 358, certified by the Commission to be a true copy, is admissible in any legal proceedings as evidence of the opinion of the inspector in relation to any matter contained in the report.

(2) A document purporting to be such a certificate as mentioned in subsection (1) shall be received in evidence and be deemed to be such a certificate, unless the contrary is proved.

369. (1) Where it appears to the Commission that there is good reason so to do, it may appoint one or more competent inspectors to investigate and report on the membership of any company, and otherwise with respect to the company, for the purpose of determining the true persons who are or have been financially interested in the success or failure (real or apparent) of the company or able to control or materially to influence the policy of the company.

(2) The appointment of an inspector under this section may define the scope of his investigation, whether in respect of the matter or the period to which it is to extend or otherwise, and in particular may limit investigation to matters connected with particular share or debenture.

(3) Where an application for an investigation under this section with respect to particular share or debenture of a company is made to the Commission by members of the company, and the number of applicants or the amount of the shares held by them is not less than that required for an application for the appointment of an inspector under section 357 (2) (*a*) and (*b*)—

(a) the Commission shall appoint an inspector to conduct that investigation, unless it is satisfied that the application is vexatious ; and

(b) the inspector's appointment is not excluded from the scope of his investigation any matter which the application seeks to include, except in so far as the Commission is satisfied that it is reasonable for the matter to be investigated.

(4) Subject to the terms of an inspector's appointment, his powers shall extend to the investigation of any circumstances suggesting the existence of an arrangement or understanding which, though not legally binding, is or was observed or likely to be observed in practice and which is relevant to the purposes of his investigation.

370.—(1) For the purposes of any investigation under section 369, the provisions of sections 359-363 apply with the necessary modifications to references to the affairs of the company or those of any body corporate, that—

(a) the said sections shall apply in relation to all persons who are or have been, or whom the inspector has reasonable cause to believe to be or have been, financially interested in the success or failure or the apparent success or failure of the company or any other body corporate whose membership is investigated with that of the company, or able to control or materially to influence the policy thereof, including persons concerned only on behalf of others, as they apply in relation to officers and agents of the company or of the other body corporate, as the case may be ; and

(b) the Commission is not bound to furnish the company or any other person with a copy of any report by an inspector appointed under this section or with a complete copy thereof if he is of the opinion that there is good reason for not divulging the contents of the report or any part thereof, but shall keep a copy of any such report, or, the parts of any report, as regards which he is not of that opinion.

(2) The expenses of any investigation under section 369 shall be defrayed out of the Consolidated Revenue Fund.

371.—(1) Where it is made to appear to the Commission that there is good reason to investigate the ownership of any share in or debenture of a company and that it is unnecessary to appoint an inspector for the purpose, the Commission may require any person who it has reasonable cause to believe to—

(a) be or to have been interested in those shares or debentures ;

(b) act or to have acted in relation to those shares or debentures as a legal practitioner or an agent of someone interested therein ; or

(c) give to the Commission any information which the person has or might reasonably be expected to obtain as to the present and past interest in those shares or debentures and the names and addresses of the persons interested, and of any persons who act or have acted on their behalf in relation to the shares or debentures.

(2) For the purposes of this section, a person is deemed to have an interest in a share or debenture if he has any right to acquire or dispose of the share or debenture or any interest therein or to vote in respect thereof, or if his consent is necessary for the exercise of any of the rights of other persons interested therein, or if other persons interested therein can be required or are accustomed to exercise their rights in accordance with his instructions.

(3) Any person who fails to give any information required of him under this section, or who, in giving any such information, makes any statement which he knows to be false, or recklessly makes any statement which is false commits an offence and liable to a penalty as the Commission shall specify in its regulations.

372.—(1) Where, in connection with an investigation under section 369 or 371, it appears to the Commission that there is difficulty in finding out the relevant facts about any share (whether issued or to be issued), and that the difficulty is due wholly or mainly to the unwillingness of the persons concerned, or any of them, to assist the investigation as required by this Act the Commission may in writing direct that the shares shall, until further notice, be subject to the restrictions imposed by this section.

(2) If shares are directed to be subject to the restrictions imposed by this section—

(a) any transfer of those shares, or in case of unissued shares, any transfer of the right to be issued therewith and any issue thereof, is void ;

(b) no voting rights are exercisable in respect of those shares ;

(c) no further shares shall be issued in right of those shares or in pursuance of any offer made to the holder of shares ; and

(d) except in a liquidation, no payment shall be made of any sums due from the company on those shares, whether in respect of capital or otherwise.

(3) Where the Commission directs shares to be subject to restrictions under this section, or refuses to direct that shares shall cease to be subject thereto, any person aggrieved

thereby may appeal to the Court, and the Court may, if it deems fit, direct that the shares shall cease to be subject to the said restrictions.

(4) Any direction or order of the Court that shares shall cease to be subject to restrictions under this section, expressed to be made with a view to permitting a transfer of those shares, may continue the restrictions mentioned in subsection (2) (*c*) and (*d*), either in whole or in part, so far as they relate to any right acquired or offer made before the transfer.

(5) Any person who—

(a) exercises or purports to exercise any right to dispose of shares which, to his knowledge, are for the time being subject to restrictions under this section,

(b) votes in respect of such shares, whether as holder or proxy, or appoints a proxy to vote in respect thereof, or

(c) being the holder of such shares, fails to notify that they are subject tothe said restrictions, commits an offence and is liable to a penalty as the Commission shall specify in its regulations.

(6) Where shares in any company are issued in contravention of the said restrictions, the company and each officer of the company who are in default commits an offence and is liable to a penalty as the Commission shall specify in its regulations.

(7) A prosecution shall not be instituted under this section except by or with the consent of the Attorney-General of the Federation.

(8) This section applies in relation to debentures as it applies in relation to shares.

373. Nothing in this Part requires disclosure to the Commission or to an inspector appointed by it, by a—

(a) legal practitioner of any privileged communication made to him in that capacity, except as regards the name and address of his client ; or

(b) company's banker as such, of any information as to the affairs of any of their customers other than the company.

CHAPTER 14—FINANCIAL STATEMENTS, AUDIT AND ACCOUNTING RECORDS

374.—(1) Every company shall cause accounting records to be kept in accordance with this section.

(2) The accounting records are sufficient to show and explain the transactions of the company and as such, are to—

(a) disclose with reasonable accuracy, at any time, the financial position of the company ; and

(b) enable the directors to ensure that any financial statements prepared under this Part comply with the requirements of this Act as to the form and content of the company's financial statements.

(3) The accounting records shall, in particular, contain—

(a) entries from day to day of all sums of money received and expended by the company, and the matters in respect of which the receipt and expenditure took place ; and

(b) a record of the assets and liabilities of the company.

(4) If the business of the company involves dealing in goods, the accounting records shall contain—

(a) statements of stocks held by the company at the end of each year of the company ;

(b) all statements of stocktakings from which any such statement of stock as is mentioned in paragraph (*a*) has been or is to be prepared ; and

(c) except in the case of goods sold by way of ordinary retail trade, statements of all goods sold and purchased, showing the goods and the buyers and sellers in sufficient detail to enable all these to be identified.

(5) A parent company that has a subsidiary undertaking in relation to which subsection (4) does not apply shall take reasonable steps to secure that the undertaking keeps such accounting records as to enable the directors of the parent company to ensure that any accounts required to be prepared under this Part comply with the requirements of this Act.

(6) Each public company shall keep its audited accounts displayed on its website.

375.—(1) The accounting records of a company shall be kept at its registered office or such other place in Nigeria as the directors think fit, and shall at all times be open to inspection by the officers of the company.

(2) Subject to any direction with respect to the disposal of records given under winding-up rules made under section 732 of this Act, accounting records which a company is required by section 374 of this Act to keep are preserved by it for six years from the date on which they were made.

(3) A company may, in addition to original hard copies, keep electronic copies or registers of any document or record it is obliged to keep or maintain under this Act, and where a company chooses to maintain electronic copies or registers of its documents or records, the company shall give sufficient consideration to the quality of the hardware and software to be used, and technical specifications such as protocol, security, anti-virus protection or encryption.

376.—(1) If a company fails to comply with any provision of section 374 or 375 (1), every officer of the company who is in default commits an offence unless he shows that he acted honestly and that in the circumstances in which the business of the company was carried on, the default was excusable.

(2) An officer of a company commits an offence if he fails to take all reasonable steps for securing compliance by the company with section 375 of this Act, or has intentionally caused any default by the company under it.

(3) A person who commits an offence under this section, is liable to a penalty as the Commission shall specify in its regulations.

377.—(1) In the case of every company, the directors shall, in respect of each year of the company, prepare financial statement for the year.

(2) Subject to subsection (3), the financial statements required under subsection (1) shall include—

(a) statement of the accounting policies ;

(b) the balance sheet or balance sheet as at the last day of the year ;

(c) a profit and loss account or, in the case of a company not trading for-profit, an income and expenditure account for the year ;

(d) notes on the accounts ;

(e) the auditors' report ;

(f) the directors' report ;

(g) a statement of the source and application of fund or statement of cash flow ;

(h) changes in equity ;

(i) a value-added statement for the year ;

(j) a five year financial summary ;
(k) in the case of a holding company, the group financial statements ; and
(l) such other matters as are required in accordance with the applicable accounting standards.
(3) The financial statements of a private company need not include the matters stated in subsection (2) (*a*), (*g*), (*h*) and (*i*).
(4) The directors shall, at their first meeting after the incorporation of the company, determine what date in each year financial statements is made up, and they shall give notice of the date to the Commission within 14 days of the determination.
(5) In the case of a holding company, the directors shall ensure that, except where in their opinion there are good reasons against it, the year of each of its subsidiaries shall coincide with the year of the company.

FORM AND CONTENT OF COMPANY, INDIVIDUAL AND GROUP FINANCIAL STATEMENTS

378.—(1) The financial statements of a company prepared under section 377 of this Act, shall comply with the requirements of the First Schedule to this Act (so far as applicable) with respect to their form and content, and with the accounting standards laid down in the statements of accounting standards issued by the Financial Reporting Council of Nigeria, provided such accounting standards do not conflict with the provisions of this Act or the First Schedule to this Act.
(2) The balance sheet shall give a true and fair view of the state of affairs of the company as at the end of the year, and the profit and loss account shall give a true and fair view of the profit or loss of the company for the year.
(3) The statement of the source and application of funds shall provide information on the generation and utilisation of funds by the company during the year.
(4) The value added statement shall report the wealth created by the company during the year and its distribution among various interest groups such as the employees, government, creditors, proprietors and the company.
(5) The five-year financial summary shall provide a report for a comparison over a period of five years or more of vital financial information.
(6) Subsection (2) overrides—
(a) the requirements of the First Schedule to this Act ; and
(b) all other requirements of this Act as to the matters to be included in the accounts of a company or in notes to those accounts, and accordingly, the provisions of subsections (7) and (8) shall have effect.
(7) If the balance sheet or profit and loss account drawn up in accordance with those requirements would not provide sufficient information to comply with subsection (2), any necessary additional information shall be provided in that balance sheet, profit and loss account or in a note to the accounts.
(8) If, owing to special circumstances in the case of any company, compliance with any such requirement in relation to the balance sheet or profit and loss account would prevent compliance with subsection (2), (even if additional information were provided in accordance with subsection (4)), the directors shall depart from that requirement in preparing the balance sheet or profit and loss account (so far as necessary) in order to comply with subsection (2).
(9) If the directors depart from any such requirement, particulars of the departure, the reasons for it and its effects shall be given in a note to the accounts.

(10) Subsections (1)-(9) do not apply to group accounts prepared under section 379 (1) and (2) apply to a company's profit and loss account (or require the notes otherwise required in relation to that account) if—

(a) the company has subsidiaries ; and

(b) the profit and loss account is framed as a consolidated account dealing with all or any of the subsidiaries of the company as well as the company—

(i) complies with the requirements of this Act relating to consolidated profit and loss account, and

(ii) shows how much of the consolidated profit and loss for the year is dealt with in the individual financial statements of the company.

(11) If group financial statements are prepared and advantage is taken of subsection (7), that fact shall be disclosed in a note to the group financial statements.

379.—(1) If, at the end of a year a company has subsidiaries, the directors shall, as well as preparing individual accounts of each subsidiary for that year, also prepare group financial statements being accounts or statements which deal with the state of affairs and profit or loss of the entire company and the subsidiaries.

(2) The provisions of subsection (1) do not apply in instances exempted under accounting standards issued by the Financial Reporting Council of Nigeria.

(3) A group financial statement may not deal with a subsidiary, if the directors of the company are of the opinion that—

(a) it is impracticable, or would be of no real value to the members, in view of the insignificant amounts involved ;

(b) it would involve expense or delay out of proportion to its value to members of the company ;

(c) the result would be misleading, or harmful to the business of the company or any of its subsidiaries ; or

(d) the business of the holding company and that of the subsidiary are so different that they cannot reasonably be treated as a single undertaking.

(4) The group financial statements of a company shall consist of a consolidated—

(a) balance sheet dealing with the state of affairs of the company and all the subsidiaries of the company ; and

(b) profit and loss account of the company and its subsidiaries.

(5) If the directors are of the opinion that it is better for the purpose of presenting the same or equivalent information about the state of affairs and profit or loss of the company and its subsidiaries, and that to so present it may be readily appreciated by the members of the company, the group financial statements may be prepared in a form not consistent with subsection (1) and in particular the group financial statement may consist of—

(a) more than one set of consolidated financial statements dealing respectively with the company and one group of subsidiaries and with other groups of subsidiaries ;

(b) separate financial statements dealing with each of the subsidiaries ; or

(c) statements expanding the information about the subsidiaries in individual financial statements of the company, or in any other form.

(6) The group financial statements may be wholly or partly incorporated in the individual balance sheet and profit and loss account of the holding company.

380.—(1) The group financial statements of a holding company shall comply with the requirements of the First Schedule to this Act, so far as applicable to group financial statements in the form in which those accounts are prepared with respect to the form and content of those statements and any additional information to be provided by way of notes to those accounts.

(2) Group financial statements together with any notes thereon shall give a true and fair view of the state of affairs and profit or loss of the company and the subsidiaries dealt with by those statements as a whole.

(3) Subsection (2) overrides—

(a) the requirements of the First Schedule to this Act ; and

(b) all the requirements of this Act as to the matters to be included in group financial statements or in notes to those statements and accordingly subsections (4) and (5) shall have effect.

(4) If group financial statements are not in accordance with the requirements of this Act by not providing sufficient information in compliance with subsection (2), any necessary additional information shall be provided in, or in a note to, the group financial statements.

(5) If, owing to special circumstances in the case of any company, compliance with any such requirements in relation to its group financial statements would prevent the statements from complying with subsection (2), (even if additional information were provided in accordance with subsection (4)), the directors may depart from that requirement in preparing the group financial statements.

381.—(1) Subject to subsection (4), a company is for the purposes of this Act deemed to be a subsidiary of another company if the company—

(a) is a member of the company and controls the composition of its board of directors;

(b) holds more than 50% in nominal value of its equity share capital ; or the first-mentioned company is a subsidiary of any company which is that other's subsidiary.

381.—(1) Subject to subsection (4), a company is for the purposes of this Act deemed to be a subsidiary of another company if the company—

(c) is a member of the company and controls the composition of its board of directors;

(d) holds more than 50% in nominal value of its equity share capital ; or

(e) the first-mentioned company is a subsidiary of any company which is that other's subsidiary.

(2) For the purposes of subsection (1), the composition of the board of directors of a company is deemed to be controlled by another company if that other company by the exercise of some power, without the consent or concurrence of any other person, can appoint or remove the holders of all or majority of the directors.

(3) For purposes of subsection (2), the other company is deemed to have power to appoint a director with respect to which any of the following conditions is satisfied that—

(a) a person cannot be appointed to it without the exercise in his favour by the other company of such power as is mentioned in this section ;

(b) the appointment of a person to the directorship follows necessarily from his appointment as director of the other company ; or

(c) the directorship is held by the other company itself or by a subsidiary of it.

(4) In determining whether one company is a subsidiary of another—

(a) any share held or power exercisable by the other in a fiduciary capacity is treated as not held or exercisable by it ;

(b) subject to paragraphs (*c*) and (*d*), any share held or power exercisable—

(i) by any person as nominee for the other (except where the other is concerned only in a fiduciary capacity), or

(ii) by, or by a nominee for, a subsidiary or the other (not being a subsidiary which is concerned only in a fiduciary capacity), is treated as held or exercisable by the other;

(c) any share held or power exercisable by any person by virtue of the provisions of any debentures of the first mentioned company or of a trust deed for securing any issue of such debentures are disregarded ; and

(d) any share held or power exercisable by, or by a nominee for, the other or its subsidiary (not being held or exercisable as mentioned in paragraph (*c*)), shall be treated as not held or exercisable by the other, if the ordinary business of the other or its subsidiary (as the case may be) includes the lending of money and the shares are held or the power is exercisable by way of security only for the purposes of a transaction entered into in the ordinary course of that business.

(5) For the purposes of this Act—

(a) a company is deemed to be the holding company of another, if the other is its subsidiary ; and

(b) a body corporate is deemed to be the wholly-owned subsidiary of another, if it has no member except that other and that other's wholly owned subsidiaries are its or their nominees.

(6) In this section, "company" includes any body corporate.

382.—(1) The additional matters contained in the Second Schedule shall be disclosed in the company's financial statements for the year; and in that Schedule, where a thing is required to be stated or shown or information is required to be given, it is construed to mean that the thing shall be stated or shown, or the information is to be given in a note to those statements.

(2) In the Second Schedule to this Act —

(a) Parts I and II deal respectively with the disclosure of particulars of the subsidiaries of the company and its shareholders ;

(b) Part III deals with the disclosure of financial information relating to subsidiaries ;

(c) Part IV requires a subsidiary company to disclose its ultimate holding company ;

(d) Part V deals with the emoluments of directors, including emoluments waived, pensions of directors and compensation for loss of office to directors and past directors ; and

Part VI deals with disclosure of the number of the employees of the company who are remunerated at higher rates.

(3) Whenever it is stated in the Second Schedule of this Act that this subsection applies to certain particulars or information, the particulars or information is annexed to the annual return first made by the company after copies of its financial statements have been laid before its shareholders in a general meeting and if a company fails to satisfy this obligation, the company and every officer of it are liable to a penalty as the Commission shall specify in its regulations.

(4) It is the duty of any director of a company to give notice to the company of such matters relating to himself as may be necessary for the purposes of Part V of the Second Schedule to this Act and this applies to persons who are or have at any time in the preceding three years been officers as it applies to directors.

(5) A person who makes default in complying with the provisions of subsection (4), is liable to a penalty as the Commission shall specify in its regulations.

383.—(1) The group financial statements of a holding company for a year shall comply with Part I of the Third Schedule (so far as applicable) as regards the disclosure of transactions, arrangements and agreements mentioned therein, including loans, quasi loans and other dealings in favour of directors.

(2) In the case of a company other than a holding company, its individual accounts shall comply with Part I of the Third Schedule (so far as applicable) as regards disclosure matters contained in the Schedule.

(3) Particulars which are required to be contained in Part I of the Third Schedule in any financial statements are required in respect of shadow directors as well as a director given by way of notes.

(4) Where by virtue of section 379 (2) or (3), a company does not prepare group financial statements for a year, it shall disclose such matters in its individual statements as would have been disclosed in group financial statements.

(5) The requirements of this section apply with such modifications as are necessary to bring them in line with Part I of the Third Schedule to this Act, (including with particulars of exceptions in respect of recognised banks it shall disclose).

384.—(1) The group financial statements of a holding company for a year shall comply with Part II of the Third Schedule to this Act, so far as applicable, as regards transactions, arrangements and agreements made by the company or its subsidiary for persons who at any time during that year were officers of the company but not directors.

(6) In respect of any failure to comply with the requirements of this Act as to the matters to be stated and the particulars to be given in the directors' report, every person who was a director of the company immediately before the end of the period prescribed for laying and delivering financial statements commits an offence and is liable on conviction to a penalty as the Commission shall specify in its regulations.

(7) In proceedings for ascertaining guilt under subsection (6), it is a defence for the person to prove that he took all reasonable steps for securing compliance with the requirements in question.

PROCEDURE ON COMPLETION OF FINANCIAL STATEMENTS

386.—(1) A company's balance sheet and every copy of it which is laid before the company in general meeting or delivered to the Commission shall be signed on behalf of the board by two of the directors of the company.

(2) If a copy of the balance sheet—

(a) is laid before the company or delivered to the Commission without being signed as required by this section, or

(b) not being a copy so laid or delivered, is issued, circulated or published in a case where the balance sheet has not been signed as so required or where (the balance sheet having been so signed) the copy does not include a copy of the signature as the case may be, the company and each officer of it are liable to a penalty as the Commission shall specify in its regulations.

(3) A company's profit and loss account and, so far as not incorporated in its individual balance sheet or profit and loss account, any group accounts of a holding company, shall be annexed to the balance sheet, and the auditors' report and the directors' report shall also be attached to the balance sheet.

(4) The balance sheet and the profit and loss account annexed to it shall be approved by the board of directors and signed on their behalf by two directors authorised to do so.

387.—(1) In the case of every company, a copy of the company's financial statements for the year shall, at least 21 days before the date of the meeting at which they are to be laid in accordance with section 388 of this Act be sent to the following persons—

(a) every member of the company (whether or not entitled to receive notice of general meetings) ;

(b) every holder of the company's debentures, (whether or not so entitled) ; and

all persons other than members and debenture holders, being persons so entitled.

(2) In the case of a company not having a share capital, subsection (1) shall not require a copy of the financial statements to be sent to a member of the company who is not entitled to receive notices of general meetings of the company, or to a holder of the company's debenture who is not so entitled.

(3) Subsection (1) shall not require copies of the financial statements to be sent to—

(a) a member of the company or a debenture holder, a person who is not entitled to receive notices of general meetings, and of whose address the company is unaware ;

(b) more than one of the joint holders of shares or debentures none of whom are entitled to receive such notices ; or

(c) those who are not entitled in the case of joint holders of shares or debentures, some of whom are not entitled to receive such notices.

(4) If copies of the financial statements are sent less than 21 days before the date of the meeting, it is, notwithstanding that fact, deemed to have been duly sent if it is so agreed by all the members entitled to attend and vote at the meeting.

(5) If default is made in complying with subsection (1), the company and each officer of it are liable to a penalty as the Commission shall specify in its regulations.

388.—(1) In respect of each year, the directors shall, at a date not later than 18 months after incorporation of the company and subsequently once at least in every year, lay before the company in general meeting copies of the financial statements of the company made up to a date not exceeding nine months previous to the date of the meeting.

(2) The auditors' report shall be read before the company in general meeting, and be open to the inspection of any member of the company.

(3) In respect of each year, the directors shall deliver with the annual return to the Commission a copy of the balance sheet, the profit and loss account and the notes on the statements which were laid before the general meeting as required by this section.

(4) In the case of an unlimited company, the directors are not required by subsection (3) to deliver a copy of the accounts if—

(a) at no time during the accounting reference period has the company been, to its knowledge, the subsidiary of a company that was then limited and at no such time, to its knowledge, have there been held or been exercisable, by or on behalf of two or more companies that were then limited, shares or powers which, if they had been held or been exercisable by one of them, would have made the company its subsidiary ; and

(b) at no such time has the company been the holding company of a company which was then limited.

(5) References in this section to a company that was limited at a particular time are to a body corporate (under whatever law incorporated) the liability of whose members was at that time limited.

389.—(1) If in a year any of the requirements of section 388 (1) or (3) are not complied with by any company, every person who immediately before the end of that period was a director of the company, in respect of each of those subsections which is not so complied with, is liable to a penalty as the Commission shall specify in its regulations.

(2) If a person is charged with an offence in respect of any of the requirements of section 384 (1) or (3), it is a defence for him to prove that he took all reasonable steps for securing that those requirements be complied with before the end of the period allowed for laying and delivering accounts.

(3) In proceedings under this section with respect to a requirement to lay a copy of a document before a company in general meeting, or to deliver a copy of a document to the Commission, it is not a defence to prove that the document in question was not in fact prepared as required by this Part of this Act.

390.—(1) If—

(a) in respect of a year, any of the requirements of section 388 (1) and(3) of this Act has not been complied with by a company before the end of the period allowed for laying and delivering financial statements, and

(b) the directors of the company fail to make good the default within 14 days after the service of a notice on them requiring compliance, the court may on application by any member or creditor of the company or by the Commission make an order directing the directors (or any of them) to make good the default within such time as may be specified in the order.

(2) The court order may provide that all costs of and incidental to the application be borne by the directors.

(3) Nothing in this section affects the provisions of section 389 of this Act.

391.—(1) If any financial statements of a company (other than its group financial statement) of which a copy is laid before the shareholders in general meeting or delivered to the Commission do not comply with the requirement of this Act as to the matters to be included in, or in a note to, those financial statements, every person who at the time when the copy is laid or delivered is a director of the company is, in respect of each contravention, liable to a penalty as the Commission shall specify in its regulations.

(2) If any group financial statements of which a copy is laid before a company in a general meeting or delivered to the Commission do not comply with section 388 (4) and (5) or section 389 and with the other requirements of this Act as to the matters to be included in or in a note to those financial statements, each person who at the time when the copy was so laid or delivered was a director of the company is liable to a penalty as the Commission shall specify in its regulations.

(3) In proceedings against a person for an offence under this section, it is a defence for him to prove that he took all reasonable steps for securing compliance with the requirements in question.

392.—(1) Any member of a company, whether or not entitled to have copies of the company's financial statements sent to him, and any holder of the company's debentures (whether or not so entitled) is entitled to be furnished on demand and without charge with a copy of the company's last financial statements.

(2) If, when a person makes a demand for a document with which he is entitled by this section to be furnished, default is made in complying with the demand within seven days after its making, the company and each officer are liable to a penalty as the Commission shall specify in its regulations, unless it is proved that the person has already made a demand for, and been furnished with, a copy of the documents.

MODIFIED FINANCIAL STATEMENTS

393.—(1) In certain cases a company's directors may, in accordance with Part 1 of the Sixth Schedule to this Act, deliver modified financial statements in respect of a year as a small company.

(2) For the purposes of sections 395-397 and the Sixth Schedule to this Act, "deliver" means deliver to the Commission.

394.—(1) A company qualifies as small in relation to its first financial year if the qualifying conditions are met in that year.

(2) A company qualifies as small in relation to a subsequent financial year if the qualifying conditions—

(a) are met in that year and the preceding financial year ;

(b) are met in that year and the company qualified as small in relation to the preceding financial year ; or

(c) were met in the preceding financial year and the company qualified as small in relation to that year.

(3) The qualifying conditions are met by a company in a year in which it satisfies the following requirements—

(a) it is a private company ;

(b) its turnover is not more than ₦120,000,000 or such amount as may be fixed by the Commission from time to time ;

(c) its net assets value is not more than ₦60,000,000 or such amount as may be fixed by the Commission from time to time ;

(d) none of its members is an alien ;

(e) none of its members is a government, government corporation or agency or its nominee ; and

(f) in the case of a company having share capital, the directors between themselves hold at least 51% of its equity share capital.

(4) For a period that is a company's financial year but not in fact a year the maximum figures for turnover shall be proportionately adjusted.

(5) The "balance sheet total" means the aggregate of the amounts shown as assets in the company's balance sheet.

(6) The "number of employees" means the average number of persons employed by the company in that year, determined as follows—

(a) find for each month in the financial year the number of persons employed under contracts of service by the company in that month (whether throughout the month or not),
(b) add together the monthly totals, and
(c) divide by the number of months in the financial year.
(7) This section is subject to section 393.
395.—(1) A parent company qualifies as a small company in relation to a financial year only if the group headed by it qualifies as a small group.
(2) A group qualifies as small in relation to the parent company's first financial year if the qualifying conditions are met in that year.
(3) A group qualifies as small in relation to a subsequent financial year of the parent company if the qualifying conditions—
(a) are met in that year and the preceding financial year ;
(b) are met in that year and the group qualified as small in relation to the preceding financial year ; or
(c) were met in the preceding financial year and the group qualified as small in relation to that year.
(4) The qualifying conditions are met by a group in a year in which it satisfies the following requirements—
(a) it is a private company ;
(b) its turnover is not more than ₦120,000,000 or such amount as may be fixed by the Commission from time to time ;
(c) its net assets value is not more than ₦60,000,000 or such amount as may be fixed by the Commission ;
(d) none of its members is an alien ;
(e) none of its members is a government or government corporation or agency or its nominee ; and
(f) in the case of a company having share capital, the directors between themselves hold at least 51% of its equity share capital.
(5) The aggregate figures are ascertained by aggregating the relevant figures determined in accordance with section 394 for each member of the group.
(6) The figures for each subsidiary undertaking are those included in its individual accounts for the relevant financial year, if—
(a) its financial year ends with that of the parent company, that financial year ;
(b) not, its financial year ending last before the end of the financial year of the parent company ; and
(c) those figures cannot be obtained without disproportionate expense or undue delay, the latest available figures shall be taken.
396.—(1) The directors of a company may (subject to section 397 where the company has subsidiaries) deliver individual financial statements modified as for a small company in the cases specified in subsections (2) and (3), and Part 1 of the Sixth Schedule apply with respect to the delivery of financial statements so modified.
(2) In respect of the company's first year the directors may deliver financial statements modified as for a small company, if in that year it qualifies as small.
(3) The directors may in respect of a company's year subsequent to the first deliver financial statements modified as for a small company,—
(a) if the company qualifies as small and it also so qualified in the preceding year ;

(b) although not qualifying in that year as small, if in the preceding year it so qualified and the directors were entitled to deliver financial statements so modified in respect of that year ; or

(c) if, in that year the company qualifies as small and the directors were entitled under paragraph (b) to deliver financial statements so modified for the preceding year (although the company did not in that year qualify as small).

397.—(1) This section applies to a holding company where in respect of a year section 379 requires the preparation of group financial statements for the company and its subsidiaries.

(2) The directors of the holding company may not under section 396 of this Act deliver financial statements modified as for a small company, unless the group (that is to say, the holding company and its subsidiaries together) is in that year a small group and the group is small if it qualifies under section 394 of this Act (applying that section as provided under subsections (3) and (4), as if it were all one company).

(3) The figures to be taken into account in determining whether the group is small are the group account figures, that is—

(a) where the group financial statements are prepared as consolidated financial statements, the figures for turnover and balance sheet total ; and

(b) where the group financial statements are not prepared as consolidated financial statements, the corresponding figures given in the group financial statements, with such adjustment as would have been made if the statements had been prepared in consolidated form, and aggregated in either case with the relevant figures for the subsidiaries (if any) omitted from the group accounts (excepting those for any subsidiary omitted under section 379 (3) (a) on the ground of impracticability).

(4) In the case of each subsidiary omitted from the group financial statements, the figures relevant as regards turnover, and balance sheet total are those which are included in the financial statements of that subsidiary prepared in respect of its relevant year (with such adjustment as would have been made if those figures had been included in group financial statements prepared in consolidated form).

(5) For the purposes of subsection (4), the relevant year of the subsidiary is—

(a) if its year ends with that of the holding company to which the group financial statements relate, that year ; and

(b) if not, the subsidiary's year ending last before the end of the year of the holding company.

(6) If the directors are entitled to deliver modified financial statements, they may also deliver modified group financial statements, and such group financial statements if—

. (a) consolidated, may be in accordance with Part II of the Sixth Schedule(while otherwise comprising or corresponding with group financial statements prepared under section 379 of this Act) ; and

(b) not consolidated, may be such as (together with any notes) give the same or equivalent information as required by paragraph (a), and Part III to the Sixth Schedule to this Act applies to modified group financial statements whether consolidated or not.

PUBLICATION OF FINANCIAL STATEMENTS

398.—(1) This section applies to the publication by a company of full individual or group financial statements, required by section 388 to be laid before the company in general meeting and delivered to the Commission, including the directors' report, unless dispensed with under paragraph 3 of the Fourth Schedule to this Act, but does not apply to interim financial statements.

(2) If a company publishes individual financial statements (modified or otherwise) for a year, it shall publish with them the relevant auditors' report.

(3) If a company required by section 379 to this Act to prepare group financial statements for a year, publishes individual financial statements for that year, it shall also publish with them its group financial statements (which may be modified financial statements but only if the individual financial statements are modified).

(4) If a company publishes group financial statements (modified or not) without its individual financial statements, it shall publish with them the relevant auditors' report.

(5) References in this section to the relevant auditor's report are to the auditors' report under section 404 or, in the case of modified financial statements (individual or group), the auditors' special report under paragraph 10 of the Sixth Schedule to this Act.

(6) If default is made in complying with any provision of this section, the company and each officer of the company are liable to a penalty as the Commission shall specify in its regulations.

399.—(1) This section applies to the publication by a company of abridged financial statements, that is to say, any balance sheet or profit and loss account relating to a year of the company or purporting to deal with any such year, otherwise than as part of full financial statements (individual or group) to which section 398 of this Act applies.

(2) The reference in subsection (1) to a balance sheet or profit and loss account, in relation to financial statements published by a holding company, includes, "an account in any form purporting to be a balance sheet or profit and loss account for the group consisting of the holding company and its subsidiaries".

(3) If the company publishes abridged financial statements, it shall publish with those statements, a statement indicating—

(a) that the statements are not full financial statements ;

(b) whether full individual or full group financial statements according as the abridged statements deal solely with the company's own affairs or with the affairs of the company and any subsidiaries have been delivered to the Commission or, in the case of an unlimited company exempted under section 388 (4), from the requirement to deliver financial statements, that the company is so exempted ;

(c) whether the company's auditors have made a report under section404 on the company's financial statements for any year with which the abridged financial statements purport to deal ; and

(d) whether any report so made was unqualified (meaning that it was a report, without qualification, to the effect that in the opinion of the person making it, the company's financial statements had been properly prepared).

(4) Where a company publishes abridged financial statements, it shall not publish with those statements any such report of the auditors as is mentioned in subsection (3) (c).

(5) If default is made in complying with any provision of this section, the company and each officer of the company are liable to a penalty as the Commission shall specify in its regulations.

SUPPLEMENTARY

400. The Minister may after consultation with the Financial Reporting Council of Nigeria by regulations in a statutory instrument—

(a) add to the classes of documents to be—

(i) comprised in a company's financial statements for a year to be laid before the company in general meeting as required by section 388, or

(ii) delivered to the Commission under that section, and make provision as to the matters to be included in any document to be added to either class ; or

(b) modify the requirements of this Act as to the matters to be stated in a document of any such class, or reduce the classes of documents to be delivered to the Commission under section 386.

CHAPTER 15—AUDIT

Appointment of auditors. 401.—(1) Every company shall at each annual general meeting appoint an auditor or auditors to audit the financial statements of the company, and to hold office from the conclusion of that, until the conclusion of the next, annual general meeting.

(2) At any annual general meeting a retiring auditor, however appointed, shall be re-appointed without any resolution being passed unless—

(a) he is not qualified for re-appointment ;

(b) a resolution has been passed at that meeting appointing some other person instead of him or providing expressly that he shall not be re-appointed ; or

(c) he has given the company notice in writing of his unwillingness to be re-appointed: Provided that where notice is given of an intended resolution to appoint some person or persons in place of a retiring auditor, and by reason of the death, incapacity or disqualification of that person or of all those persons, as the case may be, the resolution cannot be proceeded with, the retiring auditor shall not be automatically re-appointed by virtue of this subsection.

(3) Where at an annual general meeting, no auditors are appointed or reappointed, the directors may appoint a person to fill the vacancy.

(4) The company shall, within one week of the power of the directors under subsection (3) becoming exercisable, give notice of that fact to the Commission; and if a company fails to give notice as required by this subsection, the company and every officer of the company shall be liable to a penalty as the Commission shall specify in its regulations.

(5) Subject to paragraphs (a) and (b), the first auditors of a company may be appointed by the directors at any time before the company is entitled to commence business and auditors so appointed hold office until the conclusion of the next annual general meeting, provided that—

(a) the company may at a general meeting remove any such auditors and appoint in their place any other person who has been nominated for appointment by any member of the company and of whose nomination notice has been given to the members of the company at least 14 days before the date of the meeting ; and

(b) if the directors fail to exercise their powers under this subsection, the company may, in a general meeting convened for that purpose, appoint the first auditors and thereupon the said powers of the directors ceases.

(6) The directors may fill any casual vacancy in the office of auditor but while any such vacancy continues, the surviving or continuing auditor or auditors, if any, may act.

402.—(1) A company is exempt from the requirements of this Act relating to the audit of accounts in respect of a financial year if—

(a) it has not carried on any business since its incorporation ; or (b) it is a small company within the meaning of section 394.

(2) A company is not entitled to an exemption under subsection (1) if it was at any time within the financial year in question an insurance company, a bank or any other company as may be prescribed by the Commission.

403.—(1) The provisions of any Act establishing a body of accountants shall have effect in relation to any investigation or audit for the purpose of this Act and none of the following persons is qualified for appointment as auditor of a company,—

(a) an officer or servant of the company,

(b) a person who is a partner of or in the employment of an officer or servant of the company, or (c) a body corporate.

(2) References in subsection (1) to an officer or servant shall be construed as not including references to an auditor.

(3) In the application of subsection (1), the disqualification extends and applies to persons who in respect of any period of an audit were in the employment of the company or were connected therewith in any manner.

(4) A person does not qualify for appointment as an auditor of a company if he is—

(a) disqualified for appointment as auditor of any other body corporate which is that company's subsidiary or holding company or a subsidiary of that company's holding company, or would be so disqualified if the body corporate were a company;

(b) a debtor to the company or to a company that is deemed to be related to the company by virtue of interest in shares, in an amount exceeding ₦500,000 ;

(c) a shareholder or spouse of a shareholder of a company whose employee is an officer of the company ;

(d) a person who is or whose partner, employee or employer is responsible for the keeping of the register of holders of debentures of the company ; (e) an employee of or consultant to the company who has been engaged for more than one year in the maintenance of any of the company's financial records or preparation of any of its financial statements ; or

(f) under subsection (6), disqualified for appointment as auditor of any other body corporate which is that company's subsidiary or holding company or a subsidiary of that company's holding company, or would be so disqualified if the body corporate were a company.

(5) Notwithstanding subsections (1), (3) and (4), a firm is qualified for appointment as auditor of a company if, all the partners are qualified for appointment as auditors of the company.

(6) A person shall not act as auditor of a company when he knows that he is disqualified for appointment to that office and if an auditor of a company, to his knowledge, becomes so disqualified during his term of office, he shall thereupon vacate his office

and give notice in writing to the company that he has vacated it by reason of that disqualification.

(7) A person who acts as auditor in contravention of subsection (6), or fails without reasonable excuse to give notice of vacating his office as required by that subsection commits an offence and is liable to a penalty as the Commission shall specify in its regulations.

404.—(1) The auditors of a company shall make a report to its members on the accounts examined by them, and on every balance sheet and profit and loss account, and on all group financial statements, copies of which are to be laid before the company in a general meeting during the auditors' tenure of office.

(2) The auditors' report shall state the matters set out in the Fifth Schedule in addition to the report made under subsection (1), and the auditor shall in the case of a public company, make a report to an audit committee which shall be established by the public company.

(3) The audit committee referred to in subsection (2) shall consist of five members comprising of three members and two non-executive directors, the members of the audit committee are not entitled to remuneration, and are subject to election annually.

(4) The audit committee shall examine the auditors' report and make recommendations thereon to the annual general meeting as it may deem fit.

(5) All members of the audit committee shall be financially literate, and at least one member shall be a member of a professional accounting body in Nigeria established by an Act of the National Assembly.

(6) Any member may nominate another member of the company to the audit committee by giving written notice of such nomination to the secretary of the company at least 21 days before the annual general meeting and any nomination not received prior to the meeting as stipulated is invalid.

(7) Subject to such other additional functions and powers that the company's articles may stipulate, the objectives and functions of the audit committee are to—

(a) ascertain whether the accounting and reporting policies of the company are in accordance with legal requirements and agreed ethical practices ;

(b) review the scope and planning of audit requirements ;

(c) review the findings on management matters in conjunction with the external auditor and departmental responses thereon ;

(d) keep under review the effectiveness of the company's system of accounting and internal control ;

(e) make recommendations to the board with regard to the appointment, removal and remuneration of the external auditors of the company ; and

(f) authorise the internal auditor to carry out investigations into any activities of the company which may be of interest or concern to the committee.

405.—(1) The chief executive officer and chief financial officer of a company other than a small company or persons performing similar functions shall certify in each audited financial statement that the—

(a) officer who signed the audited financial statements has reviewed them, and based on the officer's knowledge the—

(i) audited financial statements do not contain any untrue statement of material fact or omit to state a material fact, which would make the statements misleading, in the light of the circumstances under which such statement was made, and
(ii) audited financial statements and all other financial information included in the statements fairly present, in all material respects, the financial condition and results of operation of the company as of and for, the periods covered by the audited financial statements ; (b) officer who signed the audited financial statements—
(i) is responsible for establishing and maintaining internal controls and has designed such internal controls to ensure that material information relating to the company and its subsidiaries is made known to the officer by other officers of the companies, particularly during the period in which the audited financial statement report is being prepared,
(ii) has evaluated the effectiveness of the company's internal controls within 90 days prior to the date of its audited financial statements, and
(iii) certifies that the company's internal controls are effective as of that date ;
(c) officer who signed the audited financial statements disclosed to the company's auditors and audit committee—
(i) all significant deficiencies in the design or operation of internal controls which could adversely affect the company's ability to record, process, summarise and report financial data, and has identified for the company's auditors any material weaknesses in internal controls, and
(ii) whether or not, there is any fraud that involves management or other employees who have a significant role in the company's internal control ; and
(d) officer who signed the report, has indicated in the report, whether or not, there were significant changes in internal controls or in other factors that could significantly affect internal controls subsequent to the date of their evaluation, including any corrective actions with regard to significant deficiencies and material weaknesses.
(2) Where a managing director, chief financial officer or person performing similar functions fails to discharge the duty imposed on him under this section, he commits an offence and is liable on conviction to a penalty as the Commission shall specify in its regulations.

406.—(1) It shall be an offence for any officer, insider, director of a company, or any other person acting under the direction of such officer, insider or director, to take any action to influence, coerce, manipulate or mislead any external auditor engaged in the performance of an audit of the financial statements of that company for the purpose of rendering such financial statements misleading.
(2) A person who commits an offence under subsection (1) is liable on conviction to a penalty as the Commission shall specify in its regulations.
(3) For the purposes of this Act, "Insider" shall have the meaning given to it under the Investments and Securities Act, or any subsequent amendments thereto.

407.—(1) The company's auditors shall, in preparing their report to carry out such investigations as may enable them to form an opinion whether—
(a) proper accounting records have been kept by the company and proper returns adequate for their audit have been received from branches not visited by them ; or
(b) the company's balance sheet and (if not consolidated) its profit and loss account are in agreement with the accounting records and returns.

(2) If the auditors are of the opinion that proper accounting records have not been received from branches not visited by them, or if the balance sheet and (if not consolidated) the profit and loss account are not in agreement with the accounting records and returns, the auditors shall state that fact in their report.

(3) Every auditor of a company has a right of access at all times to the company's books, accounts and vouchers, and be entitled to require from the company's office such information and explanations as he thinks necessary for the performance of the auditor's duties.

(4) If the requirements of Part V and VI of the Second Schedule and Parts I and II of the Third Schedule to this Act are not complied with in the accounts, it is the auditors' duty to include in their report, so far as they are reasonably able to do so, a statement giving the required particulars.

(5) The auditors' shall consider whether the information given in the directors' report for the year for which the accounts are prepared is consistent with those accounts, and if they are of opinion that it is not, they shall state that fact in their report.

408.—(1) The remuneration of the auditors of a company—

(a) in the case of an auditor appointed by the directors, may be fixed by the directors ; or

(b) shall, subject to paragraph (a), be fixed by the company in general meeting or in such manner as the company in general meeting may determine.

(2) For the purposes of subsection (1), "remuneration" includes sums paid by the company in respect of the auditors' expenses.

409.—(1) A company may by ordinary resolution remove an auditor before the expiration of his term of office, notwithstanding anything in any agreement between it and him.

(2) Where a resolution removing an auditor is passed at a general meeting of a company, the company shall within 14 days give notice of that fact in the prescribed form to the Commission and if a company fails to give the notice required by this subsection, the company and each officer of the company are liable to a penalty as the Commission shall specify in its regulations.

(3) Nothing in this section shall be taken as depriving a person removed under it of compensation or damages payable to him in respect of the termination of his appointment as auditor or of any appointment terminating with that as auditor.

410.—(1) A company's auditors are entitled to attend any general meeting of the company and to receive all notices of and other communications relating to any general meeting which a member of the company is entitled to receive and to be heard at any general meeting which they attend on any part of the business of the meeting which concerns them as auditor.

(2) An auditor of a company who has been removed is entitled to attend—

(a) the general meeting at which his term of office would otherwise have expired ; and

(b) any general meeting at which it is proposed to fill the vacancy caused by his removal, and to receive all notices of, and other communications relating to, any such meeting which any member of the company is entitled to receive, and to be heard at any such meeting which he attends on any part of the business of the meeting which concerns him as former auditor of the company.

411.—(1) A special notice is required for a resolution at a general meeting of a company—

(a) appointing as auditor a person other than a retiring auditor ;
(b) filling a casual vacancy in the office of auditor ;
(c) re-appointing as auditor a retiring auditor who was appointed by the directors to fill a casual vacancy ; or
(d) removing an auditor before the expiration of his term of office.
(2) On receipt of notice of such an intended resolution as is mentioned in subsection (1), the company shall forthwith send a copy of it—
(a) to the person proposed to be appointed or removed ;
(b) in a case within subsection (1) (a), to the retiring auditors ; and
(c) in a case within subsection (1) (b) or (c), the casual vacancy was caused by the resignation of an auditor, to the auditor who resigned.
(3) Where notice is given of such a resolution as is mentioned in subsection(1) (a) or (d) and the retiring auditor (or, the auditor proposed to be removed) makes, with respect to the intended resolution, representations in writing to the company not exceeding a reasonable length, and requests their notification to members of the company, the company shall (unless the representations are received by it too late for it to do so)—
(a) in any notice of the resolution given to members of the company, state the fact of the representations having been made ; and
(b) send a copy of the representations to every member of the company to whom notice of the meeting is or has been sent.
(4) If a copy of any such representations is not sent out as required by subsection (3) because they were received too late or because of the company's default, the auditor may (without prejudice to his right to be heard orally) require that the representations be read out at the meeting.
(5) Copies of the representations need not be sent out and the representations need not be read out at the meeting if, on the application either of the company or of any other person claiming to be aggrieved, the court is satisfied that the rights conferred by this section are being abused to secure needless publicity for defamatory matter, and the Court may order the company's costs on the application to be paid in whole or in part by the auditor, notwithstanding that he is not a party to the application.
412.—(1) An auditor of a company may resign his office by depositing Resignation a notice in writing to that effect at the company's registered office, and such of auditors. notice operates to bring his term of office to an end on the date of which the notice is deposited, or on such later date as may be specified.
(2) An auditor's notice of resignation is not effective unless it contains either—
(a) a statement to the effect that there are no circumstances connected with his resignation which he considers should be brought to the notice of the members or creditors of the company ; or
(b) a statement of any such circumstances as are mentioned above.
(3) Where a notice under this section is deposited at a company's registered office, the company shall within 14 days send a copy of the notice— (a) to the Commission ; and
(b) if the notice contained a statement under subsection (2) (b), to every person who under section 387 of this Act is entitled to be sent copies of the financial statements.

(4) The company or any person claiming to be aggrieved may, within 14 days of the receipt by the company of a notice containing a statement under subsection (2) (b), apply to the Court for an order under subsection (5).

(5) If on such an application the Court is satisfied that the auditor is using the notice to secure needless publicity for defamatory matter, it may, by order, direct that copies of the notice need not be sent out, and the Court may further order the company's costs on the application to be paid in whole or in part by the auditor, notwithstanding that he is not a party to the application.

(6) The company shall, within 14 days of the Court's decision, send to the persons mentioned in subsection (3)—

(a) if the Court makes an order under subsection (5), a statement setting out the effect of the order ; and

(b) if not, a copy of the notice containing the statement under subsection (2) (b).

(7) If default is made in complying with the provisions of subsection (3) or (6), the company and each officer of the company are liable to a penalty as the Commission shall specify in its regulations.

413.—(1) Where an auditor's notice of resignation contains a statement under section 412 (2) (b), there may be deposited with the notice a requisition signed by the auditor calling on the directors of the company forthwith to convene an extraordinary general meeting of the company for the purpose of receiving and considering such explanation of the circumstances connected with his resignation as he may wish to place before the meeting.

(2) Where an auditor's notice of resignation contains such a statement, the auditor may request the company to circulate to its members before—

(a) the general meeting at which his term of office would otherwise have expired ; or

(b) any general meeting at which it is proposed to fill the vacancy caused by his resignation or convened on his requisition, a statement in writing (not exceeding a reasonable length) of the circumstances connected with his resignation.

(3) If a resigning auditor requests the circulation of a statement by virtue of subsection (2), the company shall (unless the statement is received by it too late for it to comply)—

(a) in any notice of the meeting given to members of the company, state the fact of the statement having been made ; and

(b) send a copy of the statement to every member of the company to whom notice of the meeting is or has been sent.

(4) If the directors do not within 21 days from the date of the deposit of a requisition under this section proceed to convene a meeting for a day not more than 28 days after the date on which the notice convening the meeting is given, every director is liable to a penalty as the Commission shall specify in its regulations.

(5) If a copy of the statement mentioned in subsection (2) is not sent out as required by subsection (3) because it was received too late or because of the company's default, the auditor may (without prejudice to his right to be heard orally) require that the statement be read out at the meeting.

(6) Copies of a statement need not be sent out and the statement need not be read out at the meeting if, on the application either of the company or of any other person who claims to be aggrieved, the Court is satisfied that the rights conferred by this section are being abused to secure needless publicity for defamatory matter, and the

Court may order the company's costs on such an application to be paid in whole or in part by the auditor, notwithstanding that he is not a party to the application.

(7) An auditor who has resigned his office is entitled to attend any such meeting as is mentioned in subsection (2) (a) or (b) and to receive all notices of and other communications relating to any such meeting which any member of the company is entitled to receive, and to be heard at any such meeting which concerns him as former auditor of the company.

414.—(1) Where a company has a subsidiary, then—

(a) if the subsidiary is a body corporate, incorporated in Nigeria, it is the duty of the subsidiaries and its auditors to give the auditors of the holding company such information and explanation as those auditors may reasonably require for the purposes of their duties as auditors of the holding company ; and

(b) in any other case, it is the duty of the holding company, if required by its auditors to do so, to take all such steps as are reasonably open to it to obtain from the subsidiary such information and explanation mentioned in paragraph (a).

(2) If a subsidiary or holding company fails to comply with the provisions of subsection (1), the subsidiary or holding company, and each officer are liable to a penalty as the Commission shall specify in its regulations, and if an auditor fails without reasonable excuse to comply with subsection (1) (a), he is so liable.

415.—(1) A company's auditor shall in the performance of his duties exercise all such care, diligence and skill as is reasonably necessary in each particular circumstance.

(2) Where a company suffers loss or damage as a result of the failure of its auditor to discharge the fiduciary duty imposed on him by subsection (1), the auditor is liable for negligence and the directors may institute an action for negligence against him in the Court.

(3) If the directors fail to institute an action against the auditor under subsection (2) of this section, any member may do so after the expiration of 30 days' notice to the company of his intention to institute such action.

416.—(1) An officer of a company commits an offence if he knowingly or recklessly makes to a company's auditors a statement (whether written or oral) which—

(a) conveys or purports to convey any information or explanation which the auditors require, or are entitled to require, as auditors of the company ; and (b) is misleading, false or deceptive in a material particular.

(2) A person who commits an offence under this section is liable to a penalty as the Commission shall specify in its regulations.

CHAPTER 16—ANNUAL RETURNS

417. Every company shall, once at least in every year, make and deliver to the Commission an annual return in the form, and containing the matters specified in sections 418, 419 or 420 as may be applicable:

Provided that a company need not make a return under this section either in the year of its incorporation or, if it is not required by section 237 to hold an annual general meeting during the following year, in that year.

418.—(1) The annual return by a company having shares other than a small company shall contain with respect to the registered office of the company, registers of members and debenture holders, shares and debentures, indebtedness, past and present members, directors and secretary, the matters specified in Part I of the

Seventh Schedule to this Act, and the return shall be in the form set out in Part II of that Schedule or as near to it as circumstances admit.

(2) Where the company has converted any of its shares into stock and given notice of the conversion to the Commission, the list referred to in paragraph 5 of Part I of the Seventh Schedule to this Act shall state the amount of stock held by each of the existing members instead of the number of shares and the particulars relating to shares required by that paragraph.

(3) The return may, in any year, if the return for either of the two immediately preceding years has given, as at the date of that return, the full particulars required by the paragraph 5 of the Seventh Schedule to this Act, give only such particulars required by that paragraph as relate to persons ceasing to be or becoming members since the date of the last return and to shares transferred since that date in the amount of stock held by a member.

419. The annual return by a small company shall contain the matters specified in Part I of the Eighth Schedule to this Act and the return shall be in the form set out in Part II of that Schedule or as near to it as circumstances admit.

420.—(1) The annual return by a company limited by guarantee shall be in the form prescribed in the Ninth Schedule or as near to it as circumstances admit.

(2) There shall be annexed to the return a statement containing particulars of the total amount of the indebtedness of the company in respect of all mortgages and charges which are required to be registered with the Commission under this Act.

421.—(1) The annual return shall be completed, signed by a director and the secretary, and delivered to the Commission not later than 42 days after the annual general meeting for the year, whether or not that meeting is the first or only general meeting of the company in that year, but the company may apply to the Commission for extension of time within which to file its annual return for any given calendar year.

(2) This section does not apply to companies with only one member.

422.—(1) Subject to the provisions of section 424 of this Act, there shall be annexed to the annual return—

(a) a written copy, certified both by a director and the Secretary of the company to be a true copy, of every balance sheet and profit and loss account laid before the company in general meeting held in the year to which the return relates (including every document required by law to be annexed to the balance sheet) ; and

(b) a copy, certified in accordance with paragraph (a), of the report of the auditors on, and of the report of the directors accompanying, each such balance sheet.

(2) If any such balance sheet as mentioned in subsection (1), or document required by law to be annexed does not comply with the requirement of the law in force at the date of the audit with respect to the form of balance sheet or the documents, there shall be made such additions to and corrections in the copy as would have been required to be made in the balance sheet or document in order to comply with the requirements, and the fact that the copy has been amended shall be stated on it.

(3) Any document required to be annexed to the annual return may be delivered to the Commission either in hard copy or through electronic communications.

423.—(1) A private company shall send with the annual return required by sections 418, 419 or 420 of this Act a certificate signed both by a director and the secretary of the company that the company has not, since the date of the last return, or, in the case of a first return, since the date of the incorporation of the company, issued any

invitation to the public to subscribe for shares or debentures of the company, and, where the annual return discloses the factAnnual
that the number of members of the company exceeds 50, also a certificate so signed that the excess consists wholly of persons who under section 22 (3) of this Act are not included in reckoning the number of 50.

(2) A small company shall in addition to the certificate required under subsection (1), send with the annual return a certificate signed by a director and the secretary that—

(a) it is a private company limited by shares ;

(b) the amount of its turn-over for that year is not more than ₦120,000,000 or such amount as may be fixed by the Commission ;

(c) its net assets value is not more than ₦60,000,000 or such amount as may be fixed by the Commission ;

(d) none of its members is an alien ;

(e) none of its members is a government, a government agent or nominee ; and

(f)) the directors among them hold at least 51% of the equity share capital of the company.

424.—(1) An unlimited company shall be exempted from the requirements of section 422 of this Act as to documents to be annexed to the annual return if,—

(a) at no time during the period to which the return relates has it been, to its knowledge, the subsidiary of a company that was then limited and at no such time, to its knowledge, have there been held or exercisable by or on behalf of two or more companies that were limited, shares or powers which, had they been held or exercisable by one of them, would have made the company its subsidiary ; and

(b) at no such time has it been the holding company of a company that was then limited.

(2) A small company is exempted from the requirements imposed by section 422 provided that it complies with the provision of section 394 of this Act.

425.—(1) If a company required to comply with any of the provisions of sections 417-423 fails to do so, the company and every director or officer of the company are liable to a penalty as may be prescribed by the Commission.

(2) For the purposes of subsection (1), "officer" includes any person in accordance with whose directions or instructions the directors of the company are accustomed to act.

(3) Failure to file annual returns for a consecutive period of 10 years is a ground for striking the name of a company off the companies' register.

426.—(1) A company may, in general meeting, declare dividends in respect of any year or other period only on the recommendation of the directors.

(2) The company may from time to time pay to the members such interim dividends as appear to the directors to be justified by the profits of the company.

(3) The general meeting has power to decrease the amount of dividend recommended by the directors, but has no power to increase the recommended amount.

(4) Where the recommendation of the directors of a company with respect to the declaration of a dividend is varied in accordance with subsection (3) by the company in general meeting, a statement to that effect shall be included in the relevant annual return.

(5) Subject to the provisions of this Act, dividends is payable to the shareholders only out of the distributable profits of the company.

427.—(1) A company may pay dividends only out of profits available for the purpose.

(2) The profits of a company available for payment of dividends are its accumulated, realised profits (so far as not previously utilised by distribution or capitalisation), less - its accumulated, realised losses (so far as not previously written off in a lawfully made reduction or reorganisation of capital).

428. A company shall not declare or pay dividend if there are reasonable grounds for believing that the company is or would be, after the payment, unable to pay its liabilities as they become due.

429.—(1) Where dividends paid by a company remain unclaimed, the company shall publish in two national newspapers, a list of the unclaimed dividends and the names of the persons entitled to the dividends, and attach the list, as published in the national newspapers, to the notice that is sent to the members of the company for each subsequent annual general meeting of the company.

(2) After the expiration of three months of the publication and notice referred to in subsection (1), the company may invest the unclaimed dividend for its own benefit in investments outside the company and no interest shall accrue on the dividends against the company.

(3) Where dividends have been sent to members and there is an omission to send to some members due to the fault of the company, the dividends shall earn interest at the current bank rate from three months after the date on which they ought to have been posted.

(4) For the purpose of liability, the date of posting the dividend warrant is deemed to be the date of payment and proof of whether it has been sent is a question of fact.

430.—(1) The directors may, before recommending any dividend, set capitalisation. aside out of the profits of the company such sums as they think proper as a reserve or reserves which shall, at the discretion of the directors, be applicable for any purpose to which the profits of the company may be properly applied, and pending such application may, at the discretion, either be employed in the business of the company or be invested in such investments (other than shares of the company) as the directors think fit, and the directors may without placing the same to reserve, carry forward any profits which they may think prudent not to distribute.

(2) The company in general meeting may upon the recommendation of the directors resolve that it is desirable to capitalise any part of the amount, for the time being, standing to the credit of any of the company's reserve accounts or to the credit of the profit and loss account or available for distribution.

(3) Such sum may be set free for distribution among the members who would have been entitled to dividends in the same proportions on condition that the same be not paid in cash but be applied either on or towards paying up any amount unpaid on any shares held by such members respectively or paying up in full unissued shares or debentures of the company to be allotted and distributed to creditors as fully paid up.

(4) The company may decide by a resolution, what part shall be distributed in cash or in shares and the directors shall give effect to such resolution.

(5) Share premium account and a capital redemption reserve fund may, for the purposes of this subsection, only be applied in the paying up of unissued shares to be issued to members of the company as fully paid bonus shares.

(6) Where a resolution under subsections (2)-(5) is passed, the directors shall make all appropriations and applications of the undivided profits resolved to be capitalised

thereby, and all allotments and issues of fully-paid shares or debentures, if any, and generally do all acts and things required to give effect to it.

(7) The directors shall have power to make such provision by the issue of fractional certificates or by payment in cash or otherwise as they think fit in the case of shares or debentures becoming distributable in fractions.

(8) Any person may be authorised by the directors to enter on behalf of all the members entitled under this section into an agreement with the company to provide for the allotment to them respectively, credited as fully paid up, of any further shares or debentures to which they may be entitled upon such capitalisation, or (as the case may require) for the payment by the company on their behalf, of the amount or any part of the amount remaining unpaid on their existing shares, and any agreement made under such authority is effective and binding on all such members.

431. If under his contract of service, an employee is entitled to share in the profits of the company as an incentive, he is entitled to share in the profits of the company, whether or not dividends have been declared.

432.—(1) Dividends are special debts due to and recoverable by shareholders within 12 years, and actionable only when declared.

(2) Dividends that are unclaimed after 12 years should be included in the profits that should be distributed to the other shareholders of the company.

433.—(1) All directors who knowingly pay, or are party to the payment of dividend out of capital or in contravention of this Part, are personally liable jointly and severally to refund to the company any amount so paid.

(2) Such directors shall have the right to recover the dividend from shareholders who receive it with knowledge that the company had no power to pay it.

CHAPTER 17—COMPANY VOLUNTARY ARRANGEMENTS

434.—(1) The directors of a company may make a proposal under this Part to its creditors for a composition in satisfaction of its debts or a scheme of arrangement of its affairs (in this Act referred to in either case, as a "voluntary arrangement").

(2) A proposal under this Part is one which provides for some person ("the nominee") to act in relation to the voluntary arrangement either as trustee or otherwise for the purpose of supervising its implementation, and the nominee shall be a person who is qualified to act as an insolvency practitioner in relation to the company.

(3) Such a proposal may be made where—

(a) an administration order is in force in relation to the company, by the administrator ; and

(b) the company is being wound up, by the liquidator.

435.—(1) This section applies where the nominee under section 434 is not the liquidator or administrator of the company.

(2) The nominee shall, within 28 days (or such longer period as the Court may allow) after he is given notice of the proposal for a voluntary arrangement, submit a report to the Court stating—

(a) whether, in his opinion, meetings of the company and of its creditors should be summoned to consider the proposal ; and

(b) if, in his opinion, such meetings should be summoned, the date on which, and time and place at which, he proposes the meetings to be held.

(3) For the purposes of enabling the nominee to prepare his report, the person intending to make the proposal shall submit to the nominee—

(a) a document setting out the terms of the proposed voluntary arrangement ; and

(b) a statement of the company's affairs containing—

(i) particulars of its creditors, its debts and other liabilities and of its assets as may be prescribed, and

(ii) other information as may be prescribed.

(4) The Court may, on an application made by the person intending to make the proposal, in a case where the nominee failed to submit the report required by this section, direct that the nominee be replaced as such by another person qualified to act as an insolvency practitioner in relation to the company.

436.—(1) A proposal may also be made where the nominee is —

(a) not the liquidator or administrator, and it has been reported to the Court that such meetings should be summoned, the person making the report shall (unless the Court otherwise directs) summon those meetings for the time, date and place proposed in the report ; and

(b) the liquidator or administrator, he shall summon meetings of the company and of its creditors to consider the proposal for such a time, date and place as he thinks fit.

(2) The persons to be summoned to a creditors' meeting under this section are every creditor of the company of whose claim and address the person summoning the meeting is aware.

CONSIDERATION AND IMPLEMENTATION OF PROPOSAL

437.—(1) The meetings summoned shall decide whether to approve the proposed voluntary arrangement with or without modifications.

(2) The modifications may include conferring the functions proposed to be conferred on the nominee on another person qualified to act as an insolvency practitioner in relation to the company but shall not include any modification by virtue of which the proposal ceases to be a proposal such as is mentioned in section 434.

(3) A meeting so summoned shall not approve any proposal or modification which affects the right of a secured creditor of the company to enforce his security, except with the concurrence of the creditor concerned.

(4) A meeting so summoned shall not approve any proposal or modification under which—

(a) any preferential debt of the company is to be paid otherwise than in priority to such of its debts as are not preferential debts ; or

(b) a preferential creditor of the company is to be paid an amount in respect of a preferential debt that bears to that debt a smaller proportion than is borne to another preferential debt by the amount that is to be paid in respect of that other debt provided that the meeting may approve such a proposal or modification with the concurrence of the preferential creditor concerned.

(5) Subject to the provisions of this section, each of the meetings shall be conducted in accordance with the rules.

(6) After the conclusion of either meeting in accordance with the rules, the chairman of the meeting shall report the result of the meeting to the Court, and, immediately after reporting to the Court, shall give notice of the result of the meeting to such persons as may be prescribed.

438.—(1) This section applies to a decision, under section 437, with respect to the approval of a proposed voluntary arrangement.

(2) The decision has effect if, in accordance with the rules—

(a) it has been taken by both meetings summoned under section 436 ; or
(b) subject to any order made under subsection (4) it has been taken by the creditors' meeting summoned under that section.
(3) If the decision taken by the creditors' meeting differs from that taken by the company meeting, a member of the company may apply to the Court.
(4) An application under subsection (3) shall not be made after the end of 28 days beginning with—
(a) the day on which the decision was taken by the creditors' meeting ; or
(b) where the decision of the company meeting was taken on a later day, that day.
(5) On an application under subsection (3), the Court may—
(a) order the decision of the company meeting to have effect instead of the decision of the creditors' meeting ; or
(b) make such other order as it deems fit.
439.—(1) This section applies where a decision approving a voluntary arrangement has effect under section 437.
(2) The order of the Court that the decision of the company meeting should have effect instead of the decision of the creditors' meeting—
(a) takes effect as if made by the company at the creditors' meeting ; and(b) binds every person who, in accordance with the rules—
(i) was entitled to vote at that meeting (whether or not he was present or represented at it), or
(ii) would have been so entitled if he had had notice of it, as if he were a party to the voluntary arrangement.
(3) Where the arrangement—
(a) ceases to have effect, any amount payable, under the arrangement to a person bound by virtue of subsection (2) (b) (ii) has not been paid, and (b) did not come to an end prematurely, the company shall at that time become liable to pay to that person the amount payable under the arrangement.
(4) Where the company is being wound up or is in administration, the Court may—
(a) by order, stay all proceedings in the winding-up or provide for the appointment of the administrator to cease to have effect ; or
(b) give such directions with respect to the conduct of the winding-up or the administration as it considers appropriate for facilitating the implementation of the order of the Court that the decision of the company meeting should have effect instead of the decision of the creditors' meeting on the voluntary arrangement.
(5) The Court shall not make an order under subsection (4) (a)—
(a) at any time before the end of 28 days beginning with the first day on which each of the reports required by section 435 (2) has been made to the Court ; or
(b) at any time when an application under section 435 (4) or an appeal in respect of such an application is pending, or at any time in the period within which such an appeal may be brought.
Challenge of 440.—(1) Subject to this section, an application to the Court may be decisions. made, by any of the persons specified in subsection (2), on the ground that—
(a) a voluntary arrangement which has effect under section 437 unfairly prejudices the interests of a creditor, member or contributory of the company ; or
(b) there has been some material irregularity at or in relation to either of the meetings.

(2) The persons who may apply under subsection (1) are—

(a) persons entitled, in accordance with the rules, to vote at either of the meetings ;

(b) persons who would have been entitled, in accordance with the rules, to vote at the creditors' meeting if they had had notice of it ;

(c) the nominees or persons who replaced them under section 435 (4) or437 (2) ; and

(d) if the company is being wound up or is in administration, the liquidator or administrator.

(3) An application under this section shall not be made—

(a) after the end of 28 days beginning with the first day on which each of the reports required under section 435 (2) has been made to the Court, or

(b) on which each of the reports required by section 435 (2) has been made to the Court but (subject to that), an application made by a person within this subsection on the ground that the voluntary arrangement prejudices his interests may be made after the arrangement has ceased to have effect, unless it came to an end prematurely.

(4) Where on such an application the Court is satisfied as to either of the grounds mentioned in subsection (1), it may—

(a) revoke or suspend any decision approving the voluntary arrangement which has effect under section 437 or, in a case falling within subsection (1) (b), any decision taken by the meeting in question which has effect under that section ; or

(b) give a direction to any person for the summoning of further meetings to consider any revised proposal, the person who made the original proposal may make or, in the case falling within subsection (1) (b), a further company or creditors' meeting to reconsider the original proposal.

(5) Where after giving a direction under subsection (4)(b) for the summoning of meetings to consider a revised proposal the Court is satisfied that the person who made the original proposal does not intend to submit a revised proposal, the Court shall revoke the direction and revoke or suspend any decision approving the voluntary arrangement which has effect under section 437.

(6) Where the Court, on an application under this section with respect to any meeting—

(a) gives a direction under subsection (4) (b), or

(b) revokes or suspends an approval under subsection (4) (a) or (5), the Court may give such supplemental directions as it deems fit and, in particular, directions with respect to things done under the voluntary arrangement since it took effect.

(7) Except as provided in this section, a decision taken at a meeting summoned under section 436 is not invalidated by any irregularity at or in relation to the meeting.

A false 441.—(1) If, for the purpose of obtaining the approval of the members representation, or creditors of a company to a proposal for a voluntary arrangement, a person etc.

who is an officer of the company—

(a) makes any false representation, or

(b) fraudulently does, or omits to do anything, he commits an offence.

(2) A person who contravenes subsection (1), commits an offence and is liable on conviction to imprisonment for a term of one year or a fine as the Court deems fit or both.

Implementation approved of proposal. 442.—(1) This section applies where a voluntary arrangement by the meetings summoned under section 436 has taken effect.

(2) The person who performs, in relation to the voluntary arrangement, the functions conferred by virtue of— (a) the approval on the nominee, or

(b) section 435 (4) or 437 (3) on a person other than the nominee, shall be known as the supervisor of the voluntary arrangement.

(3) If any of the company's creditors or any other person is dissatisfied by any act, omission or decision of the supervisor, he may apply to the Court, and, on the application, the Court may—

(a) confirm, reverse or modify any act or decision of the supervisor ;

(b) give him directions ; or

(c) make such other order as it deems fit.

(4) The supervisor may apply to the Court for directions in relation to any particular matter arising under the voluntary arrangement, and is included among the persons who may apply to the Court for the winding-up of the company or for an administration order to be made in relation to it.

(5) The Court may, whenever it is—

(a) expedient to appoint a person to perform the functions of the supervisor, and

(b) it is inexpedient, difficult or impracticable for an appointment to be made without the assistance of the Court,

make an order appointing a person who is qualified to act as an insolvency practitioner in relation to the company, either in substitution for the existing supervisor or to fill a vacancy.

(6) The power conferred by subsection (5) is exercisable so as to increase the number of persons performing the functions of supervisor or, where there is more than one person performing those functions, so as to replace one or more of those persons.

CHAPTER 18—ADMINISTRATION OF COMPANIES : NATURE OF ADMINISTRATION

443.—(1) A person may be appointed as administrator of a company by—

(a) an administration order of the Court under section 449 of this Act ; (b) the holder of a floating charge under section 452 of this Act ; or (c) the company or its directors under section 459 of this Act.

(2) Where an administrator is appointed out of Court, if it is an administration that has a cross-border element, an application shall be made ex parte to the Court for approval.

(3) An extra curia administrator appointed under subsection (1) (b) may, in addition to statutory notice to the Court under section 457, also request, in an accompanying ex parte application to the Court, a formal court order.

444.—(1) The administrator of a company may do all such things as may be necessary for the management of the affairs, business and property of the company, and shall perform his functions with the objective of—

(a) rescuing the company, the whole or any part of its undertaking, as a going concern;

(b) achieving a better result for the company's creditors as a whole than would be likely if the company were wound up, without first being in administration ; or

(c) realising property in order to make a distribution to one or more secured or preferential creditors.

(2) Notwithstanding subsection (1) (b) and (c), the rescue of the company is the primary objective of the administrator in the performance of his functions, except where he is of the opinion that it is not reasonably practicable or a better result can be achieved for the company's creditors by pursuing some other course in order of priority as specified in that subsection.

(3) Subject to subsection (5), the administrator of a company shall perform his functions in the interests of the company's creditors as a whole.

(4) The administrator shall perform his functions with the objective specified in subsection (1) (a) unless he is of the opinion that— (a) it is not reasonably practicable to achieve that objective ; or

(b) the objective specified in subsection (1) (b) would achieve a better result for the company's creditors as a whole.

(5) The administrator may perform his functions with the objective specified in subsection (1) (c) only if he—

(a) is of the opinion that it is not reasonably practicable to achieve either of the objectives specified in subsection (1) (a) and (b) ; and

(b) does not unnecessarily harm the interests of the creditors of the company as a whole.

(6) The administrator shall, within 60 days of his appointment prepare a detailed schedule of assets and submit a copy to the person by whom he was appointed.

445. The administrator of a company shall perform his functions as quickly and efficiently as is reasonably practicable.

446. An Administrator is an officer of the Court, whether or not he is appointed by the Court.

447.—(1) A person may be appointed as administrator of a company only if he is qualified to act as an insolvency practitioner in relation to the company.

(2) A person shall only be appointed as administrator of a company which is in administration, subject to the provisions of sections 525-534 and 537-541 of this Act about replacement and additional administrators.

(3) A person shall not be appointed as administrator of a company which is in liquidation by virtue of—

(a) a resolution for voluntary winding-up, subject to section 475 (2) (b) of this Act ; or

(b) a winding-up order, subject to sections 474 and 475 of this Act.

(4) A person shall not be appointed as administrator of a company which—

(a) has as a liability in respect of a deposit which it accepted in accordance with relevant banking laws ; and

(b) is not an authorised deposit taker within the meaning of banking laws and regulations.

(5) A person shall not be appointed as administrator of a company which effects or carries out contracts of insurance except with the leave of the insurance regulator.

APPOINTMENT OF ADMINISTRATOR BY COURT

448. An administration order is an order appointing a person as the administrator of a company.

449. A Court may make an administration order in relation to a company, where it is satisfied that the—

(a) company is or is likely to become unable to pay its debts ; and

(b) administration order is likely to achieve the purpose of administration.

450.—(1) An application to the Court for an administration order in respect of a company (in this Act referred to as an "administration application") may be made by— (a) the company ;

(b) the directors of the company ;

(c) one or more creditors of the company ;

(d) the designated officer of the Federal High Court appointed to act as a receiver under this Act or any other law; or

(e) a combination of the persons listed in paragraphs (a)-(d).

(2) As soon as is reasonably practicable after the making of an administration application, the applicant shall notify—

(a) any Court that has appointed a receiver and any person who has appointed a receiver of the company ;

(b) a person who has, who is or who may be entitled to appoint a receiver of the company ;

(c) a person who is or may be entitled to appoint an administrator of the company under section 452 of this Act ; and

(d) such other persons as may be prescribed.

(3) An administration application shall not be withdrawn without the permission of the Court.

(4) In subsection (1), "creditor" includes a contingent creditor and a prospective creditor.

451.—(1) On hearing an administration application, the Court may—

(a) make the administration order sought ;

(b) dismiss the application ;

(c) adjourn the hearing conditionally or unconditionally ;

(d) make an interim order ;

(e) treat the application as a winding-up petition and make any order which the Court could make under section 574 of this Act ; or

(f) make any other order which the Court deems appropriate.

(2) An appointment of an administrator by an administration order takes effect—

(a) at a time appointed by the order ; or

(b) where no time is appointed by the order, when the order is made.

(3) An interim order under subsection (1) (d) may, in particular— (a) restrict the exercise of a power of the directors or the company; or

(b) make provision conferring a discretion on the Court or on a person qualified to act as an insolvency practitioner in relation to the company.

(4) This section is subject to section 573 of this Act.

452.—(1) Subject to section 450 of this Act, the holder of a floating charge in respect of a company's property may appoint an administrator of the company.

(2) For the purposes of subsection (1), a floating charge qualifies if it is created by an instrument which—

(a) states that this section applies to the floating charge ;

(b) purports to empower the holder of the floating charge to appoint an administrator of the company ; or

(c) purports to empower the holder of the floating charge to appoint a receiver within the meaning of this Part or where this Part is not applicable, the relevant provisions of this Act.

(3) For the purposes of subsection (1), a person is the holder of a floating charge in respect of a company's property if he holds one or more debentures of the company secured by—

(a) a floating charge which relates to the whole or substantially the whole of the company's property ;

(b) a number of floating charges which together relate to the whole or substantially the whole of the company's property ; or

(c) charges and other forms of security which together relate to the whole or substantially the whole of the company's property and at least one of which is a floating charge.

(4) Without prejudice to the specific terms of the instrument creating a charge, any contrary or conflicting provision of this Act or other enactments, the appointment of a receiver or manager by the holder of a floating charge is to all intents and purpose equivalent to the appointment of an administrator, and the provisions of this Part are applicable to the person qualified to act as an insolvency practitioner and appointed under the relevant instrument by the holder of a floating charge.

453.—(1) A person shall not appoint an administrator under section 452 of this Act unless—

(a) he has given at least two working days' written notice to the holder of any prior floating charge which satisfies section 452 (2) of this Act ; or

(b) the holder of any prior floating charge which satisfies section 452 (2) of this Act has consented in writing to the making of the appointment.

(2) One floating charge is prior to another for the purposes of subsection

(1) if it—

(a) was created first ; or

(b) is to be treated as having priority in accordance with an agreement to which the holder of each floating charge was party.

454. An administrator shall not be appointed under section 452 of this Act if —

(a) a floating charge on which the appointment relies is not enforceable, a holder of the unenforceable charge may apply or join as a mere creditor in an administration application under section 450 of this Act ;

(b) a provisional liquidator of the company has been appointed under section 585 of this Act ; or

(c) prior to the commencement of this Act and the coming into effect of this Chapter, a receiver or manager of the company is in office.

455.—(1) A person who appoints an administrator of a company under section 452 of this Act shall file with the Commission—

(a) a notice of appointment ; and

(b) such other documents as may be prescribed.

(2) The notice of appointment shall include a statutory declaration by or on behalf of the person who makes the appointment that—

(a) the person is the holder of a floating charge in respect of the company's property ;

(b) each floating charge relied on in making the appointment is or was enforceable on the date of the appointment ; and

(c) the appointment is in accordance with this Chapter and generally with this Act.

(3) The notice of appointment shall identify the administrator and be accompanied by a statement by the administrator—

(a) that he consents to the appointment ;
(b) that in his opinion, the purpose of administration is likely to be achieved ; and
(c) giving such other information and opinions as may be prescribed.
(4) The administrator may at his discretion elect to apply for further discretion or relief.
(5) For the purpose of a statement under subsection (3), an administrator may rely on information supplied by directors of the company, unless he has reason to doubt its accuracy.
(6) The notice of appointment and any document accompanying it shall be in the prescribed form.
(7) A statutory declaration under subsection (2) shall be made during the prescribed period.
(8) A person commits an offence, if in a statutory declaration under subsection (2), he makes a statement which—
(a) is false ; and
(b) he does not reasonably believe to be true.
456. The appointment of an administrator under section 450 of this Act takes effect when the requirements of section 447 of this Act are satisfied.
457.—(1) A person who appoints an administrator under section 450 of this Act shall notify the administrator and such other persons as may be prescribed as soon as is reasonably practicable after the requirements of section
447 of this Act are satisfied.
(2) A person who fails, without reasonable excuse, to comply with subsection (1), commits an offence.
458.—(1) This section applies where—
(a) a person purports to appoint an administrator under section 452 of this Act ; and
(b) the appointment is discovered to be invalid.
(2) The Court may order the person who purported to make the appointment to indemnify the person appointed against liability which arises solely by reason of the invalidity of the appointment.

APPOINTMENT OF ADMINISTRATOR BY COMPANY OR DIRECTORS OUT OF COURT

459.—(1) A company may appoint an administrator out of Court.
(2) The directors of a company may also appoint an administrator out of Court.
460.—(1) This section applies where an administrator of a company is appointed—
(a) under section 450 of this Act ; or
(b) on an administration application made by the company or its directors.
(2) An administrator of the company shall not be appointed under section 449 of this Act within 12 months beginning with the date on which the appointment referred to in subsection (1) ceases to have effect.
461.—(1) If a moratorium for a company under this Part and any supportive schedule ends on a date when no voluntary arrangement is in effect in respect of the company, this section applies for the period of 12 months beginning with that date.
(2) This section also applies for the period of 12 months beginning with the date on which a voluntary arrangement in respect of a company ends, where the arrangement—
(a) was made during a moratorium for the company under this Part ; and (b) ends prematurely.

(3) While this section applies, an administrator of the company shall not be appointed under section 450 of this Act.

462. An administrator of a company shall not be appointed under section 459 of this Act where—

(a) a petition for the winding-up of the company has been presented and is not yet disposed of;

(b) an administration application has been made and is not yet disposed of; or

(c) a receiver of the company is in office.

463.—(1) Except where there is no secured creditor who has, or might have the right to appoint an administrator under section 452 of this Act or a receiver or any other person as envisaged under subsection (2), a person who proposes to make an appointment under section 469 of this Act shall give at least three working days' written notice by post, personal delivery, hand delivered mail, or email to any person who is or may be entitled to appoint—

(a) a receiver of the company; and

(b) an administrator of the company under section 450 of this Act.

(2) A person who proposes to make an appointment under this section shall also give such notice as may be prescribed to such other persons as may be prescribed.

(3) A notice under this section shall—(a) identify the proposed administrator; and (b) be in the prescribed form.

464.—(1) A person who gives notice of intention to appoint under section 458 shall file with the Commission as soon as is reasonably practicable a copy of—

(a) the notice; and

(b) any document accompanying it.

(2) The copy filed under subsection (1) shall be accompanied by a statutory declaration made by or on behalf of the person who proposes to make the appointment—

(a) that the company is or is likely to become unable to pay its debts;

(b) that the company is not in liquidation;

(c) that so far as the person making the statement is able to ascertain, the appointment is not prevented by sections 453 and 454 of this Act; and

(d) to such additional effect, and giving such information, as may be prescribed.

(3) A statutory declaration under subsection (2) shall be—

(a) in the prescribed form; and (b) made during the prescribed period.

(4) A person commits an offence if, in a statutory declaration under subsection (2), he makes a statement which—

(a) is false; and

(b) he does not reasonably believe to be true.

465.—(1) An appointment shall not be made under section 459 of this Act unless the person who makes the appointment has complied with any requirement of sections 462 and 463 of this Act—

(a) the period of notice specified in section 463 (1) of this Act has expired; or

(b) each person to whom notice has been given under section 463 (1) of this Act has consented in writing to the making of the appointment.

(2) An appointment shall not be made under section 460 after the period of 10 working days beginning with the date on which the notice of intention to appoint is filed under section 463 (1) of this Act.

466.—(1) A person who appoints an administrator of a company under section 459 of this Act shall file with the Court—
(a) a notice of appointment ; and
(b) such other documents as may be prescribed.
(2) The notice of appointment shall include a statutory declaration by or on behalf of the person who makes the appointment that—
(a) the person is entitled to make an appointment under section 459 of this Act ;
(b) the appointment is in accordance with this Part ; and
(c) so far as the person making the statement is able to ascertain, the statements made and information given in the statutory declaration filed with the notice of intention to appoint remain accurate.
(3) The notice of appointment shall identify the administrator and be accompanied by a statement by the administrator—
(a) that he consents to the appointment ;
(b) that in his opinion the purpose of administration is likely to be achieved ; and
(c) giving such other information and opinions as may be prescribed.
(4) For the purpose of a statement under subsection (3), an administrator may rely on information supplied by directors of the company unless he has reason to doubt its accuracy.
(5) The notice of appointment and any document accompanying it shall be in the prescribed form.
(6) A statutory declaration under subsection (2) shall be made during the prescribed period.

467. A person commits an offence if, in a statutory declaration under section 464 (2), he makes a statement which—
(a) is false ; or
(b) he does not reasonably believe to be true.

468. Where a person is not entitled to notice of intention to appoint under section 455 (1), and section 457 of this Act, shall not apply—
(a) the statutory declaration accompanying the notice of appointment shall include the statements and information required under section 464 (2) of this Act ; and
(b) section 464 (2) (c) of this Act shall also not apply.

469. The appointment of an administrator under section 459 of this Act takes effect when the requirements of section 464 of this Act are satisfied.

470. A person who appoints an administrator under section 459 of this Act—(a) shall notify the administrator and such other persons as may be prescribed as soon as is reasonably practicable after the requirements of section 464 are satisfied ; and
(b) commits an offence if he fails, without reasonable excuse, to comply with paragraph (a).

471. Where, before the requirements of section 464 of this Act are satisfied, the company enters administration by virtue of an administration order or an appointment under section 450 of this Act—
(a) the appointment under section 459 of this Act shall not take effect ; and (b) section 467 of this Act shall not apply.

ADMINISTRATION APPLICATION—SPECIAL CASES

472.—(1) This section applies where an administration application in respect of a company—

(a) is made by the holder of a floating charge in respect of the company's property ; and
(b) includes a statement that the application is made in reliance on this section.
(2) The Court may make an administration order—
(a) whether or not satisfied that the company is or is likely to become unable to pay its debts ; and
(b) only if satisfied that the applicant could appoint an administrator under section 450 of this Act.
473.—(1) This section applies where—
(a) an administration application in respect of a company is made by a person who is not the holder of a floating charge in respect of the company's property ; and
(b) the holder of a floating charge in respect of the company's property applies to the Court to have a specified person appointed as administrator and not the person specified by the administration applicant.
(2) The Court shall grant an application under subsection (1) (b) unless the Court deems it right to refuse the application because of the particular circumstances of the case.
474.—(1) This section applies where the holder of a floating charge in respect of a company's property could appoint an administrator under section 452 of this Act but for section 452 (3) (b) of this Act.
(2) The holder of the floating charge may make an administration application.
(3) If the Court makes an administration order on hearing an application made by virtue of subsection (2), the Court— (a) shall discharge the winding-up order ;
(b) shall make provision for such matters as may be prescribed ;
(c) may make other consequential provision ; and
(d) shall specify which of the powers under this Chapter and Eleventh Schedule are to be exercisable by the administrator.
(4) This Part shall have effect with such modifications as the Court may direct.
475.—(1) The liquidator of a company may make an administration application.
(2) If the Court makes an administration order on hearing an application made by virtue of subsection (1), the Court—
(a) shall discharge any winding-up order in respect of the company ;
(b) shall make provision for such matters as may be prescribed ;
(c) may make other consequential provision ; and
(d) shall specify which of the powers under this Chapter and Tenth Schedule are to be exercisable by the administrator.
(3) This Chapter shall have effect with such modifications as the Court may direct.
476.—(1) Where there is a receiver of a company based on appointment by a holder of a fixed charge, the Court shall dismiss an administration application in respect of the company unless—
(a) the person by or on behalf of whom the receiver was appointed consents to the making of the administration order ;
(b) the Court considers that the security by virtue of which the receiver was appointed would be liable to be released or discharged under section 232 or 233 of this Act if an administration order were made ; or
(c) the Court considers that the security by virtue of which the receiver was appointed would be challengeable under section 558 or 559 of this Act.

(2) Subsection (1) applies whether or not the receiver is appointed before the making of the administration application.

EFFECT OF ADMINISTRATION

477. (1) A petition for the winding-up of a company shall be—

(a) dismissed on the making of an administration order in respect of the company ; and

(b) suspended while the company is in administration following an appointment under section 475 of this Act.

(2) The provision of subsection (1)(b) does not apply to a petition presented under grounds of public interest as may be prescribed from time to time by the Chief Judge or under an enactment.

(3) Except with the leave of the Court, subsection (1) (a) and (b) does not apply to a petition presented under special banking provisions of the Banks and Other Financial Institutions Act, Nigerian Deposit Insurance Corporation Act or any law or rule by a financial services and markets regulator.

478.—(1) When an administration order takes effect in respect of a company, a receiver of the company appointed by a holder of a floating charge or by the Court shall vacate office.

(2) Without prejudice to priority rules under this Act, where a company is in administration, any receiver of part of the company's property appointed by a secured creditor shall vacate office if the administrator requires him to.

(3) Where a receiver vacates office under this section—

(a) his remuneration shall be charged on and paid out of any property of the company which was in his custody or under his control immediately before he vacated office ; and

(b) he need not take any further steps under section 561 or 562.

(4) In the application of subsection (3) (a)—

(a) "remuneration" includes expenses properly incurred and any indemnity to which the receiver is entitled out of the assets of the company ;

(b) the charge imposed takes priority over security held by the person by whom or on whose behalf the receiver was appointed ; and (c) the provision for payment is subject to section 558.

479.—(1) This section applies to a company in administration.

(2) Where a company is in administration, no—

(a) resolution shall be passed for the winding-up of the company ; and (b) order shall be made for the winding-up of the company.

(3) Subsection (2) (b) does not apply to an order made on a petition presented under—

(a) grounds of public interest as may be prescribed from time to time by the Chief Judge or under any enactment ; or

(b) special banking and financial provisions of the Banks and Other Financial Institutions Act, the Nigerian Deposit Insurance Corporation Act, or any other financial services and markets related Acts.

(4) If a petition presented under a provision referred to in subsection (3) comes to the attention of the administrator, he shall apply to the Court for directions under section 500.

480.—(1) This section applies to a company in administration.

(2) Where a company is in administration, no step shall be taken to— (a) enforce security over the company's property except with—

(i) the consent of the administrator, or
(ii) the permission of the Court ; or
(b) repossess goods in the company's possession under a hire purchase agreement except with the—
(i) consent of the administrator, or (ii) permission of the Court.
(3) A landlord shall not exercise a right of forfeiture by peaceable re-entry in relation to premises let to the company except with the—
(a) consent of the administrator ; or (b) permission of the Court.
(4) No legal process, including legal proceedings, execution, distress and diligence shall be instituted or continued against the company or property of the company except with the—
(a) consent of the administrator ; or (b) permission of the Court.
(5) Where the Court gives permission for a transaction under this section, it may impose a condition on or a requirement in connection with the transaction. (6) In this section, "landlord" includes a person to whom rent is payable.
481.—(1) This section applies where an administration application in respect of a company has been made and the application has—
(a) not yet been granted or dismissed ; or
(b) been granted but the administration order has not yet taken effect.
(2) This section also applies when a copy of a notice in the prescribed form, of intention to appoint an administrator under section 464 of this Act is filed with the Court, until—
(a) the appointment of the administrator takes effect ; or
(b) the period of three business days beginning with the date of filing expires without an administrator having been appointed.
(3) This section also applies when a copy, in the prescribed form, of notice of intention to appoint an administrator is filed with the court under section 464 (1) of this Act, until—
(a) the appointment of the administrator takes effect ; or
(b) the period specified in subsection (2) expires without an administrator having been appointed.
(4) The provisions of sections 475 and 476 of this Act shall apply, without regard to any reference to the consent of the administrator.
(5) If there is a receiver of the company appointed by the holder of a floating charge when the administration application is made, the provisions of section 480 and this section shall not apply until the person by or on behalf of whom the receiver was appointed consents to the making of the administration order.
(6) This section does not prevent or require the permission of the Court for the—
(a) presentation of a petition for the winding-up of the company under section 451 of this Act ;
(b) appointment of an Administrator under section 452 of this Act ;
(c) appointment of a receiver of the company by the holder of a floating charge ; or
(d) performing by such a receiver, whenever appointed, of his functions.
482.—(1) If a company is in administration, every business document issued by or on behalf of the company or the administrator, and all the company's websites, shall state—
(a) the name of the administrator ; and

(b) that the affairs, business and property of the company are being managed by the administrator.

(2) An administrator, officer of the company or the company who, without reasonable excuse, authorises or permits a contravention of subsection (1), commits an offence.

(3) In subsection (1), "business document" includes—

(a) an invoice ;

(b) an order for goods or services ;

(c) a business letter ; and

(d) an order form, whether in hard copy, electronic or any other form.

PROCESS OF ADMINISTRATION

483.—(1) This section applies where a person becomes the administrator of a company.

(2) The administrator shall not later than 14 days—

(a) send a notice of his appointment to the company ;

(b) publish a notice of his appointment in the prescribed manner ;

(c) obtain a list of the company's creditors ; and

(d) send a notice of his appointment to each creditor whose claim and address he is aware of.

(3) The administrator shall send a notice of his appointment to the Commission, publicising the notice before the end of 14 working days beginning with the date specified in subsection (5).

(4) The administrator shall send a notice of his appointment to such persons as may be prescribed before the end of the prescribed period beginning with the date specified in subsection (5).

(5) The date, for the purpose of subsections (3) and (4) is, in the case of an administrator appointed—

(a) by administration order, the date of the order ;

(b) under section 452 of this Act, the date on which he receives notice under section 453 and 455 of this Act ; and

(c) under section 458 of this Act, the date on which he receives notice under section 463 and 465 of this Act.

(6) The Court may direct that subsection (2) (d) or (4)—

(a) shall not apply ; or

(b) shall apply with the substitution of a different period.

(7) A notice under this section shall—(a) contain the prescribed information; and (b) be in the prescribed form.

(8) An administrator commits an offence if he fails, without reasonable excuse, to comply with a requirement of this section.

484.—(1) As soon as is reasonably practicable after appointment, the administrator of a company shall, by notice in the prescribed form, require one or more relevant persons to provide the administrator with a statement of the affairs of the company.

(2) The statement shall—

(a) be verified by a statement on oath ;

(b) be in the prescribed form ;

(c) give particulars of the company's property, debts and liabilities ;

(d) give the names and addresses of the company's creditors ;

(e) specify the security held by each creditor ;

(f) give the date on which each security was granted ; and (g) contain such other information as may be prescribed.

(3) In subsection (1), "relevant person" means a person—

(a) who is or has been an officer of the company ;

(b) who took part in the formation of the company during the period of one year ending with the date on which the company enters administration ;

(c) employed by the company during that period ; and

(d) who is or has, during the period of one year ending with the date on which the company enters administration, been an officer or employee of a company.

(4) For the purpose of subsection (3), a reference to employment is a reference to employment through a contract of employment or a contract for services.

(5) A person commits an offence if he fails, without reasonable excuse, to comply with a requirement of this section.

485.—(1) A person required to submit a statement of affairs shall do so before the end of 11 working days beginning with the day on which he receives notice of the requirement.

(2) The administrator may—

(a) revoke a requirement under section 484 (2) of this Act ; or

(b) extend the period specified in subsection (1), before or after expiration of the period.

(3) If the administrator refuses a request to act under subsection (2) (b)— (a) the person whose request is refused may apply to the Court ; and (b) the Court may take action as specified in subsection (2).

486.—(1) The administrator of a company shall make a statement setting out proposals for achieving the purpose of the administration.

(3) A statement under subsection (1) shall, in particular—

(a) deal with such matters as may be prescribed ; and

(b) where applicable, explain why the administrator thinks that the objective mentioned in section 444 (1) (a) or (b) of this Act cannot be achieved.

(4) Proposals under this section may include—

(a) a proposal for a voluntary arrangement under Chapter 17 of this Act, but this section is without prejudice to section 435 of this Act ; and

(b) a proposal for a scheme of arrangement and compromise or reconstruction to be sanctioned under relevant Parts of this Act.

(5) The administrator shall send a copy of the statement of his proposals to—

(a) the Commission ;

(b) every creditor of the company of whose claim and address he is aware ; and

(c) every member of the company of whose address he is aware.

(5) The administrator shall comply with subsection (4) before the end of30 days beginning with the day on which the company enters administration.

(6) The administrator is deemed to comply with subsection (4) (c) if he publishes in the prescribed manner, a notice undertaking to provide a copy of the statement of proposals free of charge to any member of the company who applies in writing to a specified address.

(7) An administrator commits an offence if he fails, without reasonable excuse, to comply with subsection (5).

(8) A period specified in this section may be varied in accordance with section 546 of this Act.

487.—(1) Subject to this Part, the administrator shall summon a meeting of the creditors of the company to be known as "creditors' meeting"—

(a) in the prescribed manner ; and

(b) giving the prescribed period of notice to every creditor of the company of whose claim and address he is aware.

(2) A period prescribed under subsection (1) (b) may be varied in accordance with section 546 of this Act.

(3) A creditors' meeting shall be conducted in accordance with the prescribed rules.

488.—(1) Each copy of an administrator's statement of proposals sent to a creditor under section 486 (4) (b) of this Act shall be accompanied by an invitation to creditors' meeting (an "initial creditors' meeting").

(2) The date set for an initial creditors' meeting is 42 days beginning with the date on which the company enters administration.

(3) An administrator shall present a copy of his statement of proposals to an initial creditors' meeting.

(4) A period specified in this section may be varied in accordance with section 546.

(5) An administrator commits an offence if he fails, without reasonable excuse, to comply with a requirement of this section.

489.—(1) Section 487 (1) of this Act does not apply where the statement of proposals states that the administrator thinks that—

(a) the company has sufficient property to enable each creditor of the company to be paid in full ;

(b) the company has insufficient property to enable a distribution to be made to unsecured creditors other than by virtue of the provisions of this Act; or

(c) neither of the objectives specified in section 444 (1) (a) and (b) of this Act shall be achieved.

(2) The Administrator shall summon an initial creditors' meeting if it is requested—

(a) by creditors of the company whose debts amount to at least 10% of the total debts of the company ;

(b) in the prescribed manner ; and(c) within the prescribed period.

(3) A meeting requested under subsection (2), shall be summoned for ad ate within the prescribed period.

(4) The period prescribed under subsection (3), may be varied in accordance with section 545 of this Act.

490.—(1) An initial creditors' meeting to which an administrator's proposals are presented shall consider them and may approve them—

(a) without modification ; or

(b) with modification to which the administrator consents.

(2) After the conclusion of an initial creditors' meeting the administrator shall, as soon as is reasonably practicable, report any decision taken to—

(a) the Court ;

(b) the Commission ; and

(c) such other persons as may be prescribed by the Minister.

(3) An administrator commits an offence if he fails, without reasonable excuse, to comply with subsection (2).

491.—(1) This section applies where—
(a) an administrator's proposals have been approved with or without modification at an initial creditors' meeting ;
(b) the administrator proposes a revision to the proposals ; and
(c) the administrator thinks that the proposed revision is substantial.
(2) The administrator shall—
(a) summon a creditors' meeting ;
(b) send a statement in the prescribed form of the proposed revision with the notice of the meeting sent to each creditor ;
(c) send a copy of the statement, within the prescribed period, to each member of the company of whose address he is aware ; and (d) present a copy of the statement to the meeting.
(3) The administrator is deemed to have complied with subsection(2) (c) if he publishes a notice undertaking to provide a copy of the statement free of charge to any member of the company who applies in writing to a specified address.
(4) A notice under subsection (3) shall be published—
(a) in the prescribed manner ; and
(b) within the prescribed period.
(5) A creditors' meeting to which a proposed revision is presented shall consider it and may approve it—
(a) without modification ; or
(b) with modification to which the administrator consents.
(6) After the conclusion of a creditors' meeting, the administrator shall, as soon as is reasonably practicable, report any decision taken to—
(a) the Court ;
(b) the Commission ; and
(c) such other persons as may be prescribed by the Minister.
(7) An administrator commits an offence if he fails, without reasonable excuse, to comply with subsection (6).

492.—(1) This section applies where an administrator reports to the obtain Court that—
(a) an initial creditors' meeting has failed to approve the administrator's proposals presented to it ; or
(b) a creditors' meeting has failed to approve a revision of the administrator's proposals presented to it.
(2) The Court may—
(a) provide that the appointment of an administrator shall cease to have effect from a specified time ;
(b) adjourn the hearing conditionally or unconditionally ;
(c) make an interim order ;
(d) make an order on a petition for winding-up suspended by virtue of section 462 (b) of this Act; or
(e) make any other order, including an order making consequential provision, that the Court deems appropriate.

493.—(1) The administrator shall summon further creditors' meeting if— (a) it is requested in the prescribed manner by creditors of the company whose debts amount to at least 10% of the total debts of the company ; or (b) he is directed by the Court to summon a creditors' meeting.

(2) An administrator commits an offence if he fails, without reasonable excuse, to summon a creditors' meeting as required by this section.

494.—(1) A creditors' meeting may establish a Creditors' Committee.

(2) A Creditors' Committee shall perform functions conferred on it under this Act.

(3) A Creditors' Committee may require the administrator to—

(a) attend on the Committee at any reasonable time of which he is given at least seven days' notice ; and

(b) provide the Committee with information about the exercise of his functions.

495.—(1) Anything which is required or permitted by or under this Chapter to be done at a creditors' meeting may be done by correspondence between the administrator and creditors—

(a) in accordance with the prescribed rules ; and (b) subject to any prescribed condition.

(2) A reference in this Chapter to anything done at a creditors' meeting includes a reference to anything done in the course of correspondence in accordance with subsection (1).

(3) A requirement to hold a creditors' meeting is satisfied by correspondence in accordance with this section.

FUNCTIONS OF ADMINISTRATOR

496.—(1) The administrator of a company may do anything necessary or expedient for the management of the affairs, business and property of the company.

(2) Any provision of this Chapter which expressly permits the administrator to do a specified thing is without prejudice to subsection (1).

(3) A person who deals with the administrator of a company in good faith and for value need not inquire whether the administrator is acting within his powers.

497. The Administrator of a company shall exercise the additional powers specified in Eleventh Schedule to this Act.

498. The administrator of a company may remove or appoint a director of the company, whether or not the appointment is to fill a vacancy.

499. The administrator of a company may call a meeting of members or creditors of the company.

500. The administrator of a company may apply to the Court for directions in connection with his functions.

501.—(1) A company in administration or an officer of a company in administration shall not exercise a management power without the consent of the administrator.

(2) For the purpose of subsection (1)—

(a) "management power" means a power which could be exercised so as to interfere with the exercise of the administrator's powers ;

(b) it is immaterial whether the power is conferred by an enactment oran instrument ; and

(c) consent may be general or specific.

502.—(1) The administrator of a company may make a distribution to a creditor of the company.

(2) Section 643 applies in relation to a distribution under this section as it applies in relation to a winding-up.

(3) A payment shall not be made by way of distribution under this section to a creditor of the company who is neither secured nor preferential unless the Court gives permission.

503. The administrator may make a payment other than in accordance with section 497 or paragraph 13 of the Eleventh Schedule to this Act if he thinks it likely to assist achievement of the purpose of administration.

504. The administrator of a company shall, on his appointment take custody or control of all the property to which he thinks the company is entitled.

505.—(1) Subject to subsection (2), the administrator of a company shall manage its affairs, business and property in accordance with any—

(a) proposal approved under section 491 ;

(b) revision of those proposals which is made by him and which he does not consider substantial ; and

(c) revision of those proposals approved under section 489.

(2) If the Court gives directions to the administrator of a company in connection with any aspect of his management of the company's affairs, business or property, the administrator shall comply with the directions.

(3) The Court may give directions under subsection (2) only if—

(a) no proposal has been approved under section 492 of this Act ;

(b) the directions are consistent with any proposal or revision approved under section 486 or 491 of this Act ;

(c) the Court considers that the directions are required in order to reflect a change in circumstances since the approval of proposals or a revision under section 486 or 491 of this Act ; or

(d) the Court considers that the directions are desirable because of a misunderstanding about proposals or a revision approved under section 486 or 491 of this Act.

506. In performing his functions under this Part, the administrator of a company acts as its agent.

507.—(1) The administrator of a company may dispose of or take action relating to property which is subject to a floating charge as if it were not subject to the charge.

(2) Where property is disposed of in accordance with subsection (1), the holder of the floating charge shall have the same priority in respect of acquired property as he had in respect of the property disposed of.

(3) In subsection (2), "acquired property" means property of the company which directly or indirectly represents the property disposed of.

508.—(1) The Court may by order enable the administrator of a company to dispose of property which is subject to a security other than a floating charge as if it were not subject to the security.

(2) An order under subsection (1) may be made only—

(a) on the application of the administrator ; and

(b) where the Court considers that disposal of the property would likely promote the purpose of administration in respect of the company.

(3) An order under this section is subject to the condition that there shall be applied towards discharging the sums secured by the security—

(a) the net proceeds of disposal of the property ; and

(b) any additional money required to be added to the net proceeds so as to produce the amount determined by the Court as the net amount which would be realised on a sale of the property at market value.

(4) If an order under this section relates to more than one security, application of money under subsection (3) shall be in the order of the priorities of the securities.

(5) An administrator who makes a successful application for an order under this section shall send a copy of the order to the Commission before the end of 14 days starting with the date of the order.

(6) An administrator commits an offence if he fails, without reasonable excuse, to comply with subsection (5).

509.—(1) The Court may by order enable the administrator of a company to dispose of goods which are in the possession of the company under a hire purchase agreement as if all the rights of the owner under the agreement were vested in the company.

(2) An order under subsection (1) may be made only—

(a) on the application of the administrator ; and

(b) where the Court considers that disposal of the goods would be likely to promote the purpose of administration in respect of the company.

(3) An order under this section is subject to the condition that there shall be applied towards discharging the sums payable under the hire-purchase agreement—

(a) the net proceeds of disposal of the goods ; and

(b) any additional money required to be added to the net proceeds so as to produce the amount determined by the Court as the net amount which would be realized on a sale of the goods at market value.

(4) An administrator who makes a successful application for an order under this section shall send a copy of the order to the Commission before the end of 14 days starting with the date of the order.

(5) An administrator commits an offence if he fails, without reasonable excuse, to comply with subsection (4).

510.—(1) An administrator's statement of proposals under section 486 of this Act does not include any action which—

(a) affects the right of a secured creditor of the company to enforce his security ;

(b) would result in a preferential debt of the company being paid otherwise than in priority to its non-preferential debts ; or

(c) would result in one preferential creditor of the company being paid a smaller proportion of his debt than another.

(2) A creditor or member of a company in administration may apply to the Court claiming that the administrator is not performing his functions as quickly or as efficiently as is reasonably practicable.

(3) The Court may—

(a) grant a relief ;

(b) dismiss the application ;

(c) adjourn the hearing conditionally or unconditionally ;

(d) make an interim order ; or

(e) make any other order it considers appropriate.

(4) In particular, an order under this section may—

(a) regulate the administrator's exercise of his functions ;

(b) require the administrator to do or not do a specified thing ;

(c) require a creditors' meeting to be held for a specified purpose ;
(d) provide for the appointment of an administrator to cease to have effect ; or
(e) make consequential provision.

(5) An order may be made on a claim under subsection (1) whether or not the action complained of—

(a) is within the administrator's powers under Tenth Schedule to this Act ; or
(b) was taken in reliance on an order under section 505 or 506 of this Act.

(6) An order shall not be made under this section if it would impede or prevent the implementation of —

(a) a voluntary arrangement approved under Chapter 17 of Part B ;
(b) a proposal for a scheme of arrangement and compromise or reconstruction to be sanctioned under relevant Parts of this Act ;
(c) a proposal for a cross-border merger within the meaning of relevant legislation, including but not limited to the Investments and Securities Act ; or
(d) proposals or a revision approved under section 491 or 492 of this Act more than 28 days before the day on which the application for the order under this section is made.

512.—(1) The Court may examine the conduct of a person who—

(a) is, or purports to be, the administrator of a company ; or
(b) has been, or has purported to be, the administrator of a company.

(2) An examination under this section may be held only on the application of—

(a) the official receiver ;
(b) the administrator of the company ;
(c) the liquidator of the company ;(d) a creditor of the company ; or (e) a contributory of the company.

(3) An application under subsection (2) shall allege that the administrator has—

(a) misapplied or retained money or other property of the company ;
(b) become accountable for money or other property of the company ;(c) breached a fiduciary or other duty in relation to the company ; or (d) been guilty of misfeasance.

(4) On an examination under this section into a person's conduct, the Court may order him to—

(a) repay, restore or account for money or property ;
(b) pay interest ; or
(c) contribute a sum to the company's property by way of compensation for breach of duty or misfeasance.

(6) An application under subsection (2) may be made in respect of an administrator who has been discharged under section 523 of this Act only with the permission of the Court.

(7) In subsection (3), "administrator" includes a person who purports or has purported to be an administrator of a company.

CESSATION OF ADMINISTRATION

513.—(1) Subject to subsection (2) the appointment of an administrator shall cease to have effect at the end of the period of one year beginning with the date on which it takes effect.

(2) The term of office of an administrator may be extended for—

(a) a specified period, by an order of the Court on the application of the administrator ; or

(b) a period not exceeding six months, by consent.

514.—(1) An order of the Court under section 513 of this Act—

(a) may be made in respect of an administrator whose term of office has already been extended by order or by consent ; and

(b) shall not be made after the expiry of the administrator's term of office.

(2) Where an order is made under section 513 of this Act, the administrator shall, as soon as is reasonably practicable, notify the Commission of the order.

(3) An administrator who fails, without reasonable excuse, to comply with subsection (2) commits an offence.

515.—(1) In section 513 (2) (b) of this Act, "consent" means consent of—

(a) each secured creditor of the company ; and

(b) if the company has unsecured debts, creditors whose debts amount to more than 50% of the company's unsecured debts, without regard to the debts of any creditor who does not respond to an invitation to give or withhold consent.

(2) Where the Administrator has made a statement under section 486 of this Act, "consent", in section 513 (2) (b) of this Act, means—

(a) consent of each secured creditor of the company ; or

(b) if the administrator thinks that a distribution may be made to preferential creditors, consent of—

(i) each secured creditor of the company, and

(ii) preferential creditors whose debts amount to more than 50% of the preferential debts of the company, without regard to the debts of any creditor who does not respond to an invitation to give or withhold consent.

516.—(1) Consent, for the purposes of section 513 (2) (b) of this Act, may be—

(a) written ; or

(b) signified at a creditors' meeting.

(2) An administrator's term of office may be extended by consent only once, provided that it shall not be extended by consent after—

(a) expiry ; and

(b) extension by order of the Court.

(3) Where an administrator's term of office is extended by consent, he shall, as soon as is reasonably practicable—

(a) file notice of the extension with the Court ; and (b) notify the Commission.

(4) An administrator who fails, without reasonable excuse, to comply with subsection (3) commits an offence.

517.—(1) On the application of the administrator of a company, the Court may provide for the appointment of an administrator of the company to cease to have effect from a specified time.

(2) The administrator of a company shall make an application under this section if—

(a) he thinks the purpose of administration cannot be achieved in relation to the company ;

(b) he thinks the company should not have entered administration ; or

(c) a creditors' meeting requires him to make an application under this section.

(3) The administrator of a company shall make an application under this section if the—

(a) administration is pursuant to an administration order ; and

(b) administrator thinks that the purpose of administration has been sufficiently achieved in relation to the company.

(4) On an application under this section the Court may—

(a) adjourn the hearing conditionally or unconditionally ;

(b) dismiss the application ;

(c) make an interim order ; or

(d) make any order it considers appropriate, whether in addition to, inconsequence of or in place of the order applied for.

518.—(1) This section applies where an administrator of a company is appointed under section 443 or 448 of this Act.

(2) If the Administrator thinks that the purpose of administration has been sufficiently achieved in relation to the company he may file a notice in the prescribed form with the—

(a) Court ; and (b) Commission.

(3) The administrator's appointment ceases to have effect when the requirements of subsection (2) are satisfied.

(4) Where the administrator files a notice, he shall, within the prescribed period, send a copy to every creditor of the company of whose claim and address he is aware.

(5) The prescribed rules may provide that the administrator is taken to have complied with subsection (4) if, before the end of the prescribed period, he publishes, in the prescribed manner, a notice undertaking to provide a copy of the notice under subsection (2) to any creditor of the company who applies in writing to a specified address.

(6) An administrator who fails, without reasonable excuse, to comply with subsection (4) commits an offence.

519.—(1) On the application of a creditor of a company, the Court may provide for the appointment of an administrator of the company to cease to have effect at a specified time.

(2) An application under this section shall allege an improper motive—

(a) in the case of an administrator appointed by administration order, other part of the applicant for the order ; or

(b) in any other case, on the part of the person who appointed the administrator.

(3) On an application under this section, the Court may— (a) adjourn the hearing conditionally or unconditionally ; (b) dismiss the application ;

(c) make an interim order ; or

(d) make any order it considers appropriate, whether in addition to, inconsequence of or instead of the order applied for.

520.—(1) This section applies where a winding-up order is made for the winding-up of a company in administration on a petition presented under—

(a) grounds of public interest as may be prescribed by the Chief judge or under an enactment ; or

(b) the Banks and Other Financial Institutions Act, Nigeria Deposit Insurance Corporation Act or any other financial services and markets related Act.

(2) This section also applies where a provisional liquidator of a company in administration is appointed following the presentation of a petition under any of the provisions in subsection (1).

(3) The Court shall order that the appointment of the administrator ceases to have effect or continue to have effect.

(4) Where the Court makes an order under subsection (3) (b) of this section it may also—

(a) specify which of the powers under the Tenth Schedule to this Act are to be exercisable by the administrator ; and

(b) order that this Part shall have effect in relation to the administrator with specified modifications.

521.—(1) This section applies where the administrator of a company thinks that—

(a) the total amount which each secured creditor of the company is likely to receive has been paid to him or set aside for him ; and

(b) a distribution is made to unsecured creditors of the company, if there are any.

(2) The administrator may send to the Commission a notice that this section applies.

(3) On receipt of a notice under subsection (2), the Commission shall register the notice.

(4) After an administrator has sent a notice under subsection (2), he shall, as soon as is reasonably practicable— (a) file a copy of the notice with the Court ; and

(b) send a copy of the notice to each creditor of whose claim and address he is aware.

(5) On the registration of a notice under subsection (3) the—

(a) appointment of an administrator in respect of the company ceases to have effect ; and

(b) company shall be wound up as if a resolution for voluntary winding up under section 620 of this Act were passed on the day on which the notice is registered.

(6) The liquidator, for the purposes of the winding-up, shall be—

(a) a person nominated by the creditors of the company in the prescribed manner and within the prescribed period ; or

(b) the administrator, if no person is nominated under paragraph (a).

(8) In the application of this Chapter to a winding-up by virtue of this section—

(a) section 520 of this Act shall not apply ;

(b) this section applies as if the reference to the time of the passing of the resolution for voluntary winding-up were a reference to the beginning of the date of registration of the notice under subsection (3) ;

(c) sections 523, 532, 533 and 534 shall not apply ;

(d) subsection (5) (b) shall apply as if the reference to the time of the passing of the resolution for voluntary winding-up were a reference to the beginning of the date of registration of the notice under subsection (3) ; and

(e) any creditors' committee which is in existence immediately before the company ceases to be in administration shall continue in existence after that time as if appointed as a liquidation committee by the creditors at the creditors' meeting for the purpose of the winding-up.

522.—(1) If the administrator of a company thinks that the company has no property which might permit distribution to its creditors, he shall send a notice to that effect to the Commission.

(2) The Court may on the application of the administrator of a company, discontinue the application of subsection (1) in respect of the company.

(3) On receipt of a notice under subsection (1) the Commission shall register the notice.

(4) On the registration of a notice in respect of a company under subsection

(3) the appointment of an administrator of the company ceases to have effect.

(5) If an administrator sends a notice under subsection (1), he shall, as soon as is reasonably practicable—

(a) file a copy of the notice with the Court ; and

(b) send a copy of the notice to each creditor of whose claim and address he is aware.

(6) At the end of three months beginning with the date of registration ofa notice in respect of a company under subsection (3) the company is deemed to be dissolved.

(7) On an application in respect of a company by the administrator or another interested person, the Court may—

(a) extend the period specified in subsection (6) ;

(b) suspend that period ; or

(c) discontinue the application of subsection (6).

(8) Where an order is made under subsection (7) in respect of a company the administrator shall, as soon as is reasonably practicable, notify the Commission.

(9) An administrator commits an offence if he fails, without reasonable excuse, to comply with subsection (5).

. 523.—(1) This section applies where—

(a) the Court makes an order under this Chapter providing for the appointment of an administrator of a company to cease to have effect ; and (b) the administrator was appointed by administration order.

(2) The Court shall discharge the administration order.

524.—(1) This section applies where the Court makes an order under this Chapter providing for the appointment of an administrator to cease to have effect.

(2) The administrator shall send a copy of the order to the Commission within 14 days beginning with the date of the order.

(3) An administrator who fails, without reasonable excuse, to comply with subsection (2) commits an offence.

REPLACEMENT OF ADMINISTRATOR

525.—(1) An administrator may resign only in prescribed circumstances.

(2) An administrator may resign only where he is appointed— (a) by administration order, by notice in writing to the Court ;

(b) under section 452 of this Act, by notice in writing to the holder of the floating charge by virtue of which the appointment was made ;

(c) under section 459 (1) of this Act, by notice in writing to the company ; or

(d) under section 459 (2) of this Act, by notice in writing to the directors of the company.

526. The Court may by order remove an administrator from office.

527.—(1) The administrator of a company shall vacate office if he ceases to be qualified to act as an insolvency practitioner in relation to the company.

(2) Where an administrator vacates office by virtue of subsection (1) he shall give notice in writing, in the case of an administrator appointed—

(a) by administration order, to the Court ;

(b) under section 452 of this Act, to the holder of the floating charge by virtue of which the appointment was made ;

(c) under section 459 (1) of this Act, to the company ; or

(d) under section 459 (2) of this Act, to the directors of the company.

(3) An administrator who fails, without reasonable excuse, to comply with subsection (2) commits an offence.

528. Sections 529-535 of this Act shall apply where an administrator—

(a) dies ;

(b) resigns ;

(c) is removed from office under section 524 of this Act ; or(d) vacates office under section 523 of this Act.

529.—(1) Where the administrator was appointed by administration order, the Court may replace the administrator on an application under this subsection made by—

(a) a Creditors' Committee of the company ;

(b) the company ;

(c) the directors of the company ;

(d) one or more creditors of the company ; or

(e) where more than one person was appointed to act jointly or concurrently as the administrator or any of those persons who remains in office.

(2) An application may be made in reliance on subsection (1) (b-d) only where—

(a) there is no Creditors' Committee of the company ;

(b) the Court is satisfied that the Creditors' Committee or a remaining administrator is not taking reasonable steps to make a replacement ; or

(c) the Court is satisfied that for another reason it is right for the application to be made.

r. 530. An administrator appointed under section 452 of this Act may be replaced by the holder of the floating charge by virtue of which the appointment was made.

531.—(1) An administrator appointed under section 459 (1) of this Act, may be replaced by the company.

(2) A replacement under this section may be made only—

(a) with the consent of each person who is the holder of a floating charge in respect of the company's property ; or

(b) where consent is withheld, with the permission of the Court.

532.—(1) An administrator appointed under section 459 (2) of this Act, may be replaced by the directors of the company.

(2) A replacement under this section may be made only—

(a) with the consent of each person who is the holder of a floating charge in respect of the company's property ; or

(b) where consent is withheld, with the permission of the Court.

533. The Court may replace an administrator on the application of a person listed in section 529 (1) of this Act if the Court is satisfied that—

(a) a person who is entitled to replace the administrator under sections 525-527 of this Act is not taking reasonable steps to make a replacement ; or

(b) for any other reason which, in the opinion of the Court, it is proper to make the replacement.

534.—(1) This section applies where an administrator of a company is appointed under section 452 of this Act by the holder of a floating charge in respect of the company's property.

(2) The holder of a prior floating charge in respect of the company's property may apply to the court for the administrator to be replaced by an administrator nominated by the holder of the prior floating charge.

(3) A floating charge is prior to another for the purposes of this section if it —

(a) was first registered with the Commission or, in default of registration, it was first created ; or

(b) is to be treated as having priority in accordance with an agreement to which the holder of each floating charge was a party.

535. (1) This section applies where—

(a) an administrator of a company is appointed by a company or directors under section 459 of this Act ; and

(b) there is no holder of a floating charge in respect of the company's property.

(2) A creditors' meeting may replace the administrator.

(3) A creditors' meeting may act under subsection (2) only if the new administrator's written consent to act is presented to the meeting before the replacement is made.

536.—(1) Where a person ceases to be the administrator of a company because—

(a) he vacates office by reason of resignation, death or otherwise ;

(b) he is removed from office ; or

(c) his appointment ceases to have effect, he is discharged from liability in respect of any of his actions as Administrator.

(2) The discharge provided by subsection (1) takes effect in—

(a) the case of an administrator who dies, on the filing with the court of notice of his death ;

(b) the case of an administrator appointed under section 450 or 457 of this Act, at a time appointed by resolution of the creditors' committee or, if there is no committee, by resolution of the creditors ; or (c) any other case, at a time specified by the Court.

(3) For the purpose of the application of subsection (2) (b) in a case where the Administrator has made a statement under section 488 of this Act, a resolution is taken as passed if it is passed with the approval—

(a) each secured creditor of the company ;

(b) each secured creditor of the company ; and

(c) preferential creditors whose debts amount to more than 50% of the preferential debts of the company, disregarding debts of any creditor who does not respond to an invitation to give or withhold approval, where the administrator has made a distribution to preferential creditors or thinks that a distribution may be made to preferential creditors.

(4) In this section, "discharge"—

(a) applies to liability accrued before the discharge takes effect ; and (b) does not prevent the exercise of the court's powers under section 500.

537.—(1) This section applies where a person ceases to be the administrator of a company, whether by reason of resignation, removal from office, cessation of appointment, death or otherwise.

(2) The former administrator's remuneration and expenses shall be—

(a) charged on and payable out of property of which he had custody or control immediately before cessation ; and

(b) payable in priority to any security to which section 510 of this Act applies.

(3) A sum payable in respect of a debt or liability arising out of a contract, including a contract for post-commencement financing, entered into by the former Administrator or a predecessor before cessation shall be—

(a) charged on and payable out of property of which the former Administrator had custody or control immediately before cessation ; and (b) payable in priority to any charge arising under subsection (2).

(4) In this section—

(a) "cessation" means the time when he ceases to be the company's Administrator ;

(b) "former Administrator" means the person referred to in subsection (1) ;

(c) subsection (3) applies to a liability arising under a contract of employment which was adopted by the former administrator or a predecessor before cessation; and for that purpose—

(i) action taken within 14 days after an Administrator's appointment shall not be taken to amount or contribute to the adoption of a contract,

(ii) no account shall be taken of a liability which arises, by reference to anything which is done or which occurs before the adoption of the contract of employment, and

(iii) no account shall be taken of a liability to make a payment other than wages or salary.

(5) In subsection (4) (c) (iii), "wages or salary" includes—

(a) a sum payable in respect of a period of holiday, for which purpose, the sum shall be treated as relating to the period by reference to which the entitlement to holiday accrued ;

(b) a sum payable in respect of a period of absence through illness or other good cause ;

(c) a sum payable in lieu of holiday ;

(d) in respect of a period, a sum which would be treated as earnings for that period for the purposes of an enactment on social security ; and (e) a contribution to an occupational pension scheme.

GENERAL

538.—(1) In this Chapter a reference to the appointment of—

(a) an administrator of a company includes a reference to the appointment of a number of persons to act jointly or concurrently as the Administrator of a company ; and

(b) a person as administrator of a company includes a reference to the appointment of a person as one of a number of persons to act jointly or concurrently as the administrator of a company.

(2) The appointment of a number of persons to act as administrator of a company shall specify which functions, if any, are to be performed by—

(a) the persons appointed acting jointly ; and (b) any or all of the persons appointed.

539.—(1) This section applies where two or more persons are appointed to act jointly as the administrator of a company.

(2) A reference to the administrator of the company is a reference to those persons acting jointly.

(3) A reference to the administrator of a company in sections 523-534 of this Act is a reference to any or all of the persons appointed to act jointly.

(4) Where an offence of omission is committed by the administrator, each of the persons appointed to act jointly—

(a) commits the offence ; and

(b) may be proceeded against and punished individually.

(5) The reference in section 482(1)(a) of this Act to the name of the administrator is a reference to the name of each of the persons appointed to act jointly.

(6) Where persons are appointed to act jointly in respect of only some of the functions of the administrator of a company, this section applies only in relation to those functions.

540.—(1) This section applies where two or more persons are appointed to act concurrently as the administrator of a company.

(2) A reference to the administrator of a company in this Chapter is a reference to any of the persons appointed or any combination of them.

541.—(1) Where a company is in administration, a person may be appointed to act as administrator jointly or concurrently with the person or persons acting as the administrator of the company.

(2) Where a company entered administration by administration order, an appointment under subsection (1) shall be made by the Court on the application of—

(a) a person or group listed in section 450(1)(a-e) of this Act ; or (b) the person or persons acting as the administrator of the company.

(3) Where a company entered administration as a result of appointment under section 443 of this Act, an appointment under subsection (1) shall be made by the—

(a) holder of the floating charge by virtue of which the appointment was made ; or

(b) Court on the application of the person or persons acting as the administrator of the company.

(4) Where a company entered administration by virtue of an appointment under section 447 of this Act, an appointment under subsection (1) shall be made either by the Court on the application of the person or persons acting as the administrator of the company or—

(a) by the company ; and

(b) with the consent of each person who is the holder of a floating charge in respect of the company's property or, where consent is withheld, with the permission of the Court.

(5) Where a company entered administration by virtue of an appointment under section 452 (2) of this Act, an appointment under subsection (1) shall be made either by the Court on the application of the person or persons acting as the Administrator of the company or—

(a) by the directors of the company ; and

(b) with the consent of each person who is the holder of a floating charge in respect of the company's property or, where consent is withheld, with the permission of the Court.

(6) An appointment under subsection (1) may be made only with the consent of the person or persons acting as the administrator of the company.

542. An act of the administrator of a company is valid in spite of a defect in his appointment or qualification.

543. A reference in this Chapter to something done by the directors of a company includes a reference to the same thing done by a majority of the directors of a company.

544.—(1) Unless otherwise provided, a person who commits an offence under this Chapter is liable on conviction to a fine of at least ₦200,000.

(2) A person who commits an offence under—

(a) section 455,

(b) section 467,

(c) section 470,
(d) section 482,(e) section 483,
(f) section 484,
(g) section 486,
(h) section 488,
(i) section 491,
(j) section 493,
(k) section 508,
(l) section 509,
(m) section 514,
(n) section 516,
(o) section 518,
(p) section 522,
(q) section 524, and
(r) section 527,is liable on conviction to a daily default fine of not less than ₦5,000.

545.—(1) Where a provision of this Part provides that a period may be varied in accordance with this section, the period may be varied in respect of a company—
(a) by the Court ; and
(b) on the application of the administrator.
(2) A time period may be extended in respect of a company under this section—
(a) more than once ; and(b) after expiry.

546.—(1) A period specified in sections 483(5), 487 (1)(b), or 488 (2) of this Act may be varied in respect of a company by the administrator with consent.
(2) In subsection (1), "consent" means consent of—
(a) each secured creditor of the company ; and
(b) creditors whose debts amount to more than 50% of the company's unsecured debts, if the company has unsecured debts, disregarding debts of any creditor who does not respond to an invitation to give or withhold consent.
(3) Where the administrator has made a statement under section 486 of this Act—
"consent" means—
(a) consent of each secured creditor of the company ; or
(b) if the Administrator thinks that a distribution may be made to preferential creditors, consent of—
(i) each secured creditor of the company, and
(ii) preferential creditors whose debts amount to more than 50%of the total preferential debts of the company, disregarding debts of any creditor who does not respond to an invitation to give or withhold consent.
(4) Consent for the purposes of subsection (1) may be—
(a) written ; or
(b) signified at a creditors' meeting.
(5) The power to extend under subsection (1)— (a) may be exercised in respect of a period only once ;
(b) shall not be used to extend a period by more than 28 days ;
(c) shall not be used to extend a period which has been extended by the
Court ; and
(d) shall not be used to extend a period after expiry.

547. Where a period is extended under section 545 or 546, a reference to the period shall be taken as a reference to the period as extended.

548.—(1) The Chief Judge of the Federal High Court may by order amend a provision of this Chapter which—

(a) requires anything to be done within a specified period of time ;

(b) prevents anything from being done after a specified time ; or(c) requires a specified minimum period of notice to be given.

(2) The Chief Judge shall make procedural rules relating to administration.

(3) An order or rule under this section shall be made by statutory instrument published in the Federal Government Gazette.

549.—(1) In this Chapter—

"administrator" of a company means a person appointed under any of this Chapter. means under this Chapter to manage the company's affairs, business and property ;

"company" means—

(a) a company registered under this Act or any other special legislation relating to companies ; or

(b) any other corporate entity which is recognised under rules ororder made by the Minister ;

"correspondence" includes correspondence by telephonic or other electronic means ;

"creditors' meeting" has the meaning given under section 487 of this Act ;

"enters administration" has the meaning given to it under subsection (2) (a) ;

"floating charge" means a charge which is a floating charge on its creation ;

"in administration" has the meaning given to under subsection (2)(b) ;

"hire-purchase agreement" includes a conditional sale agreement, a chattel leasing agreement and a retention of title agreement;

"holder of a floating charge" in respect of a company's property has the meaning given under section 452 of this Act ;

"market value" means the amount which would be realised on a sale of property in the open market by a willing vendor ;

"purpose of administration" means an objective specified in section 444 of this Act ; and

"unable to pay its debts" has the meaning given by section 572 of this Act.

(2) For the purposes of this Chapter—

(a) a company "enters administration" when the appointment of an administrator takes effect ;

(b) a company is "in administration" while the appointment of an Administrator of the company has effect ;

(c) a company ceases to be in administration when the appointment of an administrator of the company ceases to have effect ; and

(d) a company does not cease to be in administration merely because an administrator vacates office (by reason of resignation, death or otherwise) or is removed from office.

(3) In this Chapter, a reference to—

(a) a thing in writing includes a reference to a thing in electronic form ; and (b) action includes a reference to inaction.

CHAPTER 19— RECEIVERS AND MANAGERS, APPOINTMENT OF RECEIVERS AND MANAGERS

550.—(1) The following persons shall not be appointed or act as receivers or managers of any property or undertaking of any company —

(a) an infant ;

(b) any person found by a competent Court to be of unsound mind ;(c) a body corporate ;

(d) an undischarged bankrupt, unless he is given leave to act as a receiver or manager of the property or undertaking of the company by the Court by which he was adjudged bankrupt ;

(e) a director or auditor of the company ; and

(f) any person convicted of any offence involving fraud, dishonesty, official corruption or moral turpitude or who is disqualified under section 280 of this Act.

(2) Any appointment made in contravention of the provisions of subsection(1) is void and if any of the persons named in paragraphs (c), (d), (e) and (f) acts as a receiver or manager, he commits an offence and is liable to a fine in such amount as the Commission shall specify in its regulations, and in the case of a body corporate or, in the case of an individual, to imprisonment for a term not exceeding six months or a fine as the Court deems fit.

(3) Where any of the persons mentioned in subsection (1) is at the commencement of this Act acting as a receiver or manager, he may be removed by a Court on an application by a person interested.

551. Where an application is made to the Court to appoint a receiver on behalf of the debenture holder or other creditors of a company which is being wound up by a court, an official receiver may be appointed.

552.—(1) Notwithstanding the provisions of section 233 (1) (d) the Court may, on the application of a person interested, appoint a receiver or a receiver and manager of the property or undertaking of a company if the—

(a) principal money borrowed by the company or the interest is in arrears ; or

(b) security or property of the company is in jeopardy.

(2) A receiver or manager of any property or undertaking of a company appointed by the Court is deemed to be an officer of the Court and not of the company and shall act in accordance with the directions and instructions of the Court.

553.—(1) A receiver or manager of any property or undertaking of a company appointed out of Court under a power contained in any instrument is, subject to section 554 of this Act, deemed to be an agent of the person or persons on whose behalf he is appointed and, if appointed manager of the whole or any part of the undertaking of a company, he is deemed to stand in a fiduciary relationship to the company and observe the utmost good faith towards it in any transaction with it or on its behalf.

(2) Such a manager—

(a) shall act at all times in what he believes to be the best interests of the company as a whole so as to preserve its assets, further its business, and promote the purposes for which it was formed, and in such manner as a faithful, diligent, careful and ordinarily skilful manager would act in the circumstances ; and

(b) in considering whether a particular transaction or course of action is in the best interest of the company as a whole, may have regard to the interests of the employees, as well as the members of the company, and, when appointed by, or as a representative of, a special class of members or creditors may give special, but not exclusive, consideration to the interests of that class.

(3) Nothing contained in the articles, or in any contract, or in any resolution of a company, shall relieve any manager from the duty to act in accordance with subsection (2) or relieve him from any liability incurred as a result of any breach of such duty.

554. A receiver or manager of the property of a company appointed under a power contained in any instrument, or the persons by whom or on whose behalf a receiver or manager has been so appointed may apply to the Court for directions in relation to any particular matter arising in connection with the performance of his functions, and on any such application the Court may give such directions or make such order declaring the rights of persons before the Court or otherwise, as it deems just.

555.—(1) Where a receiver or manager of the property of a company has been appointed, the receiver or manager shall within 14 days give notice of his appointment to the Commission indicating the terms of and remuneration for the appointment, and every invoice, order for goods or business letter issued by or on behalf of the company, receiver, manager or liquidator of the company, being a document on or in which the company's name appears, shall contain a statement that a receiver or manager has been appointed.

(2) If default is made in complying with this section, the receiver, manager, liquidator or any officer of the company who is in default, authorises or permits the default as the case may be, commits an offence and is liable to a penalty for every day during which the default continues in such amount as the Commission shall specify in its regulations.

DUTIES, POWERS AND LIABILITIES OF RECEIVERS AND MANAGERS

556.—(1) A person appointed as a receiver of any property of a company shall, subject to the rights of prior encumbrances, take possession of and protect the property, receive rents and profits and discharge all out-goings in respect thereof and realise the security for the benefit of those on whose behalf he is appointed, but unless he is an appointed manager, he does not have power to carry on any business or undertaking.

(2) A person appointed manager of the whole or any part of the undertaking of a company shall manage the same with a view to the realisation of the security of those on whose behalf he is appointed.

(3) Without prejudice to subsection (1) or (2), where a receiver or manager is appointed for the whole or substantially the whole of a company's property, the powers conferred on him by the debentures by virtue of which he was appointed are deemed to include (except they are inconsistent with any of the provisions of those debentures) the powers specified in the Eleventh Schedule to this Act.

(4) From the date of appointment of a receiver or manager, the powers of the directors or liquidators in a members' voluntary winding-up to deal with the property or undertaking over which he is appointed, shall cease, unless the receiver or manager is discharged or the security is realised.

(5) If, on the appointment of a receiver or manager, the company is being wound up under the provision relating to creditors' voluntary winding up, or the property concerned is in the hands of some other officer of the Court, the liquidator or officer

shall not be bound to relinquish control of such property to the receiver or manager except under the order of the Court.

557.—(1) A receiver or manager of any property or undertaking of a company is personally liable on any contract entered into by him except in so far as the contract otherwise expressly provides.

(2) As regards contracts entered into by a receiver or manager in the proper performance of his functions, such receiver or manager is, subject to the rights of any prior encumbrance, entitled to an indemnity in respect of liability thereon out of the property over which he has been appointed to act as a receiver or manager.

(3) A receiver or manager appointed out of Court under a power contained in any instrument is also entitled, as regards contracts entered into by him with the express or implied authority of those appointing him, to an indemnity in respect of liability thereon from those appointing him to the extent to which he is unable to recover in accordance with subsection (2).

558.—(1) The Court may, on the application of the company or the liquidator, by order fix the amount to be paid by way of remuneration to any person who, under the powers contained in any instrument, has been appointed as a receiver or manager of the property of the company.

(2) The powers of the Court under subsection (1) shall, where no previous order is made under that subsection—

(a) extend to fixing the remuneration for any period before the making of the order or the application ;

(b) be exercisable notwithstanding that the receiver or manager has died or ceased to act before the making of the order or the application ; and

(c) extend, where the receiver or manager has been paid or has retained as his remuneration for any period before the making of the order any amount in excess of that so fixed for that period, to requiring him or his personal representatives to account for the excess or such part as may be specified in the order :

Provided that the power conferred by this paragraph shall not be exercised as respects any period before the making of the application for the order unless, in the opinion of the Court there are special circumstances making it proper for the power to be exercised.

(3) The Court may, on an application made by the company, liquidator or by the receiver or manager, vary or amend an order made under subsection (1).

(4) This section applies whether the receiver or manager has been appointed before or after the commencement of this Act.

PROCEDURE AFTER APPOINTMENT

559.—(1) Where a receiver or manager of the whole or substantially the whole of the property of a company (in this section and in section 560 of this Act referred to as "the receiver") has been appointed on behalf of the holders of any debentures of the company secured by a floating charge, then, subject to the provisions of this section and of section 560 of this Act —

(a) the receiver shall immediately send notice to the company of his appointment and the terms ;

(b) there shall, within 14 days after receipt of the notice, or such longer period as may be allowed by the Court or by the receiver, be made out and submitted to the receiver in accordance with section 560 of this Act, a statement in the prescribed form as to the affairs of the company ; and

(c) the receiver shall, within two months after receipt of the statements, send to—

(i) the Commission or Court a copy of the statement and of any comments he sees fit to make thereon and in the case of the Commission also a summary of the statement and of his comments, if any,

(ii) the company a copy of any comments or if he does not think fit to make any comment, a notice to that effect, and

(iii) any trustees for the debenture holders on whose behalf he has been appointed and, so far as he is aware of their addresses, to all such debenture holders, a copy of the said summary.

(2) The receiver shall within two months, or such longer period as the Court may allow after the expiration of the period of 12 months from the date of his appointment and of every subsequent period of 12 months, and within two months, or such longer period as the Court may allow after he ceases to act as receiver or manager of the property of the company, send to the Commission, any trustee for the debenture holders of the company on whose behalf he was appointed, the company and (if he is aware of their addresses) all debenture holders (if he is aware of their addresses), an abstract in the prescribed form showing his receipts and payments during that period of 12 months, or, where he ceases to act, during the period from the end of the period to which the last preceding abstract relates up to the date of his so ceasing, and the aggregate amounts of his receipts and payments during all preceding periods since his appointment.

(3) Where the receiver is appointed under the powers contained in any instrument, this section has effect with the —

(a) omission of the references to the Court in subsection (1) ; and

(b) substitution for the references to the Court in subsection (2), of references to the Commission and in any other case references to the Court shall be taken as referring to the Court by which the receiver was appointed.

(4) Subsection (1) does not apply in relation to the appointment of a receiver or manager to act with an existing receiver or manager or in place of a receiver or manager dying or ceasing to act, except that, where that subsection applies to a receiver or manager who dies or ceases to act before it has been fully complied with, the references in paragraphs (b) and (c) to the receiver shall, subject to subsection (5), include references to his successor and to any continuing receiver or manager and nothing in this subsection shall be taken as limiting the meaning of the expression "the receiver" where used in, or in relation to, subsection (2).

(5) This section and section 560 of this Act, where the company is being wound up, apply notwithstanding that the receiver or manager and the liquidator are the same person.

(6) Nothing in subsection (2) shall be taken to prejudice the duty of the receiver to render proper accounts of his receipts and payments to the persons to whom, and at the times at which, he may be required to do so apart from that sub-section.

(7) If the receiver makes default in complying with the requirements of this section, he is liable to a penalty for every day during which the default continues in such amount as the Commission shall specify in its regulations.

560.—(1) The statements as to the affairs of a company required by section 559, to be submitted to the receiver (or his successor) shall, show as at the date of the receiver's appointment—

(a) the particulars or the company's assets, debts and liabilities ;
(b) the names, residences and occupations of its creditors ;
(c) the securities held by the directors respectively ;
(d) the dates when the securities were respectively given ; and
(e) such further or other information as may be prescribed.

(2) The statement shall be submitted, and verified by affidavit of one or more of the persons who are, at the date of the receiver's appointment, the directors and by the person who is, at that date, the secretary of the company, or by the receiver or his successor, subject to the direction of the court, may require to submit and verify the statement of who—

(a) are or have been officers of the company ;
(b) have taken part in the formation of the company at any time within one year before the date of the receiver's appointment ;
(c) are in the employment of the company, or have been in the employment of the company within the year, and are in the opinion of the receiver capable of giving the information required ; or
(d) are or have been within the said year officers of or in the employment of a company which is, or within the said year was, an officer of the company to which the statement relates.

(3) A person making the statement and affidavit is allowed, and shall be paid by the receiver (or his successor) out of his receipts, such costs and expenses incurred in the preparation and making of the statement and affidavit as the receiver or his successor may consider reasonable, subject to an appeal to the Court.

(4) Where the receiver is appointed under the powers contained in any instrument, this section has effect with the substitution for references to the Court of references to the Commission and references to an affidavit, of references to a statutory declaration and in any other case references to the Court is taken as referring to the Court by which the receiver was appointed.

(5) If any person without reasonable excuse makes default in complying with the requirements of this section, he is liable to a penalty as may be prescribed by the Regulation for every day during which the default continues.

(6) References in this section to the receiver's successor include a continuing receiver or manager.

ACCOUNTS BY RECEIVER OR MANAGER

561.—(1) Except where section 559 (2) of this Act applies, every receiver or manager of the property of a company who has been appointed under the powers contained in any instrument shall, within one month or such longer periods as the Commission may allow, after the expiration of the period of six months from the date of his appointment, and of every subsequent period of six months, and within one month after he ceases to act as receiver or manager, deliver to the Commission for registration an abstract in the prescribed form showing his receipts and his payments during that period of six months, or where he ceases to act, during the period from the end of the period to which the last preceding abstract relates, up to the date of his ceasing, and the aggregate amount of his receipts and of his payments during all preceding periods since his appointment.

(2) Every receiver or manager who makes default in complying with the provisions of this section is liable to a penalty as may be prescribed in the regulation for every day during which the default continues.

DUTY AS TO RETURNS

562.—(1) If any receiver or manager of the property of a company having—

(a) made default in filing, delivering or making any returns, account or other document, or in giving any notice which a receiver or manager is by law required to file, delivers, makes, gives or fails to make good the default within 14 days after the service on him of a notice requiring him to do so, or

(b) been appointed under the powers contained in any instrument has, after being required at any time by the liquidator of the company so to do, fails to render proper accounts of his receipts and payment and to vouch the same and to pay over to the liquidator the amount properly payable to him, the Court may, on an application made for that purpose, make an order directing the receiver or manager, as the case may be to make good the default within such time as may be specified in the order.

(2) In the case of any default under subsection (1)(a), an application may be made by any member or by the Commission, and in the case of any default under subsection (1)(b), the application shall be made by the liquidator, and in either case the order may provide that all costs shall be borne by the receiver or manager.

(3) Nothing in this section shall be taken to prejudice the operation of any enactment imposing penalties on receivers in respect of any default mentioned in subsection (1).

CONSTRUCTION OF REFERENCES

563. Any reference in this Act to—

(a) a receiver or manager of the property of a company, or to a receiver thereof, includes a reference to a receiver or manager, or to a receiver of part only of that property and to a receiver only of the income arising from that property or from part thereof; and

(b) the appointment of a receiver or manager under powers contained in any instrument, includes a reference to an appointment made under powers which, by virtue of any enactment, are implied in and have effect as if contained in an instrument.

CHAPTER 20—WINDING-UP OF COMPANIES MODES OF WINDING-UP

564.—(1) The winding-up of a company may be effected—

(a) by the Court ;

(b) voluntarily ; or

(c) subject to the supervision of the Court.

(2) The provisions of this Act with respect to winding-up apply, unless the contrary appears, to the winding-up of a company by any of those modes.

CONTRIBUTORIES

565. In the event of a company being wound up, every present and past member is liable to contribute to the assets of the company as provided in section 117 of this Act.

566. The term, "contributory" means every person liable to contribute to the assets of a company in the event of its being wound up, and for the purposes of all

proceedings prior to the final determination of the persons who are to be deemed contributories, the expression includes any person alleged to be a contributory.

567.—(1) The liability of a contributory creates a debt of the nature of an ordinary contract debt accruing and due from him at the time when his liability commenced, but payable at the time when calls are made for enforcing the liability.

(2) An action to recover a debt created by this section shall not be brought after the expiration of six years from the date on which the cause of action accrued.

568.—(1) If a contributory dies either before or after he has been placed on the list of contributories, his personal representatives, heirs and devisees, are liable in due course of administration to contribute to the assets of the company in discharge of his liability and they are contributories accordingly.

(2) Where the personal representatives are placed on the list of contributories, the heirs or devisees need not be added but they may be added as and when the Court deems fit.

(3) If the personal representatives make default in paying any money ordered to be paid by them, proceedings may be taken for administering the whole or any part of the estate of the deceased contributory, and for compelling payment out of it of the money due.

569.—(1) If a contributory becomes bankrupt, either before or after he has been placed on the list of contributories, then—

(a) his trustee in bankruptcy shall represent him for the purposes of the winding-up, and shall be a contributory accordingly, and may be called—

(i) on to admit to proof against the estate of the bankrupt, or

(ii) to allow to be paid out of his assets, any money due from the bankrupt in respect of his liability to contribute to the assets of the company ; and

(b) there may be proved against the estate of the bankrupt the estimated value of his liability to future calls as well as calls already made.

(2) The provisions of this section extend and apply with all necessary changes to the case of an insolvent person.

CHAPTER 21—WINDING-UP BY THE COURT JURISDICTION

570.—(1) The Court having jurisdiction to wind up a company is the Federal High Court within whose area of jurisdiction the registered office or head office of the company is situate.

(2) For the purpose of this section, "registered office" or "head office" means the place which has longest been the principal place of business of the company during the six months immediately preceding the presentation of the petition for winding-up.

CASES IN WHICH COMPANY MAY BE WOUND-UP BY COURT

571. A company may be wound up by the court if—

(a) the company has by special resolution resolved that the company be wound up by the Court ;

(b) default is made in delivering the statutory report to the Commission or in holding the statutory meeting ;

(c) the number of members is reduced below two in the case of companies with more than one shareholder ;

(d) the company is unable to pay its debts ;

(e) the condition precedent to the operation of the company has ceased to exist ; or

(f) the Court is of opinion that it is just and equitable that the company should be wound up.

572. A company is deemed to be unable to pay its debts if—

(a) a creditor, by assignment or otherwise, to whom the company is indebted in a sum exceeding N200,000, then due, has served on the company,

by leaving it at its registered office or head office, a demand under his hand requiring the company to pay the sum due, and the company has for three weeks thereafter neglected to pay the sum or to secure or compound for it

to the reasonable satisfaction of the creditor ;

(b) execution or other process issued on a judgment, act or order of any Court in favour of a creditor of the company is returned unsatisfied in whole or in part ; or

(c) the Court, after taking into account any contingent or prospective liability of the company, is satisfied that the company is unable to pay its debts.

PETITIONS FOR WINDING-UP AND ITS EFFECTS

. 573.—(1) An application to the court for the winding-up of a company shall be by petition presented subject to the provisions of this section, by —

(a) the company or a director ;

(b) a creditor, including a contingent or prospective creditor of the company ;

(c) the official receiver ;

(d) a contributory ;

(e) a trustee in bankruptcy to, or a personal representative of, a creditor or contributory;

(f) the Commission under section 366 of this Act ;

(g) a receiver, if authorised by the instrument under which he was appointed ; or

(h) by all or any of those parties, together or separately.

(2) Notwithstanding anything in subsection (1)—

(a) a contributory is not entitled to present a petition for winding-up a company unless the—

(i) number of members is reduced below two in the case of companies with more than one shareholder, or

(ii) shares in respect of which he is contributory or some of them, were originally allotted to him or have been held by him, and registered in his name, for at least six months during the 18 months before the commencement of the winding-up, or have devolved on him through the death of a former holder ;

(b) a winding-up petition shall not, if the ground of the petition is default in delivering the statutory report to the Commission or in holding the statutory meeting, be presented by any person except a shareholder, or before the expiration of 14 days after the last day on which the meeting should have been held ; and

(c) the Court shall not hear a winding-up petition presented by a contingent or prospective creditor until sufficient security for costs has been given, and a prima facie case for winding-up has been established to its satisfaction.

(3) Where a company is being wound up voluntarily or subject to supervision, a winding-up petition may be presented by the official receiver attached to the Court, as well as by any other person authorised under the other provisions of this section, but the Court shall not make a winding-up order on any such petition unless it is satisfied that the voluntary winding-up or winding-up subject to supervision cannot be continued with due regard to the interests of the creditors or contributories.

(4) A contributory is entitled to present a winding-up petition notwithstanding that there may not be assets available on the winding-up for distribution to contributories.

574.—(1) On hearing a winding-up petition, the Court may dismiss it, adjourn the hearing conditionally or unconditionally or make any interim order, or any other order that it deems fit, but the Court shall not refuse to make a winding-up order on the ground only that the assets of the company have been mortgaged to an amount equal to or in excess of those assets, or that the company has no assets.

(2) Unless it appears to the Court that some other remedies are available and that the petitioners are acting unreasonably in seeking a winding-up order instead of pursuing those remedies, the Court, on hearing a petition by contributory members of a company for relief by winding-up on the ground that it would be just and equitable so to do, shall make the order as prayed if it is of the opinion that the petitioners are entitled to the relief sought.

(3) Where a petition is presented on the ground of default in delivering the statutory report to the Commission or in holding the statutory meeting, the Court, instead of making a winding-up order, may direct the delivery of the statutory report or the holding of a meeting, and order the costs to be paid by the persons who, in the opinion of the Court, are responsible for the default.

575. Where a winding-up petition has been presented and an action or other proceeding against a company is instituted or pending in any Court (in this section referred to as "the Court concerned"), the company or any creditor or contributory may, before the making of the winding-up order, apply to the Court concerned for an order staying proceedings and the Court concerned may, with or without imposing terms, stay or restrain proceedings, or if it deems fit, refer the case to the Court hearing the winding-up petition.

576. In a winding-up by the Court, any disposition of the property of the company, including things in action and any transfer of shares, or alteration in the status of the members of the company, made after the commencement of the winding-up shall, unless the Court otherwise orders, be void.

577. Where a company is being wound up by the Court, any attachment, sequestration, distress or execution put in force against the estate or effects of the company after the commencement of the winding-up is void :

Provided the provisions of this section do not apply to a fixed charge or any other validly created and perfected security interest other than a floating charge.

COMMENCEMENT OF WINDING-UP

578.—(1) Where, before the presentation of a petition for the winding up of a company by the Court, a resolution has been passed by the company for voluntary winding-up, the winding-up of the company is deemed to have commenced at the time of the passing of the resolution, and unless the Court, on proof of fraud or mistake, deems it fit to direct otherwise, all proceedings taken in the voluntary winding-up are deemed to have been validly taken.

(2) In any other case, the winding-up of a company by the court is deemed to commence at the time of the presentation of the petition for the winding-up.

CONSEQUENCES OF WINDING-UP ORDER

579. On the making of a winding-up order, a copy of the order shall immediately be forwarded by the company, or otherwise as may be prescribed, to the Commission, which shall make a minute thereof in its books relating to the company.

580. If a winding-up order is made or a provisional liquidator is appointed, no action or proceeding shall proceed with or commence against the company except by leave of the Court given on such terms as the Court may impose.

581. An order for winding-up a company shall operate in favour of all the creditors and of all the contributories of the company as if made on the joint petition of a creditor and of a contributory.

OFFICIAL RECEIVER

582.—(1) For the purpose of this Act and so far as it relates to the winding-up of companies by the Court, "official receiver" means the Deputy Chief Registrar of the Federal High Court or an officer designated for that purpose by the Chief Judge of the Court.

(2) Any such officer shall, for the purpose of his duties under this Act, be called "the official receiver".

583.—(1) Where the Court has made a winding-up order or appointed a provisional liquidator there shall, unless the court deems fit to order otherwise and so orders, be made out and submitted to the official receiver a statement of affairs of the company in the prescribed form, verified by affidavit, and showing the particulars of its assets, debts and liabilities, the names, residences and occupations of its creditors, the securities held by them respectively, the dates when the securities were respectively given, the list of members and the list of charges and such further or other information as may be prescribed or as the official receiver may require.

(2) The statement shall be submitted and verified by one or more of the persons who are, at the relevant date, the directors and the person who is at that date the secretary of the company, or by the persons mentioned in this subsection as the official receiver, subject to the direction of the Court, may require to submit and verify the statement, of persons who—

(a) are or have been officers of the company ;

(b) have taken part in the formation of the company at any time within one year before the relevant date ;

(c) have been or are in the employment of the company within the said year, and are in the opinion of the official receiver capable of giving the information required ;

(d) are or have been within the said year officers of or in the employment of a company which is, or within the said year was, an officer of the company to which the statement relates.

(3) The statement shall be submitted within 14 days from the relevant date or within such extended time as the official receiver or the Court may, for special reasons, appoint.

(4) Any person making or concurring in making the statement and affidavit required by this section shall be allowed and shall be paid by the official receiver or provisional liquidator, as the case may be, out of the assets of the company such costs and expenses incurred in and about the preparation and making of the statement and affidavit as the official receiver may consider reasonable, subject to an appeal to the Court.

(5) If any person, without reasonable excuse, makes default in complying with the requirements of this section, he commits an offence and is liable to a fine of ₦100 for every day during which the default continues.

(6) Any person stating himself in writing to be a creditor or contributory of the company is entitled by himself or by his agent at all reasonable times, on a payment of the prescribed fee to inspect the statement submitted under this section, and to a copy of or extract from it.

(7) Any person who falsely states that he is a creditor or contributory is guilty of contempt of court and shall, on the application of the liquidator or of the official receiver, be punished accordingly.

(8) In this section, the expression "the relevant date" means, in a case where a provisional liquidator is appointed, the date of his appointment and in a case where no appointment is made, the date of the winding-up order.

584.—(1) If a winding-up order is made, the official receiver shall as soon as practicable after receipt of the statement to be submitted under section 583 of this Act or where the Court orders that no statement be submitted, as soon as practicable after the date of the order, submit a preliminary report to the Court—

(a) as to the amount of capital issued, subscribed and paid up, and the estimated amount of assets and liabilities ;

(b) if the company has failed, as to the causes of the failure ; and

(c) whether, in his opinion, further inquiry is desirable as to any matter relating to the promotion, formation or failure of the company.

(2) The official receiver may, if he thinks fit, make further reports stating the manner in which the company was formed and whether, in his opinion, fraud has been committed by any person in its promotion or formation, or by any officer of the company in relation to the company since its formation and the reports may include any other matters which, in his opinion, is desirable to bring to the notice of the court.

(3) If any further report under this section indicates the commission of fraud, the Court shall have the further powers provided in section 613 of this Act (which confers authority to order public examination of certain officials).

LIQUIDATORS

585.—(1) The Court may appoint a liquidator or liquidators for the purpose of conducting the proceedings in winding-up a company and performing such duties in reference to it as the court may impose and where there is a vacancy, the official receiver shall by virtue of his office, act as liquidator until such time as the vacancy is filled.

(2) At any time after the presentation of a petition and before the making of a winding-up order, the appointment shall be provisional and the Court making the appointment may limit and restrict the powers of the liquidator by the order appointing him.

(3) In the application of this section—

(a) if a provisional liquidator is to be appointed before the making of a winding-up order, the official receiver, or any other fit person, may be so appointed ;

(b) on the making of a winding-up order, if no liquidator is appointed, the official receiver shall by virtue of his office become the liquidator ;

(c) the official receiver in his capacity as provisional liquidator shall, and in any other case may, summon meetings of creditors and contributories of the company to be held separately for the purpose of determining whether or not an application is to be made to the court for appointing a liquidator in place of the official receiver ; or

(d) if a person other than the official receiver is appointed liquidator, he is not capable of acting in that capacity until he has notified his appointment to the Commission and given security in the prescribed manner to the satisfaction of the Court.

(4) If more than one liquidator of a company is appointed by the Court, the Court shall declare whether anything by this Act required or authorised to be done by a liquidator is to be done by all or any one or more of them.

(5) A liquidator appointed by the Court may resign, or, on cause shown, be removed by the Court and any vacancy in the office of a liquidator so appointed shall be filled by the Court.

(6) Where a person other than the official receiver is appointed a liquidator, he shall receive salary in an amount, or remuneration by way of percentage or otherwise, as the Court may direct and, if more than one person is appointed as a liquidator, their remuneration shall be distributed among them in such proportions as the Court directs.

(7) Where a liquidator of a company is appointed, he shall, after his individual name—

(a) if he is the official receiver, be described as "official receiver and liquidator of (add here name of the company)" ; and

(b) in any other case be described as "liquidator of (add here name of the company)".

(8) The acts of a liquidator shall be valid notwithstanding any defects that may afterwards be discovered in his appointment or qualification.

(9) If a liquidator is appointed under this section, all the powers of the directors shall cease, except so far as the Court may by order sanction the continuance thereof.

586. In a winding-up by the Court the liquidator shall take into his custody, or under his control, all the property and choses in action to which the company is or appears to be entitled.

587. Where a company is being wound up by the Court, the Court may, on the application of the liquidator, by order direct that all or any part of the property of whatsoever description belonging to the company or held by trustees on its behalf shall vest in the liquidator by his official name, and thereupon, but subject to the requirements of registration under any particular enactment, the property to which the order relates shall vest accordingly and the liquidator may, after giving such indemnity, if any, as the Court may direct, bring or defend in his official name any action or other legal proceeding which relates to that property or which it is necessary to bring or defend for the purpose of effectually winding-up the company and recovering its property.

588.—(1) The liquidator in a winding-up by the Court shall have power, with the sanction either of the court or of the committee of inspection to—

(a) bring or defend any action or other legal proceeding in the name and on behalf of the company ;

(b) carry on the business of the company so far as may be necessary for its beneficial winding-up ;

(c) appoint a legal practitioner or any other relevant professional to assist him in the performance of his duties ;

(d) pay any classes of creditors in full;

(e) make any compromise or arrangement with creditors or persons claiming to be creditors, or having or alleging themselves to have any claim, present or future, certain or contingent, ascertained or sounding only in damages against the company, or whereby the company may be rendered liable ; and

(f) compromise all calls and liabilities to calls, debts and liabilities capable of resulting in debts, and all claims, present or future, certain or contingent, ascertained or sounding only in damages, subsisting or supposed to subsist between the company and a contributory or alleged contributory or other debtor or person apprehending liability to the company, and all questions in any way relating to or affecting the assets or the winding-up of the company, on such terms as may be agreed, and take any security for the discharge of any such call, debt, liability or claim and give a complete discharge in respect of it.

(2) The liquidator in winding-up by the Court shall have power to—

(a) sell the property of the company of whatever nature by public auction or private contract, with power to transfer the whole thereof to any person or company or to sell the same in parcels ;

(b) do all acts and to execute, in the name and on behalf of the company, all deeds, receipts and other documents, and for that purpose to use, when necessary, the company's seal (where the company has a seal) ;

(c) prove, rank and claim in the bankruptcy, insolvency or sequestration of any contributory for any balance against his estate, and to receive dividends in the bankruptcy, insolvency or sequestration in respect of that balance as a separate debt due from the bankrupt or insolvent, and ratably with the other separate creditors ;

(d) draw, accept, make and indorse any bill of exchange or promissory note in the name and on behalf of the company with the same effect with respect to the liability of the company as if the bill or note had been drawn, accepted, made or indorsed by or on behalf of the company in the course of its business ;

(e) raise on the security of the assets of the company any money requisite ;

(f) take out in his official name, letters of administration to any deceased contributory, and to do in his official name any other act necessary for obtaining payment of any money due from a contributory or his estate which cannot be conveniently done in the name of the company, and in all such cases the money due shall, for the purpose of enabling the liquidator to take out the letters of administration or recover the money, be deemed to be due to the liquidator himself;

(g) appoint an agent to do any business which the liquidator is unable to do himself; and

(h) do all other things as may be necessary for winding-up the affairs of the company and distributing its assets.

(3) The exercise by the liquidator in a winding-up by the Court of the powers conferred by this section shall be subject to the control of the Court, and any creditor or contributory may apply to the Court with respect to any exercise or proposed exercise of any of those powers.

589. If during the winding-up of a company by the court a person other than the official receiver is appointed liquidator, he shall give the official receiver such information and access to and facilities for inspecting the books and documents of the company,

and generally any aid requisite or necessary for enabling that officer to perform his duties under this Act.

590.—(1) Subject to the provisions of this Act, the liquidator of a company being wound up by the Court shall, in the administration and distribution of the assets of the company among its creditors, have regard to directions given by resolution of the creditors or contributories at any general meeting, or by the

Committee of Inspection and directions given by the creditors or contributories at any general meeting shall, in case of conflict, override directions given by the Committee of Inspection.

(2) The liquidator may summon general meetings of the creditors or contributories for the purpose of ascertaining their wishes, and it shall be his duty to summon meetings at such times as the creditors or contributories by resolution either at the meeting appointing the liquidator or otherwise, may direct, or whenever requested in writing to do so by one tenth in value of the creditors or contributories, as the case maybe.

(3) The liquidator may apply to the Court in the manner prescribed for directions in relation to any particular matter arising under the winding-up.

(4) Subject to the provisions of this Act, the liquidator shall use his own discretion in the management of the estate and its distribution among the creditors.

(5) Any person aggrieved by an act or decision of the liquidator, may apply to the Court for such order as it deems just and the Court may confirm, reverse, or modify the act or decision.

591.—(1) Every liquidator of a company being wound up by the Court shall, in such manner and at such times as the Commission directs, pay moneys received by him into the public fund of the Federation kept by the Commission for the purposes of this Act known as "the Companies Liquidation Account", and the Accountant-General of the Federation shall furnish him with a certificate of receipt for the money so paid.

(2) If the Committee of Inspection satisfies the Commission that for the purpose of carrying on the business of the company or of obtaining advances, or for any other reason, it is for the advantage of the creditors or contributories that the liquidator should have an account with any bank, the Commission shall, on the application of the Committee of Inspection, authorise the liquidator to make his payments into and out of such bank in Nigeria as the committee may select, and thereupon those payments shall be made in the prescribed manner.

(3) If the liquidator of a company being wound up, at any time retains for more than 10 days an amount in excess of either ₦50,000 or such other amount as the Commission may approve, and fails to satisfy the Commission as to the need for the retention of that amount beyond that time, the liquidator shall pay interest on the amount so retained in excess, at the rate of 20% per annum, and shall be liable to—

(a) disallowance of the whole or such part of his remuneration as the Commission deems fit ; and

(b) removal from office, and in addition, he shall be liable to pay any expenses occasioned by the retention.

(4) A liquidator of a company which is being wound up by the Court shall not pay any sums received by him as liquidator into his private banking account.

592.—(1) Every liquidator of a company being wound up by the Court shall, at such times as may be prescribed, but not less than twice in each year during his tenure of office, send to the Commission an account of his receipts and payments as liquidator.

(2) The account shall be in duplicate in the prescribed form, and shall be verified by a statutory declaration in the prescribed form.

(3) The Commission shall cause the account to be audited, and for the purpose of the audit, the liquidator shall furnish the Commission with such vouchers and information as the Commission may require, and the Commission may at any time require the production of, and may inspect, any book or account kept by the liquidator.

(4) When the account has been audited, one copy shall be filed and kept by the Commission, and the other copy shall be with the Court and each shall be open to inspection by any creditor or other person interested, on payment of the prescribed fee.

(5) The Commission shall cause the account when audited, or a summary of it, to be printed, and shall send a printed copy of the account or summary by post to every creditor and contributory.

593. Every liquidator of a company which is being wound up by the Court shall, in the manner prescribed, keep proper books in which he shall cause to be made entries or minutes of proceedings at meetings and of other matters as may be prescribed, and a creditor or contributory may, subject to the control of the Court, personally or by his agent inspect the books.

594.—(1) Where the liquidator of a company being wound up by the Court has realised all the property of the company, or so much of it as may, in his opinion, be realised without needlessly protracting the liquidation, and has distributed a final dividend, if any, to the creditors, adjusted the rights of the contributories among themselves, and made a final return, if any, to the contributories, has resigned, or has been removed from his office, the Commission shall, on the application of the liquidator, cause a report on the accounts of the liquidator to be prepared.

(2) The Commission shall consider the report referred to in subsection(1) together with any objection that may be raised by a creditor, contributory, or person interested against the release of the liquidator, and may grant or withhold the release as it deems fit subject to an appeal to the Court.

(3) If the release of a liquidator is withheld, the Court may, on the application of any creditor, contributory, or person interested, make such order as it deems just, charging the liquidator with the consequences of any act or default which he may have done or made contrary to his duty.

(4) An order of the Commission releasing the liquidator shall discharge him from all liability in respect of any act done or default made by him in the administration of the affairs of the company, or otherwise in relation to his conduct as liquidator, and the order may be revoked on proof that it was obtained by fraud, suppression or concealment of any material fact.

(5) Where the liquidator has not previously resigned or been removed, his release shall operate as a removal from his office.

595.—(1) The Commission shall take cognisance of the conduct of liquidators of companies which are being wound up by the Court and if a liquidator does not faithfully perform his duties and duly observe all the requirements imposed on him by any enactment, or other- wise with respect to the performance of his duties, or if any complaint is made to the Commission by a creditor or contributory in that regard, the Commission shall inquire into the matter, and may take such action thereon as it deems fit, including the direction of a local investigation of the books and vouchers of the liquidator.

(2) The Commission may, at any time, require the liquidator of a company being wound up by the Court to answer any inquiry in relation to any winding up in which he is engaged and if the Commission deems fit, it may apply to the Court to examine the liquidator or any other person on oath concerning the winding-up.

COMMITTEE OF INSPECTION, SPECIAL MANAGER

596.—(1) Where a winding-up order is made by the Court, the separate meetings of creditors and contributories summoned for the purpose of determining whether or not to apply to the court for an order appointing a liquidator in place of the official receiver, shall determine whether or not an application should be made to the court for the appointment of a Committee of Inspection to act with the liquidator, and to determine who are to be members of the Committee, if the appointment is made.

(2) The Court may make any appointment and order required to give effect to any determination under this section and if there is a difference between the determinations of the meetings of the creditors and contributories in respect of the matters aforesaid, the court shall decide the difference and make any order it deems necessary.

597.—(1) A Committee of Inspection appointed under this Act shall consist of creditors and contributories of the company or persons holding general powers of attorney from creditors or contributories in the proportions as may be agreed on by the meetings of creditors and contributories or as, in case of difference, may be determined by the Court.

(2) A Committee of Inspection shall meet at the time appointed, and there shall be a meeting at least once in every month during its existence, but the liquidator or any member of the Committee may convene a meeting as and when necessary.

(3) A meeting of a Committee of Inspection shall be deemed convened if a majority of members are present, and at the meeting of the Committee of Inspection may act by a majority of the members present.

(4) A member of the Committee of Inspection may resign by notice in writing signed by him and delivered to the liquidator.

(5) If a member of the Committee of Inspection becomes bankrupt, compounds or arranges with his creditors, is absent from five consecutive meetings of the Committee of Inspection without leave of those members who, together with himself, represent the creditors or contributories, as the case may be, his office shall thereupon become vacant.

(6) A member of the Committee of Inspection may be removed by an ordinary resolution at a meeting of creditors if he represents creditors, or of contributories if he represents contributories, of which seven days' notice has been given, stating the object of the meeting.

(7) On a vacancy occurring in the Committee of Inspection, the liquidators hall immediately summon a meeting of creditors or contributories, as the case may

require, to fill the vacancy, and the meeting may, by resolution, reappoint the same or appoint another creditor or contributory to fill the vacancy:

Provided that if the liquidator, having regard to the position in the winding-up, is of the opinion that it is unnecessary for the vacancy to be filled he may apply to the court and the Court may make an order that the vacancy shall not be filled, or shall be filled in the circumstances as may be specified in the order.

(8) The continuing members of the Committee of Inspection, if not less than two, may act notwithstanding any vacancy in the Committee of Inspection.

598. Where, in the case of winding-up, there is no Committee of Inspection, the Commission may, on the application of the liquidator, if it deems fit, do anything or give any direction or permission which is by this Act authorised or required to be done or given by the Committee of Inspection.

599.—(1) Where the official receiver becomes the liquidator of a company, whether provisionally or otherwise, he may, if satisfied that the nature of the estate or business of the company, interests of the creditors or contributories generally, require the appointment of a special manager of the estate or business of the company other than himself, apply to the Court for an order appointing a special manager to act during such time as the Court may direct, with the powers, including those of a receiver or manager, as may be entrusted to him by the Court and the Court may make any order necessary.

(2) A special manager appointed under this section shall receive remuneration as fixed by the Court and shall give security and account in such manner as the Commission directs.

600. Where application is made to the Court to appoint a receiver on behalf of the debenture holders or other creditors of a company being wound up by the Court, the official receiver may be so appointed.

GENERAL POWERS OF COURT IN CASE OF WINDING-UP BY COURT

601.—(1) The Court may, at any time after an order for winding-up, on the application either of a liquidator, the official receiver or a creditor or contributory and on proof to the satisfaction of the Court that all proceedings in relation to the winding-up ought to be stayed, make an order staying the proceedings either altogether or for a limited time, on such terms and conditions as the Court deems fit.

(2) The Court may, at any time after an order for winding-up, on the application either of the liquidator or a creditor, and after having regard to the wishes of the creditors and contributories, make an order directing that the winding-up, ordered by the Court, shall be conducted as a creditors' voluntary winding-up, and if the Court does so, the winding-up shall be so conducted.

(3) On any application under this section, the Court may, before making an order, require the official receiver to furnish to the Court a report with respect to any facts or matters which are in his opinion relevant to the application.

(4) A copy of every order made under this section shall immediately be forwarded by the company, or otherwise as may be prescribed, to the Commission which shall make a minute of the order in its books relating to the company.

(5) If default is made in lodging a copy of an order made under this section with the Commission as required by subsection (4), every officer of the company or other person who authorises or permits the default shall be liable to a penalty as may be prescribed by regulation.

602.—(1) As soon as may be after making a winding-up order, the Court shall settle a list of contributories, and may rectify the register of members in all cases where rectification is required in under this Act, and the Court shall cause the assets of the company to be collected, and applied in discharge of its liabilities.

(2) Where it appears to the Court that it will not be necessary to make calls on or adjust the rights of contributories, the Court may dispense with the settlement of a list of contributories.

(3) In settling the list of contributories, the Court shall distinguish between persons who are contributories in their own right and persons who are contributories as being representatives of or liable for the debts of others.

603. The Court may, at any time after making a winding-up order require a contributory for the time being on the list of contributories and any trustee, receiver, banker, agent, or officer of the company to pay, deliver, convey, surrender or transfer immediately, or within such time as the Court directs, to the liquidator, money, property, or books and papers in his hands, to which the company is prima facie entitled.

604.—(1) The Court may, at any time after making a winding-up order, make an order on any contributory for the time being on the list of contributories to pay, in the manner directed by the order any money due from him or from the estate of the person whom he represents to the company, exclusive of any money payable by him or the estate by virtue of any call under this Act.

(2) The Court making an order under this section in the case of—

(a) an unlimited company, may allow to the contributory by way of setoff any money due to him or to the estate which he represents from the company of any independent dealing or contract with the company, but not any money due to him as a member of the company in respect of any dividend or profit; and

(b) a limited company, may make to any director or manager whose liability is unlimited or to his estate, the allowances in paragraph (a).

(3) In the case of any company, limited or unlimited, when all the creditors are paid in full, the money due on any account to a contributory from the company may be allowed to him by way of set-off against any subsequent call.

605.—(1) The Court may, at any time after making a winding-up order and either before or after it has ascertained the sufficiency of the assets of the company, make calls on all or any of the contributories for the time being settled on the list of the contributories to the extent of their liability, for payment of any money which the Court considers necessary to satisfy the debts and liabilities of the company, the costs, charges and expenses of winding-up, the adjustment of the rights of the contributories among themselves, and make an order for payment of the calls made.

(2) In making a call under this section, the Court shall take into consideration the probability that some of the contributories may fail, wholly or partially to pay for the call.

606.—(1) The Court may order any contributory, purchaser or other person from whom money is due to the company to pay it into the company's liquidation account referred to in section 591 of this Act to the account of the liquidator instead of directly to the liquidator and the order may be enforced in the same manner as if it had directed payment to the liquidator.

(2) Moneys and securities paid or delivered into the company's liquidation account in the event of a winding-up by the Court shall be subject in all respects to any relevant order of the Court.

607.—(1) An order made by the Court on a contributory shall, subject to any right of appeal, be conclusive evidence that money, if any thereby appearing to be due or ordered to be paid, is due.

(2) All other pertinent matters stated in the order shall be taken to be truly stated as against all persons and in all proceedings, except proceedings against the land of a deceased contributory, when the order shall be only prima facie evidence for the purpose of charging his land, unless his heirs or devisees were on the list of contributories at the time the order was made.

608. The Court may fix a time or times within which creditors are to prove their debts or claims, or be excluded from the benefit of any distribution made before those debts are proved.

609. The Court shall adjust the right of the contributories among themselves and distribute any surplus among the persons entitled thereto.

610.—(1) The Court may, at any time after making a winding-up order, make such order for inspection of the books and papers of the company by creditors and contributories as the Court deems just, and books and papers in the possession of the company may be inspected by creditors or contributories accordingly, but not further or otherwise.

(2) Nothing in this section shall be taken as excluding or restricting any statutory rights of a government department or person acting under the authority of a government department.

611. The Court may, in the event of the assets being insufficient to satisfy the liabilities, make an order as to the payment out of the assets of the costs, charges and expenses incurred in the winding-up in such order of priority as the Court deems just.

612.—(1) The Court may, at any time after the appointment of a provisional liquidator or the making of a winding-up order, summon before it any officer of the company or person known or suspected to have in his possession any property of the company or supposed to be indebted to the company, or any person who the court deems capable of giving information concerning the promotion, formation, trade, dealings, affairs or property of the company.

(2) The Court may examine on oath any person summoned concerning the matters under subsection (1) either by word of mouth or on written interrogatories, reduce his answers to writing and require him to sign them.

(3) The Court may require any person summoned under subsection (1),to produce books and papers in his custody or power relating to the company but, where the person claims a lien on books or papers produced by him, the production is without prejudice to the lien, and the court shall have jurisdiction in the winding-up to determine all questions relating to that lien.

(4) If a person summoned under subsection (1), after being tendered a reasonable sum for his expenses, refuses to come before the Court at the time appointed, not having lawful impediment (made known to the Court at the time of its sitting and allowed by it), the Court may cause him to be apprehended and brought before the Court for examination.

613.—(1) Where an order is made for winding-up a company by the Court and the official receiver makes a further report under this Act stating that in his opinion a fraud has been committed by a person in the promotion or formation of the company, or by any director or other officer of the company in relation to the company since its formation, the Court may, after consideration of the report, direct that a person who has taken part in the promotion or formation of the company, or has been a director or officer of the company, shall attend before the Court on a day appointed by the court for that purpose, and be publicly examined as to the promotion or formation or the conduct of the business of the company, or as to his conduct and dealing as director or officer thereof.

(2) The official receiver shall take part in the examination, and for that purpose may, if specially authorised by the Commission in that behalf, employ a legal practitioner.

(3) The liquidator, where the official receiver is not the liquidator, and a creditor or contributory, may also take part in the examination, either personally or by a legal practitioner.

(4) The Court may put such questions to the person examined as the Court deems fit.

(5) The person examined shall be examined on oath, and shall answer all such questions as the Court may put or allow to be put to him.

(6) A person ordered to be examined under this section shall, at his own cost, before his examination, be furnished with a copy of the official receiver's report, and may, at his own cost, employ a legal practitioner who shall be at liberty to put to him such questions as the Court may deem just for the purpose of enabling him to explain or qualify any answers given by him :

Provided that the person applies to the Court to be exculpated from charges made or suggested against him, the official receiver shall appear on the hearing of the application and call the attention of the Court to any matters which appear to the official receiver to be relevant, and if the Court after hearing any evidence given or witnesses called by the official receiver, grants the application, the Court may allow the applicant such costs as in its discretion it may deem fit.

(7) Notes of the examination shall be taken down in writing, and shall be read over to or by, and signed by, the person examined and may, thereafter be used in evidence against him and shall be open to the inspection of any creditor or contributory at all reasonable times.

(8) The Court may, if it deems fit, adjourn the examination.

(9) An examination under this section may, if the Court directs, and subject to general rules made under section 616 of this Act, be held before any magistrate, and the powers of the court under this section as to the conduct of the examination but not as to costs, may be exercised by the magistrate before whom the examination is held.

614. The Court, at any time either before or after making a winding-up order, on proof of probable cause for believing that a contributory is about to quit Nigeria or otherwise abscond, remove or conceal any of his property for the purpose of evading payment of calls, or of avoiding examination with respect to the affairs of the company, may cause the contributory to be arrested, and his books, papers and movable personal property, to be seized, and him and them to be kept safely until the time which the Court may order.

615. A power by this Act conferred on the court shall be in addition to and not in restriction of existing powers of instituting proceedings against contributory or

debtor of the company, or the estate of a contributory or debtor, for the recovery of any call or other sums.

616.—(1) Provision may be made by rules for enabling or requiring all or any of the powers and duties conferred and imposed on the Court by this Act, in respect of the matters following, to be exercised or performed by the liquidator as an officer of the Court, and subject to the control of the Court, that is to say, the powers and duties of the Court in respect of—

(a) holding and conducting of meetings to ascertain the wishes of creditors and contributories ;

(b) settling of lists of contributories and the rectifying of the register of members where required, and the collecting and applying of the assets;

(c) requiring delivery of property or documents to the liquidator;

(d) making of calls ; and

(e) fixing of a time within which debts and claims shall be proved.

(2) Nothing in this section shall authorise the liquidator, without the special leave of the Court, to rectify the register of members, or, without either the special leave of the Court or the sanction of the Committee of Inspection, to make any call.

617.—(1) If the affairs of a company have been fully wound up and the liquidator makes an application in that behalf, the court shall order the dissolution of the company and the company shall be dissolved accordingly from the date of the order.

(2) A copy of the order shall, within 14 days from the date when made, be forwarded by the liquidator to the Commission who shall make in its books a minute of the dissolution of the company.

(3) If the liquidator makes default in complying with the requirements of this section, he shall be liable to a penalty as may be prescribed by the Regulation for every day during which he is in default.

ENFORCEMENT OF AND APPEALS FROM ORDERS

618. An order made by a court under this Act may be enforced in the same manner as orders made in any action pending therein.

619. Subject to rules of Court, an appeal from any order or decision made or given in the winding-up of a company by the Court under this Act, shall lie in the same manner and subject to the same conditions as an appeal from any order or decision of the court in cases within its ordinary jurisdiction.

CHAPTER 22—VOLUNTARY WINDING-UP

RESOLUTIONS FOR AND COMMENCEMENT OF VOLUNTARY WINDING-UP

620.—(1) Any company may be wound up voluntarily—

(a) when the period, if any, fixed for the duration of the company by the articles expires, or the event, if any, occurs, on occurrence of which the articles provided that the company is to be dissolved and the company in general meeting has passed a resolution requiring the company to be wound up voluntarily ;

(b) if the company resolves by special resolution that the company be wound up.

(2) References in this Act to a "resolution for voluntary winding-up" means a resolution passed under any of the paragraphs of this section.

621.—(1) If a company passes a resolution for voluntary winding-up it shall, within 14 days after the passing of the resolution, give notice of the resolution by advertisement in the Federal Government Gazette or two daily newspapers and to the Commission.

(2) If default is made in complying with this section, the company and each officer of the company who is in default is liable to a penalty in such amount as the Commission may specify in its regulations and for the purposes of this subsection the liquidator of the company shall be deemed to be an officer of the company.

622. A voluntary winding-up shall be deemed to commence at the time of the passing of the resolution for voluntary winding-up.

623. In case of voluntary winding-up, the company shall, from the commencement of the winding-up, cease to carry on its business, except so far as may be required for the beneficial winding-up thereof:

Provided that the corporate state and powers of the company shall, notwithstanding anything to the contrary in its articles, continue until it is dissolved.

624. A transfer of shares, not being a transfer made to or with the sanction of the liquidator, and any alteration in the status of the members of the company, made after the commencement of a voluntary winding up, shall be void.

DECLARATION OF SOLVENCY

625.—(1) Where on or after the commencement of this Act, it is proposed to wind up a company voluntarily, the directors of the company or, in the case of a company having more than two directors, the majority of the directors, may at a meeting of the directors make a statutory declaration to the effect that they have made a full inquiry into the affairs of the company and that, having done so, they have formed the opinion that the company will be able to pay its debts in full within a period, not exceeding 12 months from the commencement of the winding-up, as is specified in the declaration.

(2) A declaration made under subsection (1) does not have effect for the purposes of this Act unless it—

(a) is made within the five weeks immediately preceding the date of the passing of the resolution for winding-up the company and the statutory declaration and resolution are delivered to the Commission for registration within 15 days after passing the resolution ; and

(b) embodies a statement of the company's assets and liabilities as at the latest practicable date before making the declaration.

(3) A director of a company making a declaration under this section without having reasonable grounds for the opinion that the company will be able to pay its debts in full within the period specified in the declaration, commits an offence and is liable on conviction to a fine as the Court deems fit or to imprisonment for a term of three months, or to both, and if the company is wound-up under a resolution passed within the period of five weeks after making the declaration, and if its debts are not paid or provided for in full within the period stated in the declaration, it is presumed, until the contrary is shown, that the director did not have reasonable grounds for his opinion.

(4) A winding-up in any case where a declaration has been made and delivered in accordance with this section, shall in this Act be referred to as "a members' voluntary winding-up" and a winding-up in any case where a declaration has not been made and delivered as aforesaid shall in this Act be referred to as "a creditors' voluntary winding-up".

(5) Subsections (1)-(3) shall not apply to a winding-up commenced before the commencement of this Act.

PROVISIONS APPLICABLE TO A MEMBERS' VOLUNTARY WINDING-UP

626. Sections 627-633 of this Act, subject to the alternative provision in section 632 of this Act, apply in relation to a members' voluntary winding-up.

627.—(1) The company in general meeting shall appoint one or more liquidators for the purpose of winding-up the affairs and distributing the assets of the company, and may fix the remuneration to be paid to him or them.

(2) If a liquidator is appointed under this section, all the powers of the directors shall cease, except so far as the company in general meeting or the liquidator sanctions the continuance thereof.

628.—(1) If a vacancy occurs by death, resignation or otherwise in the office of a liquidator appointed by the company, the company in general meeting may, subject to any arrangement with its creditors, fill the vacancy and for that purpose a general meeting may be convened by a contributory or, if there were more liquidators than one, by the continuing liquidators.

(2) The general meeting shall be held in the manner provided by this Act or by the articles, or in such manner as may, on application by a contributory or by the continuing liquidators, be determined by the Court.

629.—(1) If, in the case of a winding-up commenced after the commencement of this Act, the liquidator is, at any time, of the opinion that the company will not be able to pay its debts in full within the period stated in the declaration under section 625 of this Act, he shall immediately summon a meeting of the creditors, and lay before the meeting a statement of the assets and liabilities of the company.

(2) If the liquidator fails to comply with this section, he is liable to a penalty in such amount as the Commission shall specify in its regulations.

630.—(1) Subject to the provisions of section 632 of this Act, in the event of the winding-up continuing for more than one year, the liquidator shall summon a general meeting of the company at the end of the first year from the commencement of the winding-up, and of each succeeding year, or at the first convenient date within three months from the end of the year or such longer period as the Commission may allow, and shall lay before the meeting an account of his acts and dealings and of the conduct of the winding-up during the preceding year :

Provided that the account shall be sent to all the members of the company not later than 14 days before the date of the meeting.

(2) If the liquidator fails to comply with this section, he is liable to a penalty in such amount as the Commission shall specify in its regulations.

631.—(1) Subject to the provisions of section 632 of this Act, as soon as the affairs of the company are fully wound up, the liquidator shall prepare an account of the winding-up, showing how the winding-up has been conducted and the property of the company has been disposed of and when the account

is prepared, he shall call a general meeting of the company for the purpose of laying before it the account, and giving any explanation thereof.

(2) The meeting shall be called by notice published in the Federal Government Gazette and in two newspapers printed in Nigeria and circulating in the locality where the meeting is being called, specifying the time, place and object of, and published at least one month before the meeting.

(3) Within seven days after the meeting, the liquidator shall send to the Commission a copy of the account, and shall make a return to it of the holding of the meeting, its

date and if the copy is not sent or the return is not made in accordance with this subsection, the liquidator is liable to a penalty in such amount as the Commission shall specify in its regulations for every day during which the default continues:

Provided that if a quorum is not present at the meeting, the liquidator shall, in lieu of the return hereinbefore mentioned, make a return that the meeting was duly summoned and that no quorum was present and upon such a return being made, the provisions of this subsection as to the making of the return shall be deemed to have been complied with.

(4) The Commission, on receiving the account and the appropriate return, shall forthwith register them, and on the expiration of three months from the registration of the return, the company is deemed dissolved:

Provided that the Court may, on the application of the liquidator or of any other person who appears to the Court to be interested, make an order deferring the date at which the dissolution of the company is to take effect for such time as the Court deems fit.

(5) The person on whose application an order of the Court under this section is made shall, within seven days after the order is made, deliver to the Commission a certified true copy of the order for registration, and if that person fails to do so, he is liable to a penalty for every day during which the default continues in such amount as the Commission shall specify in its regulations.

(6) If the liquidator fails to call a general meeting of the company as required by this section, he is liable to a penalty in such amount as the Commission shall specify in its regulations.

632. Where section 629 of this Act has effect, sections 640 and 641 shall apply to the winding-up to the exclusion of the two last foregoing sections, as if the winding-up were a creditors' voluntary winding-up and not a members' voluntary winding-up:

Provided that the liquidator shall not be required to summon a meeting of creditors under section 640 of this Act at the end of the first year from the commencement of the winding-up, unless the meeting held under section 629 of this Act is held more than three months before the end of that year.

633.—(1) The liquidator in a members' voluntary winding-up shall—

(a) keep—

(i) proper records and books of account with respect to his acts and dealings, the conduct of the winding-up, and

(ii) all receipts and payments by him ; and

(b) if he carries on the business of the company, keep a distinct account of the trading.

(2) In the event of the winding-up continuing for more than a year, the liquidator shall summon a general meeting of the company at the end of the first year from the commencement of the winding-up and of each succeeding year, or at the first convenient date within three months of the end of the year or such longer period as the Commission may allow, and shall lay before the meeting an account of his acts and dealings and of the conduct of the winding up during the preceding year and of the trading during such time as the business of the company has been carried on, and within 28 days thereafter shall send a copy of such accounts to the Commission for registration.

(3) As soon as the affairs of the company are fully wound up, the liquidator shall prepare and send to every member of the company final accounts of the winding-up showing how the winding-up has been conducted, the result of the trading during

such time as the business of the company has been carried on, and how the property of the company has been disposed of, and thereupon shall convene a general meeting of the company for the purpose of laying before it such accounts and of giving an explanation thereof.

(4) Within 28 days after the meeting referred to in the immediately preceding subsection, the liquidator shall send to the Commission for registration copies of the accounts laid before the meeting and a statement of the holding of the meeting and of its date :

Provided that if a quorum was not present at the meeting the liquidator, in lieu of the statement hereinbefore mentioned, shall send a statement that the meeting was duly convened and that no quorum was present thereat.

(5) The records, books and accounts referred to in this section shall be in such form, if any, as the Commission may prescribe and shall give a true and fair view of the matters therein recorded and of the administration of the company's affairs and of the winding-up.

(6) The accounts referred to in subsections (2) and (3), shall be audited by the auditor of the company prior to being laid before the company in general meeting in accordance with such subsections and the auditors shall state in a report annexed thereto whether, in their opinion and to the best of their information—

(a) they have obtained all the information and explanations necessary for the purpose of their audit ; and

(b) proper books and records have been maintained by the liquidator in accordance with this Act, and such accounts are in accordance with the books and records and give all the information required by this Act in the manner therein required and give a true and fair view of the matters stated in such accounts :

Provided that such audit and auditors' report shall not be required if—

(i) the liquidator, or one of the liquidators if more than one, is duly qualified under the provisions of this Act for appointment as auditor of a public company, and

(ii) on or after his appointment as liquidator, the company resolved by special resolution that the accounts shall not be audited in accordance with this subsection.

(7) Meetings required to be convened under this section or subsection(6), shall be convened and held, in accordance with the provisions of this Act and the regulations of the company relating to general meetings.

(8) The liquidator shall preserve the books and papers of the company and of the liquidator for five years from the dissolution of the company but thereafter may destroy such books and papers unless the Commission shall otherwise direct, in which event he shall not destroy the same until the Commission consents in writing.

(9) If a liquidator fails to comply with any of the provisions of this section, he is liable to a penalty for each in such amount as the Commission shall specify in its regulations.

PROVISIONS APPLICABLE TO A CREDITORS' VOLUNTARY WINDING-UP

634. The provisions of sections 635-641 of this Act apply in relation to a creditors' voluntary winding-up.

635.—(1) The company shall cause a meeting of the creditors of the company to be summoned for the day, or the day next following, on which there is to be held the meeting at which the resolution for voluntary winding up is to be proposed, and shall cause the notices of the meeting of creditors to be sent by post to the creditors simultaneously with the sending of the notices of the meetings of the company.

(2) The company shall cause notice of the meeting of the creditors to be published once in the Federal Government *Gazette* and once at least in two daily newspapers printed in Nigeria and circulating in the district where the registered office or principal place of business of the company is situate.

(3) The directors of the company shall—

(a) cause a full statement of the position of the company's affairs, including—

(i) particulars of the company's assets,

(ii) debts and liabilities together with a list of the creditors of the company, and

(iii) the estimated amount of their claims to be forwarded to each creditor not later than 14 days before the date of the meeting to be held by the directors and at which the statement shall be laid ; and (b) appoint one of them to preside at the meeting.

(4) It is the duty of the director so appointed to attend and preside over the meeting.

(5) If the meeting of the company at which the resolution for voluntary winding-up is to be proposed, is adjourned and the resolution is passed at an adjourned meeting, any resolution passed at the meeting of the creditors held under subsection (1) shall have effect as if it had been passed immediately after the passing of the resolution for winding-up of the company.

(6) If default is made by—

(a) the company in complying with subsection (1) or (2) ;

(b) the directors of the company in complying with subsection (3) ;

(c) any director of the company appointed to preside, in complying with subsection (4),

the company, directors or director, as the case may be, shall be liable to a penalty in such amount as the Commission shall specify in its regulations and in the case of default by the company, each officer of the company is liable to the like penalty.

Appointment 636.—(1) The creditors and the company at their respective meetings of liquidator mentioned in section 635 of this Act may nominate a person to be liquidator for and cesser of the purpose of winding-up the affairs and distributing the assets of the company,

directors'

powers. and if the creditors and the company nominate different persons, the person nominated by the creditors shall be liquidator, and if no person is nominated by the creditors the person if any, nominated by the company, shall be liquidator :

Provided that in the case of different persons being nominated, any director, member or creditor of the company may, within seven days after the date on which the nomination was made by the creditors, apply to the Court for an order directing that the persons nominated as liquidator by the company shall be liquidator instead of or jointly with the person nominated by the creditors, or appointing some other person to be liquidator instead of the person appointed by the creditors.

(2) On the appointment of a liquidator, all the powers of the directors shall cease, except there is a Committee of Inspection, or if there is no such committee, the creditors shall sanction the continuance.

637. (1) The creditors, at the meeting to be held under section 635 of this Act or at any subsequent meeting, may, if they think fit, set up a Committee of Inspection consisting of not more than five persons, and if such a committee is set up, the

company may, either at the meeting at which the resolution for voluntary winding-up is passed or at any time subsequently in general meeting, appoint such number of persons as they think fit to act as members of the committee not exceeding five in number:

Provided that the creditors may, if they think fit, resolve that all or any of the persons so appointed by the company shall not be members of the Committee of Inspection, and if the creditors so resolve, the persons mentioned in the resolution shall not, unless the Court otherwise directs, be qualified to act as members of the committee, and on any application to the Court under this provision the Court may, if it thinks fit, appoint other persons to act as such members in place of the persons mentioned in the resolution.

(2) Subject to the provisions of this section and to general rules made under this Act, the provisions of section 597 of this Act (except subsection (1)), shall apply with respect to a committee of inspection appointed under this section as they apply with respect to a Committee of Inspection appointed in a winding-up by the Court.

638. The Committee of Inspection, or if there is no such committee, the creditors, may fix the remuneration to be paid to the liquidator or liquidators.

639. If a vacancy occurs, by death, resignation or otherwise, in the office of a liquidator, other than a liquidator appointed by the direction of the Court, the creditors may fill the vacancy.

640.—(1) Where the winding-up continues for more than one year, the liquidator shall summon a general meeting of the company and a meeting of the creditors at the end of the first year from the commencement of the winding-up, and of each succeeding year, or at the first convenient date within three months from the end of year, or such longer period as the Commission may allow, and shall lay before the meetings an account of his acts and dealings and of the conduct of the winding-up during the preceding year.

(2) If the liquidator fails to comply with the provisions of this section, he is liable to a penalty in such amount as the Commission shall specify in its regulations.

641.—(1) As soon as the affairs of the company are fully wound up, the liquidator shall prepare an account of the winding-up, showing how the winding up has been conducted and the property of the company has been disposed of, and thereupon he shall call a general meeting of the company and a meeting of the creditors for the purpose of laying the account before the meetings and giving any explanation thereof.

(2) Each such meeting shall be called by notice published in the Federal Government Gazette and in two daily newspapers printed in Nigeria and circulating in the locality of the registered office of the company, specifying the time, place and object thereof, and published one month at least before the meeting.

(3) Within seven days after the date of the meeting, or if the meetings are not held on the same date, after the date of the later meeting, the liquidator shall send to the Commission a copy of the account, and shall make a return to it of the holding of the meetings and of their dates, and if the copy is not sent or the return is not made in accordance with this subsection, the liquidator shall be liable to a penalty for every day during which the default continues in such amount as the Commission shall specify in its regulations:

Provided that, if a quorum is not formed at either such meetings the liquidator shall, in lieu of the return, make a return that the meeting was duly summoned and that no quorum was present, and upon such a return being made the provisions of this subsection as to the making of the return are, in respect of that meeting, deemed to have been complied with.

(4) The Commission, on receiving the account, and, in respect of each such meeting, either of the returns mentioned above, shall forthwith register them, and on the expiration of three months from the registration thereof, the company shall be deemed to be dissolved :

Provided that the Court may, on the application of the liquidator or of any other person who appears to the Court to be interested, make an order deferring the date at which the dissolution of the company is to take effect for such time as the Court thinks fit.

(5) A person on whose application an order of the Court under this section is made shall, within seven days after the making of the order, deliver to the Commission a certified true copy of the order for registration, and if that person fails to do so he is liable to a penalty as prescribed in the regulation for every day during which the default continues.

(6) If the liquidator fails to call a general meeting of the company or a meeting of the creditors as required by this section, he is liable to a penalty as prescribed in the regulation.

PROVISIONS APPLICABLE TO EVERY VOLUNTARY WINDING-UP

642. The provisions of sections 643 - 648 of this Act, apply to every voluntary winding-up, whether a members' or a creditors' winding-up.

643. Subject to the provisions of this Act as to preferential payments, the property of a company shall, on its winding-up, be applied in satisfaction of its liabilities *pari passu* and, subject to such application shall, unless the articles otherwise provide, be distributed among the members according to their rights and interests in the company.

644.—(1) The liquidator may—

(a) in the case of a members' voluntary winding-up, with the sanction of special resolution of the company, and, in the case of a creditors' voluntary winding-up, with the sanction of the court or, the committee of inspection or if there is no such committee, a meeting of the creditors, exercise any of the powers given by section 588 (1) (d), (e) and (f) of this Act to a liquidator in a winding-up by the Court ;

(b) without sanction, exercise any of the other powers given by this Act to the liquidator in a winding-up by the Court ;

(c) exercise the power of the Court under this Act of settling a list of contributories, and the list of contributories shall be prima facie evidence of the liability of the persons named therein to be contributories ;

(d) exercise the Court's power of making calls ;

(e) summon general meetings of the company for the purpose of obtaining the sanction of the company by special resolution or for any other purpose he may think fit.

(2) The liquidator shall pay the debts of the company and shall adjust the rights of the contributories among themselves.

(3) Where several liquidators are appointed, any power given by this Act may be exercised by such one or more of them as may be determined by any number not less than two of the liquidators.

645. If, in any voluntary winding-up, there is no liquidator acting, the Court may appoint a liquidator and in any case the Court may, on cause shown, remove a liquidator and appoint another liquidator.

646.—(1) The liquidator or any contributory or creditor may apply to the Court to determine any question arising in the winding-up of a company, to exercise, as respects the enforcing of calls or any other matter, all or any of the powers which the Court might exercise if the company were being wound up by the Court.

(2) If the Court is satisfied that the determination of the question or the required exercise of power is just and beneficial, it may give effect wholly or partially to the application on such terms and conditions as it deems fit, or make such other order as the case may require.

(3) A copy of an order made under this section staying the proceedings in the winding-up, shall forthwith be forwarded by the company, or otherwise as may be prescribed, to the Commission, which shall make a minute of the order in its books relating to the company.

647. All costs, charges and expenses properly incurred in the winding-up, including the remuneration of the liquidator, shall be payable out of the assets of the company in priority to all other claims.

648. The voluntary winding-up of a company shall not bar the right of any creditor or contributory to have it wound up by the Court, but where the applicant for winding-up is a contributory, an order shall not be made unless the Court is satisfied that the rights of contributories shall be prejudiced by the members' or creditors' voluntary winding-up, as the case may be.

CHAPTER 23—WINDING-UP SUBJECT TO SUPERVISION OF COURT

649. If a company passes a resolution for voluntary winding-up, the Court may on petition order that the voluntary winding-up shall continue but subject to such supervision of the Court, and with such liberty for creditors, contributories, or others to apply to the Court, and generally on such terms and conditions, as the court deems fit.

650. A petition for the continuance of a voluntary winding-up subject to the supervision of the Court shall, for the purpose of giving jurisdiction to the Court over actions, be deemed to be a petition for winding-up by the Court.

651. A winding-up subject to the supervision of the court shall, for the purposes of sections 576 and 577 of this Act, be deemed to be a winding-up by the Court.

652.—(1) Where an order is made for a winding-up subject to supervision, the Court may, by the same or any subsequent order, appoint an additional liquidator.

(2) A liquidator appointed by the Court under this section shall have the same powers, be subject to the same obligations, and in all respects stand in the same position, as if he had been duly appointed in accordance with the provisions of this Act with respect to the appointment of liquidators in a voluntary winding-up.

(3) The Court may remove any liquidator so appointed by the Court or any liquidator continued under the supervision order, and may fill any vacancy occasioned by the removal, or by death or resignation.

653.—(1) Where an order is made for a winding-up subject to supervision, the liquidator may, subject to any restrictions imposed by the Court, exercise all his powers, without the sanction or intervention of the Court, in the same manner as if the company were being wound up voluntarily :

Provided that the powers specified in section 588 (1) (d), (e) and (f) of this Act shall not be exercised by the liquidator except with the sanction of the Court or, in a case where before the order for the winding-up was a creditors' voluntary winding-up, with the sanction of the Court or the committee of inspection, or (if there is no such committee) a meeting of the creditors.

(2) A winding-up subject to the supervision of the Court shall not amount to a winding-up by the Court for the purpose of the provisions of this Act as specified in the Twelfth Schedule to this Act (dealing with provisions which do not apply in the case of winding-up subject to the supervision of the Court) but, subject to this, an order for a winding-up subject to supervision shall for all purposes be an order for winding-up by the Court :

Provided that where the order for winding-up subject to supervision of the Court was made in relation to a creditors' voluntary winding-up in which a Committee of Inspection had been appointed, the order shall be deemed to be an order for winding-up by the Court for the purposes of section 597 of this Act, (except subsection (1) of that section) unless the operation of that section is excluded in a voluntary winding-up by general rules made under this Act.

CHAPTER 24—PROVISIONS APPLICABLE TO EVERY MODE OF WINDING-UP

654.—(1) The liquidator shall, within 14 days after his appointment, publish in the Federal Government Gazette or in two daily newspapers and deliver to the Commission for registration a notice of his appointment in such form as the Commission may from time to time approve.

(2) If the liquidator fails to comply with the requirements of subsection (1), he is liable to a penalty as prescribed by the Commission in the regulation.

655. In every winding-up (subject, in the case of insolvent companies, to the application in accordance with the provisions of this Act of the law of bankruptcy), all debts payable on a contingency, and all claims against the company, present or future, certain or contingent, ascertained or sounding only in damages, shall be admissible to proof against the company, a just estimate being made, so far as possible, of the value of such debts or claims as may be subject to any contingency or sound only in damages, or for some other reasons do not bear a certain value.

656. In the winding-up of an insolvent company registered in Nigeria, the same rules shall prevail and be observed with regard to the respective rights of secured and unsecured creditors and to debts provable and to the valuation of annuities and future contingent liabilities as are in force for the time being under the law of bankruptcy in Nigeria with respect to the estates of persons adjudged bankrupt, and all persons who in any such case would be entitled to prove for and receive dividends out of the assets of the company may come in under the winding-up and make such claims against the company as they respectively are entitled to by virtue of this section:

Provided that nothing in this section shall affect the power of any secured creditor to realise or otherwise deal with his security during the winding-up of an insolvent company registered in Nigeria.

657.—(1) In a winding-up, there shall be paid in priority to all other debts—

(a) all local rates and charges due from the company at the relevant date, and having become due and payable within 12 months immediately before that date, and all pay-as-you-earn tax deductions and other assessed taxes, property or income tax assessed on or due from the company up to the annual day of assessment next before the relevant date, and in the case of pay-as-you-earn tax deductions not exceeding deductions made in respect of one year of assessment and, in any other case, not exceeding in one year's assessment ;

(b) deductions made from the remuneration of employees and contributions of the company under the Pension Reform Act ;

(c) contributions and obligations of the company under the employees' Compensation Act ;

(d) all wages or salaries of any clerk or servant in respect of services rendered to the company ;

(e) all wages of any workman or labourer, whether payable for time or for piece of work, in respect of services rendered to the company ; and

(f) all accrued holiday remuneration becoming payable to any clerk, servant, workman or labourer (or in the case of his death to any other person in his rights) on the termination of his employment before or by the effect of the winding-up order or resolution.

(2) Where any compensation under the Employees' Compensation Act No. 13, is a weekly payment, the amount due in respect thereof shall, for the purpose of subsection (1) (e), be taken to be the amount of the lump sum for which the weekly payment could, if redeemable, be redeemed, if the employer made an application for that purpose under the Act.

(3) Where any payment on account of wages or salaries has been made to any clerk, servant, workman or labourer in the employment of a company out of the money advanced by some persons for that purpose, that person shall in a winding-up have a right of priority in respect of the money so advanced and paid up to the amount by which the sum in respect of which that clerk, servant, workman or labourer would have been entitled to priority in the winding up has been diminished by reason of the payment having been made.

(4) The debts shall—

(a) rank equally among themselves after the expenses of the winding-up and shall be paid in full, unless the assets are insufficient to meet them, in which case they shall abate in equal proportions ; and

(b) if the assets of the company available for payment of general creditors are insufficient to meet them, have priority over the claims of holders of debentures under any floating charge created by the company and be paid accordingly out of any property comprised in or subject to that charge.

(5) Subject to the retention of such sums as may be necessary to discharge the costs and expenses of the winding-up, the debts shall be discharged immediately if the assets of the company are sufficient to meet them.

(6) Notwithstanding the foregoing and any other provisions of this Act and any other law applicable in Nigeria where it relates to settlement of claims in the winding-up of a company, claims of—

(a) secured creditors, as defined under this Act, shall rank in priority to all other claims, including any preferential payment under this Act or any other debts inclusive of expenses of winding-up ; and (b) the equity holders shall rank last.

(7) In this section, "the relevant date" means—

(a) in the case of a company ordered to be wound up compulsorily which had not previously commenced to be wound up voluntarily, the date of the winding-up order ; and

(b) in any other case, the date of the commencement of the winding-up.

EFFECT OF WINDING-UP AND ADMINISTRATION ON ANTECEDENT AND OTHER TRANSACTIONS

658.—(1) Where a company at any time within the period defined in subsection (6), does anything or procures anything to be done which has the effect of putting a person, being one of the company's creditors or a surety or guarantor undue advantage shall be deemed a preference of that person, and be invalid accordingly.

(2) Notwithstanding subsection (1), a preference given to any person is not invalid unless the company which gave the preference was influenced in deciding to give it by a desire to produce in relation to that person the effect mentioned in sub-section (1).

(3) A company which has given a preference to a person connected with the company (otherwise than by reason only of being its employee) at the time the preference was given is presumed, unless the contrary is shown, to have been influenced in deciding to give it by such a desire as is mentioned in subsection (2).

(4) The fact that something has been done in pursuance of the order of a Court does not, without more, prevent the doing or procuring of that thing from constituting the giving of a preference.

(5) Any conveyance or assignment by a company of all its property to trustees in furtherance of the preference for the benefit of all its creditors is void.

(6) In the case of a preference which is given to a person who is connected with the company (otherwise than by reason only of being its employee), the relevant time is the period of years ending with the onset of insolvency (which expression is defined below), and in any other case, the relevant time is the period of three months ending with the onset of insolvency.

(7) For the purpose of this section, the onset of insolvency refers to the time of the presentation of a petition for winding-up in the case of a winding up by or subject to the supervision of the Court or, the passing of a resolution for winding-up in the case of a voluntary winding-up.

(8) This section applies in the case of a company where—(a) the company enters administration ; or (b) the company goes into liquidation.

659.—(1) This section applies in the case of a company where—

(a) the company enters administration ; or (b) the company goes into liquidation.

(2) Where the company has at a relevant time entered into a transaction with any person at an undervalue, the liquidator or administrator may apply to the Court for an order under this section.

(3) The Court shall, on such an application, make such order as it deems fit for restoring the position to what it would have been if the company had not entered into that transaction.

(4) For the purposes of this section, a company enters into a transaction with a person at an undervalue if the company—

(a) makes a gift to that person or enters into a transaction with that person on terms that provide for the company to receive no consideration ; or

(b) enters into a transaction with that person for a consideration the value of which, in money or money's worth, is significantly less than the value, in money or money's worth, of the consideration provided by the company.

(5) The Court shall not make an order under this section in respect of a transaction at an undervalue if it is satisfied—

(a) that the company which entered into the transaction did so in good faith and for the purpose of carrying on its business ; and

(b) that at the time it did so there were reasonable grounds for believing that the transaction would benefit the company.

(6) Subject to subsection (7), the time at which a company enters into a transaction at an undervalue is a relevant time if the transaction is entered into—

(a) within two years ending with the onset of insolvency as defined in subsection (8) ;

(b) between the making of an administration application in respect of the company and the making of an administration order on that application; and

(c) between the filing with the Court of a copy of notice of intention to appoint an administrator under sections 456 or 464 of this Act and the making of an appointment under this paragraph.

(7) Where a company enters into a transaction at an undervalue at a time mentioned in subsection (6) (a), that time is not a relevant time for the purposes of this section unless the company —

(a) is at that time unable to pay its debts within the meaning of section572 ; or

(b) becomes unable to pay its debts within the meaning of that section inconsequence of the transaction or preference,

but the requirements of this subsection are presumed to be satisfied, unless the contrary is shown, in relation to any transaction at an undervalue which is entered into by a company with a person who is connected with the company.

(8) For the purposes of subsection (6), the onset of insolvency is, in a case where this section applies by reason of—

(a) an administrator of a company being appointed by administration order, the date on which the administration application is made ;

(b) an administrator of a company being appointed under section 456 or464 of this Act following filing with the Court of a copy of a notice of intention to appoint under that section, the date on which the copy of the notice is filed ;

(c) an administrator of a company being appointed otherwise than as mentioned in paragraph (a) or (b), the date on which the appointment takes effect;

(d) a company going into liquidation either following conversion of administration into winding-up or at the time when the appointment of an administrator ceases to have effect, the date on which the company entered administration (or, if relevant, the date on which the application for the administration order was made or a copy of the notice of intention to appoint was filed) ; and

(e) a company going into liquidation at any other time, the date of the commencement of the winding-up.

660. (1) Where anything made or done after the commencement of this Act is void under this Chapter as a fraudulent preference of a person interested in property mortgaged or charged to secure the company's debt, the person preferred shall, without prejudice to any liabilities or rights arising apart from this provision, be subject to the same liabilities, and have the same rights, as if he had undertaken to be personally liable as surety for the debt, to the extent of the charge on the property or the value of his interest, whichever is the less, and the value of the said person's interest shall be determined as at the date of the transaction constituting the fraudulent preference, and shall be determined as if the interest were free of all encumbrances other than those to which the charge for the company's debt was the subject.

(2) Where for the purposes of this section, application is made to the Court with respect to any payment on the ground that the payment was fraudulent preference of a surety or guarantor, the court shall have jurisdiction to determine any questions with respect to the payment arising between the person to whom the payment was made and the surety or guarantor, and to grant relief in respect thereof, though it is not necessary to do so for the purposes of the winding-up, and for that purpose may give leave to bring in the surety or guarantor as a third party as in the case of an action for the recovery of the sum paid.

(3) Subsection (2) applies, with the necessary modifications, in relation to transactions other than the payment of money, as it applies in relation to payments.

661. Where a company is being wound up subject to the supervision of the Court, any attachment, sequestration or execution put in force against the estate or effects of the company after the commencement of the winding-up, is void.

662. Where a company is being wound up, a floating charge on the undertaking or property of the company created within three months of the commencement of the winding-up shall, unless it is proved that the company immediately after the creation of the charge was solvent, be invalid, except to the amount of any cash paid to the company at the time of or subsequently to the creation of, and in consideration for, the charge, together with interest on that amount at the current bank rate.

663.—(1) Where any part of the property of a company which is being wound up consists of—

(a) unprofitable contracts ; or

(b) any other property that is unsaleable, or not readily saleable, or is such that it may give rise to the performance of any onerous act or a liability for the payment of any sum of money, the liquidator, notwithstanding that he has endeavoured to sell it or has taken possession of the property or exercised any act of ownership in relation thereto, may, with the leave of the Court, and subject to the provisions of this section, in writing signed by him, within 12 months after the commencement of the winding-up or such extended period as may be allowed by the Court, disclaim the property :

Provided that, where the property has not come to the knowledge of the liquidator within one month after the commencement of the winding-up, the power under this section of disclaiming the property may be exercised at any time within 12 months after he has become aware thereof or such extended period as may be allowed by the Court.

(2) A disclaimer under this section shall operate to determine, as from the date of the disclaimer, the rights, interest and liabilities of the company, in or in respect of the property disclaimed, but shall not, except it is necessary for the purpose of releasing the company from any liability, affect the rights or liabilities of any other person.
(3) The Court, before or on granting leave to disclaim under subsection(1), may require such notices to be given to persons interested, and impose such terms as a condition of granting leave, and make such other order in the matter as the Court deems just.
(4) The liquidator is not entitled to disclaim any property under this section in any case where an application in writing has been made to him by any person interested in the property requiring him to decide whether or not he will disclaim, and the liquidator has not, within 28 days after the receipt of the application or such further period as may be allowed by the Court, give notice to the applicant that he intends to apply to the Court for leave to disclaim, and, in the case of a contract, if the liquidator, after such an application, does not within that period or further period disclaim the contract, the company is deemed to have adopted it.
(5) The Court may, on the application of any person who is, as against the liquidator, entitled to the benefit or subject to the burden of a contract on such terms as to payment by or to either party, of damages for the non-performance of the contract, or otherwise as the Court deems just, and any damages payable under the order to that person may be proved by him as a debt in the winding-up.
(6) The Court may, on an application by any person who claims any interest in any property disclaimed under this section, or is under any liability not discharged by this Act in respect of any disclaimed property, and on hearing any such persons as it thinks fit, make an order for the vesting of the property in or the delivery of the property to any persons entitled thereto, or to whom it may seem just that the property should be delivered by way of compensation for such liability, or a trustee for him, and on such terms as the Court deems just and on any such vesting order being made, the property comprised therein shall vest in the person therein named in that behalf without any conveyance or assignment for the purpose.
(7) Where the property disclaimed is of a leasehold nature, the Court shall not make a vesting order in favour of any person claiming under the company, whether as an under- lessee or as a mortgagee by demise, a mortgage by way of legal charge or mortgage, as the case may be, except upon the terms of making that person—
(a) object to the same liabilities and obligations as those to which the company was subject under the lease in respect of the property at the commencement of the winding-up ; or
(b) if the Court deems fit, subject only to the same liabilities and obligations as if the lease had been assigned to that person at that date, and in either event if the case so requires, as if the lease had comprised only the property comprised in the vesting order, and any mortgagee or under lessee declining to accept a vesting order upon such terms shall be excluded from all interest in and security upon the property, and if there is no person claiming under the company who is willing to accept an order upon such terms, the Court shall have power to vest the estate and interest of the company in the property in any person liable, either personally or in a representative character, and either alone or jointly with the company, to perform the lessee's covenants in the lease, freed and discharged from all estates, encumbrances and interests created therein by the company.

664\. Any person injured by the operation of a disclaimer under section 663 is deemed to be a creditor of the company to the amount of the injury, and may accordingly prove the amount as a debt in the winding-up.

665\.—(1) This section applies in the case of a company where—

(a) the company enters administration ;

(b) a company voluntary arrangement approved under Chapter 17 has taken effect ;

(c) the company goes into liquidation ; or

(d) a provisional liquidator is appointed.

(2) If a request is made by or with the concurrence of the officeholder for the giving, after the effective date, of any of the supplies mentioned in the next subsection, the supplier—

(a) may make it a condition of the giving of the supply that the officeholder personally guarantees the payment of any charges in respect of the supply ;

(b) shall not make it a condition of the giving of the supply, or do anything which has the effect of making it a condition of the giving of the supply, that any outstanding charges in respect of a supply given to the company before the effective date are paid.

(3) For the purpose of subsection (2), "the officeholder" means the administrator, the nominee, the supervisor, the liquidator or the provisional liquidator, as the case may be.

(4) The supplies referred to in subsection (2) are a supply of—

(a) gas by a gas supplier within the meaning of legislation regulating the provision of gas, if applicable ;

(b) electricity by an electricity supplier within the meaning of legislation dealing with the provision of electricity ;

(c) water by a water provider refer to legislation if applicable ; and

(d) communications services by a provider of a public electronic communications service.

(5) The "effective date" for the purposes of this section, is the date on which the—

(a) company entered administration ;

(b) voluntary arrangement took effect ;(c) company went into liquidation ; or

(d) provisional liquidator was appointed.

(6) In subsection (4) (d), the term, "communications services" does not include electronic communications services to the extent that they are used to broadcast or otherwise transmit programme services within the meaning of the Nigerian Communications Commission Act.

666\.—(1) Where a creditor issues execution against any goods or land of a company, or attaches any debt due to the company, and the company is subsequently wound up, the creditor shall not be entitled to retain the benefit of the execution or attachment against the liquidator in the winding-up of the company, unless he has completed the execution or attachment before the commencement of the winding-up :

Provided that—

(a) where any creditor has had notice of a meeting having been called at which a resolution for voluntary winding-up is to be proposed, the date on which the creditor so had notice shall, for the purposes of this subsection, be substituted for the date of the commencement of the winding-up ;

(b) if a person purchases in good faith under a sale by the sheriff any goods of a company on which an execution has been levied, he shall acquire a good title to them against the liquidator ; and

(c) the rights conferred by this subsection on the liquidator may be set aside by the Court in favour of the creditor to such extent and subject to such terms as the court deems fit.

(2) For the purposes of this section, an execution against goods shall be taken to be completed by seizure and sale, and an attachment of a debt is deemed to be completed by receipt of the debt, and an execution against land is deemed to be completed by seizure and, in the case of an equitable interest, by the appointment of a receiver.

667.—(1) Subject to the provisions of subsection (3), where any goods of a company are taken in execution and before the sale thereof or the completion of the execution by the receipt or recovery of the full amount of the levy, notice is served on the sheriff that a provisional liquidator has been

appointed or that a winding-up order has been made or that a resolution for voluntary winding-up has been passed, the sheriff shall, on being so required, deliver the goods and any money seized or received in part satisfaction of the execution to the liquidator, but the costs of the execution shall be a first charge on the goods or money so delivered, and the liquidator may sell the goods, or a sufficient part thereof, for the purpose of satisfying that charge.

(2) Subject to the provisions of subsection (3), where under an execution in respect of a judgment for a sum exceeding ₦100,000, the goods of a company are sold or money is paid in order to avoid the sale, the sheriff shall deduct the costs of the execution from the proceeds of the sale or the money paid, and retain the balance for 14 days and if within that time notice is served on him of a petition for the winding-up of the company having been presented or of a meeting having been called at which there is to be proposed a resolution for the voluntary winding-up of the company and an order is made or a resolution is passed, as the case may be, for the winding-up of the company, the sheriff shall pay the balance to the liquidator, who shall be entitled to retain it as against the execution creditor.

(3) The rights conferred by this section on the liquidator may be set aside by the Court in favour of the creditor to such extent and subject to such terms as the Court deems fit.

(4) In this section and section 666 of this Act—

(a) "goods" includes chattels personal ; and

(b) "sheriff" includes any officer responsible for the execution of a writ or other process.

OFFENCES ANTECEDENT TO OR IN COURSE OF WINDING-UP

668.—(1) If any person, being a past or present officer of a company which at the time of the commission of the alleged offence is being wound up, whether by or under the supervision of the Court or voluntarily, or is subsequently ordered to be wound up by the Court or subsequently passes a resolution for voluntary winding-up—

(a) does not, to the best of his knowledge and belief, fully and truly discover or deliver to the liquidator all the property, landed and personal, of the company, and how and to whom, for what consideration and when, the company disposed of any part thereof, except such part as has been disposed of in the ordinary way of the business of the company;

(b) does not deliver up to the liquidator, or as he directs, all such part of the real and personal property of the company as is in his custody or under his control, which he is required by law to deliver up ;

(c) does not deliver up to the liquidator, or as he directs, all books and papers in his custody or under his control belonging to the company which he is required by law to deliver up ;

(d) within 12 months immediately preceding the commencement of the winding-up or at any time thereafter, conceals any part of the property of the company to the value of N100,000 or upwards, or conceals any debt due to or from the company ;

(e) within 12 months immediately preceding the commencement of the winding-up or at any time thereafter, fraudulently removes any part of the property of the company to the value of N100,000 or upwards ;

(f) makes any material omission in any statement relating to the affairs of the company;

(g) knowing or believing that a false debt has been proved by any person under the winding-up, fails for the period of one month to inform the liquidator thereof ;

(h) after the commencement of the winding-up, prevents the production of any book or paper affecting or relating to the property or affairs of the company ;

(i) within 12 months immediately preceding the commencement of the winding-up or at any time thereafter ;

(j) conceals, destroys, mutilates or falsifies, or is privy to the concealment, destruction, mutilation or falsification of the book or paper affecting or relating to the property or affairs of the company—

(i) makes or is privy to the making of any false entry in any book or paper affecting or relating to the property or affairs of the company,

(ii) fraudulently parts with, alters or makes any omission in, or is privy to the fraudulently parting with, altering or making any omission in any document affecting or relating to the property or affairs of the company,

(iii) at any meeting of the creditors of the company, attempts to account for any part of the property of the company by fictitious losses or expenses,

(iv) makes false representation or other fraud, obtained any property for or on behalf of the company on credit which the company does not subsequently pay for,

(v) under the false pretence that the company is carrying on its business, obtains on credit, for or on behalf of the company any property

which the company does not subsequently pay for, or

(vi) pawns, pledges or disposes of any property of the company which has been obtained on credit and has not been paid for, unless such pawning, pledging, or disposing is in the ordinary way of the business of the company ; or

(k) makes any false representation or other fraud for the purpose of obtaining the consent of the creditors of the company or any of them to an agreement with reference to the affairs of the company or to the winding-up,

commits an offence and is—

(i) in the case of the offences mentioned respectively in sub-paragraphs(iv), (v) and (vi), liable on conviction to imprisonment for a term of 12 months, and

(ii) in the case of any other offence under this subsection, is liable on conviction to imprisonment for a term of two years :

Provided it is a good defence to a charge under any of paragraphs (a), (b), (c), (d), (f) and (i) (v) and (vi) of this subsection, if the accused proves that he had no intent to defraud, and to a charge under any of paragraphs (h), (i) and (j), if he proves he had no intention to conceal the state of affairs of the company or to defeat the law.

(2) Where any person pawns, pledges or disposes of any property in circumstances which amount to an offence under subsection (1) (j) (i) and (vi), every person who takes in pawn or pledge, or otherwise receives the property knowing it to be pawned, pledged or disposed of in such circumstances, commits an offence and is liable on conviction to be punished in the same way as if he had received the property knowing it to have been obtained in circumstances amounting to an offence.

(3) For the purposes of this section, "officer" includes any person in accordance with whose directions or instructions the directors of a company have been accustomed to act.

669. An officer or contributory of any company being wound up who destroys, mutilates, alters or falsifies books, papers or securities, or makes or is privy to the making of any false or fraudulent entry in any register, book of account or document belonging to the company with intent to defraud or deceive any person, commits an offence and is liable on conviction to imprisonment for a term of two years or a fine as the Court deems fit.

670. A person who, being at the time of the commission of the alleged offence is an officer, of a company which is subsequently ordered to be wound up by the Court, or subsequently passes a resolution for voluntary winding-up—

(a) has by false pretence or by means of any other fraud induced any person to give credit to the company;

(b) with intent to defraud creditors of the company, made or caused to be made any gift or transfer of or charge on, or has cause or connive at the levying of any execution against the property of the company; or

(c) with intent to defraud creditors of the company, has concealed or removed any part of the property of the company, or within two months before the date of any unsatisfied judgment or order for payment of money obtained against the company, he commits an offence and is liable on conviction to imprisonment for a term of two years.

671.—(1) If, where a company is wound up, it is shown that proper books of account were not kept by the company throughout the period of two years immediately preceding the commencement of the winding-up or the period between the incorporation of this company and commencement of the winding-up, whichever is the shorter, each officer of the company who is in default, unless he shows that he acted honestly and that in the circumstances in which the business of the company was carried on the default was excusable, commits an offence and is liable on conviction to a fine as prescribed by the Commission in the regulation.

(2) For the purposes of this section, proper books of account shall be deemed not to have been kept in the case of any company if there have not been kept such books of accounts as are necessary to exhibit and explain the transactions and financial position of the trade or business of the company, including books containing entries from day to day in sufficient detail of all cash received and cash paid and, where the trade or business has involved dealing in goods, statements of the annual stock takings and (except in case of goods sold by way of ordinary retail trade) of all goods

sold and purchased, showing the goods and the buyers and sellers in sufficient details to enable those goods and those buyers and sellers to be identified.

672.—(1) If, in the course of the winding-up of a company, it appears that any business of the company has been carried on in a reckless manner or with intent to defraud creditors of the company or creditors of any other person, or for any fraudulent purpose, the Court, on the application of the official receiver, or the liquidator or any creditor or contributory of the company, may, if it deems proper to do so, declare that persons who were knowingly parties to the carrying on of the business in that manner, is personally responsible, without any limitation of liability for all or any of the debts or other liabilities of the company as the Court may direct.

(2) Where the Court makes a declaration as to responsibility for debts or liabilities under subsection (1), it may give any direction it deems proper for the purpose of giving effect to that declaration, and in particular the Court may make provision for making the liability of any such person under the declaration a charge on any debt or obligation due from the company to him, or on any mortgage, charge or interest in any mortgage, or charge or assets of the company held by or vested in him, or any company or person on his behalf, or any person claiming as assignee from or through the person liable or any company or person acting on his behalf, and may make any further order necessary for enforcing any charge imposed under this subsection.

(3) Where any business of a company is carried on with such intent or for such purpose as is mentioned in subsection (1) (other than recklessly), every person who was knowingly a party to the carrying on of the business in that manner, commits an offence, and is liable on conviction to a fine as the Court deems fit or to imprisonment for a term of two years or both.

(4) In its operation, this section shall have effect, so that—

(a) a declaration may be made notwithstanding that the person concerned may be criminally liable in respect of matters which are grounds for the declaration and a declaration, if made, is deemed to be a final judgment of the Court ;

(b) the official receiver or the liquidator, as the case may be, on the hearing of an application to the Court, may himself give evidence or call witnesses ;

(c) the expression "assignee" includes any person to whom or in whose favour by the direction of the person liable, the debt, obligation, mortgage, or charge was created, issued or transferred, or the interest created, other than any person being an assignee for valuable consideration given in good faith and without notice of any of the matters on the ground of which the declaration is made ; and

(d) "valuable consideration" shall not include consideration by way of marriage.

Wrongful trading.

673.—(1) Subject to subsection (3), if, in the course of the winding-up of a company, it appears that subsection (2) applies in relation to a person who is or has been a director of the company, the Court, on the application of the liquidator, may declare that that person is to be liable to make such contribution (if any) to the company's assets as the Court deems proper.

(2) This subsection applies in relation to a person if—(a) the company has gone into insolvent liquidation, (b) at some time before the commencement of the winding-up of the company, that person knew or ought to have concluded that there was no reasonable prospect that the company would avoid going into insolvent liquidation, and

(c) that person was a director of the company at that time.

(3) The Court shall not make a declaration under this section with respect to any person if it is satisfied that after the condition specified in subsection (2) (b) was first satisfied in relation to him, that person took every step with a view to minimising the potential loss to the company's creditors as (assuming him to have known that there was no reasonable prospect that the company would avoid going into insolvent liquidation) he ought to have taken.

(4) For the purposes of subsections (2) and (3), the facts which a director of a company ought to know or ascertain, the conclusions which he ought to reach and the steps which he ought to take are those which would be known or ascertained, or reached or taken, by a reasonably diligent person having both—

(a) the general knowledge, skill and experience that may reasonably be expected of a person carrying out the same functions as are carried out by that director in relation to the company ; and

(b) the general knowledge, skill and experience that that director has.

(5) The reference in subsection (4) to the functions performed in relation to a company by a director of the company includes any function which he does not perform but which has been entrusted to him.

(6) For the purposes of this section, a company goes into insolvent liquidation if it goes into liquidation at a time when its assets are insufficient for the payment of its debts and other liabilities and the expenses of the winding-up.

674.—(1) If, in the course of winding-up a company, it appears that any person who has taken part in the formation or promotion of the company, or any past or present director, manager or liquidator, or any officer of the company, has misapplied or retained or become liable or accountable for any money or property of the company, or been guilty of any misfeasance or breach of duty in relation to the company which would involve civil liability at the suit of the company, the Court may, on the application of the official receiver, liquidator, creditor or contributory, examine into the conduct of the promoter, director, liquidator or officer, and compel him to repay or restore the money or property or any part thereof respectively with interest at such rates as the Court deems just, or to contribute such sum to the assets of the company by way of compensation in respect of the misapplication, retainer, misfeasance or breach of trust as the Court deems just.

(2) The provisions of this section extend to any receiver of the property of a company, and, shall, in any case, have effect notwithstanding that the offence is one for which the offender may be criminally liable.

(3) Where an order for payment of money is made under this section, the order is deemed to be a final judgment of the Court.

PROSECUTION OF DELINQUENT OFFICERS AND MEMBERS OF A COMPANY

675.—(1) If it appears to the Court, in the course of winding-up by, or subject to the supervision of the Court, that any past or present officer, or any member of the company has been guilty of any offence in relation to the company for which he is criminally liable, the Court may, either on the application of any person interested in the winding-up or of its own motion, direct the liquidator to refer the matter to the Attorney-General of the Federation.

(2) If it appears to the liquidator, in the course of a voluntary winding-up, that any past or present officer, or any member of the company has been guilty of any offence in

relation to the company for which he is criminally liable, he shall report the matter to the Attorney-General of the Federation and shall furnish him such information and give to him such access to and facilities for inspecting and taking copies of any document, being information or document in the possession or under the control of the liquidator and relating to the matter in question, as he may require.

(3) Where any report is made under subsection (2) to the Attorney General of the Federation, he may, if he thinks fit, apply to the Court for—

(a) an order conferring on him or any person designated by him for the purpose with respect to the company concerned ; and

(b) all such powers of investigating the affairs of the company as are provided by this Act in the case of a winding-up by the Court.

(4) If it appears to the Court, in the course of a voluntary winding-up, that any past or present officer, or any member of the company has been guilty, and that no report with respect to the matter has been made by the liquidator to the Attorney-General of the Federation under subsection (2), the Court may, on the application of any person interested in the winding-up or of its own motion, direct the liquidator to make such a report, and on a report being made accordingly, the provisions of this section shall have effect as though the report had been made under subsection (2).

(5) If, any matter is reported or referred to the Attorney-General of the Federation under this section, and he considers that the case is one in which a prosecution ought to be instituted, the Attorney-General of the Federation shall institute proceedings accordingly, and it is the duty of the liquidator and of every other officer and agent of the company past and present (other than the defendant in the proceedings) to give him all assistance in connection with the prosecution which he is reasonably able to give.

(6) For the purposes of subsection (5), the word, "agent" in relation to a company includes any—

(a) banker or solicitor of the company ; and

(b) person employed by the company as auditor, whether that person is or is not an officer of the company.

(7) If a person fails or neglects to give assistance in the manner required by subsection (5), the Court may, on the application of the Attorney-General of the Federation, direct that person to comply with the requirements of the subsection (5), and where any such application is made with respect to a liquidator, the Court, may, unless it appears that the failure or neglect to comply was due to the liquidator not having in his hands sufficient assets of the company to enable him to do so, direct that the costs of the application shall be borne by the liquidator personally.

SUPPLEMENTARY PROVISIONS AS TO WINDING-UP

676.—(1) The following persons shall not be competent to be appointed or to act as liquidator of a company, whether in a winding-up by, or under the supervision of the Court, or in a voluntary winding-up—

(a) an infant ;

(b) anyone found by the Court to be of unsound mind ;

(c) a body corporate ;

(d) an undischarged bankrupt ;

(e) any director of the company under liquidation ; and

(f)) any person convicted of any offence involving fraud, dishonesty, official corruption or moral turpitude and in respect of whom there is a subsisting order under section 672 and 280 of this Act.

(2) Any appointment made that is contrary to subsection (1) is void and if any of the persons named in subsection (1) (c)-(f) act as a liquidator of the company, he commits an offence and is liable to a fine as prescribed by the Commission in the Regulations in the case of a body corporate or, in the case of an individual, to imprisonment for a term not exceeding six months or to a fine as the Court deems fit or both.

677. Any person who gives, agrees or offers to give to any member or creditor of a company any valuable consideration with a view to securing his own appointment or nomination, or to securing or preventing the appointment or nomination of a person other than himself as the company's liquidator, commits an offence and is liable to a fine as the Court deems fit.

678.—(1) If a liquidator makes default in filing, delivering or making any return, account or other document, or in giving any notice which he is by law required to file, deliver, make or give, and fails to make good the default within 14 days after the service on him of a notice requiring him to do so, the Court may, on an application made to the Court by any contributory or creditor of the company or by the Commission, make an order directing the liquidator to make good the default within such time as is specified in the order.

(2) Any order under this section may provide that the costs of any expenses incidental to the application shall be borne by the liquidator, and nothing in this section shall be taken to prejudice the operation of any enactment imposing penalties on a liquidator in respect of any such default.

679.—(1) Where a company is being wound up, whether by, or under the supervision of, the Court or voluntarily, every invoice, order for goods or business letter issued by, or on behalf of, the company or a liquidator of the company, or a receiver or manager of the property of the company, being a document on or in which the name of the company appears, shall contain a statement that the company is being wound up.

(2) If default is made in complying with the provisions of this section—

(a) the company,

(b) any officer of the company,

(c) any liquidator of the company, and

(d) any receiver or manager, are liable to a penalty as prescribed by the Commission in the regulations.

680.—(1) In the case of a winding-up by the Court or a creditors' voluntary winding-up —

(a) every assurance relating to any property of the company, or to any mortgage, charge or other encumbrance or any right or interest in any property, in any event forming part of the assets of the company and which, after the execution of the assurance, either at law or in equity is, or remains part of the assets of the company; and

(b) every power of attorney, proxy paper, writ, order, certificate, affidavit, bond or other instrument or writing relating solely to the property of any company which is being so wound up, or to any proceeding under any such winding-up, shall be exempted from duties chargeable under any law or enactment relating to stamp duties.

(2) In this section, "assurance" includes any deed, conveyance, instrument, discharge, assignment or surrender.

681. Where a company is being wound up, all books and papers of the company and of the liquidators shall, as between the contributories of the company, be prima facie evidence of the truth of all matters purported to be recorded.

682.—(1) Where a company is being wound up and is about to be dissolved, the books and papers of the company and of the liquidators may be disposed of in the following manner—

(a) in the case of a winding-up by, or under the supervision of, the court in such way as the Court directs ;

(b) in the case of a members' voluntary winding-up, in such a way as the company by special resolution directs ; and

(c) in the case of a creditors' voluntary winding-up, in such way as the Committee of Inspection or, if there is no such committee, as the creditors of the company, may direct.

(2) After five years from the dissolution of the company no responsibility shall rest on the company, the liquidators, or any person to whom the custody of the books and papers has been committed, by reason of any book or paper not being forthcoming to any person claiming to be interested therein.

(3) Provisions may be made by general rules for enabling the Commission to prevent, for such period (not exceeding five years from the dissolution of the company) as it may consider proper, the destruction of the books and papers of a company which has been wound up, and for enabling any creditor or contributory of the company to make representations to it and to appeal to the Court from any direction which may be given by it in the matter.

(4) A person who acts in contravention of any general rule made for the purposes of this section or any direction of the Commission, is liable to a penalty as prescribed by the Commission in the Regulations.

683.—(1) Where a company is being wound up, and the winding-up is not concluded within one year after its commencement, the liquidator shall, at such intervals as may be prescribed until the winding-up is concluded, send to the Commission a statement in the prescribed form containing the prescribed particulars with respect to the proceedings in, and position of, the liquidation.

(2) Any person stating himself in writing to be a creditor or contributory of the company is entitled, by himself or his agent, at all reasonable times and on payment of the prescribed fee, to inspect the statement, and receive a copy or extract of the statement, but a person who falsely states himself to be creditor or contributory is liable to contempt of Court, and is punishable on the application of the liquidator or official receiver.

(3) If a liquidator fails to comply with the requirements of this section, he is liable to a penalty as prescribed by the Commission in the Regulations.

(4) If it appears from any such statement or otherwise that a liquidator has in his custody or under his control any money representing unclaimed or undistributed assets of the company which have remained unclaimed or undistributed for six months after the date of their receipt, the liquidator shall immediately pay the same to the companies liquidation account mentioned in section 591 of this Act and is

entitled to a certificate of receipt in the prescribed form for the money so paid, which is an effectual discharge to him.

(5) For the purposes of ascertaining and getting in any money payable into the companies liquidation account under this section—

(a) the Commission may at any time order any such liquidator to submit to it an account verified by affidavit of the sums received and paid by him under or in pursuance of the liquidation, and may direct and enforce an audit of the account and if the liquidator fails to submit the account within such reasonable time as the Commission directs, he shall be liable to contempt of Court and may, on the application of the Commission to the Court made for the purpose, be punished accordingly ; and

(b) the Court may, if default is made in submitting the account referred to under this section—

(i) by warrant addressed to any police officer, cause the liquidator to be arrested, and all books, papers and money or goods, relating to the liquidation in his possession to be seized and him and them to be safely kept until such time as the Court may order,

(ii) at any time by order addressed to the Postmaster-General of the Nigerian Postal Service require that, for a period of not more than three months, letters addressed to the liquidator and sent through the post, be in course of post, redirected, sent or delivered to or at any place or places mentioned in the order,

(iii) summon the liquidator or his wife, or any person known or suspected to have in his possession any book or paper relating to the liquidation, and any money or goods belonging to the liquidator or representing any unclaimed or undistributed assets of the company, or summon any person whom the Court deems capable of giving information respecting any book, paper, money, goods or other asset, and require any person summoned under this paragraph to produce documents in his custody or under his control relating to the liquidator's dealings with the property of the company,

(iv) where any person on examination before it admits that he is indebted to the company, by order made on the application of the official receiver or liquidator, direct payment to the official receiver or liquidator, as the case may be, of the amount admitted, or any part, either in full discharge of the whole amount in question or not at such time and in such manner as the Court deems fit, with or without costs of the examination,

(v) examine on oath, either by word of mouth or written interrogatories, any person so brought before it concerning the liquidator and his dealings

with the property of the company, and

(vi) if any person on examination before the Court admits that he has in his possession any money properly payable into the company's liquidation account under this section, order him to pay any such money into that account.

(6) A person claiming to be entitled to money paid into the company's liquidation account under this section may apply to the Commission for payment, and the Commission, if the liquidator certifies the claim, may make an order for payment accordingly.

(7) An appeal shall lie to the Court by any person claiming to be dissatisfied with the decision of the Commission in respect of any claim made under this section.

. 684. Where a resolution is passed at an adjourned meeting of creditors or contributories of a company, the resolution shall, for all purposes, be treated as having been passed on the date on which it was in fact passed, and is not deemed to have been passed on any earlier date.

685.—(1) On the winding-up of a company, whether by the Court or voluntarily, the liquidator may, subject to subsections (2)–(4), make any payment which the company has, before the commencement of the winding up, decided to make under section 745 of this Act.

(2) The power which a company may exercise by virtue of section 745 of this Act may be exercised by the liquidator after the winding-up has commenced if, after the company's liabilities have been fully satisfied and provision has been made for the costs of the winding-up, the exercise of that power has been sanctioned by such resolution of the company as would be required of the company itself by section 745 (3) of this Act before that commencement, as if paragraph (b) of that subsection were omitted and any other requirement applicable to its exercise by the company had been met.

(3) Any payment which may be made by a company under this section may be made out of the company's assets which are available to the members on the winding-up.

(4) On a winding-up by the Court, the exercise by the liquidator of his powers under this section shall be subject to the Court's control and any creditor or contributory may apply to the Court with respect to any exercise or proposed exercise of the power.

(5) Subsections (1) and (2) shall have effect notwithstanding any other rule or law.

SUPPLEMENTARY POWERS OF COURT

686.—(1) The Court may, as to all matters relating to the winding-up of a company, have regard to the wishes of the creditors or contributories of the company, as proved to it by any sufficient evidence, and may, if it deems fit, for the purposes of ascertaining those wishes, direct meetings of the creditors or contributories to be called, held and conducted in such manner as the Court directs and may appoint a person to act as chairman of any such meeting and to report the result to the Court.

(2) In the case of creditors, regard shall be had to the value of each creditor's debt.

(3) In the case of contributories, regard shall be had to the number of votes conferred on each contributory by this Act or the articles.

687. In all proceedings under this Part of this Act, all Courts, Judges, and persons judicially acting, and all officers, judicial or ministerial, of any Court or employed in enforcing the process of any Court, shall take judicial notice of the signature of any officer of Court and also of the official seal or stamp of a Court appended to or impressed on any document made, issued or signed under this Part of this Act, or on any official copy of any such document.

688.—(1) Documents purporting to be orders or certificates made or issued by the Attorney-General of the Federation or the Commission for the purposes of this Act and to be signed by the Attorney-General of the Federation or the Accountant-General of the Federation, or under the seal of the Commission or signed by any person authorised in that behalf by them, and, in proper case, to be sealed where necessary, shall be received in evidence and deemed to be such orders, or certificates without further proof, unless the contrary is shown.

(2) A certificate signed by the Attorney-General for the Federation, Accountant-General of the Federation or under the seal of the Commission that any order made, certificate issued, or act done, is the order, certificate or act of the Attorney-General of the Federation, Accountant-General of the Federation or the Commission, as the case may be, shall be conclusive of the fact so certified.

689.—(1) Where a company is in course of being wound up, all magistrates shall be commissioners for the purpose of taking evidence under this Act and the Court may refer the whole or any part of the examination of any witnesses under this Act to any person appointed commissioner.

(2) Every commissioner shall, in addition to any power which he might lawfully exercise as a magistrate, have in the matter so referred to him the same powers as the Court, of—

(a) summoning and examining witnesses ;

(b) requiring the production or delivery of documents;(c) punishing defaults by witnesses; and

(d) allowing costs and expenses to witnesses.

(3) The examination so taken shall be returned or reported to the Court in such manner as that Court directs.

690. An affidavit required to be sworn under the provisions or for the purposes of this Part of this Act may be sworn in Nigeria or elsewhere in accordance with the provisions of the Oaths Act or under any other enactment or law providing for the administration of oaths and all Courts, Judges, commissioners, and persons acting judicially shall take judicial notice of the seal or stamp or signatures, as the case may be, of any Court, Judge, person, consul, or vice-consul, attached, appended, or subscribed to any such affidavit, or to any other document to be used for the purposes of this Part of this Act.

PROVISIONS AS TO DISSOLUTION

691.—(1) Where a company has been dissolved, the Court may, at any time within two years of the date of the dissolution, on an application being made for the purpose by the liquidator of the company or by any other person who appears to the Court to be interested, make an order, upon such terms as the Court may deem fit, declaring the dissolution to have been void, and thereupon such proceedings may be taken as might have been taken if the company had not been dissolved.

(2) A person on whose application the order was made, shall, within seven days after the making of the order or such further time as the Court may allow, deliver to the Commission for registration an office copy of the order, and if that person fails to do so he is liable to a penalty as prescribed by the Commission in the regulations.

692.—(1) The Commission may strike off the name of a company from the register of companies if—

(a) a special resolution has been passed by the company that the name of the company be struck off the register ;

(b) an application has been made to the Commission that the name of the company be struck off the register ;

(c) advertisement has been made in three national daily newspapers within 28 days of passing the resolution, calling for objections, if any, to the application ; and

(d) the Commission is satisfied that—

(i) the reasons given for the application are sufficient to justify the striking off,

(ii) the company has not commenced business and has no undischarged obligations, and

(iii) no reasonable objection has been received within 28 days of the publication of the advertisement mentioned in paragraph (c).

(2) Any person aggrieved by the striking off of the name of the company under this subsection may apply to the Court, at any time before the expiration of two years from the date of the striking off, and if the Court is satisfied that it is just to restore it to the register, the Court may order the name of the company to be so restored.

(3) Where the Commission observes or has reasonable cause to believe that a company is not carrying on business or has not been in operation for 10 years or has not complied with provisions of this Act for a consecutive period of 10 years, the Commission may cause to be published, in at least three national daily newspapers, a notice of its intention to strike off the company from the register.

(4) Where the Commission does not, within 90 days of the last publication, receive any response from the company that it is carrying on business or in operation, it may strike off the name of the company.

(5) Where a company has been struck off in accordance with the provisions of this section, the Commission shall cause to be published in at least three national daily newspapers, the name and date of the striking off of the company, provided that—

(a) the liability, if any, of every director, managing officer and member of the company shall continue and may be enforced as if the company has not been struck off ; and

(b) nothing in this subsection shall affect the power of the Court to windup a company the name of which has been struck off the register.

(6) Any company, member or creditor aggrieved by the striking off from the register under subsection (4) may apply to the Court, at any time before the expiration of 10 years from the publication of the notice under subsection (5), for an order restoring the company to the register, and if the Court is satisfied that, at the time of the striking off, the company was carrying on business or in operation, or that otherwise it is just to restore it to the register, the Court may order the name of the company to be restored to the register, and an order under this subsection may include any directions, the Court deems fit, and provision may be made therein for placing the company and all other persons in the same position, as nearly as may be, as if the name of the company had not been struck off the register, and upon delivery of an office copy to the Commission for registration, the order shall have effect according to its tenor, and may be registered accordingly.

(7) Any notice to a liquidator to be sent under this section may be addressed to the liquidator at his last known place of business, and any letter or notice to be sent under this section to a company may be addressed to the company at its registered or head office.

693. Where a company is dissolved, all property and rights whatsoever vested in or held on trust for the company immediately before its dissolution, including leasehold property (but not including property held by the company on trust for any other person) shall, subject and without prejudice to any order which may at any time be made by the Court under section 691 or 692 of this Act, be deemed to be vested in the State without further assurance, as *bona vacantia.*

CENTRAL ACCOUNTS

694.—(1) There shall continue to be an account called the Companies Liquidation Account, kept on behalf of the Commission by the Accountant General of the Federation, into which shall be paid all money received by the Commission in respect of proceedings under this Act in connection with the winding-up of companies.

(2) All payments out of money standing to the credit of the Commission in the Companies Liquidation Account shall be made by the Accountant-General in the prescribed manner.

695.—(1) If the cash balance standing to the credit of the Companies Liquidation Account is in excess of the amount which in the opinion of the Commission is required for the time being to answer demands in respect of companies' estates, the Commission shall notify the excess to the Accountant General of the Federation and the Accountant-General of the Federation, may invest the excess or any part thereof, in Government securities, to be placed to the credit of such account as he may deem fit in the circumstances.

(2) If any part of the money so invested is, in the opinion of the Commission, required to answer any demand in respect of companies' estates, the Commission shall notify the Accountant-General of the Federation the amount so required, and the Accountant-General of the Federation shall thereupon repay to the Commission such sum as may be required to the credit of the Companies Liquidation Account, and for that purpose may direct the sale of such part of the securities as may be necessary.

(3) The dividends on investments under this section shall be paid to such account as the Accountant-General of the Federation may direct, and regard shall be had to the amount thus derived in fixing the fees payable in respect of proceedings in the winding-up of companies.

696.—(1) The Commission shall keep an account of the receipts and payments in the winding-up of each company, and, when the cash balance standing to the credit of the account of any company is in excess of the amount which, in the opinion of the Committee of Inspection, is required for the time being to answer demands in respect of that company's estate, the Commission shall, on the request of the committee, invest the amount not so required in Government securities, to be placed to the credit of the said account for the benefit of the company.

(2) If any part of the money so invested is, in the opinion of the Committee of Inspection, required to answer any demands in respect of the estate of the company, the Commission shall, on the request of that committee, raise such sum as may be required by the sale of such part of the said securities as may be necessary.

(3) The dividends on investments under this section shall be paid to the credit of the company.

(4) Where the balance at the credit of any company's account in the hands of the Commission exceeds ₦1,000,000 and the liquidator gives notice to the Commission that the excess is not required for the purposes of the liquidation, the company is entitled to interest on the excess at the current bank rate.

RETURNS BY OFFICERS OF COURT

697. The officers of the Courts acting in the winding-up of companies shall make to the Commission such returns of the business of their respective Courts and offices, at

such times, and in such manner and form as may be prescribed, and from those returns the Commission shall cause books to be prepared which shall be opened for public information and searches.

ACCOUNTS TO BE PREPARED ANNUALLY

698.—(1) The Commission and every officer by whom fees are taken under this Act in relation to the winding-up of companies, shall make returns and give information to the Accountant-General of the Federation in such form as he may require and the accounts of the Commission relating to the winding-up of companies shall be audited at the end of each year in the manner prescribed by the Constitution.

(2) The Accountant-General of the Federation shall, before the end of each year in which the audit is made, prepare for submission to the President an account of the winding-up of companies, as audited by the Accountant General for the Federation, showing in respect of such winding-up, the receipts and expenditure during the previous year, and any other matter which the President or the Minister, as the case may be, may require.

CHAPTER 25—WINDING-UP OF UNREGISTERED COMPANIES

699. Subject to the provisions of this Part of this Act, an unregistered company may be wound up under this Act and all the provisions of this Act, with respect to winding-up shall apply to an unregistered company, with the following exceptions—

(a) the principal place of business of an unregistered company shall, for all the purposes of the winding-up, be deemed to be the registered office of the company ;

(b) an unregistered company shall not be wound up under this Act voluntarily or subject to supervision ;

(c) an unregistered company may be wound up if—

(i) the company is dissolved, or has ceased to carry on business or is carrying on business only for the purpose of winding-up its affairs,

(ii) the company is unable to pay its debts, or

(iii) the Court is of opinion that it is just and equitable that the company should be wound up ; or

(d) an unregistered company shall, for purposes of this Act, be deemed to be unable to pay its debts if—

(i) a creditor, by assignment or otherwise, to whom the company is indebted in a sum exceeding ₦100,000 then due, has served on the company, by leaving at its principal place of business, or by delivering to the secretary or some director, manager, or principal officer of the company, or by otherwise serving in such manner as the Court may approve or direct, a demand under his hand requiring the company to pay the sum so due, and the company has for 21 days after the service of the demand neglected to pay the sum, or to secure or compound for it to the satisfaction of the creditor,

(ii) any action or other proceedings has been instituted against any member for any debt or demand due from the company, or from him in his capacity as a member, and notice in writing of the institution of the action or proceeding having been served on the company by leaving it at its principal place of business, or by delivering it to the secretary, or some director, manager, or principal officer of the company, or by otherwise serving the notice in such manner as the court may approve or direct, the company has not within 28 days after service of the notice secured or compounded for the debt or demand or procured the action or proceeding to be stayed, or within that period has not indemnified the defendant to his reasonable satisfaction against the action or proceeding, and against all costs, damages and expenses to be incurred by him by reason of the same, or

(iii) execution or other process issued on a judgment, act or order obtained in any Court in favour of a creditor against the company, or any of its members or any person authorised to be sued as nominal defendant on behalf of the company, is returned unsatisfied and it is otherwise proved to the satisfaction of the Court that the company is unable to pay its debts.

700.—(1) In the event of an unregistered company being wound up—

(a) every person is deemed to be a contributory, who is liable to pay or contribute to the payment of—

(i) any debt or liability of the company,

(ii) any sum for the adjustment of the rights of the members among themselves,

(iii) the costs and expenses of winding-up the company, and

(b) every contributory is liable to contribute to the assets of the company all sums due from him in respect of any such liability.

(2) In the event of the death, bankruptcy, or insolvency of any contributory, the provisions of this Act with respect to the personal representatives, heirs, and devisees of deceased contributories, and the trustees of bankrupt or insolvent contributories, as the case may be, shall apply.

701. The provisions of this Act with respect to staying and restraining actions and proceedings against a company at any time after the presentation of a petition for winding-up and before the making of a winding-up order shall, in the case of an unregistered company, where the application to stay or restrain is by a creditor, extend to actions and proceedings against any contributory of the company.

702. Where an order has been made for winding-up an unregistered company, no action or proceeding shall be proceeded with or commenced against any contributory of the company in respect of any debt of the company except by leave of the Court, and subject to such terms as the Court may impose.

703. The provisions of this Chapter of this Act with respect to unregistered companies shall be in addition to and not in restriction of any provision under this Act, contained with respect to winding-up companies by the Court, and the Court or liquidator may exercise any power to do any act in the case of unregistered companies which might be exercised or done by it or him in winding-up companies formed and registered under this Act, but an unregistered company shall not, except in the event of its being wound up, be deemed to be a company under this Act, and then only to the extent provided by this Chapter of this Act.

CHAPTER 26—MISCELLANEOUS PROVISIONS APPLYING TO COMPANIES WHICH ARE INSOLVENT

704. A person acts as an insolvency practitioner in relation to a company by acting as its—

(a) liquidator, provisional liquidator or official receiver ;

(b) administrator or administrative receiver ; or

(c) receiver and manager, or as nominee or supervisor of a company's voluntary arrangement.

705.—(1) A person is only qualified to act as an insolvency practitioner where he—

(a) has obtained a degree in law, accountancy or such other relevant discipline from any recognised University or Polytechnic ;

(b) has a minimum of five years post qualification experience in matters relating to insolvency ;

(c) is authorised to so act by virtue of a certificate of membership issued by Business Recovery and Insolvency Practitioners Association of Nigeria (BRIPAN), or his membership of any other professional body recognised by the Commission, being permitted to act by or under the rules of that body ; and

(d) holds an authorisation granted by the Commission.

(2) The Commission may prescribe in its regulations such other additional qualifications as may be considered necessary.

706.—(1) The Commission may, by an instrument or order, declare a body which appears to it to fall within subsection (2), to be a recognised professional body for the purposes of this section.

(2) A body may be recognised if it regulates the practice of a profession and maintains and enforces rules for securing that its members—

(a) are permitted by or under the rules to act as insolvency practitioners ; (b) are fit and proper persons to act ; and

(c) meet acceptable requirements as to education and practical training and experience.

(3) References to members of a recognised professional body are to persons who, whether members of that body or not, are subject to its rules in the practice of the profession in question.

(4) An instrument or order made under subsection (1) in relation to a professional body may be revoked by a further order if it appears to the Commission that the body no longer falls within subsection (2).

707.—(1) Application may be made to the Commission for authorisation to act as an insolvency practitioner, and the application shall—

(a) be made in such manner as the Commission may specify ;

(b) contain or be accompanied with a certificate of membership issued by BRIPAN or any other professional body approved by the Commission and such information as the Commission may reasonably require for the purpose of determining the application ; and

(c) be accompanied by the prescribed fee in the regulations issued by the Commission.

(2) At any time after receiving the application and before determining it, the Commission may require the applicant to furnish additional information.

(3) An application may be withdrawn before it is granted or refused.

708.—(1) The Commission may, on an application duly made and after being furnished with all such information as it may require, grant or refuse the application.

(2) The Commission shall grant the application if it appears to it from the information furnished by the applicant and having regard to such other information, if any, that the applicant—

(a) is a fit and proper person to act as an insolvency practitioner, and

(b) meets the prescribed requirements with respect to education and practical training and experience.

(3) An authorisation granted pursuant to the application shall take effect from the date of grant by the Commission.

(4) Authorisation granted may be withdrawn by the Commission if it appears to it that the holder of the authorisation is no longer a fit and proper person to act as an insolvency practitioner.

(5) An authorisation granted may be withdrawn by the Commission at the request or with the consent of the holder of the authorisation.

709.—(1) Where the Commission refuses an application or withdraws an authorisation it shall within seven days notify the party in writing stating the reasons for the refusal or withdrawal of the authorisation, and the party affected within 21 days of the receipt of the notification may apply by summons on notice to the Court having jurisdiction in insolvency matter, for a review of the decision of the Commission and the Court, upon hearing the summons, may refuse or grant the summons on such terms as it deems fit.

(2) An appeal from the decision of the Court shall lie to the Court of Appeal and the decision of the Court of Appeal is final.

CHAPTER 27—ARRANGEMENTS AND COMPROMISE

710. In this Chapter, the word "arrangement" means any change in the rights or liabilities of members, debenture holders or creditors of a company or any class of them or in the regulation of a company, other than a change effected under any other provision of this Act or by the unanimous agreement of all parties affected.

711.—(1) Where under a scheme proposed for a compromise, arrangement or reconstruction between two or more companies or the merger of any two or more companies, the whole or any part of the undertaking or the property of any company concerned in the scheme (in this section referred to as "the transfer of company") is to be transferred to another company, the Court may, on the application in summary of any of the companies to be affected, order separate meetings of the companies to be summoned in such manner as the Court may direct.

(2) If a majority representing at least three-quarter in value of the share of members being present and voting either in person or by proxy at each of the separate meetings, agree to the scheme, an application may be made to the Court by one or more of the companies, and the Court shall sanction the scheme.

(3) When the scheme is sanctioned by the Court, it becomes binding on the companies, and the Court may, by the order sanctioning the scheme or by any subsequent order, make provision for—

(a) the transfer to the transferee company of the whole or any part of the undertaking and of the property or liabilities of any transferor company ;

(b) the allotting or appropriation by the transferee company of shares, debentures, policies or other like interests in that company which under the compromise or arrangement are to be allotted or appropriated by that company to or for any person;

(c) the continuation by or against the transferee company of legal proceedings pending by or against any transferor company ;

(d) the dissolution, without winding-up, of any transferor company ;

(e) the provision to be made for any persons who in such manner as the court may direct, dissent from the compromise or arrangement ; and

(f) such incidental, consequential and supplemental matters as are necessary to secure that the reconstruction or merger shall be fully and effectively carried out.

(4) An order under subsection (3) (d) shall not be made unless—

(a) the whole of the undertaking and the property, assets and liabilities of the transferor company are being transferred into the transferee company ; and

(b) the Court is satisfied that adequate provision by way of compensation or otherwise have been made with respect to the employees of the company to be dissolved.

(5) Where an order under this section provides for the transfer of property or liabilities, that property or liabilities shall, by virtue of the order, be transferred to and become the property or liabilities of the transferee company, and in the case of any property, if the order so directs, freed from any charge which is by virtue of the compromise or arrangement to cease to have effect.

(6) Where an order is made under this section, every company in relation to which the order is made shall cause an office copy of the order to be delivered to the Commission for registration within seven days after the making of the order, and a notice of the order shall be published in the Federal Government Gazette and in at least one national newspaper and if in default shall be liable to a fine in such amount as may be prescribed by the Commission in its regulations.

(7) In this section—

(a) "property" includes property rights and powers of every description; (b) "liabilities" includes rights, powers and duties of every description notwithstanding that such rights, powers and duties are of a personal character which could not generally be assigned or performed vicariously; and (c)"company" where used in this section does not include any company other than a company within the meaning of this Act.

712. (1) Where a scheme or contract, not being a take-over bid under the Investment and Securities Act involving the transfer of shares or any class of shares in a company (in this section referred to as "the transfer of company") to another company, whether a company within the meaning of this Act or not (in this section referred to as 'the transferee company') has, within four months after the making of the offer in that behalf by the transferee company been approved by the holders of at least nine-tenth in value of the shares of the company (other than shares already held at the date of the offer by a nominee for the transferee company, or its subsidiary), the transferee company may at any time within two months after the expiration of the said four months give notice in the prescribed manner to any dissenting shareholder that it desires to acquire his shares.

(2) When a notice under subsection (1) is given, the transferee company is, unless on an application made by the dissenting shareholder within one month from the date on which the notice was given, unless the Court deems fit to order otherwise, entitled and bound to acquire those shares on the terms on which, under the scheme or contract, the shares of the approving shareholders are to be transferred to the transferee company.

(3) Where shares in the transferor company of the said class or classes as the shares whose transfer is involved are already held as specified in subsection (1) to a value greater than one-tenth of the aggregate of their value and that of the share (other than those already held as specified in that subsection) whose transfer is involved, the provisions of this section do not apply unless—

(a) the transferee company offers the same terms to all holders of the shares (other than those already held) whose transfer is involved, or where those shares include shares of different classes, of each class of them ; and

(b) the holders who approve the scheme or contracts besides holding at least nine-tenth in value of the shares (other than those already held as aforesaid) whose transfer is involved, shall be at least three- quarters in number of the holders of those shares.

(4) Where a notice has been given by the transferee company under subsection (1) and the Court has not, on an application made by the dissenting shareholder, ordered to the contrary, the transferee company shall—

(a) on the expiration of one month from the date on which the notice has been given or if an application to the Court by the dissenting shareholder is then pending after that application has been disposed of, transmit a copy of the notice to the transferor company together with an instrument of transfer executed on behalf of the shareholder by any person appointed by the transferee company and on its behalf by the transferee company; and

(b) pay or transfer to the transferor company the amount or other consideration representing the price payable by the transferee company for the shares which by virtue of this section that company is entitled to acquire, and the transferor company shall thereupon register the transferee company as the holder of those shares.

(5) Any sum received by the transferor company under this section shall be paid into a separate bank account, and such sums and any other consideration so received shall be held by that company on trust for the several persons entitled to the shares in respect of which the said sums or other consideration, were respectively received.

(6) In this section, "dissenting shareholder" includes a shareholder who has not assented to the scheme or contract and any shareholder who has failed or refused to transfer to the transferee company in accordance with the scheme or contract.

713. (1) This section applies where, in pursuance of any such scheme or contract, shares in a company are transferred to another company or its nominee, and those shares together with any other shares in the first mentioned company held by, or by a nominee for the transferee company or its subsidiary at the date of the transfer comprise or include nine-tenth in value of the shares in the first mentioned company or of a class of those shares.

(2) The transferee company shall, within one month from the date of the transfer (unless on a previous transfer in pursuance of the scheme or contract it has already complied with this requirement), give notice of that fact in the prescribed manner to the holder of the remaining shares or of the remaining shares of that class, as the case may be, who have not assented to the scheme or contract.

(3) A holder may, within three months from the giving of the notice to him, require the transferee company to acquire the shares in question.

(4) If a shareholder gives notice under subsection (3) with respect to any share, the transferee company is entitled and bound to acquire those shares on the terms on which under the scheme or contract the shares of the approving shareholders were transferred to it, or on such other terms as may be agreed on as the Court hearing the application of either the transferee company or the shareholder deems fit.

714.—(1) With a view to effecting any arrangement, a company may by special resolution resolve that the company be put into members' voluntary winding-up and that the liquidator be authorised to sell the whole or part of its undertaking or assets to another body corporate, whether a company within the meaning of this Act or not (in this section called "the transferee company") in consideration or part consideration of fully paid shares, and to distribute the same in specie among the members of the company in accordance with their rights in the liquidation.

(2) Any sale or distribution in pursuance of a special resolution under this section is binding on the company and all its members and each member shall be deemed to have agreed with the transferee company to accept the fully paid shares, debentures, policies, cash or other like interests to which he is entitled under such distribution : Provided that if—

(a) within one year from the date of the passing of any special resolution as is referred to in subsection (1), an order is made under sections 353-355 of this Act dealing with relief on the grounds of unfairly prejudicial and oppressive conduct or for the winding-up of the company under a creditors' voluntary winding-up, the arrangement for the sale and distribution shall not be valid unless sanctioned by the Court; or

(b) any member of the company, by writing addressed to the liquidator and left at the registered office or head office of the company, within 30 days after the passing of the resolution, dissents in respect of any of the shares held by him, the liquidator shall either abstain from carrying the resolution into effect or shall purchase such shares at a price to be determined in the manner provided by subsection (4).

(3) Any member who fails to signify his dissent in accordance with subsection (2) is deemed to have accepted the resolution.

(4) If the liquidator elects to purchase the shares of any member who has expressed his dissent in accordance with subsection (2), the price payable shall be determined by agreement in the case of a private company in which aliens do not participate, and in the case of a public company or a private company in which aliens participate, by the Securities and Exchange Commission :

Provided that in the case of a private company in which no aliens participate—

(a) such price is determined by estimating what the member concerned would have received had the whole of the undertaking of the company been sold as a going concern for cash to a willing buyer and the proceeds, less the cost of winding-up, been divided amongst the members in accordance with their rights ; and

(b) the purchase money is paid by the company before the company is dissolved and be raised by the liquidator or, in default of any direction in the special resolution, in such manner as he may think fit as part of the expenses of the winding-up.

(5) Nothing contained in this section authorises any variation or abrogation of the rights of any creditor of the company.

(6) If any company, otherwise than under this section, sells or resolves to sell the whole or part of its undertaking or assets to another body corporate in consideration or part consideration of any shares, debentures, policies or other like interest in that body corporate, and resolves to distribute the same in specie among members of the company (whether in liquidation or by way of dividend), any member of the company may by notice in writing addressed to the company and left at the registered office or head office of the company within 30 days after the passing of the resolution authorising such distribution, require the company either to abstain

from carrying the resolution into effect or to purchase any of his shares at a price to be determined in the manner provided by subsection (4).

(7) Nothing contained in subsection (6) authorises any company to purchase its own shares or make any distributions to its shareholders except in accordance with the provisions of this Act.

715. (1) Where a compromise or arrangement is proposed between a company and its creditors or any class of them, the Court may, on the application, in a summary way, of the company or any of its creditors or members or, in the case of a company being wound up, of the liquidator, order a meeting of the creditors or class of creditors, or of the members of the company, or class of members, as the case may be, to be summoned in such a manner as the Court directs.

(2) If a majority representing at least three quarters in value of the shares of members or class of members, or of the interest of creditors or class of creditors, as the case may be, being present and voting either in person or by proxy at the meeting, agree to any compromise or arrangement, the compromise or arrangement may be referred by the Court to the Securities and Exchange Commission which shall appoint one or more inspectors to investigate the fairness of the compromise or arrangement and to make a written report on it to the Court within a time specified by the Court.

(3) If the Court is satisfied as to the fairness of the compromise or arrangement, it shall sanction the same and the compromise or arrangement shall be binding on all the creditors or the class of creditors or on the members or the class of members as the case may be, and also the company or in the case of a company in the course of being wound up, on the liquidator and contributories of the company.

(4) An order made under subsection (3) shall have no effect until a certified true copy of the order has been delivered by the company to the Commission for registration and a copy of every order shall be annexed to every copy of the memorandum of the company issued after the order has been made.

(5) If a company defaults in complying with subsection (4), the company and each officer of the company is liable to a penalty as prescribed by the Commission in the regulations.

(6) In this section and section 716 of this Act, "company" means any company liable to be wound up under this Act.

716.—(1) Where a meeting of creditors or any class of creditors or of members or any class of members is summoned under section 715 of this Act, there shall—

(a) with every notice summoning the meeting which is sent to a creditor or member, be sent also a statement explaining the effect of the compromise or arrangement and in particular stating any material interests of the directors of the company, whether as directors or as members or as creditors of the company or otherwise, and the effect of the compromise or arrangement in so far as it is different from the effect on the like interest of other persons ; and

(b) in every notice summoning the meeting which is given by advertisement, be included such a statement, or a notification of the place at which and the manner in which creditors or members entitled to attend the meeting may obtain copies of such a statement.

(2) Where the compromise or arrangement affects the rights of debenture holders of the company, the statement shall give the like explanation as respects the trustees of

any deed for securing the issue of the debenture as it is required to give as respects the company's directors.

(3) Where a notice given by advertisement includes a notification that copies of a statement explaining the effects of the compromise or arrangement proposed can be obtained by creditors or members entitled to attend the meeting, every such creditor or member shall, on making application in the manner indicated by the notice, be furnished by the company free of charge with a copy of the statement.

(4) Where a company makes default in complying with any requirement of this section, the company and every officer of the company are liable to a penalty as prescribed by the Commission in the regulations and for the purpose of this subsection any liquidator of the company and any trustee of a deed for securing the issue of debentures of the company shall be deemed to be an officer of the company :

Provided that a person is not liable under this subsection, if that person shows that the default was due to refusal of any other person, being a director or trustee for debenture holders, to supply the necessary particulars as to his interests.

(5) A director of the company and any trustee for debenture holders of the company shall give notice to the company of such matters relating to himself as may be necessary for the purpose of this section, and any person who defaults in complying with this subsection is liable to a penalty as prescribed by the Commission in the regulations.

717.—(1) No winding-up petition or enforcement action by a creditor (secured or unsecured) shall be entertained against any company or its assets that has commenced a process of arrangement and compromise with its creditors for six months from the time that the company by way of affidavit provides the following documents to the Court—

(a) a document setting out the terms intended to be proposed to the creditors in an arrangement or compromise ;

(b) a statement of the company's affairs containing the particulars of the company's creditors and its debts and other liabilities and of its assets;

(c) such other information as the Court may require; and

(d) a statement that the company desires a protection from a winding-up process pending the completion of the arrangement or compromise.

(2) Notwithstanding the provisions of subsection (1), a secured creditor may, by application to the Court filed within 30 days of notice of the arrangement and compromise, discharge the six months moratorium period provided in subsection (1) if—

(a) the asset of the company sought to be enforced by the creditor does not form part of the company's pool of assets to be considered under the arrangement and compromise proceeding ;

(b) the asset sought to be enforced by the creditor is a perishable goods or commodities which may depreciate or dissipate before expiration of the six months moratorium period ;

(c) the secured creditor enforces its security over the assets before receiving notice of the company's proposed arrangement and compromise ; or

(d) the company consents in writing for a secured creditor to enforce its right over the company's asset within the six months moratorium period :

Provided that the company, upon the approval or consent shall file a further affidavit updating the Court of the dissipation of the said asset.

CHAPTER 28—NETTING

718. In this Chapter—

"financial regulatory authority" means—

(a) the Central Bank of Nigeria ;

(b) the Securities and Exchange Commission ;

(c) the National Insurance Commission ;

(d) the National Pension Commission ; and

(e) any other financial regulatory authority established by an Act of the National Assembly ;

"cash" means money credited to an account in any currency or a similar claim for repayment of money, such as a money market deposit ;

"collateral" means any—

(a) cash in any currency ;

(b) securities of any kind, including debt and equity securities ;

(c) guarantees, letters of credit and obligations to reimburse ; and

(d) any asset commonly used as collateral in Nigeria;

"collateral arrangement" means any margin, collateral, security arrangement or other credit enhancement related to or forming part of a netting agreement or one or more qualified financial contracts entered into thereunder, including—

(a) a pledge, charge or any other form of security interest in collateral, whether possessory or non-possessory ; (b) a title transfer collateral arrangement;

(c) a security interest collateral arrangement ; and

(d) any guarantee, letter of credit or reimbursement obligation by or to a party to one or more qualified financial contracts, in respect of those qualified financial contracts

"insolvent party" means the party in relation to which an insolvency proceeding under the laws of Nigeria has been instituted ;

"liquidator" means the liquidator, administrator, nominee, supervisor, receiver, trustee, conservator or other individual, person or entity which administers the affairs of an insolvent party during an insolvency proceeding under the laws of Nigeria ;

"netting" means the occurrence of the following—

(a) termination, liquidation or acceleration of any payment or delivery obligation or entitlement under one or more qualified financial contracts entered into under a netting agreement;

(b) calculation or estimation of a close-out value, market value, liquidation value or replacement value in respect of each obligation or entitlement or group of obligations or entitlements terminated, liquidated or accelerated under paragraph (a) ;

(c) conversion of any values calculated or estimated under paragraph (b) into a single currency ; and

(d) determination of the net balance of the values calculated under paragraph (b), as converted under paragraph (c), whether by operation of set-off or otherwise ;

"netting agreement" means any—

(a) agreement between two parties that provides for netting of present or future payment or delivery obligations or entitlements arising under or in connection with one or more qualified financial contracts entered into under the agreement by the parties to the agreement (a "master netting agreement") ;

(b) master agreement between two parties that provides for netting of the amounts due under two or more master netting agreements (a "master-master netting agreement") ; and

(c) collateral arrangement related to or forming part of one or more of the foregoing ;

"non-insolvent party" means the party other than the insolvent party;

"party" means a person constituting one of the parties to a netting agreement ;

"person" includes partnerships, companies, regulated entities such as banks, insurance companies and pension fund administrators, or any other body corporate (including statutory corporations or statutory bodies) whether organised under the laws of Nigeria or under the laws of any other jurisdiction, and any international or regional development bank or other international or regional organisation ;

"qualified financial contract" means any financial agreement, contract or transaction, including any terms and conditions incorporated by reference in any financial agreement, contract or transaction, pursuant to which payment or delivery obligations are due to be performed at a certain time or within a certain period of time and whether or not subject to any condition or contingency and includes—

(a) a currency, cross-currency or interest rate swap ;

(b) a basis swap ;

(c) a spot, future, forward or other foreign exchange transaction ;

(d) a cap, collar or floor transaction ;

(e) a commodity swap ;

(f) a forward rate agreement ;

(g) a currency or interest rate future ;

(h) a currency or interest rate option ;

(i) an equity derivative, such as an equity or equity index swap, equity forward, equity option or equity index option ;

(j) a derivative relating to bonds or other debt securities or to a bond or debt security index, such as a total return swap, index swap, forward, option or index option ;

(k) a credit derivative, such as a credit default swap, credit default basket swap, total return swap or credit default option ;

(l) an energy derivative, such as an electricity derivative, oil derivative, coal derivative or gas derivative ;

(m) a weather derivative, such as a weather swap or weather option ;

(n) a bandwidth derivative ;

(o) a freight derivative ;

(p) an emissions derivative, such as an emissions allowance or emissions reduction transaction ;

(q) an economic statistics derivative, such as an inflation derivative ;

(r) a property index derivative ;

(s) a spot, future, forward or other securities or commodities transaction ;(t) a securities contract, including a margin loan and an agreement to buy, sell, borrow or lend securities, such as a securities repurchase or reverse repurchase agreement, a securities lending agreement or a securities buy or sell back agreement, including any such contract or agreement relating to mortgage loans, interests in mortgage loans or mortgage-related securities;

(u) a commodities contract, including an agreement to buy, sell, borrow or lend commodities, such as a commodities repurchase or reverse repurchase agreement, a commodities lending agreement or a commodities buy or sell back agreement ;

(v) a collateral arrangement ;

(w) an agreement to clear or settle securities transactions or to act as a depository for securities ;

(x) any other agreement, contract or transaction similar to any agreement, contract or transaction referred to in paragraphs (a) - (w) with respect to one or more reference items or indices relating to interest rates, currencies, commodities, energy products, electricity, equities, weather, bonds and other debt instruments, precious metals, quantitative measures associated with an occurrence, extent of an occurrence, or contingency associated with a financial, commercial or economic consequence, or economic or financial indices or measures of economic or financial risk or value ;

(y) any swap, forward, option, contract for differences or other derivative in respect of, or combination of, one or more agreements or contracts referred to in paragraphs (a-x) ; and

(z) any agreement, contract or transaction designated as such by the financial regulatory authority under this Act ;

"security interest collateral arrangement" means "security financial collateral arrangement" as defined in Chapter 9 (Debentures) of this Act and includes charges ; and

"title transfer collateral arrangement" means a margin, collateral or security arrangement related to a netting agreement based on the transfer of title to collateral, whether by outright sale or by way of security, including a sale and repurchase agreement, securities lending agreement, or securities buy or sell-back agreement.

719. A financial regulatory authority may, in relation to the relevant sector it regulates, by notice issued under this section, designate as "qualified financial contracts" any agreement, contract or transaction, or type of agreement, contract or transaction, in addition to those listed in this section.

720. A qualified financial contract shall not be and shall be deemed never to have been void or unenforceable by reason of the Gaming Machines (Prohibition) Act or any other laws relating to games, gaming, gambling, wagering or lotteries.

721.—(1) The provisions of a netting agreement is enforceable in accordance with their terms, including against an insolvent party, and, where applicable, against a guarantor or other person providing security for a party and shall not be stayed, avoided or otherwise limited by—

(a) any action of the liquidator ;

(b) any other provision of law relating to bankruptcy, reorganisation, composition with creditors, receivership or any other insolvency proceeding an insolvent party may be subject to ; or

(c) any other provision of law that may be applicable to an insolvent party, subject to the conditions contained in the applicable netting agreement.

(2) After commencement of insolvency proceedings in relation to a party, the only obligation, if any, of either party to make payment or delivery under a netting agreement shall be equal to its net obligation to the other party as determined in accordance with the terms of the applicable netting agreement.

(3) After commencement of insolvency proceedings in relation to a party, the only right, if any, of either party to receive payment or delivery under a netting agreement shall be equal to its net entitlement with respect to the other party as determined in accordance with the terms of the applicable netting agreement.

(4) Any power of the liquidator to assume or repudiate individual contracts or transactions will not prevent the termination, liquidation or acceleration of all payment or delivery obligations or entitlements under one or more qualified financial contracts entered into under or in connection with a netting agreement, and applies, if at all, only to the net amount due in respect of all of such qualified financial contracts in accordance with the terms of such netting agreement.

(5) The provisions of a netting agreement which provide for the determination of a net balance of the close-out values, market values, liquidation values or replacement values calculated in respect of accelerated or terminated payment or delivery obligations or entitlements under one or more qualified financial contracts entered into is not affected by any applicable insolvency law limiting the rights to set off, offset or net out obligations, payment amounts or termination values owed between an insolvent party and another party.

(6) The liquidator of an insolvent party may not avoid—

(a) any transfer, substitution or exchange of cash, collateral or any other interests under or in connection with a netting agreement from the insolvent party to the non-insolvent party ; or

(b) any payment or delivery obligation incurred by the insolvent party and owing to the non-insolvent party under or in connection with a netting agreement on the grounds of it constituting a preference by the insolvent party to the non-insolvent party, unless there is clear and convincing evidence that the non-insolvent party—

(i) made such transfer,

(ii) incurred such obligation with actual intent to hinder, delay, or defraud any entity to which the insolvent party was indebted or became indebted, on or after the date that such transfer was made or such obligation was incurred.

(7) Reasonable notice to interested parties, individuals, persons or entities shall be required for the realisation, appropriation or liquidation of collateral under a collateral arrangement unless otherwise agreed by the parties:

Provided that this subsection is without prejudice to any applicable provision of law requiring that realisation, appropriation or liquidation of collateral is conducted in a commercially reasonable manner.

(8) For the purposes of this section—

(a) a netting agreement is deemed to be a netting agreement notwithstanding the fact that the netting agreement may contain provisions relating to agreements, contracts or transactions that are not qualified financial contracts defined in section 718, provided, however, that, for the purposes of this section, such netting agreement shall be deemed to be a netting agreement only with respect to those agreements , contracts or transactions that fall within the definition of "qualified financial contract" in this Chapter ;

(b) a collateral arrangement is deemed to be a collateral arrangement notwithstanding the fact that such collateral arrangement may contain provisions relating to agreements, contracts or transactions that are not a netting agreement or qualified financial contracts as defined in section 718 of this Act, provided, however, that, for the purposes of this section, such collateral arrangement shall be deemed to be a collateral arrangement only with respect to those agreements, contracts or transactions that fall within the definition of "netting agreement" or "qualified financial contract" as defined in section 718 of this Act ; and

(c) a netting agreement and all qualified financial contracts entered into shall constitute a single agreement.

CHAPTER 29—MISCELLANEOUS AND SUPPLEMENTAL

APPLICATION OF THIS PART

722.—(1) Except as otherwise provided, Part B of this Act, applies to— Application of this Part.

(a) all companies formed and registered under this Act ;

(b) all existing companies ;

(c) all companies incorporated, formed or registered under other enactments ; and

(d) unregistered companies.

(2) This Act does not apply to unions of workers or of employers.

723.—(1) Except as otherwise expressly provided in this Act—

(a) the provisions of this Act shall have effect notwithstanding anything to the contrary contained in the memorandum or articles of a company, or in any agreement executed, by it, or in any resolution passed by the company in general meeting or by its board of directors whether the same be registered, executed or passed, as the case may be, before or after the commencement of this Act ; and

(b) any provision contained in the memorandum or articles, agreement or resolution as in paragraph (a) shall, to the extent to which it is repugnant to the provisions of this Act, become or be void, as the case may be.

(2) Any provision of this Act overriding or interpreting a company's articles shall, except as provided by this Act, apply in relation to articles in force at the commencement of this Act, as well as to articles coming into force thereafter, and shall apply also in relation to a company's memorandum as it applies in relation to its articles.

724. In its application to existing companies, this Act shall apply in the same manner—

(a) in the case of a limited company, other than a company limited by guarantee, as if the company had been formed and registered under this Act as a company limited by shares ;

(b) in the case of a company limited by guarantee, as if the company has been formed and registered under this Act as a company limited by guarantee ; and

(c) in the case of a company, other than a limited company, as if the company had been formed and registered under this Act as an unlimited company :

Provided that reference, express or implied, to the date of registration shall be construed as a reference to the date at which the company was registered under the Companies Act, 1912 as the first Nigerian enactment in respect of companies, or as the case may be, any enactment relating to companies thereafter in force in Nigeria before the commencement of this Act.

725. This Act applies to every company registered but not formed under the Companies Act, 1912 referred to in section 724 of this Act or, as the case may be, any enactment relating to companies in force in Nigeria before the commencement of this Act :

Provided that reference, express or implied, to the date of registration shall be construed as a reference to the date at which the company was registered under the enactment in force in Nigeria at the date when it was registered.

726. This Act applies to every unlimited company registered as a limited company under section 52 of the Companies and Allied Matters Act, 1990 or of any enactment replaced by that section, as the case may be, in the same manner as it applies to an unlimited company registered under this Act as a limited company:

Provided that reference, express or implied, to the date of registration shall be construed as a reference to the date at which the company was registered as a limited company under section 52 of the 1990 Act or any enactment replaced by that section, as the case may be.

727.—(1) The provisions of this Act specified in the Second Column of the Thirteenth Schedule to this Act (which respectively related to all bodies corporate, incorporated in and having a principal place of business in Nigeria, other than those mentioned in subsection (2) as if they were companies registered under this Act, but subject to any limitations mentioned in relation to those provisions respectively in the Third Column of that Schedule and to such adaptation and modifications (if any) as may be specified by order made by the Minister and published in the Federal Government Gazette.

(2) The provisions of subsection (1) shall not apply by virtue of this section to any body—

(a) incorporated under any enactment other than this Act ;

(b) not formed for the purpose of carrying on a business which has for its objects the acquisition of gain by the body or by the individual members thereof ; and

(c) for the time being exempted by the direction of the Minister.

(3) This section does not repeal or revoke in whole or in part any enactment or other instrument constituting or regulating anybody in relation to which the said provisions are applied by virtue of this section, but in relation to any such body, the operation of any such enactment or instrument shall be suspended in so far as it is inconsistent with any of the said provisions as they apply for the time being to that body.

ADMINISTRATION

728.—(1) The address of the registered or head office of a company given to the Commission in accordance with section 36 (2) (b) of this Act or any change in the address made in accordance with the provisions of this section, shall be the office to which all communications and notices to the company may be addressed.

(2) Notice of any change in the address of the registered or head office of the company shall be given within 14 days of the change to the Commission which shall record the same :

Provided that a postal box address or a private mailbag address shall not be accepted by the Commission as the registered or head office.

(3) If a company carries on business without complying with subsection (2),the company and each officer of the company shall be liable to a penalty prescribed in the regulations every day during which the company so carries on business.

(4) The fact that a change in the address of a company is included in its annual return shall not be taken to satisfy the obligation imposed by this section.

(5) Where a company incorporated before the commencement of this Act has provided an address not in accordance with this section or section 36 of this Act, as the case may be, it shall within 14 days after such commencement comply with the requirements of this section and the failure shall be an offence liable to a penalty as prescribed in the regulations.

729.—(1) Every company, after incorporation, shall—

(a) paint or affix, and keep painted or affixed, its name and registration number on the outside of every office or place in which its business is carried on, in a conspicuous position, in letters easily legible;

(b) have its name engraved in legible characters on its seal, where the company has a seal ; and

(c) have its name and registration number mentioned in legible characters in all business letters of the company and in all notices, advertisements, and other official publications of the company, and in all bills of exchange, promissory notes, endorsements, cheques, and orders for money or goods purporting to be signed by or on behalf of the company, and in all bills or parcels, invoices, receipts, and letters of credit of the company.

(2) If a company makes default in complying with subsection (1), it is liable to a penalty prescribed in the Regulations for everyday during which the default continues and every director and manager of the company are liable to the like penalty.

(3) If an officer of a company or any person on its behalf—

(a) uses or authorises the use of any seal purporting to be a seal of the company where on its name is not so engraved,

(b) issues or authorises the issue of any business letter of the company or any notice, or other official publication of the company, or signs or authorises to be signed on behalf of the company any bill of exchange, promissory note, endorsement, cheque or order for money or goods wherein its name is not mentioned in that manner, or

(c) issues or authorises to be issued any bill or parcel, invoice, receipt, or letter of credit of the company, wherein its name is not mentioned in the manner,

he is liable to a penalty prescribed in the Regulations and shall further be personally liable to the holder of any such bill of exchange, promissory note, cheque, or order for money or goods, for the amount thereof, unless it is duly paid by the company.

730.—(1) Any fee paid to the Commission before the commencement of this Act, is deemed to have been validly paid under this Act.

(2) All fees paid to the Commission, and not otherwise directed by this Act for payment into a particular account, shall be paid into the Consolidated Revenue Fund of the Federation.

731.—(1) Any register, record, index, minute book or book of account required by this Act to be made and kept by a company may be made by making entries in bound books or in loose leaves, whether pasted or not, or in a photographic film form, or may be entered or recorded by any information storage device that is capable of reproducing the required information in intelligible written form within a reasonable time, or by recording the matters in question in any other manner in accordance with accepted commercial usage.

(2) Where any such register, record, index, minute book or book of account is not kept by making entries in a bound book, but by some other means including electronic means, adequate precautions shall be taken for guarding against falsification and for

facilitating its discovery and where default is made in complying with the provisions of this subsection, the company and each officer of the company is liable to a penalty prescribed in the regulations and where the offence is a continuing one, it shall, in addition be liable to a fine to be prescribed in the regulations for every day during which the default continues.

(3) The power conferred on a company by subsection (1) to keep a register, or other record by recording the matters in question otherwise than by making entries in bound books, includes power to keep the register or other record by recording those matters otherwise than in legible form, so long as the recording is capable of being reproduced in a legible form.

(4) If any such register or other record of a company as is mentioned in subsection (2) or a register of holders of a company's debentures, is kept by the company by recording the matters in question otherwise than in a legible form, the duty imposed on the company by this Act to allow inspection of or to furnish a copy of the register or other record or any part of it, shall be treated as a duty to allow inspection of, or to furnish a reproduction of the recording or of the relevant part of it in a legible form.

. 732.—(1) The Chief Judge of the Federal High Court or of any Court designated by an Act of the National Assembly as being vested with the jurisdiction to hear cases arising out of this Act may make rules of court for carrying into effect the objects of this Act so far as they relate to the winding-up of companies or generally in respect of other applications to a court under this Act.

(2) For the purpose of this section, rules made for the purpose of any enactment passed or made on or before, or to have effect on or after, the commencement of this Act shall, on its commencement, ensure and have effect where they are not inconsistent with rules of court made or deemed to have been made, under this section.

733.—(1) Every banking company, insurance company or a deposit, provident or benefit society shall, before it commences business, and also on the first Monday in February and the first Tuesday in August in every year during which it carries on business, submit to the Commission a statement in the form in the Fourteenth Schedule to this Act or as near thereto as circumstances may admit.

(2) A copy of the statement shall be put up in a conspicuous place in the registered office of the company, and in every branch office or place where the business of the company is carried on.

(3) Every member or creditor of the company is entitled to a copy of the statement, on payment of a sum prescribed in the regulation.

(4) If default, is made in complying with this section, the company and every director and manager of the company is liable to a penalty prescribed in the regulation for everyday during which the default continues.

(5) For the purposes of this Act, a company that carries on the business of insurance in common with any other business or businesses is deemed to be an insurance company.

LEGAL PROCEEDINGS, ETC

734.—(1) All offences under this Act may be tried by a court of competent jurisdiction in the place where the offence is alleged to have been committed.

(2) Where provision is made in this Act for a criminal sanction to be imposed in case of an act, omission or default without reference to the default being an offence, or without reference to conviction in a court, as the case may be, the—

(a) reference to the act, omission or default shall be construed as referable to an offence; and

(b) expression "offences" as used in this section shall have effect in relation to any such act, omission or default.

735.—(1) If, on application made to a Judge of the Federal High Court in Chambers by the Attorney-General of the Federation, there is shown to be reasonable cause to believe that a person has, while an officer of a company, committed an offence in connection with the management of the company's affairs and that evidence of the commission of the offence is to be found in any document in the possession or under the control of the company, an order may be made—

(a) authorising any person named in the order to inspect the documents or any of them for the purpose of investigating and obtaining evidence of the offence ; or

(b) requiring the secretary or any other officer of the company as maybe named in the order to produce the said documents, to a person and at a place named in the order.

(2) The provisions of subsection (1) shall apply also in relation to any document of a person carrying on the business of banking if they relate to the company's affairs, as it applies to any document in the possession or under the control of the company, except that no such order as is referred to in subsection (1) (b) shall be made by virtue of this subsection.

(3) In this section, "document" includes an instrument on which information is recorded by means of letters, figures or marks.

736. Where a limited company is the plaintiff in an action or other legal proceedings, a judge having jurisdiction in the matter may, if it appears by credible testimony that there is reason to believe that the company may be unable to pay the costs of the defendant if successful in his defence, require sufficient security to be given for those costs and may stay all proceedings until the security is given.

737. Where proceedings are instituted under this Act against any person by the Attorney-General of the Federation, nothing in this Act shall be taken to require any person who has acted as legal practitioner for the defendant to disclose any privileged communication made to him in that capacity.

738.—(1) If in any proceeding for negligence, default or breach of duty or trust against an officer of a company or a person employed by a company as auditor, it appears to the Court hearing the case that the officer or person is or may be liable but that he has acted honestly and reasonably and that, having regard to all the circumstances of the case, including those connected with his appointment he ought fairly to be excused, the Court may relieve him, either wholly or partly, from liability on such terms as it may deem fit.

(2) When any such officer or person has reasonable apprehension that a claim may be made against him in respect of any negligence, default, breach of duty or trust, he may apply to the Court for relief, and the Court on the application shall have the same power to relieve him as under this section it would have had if it had been a court before which proceedings against that person for negligence, default, breach of duty or breach of trust had been brought.

739. Where a person trades or carries on business under any name or title of which the last word or words are "Unlimited", "Limited", "Public Limited Company" or "Limited by Guarantee" or their abbreviations, he is, unless duly incorporated as an unlimited company, a private company limited by shares, a public company limited by shares, or a company limited by guarantee, respectively, liable to a penalty prescribed in the Regulation for every day during which the name or title is used.

740. The provisions of section 672 (3) of this Act which imposes a penalty for certain offences connected with fraudulent trading discovered on the winding-up of a company shall extend and apply to cases where fraudulent trading is discovered in circumstances other than on the winding-up of a company.

741. A court imposing a fine under this Act may direct that the whole or any part thereof be applied in or towards payment of the costs of the proceedings, or in or towards rewarding the person on whose information or at whose suit the fine is recovered and subject to the direction, all fines under this Act shall, notwithstanding anything in any other enactment, be paid into the Consolidated Revenue Fund.

742.—(1) The Commission may apply to the Court for directions in respect of any matter concerning its duties, powers and functions under this Act and, on any such application, the Court may give directions and make further order as it deems fit in the circumstances.

(2) Notwithstanding the provision of subsection (1), the Commission may conduct enquiries with respect to the compliance with the provisions of this Act by any person or company.

MISCELLANEOUS

743.—(1) The Commission may, with the approval of the Minister, by regulation or order, published in the Federal Government Gazette, add to, delete from or otherwise alter the whole or any part of any of the Schedules, Tables or Forms prescribed or under this Act.

(2) Until regulations, rules or orders are made under, and for the purpose of this Act prescribing forms for use, the forms in force at the commencement of this Act shall be deemed to have been made under it and shall have effect accordingly.

744.—(1) If a company, having made default in complying with any provision of this Act requiring it to file with, deliver or send to the Commission any return, account or other document, or to give notice to it of any matter, fails to make good the default within 14 days after the service of a notice on the company requiring it to do so, the Court may, on the application of any member or creditor of the company or of the Commission, order the company and any officer to make good the default within the time as may be specified in the order.

(2) Any order under this section may provide that all costs of or incidental to the application shall be borne by the company or by any officer of the company responsible for the default.

(3) Nothing in this section shall be taken to prejudice the operation of any enactment imposing penalties on a company or its officers in respect of any such default.

745.—(1) The powers of a company include if they would not otherwise do so apart from this section power to make for the benefit of persons employed or formerly employed by the company or any of its subsidiaries provision in connection with the cessation or the transfer to any person of the whole or part of the undertaking of the company or subsidiary.

(2) The power conferred under subsection (1) is exercisable even if its exercise is not in the best interest of the company.

(3) The power which a company may exercise under subsection (1) is exercised by the company if sanctioned—

(a) in a case not falling within paragraph (b) or (c), by a resolution of the company ;

(b) if so authorised by the memorandum or articles, a resolution of the directors ; or

(c) if the memorandum or articles require the exercise of the power to be sanctioned by a resolution other than a simple resolution of the company, with the sanction of that other resolution.

(4) Any payment which may be made by a company under this section may, if made before the commencement of any winding-up of the company, be made out of profits of the company which are available for dividend.

PART C—THE LIMITED LIABILITY PARTNERSHIP

CHAPTER 1—NATURE OF LIMITED LIABILITY PARTNERSHIP

746.—(1) A limited liability partnership is a body corporate formed and incorporated under this Act and is a legal entity separate from the partners.

(2) A limited liability partnership shall have perpetual succession.

(3) Any change in the partners of a limited liability partnership does not affect the existence, rights or liabilities of the limited liability partnership.

747. Any individual or body corporate may be a partner in a limited liability partnership provided that an individual shall not be capable of becoming a partner of a limited liability partnership, if he is—

(a) of unsound mind and has been so found by a court in Nigeria or elsewhere ;

(b) an undischarged bankrupt.

748.—(1) Every limited liability partnership shall have at least two partners.

(2) If at any time the number of partners of a limited liability partnership is reduced below two and the limited liability partnership carries on business for more than six months while the number is so reduced, the person, who is the only partner of the limited liability partnership during the time that it carries on business after those six months and has the knowledge of the fact that it is carrying on business with him alone, is liable personally for the obligations of the limited liability partnership incurred during that period.

749.—(1) Every limited liability partnership shall have at least two designated partners who are individuals and at least one of them shall be resident in Nigeria:

Provided that in case of a limited liability partnership in which all the partners are bodies corporate or in which one or more partners are individuals and bodies corporate, at least two individuals who are partners of the limited liability partnership or nominees of the bodies corporate shall act as designated partners.

(2) Subject to the provisions of subsection (1)—

(a) if the incorporation document—

(i) specifies who are to be designated partners, the persons is designated partners on incorporation, or

(ii) states that each of the partners of a limited liability partnership isto be designated partner, every such partner is a designated partner; or (b) any partner may become a designated partner in accordance with the limited liability partnership agreement and a partner may cease to be a designated partner in accordance with the limited liability partnership agreement.

(3) An individual does not become a designated partner in any limited liability partnership unless he has given his prior written consent to act as such to the limited liability partnership.

(4) Every limited liability partnership shall file with the Commission the particulars of every individual who has given his consent to act as designated partner within 30 days of his appointment.

(5) A person ceases to be a designated partner if he ceases to be a partner.

750. Unless expressly provided otherwise in this Act, a designated partner is—

(a) responsible for the doing of all acts, matters and things as are required to be done by the limited liability partnership in respect of compliance of the provisions of this Act including filing of any document, return, statement and other report under this Act and as may be specified in the limited liability partnership agreement ; and

(b) liable to all penalties imposed on the limited liability partnership for any contravention of those provisions.

751. A limited liability partnership shall appoint a designated partner within 30 days of a vacancy arising for any reason and the provisions of section 749 (4) shall apply in respect of such new designated partner: Provided that if no designated partner is appointed, or if at any time there is only one designated partner, each partner is deemed to be a designated partner.

752. If default is made in complying with the provisions of sections749-751 the limited liability partnership and each of its partners is liable to a penalty in the amount as the Commission shall specify in its regulation.

CHAPTER 2—INCORPORATION OF LIMITED LIABILITY PARTNERSHIP AND INCIDENTAL MATTERS

753.—(1) For a limited liability partnership to be incorporated—

(a) two or more persons associated for carrying on a lawful business with a view to profit shall subscribe their names to an incorporation document ; and

(b) the incorporation documents shall be filed in the manner and with the fees, as may be prescribed by the Commission from time to time.

(2) The incorporation documents shall be in the form as prescribed by the Commission and shall—

(a) state the name of the limited liability partnership ;

(b) state the proposed business of the limited liability partnership ;

(c) state the address of the registered office of the limited liability partnership ;

(d) state the name and address of each of the persons who are partners of the limited liability partnership on incorporation ;

(e) state the name and address of the persons who are to be designated partners of the limited liability partnership on incorporation ;

(f) contain other information concerning the proposed limited liability partnership as the Commission may prescribe.

(3) If a person knowingly makes a statement under subsection (2) which is false, he commits an offence and is liable on conviction to imprisonment for a term of three months or a fine as the Court deems fit or both.

Incorporation 754. (1) When the requirements imposed under section 753 (1) and (2) by have been complied with, the Commission shall, within 14 days— registration.

(a) register the incorporation document ; and

(b) give a certificate that the limited liability partnership is incorporated by the name specified in the certificate.

(2) The Commission may accept the statement delivered under section753 (2) (c) as sufficient evidence that the requirement imposed under section 753 (1) (a) has been complied with.

(3) The certificate issued under subsection (1) (b) shall be signed by the Commission and authenticated by its official seal.

(4) The certificate shall state—

(a) the name of the limited liability partnership given in the incorporation document ;

(b) the limited liability partnership's registration number ;

(c) the date of registration ; and

(d) that the limited liability partnership is incorporated as a limited liability partnership under this Act.

(5) The certificate shall be prima facie evidence that the limited liability partnership is incorporated by the name specified in it.

755.—(1) Every limited liability partnership shall have a registered office to which all communications and notices may be addressed and where they shall be received.

(2) A document may be served on a limited liability partnership, partner or designated partner of the partnership by sending it by post under a certificate of posting, registered post or by any other manner as may be prescribed, at the registered office or any other address specifically declared by the limited liability partnership for the purpose in such form and manner as may be prescribed.

(3) A limited liability partnership may by resolution change the place of its registered office.

(4) Where a limited liability partnership changes the place of its registered address, the change shall not take effect unless notice of the change has been delivered to the Commission not later than 14 days after the passing of the resolution.

(5) Where a limited liability partnership makes default in complying with the provisions of this section, the limited liability partnership and each partner shall each be liable to a penalty for every day that the default continues and the penalty shall be in the amount as the Commission shall specify in the regulations.

756. On registration, a limited liability partnership may—

(a) sue and be sued in its name ;

(b) acquire, own, hold and develop or dispose of property, whether movable or immovable, tangible or intangible ;

(c) if it decides to have one, have a common seal,; and

(d) do and suffer such other acts and things as bodies corporate may lawfully do and suffer.

757.—(1) Every limited liability partnership shall have either the words, "limited liability partnership" or the acronym, "LLP" as the last words of its name.

(2) A limited liability partnership shall not be registered by a name which, in the opinion of the Commission is—

(a) undesirable ; or

(b) identical or too nearly resembles that of any other partnership, business name, limited liability partnership, body corporate, or a registered trade mark.

758. The provisions of sections 30 and 31 of this Act are applicable in relation to the reservation of name or change of name of a limited liability partnership.

759. Where a person carries on business under a name or title of which the words "Limited Liability Partnership" or "LLP" or any contraction or imitation is or are the last word or words, that person or each of those persons shall, unless duly incorporated as limited liability partnership, be liable to a penalty in the amount as the Commission shall specify in the regulation.

760.—(1) Every limited liability partnership shall ensure that its invoices, official correspondence and publications bear—

(a) the name, address of its registered office and registration number of the limited liability partnership ; and

(b) a statement that it is registered with limited liability.

(2) Where a limited liability partnership makes default in complying with the provisions of this section, the limited liability partnership and every partner shall each be liable to a penalty for every day the default continues in the amount as the Commission shall specify in the regulation.

CHAPTER 3—PARTNERS AND THEIR RELATIONS

761. On the incorporation of a limited liability partnership, the persons who subscribed their names to the incorporation documents shall be its partners and any other person may become a partner of the limited liability partnership in accordance with the limited liability partnership agreement.

762.—(1) Except as otherwise provided by this Act, the mutual rights and duties of the partners of a limited liability partnership, and the mutual rights and duties of a limited liability partnership and its partners, shall be governed by the limited liability partnership agreement between the partners, or between the limited liability partnership and its partners.

(2) The limited liability partnership agreement and any changes, made in it shall be—

(a) filed with the Commission in the form and manner ; and (b) accompanied by the fees as may be prescribed.

(3) An agreement in writing made before the incorporation of a limited liability partnership between the persons who subscribe their names to the incorporation documents may impose obligations on the limited liability partnership if that agreement is ratified by all the partners after the incorporation of the limited liability partnership.

(4) In the absence of agreement as to any matter, the mutual rights and duties of the partners and the mutual rights and duties of the limited liability partnership and the partners shall be determined by the provisions relating to that matter as are set out in the Fifteenth Schedule.

763.—(1) A person may cease to be a partner of a limited liability partnership in accordance with an agreement with the other partners or, in the absence of agreement with the other partners as to cessation of being a partner, by giving a notice in writing of at least 30 days to the other partners of his intention to resign as partner.

(2) A person shall cease to be a partner of a limited liability partnership—

(a) on his death or dissolution of the limited liability partnership ; or (b) if he is declared to be of unsound mind by a competent court ; or (c) if he has applied to be adjudged or declared as an insolvent.

(3) Where a person has ceased to be a partner of a limited liability partnership (in this Act referred to as "former partner"), the former partner is to be regarded, in relation

to any person dealing with the limited liability partnership as still being a partner of the limited liability partnership unless—

(a) the person has notice that the former partner has ceased to be a partner of the limited liability partnership ; or

(b) notice that the former partner has ceased to be a partner of the limited liability partnership has been delivered to the Commission.

(4) The cessation of a partner from the limited liability partnership does not by itself discharge the partner from any obligation to the limited liability partnership, the other partners or any other person which he incurred while being a partner.

(5) Where a partner of a limited liability partnership ceases to be a partner, unless otherwise provided in the limited liability partnership agreement, the former partner or a person entitled to his share as a result of death or insolvency of the former partner, is entitled to receive from the limited liability partnership—

(a) an amount equal to the capital contribution the former partner actually made to the limited liability partnership ; and

(b) his right to share in the accumulated profits of the limited liability partnership, after the deduction of accumulated losses of the limited liability partnership, determined as at the date the former partner ceased to be a partner.

(6) A former partner or a person entitled to his share as a result of death or insolvency of the former partner shall not have any right to interfere in the management of the limited liability partnership.

764.—(1) Every partner shall inform the limited liability partnership of any change in his name or address within 15 days of the change.

(2) A limited liability partnership shall—

(a) where a person becomes or ceases to be a partner, file a notice with the Commission within 30 days from the date he becomes or ceases to be a partner ; and

(b) where there is a change in the name or address of a partner, file a notice with the Commission within 30 days of the change.

(3) A notice filed with the Commission under subsection (2)—

(a) shall be in such form and accompanied by such fees as may be prescribed ;

(b) shall be signed by the designated partner of the limited liability partnership ; and

(c) if it relates to an incoming partner, shall contain a statement by the partner that he consents to becoming a partner and signed by him.

(4) Where default is made by any limited liability partnership in complying with subsection (2), the limited liability partnership and every designated partner of the limited liability partnership shall each be liable to a penalty for each day the default continues in the amount as the Commission shall specify in its regulations.

(5) If any partner contravenes the provisions of subsection (1), the partner shall be liable to a penalty in such amount as the Commission shall specify in its regulations.

(6) A person who ceases to be a partner of a limited liability partnership may himself file with the Commission the notice referred to in subsection (3) if he has reasonable cause to believe that the limited liability partnership may not file the notice with the Commission and in case of any such notice filed by a partner, the Commission shall obtain a confirmation to this effect from the limited liability partnership unless the limited liability partnership has also filed such notice.

(7) Where no confirmation is given by the limited liability partnership within 15 days, the Commission shall register the notice made by a person ceasing to be a partner under this section.

CHAPTER 4—EXTENT AND LIMITATION OF LIABILITY OF LIMITED LIABILITY PARTNERSHIP AND PARTNERS

765. A partner of a limited liability partnership is, for the purpose of the business of the limited liability partnership, the agent of the limited liability partnership, but not of other partners.

766.—(1) A limited liability partnership is not bound by anything done by a partner in dealing with a person if the—

(a) partner in fact has no authority to act for the limited liability partnership in doing a particular act ; and

(b) person knows that he has no authority, does not know or believe him to be a partner of the limited liability partnership.

(2) A limited liability partnership is liable if a partner of the limited liability partnership is liable to any person as a result of a wrongful act or omission on his part in the course of the business of the limited liability partnership or with its authority.

(3) An obligation of the limited liability partnership whether arising in contract or otherwise, shall be solely the obligation of the limited liability partnership.

(4) The liabilities of a limited liability partnership shall be met out of the property of the limited liability partnership.

767.—(1) A partner is not personally liable, directly or indirectly for an obligation referred to in section 766 (3) solely by reason of being a partner of the limited liability partnership.

(2) The provisions of section 766 (3) and subsection (1) of this section shall not affect the personal liability of a partner for his own wrongful act or omission, and a partner shall not be personally liable for the wrongful act or omission of any other partner of the limited liability partnership.

768.—(1) A person who by words spoken or written or by conduct, represents himself, or knowingly permits himself to be represented to be a partner in a limited liability partnership is liable to any person who has on the faith of the representation given credit to the limited liability partnership, whether the person representing himself or represented to be a partner does or does not know that the representation has reached the person giving credit : Provided that where any credit is received by the limited liability partnership as a result of representation in subsection (1), the limited liability partnership shall, without prejudice to the liability of the person so representing himself or represented to be a partner, be liable to the extent of credit received by it or any financial benefit derived thereon.

(2) Where after a partner's death the business is continued in the same limited liability partnership name, the continued use of that name or of the deceased partner's name as a part thereof shall not of itself make his legal representative or his estate liable for any act of the limited liability partnership done after his death.

769.—(1) In the event of an act carried out by a limited liability partnership, or any of its partners, with intent to defraud creditors of the limited liability partnership or any other person, or for any fraudulent purpose, the liability of the limited liability partnership and partners who acted with intent to defraud creditors or for any fraudulent purpose shall be unlimited for all or any of the debts or other liabilities of the limited liability partnership:

Provided that where any act is carried out by a partner, the limited liability partnership is liable to the same extent as the partner unless it is established by the limited liability partnership that the act was carried out without the knowledge or the authority of the limited liability partnership.

(2) Where any business is carried on with such intent or for such purpose as mentioned in subsection (1), every person who was knowingly a party to the carrying on of the business in the manner stated, commits an offence and is liable on conviction to imprisonment for a term which may extend to two years or a fine as the court deems fit or to both.

(3) Where a limited liability partnership or any partner or designated partner or employee of the limited liability partnership has conducted the affairs of the limited liability partnership in a fraudulent manner, then without prejudice to any criminal proceedings which may arise under any law for the time being in force, the limited liability partnership and any such partner or designated partner or employee shall be liable to pay compensation to any person who has suffered any loss or damage by reason of the conduct, but the limited liability partnership shall not be liable if any such partner or designated partner or employee has acted fraudulently without the knowledge of the limited liability partnership.

CHAPTER 5—CONTRIBUTIONS

770.—(1) A partner's contribution may consist of tangible, intangible, movable, immovable or property or other benefit to the limited liability partnership, including money, promissory notes, other agreements to contribute cash or property, and contracts for services performed or to be performed.

(2) The monetary value of contribution of each partner shall be accounted for and disclosed in the accounts of the limited liability partnership in the manner as may be prescribed.

771.—(1) An obligation of a partner to contribute money, property or other benefit or to perform services for a limited liability partnership shall be in accordance with the limited liability partnership agreement.

(2) A creditor of a limited liability partnership, which extends credit or otherwise acts in reliance on an obligation described in that agreement, without notice of any compromise between partners, may enforce the original obligation against such partner.

CHAPTER 6—FINANCIAL DISCLOSURES

772.—(1) The limited liability partnership shall maintain such proper books of account as may be prescribed relating to its affairs for each year of its existence on cash basis or accrual basis and according to double entry system of accounting and shall maintain the same at its registered office for such period as may be prescribed.

(2) Every limited liability partnership shall, within six months from the end of each financial year, prepare a statement of account and solvency for the financial year as at the last day of the financial year in such form as may be prescribed, and the statement shall be signed by the designated partners of the limited liability partnership.

(3) A limited liability partnership shall file within the prescribed time, the Statement of Account and Solvency prepared under subsection (2) with the Commission every year in the form and manner and accompanied by the fees as may be prescribed.

(4) The accounts of limited liability partnerships shall be audited in accordance with such rules as may be prescribed and the Minister may, by regulation, exempt any class or classes of limited liability partnerships from the requirements of this subsection.

(5) Where default is made in complying with the provisions of this section, the limited liability partnership and each designated partner of the limited liability partnership shall each be liable to a penalty in such amount as the Commission shall specify in its regulations.

773.—(1) A limited liability partnership shall file an annual return with the Commission within 60 days of closure of its financial year in the form and manner and accompanied by such fee as may be prescribed.

(2) Where default is made in complying with the provisions of this section, the limited liability partnership and each designated partner of the limited liability partnership shall each be liable to a penalty in such amount as the Commission shall specify in its regulations.

CHAPTER 7—ASSIGNMENT AND TRANSFER OF PARTNERSHIP RIGHTS

774.—(1) Unless otherwise provided in the limited liability partnership agreement, the rights of a partner to a share of the profits and losses of a limited liability partnership and to receive distributions in accordance with the limited liability partnership agreement are transferable either wholly or in part.

(2) The transfer of any right by any partner under subsection (1) does not by itself cause the disassociation of the partner or a dissolution and winding up of the limited liability partnership.

(3) The transfer of a right under this section does not, by itself, entitle the transferee or assignee to participate in the management or conduct of the activities of the limited liability partnership, or grant access to information concerning the transactions of the limited liability partnership.

CHAPTER 8—INVESTIGATION

775.—(1) Where a court, by order, declares that the affairs of a limited liability partnership ought to be investigated, the Commission shall appoint one or more competent persons as inspectors to investigate the affairs of a limited liability partnership and to report thereon in such manner as it may direct.

(2) Notwithstanding the provisions of subsection (1), the Commission may appoint one or more competent persons as inspectors to investigate the affairs of a limited liability partnership and to report on them in such manner as it may direct.

(3) The appointment of inspectors under subsection (2) may only be made if—

(a) at least one-fifth of the total number of partners of the limited liability partnership make an application along with supporting evidence and security amount as may be prescribed ;

(b) the limited liability partnership makes an application that the affairs of the limited liability partnership ought to be investigated ; or

(c) in the opinion of the Commission, there are circumstances suggesting—

(i) that the business of the limited liability partnership is being or has been conducted with an intent to defraud its creditors, partners or any other person, or otherwise for a fraudulent or unlawful purpose,

(ii) that the business of the limited liability partnership is being or has been conducted in a manner oppressive or unfairly prejudicial to some or any of its partners, or that the limited liability partnership was formed for any fraudulent or unlawful purpose,

(iii) that the affairs of the limited liability partnership are not being conducted in line with the provisions of this Act, or

(iv) that, on receipt of a report of the Commission or any other investigating or regulatory agency, there are sufficient reasons to show that the affairs of the limited liability partnership ought to be investigated.

776. An application by the partners of the limited liability partnership under section 775 (3) shall be supported by such evidence as the Commission may require for the purpose of showing that the applicants have good reason for requiring the investigation and the Commission may, before appointing an inspector, require the applicants to give security, of such amount as may be prescribed, for payment of costs of the investigation.

777. No firm, body corporate or other association shall be appointed asan inspector.

778.—(1) If an inspector appointed by the Commission to investigate the affairs of a limited liability partnership thinks it necessary for the purposes of his investigation to also investigate the affairs of an entity which has been associated in the past or is presently associated with the limited liability partnership or any present or former partner or designated partner of the limited liability partnership, the inspector shall have the power to do so and shall report on the affairs of the other entity or partner or designated partner, so far as he thinks that the results of his investigation are relevant to the investigation of the affairs of the limited liability partnership.

(2) In the case of any entity or partner or designated partner referred to in subsection (1), the inspector shall not exercise the power of investigating into, and reporting on, its or his affairs without obtaining the prior approval of the Commission.

(3) Before giving approval under this subsection, the Commission shall give the entity, partner or designated partner a reasonable opportunity to show cause why the approval should not be accorded.

779.—(1) The designated partner and partners of the limited liability partnership shall—

(a) preserve and produce before an inspector or any person authorised by him in that behalf with the or approval of the Commission, all books and papers of, or relating to, the limited liability partnership or the other entity, as the case may be, which are in their custody or power ; and

(b) give the inspector all assistance in connection with the investigation which they are reasonably able to give.

(2) The inspector may, with the previous approval of the Commission, require any entity, other than an entity referred to in subsection (1), to furnish such information to, or produce such books and papers before him or any person authorised by him in that behalf, with the previous approval of the Commission, as he may consider necessary, if the furnishing of such information or the production of such books and papers is relevant or necessary for the purposes of his investigation.

(3) The inspector may keep in his custody any books and papers produced under subsections (1) or (2) for 30 days and thereafter shall return the same to the limited liability partnership, other entity or individual by whom or on whose behalf the books and papers are produced :

Provided that the inspector may call for the books and papers if they are needed again and that if certified copies of the books and papers produced under subsection (2) are furnished to the inspector, he shall return those books and papers to the entity or person concerned.

(4) An inspector may—

(a) examine on oath—

(i) any of the persons referred to in subsection (1),

(ii) with the prior approval of the Commission, any other person in relation to the affairs of the limited liability partnership or any other entity, as the case may be; and

(b) administer an oath accordingly and for that purpose may require any of those persons to appear before him personally ;

(c) if any person fails without reasonable cause or refuses to—

(i) produce before an inspector or any person authorised by him in that behalf, with the prior approval of the Commission, any book or paper which it is his duty under subsections (1) or (2) to produce,

(ii) furnish any information which is his duty under subsection (2) to furnish,

(iii) appear before the inspector personally when required to do so under this subsection or to answer any question which is put to him by the inspector under that subsection, or

(iv) to sign the notes of any examination, the inspector shall certify the refusal in writing and apply to the Court for contempt proceedings against the person, the Court may thereupon enquire into the case, and after hearing any witnesses who may be produced against or on behalf of the alleged offender or any statement which may be offered in defence, the Court may punish the offender in like manner as if he had been guilty of contempt of the court.

(5) The notes of any examination under subsection (4) shall be written and signed by the person whose examination was made on oath and a copy of such notes shall be given to the person so examined on oath and thereafter be used as evidence by the inspector.

780.—(1) Where in the course of investigation, the inspector has reasonable ground to believe that the books and papers of, or relating to, the limited liability partnership, other entity, partner or designated partner of such limited liability partnership may be destroyed, mutilated, altered, falsified or secreted, the inspector may make an application to the Court having jurisdiction, for an order for the seizure of such books and papers.

(2) After considering the application and hearing the inspector, if necessary, the court may, by order, authorise the inspector to—

(a) enter, with such assistance, as may be required, the place or places where such books and papers are kept ;

(b) search that place or those places in the manner specified in the order ; and

(c) seize books and papers which the inspector considers necessary for the purposes of his investigation.

(3) The inspector shall keep in his custody the books and papers seized under this section for such period not later than the conclusion of the investigation as he considers necessary and thereafter shall return the same to the concerned entity or person from whose custody or power they were seized and inform the court of such return, provided the books and papers shall not be seized for a continuous period of more than six months and the inspector may, before returning the books and papers as, place identification marks on them or any part thereof.

781.—(1) The Inspector may, and if so directed by the Commission, make interim reports to the Commission, and shall, on the conclusion of the investigation, make a final report to the Commission and any such report shall be printed.

(2) The Commission—

(a) shall forward a copy of any report other than an interim report, made by the inspectors to the limited liability partnership at its registered office, and also to any other entity or person dealt with or related to the report ; and

(b) may, if it deems fit, furnish a copy of the report, on request and on payment of the prescribed fee, to any person or entity related to or affected by the report.

782.—(1) If, from any report made under section 781 of this Act, it appears to the Commission that any civil proceedings ought in the public interest to be brought by the limited liability partnership or anybody corporate, the Commission may itself bring such proceedings in the name and on behalf of the limited liability partnership or the body corporate.

(2) The Commission shall indemnify the body corporate against any cost or expenses incurred by it or in connection with proceedings brought under this section, and any cost or expenses so incurred shall, if not otherwise recoverable, be defrayed out of the Consolidated Revenue Fund.

783. (1) If, from any report made under section 781 of this Act, it appears that a person has been convicted of an offence for which he is criminally liable, the report shall be referred to the Attorney-General of the Federation.

(2) Where the Attorney-General of the Federation considers that the case referred to him is one in which a prosecution ought to be instituted, he shall direct action accordingly, and all past and present officers and agents of the limited liability partnership or other body corporate, as the case may be, other than the defendant in the proceedings, shall give all assistance in connection with the prosecution which they are reasonably able to give.

(3) Where, from any report made under section 781 of this Act, it appears to the Commission that proceedings ought, in the public interest, to be brought by any body corporate dealt with by the report for the recovery of damages, in respect of fraud, misfeasance or other misconduct in connection with the promotion or formation of that body corporate or the management of its affairs, or for the recovery of any property of the body corporate which has been misapplied or wrongfully retained, it may refer the case to the Attorney-General of the Federation for his opinion as to the bringing of proceedings for that purpose in the name of the body corporate if proceedings are brought, all past and present officers and agents of the limited liability partnership or other body corporate as the case may be, other than the defendants in proceedings, to give him all assistance in connection with the proceedings which they are reasonably able to give.

(4) Cost and expenses incurred by a body corporate in or in connection with any proceedings brought by it under subsection (3) shall, if not otherwise recoverable, be defrayed out of the Consolidated Revenue Fund.

784. If, in the case of a body corporate liable to be wound up under this Act, it appears to the Commission from a report made by an inspector under section 781 of this Act that it is expedient in the public interest that the body corporate should be wound up, the Commission may, unless the body corporate is already wound up by the court present a petition for it to be wound up if the Court deems it just and equitable to do so.

785.—(1) The expenses of, and incidental to, an investigation by an inspector appointed by the Commission under the foregoing provisions of this Act, shall be defrayed in the first instance out of the Consolidated Revenue Fund, but the following persons shall, to the extent mentioned, be liable to repay—

(a) any person who is convicted in a prosecution instituted, as a result of the investigation report by the Attorney-General of the Federation, or who is ordered to pay damages or restore any property in proceedings brought by virtue of section 783 (3) of this Act, may in the same proceedings be ordered to pay the said expenses to such extent as specified in the order;

(b) a body corporate in whose name proceedings are brought as aforesaid is liable to the extent of the amount or value of any sums or property recovered by it as a result of those proceedings ;

(c) unless as the result of the investigation a prosecution is instituted by the Attorney-General of the Federation, the applicants for the investigation, where the inspector was appointed under section 775 (3) of this Act, shall be liable to such extent, if any, as the Commission may direct, and any amount for which a body corporate is liable by virtue of paragraph (b), shall be a first charge on the sums or property mentioned in that paragraph.

(2) For the purposes of this section, any costs or expenses incurred by the Commission in or in connection with proceedings brought by virtue of section 781 (2) of this Act, shall be treated as expenses of the investigation giving rise to the proceedings.

(3) Expenses to be defrayed by the Commission under this section shall, so far as not recovered thereunder, be paid out of the Consolidated Revenue Fund.

786. Where a limited liability partnership is liable to be wound up under this Act or any other law for the time being in force, it appears to the Commission from a report under section 781 that it is expedient to do so, the Commission may, unless the limited liability partnership is already being wound up by the court, cause to be presented to the court by any person authorised by the Commission in that behalf, a petition for the winding-up of the limited liability partnership on the ground that it is just and equitable that it should be wound up.

787. A copy of the report of any inspector or inspectors appointed under the provisions of this Act, authenticated in such manner, as may be prescribed shall be admissible in any legal proceeding as evidence in relation to any matter contained in the report.

CHAPTER 9—FOREIGN LIMITED LIABILITY PARTNERSHIP

788.—(1) A foreign limited liability partnership which before or after the commencement of this Act was incorporated outside Nigeria, and having the intention of carrying on business in Nigeria, shall take all steps necessary to be incorporated as a separate entity in Nigeria for that purpose, but until so incorporated, the foreign limited liability partnership shall not carry on business in Nigeria or exercise any of the powers of a corporate body registered under this Act and shall not have a place of business or an address for service of documents or processes in Nigeria for any purpose other than the receipt of notices and other documents, as matters preliminary to incorporation under this Act.

(2) The Minister may, by regulation, exempt a foreign limited liability partnership from the requirement of incorporation under subsection (1).

CHAPTER 10—WINDING-UP AND DISSOLUTION

789. The winding-up of a limited liability partnership may be either voluntary or by the Court and limited liability partnership, so wound up may be dissolved.

790. A limited liability partnership may be wound up by the Court if—

(a) all the partners decide that the limited liability partnership be so wound-up by the Court ;

(b) for a period of more than six months, the number of partners of the limited liability partnership falls below two ;

(c) the limited liability partnership is unable to pay its debts ;

(d) the limited liability partnership has acted against the interests of the sovereignty and integrity of Nigeria or against her security or public order ;

(e) the limited liability partnership has made a default in filing with the Commission, the Statement of Account and Solvency or annual return for any 10 consecutive financial years ; or

(f) the Court is of the opinion that it is just and equitable that the limited liability partnership be wound up.

CHAPTER 11—MISCELLANEOUS

791.—(1) A person with significant control over a limited liability partnership shall within seven days of becoming such a person, indicate to the limited liability partnership in writing the particulars of such control.

(2) A limited liability partnership after receiving or coming into possession of the information required under subsection (1), shall, not later than one month from the receipt of the information or any change therein, notify the Commission of that information, provided that a company shall in every annual return, disclose the information required under subsection (1) in respect of the year for which the return is made.

(3) The Commission shall maintain a register of persons with significant control in which it shall enter the information received from the limited liability partnership or any change therein under subsection (2).

(4) A limited liability partnership shall inscribe against the name of every member in the register of members, the information received in pursuance of the requirements of this section.

(5) If default is made by any person or limited liability partnership in complying with subsections (1), (2) and (4), the person or limited liability partnership and each officer of the limited liability partnership is liable to such fines as the Commission may prescribe by regulation for every day during which the default continues.

(6) If default is made by any partner in complying with subsection (1) or in purported compliance, makes any statement which he knows to be false in a material particular or recklessly makes any statement which is false, he commits an offence and is liable to a term of imprisonment for six months or a fine as the court deems fit.

(7) If default is made by any limited liability partnership in complying with subsection (3), the limited liability partnership and each officer of the limited liability partnership is liable to a penalty in such amount as the Commission shall specify in its regulations for every day during which the default continues.

792. A partner may lend money to and transact other business with the limited liability partnership and has the same rights and obligations with respect to the loan or other transactions as a person who is not a partner.

793. Where the Commission has reasonable cause to believe that a limited liability partnership is not carrying on business or operation, in accordance with the provisions of this Act, the name of limited liability partnership may be struck off the register of limited liability partnerships in accordance with the procedures provided under section 692 of this Act.

Power of Commission to strike defunct limited liability partnership off register.

. 794. The Commission may make rules or regulations concerning any of the following matters—

(a) the fees to be paid to the Commission under this Part ;

(b) the duties or additional duties to be performed by the Commission for the purposes of this Part ;

(c) the forms to be used for the purposes of this Part ; and

(d) generally the conduct and regulation of registration under this Part and any matter incidental thereto.

PART D—THE LIMITED PARTNERSHIP

CHAPTER 1—NATURE OF LIMITED PARTNERSHIP

795.—(1) Limited partnerships may be formed in the manner and subject to the conditions set out in this Part.

(2) A limited partnership shall not consist of more than 20 persons.

(3) A limited partnership shall consist of one or more persons called general partners, who shall be liable for all debts and obligations of the firm, and one or more persons called limited partners.

(4) Each limited partner shall at the time of entering into the partnership contribute, or agree to contribute, thereto a sum or sums as capital or property valued at a stated amount and shall not be liable for the debts of obligations of the firm, beyond the amount so contributed or agreed to be contributed :

Provided that a limited partner is not under obligation to contribute any capital or property to the partnership where the partners have so agreed in writing.

(5) Unless otherwise agreed in writing by the partners, a limited partner shall not, during the continuance of the partnership, either directly or indirectly, draw out or receive back any part of his contribution and if he draws, out or receives back any such part, is liable for the debts and obligations of the partnership up to the amount so drawn out or received back.

796. An individual or body corporate may be a partner in a limited partnership: Provided that an individual shall not become a partner of a limited partnership, if he is—

(a) of unsound mind and has been so found by a court in Nigeria or elsewhere ; or

(b) an undischarged bankrupt.

CHAPTER 2—REGISTRATION OF LIMITED PARTNERSHIP AND INCIDENTAL MATTERS

797.—(1) A partnership carrying on business as a limited partnership must be registered as such in accordance with the provisions of this Part.

(2) A partnership not registered as prescribed in subsection (1) shall be deemed to be a general partnership and every limited partner shall be deemed to be a general partner.

798.—(1) An application for registration as a limited partnership shall be in the form as prescribed by the Commission and shall—

(a) specify the name under which the limited partnership is to be registered ;
(b) be signed or otherwise authenticated by or on behalf of each partner, and
(c) include a statement containing the details listed in subsection (2).

(2) The application for registration of a limited partnership shall include a statement signed by the partners which shall contain —

(a) the name of the limited partnership ;
(b) the general nature of the business ;
(c) the principal place of business ;
(d) the full name and address of each general partner ;
(e) the full name and address of each limited partner ;
(f) the term if any, for which the partnership is entered into and the date of its commencement ;
(g) a statement that the partnership is limited and the description of every limited partner as such ; and
(h) the sum contributed, or agreed to be contributed by each limited partner and whether paid, or to be paid in cash or in another specified form.

799.—(1) When the requirements imposed by section 798 (1) and (2) have been complied with, the Commission shall,— (a) register the limited partnership ; and (b) issue a certificate of registration.

(2) The certificate shall be signed by the Commission and authenticated by his official seal.

(3) The certificate shall state—

(a) the name of the limited partnership given in the application for registration ;
(b) the limited partnership's registration number ;
(c) the date of registration ; and
(d) that the limited partnership is registered as a limited partnership under this Act.

(4) The certificate shall be prima facie evidence that a limited partnership came into existence on the date of registration.

800.—(1) If during the continuance of a limited partnership any change is made or occurs in the—

(a) firm,
(b) general nature of the business,
(c) principal place of business,
(d) partners or the name of any partner,
(e) terms or character of the partnership,
(f) sum contributed or to be contributed by any limited partner, or
(g) liability of any partner by reason of his becoming a limited partner instead of a general partner or a general partner instead of a limited partner, a statement signed

by the firm specifying the nature of the change shall within seven days be delivered to the Commission.

(2) If default is made in compliance with the requirements of this section, each of the general partners is liable to a fine as shall be prescribed by the Commission in its regulations.

801.—(1) Notice of any arrangement or transaction under which a person will cease to be a general partner in a firm and will become a limited partner in that firm or under which the share of a limited partner in a firm will be assigned to any person shall, be filed with the Commission within five days of such change.

(2) Until the notice of the arrangement or transaction referred to in subsection (1) is filed with the Commission, the arrangement or transaction shall for the purposes of this Part, be deemed to be of no effect.

(3) If default is made in compliance with the requirements of subsection (1), each of the general partners is liable to a fine as shall be prescribed by the Commission in its Regulations.

802. The name of a limited partnership must end with the words "limited partnership" (upper or lower case, or any combination), or the abbreviation "LP" (upper or lower case, or any combination, with or without punctuation).

.(2) A limited partnership shall not be dissolved by the death or bankruptcy of a limited partner and the lunacy of a limited partner shall not be a ground for the dissolution of the partnership by the Court, unless the lunatic's share cannot be otherwise ascertained and realised.

(3) In the event of the dissolution of a limited partnership its affairs shall be wound up by the general partners unless the Court orders otherwise.

(4) Subject to any agreement, express or implied, between the partners—

(a) any difference arising as to ordinary matters connected with the partnership business may be decided by a majority of the general partners ;

(b) a limited partner may, with the consent of the general partners, assign his share in the partnership and upon such an assignment the assignee shall become a limited partner with all the rights of the assignor ;

(c) the other partners shall not be entitled to dissolve the partnership by reason of any limited partner suffering his share to be charged for his separate debt ;

(d) a person may be introduced as a partner without the consent of the existing limited partners ; and

(e) a limited partner shall not be entitled to dissolve the partnership by notice.

807. The provisions of Part C of this Act relating to limited liability partnerships shall apply to limited partnership except so far as they are inconsistent with the express provisions of this Part.

808. Subject to the provisions of this Act, the provisions of the Partnership Act 1890, except so far as they are inconsistent with the express provisions of this Act, shall apply to limited partnerships.

809.—(1) A person may inspect the statements filed by the Commission upon payment of such fees as maybe prescribed by the Commission in its regulations and any person may require a certificate of the registration of a limited partnership or a copy of an extract from any registered statement, to be certified by the Registrar.

(2) A certificate of registration or a copy of an extract from any statement registered under this Part, if duly certified to be a true copy under the hand of the Registrar,

whom it shall not be necessary to prove to be the Registrar shall, in all legal proceedings, civil or criminal, and in all cases be received in evidence.

810. If any statement required to be furnished under this Part of this Act contains any matter which is false to the knowledge of any person signing it, such person commits an offence and is liable on conviction to imprisonment for a term of not more than one year or a fine as the Court deems fit and in addition, he shall be liable to pay such additional fines as the Commission may specify by regulation.

PART E—BUSINESS NAMES

CHAPTER 1—ESTABLISHMENT OF BUSINESS NAMES REGISTRY: APPOINTMENT AND FUNCTIONS OF HEAD OF OFFICE AND OTHER OFFICERS

811. There shall be established in each State of the Federation, a registry of business names where there shall be kept a register in the prescribed form in which shall be entered such matters as are required by this Act or any regulation made under it to be entered in it.

812.—(1) The Registrar-General appointed under section 9 of this Act shall be the Registrar of Business Names.

(2) Suitable staff of the Commission may be appointed from time to time to be head of office and other officers of the Business Names Registry in each State of the Federation as may be necessary for the administration of this Part of this Act.

813.—(1) The Registrar shall cause business names to be registered in accordance with the provisions of this part of this Act.

(2) For the purpose of the registration under this Part, of the business names of a firm, individual or corporation at any of the offices for business names, any head of office may, subject to any direction that the Commission may give, perform any act or discharge any duty which the Registrar may lawfully perform or discharge or is required by this Act to perform or discharge, and, subject to that, any reference in this Part to the Registrar, unless the context otherwise admits, shall accordingly be deemed to include a reference to a head of office.

(3) Without prejudice to the generality of the foregoing provisions of subsection (1), a head of office may be assigned to the Business Names Registry in a State for the purpose of registering business names and keeping a register of business names.

CHAPTER 2—REGISTRATION OF BUSINESS NAMES

814.—(1) Every individual, firm or Corporation having a place of business in Nigeria and carrying on business under a business name shall be registered in the manner provided in this Part if—

(a) in the case of a firm, the name does not consist of the true surname of all partners without any addition other than the true forenames of the individual partners or the initials of such forenames ;

(b) in the case of an individual, the name does not consist of his true surname without any addition other than his true forenames or the initials thereof ; or

(c) in the case of a company, whether or not registered under this Act, the name does not consist of its corporate name without any addition.

(2) Notwithstanding subsection (1) where —

(a) the addition merely indicates that the business is carried on in succession to a former owner of the business, that addition shall not of itself render registration necessary;

(b) two or more individual partners have the same surname, the addition of an "s" at the end of that surname shall not of itself render registration necessary ; and

(c) the business is carried on by a receiver or manager appointed by any court, registration shall not be necessary.

815.—(1) Every individual, firm or company required under this Act to be registered shall, within 28 days after the individual, firm or corporation commences the business in respect of which registration is required, furnish to the Registrar at the registry in the State in which the principal place of business of the individual, firm or company is situated, a statement in writing in the prescribed form, signed as required by this section and containing the following particulars—

(a) the business name or, if the business is carried on under two or more business names, each of those business names ;

(b) the general nature of the business ;

(c) the full postal address of the principal place of business ;

(d) the full postal address of every other place of business ;

(e) where the registration to be effected is that of a firm—

(i) the present forenames and surname, any former forenames or surname, the nationality and, if that nationality is not the nationality of origin, the nationality of origin, the age, the sex, the usual residence and any other business occupation of each of the individuals who are partners ; and

(ii) the corporate name and registered office of such company which is a partner ;

(f) where the registration to be effected is that of an individual, the present forenames and surname, any former forenames or surnames, the nationality and, if that nationality is not the nationality of origin, the nationality of origin, the age, the sex, the usual residence and any other business occupation of the individual ;

(g) where the registration to be effected is that of a company, the name and registered office of the company ; and

(h) the date of commencement of the business, whether before or after the coming into operation of this Act.

(2) Where the registration to be effected is that of an individual or a firm, some or all of whose partners are individuals, there shall be submitted to the Registrar copies of the passport photographs of the individual certified in a manner required by the Registrar.

(3) Where the registration to be effected is that of a firm or individual carrying on business on behalf of another individual, firm or corporation whether as nominee or trustee, the statement required by subsection (1) to be furnished shall contain the following particulars in addition to the particulars required by that subsection—

(a) the present forenames and surname, any former forenames or surname, the nationality and, if that nationality is not the nationality of origin, the nationality of origin and the usual residence of each individual on whose behalf the business is carried on ; and

(b) the name of each firm or corporation on whose behalf the business is carried on.

(4) Where the registration to be effected is that of a firm or individual carrying on business as general agent for any concern carrying on business outside Nigeria and not having a place of business in Nigeria, the statement required by subsection (1) to be furnished shall, in addition to the particulars required by that subsection, state the name and full postal address of each such concern, provided that in the case of

a firm or individual carrying on business as general agent for three or more such concerns, it shall be sufficient to state the fact that the business is so carried on and the countries in which the concerns carry on business.

(5) A statement furnished in accordance with subsections (1) - (4) shall in the case of a—

(a) statement furnished by an individual, be signed by him ;

(b) statement furnished by a firm, be signed by each individual who is a partner and by a director or the secretary of each Corporation which is partner ; and

(c) corporation, be signed by a director or the secretary :

Provided that, if the statement is accompanied by a statutory declaration made by any person to the effect that he is a partner of the firm or is a director or the secretary of a corporation which is a partner of the firm, the statement may be signed by that person alone.

(6) A statement furnished in accordance with subsections (1) - (4) by an individual who is a minor or by a firm of which one of the partners is a minor shall, in addition to the requirements of subsection (1), be signed by a magistrate, legal practitioner or police officer of, or above the rank of Assistant Superintendent of Police.

(7) If an individual, firm or corporation makes default in complying with the provisions of this section, the individual, corporation or every partner in the firm commits an offence and is liable on conviction to a fine prescribed in the Commission's regulations for every day during which the default continues, and the Court shall order a statement of the required particulars to be furnished to the Registrar within such time as may be specified in the order.

816.—(1) On receipt by the Registrar of the statement of particulars required to be furnished under section 815 of this Act, he shall, subject to subsection (2) and to the provisions of any regulations made under this Act, cause to be entered in the register the business name of the individual, company or firm and file the statement.

(2) The Registrar shall add to the business name in the register the identification letters of the State which shall be in brackets at the end of the business name, and these shall form part of the business name.

817.—(1) On the registration of any individual, firm or corporation under this Act, the Registrar shall issue a certificate in the prescribed form containing the business name of the individual, firm or corporation.

(2) On the registration of any change in the particulars registered in respect of any firm, corporation or individual, the Registrar may in his discretion either amend the certificate previously issued or issue a fresh certificate.

(3) A certificate issued under this section shall be sent by registered post or delivered to an individual, firm or corporation registering, who shall thereupon exhibit and thereafter maintain the same in a conspicuous position at the principal place of the business so registered:

Provided that—

(a) where a fresh certificate has been issued under subsection (2), the provisions of this subsection shall apply to such fresh certificate ; and

(b) where any certificate has been lost or destroyed or rendered illegible, a copy of such certificate certified by the Registrar may be exhibited in place of the original.

(4) Where an individual, firm or corporation registered under this Act has more than one place of business, the original certificate shall be exhibited and maintained as

required by subsection (3) at the principal place of business and a copy of the certificate certified by the Registrar shall be exhibited and thereafter maintained in a conspicuous position in each of the other places of business.

(5) If an individual, firm or company makes default in complying with the provisions of subsection (3) or subsection (4), the individual, corporation or every partner in the firm is liable to a penalty for every day during which the default continues, the penalty shall be determined in accordance with regulations made by the Commission from time to time.

818. (1) Whenever a change is made or occurs in the particulars required by section 815 of this Act to be furnished in respect of any individual, firm or corporation registered under that section, other than particulars as to the age of an individual, the individual, firm or corporation shall within 28 days after such change notify the change to the registrar.

(2) The notice required under subsection (1) shall be in writing signed as provided in section 815 of this Act.

(3) If an individual, firm or corporation makes default in complying with the provisions of this section, the individual, corporation or every partner in the firm is liable to a penalty for every day during which the default continues, the penalty shall be determined in accordance with regulations made by the Commission from time to time.

CHAPTER 3—REMOVAL OF BUSINESS NAME FROM REGISTER

819.—(1) If an individual, firm or corporation registered under this Act ceases to carry on business, it shall be the duty of the individual or if he is dead, his personal representative, or of a partner in the firm at the time it ceased to carry on business, the director or liquidator of the corporation, within three months after the business has ceased to be carried on, to send by post or deliver to the Registrar a notice, stating that the individual, firm or corporation has ceased to carry on business.

(2) On receipt of such a notice as mentioned in subsection (1), the Registrar may remove the individual, firm or corporation from the register.

(3) Where the Registrar has reasonable cause to believe that any individual, firm or corporation registered under this Act is not carrying on business, he may send a notice by registered post to the individual, firm or corporation, unless an answer is received to such notice within two months from the date thereof, the individual, firm or corporation may be removed from the register.

(4) If the Registrar either receives an answer from the individual, firm or corporation to the effect that the individual, firm or corporation is not carrying on business or does not within two months from the date of the notice receive an answer, he may remove the individual, firm or corporation from the register.

(5) If any person whose duty it is under subsection (1) to give notice that any individual, firm or corporation has ceased to carry on business fails to comply with the provisions of that subsection, he commits an offence and is liable on conviction to a fine in such amount as the Commission shall specify in its regulations.

CHAPTER 4—MISCELLANEOUS AND SUPPLEMENTAL

820.—(1) Every individual, firm or corporation required by this Act to of true be registered shall in all trade catalogues, trade circulars, show cards, name. complimentary cards, notices, bills of exchange, promissory notes, endorsements, cheques, orders for money or goods, invoices, receipts, letters of credits, advertisements, business letters and other official documents issued or sent by the individual or firm to any person, have mentioned in legible characters—

(a) in the case of an individual, his present forenames or the initials thereof and present surname and any former forenames or surname and his nationality ; and

(b) in the case of a firm, the present forenames or the initials thereof and present surname, and any former forenames or surnames and the nationality of all the partners in the firm or in the case of a company being a partner, the corporate name ; and

(c) the registration number of the business name.

(2) Without prejudice to section 19, the provisions of subsection (1) do not apply in relation to a document issued by a firm with more than 20 partners if the following conditions are met—

(a) the partnership maintains at its principal place of business a list of names of all the partners ;

(b) no partners' name appears in the document, except in text or as a signatory ; and

(c) the document states in legible characters the address of the firm's principal place of business and that the list of the partner's names is open to inspection there.

(3) Where a firm maintains a list of the partners' names for the purposes of this section, any person may inspect the list during ordinary business hours.

(4) Any member of the firm, who, without reasonable justification, refuses or sanctions the refusal of an inspection required by a person in accordance with this section, commits an offence and is liable to a fine in such amount as the Commission shall specify in its regulations.

(5) Where an individual referred to in subsection (1) is a minor, the words "a minor" shall be added, in brackets, after his name.

(6) If an individual, firm or corporation fails to comply with this section, the individual or each partner in the firm is liable to a penalty in such amount as the Commission shall specify in its regulations.

821. Where any firm or individual required under this Act to furnish a statement of particulars or of any change in particulars, makes default in so doing, the rights of such defaulter under or arising out of any contract made or entered into by or on behalf of such defaulter in relation to the business in respect of which particulars where required at any time while he is in default, shall not be enforceable by action or other legal proceedings either in the business name or otherwise:

Provided that—

(a) the defaulter may apply to a High Court in which any such contract would otherwise be enforceable for relief against the disability imposed by this section and a High Court in which any such contract would otherwise be enforceable, on being satisfied that the default was accidental, or due to inadvertence, or some other sufficient cause, or that on other grounds it is just and equitable to grant relief, may grant such relief either generally as regards all contracts enforceable by the court or as respect any particular contract and on such conditions as the court may impose ; and

(b) nothing shall prejudice the rights of any other parties as against the defaulter in respect of such contract, if any action or proceeding shall be commenced by any other party against the defaulter to enforce the rights of such party in respect of such contract, nothing shall preclude the defaulter from enforcing in that action or proceeding by way of counterclaim, set-off or otherwise such rights as he may have against that party in respect of such contract.

822.—(1) Every individual, firm or corporation carrying on business under a registered business name shall, not later than the 30th day of June in each year, except the calendar year in which the business name is registered, deliver to the Commission a return in a prescribed form showing the particulars of the individual, firm or corporation and the nature of the business carried on.

(2) The returns shall be accompanied by the financial statement of the individual, firm or corporation in the business during the preceding period of January 1 to December 31.

(3) The returns and the accompanying financial statement shall be signed, in the case of an individual or firm consisting only of individuals, by the individuals and in the case of a corporation or a partner who is a corporation, by a director and the secretary.

(4) Every individual, firm or corporation that fails to comply with any of the provisions of this section is liable to a penalty and a daily default penalty prescribed in the Commission's regulations.

PART F—INCORPORATED TRUSTEES

CHAPTER 1—INCORPORATED TRUSTEES

823.—(1) Where two or more trustees are appointed by any community of persons bound together by custom, religion, kinship or nationality or by anybody or association of persons established for any religious, educational, literary, scientific, social, development, cultural, sporting or charitable purpose, they may, if so authorised by the community, body or association (in this Act referred to as "the association") apply to the Commission in the manner provided for registration under this Act as a corporate body.

(2) Upon being so registered by the Commission, the trustees shall become a corporate body in accordance with the provisions of section 830 of this Part.

824. The Commission shall determine the classification of associations to be registered under this Part in accordance with the aims and objects of the association.

825.—(1) Application under section 823 shall be in the form prescribed by the Commission and shall state the—

(a) name of the proposed corporate body which must contain the words "Incorporated Trustees of" ;

(b) aims and objects of the association which shall be for the advancement of any religious, educational, literary, scientific, social, development, cultural, sporting or charitable purpose, and shall be lawful ; and

(c) names, addresses and occupations of the secretary of the association, if any.

(2) There shall be attached to the application—

(a) two printed copies of the constitution of the association ;

(b) duly signed copies of the minutes of the meeting appointing the trustees and authorising the application showing the people present and the votes scored ; and

(c) the impression or drawing of the proposed common seal, if there is one.(3) The application shall be signed by the person making it.

(4) The Commission may require such declaration or other evidence in verification of the statements and particulars in the application, and such other, information and evidence, if any, as it may deem fit.

(5) If any person knowingly makes any false statement or gives any false information for the purpose of incorporating trustees under this Part, he commits an offence and is liable on conviction to imprisonment for one year or to a fine as the Court deems fit.

826.—(1) A person shall not be qualified to be appointed or act as a trustee if—

(a) he is an infant ;

(b) he is a person of unsound mind having been so found by a court ;(c) he is an undischarged bankrupt ; or

(d) he has been convicted of an offence involving fraud or dishonesty within five years of his proposed appointment.

(2) If a person disqualified under subsection (1) (c) or (d) acts as a trustee, he shall be liable to a penalty for every day during which he so acts, the penalty shall be determined in accordance with regulations made by the Commission from time to time.

827. The constitution of the association shall in addition to any other matter—

(a) state the name or title of the association ;

(b) the aims and objects of the association ; and

(c) make provisions, in respect of the following—

(i) appointment, powers, duties, tenure of office and replacement of the trustees,

(ii) the use and custody of the common seal, if there is one,

(iii) the meetings of the association,

(iv) the number of members of the governing body, if any, the procedure for their appointment and removal, and their powers, and

where subscriptions and other contributions are to be collected, the procedure for disbursement of the funds of the association, the keeping of accounts and the auditing of such accounts.

828.—(1) If the Commission is satisfied that the application has complied with the provisions of sections 825-827 of this Act, it shall cause the application to be published in a prescribed form in two daily newspapers circulating in the area where the association is to be situated and at least one of the newspapers shall be a national newspaper.

(2) The advertisement shall invite objections, if any, to the registration of the body.

(3) The objection shall state the grounds on which it is made and shall be forwarded to reach the Commission within 28 days of the date of the last of the publications in the newspapers.

(4) If objections are made, the Commission shall consider them and may require the objections and applicants, to furnish further information or explanation, and may uphold or reject the objections as it deems fit and inform the applicant accordingly. 829.—(1) If, after the advertisement, no objection is received within the period specified in section 828 of this Act or, where any objection is received and the same is rejected, the Commission, having regard to all the circumstances, may assent to the application or withhold its assent.

(2) If the Commission assents to the application, it shall register the trustees and issue a certificate in the prescribed form.

830.—(1) From the date of registration, the trustees shall become a body corporate by the name described in the certificate, and shall have—

(a) perpetual succession ;

(b) a common seal if they so wish ;

(c) power to sue and be sued in its corporate name as such trustees ; and

(d) subject to section 836 of this Part, power to hold and acquire, and transfer, assign or dispose of any property, or interests therein belonging to, or held for the benefit of such association, in such manner and subject to such restrictions and provisions as the trustees might without incorporation, hold or acquire, transfer, assign or otherwise dispose of the same for the purposes of such community, body or association of persons.

(2) The certificate of incorporation shall vest in the body corporate all property and interests of whatever nature or tenure belonging to or held by any person in trust for such community, body or association of persons.

(3) A certificate of incorporation when granted shall be *prima facie* evidence that all the preliminary requisitions herein contained and required in respect of such incorporation have been complied with, and the date of incorporation mentioned in such certificate shall be deemed to be the date on which incorporation has taken place.

831. Without prejudice to the provisions of section 849 of this Act, the Commission may direct that for all or any of the purposes of this Act—

(i) an association be treated as forming part of an already registered association ; and

(ii) any two or more associations having the same trustees be treated as a single association.

CHAPTER 2—CHANGES IN REGISTERED PARTICULARS OF INCORPORATED TRUSTEES

832.—(1) Where the association is desirous of changing, altering its name, objects or any of them, the trustees shall apply to the Commission in the prescribed form setting out the alterations desired and attaching a copy of the resolution approving the change and duly certified by the trustees.

(2) The Commission on receipt of the application shall consider it and, if satisfied that the change or alteration is prima facie lawful shall—

(a) cause the application to be published in two daily newspapers in the manner specified in section 828 (1) of this Act ; and

(b) direct the corporation to display for at least 28 days a notice of the proposed change or alteration conspicuously mounted at the corporation headquarters, or at any branch office, or any such place where a majority of the members are likely to see it, as the Commission may require.

(3) The publication and notices shall call for objections which, if any, shall state the grounds of objection and be forwarded to reach the Commission not later than 28 days after the last of the publications in the newspapers.

(4) The provisions of section 827 and of section 825 (1) of this Part of this Act shall apply to this section as they apply to an application for registration.

(5) If the Commission assents to the application, the alterations shall be made and in the case of a change of name, the Commission shall issue a new certificate in the new name in place of the former certificate.

833. Subject to sections 827 and 828 of this Part, an association whose trustees are incorporated under this Part may alter its constitution by resolution passed by simple majority of its members and approved by the Commission.

834.—(1) Where a body or association intends to replace some or all its trustees or to appoint additional trustees, it may by resolution at a general meeting do so and apply in the prescribed form for the approval of the Commission.

(2) Upon such application, the provisions of section 832 (2) - (4) of this Act shall apply to this section as they apply to the change of name or object.

(3) If the Commission assents to the application, it shall signify its assent in writing to the board or association and the appointment shall become valid as from the date of the resolution appointing the trustees.

835. Any change or alteration purported to be made in contravention of section 832, 833 or 834 of this Part of this Act void.

CHAPTER 3—COUNCIL, POWERS, INCOME AND PROPERTY

836. The association may appoint a council, or governing body, which shall include the trustees and may, subject to the provisions of this Part, assign to it such administrative and management functions as it deems expedient.

837. The powers vested in the trustees by or under this Act shall be exercised subject to the directions of the associations, or the council or governing body appointed under section 836 of this Part.

838.—(1) The income and property of a body or association whose trustees are incorporated under this Part of this Act shall be applied solely towards—

(a) the promotion of the objects of the body as set forth in its constitution; and

(b) no portion from it shall be paid or transferred directly or indirectly, byway of dividend, bonus, or otherwise by way of profit to any of the members of the association.

(2) Nothing in subsection (1) (b) shall prevent the payment, in good faith, of reasonable and proper remuneration to an officer or servant of the body in return for any service actually rendered to the body or association:

Provided that—

(a) with the exception of ex-officio members of the governing council, no member of a council or governing body shall be appointed to any salaried office of the body or any office of the body paid by fees ; and

(b) no remuneration or other benefit in money or money's worth shall be given by the body to any member of such council or governing body, except repayment of out-of-pocket expenses, reasonable rent for premises demised or let to the body or reasonable fee for services rendered.

(3) A person who knowingly acts or joins in acting in contravention of this section, he is liable to refund such income or property so misapplied to the association.

CHAPTER 4—SUSPENSION OF TRUSTEES, APPOINTMENT OF INTERIM MANAGERS, ETC.

839.—(1) The Commission may by order suspend the trustees of an association and appoint an interim manager or managers to manage the affairs of an association where it reasonably believes that—

(a) there is or has been any misconduct or mismanagement in the administration of the association ;

(b) it is necessary or desirable for the purpose of—(i) protecting the property of the association,

(ii) securing a proper application for the property of the association towards achieving the objects of the association, the purposes of the association of that property or of the property coming to the association, (iii) public interest ; or

(c) the affairs of the association are being run fraudulently.

(2) The trustees shall be suspended by an order of Court upon the petition of the Commission or members consisting one-fifth of the association and the petitioners shall present all reasonable evidence or such evidence as requested by the Court in respect of the petition.

(3) Upon the hearing of the petition and the appointment of the interim manager, the Court, with the assistance of the Commission, may make provision with respect to the functions to be performed by the interim manager or managers appointed by the order—

(a) the powers and duties of the interim manager or managers which may include the powers and duties of the trustees of the association concerned ; and

(b) any power or duty specified under paragraph (a) to be exercisable or discharged by the interim manager or managers to the exclusion of the trustees.

(4) The functions shall be performed by the interim manager or managers under the supervision of the Commission.

(5) The reference in subsection (1) to misconduct or mismanagement extends to the employment for—

(a) the remuneration or reward of persons acting in the affairs of the association, or

(b) other administrative purposes, of sums which are excessive in relation to the property which is or is likely to be applied or applicable for the purposes of the association.

(6) A court of competent jurisdiction may, upon the petition of the Commission or members of the association—

(a) order or suspend any person, officer, agent or employee of the association from office or employment, provided that such suspension does not exceed 12 months from the date of the order or suspension;

(b) by order appoint such number of additional trustees as it considers necessary for the proper administration of the association ;

(c) by order—

(i) vest any property held by or in trust for the association in the official custodian, who shall be a person so designated by the court from time to time ;

(ii) require the persons in whom any such property is vested to transfer it to the official custodian who will be an individual as the court may, from time to time designate, or

(iii) appoint any person to transfer any such property to the official custodian ;

(d) order any person who holds any property on behalf of the association, or of any trustee for it, not to part with the property without the approval of the Court ;

(e) order any debtor of the association not to make any payment in or towards the discharge of the debtor's liability directly to the association but to make such payment into an interest yielding account held by the Commission for the benefit of the association ;

(f) by order restrict (regardless of anything in the trusts of the association) the transactions which may be entered into, or the nature or amount of the payments which may be made, in the administration of the association without the approval of the court ; or

(g) by order appoint an interim manager to act as receiver and manager in respect of the property and affairs of the association.

(7) Where, at any time after the Commission has made an enquiry into the affairs of the association, it is satisfied as to the matters mentioned in subsection (1), it may suspend or remove—

(a) any trustee who has been responsible for or privy to the misconduct or mismanagement or whose conduct contributed to or facilitated it ; or

(b) by order of the Court, establish a scheme for the administration of the association.

(8) The court may by order replace a trustee removed under subsection (7).

(9) A person who contravenes an order under subsection (6) (d), (e) and (f) commits an offence and is liable on conviction to fine as the Court deems fit or imprisonment for a term of 6 months or to both.

(10) The Commission may make regulations in respect of—

(a) the functions, powers and remuneration of the interim manager and the manner in which the interim manager shall make reports to the Commission ; and

(b) making reports to the Commission, and such other things as may be necessary for the effective administration of the association during the period of its interim administration.

(11) The Commission shall only exercise its power under this section in respect of any association with the approval of the Minister.

CHAPTER 5—COMMON SEAL AND CONTRACT

840. The common seal, if any of the body corporate shall have such device as may be specified in the constitution, and any instrument to which the common seal of the corporate body has been affixed in apparent compliance with the regulations for the use of the common seal shall be binding on the corporate body, notwithstanding any defect or circumstance affecting the execution of such instrument.

841. Subject to the provisions of this Part of this Act and of the constitution of the association, the corporate body may contract in the same form and manner as an individual.

CHAPTER 6—ACCOUNTS AND ANNUAL RETURNS

POWER TO DIRECT TRANSFER OF CREDITS IN DORMANT BANK

842. (1) Where a bank holds one or more accounts in the name of or on behalf of the incorporated trustees of a particular association, and the account, or, if it holds two or more accounts, and each of the accounts is dormant (as defined under the relevant banking regulation), the bank shall without delay notify the Commission of these facts.

(2) Where the Commission receives a notice under subsection (1), the Commission may request that the association provide evidence of its activities, and where the association fails to respond satisfactorily within 15 days of the request, the Commission may dissolve the association in accordance with section 850, and where

an association is so dissolved, the Commission may give a direction to the bank concerned to transfer—

(a) the amount, or, as the case may be, the aggregate amount, standing to the credit of the relevant association in the account or accounts in question

Cto such other association as is specified in the direction in accordance with subsection (3) of this section to the bank; or

(b) to each of two or more other associations so specified in the direction, such part of that amount or aggregate amount as is there specified in relation to that association.

(3) The provisions of subsection (2) shall also apply where the Commission is unable, after making reasonable inquiries, to locate an association registered under this Act or any of its trustees.

(4) The Commission may specify in a direction under subsection (2) such other association or charity as it considers appropriate, having regard to the purposes of that association or charity:

Provided that before any association may be so specified by the Commission, the trustees of such an association shall, by a written memorandum to the Commission, indicate its willingness to accept such amount to be transferred to it.

(5) Any amount received by an association by virtue of this section is to be received by the association on terms that—

(a) it is to be held and applied by the association for the purposes of the association ;

(b) as property of the association, it is nevertheless subject to any restrictions on expenditure to which it was subject as property of the relevant association ; and

(c) the receipt of a trustee for an association in respect of any amount received from a relevant bank by virtue of this section is a complete discharge of the bank in respect of that amount.

(6) The Commission shall only exercise its power under this section in respect of any association with the approval of the Minister.

843. Where any bank has given notice to the Commission under section 842(1) of this Act, it shall, subject to any contrary provision under the relevant banking enactment, not re-activate the dormant accounts, without first notifying the Commission—

(a) if before any transfer is made by the bank in pursuance of a direction under section 842 (2) of this Act, the bank has cause to believe that the account or accounts held by it in the name of or on behalf of an association is no longer dormant, the bank shall without delay notify the Commission that the account or accounts have ceased to be dormant.

(b) if it appears to the Commission that the account or accounts in question is or are no longer dormant, or where the Commission receives satisfactory account of the activities of the association pursuant to section 842 (2), it shall revoke any direction made to the bank under section 842 (2) of this Act with respect to any such account.

844.—(1) No obligation as to secrecy or other restriction on disclosure, however imposed, shall preclude a relevant bank from disclosing any information on the status of dormant bank accounts to the Commission for the purpose of enabling the Commission to discharge its functions under sections 842 and 843 of this Act.

(2) For the purposes of this section and sections 842 and 843 of this Act, an account is dormant if no transaction, other than—

(a) a transaction consisting of a payment into the account, or

(b) a transaction which the bank holding the account has itself caused to be effected, has been effected in relation to the account within the period of five years immediately preceding the date when the Commission is informed as mentioned in section 842 (1) of this Act.

(3) For the purposes of sections 842 and 843 of this Act, the term "bank" and in this section, a "relevant bank" means—

(a) any Central Bank of Nigeria designated money deposit institution ; or

(b) such other person or organisation who may lawfully accept deposits as may be prescribed by the Minister.

(4) For the purposes of sections 842 and 843 of this Act, references to the transfer of any amount to an association are deemed to be references to any of its transfers made to—

(a) the trustees of the association, or

(b) any trustee of the association, as the trustees of the association may determine, and any reference to any amount received by an association is to be read accordingly.

845.—(1) The trustees of an association shall submit to the Commission a bi-annual statement of affairs of the association, as the Commission shall specify in its regulations.

(2) If the trustees fail to comply with subsection (1), each trustee shall be liable to a penalty for every day during which the default continues in such amount as the Commission shall specify in its regulations.

846.—(1) The trustees of an association shall ensure that accounting records are kept in respect of the association and such accounting records shall be sufficient to show and explain the transactions of the association, and—

(a) disclose at any time, with reasonable accuracy, the financial position of the association at that time ; and

(b) enable the trustees to ensure that statements of accounts prepared by them comply with subsection (3).

(2) The accounting records shall, in particular, contain—

(a) entries showing from day to day, all sums of money received and expended by the association, and the matters in respect of which the receipt and expenditure took place ; and

(b) a record of the assets and liabilities of the association.

(3) The Commission may make regulations generally for the purpose of this Part and, in particular, without prejudice to the generality of the foregoing provisions, make regulations—

(a) prescribing the forms, returns and other information required under this Part ;

(b) prescribing the procedure for obtaining any information required under this Part ;

(c) requiring returns to be made within the period specified therein by any body corporate to which this Part applies ; and

(d) prescribing relevant accounting principles or standards to be adopted by the association.

(4) Regulations under subsection (3) may in particular provide—

(a) for the statement to be prepared in accordance with methods and principles as are specified or referred to in the regulations ; and

(b) any information to be provided by way of notes to the accounts.

(5) The financial year of an association shall be determined by the Commission through regulations issued under subsection (3) and the Commission may also make provision for determining the financial years of an association for the purposes of this Act and any regulation made under it.

847. The accounting records of an association shall be preserved by it for six years from the date on which they were made.

848.—(1) The trustees of the association shall, not earlier than 30th June or later than 31st December each year (other than the year in which it is incorporated), submit to the Commission a return showing the name of the association, the names, addresses and occupations of the trustees, and members of the council or governing body, particulars of any land held by the corporate body during the year, and of any change which has taken place in the constitution of the association during the preceding year.

(2) The return referred to in subsection (1) shall be accompanied by the audited statement of accounts for the year of return.

(3) If default is made in complying with this section, the corporate body is liable to a penalty as may be prescribed by regulation.

CHAPTER 7—MERGER AND DISSOLUTION

849. Two or more associations with similar aims and objects may merge under terms and conditions as the Commission may prescribe by regulation.

850.—(1) A body corporate formed under this Part may be dissolved by the Court on a petition brought for that purpose by—

(a) the governing body or council ;

(b) one or more trustees ;

(c) members of the association constituting at least 50% of the total membership ; or

(d) the Commission.

(2) The grounds on which the body corporate may be dissolved are that—

(a) the aims and objects for which it was established have been fully realised and no useful purpose would be served by keeping the corporation alive ;

(b) the body corporate is formed to exist for a specified period, that period has expired and it is not necessary for it to continue to exist ;

(c) all the aims and objects of the association have become illegal or otherwise contrary to public policy ;

(d) it is just and equitable in all the circumstances that the body corporate be dissolved ; and

(e) the certificate of registration of the association has been withdrawn, cancelled or revoked by the Commission.

(3) At the hearing of the petition, all persons whose interests or rights may, in the opinion of the Court, be affected by the dissolution shall be put on notice.

(4) If in the event of a winding-up or dissolution of the corporate body there remains, after the satisfaction of all its debts and liabilities, any property whatsoever, the same shall not be paid to or distributed among the members of the association, but shall be given or transferred to some other institutions having objects similar to the objects of the association:

Provided that the institution shall be determined by the members of the association at or before the time of dissolution.

(5) If effect cannot be given to the provisions of subsection (4), the remaining property shall be transferred to some charitable object.

PART G—GENERAL

CHAPTER 1 — ESTABLISHMENT OF ADMINISTRATIVE PROCEEDINGS COMMITTEE

851.—(1) The Commission shall establish an Administrative Proceedings Committee (in this Act referred to as "the Administrative Committee") comprising—

(a) the Registrar-General who shall be the Chairman of the Administrative Committee;

(b) five representatives from the operational departments of the Commission, not below the grade level of a director, one of whom shall be from the Compliance Department of the Commission ; and

(c) a representative of the Federal Ministry of Industry, Trade and Investment not below the grade level of a director.

(2) The Administrative Committee may co-opt persons, at any of its meetings, as observers, representatives of relevant associations, including associations of shareholders, registrars or trustees, as are considered necessary, and members so co-opted shall not count towards a quorum or have the right to vote in respect of any decision taken by the Administrative Committee.

(3) The Commission shall designate an officer of the Commission with at least 10 years post-call experience in the legal profession who shall be the secretary of the Administrative Committee.

(4) The Administrative Committee shall—

(a) provide the opportunity of being heard for persons alleged to have contravened the provisions of this Act or its regulations ;

(b) resolve disputes or grievances arising from the operations of this Actor its regulations ; and

(c) impose administrative penalties for contravention of the provisions of this Act or its regulations in the settlement of matters before it.

(5) The chairman shall preside at every meeting of the Administrative Committee and in his absence the members present at the meeting shall select one of their numbers to preside over the meeting.

(6) The quorum at a sitting of the Administrative Committee is four members present while the determination of issue shall be by simple majority of members present and where there is equality of votes, the chairman or the member presiding shall be entitled to a casting vote.

(7) Parties shall attend the sitting of the Administrative Committee in person or be represented by a legal practitioner.

(8) Proceedings of the Administrative Committee shall be recorded on audio or visual tape or such other electronic device.

(9) Decisions reached on any matter before the Administrative Committee shall be forwarded to the parties not later than 14 days after the confirmation by the Board.

(10) The sanctions that may be imposed by the Administrative Committee, include—

(a) imposition of administrative penalties ;

(b) suspension or revocation of registration; or

(c) recommendation for criminal prosecution if matters brought before it reveals any criminal act or conduct.

(11) Decisions of the Administrative Committee are subject to confirmation by the Board.

(12) Parties dissatisfied with decisions of the Administrative Committee may appeal to the Federal High Court.

(13) Subject to the provisions of this section, the Administrative Committee to regulate its proceedings.

852.—(1) No company, limited liability partnership, limited partnership, business name or incorporated trustee shall be registered under this Act by a name or trade mark which—

(a) is identical with that by which a company or limited liability partnership in existence is already registered, or so nearly resembles that name as to be calculated to deceive, except where the company or limited liability partnership in existence is in the course of being dissolved and signifies its consent in such manner as the Commission requires;

(b) contains the words "Chamber of Commerce" unless it is a company limited by guarantee ;

(c) in the opinion of the Commission, is capable of misleading as to the nature or extent of its activities or is undesirable, offensive or otherwise contrary to public policy ;

(d) in the opinion of the Commission, would violate or conflict with any existing trademark or business name registered in Nigeria or body corporate formed under this Act unless the consent of the owner of the trade mark, business name or trustees of the body corporate has been obtained ;

(e) contains any word which, in the opinion of the Commission, is likely to mislead the public as to the nationality, race or religion of the persons by whom the business is wholly or mainly owned or controlled ;

(f) is, in the opinion of the Commission, deceptive or objectionable in that it contains a reference or suggests association with any practice, institution, personage, foreign state or government, international organisation or international brand or is otherwise unsuitable ; or

(g) is capable of undermining public peace and national security.

(2) Except with the consent of the Commission, no company, limited liability partnership, limited partnership, business name or incorporated trustees shall be registered by a name which—

(a) includes the word "Federal", "National", "Regional", "State" ;

(b) "Government", or any other word which, in the opinion of the Commission suggests or is calculated to suggest that it enjoys the patronage of the Government of the Federation, the Government of a State in Nigeria, any Ministry or Department of Government, or contains the word "Municipal" or "Chartered" or in the opinion of the Commission, suggests or is calculated to suggest, connection with any municipality or other local authority ;

(c) contains the word "Cooperative" or its equivalent in any other language or any abbreviation; or of the words "Building Society" ; or (d) contains the word "Group" or "Holding".

(3) No individual or firm shall be registered under PART D or E of this Act if the age of the individual or any individual who is a partner is stated in the statement furnished

under section 796 of this Act to be less than 18 years, unless the statement shows at least two other individuals aged above 18 years.

(4) No company, business name or incorporated trustee shall be registered where there is irrefutable evidence to the effect that the company, business name or incorporated trustee has previously been involved in fraudulent trade malpractices, either in local or international trade.

853. (1) The Commission may, by regulations, require that in connection with an application for the approval of the Commission under section 852 the applicant must seek the view of a specified Government Department or other body.

(2) Where such a requirement applies, the applicant must request the specified Department or other body in writing to indicate whether (and if so why) it has any objections to the proposed name.

(3) Where a request under this section is made in connection with an application for the registration of a company, limited liability partnership, business name or incorporated trustees under this Act, the application must— (a) include a statement that a request under this section has been made ; and (b) be accompanied by a copy of any response received.

(4) Where a request under this section is made in connection with a change in the name of a company, limited liability partnership, business name or incorporated trustees, the notice of the change sent to the Commission must be accompanied by—

(a) a statement by a director, partner, incorporated trustees or their secretary that a request under this section has been made ; and (b) a copy of any response received.

854.—(1) The Minister may make provision by regulations—

(a) as to the letters or other characters, signs or symbols (including accents and other diacritical marks) and punctuation that may be used in the name of a company, limited liability partnership, business name or

incorporated trustee registered under this Act ; and

(b) specifying a standard style or format for the name of a company, limited liability partnership, business name or incorporated trustee for the purposes of registration.

(2) The regulations may prohibit the use of specified characters, signs or symbols when appearing in a specified position (in particular, at the beginning of a name).

(3) A company, limited liability partnership, business name or incorporated trustee may not be registered under this Act by a name that consists of or includes anything that is not permitted in accordance with regulations under this section.

855.—(1) If it appears to the Commission that—

(a) misleading information has been given for the purposes of a company, limited liability partnership, business name or incorporated trustee registration by a particular name ; or

(b) an undertaking or assurance has been given for that purpose and has not been fulfilled,

the Commission may direct the company, limited liability partnership, business name or incorporated trustee to change its name.

(2) The direction shall—

(a) be given within five years of the company, limited liability partnership, business name or incorporated trustees registration by that name ; and

(b) specify the period within which the company, limited liability partnership, business name or incorporated trustee is to change its name.

(3) The Commission may, by a further direction, extend the period within which the company, limited liability partnership, business name or incorporated trustee is to change its name provided that the direction shall be given before the end of the period for the time being specified.

(4) A direction under this section shall be in writing.

(5) Where a company, limited liability partnership, business name or incorporated trustee fails to comply with a direction of the Commission under this section, the company, limited liability partnership and incorporated trustees together with every of the officers or each partner in the case of a business name shall each be liable to a penalty for every day the failure continues in such amount as the Commission shall specify in its regulations.

(6) In this section, "officer" of the company, limited liability partnership or incorporated trustee means the directors (including a shadow director), partners or trustees whichever is applicable.

856.—(1) If, in the opinion of the Commission, the name by which a company, limited liability partnership, business name or incorporated trustee is registered is misleading as to the nature of its activities as to be likely to cause harm to the public, the Commission may direct the company, limited liability partnership, business name or incorporated trustee in writing to change its name.

(2) The direction must be complied with within six weeks from the date of the direction or such longer period as the Commission may deem fit.

(3) Where a company, limited liability partnership, business name or incorporated trustee fails to comply with a direction of the Commission under this section, the company, limited liability partnership or incorporated trustees together with every of its officers or each partner, in the case of a business, shall each be liable to a penalty for every day the failure continues in such amount as the Commission shall specify in its regulations.

(4) In this section, "officer" of the company or incorporated trustees means the directors (including a shadow director) or trustees.

857.—(1) A person ("the applicant") may object to the registered name of a company, limited liability partnership, limited partnership, business name or incorporated trustees on the ground that it is—

(a) the same as a name associated with the applicant in which he has goodwill ; or

(b) sufficiently similar to such a name that its use in Nigeria would be likely to mislead by suggesting a connection between the company, limited liability partnership, limited partnership, business name or incorporated trustee and the applicant.

(2) The objection must be made by application to the Administrative Proceedings committee established under this Act.

(3) The company, limited liability partnership, limited partnership, business name proprietor or partners or incorporated trustees concerned shall be the primary respondent to the application provided that any of its members or directors may be joined as respondents.

(4) If the ground specified in subsection (1) (a) or (b) is established, it is for the respondents to show that the—

(a) name was registered before the commencement of the activities on which the applicant relies to show goodwill ;

(b) company, limited liability partnership, limited partnership, business name or incorporated trustee— (i) is operating under the name,
(ii) is proposing to do so and has incurred substantial start-up costs in preparation, or
(iii) was formerly operating under the name and is now dormant ;
(c) name was adopted in good faith ; or
(d) interests of the applicant are not adversely affected to any significant extent.
(5) If the facts mentioned in subsection (4) (a) or (b) are established, the objection shall nevertheless be upheld if the applicant shows that the main purpose of the respondents (or any of them) in registering the name was to obtain money (or other consideration) from the applicant or prevent him from registering the name.
(6) If the objection is not upheld under subsection (4) or (5), it shall be dismissed.
(7) In this section "goodwill" includes reputation of any description.
858. The Administrative Proceedings Committee shall within 30 days of determining an application under section 857, make its decision and reasons for it available to the public.

CHAPTER 2—MISCELLANEOUS AND SUPPLEMENTAL

859.—(1) In the case where any document filed with the Commission is lost or destroyed, the company, limited liability partnership, limited partnership, business name or incorporated trustees may apply to the Commission for leave to submit a copy of the document as originally filed.
(2) On such application being made, the Commission may direct notice of it to be given to such persons and in such manners as it deems fit.
(3) The Commission shall upon being satisfied—
(a) that the original document has been lost or destroyed,
(b) of the date of the filing it with the Commission, and
(c) that the copy of such document produced to the Commission is a correct copy,
may certify upon that copy that he is so satisfied and direct that the copy be submitted in the manner required by law in respect of the original.
(4) Upon submission under this section, the copy shall have the same effect as the original.
(5) The Court may, by order upon application by any person aggrieved and after notice to any other person whom the Court directs, confirm, vary or rescind the certification by the Commission.
(6) A copy of the Court order shall be delivered by the applicant under subsection (5) to the Commission for registration within seven days of its making.
(7) Any payment, contract, dealing, act or thing made, had or done in good faith before the registration of such order and upon the faith of and in reliance upon the certification by the Commission under subsection (3) shall not be invalidated by the court order varying or rescinding the certification.
(8) Submission of a document under subsection (3) shall be at no fee.
(9) If default is made in complying with subsection (6), the applicant is liable to a fine as the Commission may by regulation prescribe for the default and for every day the default continues.
860.—(1) Any document required to be filed with the Commission for registration may be filed electronically.
(2) A copy or extract from any document electronically filed with the Commission or issued by the Commission and certified to be a true copy or extract shall in any

proceedings be admissible in evidence as of equal validity with the original documents.

(3) Any information supplied by the Commission and certified to be a true extract from any document filed with it shall be admissible in evidence and presumed, unless evidence to the contrary is adduced, to be a true extract from such document.

861.—(1) The Commission shall preserve all documents delivered to it under this Act.

(2) Any person may, on application to the Commission, be permitted to inspect the documents kept under subsection (1) on payment of a prescribed fee and may require a copy or extract of any such document to be certified by the Commission on payment of a prescribed fee.

(3) Where a copy or extract from any document registered under this Act, is certified by the Commission to be a true copy or extract, it shall in all proceedings be admissible in evidence as of equal validity with the original document, and it shall be unnecessary to prove the official position of the person certifying the copy or extract.

(4) No process for compelling the production of any document kept by the Commission shall issue from any court, except with the leave of that court, and such process, if issued, shall bear a statement that it is issued with the leave of the Court.

862.—(1) Subject to the provisions of subsections (2) and (3), if any person in any return, report, certificate, balance sheet, or other document required by, or for the purpose of any of the provisions of this Act, wilfully makes a statement which is false in any material particular knowing it to be false, he commits an offence and is liable on conviction—

(a) to imprisonment for a term of two years ; and

(b) in the case of a company, to fine as the Court deems fit for every day the default continues.

(2) A company which makes a statement in its annual returns which is false in any material particular shall in respect of each year of any such returns be liable to a penalty prescribed in the Commission's regulations if it is a small company or in any other case.

(3) Nothing in this section shall affect the provisions of any enactment imposing penalties in respect of perjury in force in Nigeria.

863.—(1) A person or association of persons shall not carry on business in Nigeria as a company, limited liability partnership, limited partnership or under a business name without being registered under this Act.

(2) If an individual, corporation or association of persons required under this Act to be registered carries on business without registration or under a name registration of which has been refused or cancelled under this Act, the individual, corporation or every partner in the firm commits an offence and is liable on conviction to a fine prescribed in the Commission's regulations from time to time, of ₦200.00 for every day during which the default continues, and the Court shall order a statement of the required particulars for the registration of the business to be furnished to the Commission for registration within such time as may be specified in the order.

864. Companies, firms and corporate bodies registered under this Act shall retain documents stored in pursuance of the provisions of this Act in soft copies for six years from the date of storage.

865.—(1) An authorised officer of the Commission shall at all reasonable times have access to premises, buildings, offices, places, books or documents in the custody or under the control of any officer of the company, firm, corporation or any other individual for the purpose of inspecting books or documents or where there is reason to believe that the provisions of this Act are being contravened.

(2) The powers of an authorised officer under this section shall also extend to the inspection of books or documents, including those stored or maintained in computers or on digital, magnetic, optical or electronic media and any other property, process or matter found on the premises, building, offices or place which the officer considers necessary or relevant for the purpose of any inspection and may without the payment of any fee, make extract from, or copies from such books or documents.

(3) The occupier of the premises, building or place that is entered upon or proposed to be entered upon shall—

(a) provide the authorised officer with all reasonable facilities and assistance for the exercise of the powers under this section ;

(b) answer questions relating to the effective exercise of the powers under this section, orally or if required by the authorised officer, in writing or by statutory declaration.

(4) The Commission may engage the services of any of the law enforcement agencies in the discharge of its functions under this section.

(5) Any person who—

(a) obstructs, hinders, prevents or assaults an authorised officer in the performance of any function or the exercise of any power under this section ;

(b) does anything which impedes or is intended to impede the sealing up of premises or removal of books or documents or any other article for the purpose of investigation of any contravention of the provisions of this Act or its regulations,

(c) does anything intended to prevent the procuring or giving of evidence in connection with the prosecution for any breach of the provisions of this Act, or

(d) prevents the arrest of any person by a person duly engaged for that purpose or rescues any person so arrested,

commits an offence and be liable on conviction to a fine as the Court deems fit or imprisonment for a term not exceeding 12 months or to both.

866. The Commission shall have power to compound any administrative offence under this Act by accepting such sums of money as it deems fit in the circumstance but not exceeding the maximum fine to which the offender would have been liable if he had been convicted of the offence.

867. The Commission may, with the approval of the Minister, make regulations generally for the purpose of this Act and in particular, make regulations—

(a) prescribing the forms, returns and other information required under this Act ;

(b) prescribing the procedure for obtaining any information required under this Act ;

(c) requiring returns to be made within the period specified by any company, limited liability partnership, limited partnership, business name proprietors or incorporated trustees to which this Act applies ;

(d) prescribing any fees payable under this Act ; and

(e) generally for the conduct and regulation of registration under this Act.

Interpretation.

868.—(1) In this Act—

"agent" does not include a legal practitioner acting as counsel for any person ;

"alien" means a person or association, whether corporate or unincorporated, other than a Nigerian citizen or association a company, business name or association incorporated or registered in Nigeria ;

"annual return" means the return required to be made in the case of—

(a) a company limited by shares, under sections 418-419 of this Act ;

(b) a company limited by guarantee, under section 420 of this Act ;

(c) a business name, under section 822 of this Act ; and

(d) incorporated trustees, under section 848 of this Act ;

"arrangement" has the meaning assigned to it under section 710 of this Act ;

"articles" means the articles of association of a company, as originally framed or as altered by special resolution ;

"book and paper" and "book or paper" include accounts, deeds, writings, and documents ;

"business" includes any trade, industry and profession and any occupation carried on for profit ;

"business name" means the name or style under which any business is carried on whether in partnership or otherwise ;

"circulating capital" means a portion of the subscribed capital of the company intended to be used by being temporarily parted with and circulated in business, in the form of money, goods and other assets, and which, or the proceeds of which, are intended to return to the company with an increment, and are intended to be used again and again, and to always return with some accretion;

"Commission" means the Corporate Affairs Commission established under this Act;

"company" or "existing company" means a company formed and registered under this Act or, as the case may be, formed and registered in Nigeria before and in existence on the commencement of this Act ;

"company limited by guarantee" and "company limited by shares" have the meanings assigned to them respectively by section 21 of this Act;

"companies liquidation account" means the account kept on behalf of the Commission pursuant to section 591 of this Act ;

"contributory" means every person liable to contribute to the assets of a company in the event of its being wound up and for the purposes of all proceedings for determining, and all proceedings prior to the final determination of, the persons who are to be deemed contributories, the expression includes any person alleged to be contributory ;

"Court" or "the Court" used in relation to a company, means the Federal High Court, and to the extent to which application may be made to it as; court includes the Court of Appeal and the Supreme Court of Nigeria ;

"creditor" means any person who is owed an obligation (secured or unsecured) accruing on a debt, liability or performance under a contract (express or implied), or in tort, by another person ;

"creditors voluntary winding-up" has the meaning assigned to it by section 625 (4) of this Act ;

"debenture" means a written acknowledgment of indebtedness by the company, setting out the terms and conditions of the indebtedness, and includes debenture stock, bonds and any other securities of a company whether constituting a charge on the assets of the company or not ;

"designated partner" means any partner designated as such pursuant to section 749 ;

"director" includes any person occupying the position of director by whatever name called; and includes any person in accordance with whose directions or instructions the directors of the company are accustomed to act ;

"dividend" means a proportion of the distributed profits of the company which may be a fixed annual percentage, as in the case of preference shares, or it may be variable according to the prosperity or other circumstances of the company, as in the case of equity shares ;

"document" includes information recorded in any form, summons, notice, order and other legal process, and register ;

"equity capital" shall be construed accordingly ;

"equity share" means a share other than a preference share ; and

"firm" means an unincorporated body of two or more individuals or one or more individual and one or more corporations, or two or more corporations, who or which have entered into partnership with one another with a view to carrying on business for profit ;

"fixed capital" means that capital which a company retains in the form of assets upon which the subscribed capital or other sum has been expended, and which assets either themselves produced income, independent of any further action by the company, or being retained by the company are made use of to produce income or gain profits ;

"foreign company" means a company incorporated elsewhere than in Nigeria ;

"foreign limited liability partnership" means a limited liability partnership formed, incorporated or registered outside Nigeria ;

"forename" includes a Christian name and a personal name and when used with a surname includes any first name, and "surname" includes a patronymic ;

"Gazette" or "Federal Gazette" means the official Gazette of the Federation ;

"group financial statements" has the meaning assigned to it by section 379 (1) of this Act ;

"holding company" means a holding company as defined by section 381 of this Act ;

"inability to pay debts" in relation to a company has the meaning assigned by section 572 of this Act ;

"initials" includes any recognised abbreviation of a forename ;

"insolvent person" where used in this Act means any person in Nigeria who, in respect of any judgment, Act or court order against him, is unable to satisfy execution or other process issued in favour of a creditor, and the execution or other process remains unsatisfied for not less than six weeks ;

"insolvency practitioner" means a legal practitioner within the meaning of the Legal Practitioners Act or a member of the Institute of Chartered Accountants of Nigeria or such other professional bodies of accountants as are established by an Act of the National Assembly ;

"issued generally" means, in relation to a prospectus, issued to persons who are not existing members or debenture holders of the company ;

"issued share capital" in relation to any reduction has the meaning assigned by section 124 (2) of this Act ;

"legal practitioner" has the meaning assigned to it by the Legal Practitioners Act ;

"limited liability partnership" means a partnership formed and registered under this Act ;

"limited liability partnership agreement" means any written agreement between the partners of the limited liability partnership or between the limited liability partnership and its partners which determines the mutual rights and duties of the partners and their rights and duties in relation to that limited liability partnership ;

"member" includes the heir, executor, administrator or other personal representative, as the case may be, of the member ;

"members' voluntary winding-up" has the meaning assigned to it by section 625 (4) of this Act ;

"memorandum" means the memorandum of association of a company as originally framed or as altered in pursuance of any enactment ;

"minimum issued share capital" means the respective amounts stated in section 27 (2) (a) of this Act ;

"Minister" means the Minister charged with responsibility for trade; and

"Ministry" shall be construed accordingly;

"minor" means a person who has not attained the age of 18 years ;

"non-cash asset" means any property or interest in property other than cash and for this purpose, cash includes foreign currency ;

"officer" in relation to a body corporate, includes a director, manager or secretary ;

"official receiver" means the officer by whatever name called or known charged with control of affairs in bankruptcy and if the appointment is vacant for any reason whatsoever, means the sheriff ;

"partner" means a co-owner, member, or investor in a partnership, and shall include a person who joins with others to form a partnership and in relation to a limited liability partnership, means any person who becomes a partner in the limited liability partnership, in accordance with the partnership agreement ;

"person" includes an individual, company, or other entity, which has legal rights and is subject to obligations ;

"personal representative" where customary law is applicable, includes successors appointed in respect of deceased contributories ;

"person with significant control" means any person—

(a) directly or indirectly holding at least 5% of the shares or interest in a company or limited liability partnership ;

(b) directly or indirectly holding at least 5% of the voting rights in a company or limited liability partnership ;

(c) directly or indirectly holding the right to appoint or remove a majority of the directors or partners in a company or limited liability partnership ;

(d) otherwise having the right to exercise or actually exercising significant influence or control over a company or limited liability partnership ; or

(e) having the right to exercise, or actually exercising significant influence or control over the activities of a trust or firm whether or not it is a legal entity, but would itself satisfy any of the first four conditions if it were an individual ;

"preference share" means a share, by whatever name designated, which does not entitle the holder of it to any right to participate beyond a specified amount in any distribution whether by way of dividend or on redemption, in a winding-up, or otherwise ;

"prescribed" means, as respects the provisions of this Act (other than as to the winding-up of companies), prescribed by court or, as the case may be, by other proper authority by regulations or order, and as to winding-up, means as prescribed by rules of court, or deemed so to be ;

"private company" has the meaning assigned to it by section 22 (1) of this Act ;

"prospectus" means any prospectus, notice, circular, advertisement, or other invitation, offering to the public for subscription or purchase any shares or debentures of a company and includes any document which, save to the extent that it offers securities for a consideration other than cash, is a prospectus ;

"receiver" includes a manager ;

"recognised stock exchange" means any body of persons for the time being recognised by the Securities and Exchange Commission as a stock exchange dealing in shares, debentures and other securities ;

"registered company" means a company incorporated or deemed to be incorporated under this Act ;

"Registrar-General" means the Registrar-General appointed under this Act ;

"resolution for reducing share capital" has the meaning assigned to it by section 131 of this Act ;

"resolution for voluntary winding-up" has the meaning assigned to it by section 620 of this Act ;

"rules" includes rules made by the Chief Judge of the Federal High Court for the purpose of section 616 or 683 of this Act and all incidental forms together with rules made by the Corporate Affairs Commission ;

"secured creditor" means a creditor who has been granted a security interest in any property, asset or assets for the purpose of securing the performance of a debt or guarantee obligation ;

"securities" includes shares, debentures, debenture stock, bonds, notes (other than promissory notes) and units under a unit trust scheme ;

"share" means the interests in a company's share capital of a member who is entitled to share in the capital or income of such company; and except where a distinction between stock and shares is expressed or implied, includes stock ;

"share capital" means the issued share capital of a company at any given time ;

"show cards" means a card containing or exhibiting articles dealt with, or samples or representations thereof ;

"small company" has the meaning assigned to it under section 394 of this Act ;

"statutory declaration" means a declaration voluntarily made under the Oaths Act and in Nigeria includes one so made under any other enactment or law providing for the taking of a voluntary declaration ;

"statutory meeting" means the meeting required to be held by section 235 (1) of this Act ;

"statutory report" has the meaning assigned to it by section 235 (2) of this Act ;

"subsidiary" means, in relation to a body corporate, a subsidiary as defined by section 381 of this Act ;

"treasury share" means a share in a company's share capital which the company itself holds in a proprietary capacity and enjoys legal, beneficial and economic interest of;

"unlimited company" has the meaning assigned to it by section 21 (1) of this Act ;
"unregistered company" where used in Chapters 20-27 of Part B of this Act, includes any partnership, association or company with the following exceptions—

(a) a company and any existing company registered under this Act ; and (b) a partnership, association or company which consists of less than eight members and is not a foreign partnership, association or company ; "unsecured creditors" means any creditor who is not a secured creditor ;

(2) The Registration of a business name under this Act shall not be construed as authorising the use of that name if, apart from such registration, the use could be prohibited.

(3) References in this Act to bodies corporate or to corporations exclude corporations sole; but unless the context otherwise requires, they shall include references to companies incorporated outside Nigeria.

869.—(1) Subject to the provisions of this section, the Companies and Repeal and Allied Matters Act, 1990, the Companies and Allied Matters (Amendment) savings.
Act 1990, the Companies and Allied Matters (Amendment) Act, 1991, the Companies and Allied Matters (Amendment) Act, 1992 and the Companies and Allied Matters (Amendment) Act, 1998 are, on the commencement of this Act, repealed.

(2) Nothing in this Act shall affect any order, rule, regulation, appointment, conveyance, mortgage, deed or agreement, made, resolution passed, direction given, proceeding taken, instrument issued or thing done under the enactment hereby repealed; but any such order, rule, regulation, appointment, conveyance, mortgage, deed, agreement, resolution, direction, proceeding, instrument or thing if in force immediately before the commencement of this Act shall, on the commencement of this Act, continue in force, and so far as it could have been made, passed, given, taken, issued or done under this Act shall have effect as if so made, passed, given, taken, issued or done.

(3) Nothing in this Act shall be construed so as to prohibit the continuation of an inspection by inspectors appointed under any enactment repealed, begun before the commencement of this Act, and section 358 of this Act shall apply to a report of inspectors appointed under any enactment repealed as it applies to a report of inspectors appointed under section 357 of this Act.

(4) A register kept under the enactment repealed shall be deemed to be kept under the corresponding provisions of this Act.

(5) Funds and accounts constituted under this Act shall be deemed to be in continuation of the corresponding funds and accounts constituted under the enactment repealed.

(6) Nothing in this Act shall affect the incorporation of any company registered under any enactment repealed.

(7) Any individual, firm or company who immediately before the cominginto operation of this Act was registered as a business name under the enactment repealed, shall be deemed to be registered under and in accordance with the repealed Act.

Citation.870. This Act may be cited as the Companies and Allied Matters Act, 2020.

SCHEDULES

FIRST SCHEDULE Sections 378 and 380

FORM AND CONTENT OF COMPANY'S FINANCIAL STATEMENTS

PART I—GENERAL INFORMATION TO BE DISCLOSED GENERAL RULES AND FORMATS

SECTION A—GENERAL INFORMATION TO BE DISCLOSED

1. All accounting information that assist users to assess the financial liquidity, profitability and viability of a company should be disclosed and presented in a logical, clear and understandable manner.
2. The financial statements of a company shall state—
(a) the name of the company ;
(b) the period covered ;
(c) a brief description of its activities ;
(d) its legal form ; and
(e) its relationship with its significant local and overseas suppliers (ifany) including the immediate and ultimate parent, associated or affiliated company.
3. Financial statements shall include the—
(a) statement of accounting policies ;
(b) balance sheet ;
(c) profit and loss account or income statement ;
(d) notes on the accounts ;
(e) statement of source and application of funds ;
(f) value added statement ; and (g) five-year financial summary.
4. Financial implication of inter-company transfer and technical management agreements between the company and its significant local and overseas suppliers (if any), including its immediate and ultimate, associated, affiliated company shall be disclosed.
5. Financial statements shall show corresponding figures for the preceding period.

SECTION B—GENERAL RULES

6. (1) Subject to the following provisions of this Schedule, every—
(a) balance sheet of a company shall show the items listed in either of the balance sheet formats set out in section C of this Part ; and
(b) profit and loss account of a company shall show the items listed in any one of the profit and loss account formats so set out, in either case, in the order and under the headings and subheadings given in the format adopted.
(2) Subparagraph (1) is not to be read as requiring the heading or subheading for any items to be distinguished by any letter or number assigned to that item in the format adopted.

7.—(1) Where, in accordance with paragraph 6 (1), a company's balance sheet or profit and loss account for any year has been prepared by reference to one of the formats set out in section C of this Schedule, the directors of the company shall adopt the same format in preparing the accounts for subsequent years of the company unless in their opinion there are special reasons for a change.
(2) Particulars of any change in the format adopted in preparing a company's balance sheet or profit and loss account in accordance with paragraph 6 (1) shall be disclosed, and the reasons for the change shall be explained in a note to the accounts in which the new format is first adopted.

8.—(1) Any item required in accordance with paragraph 6 (1) to be shown in a company's balance sheet or profit and loss account, may be shown in greater detail than required by the format adopted.

(2) A company's balance sheet or profit and loss account may include an item representing or covering any asset or liability, income or expenditure not otherwise covered by any of the items listed in the format adopted, but the following shall not be treated as assets in any company's balance sheet—

(a) preliminary expenses ;

(b) expenses or commission on any issue of shares or debentures ; and(c) research and development costs.

(3) In preparing a company's balance sheet or profit and loss account, the directors of the company shall adopt the arrangement and subheadings otherwise required under subparagraph (1) in respect of the items to which an Arabic number is assigned in the format adopted, in any case where the special nature of the company's business requires such adaptation.

(4) Items to which Arabic numbers are assigned in any of the formats set out in section C may be combined in a company's accounts for any year if either—

(a) their individual amounts are not material to assessing the state of affairs or profit or loss of the company for that year ; or (b) the combination facilitates that assessment:

Provided that in a case within paragraph (a) the individual amounts of any item so combined shall be disclosed in a note to the accounts.

(5) Subject to paragraph 9 (3), a heading or subheading corresponding to an item listed in the format adopted in preparing a company's balance sheet or profit and loss account shall not be included if there is no amount to be shown for that item in respect of the year to which the balance sheet or profit and loss account relates.

(6) Every profit and loss account of a company shall show separately as additional items—

(a) an amount set aside or proposed to be set aside to, or withdrawn or proposed to be withdrawn from, reserves ; and

(b) the aggregate amount of any dividend paid and proposed.

9.—(1) In respect of every item shown in a company's balance sheet or profit and loss account, the corresponding amount for the year immediately preceding that to which the balance sheet or profit and loss account relates shall also be shown.

(2) Where that corresponding amount is not comparable with the amount to be shown for the item in question in respect of the year to which the balance sheet or profit and loss account relates, the former amount shall be adjusted and particulars of the adjustment and the reasons for it shall be disclosed in a note to the accounts.

(3) Paragraph 8 (5) does not apply in any case where an amount can be shown for the item in question in respect of the year immediately preceding that to which the balance sheet or profit and loss account relates, and that amount shall be shown under the heading or subheading required under subparagraph (1) for that item.

10. The amounts in respect of items representing assets or income may not be set off against amounts in respect of items representing liabilities or expenditure (as the case may be), or vice versa.

SECTION C—THE REQUIRED FORMATS FOR ACCOUNTS Preliminary

11. References in this Part of this Schedule to the items listed in any of the Formats set out below are to those items read together with any of the notes following the Formats which apply to any of those items, and the requirement imposed by subparagraph 8 (1) to show the items, listed in any such Format in the order adopted

in the Format, is subject to any provision in those notes for alternative positions for any particular items.

12. A number in brackets following any item in any of the Formats set out under Format 1 is a reference to the note of that number in the notes following the Formats.

13. In the notes following the Formats—

(a) the heading of each note gives the required heading or subheading for the item to which it applies and a reference to any letter and number assigned to that item in the Formats set out below (taking a reference in the case of Format 2 of the balance sheet Formats to the item listed under assets or under liabilities as the case may require) ; and

(b) references to a numbered Format are to the balance sheet Formator, as the case may require, to the profit and loss account Format of that number set out under Format 1.

Balance Sheet Formats

FORMAT I

A. CALLED UP SHARE CAPITAL NOT PAID (1)

B. FIXED ASSETS

1. Land and buildings.
2. Plant and machinery.
3. Fixtures, fittings, tools and equipment.
4. Construction-in-progress.
5. Pre-payment for stocks in-transit.

C. LONG-TERM INVESTMENTS

1. Shares in group companies.
2. Loans to group companies.
3. Shares in related companies.
4. Loans to related companies.
5. Investments other than loans.
6. Loans.
7. Own shares (treasury shares) (4).
8. Bonds, debentures and Federal Government Development Stocks.

D. DEFERRED CHARGES

1. Development costs.
2. Concessions, patents, licences, franchise, trademarks and similar rightsand assets (2).
3. Goodwill (3).
4. Pre-payment for services to be received.

E. CURRENT ASSETS

I. CURRENT ASSETS

1. Stocks
2. Raw materials and consumables.
3. Work-in-progress.
4. Finished goods and goods awaiting sale.
5. Pre-payment for stocks in transit.

II. DEBTORS (5)

1. Trade debtors.
2. Amount owed by group companies.

3. Amount owed by related companies.
4. Other debtors.
5. Called up share capital not paid (1). 6. Pre-payments and accrued income.

III. SHORT-TERM INVESTMENT

1. Shares in group companies.
2. Own shares (Treasury shares) (4).
3. Other investments.

IV. CASH IN BANK AND AT HAND

F. PREPAYMENTS AND ACCRUED INCOME(6)

G. CREDITORS : AMOUNTS FALLING DUE WITHIN ONE YEAR

1. Debenture loans (7).
2. Bank loans and overdrafts.
3. Payments received on account (8).
4. Trade creditors.
5. Bills of exchange payable.
6. Amounts owed to group companies.
7. Amounts owed to related companies.
8. Other creditors including taxation (P.A.Y.E.) and National ProvidentFund (social security) (9).
9. Accruals and deferred income (10).

H. NET CURRENT ASSETS (LIABILITIES) (11)

I. TOTAL ASSETS LESS CURRENT LIABILITIES

J. CREDITORS : AMOUNT FALLING DUE AFTER MORE THAN ONE YEAR

1. Debenture loans (7).
2. Bank loans and overdrafts.
3. Payments received on account (8).
4. Trade creditors.
5. Bills of exchange payable.
6. Amounts owed to group companies.
7. Amounts owed to related companies.
8. Other creditors including taxation and social security (9).
9. Accruals and deferred income (10).

K. PROVISIONS FOR LIABILITIES AND CHARGES

1. Pensions and similar obligations.
2. Taxation, including deferred taxation.
3. Other provisions.

L. ACCRUALS AND DEFERRED INCOME (10)

M. CAPITAL AND RESERVES

1. Called up share capital (12)
2. Share premium account
3. Revaluation reserves
4. Other reserves1. Capital redemption reserve.
2. Reserve for own shares.
3. Reserves provided for by the articles of association.
4. Other reserves.

V. PROFIT AND LOSS TRANSFERRED FROM PROFIT AND LOSS ACCOUNT OR INCOME

STATEMENT

Balance Sheet Formats

FORMAT 2

ASSETS

A. CALLED UP SHARE CAPITAL NOT PAID (1)

B. TANGIBLE ASSETS

1. Land and buildings.
2. Plant and machinery.
3. Fixtures, fittings, tools and equipment.
4. Payments on account and assets in course of construction.

C. LONG-TERM INVESTMENT

1. Shares in group companies.
2. Loans to group companies.
3. Shares in related companies.
4. Loans to related companies.
5. Other investments other than loans.
6. Other loans.
7. Own shares (treasury shares) (4).

D. DEFERRED CHARGES

1. Development costs.
2. Concessions, patents, licences, trademarks and similar rights andassets (2).
3. Goodwill (3).
4. Payments on account.

E. CURRENT ASSETS

I. STOCKS

1. Raw materials and consumables.
2. Work-in-progress.
3. Finished goods and goods awaiting sale.
4. Payments for stocks in transit.

II. DEBTORS (5)

1. Trade debtors.
2. Amounts owed by group companies.
3. Amounts owed by related companies.
4. Other debtors.
5. Called up share capital not paid (1).
6. Pre-payments and accrued income (6).

III. SHORT-TERM INVESTMENTS

1. Shares in group companies.
2. Own shares (Treasury Shares) (4).
3. Other investments.

IV. CASH IN BANK AND AT HAND

F. PRE-PAYMENTS AND ACCRUED INCOME (6)

CAPITAL AND LIABILITIES

A. CAPITAL AND RESERVES

I. CALLED UP SHARE CAPITAL(12) II. SHARE PREMIUM ACCOUNT

III. REVALUATION RESERVE

IV. OTHER RESERVES

1. Capital redemption reserves.
2. Reserve for own shares (12A).
3. Reserves provided for by the articles of association.
4. Other reserves.

V. PROFIT AND LOSS ACCOUNT (RETAINED EARNINGS) (12B)

B. CURRENT LIABILITIES

1. Debenture loans (7).
2. Trade creditors.
3. Bank loans and overdrafts.
4. Payments received in advance (8).
5. Bills of exchange payable.

C. NON-TRADE CURRENT LIABILITIES

1. Provision for pension and other similar obligations.
2. Provisions for taxation including deferred taxes, National ProvidentFund (social security) (9).
3. Other provisions.
4. Accruals and deferred income (10).
5. Transactions between and within group :

(a) Amount owed to group companies.

(b) Amount owed to related companies.(c) Others.

Portions of Long-Term Liabilities due in the Current Period.

D. LONG-TERM LIABILITIES

4. Debenture loans (portions not due next year).
5. Bonds (portion not due next year).
6. Other long-term debts (portion not due next year).

NOTES ON THE BALANCE SHEET FORMATS

(1) Called up hare capital not paid (Formats 1 and 2, items A and E II 5)—

This item may be shown in either of the two positions given in Formats 1 and 2.

(2) Concessions, patents, licences, trademarks and similar rights and assets (Formats 1 and 2, item D2)—Amounts in respect of assets shall only be included in a company's balance sheet under this item if either—

(a) the assets were acquired for valuable consideration and are not required to be shown under goodwill ; or

(b) the assets in question were created by the company itself.

(3) Goodwill (Formats 1 and 2, items D 3)—Amounts representing goodwill shall only be included to the extent that the goodwill was acquired for valuable consideration.

(4) Own shares (Formats 1 and 2, items C 7 and E III 2)—The nominal value of the shares held shall be shown separately.

(5) Debtors (Formats 1 and 2, items E II 1-6)—The amount falling due after more than one year shall be shown separately for each item included under debtors.

(6) Pre-payments and accrued income (Formats 1 and 2, items E II 6 and F)—This item may be shown in either of the two positions given in Formats 1 and 2.

(7) Debenture loans (7) (Format 1, items G 1 and B 1 and Format 2, itemC 1)—The amount of any convertible loans shall be shown separately.

(8) Payments received on account (Format 1, items G 3 and J 3 and Format2, item C 3)—Payments received on account of orders shall be shown for each of these items in so far as they are not shown as deductions from stocks.

(9) Other creditors including taxation (Format 1, items G 8 and J 8 and Format 2, item C 2)—The amount for creditors in respect of taxation shall be shown separately from the amount for other creditors.

(10) Accruals and deferred income (Format 1, items G 9, J 9 and L 1 and Format 2, item C 4)—The two positions given for this item in Format I at E 9 and H 9 are an alternative to the position at J, but if the item is not shown in a position corresponding to that at J, it may be shown in either or both of the other two positions (as the case may require). The two positions given for this item in Format 2 are alternatives.

(11) Net current assets (liabilities) (Format 1, item H)—In determining the amount to be shown for this item any amounts shown under pre-payments and accrued income shall be taken into account wherever shown.

(12) Called up share capital (Format 1, item K 1 and Format 2, item A)—The amount of allotted share capital and the amount of called up share capital which has been paid up shall be shown separately.

(13) Creditors—Amounts falling due within one year and after one year shall be shown separately for each of these items and their aggregate shall be shown separately for all of these items.

Profit and Loss Account Formats

FORMAT 1

(See note (17) below)

1. Turnover.
2. Cost of sales (14).
3. Gross profit or loss.
4. Distribution expenses (14).
5. Administration expenses (14).
6. Other operating income (14).
7. Income from shares in group companies.
8. Income from shares in related companies.
9. Income from other fixed asset investments (15).
10. Other interest receivable and similar income (15).
11. Amounts written off investments.
12. Accrued interest expense and similar charges.
13. Tax on profit or loss on ordinary activities.
14. Profit or loss on ordinary activities after taxation.
15. Extraordinary income.
16. Extraordinary charges.
17. Extraordinary profit or loss.
18. Tax on extraordinary profit or loss.
19. Other taxes under the above items.
20. Profit or loss for the financial year.
21. Earnings per share.
22. Dividend per share.

Profit and Loss Account Formats

FORMAT 2

1. Sales or revenue.
2. Change in stocks of finished goods and in work-in-progress.

3. Own work capitalised.
4. Other operating income.
5. (a) Raw materials and consumables. (b) Other external charges.
6. Staff costs :
(a) wages and salaries;(b) other pension costs.
7. (a) Depreciation of fixed assets, depletion and amortisation of wasting and intangible assets ;
(b) Exceptional amounts written off current assets.
8. Other operating charges.
9. Income from shares in group companies.
10. Income from shares in related companies.
11. Income from other fixed asset investments (15).
12. Other interest receivable and similar income (15).
13. Amounts written off investments.
14. Interest payable and similar charges (16).
15. Tax on profit or loss on ordinary activities.
16. Profit or loss on ordinary activities after taxation.
17. Extraordinary income.
18. Extraordinary charges.
19. Extraordinary profit or loss.
20. Tax on extraordinary profit or loss.
21. Other taxes not shown under the above item.
22. Profit or loss for the current year transferred to Retained Earnings orReserve.

Profit and Loss Account Formats

FORMAT 3

(See note (17) below)

A. CHARGES

1. Cost of sales (14).
2. Distribution costs (14).
3. Administrative expenses (14).
4. Amounts written off investments.
5. Interest payable and similar charges (16).
6. Tax on profit or loss on ordinary activities.
7. Profit or loss on ordinary activities after taxation.
8. Extraordinary charges.
9. Tax on extraordinary profit or loss.
10. Other taxes not shown under the above items.
11. Profit or loss for the financial year.

B. INCOME

1. Turnover.
2. Other operating income.
3. Income from shares in group companies.
4. Income from shares in related companies.
5. Income from other fixed asset investments (15).
6. Other interest receivable and similar income (15).
7. Profit or loss on ordinary activities after taxation.
8. Extraordinary income.

9. Profit or loss for the financial year.

Profit and Loss Account Formats

FORMAT 4

A. CHARGES

1. Reduction in stocks of finished goods and in work-in-progress.
2. (a) Raw materials and consumables ; (b) Other external charges.
3. Staff Costs : (a) wages and salaries ; (b) other pension costs.
4. (a) Depreciation and other amounts written off tangible and intangible fixed assets ;

(b) Exceptional amounts written off current assets.

5. Other operating charges.
6. Amounts written off investments.
7. Interest payable and similar charges (16).
8. Tax on profit or loss on ordinary activities.
9. Profit or loss on ordinary activities after taxation.
10. Extraordinary charges.
11. Tax on extraordinary profit or loss.
12. Other taxes not shown under the above items.
13. Profit or loss for the financial year.

B. INCOME

1. Turnover.
2. Increase in stocks of finished goods and in work-in-progress.
3. Own work capitalised.
4. Other operating income.
5. Income from shares in group companies.
6. Income from shares in related companies.
7. Income from other fixed asset investments (15).
8. Other interest receivable and similar income (15).
9. Profit or loss on ordinary activities after taxation.
10. Extraordinary income.
11. Profit or loss for the financial year.

Notes on the Profit and Loss Account Format

(14) Cost of sales : distribution costs : administrative expenses—(Format1, items 2, 4 and 5 and Format 3, items A 1, 2 and 3)—These items shall be stated after taking into account any necessary provisions for depreciation or diminution in value of assets.

(15) Income from other fixed asset investments : other interest receivableand similar income (Format 1, items 9 and 10: Format 2, items 11 and 12: Format 3, items B 5 and 6: Format 4, items B 7 and 8) — Income and interest derived from group companies shall be shown separately from income and interest derived from other sources.

(16) Interest payable and similar charges - (Format 1, item 12: Format 2,item 14 : Format 3, item A 5: Format 1, item A 7) — The amount payable to group companies shall be shown separately.

(17) Formats 1 and 3 — The amount of any provisions for depreciationand diminution in value of tangible and intangible fixed assets falling to be shown under items 7 (a) and A 4 (a) respectively in Formats 2 and 4, shall be disclosed in a note

to the accounts in any case where the profit and loss account is prepared by reference to Format 1 or Format 3.

PART II—ACCOUNTING PRINCIPLES AND RULES

SECTION A—ACCOUNTING PRINCIPLES

Preliminary

14. Subject to paragraph 15, the amounts to be included in respect of allitems shown in a company's financial statements shall be determined in accordance with generally accepted accounting principles, and with the accounting standards laid down from time to time by the Financial Reporting Council of Nigeria.

Departure from the Accounting Principles

15. If it appears to the directors of a company that there are specialreasons for departing from any of the principles stated above in preparing the company's financial statements in respect of any financial year they may do so, but particulars of the departure, the reasons for it and its effect shall be given in a note to the accounts.

SECTION A—HISTORICAL COST ACCOUNTING RULES

Preliminary

16. Subject to section C of this Part of this Schedule, the amounts to be included in respect of all items shown in a company's financial statements shall be determined in accordance with the rules set out in paragraphs17-28.

Fixed Assets

17. Subject to any provision for depreciation or diminution in value made in accordance with paragraph 18 or 19, the amount to be included in respect of any fixed asset shall be its purchase price or production cost.

18. In the case of any fixed asset which has a limited useful economic life, the amount of—

(a) its purchase price or production cost ; or

(b) where it is estimated that the assets have a residual value at the end of the period of its useful economic life, its purchase price or production cost less that estimated residual value, shall be reduced by provisions for depreciation calculated to write off that amount systematically over the period of the asset's useful economic life.

19.—(1) Where a fixed asset investment of a description falling to be included under item B III of either the balance sheet formats set out in Part I of this Schedule had diminished in value, provisions for diminution in value may be made in respect of it and the amount to be included in respect of it may be reduced accordingly, and such provisions which are not shown in the profit and loss account shall be disclosed (either separately or in aggregate) in a note to the accounts.

(2) Provisions for diminution in value shall be made in respect of any fixed asset which had diminished in value if the reduction in its value is expected to be permanent (whether its useful economic life is limited or not), and the amount to be included in respect of it shall be reduced accordingly, and such provisions which are not shown in the profit and loss account, shall be disclosed (either separately or in aggregate) in a note to the accounts.

(3) Where the reasons for which any provision was made in accordance with subparagraph (1) or (2) have ceased to apply to any extent, that provision shall be written back to the extent that it is no longer necessary, and any amounts written back in accordance with this subparagraph which are not shown in the profit and

loss account, shall be disclosed (either separately or in aggregate) in a note to the accounts.

Rules for determining particular Fixed Asset items

20.—(1) Notwithstanding that an item in respect of development costs is included under fixed assets in the balance sheet formats set out in Part I of this Schedule, an amount may only be included in a company's balance sheet in respect of development costs in special circumstances.

(2) If any amount is included in a company's balance sheet in respect of development costs the following information shall be given in a note to the accounts—

(a) the period over which the amount of those costs originally capitalised is being or is to be written off ; and

(b) the reason for capitalising the development costs in question.

21.—(1) The application of paragraphs 17 - 19 in relation to goodwill (in any case where goodwill is treated as an asset) is subject to the following provisions of this paragraph.

(2) The amount of the consideration for goodwill acquired by a company shall be reduced by provision for amortisation calculated to write off that amount systematically over a period of five years or less as may be determined by the directors of the company.

(3) In any case where any goodwill acquired by a company is shown or included as an asset in the company's balance sheet, the period chosen for writing off the consideration for that goodwill and the reasons for choosing that period shall be disclosed in a note to the accounts.

Current Assets

22. Subject to paragraph 23, the amount to be included in respect of any current asset shall be its purchase price or production cost.

23.—(1) If the net realisable value of any current asset is lower than its purchase price or production cost, the amount to be included in respect of that asset shall be the net realisable value

(2) Where the reasons for which any provision for diminution in value was made in accordance with subparagraph (1) have ceased to apply to any extent, that provision shall be written back to the extent that it is no longer necessary.

Miscellaneous and Supplementary Provision

Excess of money owed over value received as an Asset item

24.—(1) Where the amount repayable on any debt owed by a company is greater than the value of the consideration received in the transaction giving rise to the debt, the difference may be treated as an asset.

(2) Where any such amount is so treated—

(a) reasonable amounts shall be completely written off each year before repayment of the debt ; and

(b) if the current amount is not shown as a separate item in the company's balance sheet, it shall be disclosed in a note to the accounts.

Assets included at a fixed amount

25.—(1) The assets which fall to be included among the—

(a) fixed assets of a company under the item, "tangible assets", or

(b) current assets of a company under the item, "raw material and consumables",

may be included at a fixed quantity and value.

(2) Subparagraph (1) applies to assets of a kind which are constantly being replaced, where—

(a) their overall value is not material to assessing the company's state of affairs ; and

(b) their quantity, value and composition are not subject to material variation.

Determination of purchase Price or Production Cost

26.—(1) The purchase price of an asset shall be determined by adding to the actual price paid any expenses incidental to its acquisition.

(2) The production cost of an asset shall be determined by adding to the purchase price of the raw materials and consumables used, the amount of the costs incurred by the company which are directly attributable to the production of that asset.

(3) In addition, there may be included in the production cost of an asset—

(a) a reasonable proportion of the costs incurred by the company which are only indirectly attributable to the production of that asset, but only to the extent that they relate to the period of production ; and

(b) interest on capital borrowed to finance the production of that asset, to the extent that it accrues in respect of the period of production :

Provided that in a case within paragraph (a), that the inclusion of the interest in determining the cost of that asset and the amount of the interest so included is disclosed in a note to the accounts.

(4) In the case of current assets distribution, costs may not be included in production costs.

27.—(1) Subject to the qualification mentioned, the purchase price or production of—

(a) any assets which fall to be included under any item shown in a company's balance sheet under the general item "stocks"; and

(b) any assets which are tangible assets (including investments), may be determined by the application of any of the methods mentioned in subparagraph (2) in relation to any such assets of the same class, and the method chosen must be one which appears to the directors to be appropriate in the circumstances of the company.

(2) Those methods are—

(a) the method known as "first in, first out" (FIFO) ;

(b) the method known as "last in, first out" (LIFO) ;

(c) a weighted average price ; and

(d) any other method similar to any of the methods mentioned above.

(3) Where in the case of any company—

(a) the purchase price or production cost of assets falling to be included under any item shown in the company's balance sheet has been determined by the application of any method permitted by this paragraph, and

(b) the amount shown in respect of that item differs materially from the relevant alternative amount given below in this paragraph,

the difference shall be disclosed in a note to the accounts.

(4) Subject to subparagraph (5) below, for the purposes of subparagraph(3) (b), the relevant alternative amount, in relation to any item shown in a company's balance sheet, is the amount which would have been shown in respect of that item if assets of any class included under that item at an amount determined by any method permitted by this paragraph had instead been included at their replacement cost as at the balance sheet date.

(5) The relevant alternative amount may be determined by reference to the most recent actual purchase price or production cost before the balance sheet date of the assets of any class included under the item in question instead of by reference to their replacement cost as at that date, but only if the former appears to the directors of the company to constitute the more appropriate standard of comparison in the case of assets of that class.

(6) For the purposes of this paragraph, assets of any description shall be regarded as tangible if assets of that description are substantially indistinguishable one from another.

Substitution of original stated amount where price or cost unknown

28. Where there is no record of the purchase price or production cost of any assets of a company or of any price, expenses or costs relevant for determining its purchase price or production cost in accordance with paragraph 26, or any such record cannot be obtained without unreasonable expense or delay, its purchase price or production cost shall be taken for the purposes of paragraph 17-23 to be the value record of its value made on or after its acquisition or production by the company.

SECTION C

ALTERNATIVE ACCOUNTING RULES

Preliminary

29.—(1) The rules set out in section B are referred to in this Schedule as the historical cost accounting rules.

(2) Those rules, with the omission of paragraphs 16, 21 and 25 - 28, are referred to in this Part of the Schedule as the depreciation rules, and references in this Schedule to the historical cost accounting rules do not include the depreciation rules as they apply by virtue of paragraph 32.

30. Subject to paragraph 32-34, the amount to be included in respect of assets of any description mentioned in paragraph 26 may be determined on any basis so mentioned.

Alternative Accounting Rules

31.—(1) Intangible fixed assets, other than goodwill, may be included at their current cost.

(2) Tangible fixed assets may be included at a market value determined as at the date of their valuation or at their current cost.

(3) Investment of any description falling to be included under item B III of either of the balance sheet formats set out in Part I of this Schedule may be included either—

(a) at a market value determined as at the date of their last valuation, or (b) at a value determined on any basis which appears to the directors to be appropriate in the circumstances of the company, but in the latter case particulars of the method of valuation adopted and of the reasons for adopting it shall be disclosed in a note to the accounts.

(4) Investments of any description falling to be included under item CIII of either of the balance sheet formats set out in Part I of this Schedule may be included at their current cost.

(5) Stocks may be included at their current cost.

Application of the Depreciation Rules

32.—(1) Where the value of any assets of a company is determined on any basis mentioned in paragraph 31, that value shall be, or (as the case may require) be the starting point for determining, the amount to be included in respect of that asset in the company's accounts, instead of its purchase price or production cost or any value previously so determined for that asset; and the depreciation rules shall apply accordingly in relation to any such asset with the substitution for any reference to its purchase price or production cost of a reference to the value most recently determined for that asset on any basis mentioned in paragraph 31.

(2) The amount of any provision for depreciation required in the case of any fixed asset by paragraph 18 or 19 as it applies by virtue of sub-paragraph (1) is referred to below in this paragraph as the adjusted amount, and the amount of any provision which would be required by that paragraph in the case of that asset according to the historical cost accounting rules, is referred to as the historical cost amount.

(3) Where subparagraph (1) applies in the case of any fixed asset, the amount of any provision for depreciation in respect of that asset—

(a) included in any item shown in the profit and loss account in respect of amounts written off assets of the description in question ; or

(b) taken into account in stating any item so shown which is required by note (14) of the notes on the profit and loss account formats set out in Part I of this Schedule to be stated after taking into account any necessary provisions for depreciation or diminution in value of assets included under it, may be the historical cost amount instead of the adjusted amount provided that the amount of any difference between the two is shown separately in the profit and loss account or in a note to the accounts.

Additional information to be provided in case of departure from historical costs accounting rules

33. (1) This paragraph applies where the amount to be included in respect of assets covered by any item shown in a company's accounts have been determined on any basis mentioned in paragraph 31.

(2) The items affected and the basis of valuation adopted in determining the amounts of the assets in question in the case of such item shall be disclosed in a note to the accounts.

(3) In the case of each balance sheet item affected (except stocks) either—

(a) the comparable amounts determined according to the historical cost accounting rules ; or

(b) the differences between those amount and the corresponding amounts actually shown in the balance sheet in respect of that item, shall be shown separately in the balance sheet or in a note to the accounts.

(4) In subparagraph (3), references in relation to any item to the comparable amounts determined as there mentioned are references to—

(a) the aggregate amount which would be required to be shown in respect of that item if the amounts to be included in respect of all the assets covered by that item were determined according to the historical cost accounting rules ; and

(b) the aggregate amount of the cumulative provisions for depreciation or diminution in value which would be permitted or required in determining those amounts according to those rules.

Revaluation reserve

34.—(1) With respect to any determination of the value of an asset of a company on any basis mentioned in paragraph 31, the amount of any profit or loss arising from that determination (after allowing, where appropriate, for any provisions for depreciation or diminution in value made otherwise than by reference to the value to be determined and any adjustment of any such provisions made in the light of that determination) shall be credited or (as the case may be) debited to a separate reserve ("the revaluation reserve").

(2) The amount of the revaluation reserve shall be shown in the company's balance sheet under a separate subheading in the position given for the item "revaluation reserve" in Format 1 or 2 of the balance sheet formats set out in Part 1 of this Schedule, but need not be shown under that name.

(3) The revaluation reserve shall be reduced to the extent that the amount standing to the credit of the reserve are in the opinion of the directors of the company no longer necessary for the purpose of the accounting policies adopted by the company, but an amount may only be transferred from the reserve to the profit and loss account if either—

(a) the amount in question was previously charged to that account ; or (b) it represents realised profit.

(4) The treatment for taxation purposes of amount credited or debited to the revaluation reserve shall be disclosed in a note to the accounts.

PART III—NOTES TO THE ACCOUNTS

Preliminary

35. Any information required in the case of any company by the following provisions of this Part of the Schedule shall (if not given in the company's accounts) be given by way of a note to those accounts.

Disclosure of Accounting Policies

36. The accounting policies adopted by the company in determining the amounts to be included in respect of item shown in the balance sheet and in determining the profit or loss of the company shall be stated (including such policies with respect to the depreciation and diminution in value of assets).

Information Supplementing the Balance Sheet

37. Paragraphs 38-50 require information which either supplement the information given with respect to any particular items shown in the balance sheet or is otherwise relevant to assessing the company's state of affairs in the light of the information so given.

Share Capital and Debentures

38.—(1) The following information shall be given with respect to the company's share capital—

(a) the authorised share capital ; and

(b) where shares of more than one class have been allotted, the number and aggregate nominal value or shares of each class allotted.

(2) In the case of any part of the allotted share capital that consists of redeemable shares, the following information shall be given—

(a) the earliest and latest dates on which the company has power to redeem those shares;

(b) whether those shares must be redeemed in any event or are liable tobe redeemed at the option of the company or of the shareholder ; and

(c) whether any (and, if so, what) premium is payable on redemption.

39.—(1) If the company has allotted any shares during the financial year, the following information shall be given—

(a) the reason for making the allotment ;
(b) the classes of shares allotted ; and
(c) as regards each class of shares, the number allotted, their aggregate nominal value, and the consideration received by the company for the allotment.
(2) With respect to any contingent right to the allotment of shares in the company, the following particulars shall be given—
(a) the number, description and amount of the shares in relation to which the right is exercisable ;
(b) the period during which it is exercisable ; and(c) the price to be paid for the shares allotted.
(3) In subparagraph (2) "contingent right to the allotment of shares "means any option to subscribe for shares and any other right to require the allotment of shares and to any person whether arising on the conversion into shares of securities of any other description or otherwise.
40.—(1) If the company has issued any debenture during the financial year to which the accounts relate, the following information shall be given —
(a) the reason for making the issue ;
(b) the classes of debentures issued ; and
(c) as respect each class of debentures, the amount issued and consideration received by the company for the issue.
(2) Particulars of any redeemed debenture which the company has power to re-issue shall also be given.
(3) Where any of the company's debenture are held by a nominee of or trustee for the company, the nominal amount of the debentures and the amount at which they are stated in the accounting records kept by the company in accordance with section 374 of this Act shall be stated.

Fixed Assets

41.—(1) In respect of each item which is or would but for paragraph 8 (4) (b) be shown under the general item "fixed assets" in the company's balance sheet, the following information shall be given—
(a) the appropriate amount in respect of that item as at the date of the beginning of the financial year and as at the balance sheet date respectively ;
(b) the effect on any amount shown in the balance sheet in respect of that item of—
(i) any revision of the amount in respect of any asset included under that item made during,
(ii) that year on any basis mentioned in paragraph 31,
(iii) acquisitions during that year of any asset,
(iv) disposals during that year of any assets, and
(v) any transfer of assets of the company to and from that item during that year.
(2) The reference in subparagraph (1) (a) to the appropriate amount in respect of any item as at any date there mentioned, is a reference to amounts representing the aggregate amounts determined, as at that date, in respect of assets falling to be included under that item on either of the following basis, that is to say—
(a) on the basis of purchase price or production cost (determined in accordance with paragraphs 26 and 27) ; or
(b) on any basis mentioned in paragraph 31 (leaving out of account in either case any provision for depreciation or diminution in value).

(3) In respect of each item within subparagraph (1)—
(a) the cumulative amount of provisions for depreciation or diminution in value of assets included under that item as at each date mentioned in subparagraph (1) (a);
(b) the amount of any such provisions made in respect of the financial year ;
(c) the amount of any adjustment made in respect of any such provisions during that year in consequence of the disposal of any assets ; and
(d) the amount of any other adjustments made in respect of any such provisions during that year, shall also be stated.

42. Where any fixed asset of the company, other than listed investments, are included under any item shown in the company's balance sheet at an amount determined on any basis mentioned in paragraph 31, the following information shall be given—
(a) the years (if they are known to the directors) in which the assets were severally valued and the several values ; and
(b) in the case of assets that have been valued during the financial year, the name of the persons who valued them or particulars of their qualification for doing so and (whichever is stated) the bases of valuation used by them.

43. In relation to any amount which is or would but for paragraph 8 (4) (b) be shown in respect of the item "land and buildings" in the company's balance sheet, there shall be stated—
(a) how much of the amount is ascribable to land held under statutory right of occupancy and how much to land held under a sublease ; and
(b) how much of the amount ascribable to land held under a sublease is ascribable to land held on long lease and how much to land held on short lease.

44.—(1) In respect of the amount of each item which is or may for paragraph 8 (4) (b) be shown in the company's balance sheet under the general item " in "investments" (whether as fixed assets or as current assets) shall be stated—
(a) how much of that amount is ascribable to listed investments ; and
(b) how much of any amount so ascribable is ascribable to investments as respects which there has been granted a listing on a recognised stock exchange and how much to other listed investments.

(2) Where the amount of any listed investments is stated for any item in accordance with subparagraph (1) (a), the following amounts shall also be stated—
(a) the aggregate market value of those investments where it differs from the amount stated ; and
(b) both the market value and the stock exchange value of any investments of which the former value is, for the purposes of the accounts, taken as being higher than the latter

Reserves and Provisions

45.—(1) Where any amount is transferred—
(a) to or from any reserves ;
(b) to any provisions for liabilities and charges ; or
(c) from any provisions for liabilities and charges otherwise than for the purpose for which the provision was established, and the reserves or provisions are or will but for paragraph 8 (4) (b) be shown as separate items in the company's balance sheet, the information mentioned in the following subparagraph shall be given in respect of the aggregate of reserves or provisions included in the same item.

(2) That information is—

(a) the amount of the reserves or provisions as at the date of the beginning of the year and as at the balance sheet date respectively ;
(b) any amount transferred to or from the reserves or provisions during that year ; and
(c) the source and application respectively of any amount so transferred.
(3) Particulars shall be given of each provision included in the item "other provisions" in the company's balance sheet in any case where the amount of that provision is material.

Provision for Taxation.

46. The amount of any provisions for taxation other than deferred taxation shall be stated.

Details of indebtedness

47. (1) In respect of each item shown under "creditors" in the company's balance sheet there shall be stated—
(a) the aggregate amount of any debt included under that item which are payable or repayable otherwise than by instalments and fall due for payment or repayment after the end of five years beginning with the day next following the end of the financial year ; and
(b) the aggregate amount of any debt so included which are payable or repayable by instalments and any of which fall due for payment after the end of that period, and in the case of debts within paragraph (a), the aggregate amount of instalments falling due after the end of that period shall also be disclosed for each such item.
(2) Subject to subparagraph (3), in relation to each debt falling to be taken into account under subparagraph (1), the terms of payments or repayment and the rate of any interest payable on debt shall be stated.
(3) If the number of debts is such that, in the opinion of the directors, compliance with subparagraph (2) would result in a statement of excessive length, it shall be sufficient to give a general indication of the terms of payment or repayment and the rates of any interest payable on the debts.
(4) In respect of each item shown under "creditors" in the company's balance sheet there shall be stated—
(a) the aggregate amount of any debt included under that item in respect of which any security has been given by the company ; and
(b) an indication of the nature of the securities so given.
(5) References in this paragraph to an item shown under "creditors" in the company's balance sheet include references where amounts falling due to creditors within one year and after more than one year are distinguished in the balance sheet—
(a) in a case within subparagraph (1), to an item shown under the latter of those categories ; and
(b) in a case within subparagraph (4), to an item shown under either of those categories, and references to items shown under "creditors" include references to items which would, but for paragraph 8 (4) (b), be shown under that heading.

48. If any fixed cumulative dividends on the company's shares are in arrears, there shall be stated— (a) the amount of the arrears; and
(b) the period for which the dividends or, if there is more than one class, each class of them is in arrears.

Guarantee and other financial commitments

49.—(1) Particulars shall be given of any charge on the assets of the company to secure the liabilities of any other person, including where practicable, the amount secured.

(2) The following information shall be given with respect to any other contingent liability not provided for—

(a) the amount or estimated amount of that liability ;

(b) its legal nature ; and

(c) whether any valuable security has been provided by the company in connection with that liability and if so, what.

(3) There shall be stated, where practicable—

(a) the aggregate amount or estimated amount of contracts for capital expenditure, if not provided for ; and

(b) the aggregate amount or estimated amount of capital expenditure authorised by the directors which has not been contracted.

(4) Particulars shall be given of any—

(a) pension commitments included under any provision shown in the company's balance sheet ; and

(b) such commitment for which no provision has been made, and where any such commitment relates wholly or partly to pensions payable to past directors of the company, separate particulars shall be given of that commitment so far as it relates to such pensions.

(5) Particulars shall also be given of any other financial commitment which—

(a) have not been provided for ; and

(b) are relevant to assessing the company's state of affairs.

(6) Commitments within any of the preceding subparagraphs undertaken on behalf of or for the benefit of—

(a) any holding company or fellow subsidiary of the company, or

(b) any subsidiary of the company, shall be stated separately from the other commitments within that subparagraph and commitments within paragraph (a) shall be stated separately from those within paragraph (b).

Miscellaneous Matters

50.—(1) Particulars shall be given of any case where the purchase price or production cost of any asset is for the first time determined under paragraph 28.

(2) Where any outstanding loan made under the authority of section 183 (3) (b) or (c) of this Act (various cases of financial assistance by a company for purchase of its own shares) are included under any item shown in the company's balance sheet, the aggregate amount of those loans shall be disclosed for each item in question.

(3) The aggregate amount which is recommended for distribution byway of dividend shall be stated.

Information supplementing the Profit and Loss Account

51. Paragraphs 52-56 require information which either supplements the information given with respect to any particular items shown in the profit and loss account or otherwise provides particulars of income or expenditure of the company or of circumstances affecting the items shown in the profit and loss account.

Separate statement of certain items of income and expenditure

52.—(1) Subject to the provisions of this paragraph, each of the amounts mentioned in this paragraph shall be stated.

(2) The amount of the interest on or any similar charges in respect of—

(a) bank loans and overdrafts, and loans made to the company (other than bank loans and overdrafts) which are repayable—

(i) than by instalments and fall due for repayment before the end of five years beginning with the day next following the end of the financial year ; or

(ii) by instalments the last of which falls due for payment before the end of that period ; and

(b) loans of any other kind made to the company, but this sub-paragraph shall not apply to interest or charges on loans to the company from group companies, but with that exception, it applies to interest or charges on all loans, whether made on the security of debentures or not.

(3) The amounts respectively set aside for redemption of share CapitaLand for redemption of loans.

(4) The amount of income from list investments.

(5) The amount of rents from land (after deduction of ground rents, rates and other outgoings). This amount need only be stated if a substantial part of the company's revenue for the financial year consists of rents from land.

(6) The amount charged to revenue in respect of sum payable in respect of the hire of plant and machinery.

(7) The amount of the remuneration of the auditors (taking "remuneration" for the purposes of this subparagraph, as including any sums paid by the company in respect of the auditors' expenses).

53. (1) The basis on which the charge for Nigerian corporation tax and Nigerian income tax is computed shall be stated.

(2) Particulars shall be given of any special circumstances affecting liability in respect of taxation of profits, income or capital gains for the financial year or liability in respect of taxation of profits, income or capital gains for succeeding financial years.

(3) The following amount shall be stated—

(a) the amount of the charge for Nigerian corporation tax ;

(b) if that amount would have been greater but for relief from double taxation, the amount which it would have been but for such relief ;

(c) the amount of the charge for Nigerian income tax ; and

(d) the amount of the charge for taxation imposed outside Nigeria profits, income and (so far as charged to revenue) capital gains, and these amounts shall be stated separately in respect of the amount which is or would but for paragraph 8 (4) (b) be shown under the following items in the profit and loss account, that is to say "tax on profit or loss on ordinary activities" and "tax on extraordinary profit or loss".

Particulars of turnover

54.—(1) If in the course of the financial year the company has carried on business of two or more lines that, in the opinion of the directors, differ substantially from each other, there shall be stated in respect of each line (describing it)—

(a) the amount of the turnover attributable to that line ; and

(b) the amount of the profit or loss of the company before taxation which is in the opinion of the directors attributable to that line.

(2) If in the course of the financial year the company has supplied markets that in the opinion of the directors, differ substantially from each other, the turnover attributable to each such market shall also be stated.

(3) In this paragraph "market" means a market delimited by geographical bounds.

(4) The source, in terms of business or in terms of market, of turnover or (as the case may be), of profit or loss, the directors of the company shall have regard to the manner in which the company's activities are organised.

(5) For the purposes of this paragraph—

(a) classes of business which, in the opinion of the directors, do not differ substantially from each other shall be treated as one class ; and

(b) markets which, in the opinion of the directors, do not differ substantially from each other shall be treated as one market, and any amount properly attributable to one line of business or (as the case may be) to one market which are not material, may be included in the amount stated in respect of another.

Particulars of Staff

55.—(1) The following information shall be given with respect to the employees of the company—

(a) the average number of persons employed by the company in the financial year ; and

(b) the average number of persons so employed within each category of persons employed by the company.

(2) The average number required by sub-paragraph (1) (a) or (b) shall be determined by dividing the relevant annual number by the number of weeks in the financial year.

(3) The relevant annual number shall be determined by ascertaining foreach week in the financial year for the purposes of—

(a) subparagraph (1) (a), the number of persons employed under contracts of service by the company in that week (whether throughout the week ; or

(b) subparagraph (1) (b), the number of persons in the category in question of persons so employed, and in either case, adding together all the weekly numbers.

(4) In respect of all persons employed by the company during the financial year who are taken into account in determining the relevant annual number for the purposes of subparagraph (1) (a), there shall be stated the aggregate amounts respectively of—

(a) wages and salaries paid or payable in respect of that behalf; and

(b) other pension costs so incurred, save in if those amounts or any of them are stated in the profit and loss account.

(5) The categories of persons employed by the company by reference to which the number required to be disclosed by sub-paragraph (1) (b) is to be determined, shall be such as the directors may select, having regard to the manner in which the company's activities are organised.

Miscellaneous Matters

56.—(1) Where any amount relating to any preceding year is included in any item in the profit and loss account, the effect shall be stated.

(2) Particulars shall be given of any extraordinary income or charges arising in the year.

(3) The effect shall be stated of any transaction that are exceptional by virtue of size or incidence though they fall within the ordinary activities of the company.

General

57.—(1) Where sums originally denominated in foreign currencies have been brought into account under any item shown in the balance sheet or profit and loss account, the basis on which those sums have been translated into Nigerian currency shall be stated.

(2) Subject to the following subparagraph, in respect of every item stated in a note to the accounts, the corresponding amount for the financial year immediately preceding that to which the accounts relate shall also be stated and where the corresponding amount is not comparable, it shall be adjusted and particulars of the adjustment and the reasons for it shall be given.

(3) Subparagraph (2) shall not apply in relation to any amount stated by virtue of any of the following provisions of this Act—

(a) section 382 as it applies to Parts I and II of the Third Schedule(proportion of share capital of subsidiaries and other bodies corporate held by the company, etc.) ;

(b) sections 383 and 384 and the Third Schedule to this Act (particulars of loans to directors, etc.) ; and (c) paragraphs 41 and 45.

PART IV—SPECIAL PROVISIONS WHERE THE COMPANY IS A HOLDING OR SUBSIDIARY COMPANY

Company's own Financial Statements

58. Where a company is a holding company or a subsidiary of another body corporate and any item required by Part I of this Schedule to be shown in the company's balance sheet in relation to group companies includes —

(a) amounts attributable to dealings with or interests in any holding company or fellow subsidiary of the company ; or

(b) amounts attributable to dealings with or interests in any subsidiary of the company, the aggregate amounts within paragraphs (a) and (b) respectively shall be shown as separate items, either by way of sub-division of the relevant item in the balance sheet or in a note to the company's accounts.

59.—(1) Subject to the following sub-paragraph, where the company is a holding company, the number, description and amount of the shares in and debentures of the company held by its subsidiaries or their nominees shall be disclosed in a note to the company's accounts.

(2) Subparagraph (1) shall not apply in relation to any shares or debentures—

(a) in the case of which the subsidiary is concerned as personal representative ; or

(b) in the case of which it is concerned as trustee, provided that in the latter case neither the company nor any subsidiary of the company is beneficially interested under the trust, otherwise than by way of security only for the purposes of a transaction entered into by the ordinary course of a business which includes the lending of money.

The Second Schedule to this Act has effect for the interpretation of the reference in this sub-paragraph to a beneficial interest under a trust.

Consolidated accounts of holding company and subsidiaries

60. Subject to paragraphs 62 and 65, the consolidated balance sheet and profit and loss account shall combine the information contained in the separate balance sheets and profit and loss accounts of the holding company and of the subsidiaries dealt with by the consolidated accounts, but with such adjustments (if any) as the directors of the holding company think necessary.

61. Subject to paragraphs 62-65, and to Part V of this Schedule, the consolidated accounts shall, in giving the information required by paragraph 60, comply so far as practicable with the requirements of this Schedule and with the other requirements of this Act as if they were the accounts of an actual company.

62. The following provisions of this Act, namely—(a) section 382 as it applies to the Sixth Schedule; and
(b) sections 578-579 and the Sixth Schedule, if relating to accounts, other than group accounts, shall not, by virtue of paragraphs 60 and 61, apply for the purposes of the consolidated accounts.
63. Paragraph 61 is without prejudice to any requirement of this Act which applies (otherwise than by virtue of paragraph 61 or 62) to group accounts.
64.—(1) Notwithstanding paragraph 61, the consolidated accounts prepared by a holding company may deal with an investment of any member of the group in the shares of anybody corporate by way of the equity method of accounting in any case where it appears to the directors of the holding company that that body corporate is so closely associated with any member of the group as to justify the use of that method in dealing with investments by that or any other member of the group in the shares of that body corporate.
(2) In this paragraph, references to the group, in relation to consolidated accounts prepared by a holding company, are references to the holding company and the subsidiaries dealt with by the accounts.
65. Notwithstanding paragraphs 60 and 61, paragraphs 17 - 19 and 21 shall not apply to any amount shown in the consolidated balance sheet in respect of goodwill arising on consolidation.
66. In relation to any subsidiaries of the holding company not dealt with by the consolidated accounts, paragraphs 58 and 59 shall apply for the purpose of those accounts as if those accounts were the accounts of an actual company of which they were subsidiaries.

Group Financial Statements not prepared as Consolidated Financial Statements

67. Group financial statements which are not prepared as consolidated statements, together with any notes to those statements, shall give the same equivalent information as that required to be given by consolidated financial statements by virtue of paragraphs 60-66.

Provisions of General Application

68.—(1) This paragraph applies where the company is a holding company and either—
(a) does not prepare group accounts ; or
(b) prepares group accounts which do not deal with one or more of its subsidiaries, and references in this paragraph to the company's subsidiaries shall be read in a case within this subparagraph as references to such of the company's subsidiaries as are excluded from the group accounts.
(2) Subject to the provisions of this paragraph—
(a) the reasons why the subsidiaries are not dealt with in group accounts ; and
(b) a statement showing any qualification contained in the reports of the auditors of the subsidiaries on their accounts for their respective years ending with or during the year of the company, and any note or saving contained in those accounts to call attention to a matter which, apart from the note or saving, would properly have been referred to in such a qualification, in so far as the matter which is the subject of the qualification or note is not covered by the company's own accounts and is material from the point of view of its members, shall be given in a note to the company's accounts.

(3) Subject to the following provisions of this paragraph, the aggregate amount of the total investment of the holding company in the shares of the subsidiaries under the equity method of valuation shall be stated in a note to the company's financial statements.

(4) Subparagraph (3) shall not apply where the company is a wholly owned subsidiary of another body corporate incorporated in Nigeria if there is indeed in a note to the company's accounts a statement that in the opinion of the directors of the company the aggregate value of the assets of the company consisting of shares in or amounts owing (whether on account of a loan or otherwise) from, the company's subsidiaries is not less than the aggregate of the amounts at which those assets are stated or included in the company's balance sheet.

(5) In so far as information required by any of the preceding provisions of this paragraph to be stated in a note to the company's accounts is not obtainable, a statement to that effect shall be given instead in a note to those accounts.

(6) The Commission may, on the application or with the consent of a company's directors, direct that in relation to any subsidiary, subparagraphs (2) and (3) shall not apply or shall apply only to such extent as may be provided by the direction.

(7) Where in any case within subparagraph (1) (b) the group accounts are consolidated accounts, references above in this paragraph to the company's accounts and the company's balance sheet respectively, shall be read as references to the consolidated accounts and the consolidated balance sheet.

69. Where a company has subsidiaries whose years did not end with that of the company, the following information shall be given in relation to each such subsidiary (whether or not dealt with in any group accounts prepared by the company) by way of a note to the company's accounts or (where group accounts are prepared) to the group accounts, that is to say—

(a) the reasons why the company's directors consider that the subsidiaries' years should not end with that of the company ;

(b) the dates of which the subsidiaries' year ending last before that of the company respectively ended or the earliest and latest of those dates ; and

(c) the date immediately following the last statements when the accounts will be consolidated or be re-classified where appropriate as investment properties (long time investments).

PART V—INTERPRETATION OF SCHEDULE

70. The following paragraphs apply for the purposes of this Schedule and its interpretation.

Assets : Fixed or Current

71. Assets of a company are taken to be fixed assets if they are intended for use on a continuing basis in the company's activities and any assets not intended for such use shall be taken to be current assets.

Balance Sheet Date

72. "Balance sheet date" in relation to a balance sheet, means the dates at which the balance sheet was prepared.

Capitalisation

73. References to capitalising any work or costs are to treating that work or those costs as a fixed asset.

Fellow Subsidiary

74. A body corporate is treated as a fellow subsidiary of another body corporate if both are subsidiaries of the same body corporate but neither is the other's.

Group Companies

75. "Group company" in relation to any company, means anybody corporate which is that company's subsidiary or holding company, or a subsidiary of that company's holding company.

Historical Cost Accounting Rules

76. References to the historical cost accounting rules shall be read in accordance with paragraph 29.

Leases

77. (1) "Long Lease" means a lease with respect to which the portion of the term for which it was granted remaining unexpired at the end of the year is—

(a) in case of a right of occupancy to land, not less than 50 years ; and (b) in any other case, not less than 12 months.

(2) "Short Lease" means a lease which is not a long lease.

(3) "Lease" includes an agreement for a lease.

Listed Investment

78. "Listed investment" means an investment as respects which there has been granted a listing on a recognised stock exchange, or on any stock exchange of repute (other than a recognised stock exchange) outside Nigeria.

Loan

79. A loan is treated as falling due for repayment, and an instalment of a loan is treated as falling due for payment, on the earliest date on which the lender could require repayment or (as the case may be) payment, if he exercised all options and rights available to him.

Materiality

80. Amounts which in the particular context of any provision of this Schedule, the disclosure of which will influence the opinion of the reader or user of financial statements, and which are not material may be disregarded for the purposes of that provision.

Notes to the Accounts

81. Notes to a company's accounts may be contained in the accounts or in a separate document annexed to the accounts.

Provisions

82.—(1) References to provisions for depreciation or diminution in value of assets are to any amount written off by way of providing for depreciation or diminution in value of assets.

(2) Any reference in the profit and loss account formats set out in Part I of this Schedule to the depreciation of, or amounts written off, assets of any description is to any provision for depreciation or diminution in value of assets of that description.

83. References to provisions for liabilities or charges are to any amount retained as reasonably necessary for the purpose of providing for any liability or loss which is either likely to be incurred, or certain to be incurred, but uncertain as to amount or as to the date on which it will arise.

Purchase Price

84. References (however expressed) to the purchase price of any asset of a company or of any raw materials or consumables used in the production of any such asset,

include any consideration (whether in cash or otherwise) given by the company in respect of that asset or in respect of those materials or consumables (as the case may require). This includes the costs of putting it into condition ready for its intended use.

Realised profits

85. Without prejudice to—

(a) the construction of any other expression (where appropriate) by reference to accepted accounting principles or practice ; or

(b) any specific provision for the treatment of profits of any description as realised,

it is declared for the avoidance of doubt that references in this Schedule to realised profits, in relation to a company's accounts, are to such profits of the company's, fall to be treated as realised profits for the purposes of those accounts in accordance with principles generally accepted with respect to the determination, for accounting purposes, of realised profits at the time when accounts are prepared.

Related Companies

86.—(1) "Related company", in relation to any company, means anybody corporate (other than one which is a group company in relation to that company) in which that company holds on a long-term basis a qualifying capital interest for the purpose of securing a contribution to that company's own activities by the exercise of any control or influence arising from that interest.

(2) In this paragraph "qualifying capital interest" means, in relation to anybody corporate, an interest in shares comprised in the equity share capital of that body corporate of a class carrying rights to vote in all circumstances at general meetings of that body corporate.

(3) Where—

(a) a company holds a qualifying capital interest in a body corporate ;

(b) a company exercises material influence in matters relating to dividends, commercial and financial policies ; and

(c) the nominal value of any relevant shares in that body corporate held by that company is equal to twenty per cent or more of the nominal value of all relevant shares in that body corporate, it shall be presumed to hold that interest on the basis and for the purpose mentioned in subparagraph (1), unless the contrary is shown.

(4) In subparagraph (3) "relevant shares" means, in relation to anybody corporate, any such shares in that body corporate as are mentioned in subparagraph (c).

Staff costs

87.—(1) "Pension costs" includes any (past or present) costs, other contributions by the company for the purposes of any pension scheme established for the purpose of providing pensions for persons employed by the company, any sums set aside for that purpose and any amounts paid by the company in respect of pensions without first being so set aside.

(2) Any amount stated in respect of either of the above items or in respect of the item "wages and salaries" in the company's profit and loss account shall be determined by reference to payments made or costs incurred in respect of all persons employed by the company during the year who are taken into account in determining the relevant annual number for the purposes of paragraph 55 (1) (a).

Turnover

88. "Turnover", in relation to a company, means the amounts derived from the provision of goods and services falling within the company's ordinary activities, after deduction of—
(a) trade discounts ;
(b) value added tax ; and
(c) any other taxes based on the amounts so derived.

SECOND SCHEDULE

Sections 361 (1) (a), 382 and 407 (4)

MISCELLANEOUS MATTERS TO BE DISCLOSED IN NOTES TO COMPANY FINANCIAL STATEMENTS

PART I — PARTICULARS OF SUBSIDIARIES

1. If, at the end of the year, the company has subsidiaries there shall, in the case of each subsidiary, be stated—
(a) the name of the subsidiary—
(i) if it is incorporated in Nigeria, the address of its registered office, and
(ii) if it is incorporated outside Nigeria, the country in which it is incorporated and the address of its registered office ; and
(b) in relation to shares of each class of the subsidiary held by the company, the identity of the class and the proportion of the nominal value of the allotted shares of that class represented by the shares held.
2. The particulars required under paragraph 1 include, with reference to the proportion of the nominal value of the allotted shares of a class represented by shares held by the company, a statement of the extent (if any) to which it consists in shares held by, or by a nominee for, a subsidiary of the company and the extent (if any) to which it consists in shares held by, or by a nominee for, the company itself.
3. Paragraph 1 does not require the disclosure of information with respect to a body corporate which is the subsidiary of another and is incorporated outside Nigeria or, being incorporated in Nigeria, carries on business outside it if the disclosure would, in the opinion of the Minister, be harmful or jeopardise national interest.
4. If, at the end of its financial year, the company has subsidiaries and the directors are of the opinion that the number of them is such that compliance with paragraph 1 would result in particulars of excessive length being given, compliance with that paragraph shall be required only in the case of the subsidiaries carrying on the business, the results of the carrying on of which (in the opinion of the directors), principally affected the amount of the profit or loss of the company and its subsidiaries or the amount of the assets of the company and its subsidiaries.
5. If advantage is taken of paragraph 4, there shall be included in the statement required by this Part the information that it deals only with the subsidiaries carrying on such businesses as are referred to in that paragraph; and in that case section 382 (3) of this Act (subsequent disclosure with annual return) applies to the particulars given in compliance with paragraph 1, together with those which (but for the fact that advantage is taken) would have to be given.
6. For purposes of this Part, shares of a body corporate are treated as held, or not held, by another body if they would, by virtue of section 381 (4) of this Act be treated as being held or (as the case may be) not held by that other body for the purpose of determining whether the first mentioned body is its subsidiary.

PART II—SHAREHOLDING IN COMPANIES OTHER THAN SUBSIDIARIES

7. If, at the end of a year, the company holds shares of any class comprised in the equity share capital of another body corporate (not being its subsidiary) exceeding in nominal value 20% of the nominal value of the allotted shares of that class, there shall be stated—
(a) the name of that other body corporate, if it is incorporated—
(i) in Nigeria and if it is registered in Nigeria, the part of Nigeria in which it is registered ; and
(ii) outside Nigeria, the country in which it is incorporated ;
(b) the identity of the class and the proportion of the nominal value of the allotted shares of that class represented by the shares held ;
(c) if the company also holds shares in that other body corporate or another class (whether or not comprised in its equity share capital), or of other classes (whether or not so comprised), the like particulars as respects that other class or (as the case may be) those other classes ; and (d) the accounting treatment, (the equity or costs).
8. If, at the end of its year, the company holds shares comprised in the share capital of another body corporate (not being its subsidiary) exceeding in nominal value one-tenth of the allotted share capital of that other body, there shall be stated—
(a) with respect to that other body corporate, the same information as is required by paragraph 7 (a) ; and
(b) the identity of each class of such shares held and the proportion of the nominal value of the allotted shares of that class represented by the shares of that class held by the company.
9. If, at the end of its year, the company holds shares in another body corporate (not being its subsidiary) and the amount of all shares in it which the company holds (as stated or included in the company accounts) exceeds one-tenth of the amount of the company's assets (as so stated), there shall be stated—
(a) with respect to the other body corporate, the same information as is required by paragraph 7(a) ; and
(b) in relation to shares in that other body corporate of each class held, the identity of the class and the proportion of the nominal value of the allotted shares of that class represented by the shares held.
10. None of the provisions of this Part requires the disclosure by a company of information with respect to another body corporate if that other is incorporated outside Nigeria or, being incorporated in Nigeria, carries on business outside it if the disclosure would, in the opinion of the company's directors, be harmful to the business of the company or of that other body and the Minister agrees that the information need not be disclosed.
11. If, at the end of its year, the company falls within paragraph 7 or 8 in relation to more bodies corporate than one, and the number of them is such that, in the directors' opinion, compliance with either or both of those paragraphs would result in particulars of excessive length being given, compliance with paragraph 7 or (as the case may be) paragraph 8, is not required except in the case of bodies carrying on the business the results of the carrying on of which (in the directors' opinion) principally affected the amount of the profit or loss of the company or the amount of its assets.
12. If advantage is taken of paragraph 11, there shall be included in the statement dealing with the bodies last mentioned in that paragraph, the information that it

deals with them ; and section 382 (3) of this Act (subsequent disclosure in annual return) applies to the particulars given in compliance with paragraph 7 or 8 (as the case may be), together with those which, but, for the fact that advantage is so taken, would have to be so given.

13. For the purposes of this Part, shares of a body corporate are treated as held, or not held, by another such body if they would, by virtue of section 381 (4) of this Act (but on the assumption that paragraph (b)(ii) were omitted from that subsection) be treated as being held or (as the case may be), not held, by that other body for the purpose of determining whether the first mentioned body is its subsidiary.

PART III—FINANCIAL INFORMATION ABOUT SUBSIDIARIES

14. If—

(a) at the end of its year the company has subsidiaries ; and

(b) it is required under paragraph 1 in Part I to disclose particulars with respect to any of those subsidiaries, the additional information specified below shall be given with respect to each subsidiary to which the requirement under paragraph 1 applies.

15. If—

(a) at the end of the year the company holds shares in another body corporate ;

(b) it is required under paragraph 8 in Part II above to disclose particulars with respect to that body corporate ; and

(c) the shares held by the company in that body corporate exceed in nominal value 50% of the allotted share capital of that body,

the additional information specified below shall be given with respect to that body corporate.

16. The information required under paragraph 10, shall, in relation to anybody corporate (whether a subsidiary of the company or not), contain the aggregate amount of the capital and reserves of that body corporate as at the end of its relevant year, and its profit or loss for that year; and for this purpose, the relevant year is, if—

(a) the year of the body corporate ends with that of the company giving the information in a note to its accounts, that financial year ; and

(b) not, the body corporate's financial year ending last before the end of the year of the company giving that information ; this is subject to the exceptions and other provisions of paragraph 17.

17.—(1) Information otherwise required by paragraph 16 need not be given in respect of a subsidiary of a company if, either—

(a) the company is exempt under this Act from the requirement to prepare group accounts, as being at the end of its year the wholly-owned subsidiary of another body corporate incorporated in Nigeria, or the company prepares group accounts and—

(i) the accounts of the subsidiary are included in the group accounts, or (ii) the investment of the company in the shares of the subsidiary is included in, or in a not to, the company's accounts by way of the equity method of valuation.

(2) The information under subparagraph (1) need not be given in respect of another body corporate in which the company holds shares if the company's investment in those shares is included in, or in a note to, the accounts by way of the equity method of valuation.

(3) The information under subparagraph (1) need not be given in respect of anybody corporate if—

(a) that body is not required by any provision of this Act to deliver a copy of its balance sheet for its relevant year mentioned in paragraph 16, and does not otherwise publish that balance sheet in Nigeria or elsewhere; and (b) the shares held by the company in that body do not amount to at least 50% in nominal value of the body's allotted share capital.

(4) The Information required by paragraph 16 need not be given if it is not material.

18. Where, with respect to any subsidiary of the company or any other body corporate, particulars which would be required under paragraph 1 in Part I or paragraph 8 in Part II of this Schedule to be stated in a note to the company's accounts are omitted by virtue of paragraph 4 or (as the case may be) paragraph 11, section 382 (3) of this Act (subsequent disclosure in next annual return) shall apply to any information—

(a) with respect to any other subsidiary or body corporate which is given in a note to the company's accounts in accordance with this Part ; and

(b) which would have been required by this Part to be given in relation to a subsidiary or other body corporate but for the exemption under paragraph 4 or11.

19. For the purposes of this Part, shares of a body corporate shall be treated as held, or not held, by the company if they would, by virtue of section 381 (4) of this Act (but on the assumption that section 381 (4) (b) (ii) were omitted from that subsection), be treated as being held or (as the case may be), not held by the company for the purpose of determining whether that body corporate is the company's subsidiary.

PART IV—IDENTIFICATION OF ULTIMATE HOLDING COMPANY

20. If, at the end of its year, the company is the subsidiary of another body corporate, there shall be stated the name of the body corporate regarded by the directors as being the company's ultimate holding company and, if known to them, the country in which it is incorporated.

21. Paragraph 20 does not require the disclosure by a company which carries on business outside Nigeria of information with respect to the body corporate regarded by the Minister as being its ultimate holding company if the disclosure would, in his opinion, be harmful to or jeopardise national interest.

PART V—CHAIRMAN'S AND DIRECTORS' EMOLUMENTS, PENSIONS AND COMPENSATION FOR LOSS OF OFFICE EMOLUMENTS

22.—(1) There shall be shown the aggregate amount of the directors' emoluments.

(2) This amount—

(a) includes any emolument paid to or receivable by a person in respect of his services as director of the company or in respect of his services, while director of the company, as director of any subsidiary of it or in connection with the management of the affairs of the company or any subsidiary of it ; and

(b) shall distinguish between emoluments in respect of services of a director, whether of the company or its subsidiary, and other emoluments.

(3) For the purposes of this paragraph, "emolument" in relation to a director, includes fees and percentages, any sums paid by way of expenses, allowances, (in so far as those sum are charged to Nigerian income tax), any contribution paid in respect of him under any pensions scheme and estimated money value of any other benefit received by him otherwise than in cash.

23. A company which is neither a holding company nor a subsidiary of another body corporate need not comply with paragraphs 24-27 as respects a year in the case of which the amount shown in compliance with paragraph 22 does not exceed ₦120,000.

24.—(1) This paragraph applies to the emoluments of the company's chairman, and for this purpose "chairman" means the person elected by the directors to be chairman of their meetings and includes a person, who, though not so elected, holds any office (however designated) which, in accordance with the company's constitution, carries with it functions substantially similar to those discharged by a person so elected.

(2) If one person has been chairman throughout the year, there shall be shown with respect to that person during the year, his emoluments so far as attributable to the period during which he was chairman, unless his duties as chairman were wholly or mainly discharged outside Nigeria.

(3) There shall be shown with respect to each person who has been chairman during the year, his emoluments so far as attributable to the period during which he was chairman, unless his duties as chairman were wholly or mainly discharged outside Nigeria.

25.—(1) This paragraph applies to the emoluments of directors.

(2) With respect to all directors (other than any who discharged their duties as such wholly or mainly outside Nigeria), there shall be shown—

(a) the number (if any) who had no emoluments or whose several emoluments amounted to not more than N10,000 ; and

(b) by reference to each pair of adjacent points on a scale whereon the lowest point is N10,000 and the succeeding ones are successive integral multiples of N10,000, the number (if any) whose several emoluments exceeded the lowest point but did not exceed the higher.

(3) If, one of the directors (other than any who discharged his or their duties as such wholly or mainly outside Nigeria), the emoluments of each of two or more exceed the relevant amount, the emoluments (or, in the case of equality) who had the greater or, as the case may be, the greatest, shall also be shown.

(4) If, one of the directors (other than any who discharged his or their duties as such wholly or mainly outside Nigeria), the emoluments of each of two or more exceed the relevant amount, his or their emoluments (or, in the case of equality) who had the greater or, as the case may be, the least, shall also be shown.

(5) The "relevant amount"—

(a) if one person has been chairman throughout the year, means the amounts emoluments ; and

(b) otherwise, means an amount equal to the aggregate of the emoluments, so far as attributable to the period during than contributions paid in respect of him under pension scheme) as in his case are to be included in the payment shown under the paragraph 22.

26. There shall, under paragraphs 24 and 25, be brought into account as emoluments of a person all such amounts (other than contributions paid in respect of him under a pension scheme) as in his case are to be included in the payment shown under paragraph 22.

Emoluments Waived

27. There shall be shown—

(a) the number of directors who have waived rights to receive emoluments which, but for the waiver, would have fallen to be included in the payment

shown under paragraph 22 ; and

(b) a sum not so receivable that was payable only on demand, being a sum the right to receive which has been waived, is deemed to have been due for payment at the time of the waiver.

Pensions of Directors and past Directors.

28.—(1) There shall be shown the aggregate amount of directors' or past director's pensions.

(2) This amount does not include any pension paid or receivable under a pension scheme if the scheme is such that the contributions under it are substantially adequate for the maintenance of the scheme, but, subject to this scheme, it includes any pension paid or receivable in respect of such services of a director or past director as are mentioned in paragraph 22 (2) whether to or by him or, on his nomination or by virtue of dependence on or other connection with him, to or by any other person.

(3) The amount shown shall distinguish between pensions in respect of services as director, whether of the company or its subsidiary, and other pensions.

Compensation to directors for loss of office.

29.—(1) There shall be shown the aggregate amount of any compensation to directors or past directors in respect of loss of office.

(2) This amount—

(a) includes any sums paid to or receivable by a director or past director by way of compensation for the loss of office as director of the company or for the loss, while director of the company or on or in connection with his ceasing to be a director of it, or of any other office in connection with the management of the company's affairs or of any office as director or in connection with the management of the affairs of any subsidiary of the company ; and

(b) shall distinguish between compensation in respect of the office of director, whether of the company or its subsidiary, and compensation in respect of other offices.

(3) References to compensation for loss of office includes sums paid as consideration for or in connection with a person's retirement from office.

Supplementary

30.—(1) This paragraph applies with respect to the amounts shown under paragraphs 22, 28 and 29.

(2) The amount in each case includes all relevant sums paid by or receivable from—

(a) the company ;

(b) the company's subsidiaries ; and

(c) any other person, except sums to be accounted for to the company or any of its subsidiaries, to past or present members of the company or any of its subsidiaries or any class of those members.

(3) The amount shown under paragraph 29 shall distinguish between the sums respectively paid by or receivable from the company, the company's subsidiaries and persons other than the company and its subsidiaries.

31.—(1) The amounts shown for any year under paragraphs 22, 28 and 29 are the sums receivable in respect of that year (whenever paid) or, in the case of sums not receivable in respect of a period, the sums paid during that year.

(2) Where the sums—

(a) are not shown in a note to the accounts for the relevant year on the ground that the person receiving them is liable to account for them as mentioned in paragraph 30 (2), but the liability is thereafter wholly or partly released or is not enforced within a period of two years, or

(b) paid by way of expenses allowance are charged to income tax after the end of the relevant year,

those sums shall, to the extent to which the liability is released or not enforced or they are charged as mentioned above (as the case may be), be shown in a note to the first accounts in which it is practicable to show them, and shall be distinguished from the amounts to be shown apart from this provision.

32. Where it is necessary to do so for the purpose of making any distinction required by the preceding paragraphs in an amount shown in compliance with this Part, the directors may apportion any payment between the matters in respect of which these have been paid or are receivable in such manner as they think appropriate.

Interpretation

33.—(1) This paragraph applies for the interpretation of paragraphs 22-32.

(2) A reference to the company's subsidiary—

(a) in relation to a person who is or was, while a director of the company, a director also, by virtue of the company's nomination (direct or indirect) or any other body corporate includes, (subject to subparagraph (2) that body corporate, whether or not it is or was in fact the company's subsidiary ; and

(b) for the purposes of paragraphs 22-28 (including any provision of this Part referring to paragraph 22) is to a subsidiary at the time the services were rendered, and for the purposes of paragraph 29, to a subsidiary immediately before the loss of office as director.

(3) For the purpose of this paragraph—

(a) "pension" includes any superannuation allowance, superannuation gratuity or similar payment ;

(b) "pension scheme" means a scheme for the provision of pension in respect of services as director or otherwise which is maintained in whole or in part by means of contributions ; and

(c) "contribution", in relation to a pension scheme, means any payment (including an insurance premium) paid for the purposes of the scheme by or in respect of persons rendering services in respect of which pensions become payable under the scheme, except that it does not include any payment in respect of two or more persons if the amount paid in respect of each of them is not ascertainable.

Supplementary

34. This Part of the Schedule requires information to be given only if it is contained in the company's books and papers or the company has the right to obtain it from the persons concerned.

PART VI—PARTICULARS RELATING TO NUMBER OF EMPLOYEES REMUNERATED AT HIGHER RATES

35.—(1) There shall be shown by reference to each pair of adjacent points on a scale whereon the lowest point is ₦60,000 and the succeeding ones are successive integral multiples of ₦10,000 beginning with that in the case of which the multiplier is seven, the number (if any) of persons in the company's employment whose several emoluments exceeded the lower point but did not exceed the higher.

(2) The persons whose emoluments are to be taken into account for this purpose shall not include—

(a) directors of the company ; or

(b) persons (other than directors of the company) who if employed by the company—

(i) throughout the financial year, worked wholly or mainly during that year outside Nigeria, or

(ii) for part only of that year, worked wholly or mainly during that part outside Nigeria.

36.—(1) For the purpose of paragraph 35, a person's emoluments include any sum paid to or receivable by him from the company, the company's subsidiaries and any other person in respect of his services as a person in the employment of the company or a subsidiary of it or as a director of a subsidiary of the company (except sums to be accounted for to the company or any of its subsidiaries).

(2) In this paragraph, "Emoluments" includes fees and percentages, any sums paid by way of expenses allowances if those sums are charged to Nigerian income tax, and the estimated money value of any other benefits received by a person otherwise than in cash.

(3) The amounts to be brought into account for the purpose of complying with paragraph 35, are the sums receivable in respect of the year (whenever paid) or, in the case of sums not receivable sums in respect of a period, the sums paid during that year.

(4) The sums—

(a) are not brought into account for that year on the ground that the person receiving them is liable to account for them as mentioned in subparagraph (1), but the liability is wholly or partly released or is not enforced within a period of two years ; or

(b) paid to a person by way of expenses allowance, are charged to Nigerian income tax after the end of the year, those sums shall, to the extent to which the liability is released or not enforced or they are charged as above mentioned (as the case may be), be brought into account for the purpose of complying with paragraph 25 on the first occasion on which it is practicable to do so.

37. References in paragraph 36 to a company's subsidiary—

(a) in relation to a person who is or was, while employed by the company, a director, by virtue of the company's nomination (direct or indirect), of any other body corporate, include that body corporate (but subject to subparagraph (b), whether or not it is or was in fact the company's subsidiary ; and

(b) are to be taken as referring to a subsidiary at the time the services were rendered.

THIRD SCHEDULE

Sections 383, 384 and 407 (4)

PARTICULARS IN COMPANY FINANCIAL STATEMENTS OF LOAN AND OTHER TRANSACTIONS FAVOURING DIRECTORS AND OFFICERS

PART I—MATTERS TO BE DISCLOSED UNDER SECTION 383

1. Group financial statements shall contain the particulars required by this Schedule of—

(a) any transaction or arrangement of a kind described in section 296 of this Act entered into by the company or by a subsidiary of the company for a person who at any time during the year was a director of the company or its holding company, or was connected with such a director ;

(b) an agreement by the company or by a subsidiary of the company to enter into any such transaction or arrangement for a person who was at any time during the year a director of the company or its holding company, or was connected with such a director ; and

(c) any other transaction or arrangement with the company or subsidiary of it in which a person who at any time during the year was a director of the company or its holding company had, directly or indirectly, a material interest.

2. The accounts prepared by a company other than a holding company shall contain the particulars required by this Schedule of—

(a) any transaction or arrangement of a kind described in section 296 of this Act entered into by the company for a person who at any time during the year was a director of it or of its holding company or was connected with such a director ;

(b) an agreement by the company to enter into any such transaction or arrangement for a person who at any time during the year was a director of the company or its holding company or was connected with such a director ; and

(c) any other transaction or arrangement with the company in which a person who, at any time during the year, was a director of the company or of its holding company had, directly or indirectly, a material interest.

3.—(1) For purposes of paragraphs 1 (c) and 2 (c), a transaction or arrangement between a company and a director of it or of its holding company, or a person connected with such a director, is to be treated, as a transaction, arrangement or agreement in which that director is interested.

(2) An interest in such a transaction or arrangement is not material for purposes of subparagraph (1) and this subparagraph if, in the board's opinion it is not so, but this shall be without prejudice to the question whether or not such an interest is material in a case where the board has not considered the matter.

(3) For the purpose of subparagraph (2), the board" means the directors of the company preparing the accounts, or a majority of those directors, but excluding, in either case, the director whose interest it is.

(4) Paragraphs 1 and 2 shall not apply, for the purposes of accounts prepared by a company which is, or is the holding company of a recognised bank, in relation to a transaction or arrangement of a kind described in section 296 of this Act or an agreement to enter into such a transaction or arrangement, to which that recognised bank is a party.

(5) Paragraphs 1 and 2 shall not apply in relation to—

(a) a transaction, arrangement or agreement between one company and another in which a director of the former or of its subsidiary or holding company is interested only by virtue of his being a director of the latter ;

(b) a contract of service between a company and one of its directors or a director of its holding company, or between a director of a company and any of that company's subsidiaries ; or

(c) a transaction, arrangement or agreement which was not entered into during the year and which did not subsist at any time during that year.

(6) Paragraphs 1 and 2 shall apply whether or not—

(a) the transaction or arrangement was prohibited by section 296 of this Act ;

(b) the person for whom it was made was a director of the company or was connected with a director of it at the time it was made ; and

(c) in the case of a transaction or arrangement made by a company which at any time during a financial year is a subsidiary of another company, it was a subsidiary of that other company at the time the transaction or arrangement was made.

(7) Neither paragraph 1 (c) nor 2 (c) applies in relation to any transaction or arrangement if—

(a) each party to the transaction or arrangement which is a member of the same group of companies (meaning a holding company and its subsidiaries) as the company entered into the transaction or arrangement in the ordinary course of business ; or

(b) the terms of the transaction or arrangement are not less favourable to any such party than it would be reasonable to expect if the interest mentioned in that subparagraph had not been an interest of a person who was a director of the company or of its holding company.

(8) Neither paragraph 1(c) nor 2 (c) applies in relation to any transaction or arrangement if—

(a) the company is a member of a group of companies (meaning a holding company and its subsidiaries) ;

(b) either the company is a wholly-owned subsidiary or no body corporate(other than the company or a subsidiary of the company) which is a member of the group of companies, which includes the company's ultimate holding company, was a party to the transaction or arrangement ;

(c) the director in question was at some time during the relevant period associated with the company ; and

(d) the material interest of the director in question in the transaction or arrangement would not have risen if he had not been associated with the company at any time during the relevant period.

THE PARTICULARS REQUIRED BY THIS PART

(9) (1) Subject to paragraph 10, the particulars required by this Part are those of the principal terms of the transaction, arrangement or agreement.

(2) Without prejudice to the generality of subparagraph (1), the following particulars are required—

(a) a statement of the fact either that the transaction, arrangement or agreement was made or subsisted (as the case may be) during the year ;

(b) the name of the person for whom it was made and, where that person is or was connected with a director of the company or of its holding company, the name of that director ;

(c) in a case where paragraph 1(c) or 2(c) applies, the name of the director with the material interest and the nature of that interest ;

(d) in the case of a loan or an agreement for a loan or an arrangement within section 296 of this Act relating to a loan—

(i) the amount of the liability of the person to whom the loan was or was agreed to be made, in respect of principal and interest, at the beginning and at the end of the year,

(ii) the maximum amount of that liability during that year,

(iii) the amount of any interest which, having fallen due, has not been paid, and

(iv) the amount of any provision (within the meaning of the First Schedule to this Act), made in respect of any failure or anticipated failure by the borrower to repay the whole or part of the loan or to pay the whole or part of any interest on it ;

(e) in the case of a guarantee, security or an arrangement within section 296 of this Act relating to a guarantee or security—

(i) the amount for which the company (or its subsidiary) was liable under the guarantee or in respect of the security both at the beginning and at the end of the year,

(ii) the maximum amount for which the company (or its subsidiary) may become so liable, and

(iii) any amount paid and any liability incurred by the company (or its subsidiary) for the purpose of fulfilling the guarantee or discharging the security (including any loss incurred by reason of the enforcement of the guarantee or security) ; and

(f) in the case of any transaction, arrangement or agreement other than those mentioned in paragraphs 11 (2).

(10) Paragraph 9 (2) (c)-(f) shall not apply in the case of a loan or quasi-loan made or agreed to be made by a company to or for a body corporate which is either—

(a) a body corporate of which that company is a wholly-owned subsidiary ;

(b) a wholly-owned subsidiary of a body corporate of which that company is a wholly-owned subsidiary ; or

(c) a wholly-owned subsidiary of that company, if particulars of that loan, quasi- loan or agreement for it would not have been required to be included in that company's annual accounts if the first-mentioned body corporate had not been associated with a director of that company at any time during the relevant period.

Transactions excluded from Section 383

11.—(1) In relation to a company's accounts for a year, compliance with this Part is not required in the case of transactions of a kind mentioned in subparagraph (2) which are made by the company or a subsidiary of it for a person who at any time during that financial year was a director of the company or of its holding company, or was connected with such a director, if the aggregate of the values of each transaction, arrangement or agreement so made for that director or any person connected with him, less the amount (if any) by which the liabilities of the person for whom the transaction or arrangement was made has been reduced, did not at any time during the year exceed N10,000.

(2) The transactions in question are—

(a) credit transactions ;

(b) guarantees provided or securities entered into in connection with credit transactions;

(c) arrangements within section 296 of this Act relating to credit transactions ; and

(d) agreements to enter into credit transactions.

12. In relation to a company's accounts for a financial year, compliance with this Part shall not be required by virtue of paragraph 1 (c) or 2 (c) in the case of any transaction or arrangement with a company or any of its subsidiaries in which a director of the company or its holding company had, directly or indirectly, a material interest if the—

(a) value of each transaction or arrangement within paragraph 1 (c) or 2 (c) (as the case may be) in which that director had (directly or indirectly) a material interest and which was made after the commencement of the year with the company or any of its subsidiaries ; and

(b) value of each such transaction or arrangement which was made before the commencement of the year less the amount (if any) by which the liabilities of the person for whom the transaction or arrangement was made have been reduced, did not at any time during the year exceed in the aggregate ₦3,000 or, if more, did not exceed ₦19,000 or one per cent of the value of the net assets of the company preparing the accounts in question as at the end of the year, whichever is less.

For this purpose, a company's net assets are the aggregate of its assets less the aggregate of its liabilities ("liabilities" to include any provision for liabilities or charges within paragraph 83 of the First Schedule to this Act).

PART II—MATTERS TO BE DISCLOSED UNDER SECTION 384

13. This Part of this Schedule shall apply in relation to the following classes of transactions, arrangements and agreements—

(a) loans, guarantees and securities relating to loans, arrangements of a kind described under section 296 of this Act relating to loans and agreements to enter into any of the foregoing transactions and agreements ;

(b) quasi-loans, guarantees and securities relating to quasi-loans, arrangements of a kind described in either of those subsections relating to quasi-loans and agreements to enter into any of the foregoing transactions and arrangements ;

(c) credit transactions, guarantees and securities relating to credit transactions and arrangements of a kind described in either of those subsections relating to credit transactions and agreements to enter into any of the foregoing transactions and arrangements.

14.—(1) To comply with this Part of this Schedule, the accounts must contain a statement, in relation to transactions, arrangements and agreements, made as mentioned in section 296 (1) of this Act—

(a) the aggregate amounts outstanding at the end of the financial year under transactions, arrangements and agreements within subparagraphs 13 (a), (b) and (c) ; and

(b) the number of officers for whom the transactions, arrangements and agreements falling within each of those sub-paragraphs, were made.

(2) This paragraph does not apply to transactions, arrangements and agreements made by the company or any of its subsidiaries for an officer of the company if the aggregate amount outstanding at the end of the year under such transactions, arrangements, and agreements do not exceed ₦5,000.

FOURTH SCHEDULE

Sections 385 and 398 (5)

MATTERS TO BE DEALT WITH IN DIRECTORS' REPORT

PART I—MATTERS OF A GENERAL NATURE ASSET VALUES

1.—(1) If significant changes in the fixed assets of the company or of any of its subsidiaries have occurred in the financial year, the report shall contain particulars of the changes.

(2) If, in the case of such assets which consist of interests in land, their market value (as at the end of the year) differs substantially, from the amount at which they are included in the balance sheet, and the difference is, in the directors' opinion, of such significance as to require that the attention of members of the company or of holders

of its debentures should be drawn to it, the report shall indicate the difference with such degree of precision as is practicable.

Directors' Interests

2.—(1) The report shall state, with respect to each person who, at the end of the year, was a director of the company—

(a) whether or not, according to the register kept by the company for the purposes of sections 302 and 303 of this Act (director's obligation to notify his interests in the company and companies in the same group), he was at the end of that year interested in shares in, or debentures of, the company or any other body corporate, being the company's subsidiary or holding company or a subsidiary of the company's holding company ;

(b) if he was so interested—

(i) the number and amount of shares in, and debentures of, each body

(specifying it) in which, according to that register, he was then interested,

(ii) whether or not (according to that register) he was, at the beginning of that year or, if he was not then a director, when he became one, interested in shares in, or debentures of, the company or any other such body corporate, and

(iii) if he was, the number and amount of shares in and debentures of, each body (specifying it) in which, according to that register, he was interested at the beginning of the year or (as the case may be) when he became a director.

(2) An interest in shares or debentures which, under sections 302 and303 of this Act, falls to be treated as being the interest of a director is so treated for the purposes of this paragraph, and the references above to the time when a person became a director, in the case of a person who became director on more than one occasion, is the time when he first became a director.

(3) The particulars required by this paragraph may be given by way ofnotes to the company's accounts in respect of the year, instead of being stated in the directors' report.

Charitable Gifts

3.—(1) Money given for charitable purposes to a person who, when it was given, was ordinarily resident outside Nigeria is to be left out of the account.

(2) For the purpose of subparagraph (1),"Charitable purposes" means purposes which are exclusively charitable.

Miscellaneous

4. The directors' report shall contain—

(a) particulars of any important event affecting the company or any of its subsidiaries which have occurred since the end of the year ;

(b) an indication of likely future developments in the business of the company and of its subsidiaries ;

(c) an indication of the activities (if any) of the company and its subsidiaries in the field of research and development ; (d) names of distributors of the company's products ; and (e) particulars of donations and gifts made for any purpose.

PART II—DISCLOSURE REQUIRED BY COMPANY ACQUIRING ITS OWN SHARES

5. This Part of this Schedule applies where shares in a company are—

(a) purchased by the company or are acquired by it by forfeiture or surrender in lieu of forfeiture, or in pursuance of section 184 of this Act (acquisition of own shares by company limited by shares) ;

(b) required by another person in circumstances where section 183 (3) (b) or (c) of this Act applies (acquisition by company's nominee, or by another with company financial assistance, the company having a beneficial interest); or

(c) made subject to a lien or other charges taken (whether expressly or otherwise) by the company and permitted by section 164 (1) or (4) of this Act.

6. The directors' report with respect to a year shall state—

(a) the number and nominal value of the shares so purchased, the aggregate amount of the consideration paid by the company for such shares and the reasons for their purchase ;

(b) the number and nominal value of the shares so acquired by the company, acquired by another person in such circumstances and so charged respectively during the year ;

(c) the maximum number and nominal value of shares which, having been so acquired by the company, acquired by another person in such circumstances or so charged (whether or not during that year) are held at any time by the company or that other person during the year ;

(d) where the number and nominal value of the shares of any particular description are stated in pursuance of any of the preceding sub-paragraphs, the percentage of the called up share which shares of that description represent ;

(e) where any of the shares has been so charged, the amount of the charge in each case ;

(f) where any of the shares has been disposed of by the company or the person who acquired them in such circumstances for money or money's worth, the amount or value of the consideration in each case ; and

(g) the excess of the selling price over the purchase price of each share resold or the excess of the cost over the selling price which was taken to capital reserve.

PART III—EMPLOYMENT AND EMPLOYEES

Employment of Disabled Persons

7. The directors' report shall contain a statement showing how many disabled persons were employed during the year and describing the policy which the company has applied during the year—

(a) for giving full and fair consideration to applications for employment by the company made by disabled persons, having regard to their particular aptitudes and abilities ;

(b) for continuing the employment of, and for arranging appropriate training for, employees of the company who have become disabled persons during the period when they were employed by the company ; and

(c) otherwise for the training, career development and promotion of disabled persons employed by the company.

Health, Safety and Welfare at work of Company's Employees

8. The directors' report shall contain a statement as to the arrangement in force in the year for securing the health, safety and welfare at work of employees of the company and its subsidiaries, and for protecting other persons against risks to health or safety arising out of or in connection with the activities at work of those employees.

Employee Involvement and Training

9. The directors' report shall contain a statement describing the action that has been taken during the year to introduce, maintain or develop arrangements aimed at—

(a) providing employees systematically with information on matters of concern to them as employees ;

(b) consulting employees or their representatives on a regular basis so that the views of employees can be taken into account in making decisions

which are likely to affect their interests ;

(c) encouraging the involvement of employees in the company's performance through an employees' share scheme or by some other means ;

(d) achieving a common awareness on the part of all employees of the financial and economic factors affecting the performance of the company ; and

(e) showing the arrangements made or facilities provided by the company for the training of employees during the year.

FIFTH SCHEDULE Section 404 (2)

MATTERS TO BE EXPRESSLY STATED IN AUDITORS' REPORT

1. Whether the auditors have obtained all the information and explanations which, to the best of their knowledge and belief, were necessary for the purpose of their audit.

2. Whether, in the auditors' opinion, proper books of account have been kept by the company, so far as appears from their examination of those books, and proper returns adequate for the purposes of their audit have been received from branches not visited by them.

3.—(1) Whether the company's balance sheet and (unless it is framed as a consolidated profit and loss account) profit and loss account dealt with by the report are in agreement with the books of account and returns.

(2) Whether, in the auditors' opinion and to the best of their information and according to the explanations given them, the said statements give the information required by this Act in the manner so required and give a true and fair view in the case of the—

(a) balance sheet, of the state of the company's affairs as at the end of its year ; and

(b) profit and loss account, of the profit and loss for its year; or as the case may be, give a true and fair view thereof subject to the non- disclosure of any matters (to be indicated in the report) which, by virtue of Part I of the First Schedule to this Act, are not required to be disclosed.

4. In the case of a holding company, submitting group financial statements whether, in their opinion, the group financial statements have been properly prepared in accordance with the provisions of this Act so as to give a true and fair view of the state of affairs and profit or loss of the company and its subsidiaries and associates dealt with where it, so far as it concerns members of the company, or the case may so as to give a true and fair view thereof subject to the non-disclosure of any matter to be indicated in the report which by virtue of Part I of the First Schedule to this Act are not required to be disclosed.

SIXTH SCHEDULE

Sections 393, 396 (1), 397 (6)(a) and 398 (5)

MODIFIED FINANCIAL STATEMENTS OF COMPANIES QUALIFYING AS SMALL COMPANIES

PART I—MODIFIED FINANCIAL STATEMENTS INTRODUCTORY

Accounts modified as for a small company

1.—(1) In respect of the relevant financial year, there may be delivered a copy of a modified balance sheet, instead of the full balance sheet.

(2) The modified balance sheet shall be an abbreviated version of the full balance sheet, showing only those items to which a letter or Roman number is assigned in the balance sheet format adopted under Part I of the First Schedule to this Act but in other respects corresponding to the full balance sheet.

(3) The copy of the modified balance sheet shall be signed as required by section 386 of this Act.

2. A copy of the company's profit and loss account need not be delivered nor a copy of the directors' report otherwise required by section 388 of this Act.

3. The information required by Parts III and IV of the First Schedule to this Act need not be given.

4. The information required by the First Schedule to this Act to be given in notes to the accounts need not be given, with the exception of any information required by the following provisions of that Schedule—

(a) paragraph 36 (accounting policies) ;

(b) paragraph 38 (share capital) ;

(c) paragraph 39 (particulars of allotments) ;

(d) paragraph 47 (1) and (4) (particulars of debts) ;

(e) paragraph 57 (1) (basis of translation of foreign currency amounts into naira) ; and

(f) paragraph 57 (2) (corresponding amounts for preceding year), and the reference here to paragraph 57 (2) includes that subparagraph as applied to any item stated in a note to the company's accounts, whether by virtue of a requirement of the Third Schedule or under any other provision of this Act.

5. If a modified balance sheet is delivered, there shall be disclosed in it (or in a note to the company's accounts delivered) —

(a) the aggregate of the amounts required by note (5) of the notes on the balance sheet formats set out in Part I of the First Schedule to be shown separately for each item included under debtors (amounts falling due after one year) ;and

(b) the aggregate of the amounts required by note 13 of those notes to be shown separately for each item included under creditors in format 2 (amounts falling due within one year or after more than one year).

6. The company's balance sheet shall contain a statement by the directors that they—

(a) rely on sections 393 to 397 of this Act as entitling them to deliver modified accounts ; and

(b) do so on the ground that the company is entitled to the benefit of those sections as a small company, and the statement shall appear in the balance sheet immediately above the signatures of the directors.

7.—(1) The accounts delivered shall be accompanied by a special report of the auditors stating that in their opinion—

(a) the directors are entitled to deliver modified accounts in respect of the financial year as claimed in the directors' statement ; and

(b) any account comprised in the documents delivered as modified account is properly prepared as such in accordance with this Schedule.

(2) A copy of the auditors' report under section 404 of this Act need not be delivered; but the full text of it shall be reproduced in the special report under this paragraph.

(3) If the directors propose to rely on sections 393-397 of this Act as entitling them to deliver modified accounts, it shall be the auditors' duty to provide them with a report stating whether, in their opinion, the directors are so entitled, and whether the documents to be delivered as modified accounts are properly prepared.

8. Where the directors rely on sections 393 to 397 of this Act in delivering any document, and—

(a) the company is entitled to the benefit of those sections on the ground claimed by the directors in their statement under paragraph 6 ; and

(b) the accounts comprised in the documents are properly prepared in accordance with this Schedule, then section 389 (3) of this Act shall have effect as if any document which, by virtue of this Part of this Schedule, is included in or omitted from the documents delivered as modified accounts were (or, as the case may be), not required by this Act to be comprised in the company's accounts in respect of the year.

PART II—MODIFIED GROUP FINANCIAL STATEMENTS (IN CONSOLIDATED FORM) FOR SMALL COMPANIES

Introductory

9. In this Part of this Schedule, paragraphs 10-16 relate to modified financial statements for a small group.

Small Groups.

10.—(1) In respect of the relevant year, there may be delivered a copy of a modified balance sheet, instead of the full consolidated balance sheet.

(2) The modified balance sheet shall be an abbreviated version of the full consolidated balance sheet, showing only those items to which a letter or Roman numeral is assigned in the balance sheet format adopted under Part I of the First Schedule, but in other respects corresponding to the full consolidated balance sheet.

(11) Neither copy of the profit and loss account nor a copy of the directors 'report otherwise required by section 386 of this Act need not be delivered.

(12) The information required by the First Schedule to this Act to be given in notes to group financial statements need not be given, with the exception of any information required by provisions of that Schedule listed in paragraph 4.

(13) There shall be disclosed in the modified balance sheet, or in a note to the group accounts delivered, aggregate amounts corresponding to those specified in paragraph 5 above.

(14) The information required by Part III and IV of the Second Schedule need not be given.

PART III—MODIFIED GROUP ACCOUNTS CONSOLIDATED OR OTHERS

(15) If modified group accounts are delivered, paragraphs 16 -18 apply.

(16) The directors' statement required by paragraph 6 to be contained in the balance sheet include a statement that the documents delivered include modified group accounts, in reliance on section 397 of this Act.

17.—(1) The auditors' special report under paragraph 7 shall include a statement that, in their opinion—

(a) the directors are entitled to deliver modified group accounts, as claimed in their statement in the balance sheet ; and

(b) any account comprised in the documents delivered as modified group financial statements are properly prepared as such in accordance with this Schedule.

(2) A copy of the auditors' report under section 404 need not be delivered; but the full text of it shall be reproduced in the special report under paragraph 7.

(3) If the directors propose to rely on section 397 as entitling them to deliver modified group financial statements, it is the auditors' duty to provide them with a report stating whether, in their opinion, the directors are so entitled, and whether the documents to be delivered as modified group financial statements are properly prepared in accordance with this Schedule.

18. Where the directors rely on section 397 in delivering any documents, and—

(a) the company is entitled to the benefit of that section on the ground claimed by the directors in their statement in the balance sheet, and

(b) the accounts comprised in the documents delivered as modified financial statements are properly prepared in accordance with this Schedule, then section 388 (3) has effect as if any document which by virtue of this Schedule is included in or omitted from the documents delivered as modified group financial statements were (or, were not) required by this Act to be comprised in the company's financial statements in respect of the year.

SEVENTH SCHEDULE Section 418 (3)

CONTENTS AND FORM OF ANNUAL RETURNS OF A COMPANY HAVING SHARES OTHER THAN A SMALL COMPANY

PART I

Contents

1. The address of the registered office of the company.

2.—(1) If the register of members is, under the provisions of this Act, kept elsewhere than at the registered office of the company, the address of the place where it is kept.

(2) If any register of holders of debentures of the company or any duplicate of any such register or part of any such register is, under the provisions of this Act kept elsewhere than at the registered office of the company, the address of the place where it is kept.

3. A summary, distinguishing between shares issued for cash and shares issued as fully or partly paid or otherwise than in cash, specifying the following particulars—

(a) the amount of the share capital of the company and the number of shares into which it is divided ;

(b) the number of shares taken from the commencement of the company up to the date of the return ;

(c) the amount called up on each share ;

(d) the total amount of calls received ;

(e) the total amount of calls unpaid ;

(f) total amount of the sums (if any) paid by way of commission in respect of any shares or debentures ;

(g) the discount allowed on the issue of any shares issued at a discount or so much of that discount as has not been written off at the date on which the return is made ;

(h) the total amount of the sums (if any) allowed by way of discount in respect of any debentures since the date of the last return ; and (i) the total number of shares forfeited.

4. Particulars of the total amount of the indebtedness of the company in respect of all mortgages and charges which are required to be registered with the Commission under this Act.

5. A list—
(a) containing the names and addresses of all persons who, on the fourteenth day after the company's annual general meeting for the year, are members of the company, and of persons who have ceased to be members since the date of the last return or, in the case of the first return, since the incorporation of the company ;
(b) stating the number of shares held by each of the existing members at the date of the return, specifying shares transferred since the date of the last return (or, in the case of the first return, since the incorporation of the company) by persons who are still members and have ceased to be members respectively, and the dates of registration of the transfers ;
(c) if the names aforesaid are not arranged in alphabetical order, havingannexed thereto an index sufficient to enable the name of any person therein to be easily found.
6. All such particulars with respect to the persons who at the date of the return are the directors of the company and any person who at that date is the secretary of the company as are by this Act required to be contained with respect to directors and the secretary respectively in the register of the directors and secretaries of a company.

PART II

Form

ANNUAL RETURN OF.. Limited made up to the day of 20..............................(being the fourteenth day after the date of the annual general meeting for the year........................... 20.........................)

1. Address ....
(Address of the Registered Office of the Company)
2. Situation of registers of members and debenture holders.
(a) (Address of place at which the register of members is kept, if other than the registered office of the company).
(b) (Address of any place in Nigeria other than the registered office of the company at which is kept any register of holders of debentures of the company or any duplicate of any such register or part of any such register).
3. Summary of share capital and debentures.
(a) Nominal share capital
Nominal share capital N divided into :
(Insert number and class)
.... shares of .... each
.... shares of .... each
.... shares of .... each
(b) Issued share capital and debentures
Number
Number of shares of each class taken up to the date of this return (which number must agree with the total shown in the list as held by existing members).
Number of shares of each class issued subject to payment wholly in cash.

Number of shares of each class issued as partly paid up shares issued as paid up for a consideration other than cash and extent

which to the extent of to which each such shares issued as paid up share is so paid up.

Number of shares (if any) of each class issued at a discount. to the extent of # per share

Amount of discount on the issue of shares which has not been written off at the date of this return. N

Amount called N.......................... per share on ....shares up on number N.............................. per share on .... shares of shares of N................................ share on .... shares each class N............................... per share .... shares

Total amount of calls received, including payments N on application and allotment and any sums received on shares forfeited.

Total amount (if any) agreed to be considered as paid on shares the number of shares each class issued as fully paid.....

up for a consideration.. shares paid other than cash.. ....shares Total amount (if any) agreed as.. ....shares

N... to be considered shares paid on number of shares of each class issued as partly paid up for a consideration other than cash .... shares

Total amount of calls unpaid N

Total amount of the sums (if any) paid by way of commission in respect of any shares or debentures........................ N

Total amount of the sums (if any) allowed by way of discount in respect of any debentures since the date of the last return............ N Total number of shares of each class forfeited ....shares

4. Particulars of Indebtedness.

Total amount of indebtedness of the company in respect of all mortgages and charges which are required to be registered with the Commission under the Companies and Allied Matters Act.

5. List of Past and Present Members

List of persons holding shares or stock in the company on the fourteenth day after the annual general meeting for 20 and of persons who have held shares or stock therein at any time since the date of the last return, or, in the case of the first return, of the incorporation of the company.

Folio in register containing particulars	Name and addresses	Number of shares held by existing members at date of return*	Account of share	Remarks

Particulars of shares transferred since the date of the last return, of the incorporation of the company by (a) persons who are still members and (b) person who have ceased to be members*

Number (a)	(b)	Date of registration of transfer

*The aggregate number of shares held by each member must be stated, and the aggregate must be added up so as to agree with the number of shares stated in the Summary of Share Capital and Debentures to have been taken up.

When the shares are of different classes these columns should be subdivided so that the number of each class held, or transferred, may be shown separately. Where any shares have been converted into stock, the amount of stock held by each member must be shown.

The date of registration of each transfer should be given as well as the number of shares transferred on each date. The particulars should be placed together with that of the transferee, but the name of the transferee may be inserted in the remarks column immediately opposite the particulars of each transfer.

(i) If the return for either of the two immediately preceding years has given as at the date of that return the full particulars required as to past and present members and the shares and stock held and transferred by them, only such of the particulars need be given as relate to persons ceasing to be or becoming members since the date of the last return and to shares transferred since that date or to changes as compared with the date in the amount of stock held by a member.

(ii) If the names in the list are not arranged in alphabetical order, an index sufficient to enable the name of any person to be readily found must be annexed.

6. Particulars of directors and secretaries.

Particulars of the persons who are directors of the company at the date of this return

Present Any former Usual Business Date of
Forename or forenames or Nationality Residential Occupation
Birth
Names and Names and Address and
Surname Surnames particulars of other
Directorships

Particulars of the persons who is secretary of the company at the date of this return

Name
(In the case of an individual present Any former forenames Usual residential address (in
forename or names and surname, or surnames the case of a corporation, the
in the case of a corporation, the corporate name) registered or principal office)

Signed..Director

Notes

"Directors" includes any person who occupies the position of a director by whatsoever name called and any person in accordance with whose directions or instructions the directors of the company are accustomed to act.

"Former forename" and "former surname" do not include in the case of a married woman the name or surname by which she was known prior to the marriage.

The names of all bodies corporate of which the company making the return is the wholly- owned subsidiary or bodies corporate which are the wholly-owned subsidiaries either of the company or of another company of which the company is a subsidiary of another if it has no members except that other and that other's wholly-owned subsidiaries and its or their nominees. If the space provided in the form is insufficient, particulars of both directorships should be listed on a separate statement attached to the return.

Where all the partners in a firm are joint secretaries, the name and principal office of the firm may be stated.

*Delivered for filing by……………………..……………………………

*This should be printed at the bottom of the first page of the return.

CERTIFICATES AND OTHER DOCUMENTS ACCOMPANYING ANNUAL RETURNS Certificate to be given by a director and the secretary of every private company

We certify that the company has not since the date of the incorporation of the company/the last annual return, issued any invitation to the public to subscribe for any shares or debentures in the company.

Signed………………………….. Director

Signed…………………………. Secretary

Further certificate to be given as aforesaid if the number of members of the company exceeds fifty.

We certify that the excess of the number of members of the company over fifty consists wholly of persons who, under subsection (3) of section 22 of the Companies and Allied Matters Act, are not to be included in reckoning the number fifty.

Signed………………………….. Director

Signed…………………………. Secretary

Certified Copies of Accounts

There shall be annexed to this return a written copy, certified both by a director and by the secretary of the company to be a true copy, of every balance sheet laid before the company in general meeting during the period to which this return relates (including every document required by law to be annexed to the balance sheet) and a copy (certified as aforesaid) of the report of the directors accompanying each such balance sheet. If any such balance sheet or document required by law to be annexed thereto is in a foreign language, there must also be annexed to that balance sheet a translation in English of the balance sheet or document certified in a prescribed manner to be a correct translation. If any such balance sheet as aforesaid or document required by law to be annexed thereto did not comply with the requirements of the law as in force at the date of audit with respect to the form of balance sheet or documents aforesaid, as the case may be, there shall be made such additions to and corrections in the copy as would have been required to be made in the balance sheet or document in order to make it comply with the said requirements, and the fact that the copy has been amended must be stated thereon.

EIGHTH SCHEDULE Section 419

Annual return of a small company

PART I

Contents

1. The name and address of the registered office of the company.

2. If the register of members is, under the provisions of this Act, kept elsewhere than at the registered office of the company, the address of the place where it is kept.
3. If any register of holders of debentures of the company or any such register or part of any such register is, under the provisions of this Act, kept elsewhere than at the registered office of the company, the address of the place where it is kept.
4. The authorised share capital of the company.
5. The issued capital.
6. The total paid-up capital.
7. Particulars of the total amount of the indebtedness of the company in respect of all mortgages and charges which are required to be registered with the Registrar under the Act.
8. Particulars of the directors and secretary.

PART II

ANNUAL RETURN OF.. Limited made up to the day of......................... 20.................... (being the fourteenth day after the date of the annual general meeting for the year 20...........................)

1. Name..
2. Address...

(Address of the registered office of the company)

3. Situation of registers of members and debenture holders.

(a) (Address of place at which the register of members is kept, if other than the registered office of the company).

(b) (Address of any place in Nigeria other than the registered office of the company at which is kept any register of holders of debentures of the company or any duplicate of any such register or part of any such register).

4. Particulars of indebtedness.

Total amount of indebtedness of the company in respect of all mortgages and charges which are required to be registered with the Commission under the Companies and Allied Matters Act, the particulars of which are set in the annexed statement. N

....

5. Particulars of directors and secretaries.

FORMS—Continued

Particulars of the persons who are directors of the company at the date of this return

Present Forename or Names and Surname	Any former forenames or Names and Surnames	Usual Nationality	Business Address	Date of Birth	Residential	Occupation and particulars of other Directorships

Particulars of the persons who is secretary of the company at the date of this return

Name

(In the case of an individual present Any former forenames Usual residential address (in forename or names and surname, or surnames in the case of a corporation, the corporate name) the case of a corporation, the registered or principal office)

Signed...Director

"Directors" includes any person who is appointed a director by the company, or is described as a director by the company, and any person in accordance with whose directions or instructions the directors of the company are accustomed to act.

"Former forename" and "former surname" do not include in the case of a married woman the name or surname by which she was known previous to the marriage.

The names of all bodies corporate incorporated in Nigeria of which the director is also a director should be given, except bodies corporate of which the company making the return is the wholly-owned subsidiary or bodies corporate which are the wholly-owned subsidiaries either of the company or of another company of which the company is the wholly-owned subsidiary. A body corporate is deemed to be the wholly-owned subsidiary of another if it has no members except that other and that other's wholly-owned subsidiaries and its or their nominees. If the space provided in the form is insufficient, particulars of other directorships should be listed on a separate statement attached to this return.

Where all the partners in a firm are joint secretaries, the name and principal office of the firm should be stated.

*Delivered for filing by...

*This should be printed at the bottom of the first page of the return.

CERTIFICATES AND OTHER DOCUMENTS ACCOMPANYING ANNUAL RETURN Certificate to be given by a director and the secretary of every private company

We certify that the company has not since the date of the incorporation of the company/the last annual return, issued any invitation to the public to subscribe for any shares or debentures of the company.

Signed........................ Director

Signed...................... Secretary

Further certificate to be given as aforesaid if the number of members of the company exceeds fifty.

We certify that the excess of the number of members of the company over fifty consists wholly of persons, who under section 22 (3) of the Companies and Allied Matters Act, are not to be included in reckoning the number of fifty, and we also certify that the company still retains its smallness.

Signed.................................... Director

Signed.................................. Secretary

Certified copies of Accounts

There shall be annexed to this return a written copy, certified both by a director and by the secretary of the company to be a true copy, of every balance sheet laid before the company in general meeting during the period to which this return relates (including every document required by law to be annexed to the balance sheet) and a copy (certified as aforesaid) of the report of the directors accompanying each such balance sheet. If any such balance sheet or document required by law to be annexed thereto is in a foreign language, there must also be annexed to that balance sheet a translation in English of the balance sheet or document certified in prescribed manner to be a correct translation. If any such balance sheet as aforesaid or document required by law to be annexed thereto did not comply with the requirements of the law as in force at the date of audit with respect to the form of balance sheets or documents aforesaid, as the case may be, there shall be made such additions to and corrections in the copy as would have been required to be made in the balance sheet or document in order to make it comply with the said requirements, and the fact that the copy has been amended must be stated thereon.

NINTH SCHEDULE Section 420

Annual return of a company limited by guarantee

(Under the Companies and Allied Matters Act)

ANNUAL RETURN OF.. Limited made up to the day of 20....................... (being the fourteenth day after the date of the annual general meeting for the year ....20.........)

1. Address...

(Address of the registered office of the company)

2. Situation of registers of members and debenture holders.

(a) (Address of place at which the register of members is kept, if other than the registered office of the company).

(b) (Address of any place in Nigeria other than the registered office of the company at which is kept any register of holders of debentures of the company or any duplicate of any such register or part of any such register). 3. Particulars of indebtedness.

Total amount of indebtedness of the company in respect of all mortgages and charges which are required to be registered with the Commission under this Act, the particulars of which are set in the annexed statement. N..........................

4. Particulars of directors and secretaries.

Particulars of the persons who are Directors of the Company at the date of this return

Name Present Forename or Name and Surname	Any former forenames or Names and Surnames	Nationality	Usual Residential Address	Business Occupation and particulars of other Directorships	Date of Birth

Particulars of the persons who is Secretary of the Company at the date of this return

Name (In the case of an individual present forename or names and surname, in the case of a corporation, the corporate name)	Any former forenames or surnames	Usual residential address (in the case of a corporation, the registered or principal office)

Signed..Director

Notes

"Directors" includes any person who occupies the position of a director by whatsoever name called and any person in accordance with whose directions or instructions the directors of the company are accustomed to act.

"Former forename" and "former surname" do not include in the case of a married woman the name or surname by which she was known previous to the marriage.

The names of all bodies corporate incorporated in Nigeria of which the director is also a director, should be given, except bodies corporate of which the company making the return is the wholly-owned subsidiary of bodies corporate which are the wholly-owned subsidiaries either of the company or of another company of which the company is the wholly-owned subsidiary of another if it has no members except that other and that other's wholly-owned subsidiaries and its or their nominees. If the space provided in the form is insufficient, particulars of both directorships should be listed on a separate statement attached to the return.

Where all partners in a firm are joint secretaries, the name and principal office of the firm should be stated.

*Delivered for filing by..

*This should be printed at the bottom of the first page of the return.

Certificates and Other Documents Accompanying Annual Return

Certificate to be given by a director and the

Secretary of every private company

We certify that the company has not since the date of the incorporation of the company or the last annual return, issued any invitation to the public to subscribe for any shares or debentures of the company.

Signed.. Director

Signed.................................... Secretary

Further certificate to be given as aforesaid if the number of members of the company exceeds fifty.

We certify that the excess of the number of members of the company over fifty consists wholly of persons who, under section 22 (3) of the Companies and Allied Matters Act, are not to be included in reckoning the number of fifty.

Signed................................ Director

Signed.............................. Secretary

Certified Copies of Accounts

There shall be annexed to this return a written copy, certified both by a director and by the secretary of the company to be a true copy, of every balance sheet laid before the company in general meeting during the period to which this return relates (including every document required by law to be annexed to the balance sheet) and a copy (certified as aforesaid) of the report of the directors accompanying each such balance sheet. If any such balance sheet or document required by law to be annexed thereto is in a foreign language, there must also be annexed to that balance sheet a translation in English of the balance sheet or document certified in prescribed manner to be a correct translation. If any such balance sheet as aforesaid or document required by law to be annexed thereto did not comply with the requirements of the law as in force at the date of audit with respect to the form of balance sheets or documents aforesaid, as the case may be, there must be made such additions to and corrections in the copy as would have been required to be made in the balance sheet or document in order to make it comply with the said requirements, and the fact that the copy has been amended must be stated thereon.

TENTH SCHEDULE

Sections 475 (2)(d), 511 (5)(a) and 520 (4)(a)

Powers of Administrator

1. Power to take possession of, collect and get in the property of the company and, for that purpose, to take such proceedings as may seem to him expedient.
2. Power to sell or otherwise dispose of the property of the company.
3. Power to raise or borrow money and grant security therefor over the property of the company.
4. Power to appoint a solicitor or accountant or other professionally qualified person to assist him in the performance of his functions.
5. Power to bring or defend any action or other legal proceedings in the name and on behalf of the company.
6. Power to refer to arbitration any question affecting the company.
7. Power to effect and maintain insurances in respect of the business and property of the company.
8. Power to use the company's seal.
9. Power to do all acts and to execute in the name and on behalf of the company any deed, receipt or other document.
10. Power to draw, accept, make and endorse any bill of exchange or promissory note in the name and on behalf of the company.
11. Power to appoint any agent to do any business which he is unable to do himself or which can more conveniently be done by an agent and power to employ and dismiss employees.
12. Power to do all such things (including the carrying out of works) as may be necessary for the realisation of the property of the company.
13. Power to make any payment which is necessary or incidental to the performance of his functions.
14. Power to carry on the business of the company.
15. Power to establish subsidiaries of the company.
16. Power to transfer to subsidiaries of the company the whole or any part of the business and property of the company.
17. Power to grant or accept a surrender of a lease or tenancy of any of the property of the company, and to take a lease or tenancy of any property required or convenient for the business of the company.
18. Power to make any arrangement or compromise on behalf of the company.
19. Power to call up any uncalled capital of the company.
20. Power to rank and claim in the bankruptcy, insolvency, sequestration or liquidation of any person indebted to the company and to receive dividends, and to accede to trust deeds for the creditors of any such person.
21. Power to present or defend a petition for the winding-up of the company.
22. Power to change the situation of the company's registered office.
23. Power to do all other things incidental to the exercise of the foregoing powers.

ELEVENTH SCHEDULE

Section 474 (3)(d), 497, 503, 556(3)

Powers of receivers and managers of the whole or Substantially the whole of the company's property

1. Power to take possession of, collect and get in the property of the company and, for that purpose, to take such proceedings as may seem to him expedient.
2. Power to sell or otherwise dispose of the property of the company by public auction or private contract.
3. Power to raise or borrow money and grant security therefor over the property of the company.
4. Power to appoint a solicitor or accountant or other professionally qualified person to assist him in the performance of his functions.
5. Power to bring or defend any action or other legal proceedings in the name and on behalf of the company.
6. Power to refer to arbitration any question affecting the company.
7. Power to effect and maintain insurances in respect of the business and property of the company.
8. Power to use the company's seal.
9. Power to do all acts and to execute in the name and on behalf of the company any deed, receipt or other document.
10. Power to draw, accept, make and endorse any bill of exchange or promissory note in the name and on behalf of the company.
11. Power to appoint any agent to do any business which he is unable to do himself or which can more conveniently be done by an agent and power to employ and dismiss employees.
12. Power to do all such things (including the carrying out of works) as may be necessary for the realisation of the property of the company.
13. Power to make any payment which is necessary or incidental to the performance of his functions.
14. Power to carry on the business of the company.
15. Power to establish subsidiaries of the company.
16. Power to transfer to subsidiaries of the company the whole or any part of the business and property of the company.
17. Power to grant or accept a surrender of a lease or tenancy of any of the property of the company, and to take a lease or tenancy of any property required or convenient for the business of the company.
18. Power to make any arrangement or compromises on behalf of the company.
19. Power to call up any uncalled capital of the company.
20. Power to rank and claim in the bankruptcy, insolvency, sequestration or liquidation of any person indebted to the company and to receive dividends, and to accede to trust deeds for the creditors of any such person.
21. Power to present or defend a petition for the winding-up of the company.
22. Power to change the situation of the company's registered office.
23. Power to do all other things incidental to the exercise of the foregoing powers.

TWELFTH SCHEDULE

Section 653

Provisions not applicable on winding-up under supervision of the court

Section Subject Matter
551Power to appoint official receiver for debenture holders and others.
583Statement of company's affairs to be submitted to official receiver.
584Report by official receiver.
585Appointment, remuneration and title of liquidators (except subsection 8).
590Exercise and control of liquidator's powers.
591Payments by liquidator into companies liquidation account.
592Audit, etc., of liquidator's account.
593Books to be kept by liquidator.
594Release of liquidator.
595Control over liquidators.
596Power to appoint committee of inspection, etc.
597Powers, etc., of committee of inspection.
598Powers where no committee of inspection is appointed.
599Power to appoint special manager.
613Power to order public examination of promoters, etc.
616Delegation to liquidator of certain powers of the court.

THIRTEENTH SCHEDULE Section 727 (1)

Provision of this Act applying to unregistered companies

Provisions of this Act Applied Subject Matter Limitation on Application
Sections 417 to 425 and Seventh, Eighth and Ninth Schedules
Section 374 to 416 and Fourth to Eighth Schedules
Sections 314 to 330
Sections 357 to 373, 301,
302, 303, 727, 731, 733,
738, 740 (1), 742 Annual return
Accounts and audit
Investigations
Registration of
Documents, enforcement and supplemental matters Not to apply so as to require particulars in respect of any period before the commencement of this Act, and as respects any period thereafter to apply so far only as may be specified as aforesaid and to such bodies corporate as may be so specified.

To apply so far as may be specified as aforesaid and to such bodies corporate as may be so specified.

To apply so far only as they have effect in relation to provisions applying by virtue of the foregoing entries in this schedules

FOURTEENTH SCHEDULE Section 733 (1)

Forms of statement to be published by banking and insurance companies and deposit, provident or benefit societies

The share capital is.......................divided into......................shares of.......... .... each.

The number of shares issued is...

Calls to the amount of.......................... naira per share have been made, under which the sum of................................... naira has been received.

The liabilities of the company on the first day of January (or July) were—

Debts owing to sundry persons by the company—

On judgment, N
On specialty N
On notes or bills, N
On simple contracts, N
On estimated liabilities, N
The assets of the company on that day were—
Government securities (stating them), N Bills of exchange and promissory notes, N
Cash at the bankers, N
Other securities, N
*If the company has no share capital, the portion of the statement relating to capital and shares must be omitted.

FIFTEENTH SCHEDULE Section 762 (4)

Provisions regarding matters relating to mutual rights and duties of partners and limited liability partnership and its partners applicable in the absence of any agreement on such matters

1. The mutual rights and duties of the partners and the mutual rights and duties of the limited liability partnership and its partners shall be determined, subject to the terms of any limited liability partnership agreement or in the absence of any such agreement on any matter, by the provisions of this schedule.
2. All the partners of a limited liability partnership are entitled to share equally in the capital, profits and losses of the limited liability partnership
3. The limited liability partnership shall indemnify each partner in respect of payments made and personal liability incurred by him –
(a) in the ordinary and proper conduct of the limited liability partnership ; or
(b) in or about anything necessarily done for the preservation of the business or property of the limited liability partnership.
4. Every partner shall indemnify the limited liability partnership for any loss caused to it by his fraud in the conduct of the business of the limited liability partnership.
5. Every partner may take part in the management of the limited liability partnership.
6. No partner shall be entitled to remuneration for acting in the business or management of the limited liability partnership.
7. No person may be introduced as a partner without the consent of all the existing partners.
8. Any matter or issue relating to the limited liability partnership shall be decided by a resolution passed by a majority in number of the partners, and for this purpose, each partner shall have one vote. However, no change may be made in the nature of business of the limited liability partnership without the consent of all the partners.
9. Every limited liability partnership shall ensure that decisions taken byit are recorded in the minutes within 30 days of taking such decisions are kept and maintained at the registered office of the limited liability partnership.
10. Each partner shall render true accounts and full information of all things affecting the limited liability partnership to any partner or his legal representative.
11. If a partner, without the consent of the limited liability partnership, carries on any business of the same nature as and competing with the limited liability partnership, he must account for and pay over to the limited liability partnership all profits made by him in that business.

12. Every partner shall account to the limited liability partnership for any benefit derived by him without the consent of the limited liability partnership from any transaction concerning the limited liability partnership, or from any use by him of the property, name or any business connection of the limited liability.
13. No majority of the partners can expel any partner unless a power to do so has been conferred by express agreement between the partners.
14. All disputes between the partners arising out of the limited liability partnership agreement which cannot be resolved in terms of such agreement shall be referred for arbitration as per the provisions of the Arbitration and Conciliation Act.
15. The limited liability partnership shall not, without the consent of all partners, sell assets having a value of more than 50% of the total value of assets of the limited liability partnership.
16. A partner shall not sell or agree to sell his interest in the partnership to a non-partner without first offering his interest to existing partners.
17. A partner or group of partners acting together, shall not sell or agreed sell more than 50% of interest or combined interest in the partnership unless that non-partner has offered to buy all of the partners' interests and on the same terms.

I, certify, in accordance with Section 2 (1) of the Acts Authentication Act, Cap. A2, Laws of the Federation of Nigeria 2004, that this is a true copy of the Bill passed by both Houses of the National Assembly.

MOHAMMED ATABA SANI-OMOLORI

Clerk to the National Assembly

9th Day of July, 2020

EXPLANATORY MEMORANDUM

This Act repeals the Companies and Allied Matters Act, Cap. C20, Laws of the Federation of Nigeria, 2004 and enacts the Companies and Allied Matters Act, 2020 to provide for the incorporation of companies, limited liability partnerships, limited partnerships, registration of business names together with incorporation of trustees of certain communities, bodies, associations.

A 528 2020 No. 3 Companies and Allied Matters Act, 2020

www.ingramcontent.com/pod-product-compliance
Lightning Source LLC
LaVergne TN
LVHW052013200926
848481LV00005B/1481
* 9 7 8 9 7 8 6 0 2 0 3 4 1 *